Profiting
from Peace

A project of the International Peace Academy

Profiting from Peace

Managing the Resource Dimensions of Civil War

EDITED BY
Karen Ballentine
Heiko Nitzschke

LYNNE
RIENNER
PUBLISHERS

BOULDER
LONDON

Published in the United States of America in 2005 by
Lynne Rienner Publishers, Inc.
1800 30th Street, Boulder, Colorado 80301
www.rienner.com

and in the United Kingdom by
Lynne Rienner Publishers, Inc.
3 Henrietta Street, Covent Garden, London WC2E 8LU

Library of Congress Cataloging-in-Publication Data
Profiting from peace : managing the resource dimensions of civil war /
    Karen Ballentine and Heiko Nitzschke (eds.).
        p. cm. — (A project of the International Peace Academy.)
    Includes bibliographical references and index.
    ISBN 1-58826-262-6 (hardcover : alk. paper) —ISBN 1-58826-287-1
(pbk. : alk. paper) 1. Civil war—Economic aspects. 2. Natural
resources. 3. Conflict management. 4. Peace. I. Ballentine, Karen.
II. Nitzschke, Heiko. III. Series: Project of the International Peace
Academy.
HB195.P765 2005 330—dc22

                                                            2004029657

British Cataloguing in Publication Data
A Cataloguing in Publication record for this book
is available from the British Library.

Printed and bound in the United States of America

The paper used in this publication meets the requirements
of the American National Standard for Permanence of
Paper for Printed Library Materials Z39.48-1992.

5   4   3   2   1

Contents

Foreword

David M. Malone

In recent years, the economic dimensions of intrastate armed conflict have become the subject of increased academic study and policy action. The Economic Agendas in Civil Wars (EACW) Program of the International Peace Academy in particular has been influential in bringing analysis of the political economy of armed conflict to bear upon policies of conflict prevention and conflict management. The widely cited volume *Greed and Grievance: Economic Agendas in Civil Wars* proved instrumental in highlighting the importance to conflict resolution of this groundbreaking strand of policy research. A subsequently commissioned case study volume, *The Political Economy of Armed Conflict: Beyond Greed and Grievance,* qualified and extended our understanding of economic dimensions of the onset, character, and duration of contemporary conflicts. A further publication, *The Democratic Republic of Congo: Economic Dimensions of War and Peace,* sheds light on the underresearched question of how to integrate the accumulated knowledge about the economic dimensions of armed conflict into international peacemaking and postconflict peacebuilding efforts.

Building on the substantive research generated by the International Peace Academy and others, this volume identifies and assesses existing and emerging policy—the regulatory, legal, and market-based mechanisms that may be applied to more effectively redress the conflict-promoting aspects of economic activity in vulnerable or war-torn states. Specific attention is paid to the complex connections among natural resource exploitation, global financial flows, and armed intrastate conflict. Research has shown that local war economies are highly dependent upon combatants' access to global commodity and financial markets, gained variously through transnational criminal networks, legitimate but poorly regulated private sector actors, and financial institutions. Consequently, curtailing these economic transactions has become a matter of priority for those seeking to resolve and prevent violent conflict. At the same time it has become clear that the manner in which natural resources are exploited—and whether the revenues generated benefit the people rather than elites—can have an important role for conflict prevention and postconflict reconstruction. Furthermore, regulatory and legal regimes can provide promising mechanisms for regulating conflict entrepreneurs and ending impunity for those "rogue actors" benefiting from war, while protecting otherwise beneficial and legitimate trade and investment.

Clearly, the development of such tools and strategies is a long-term goal. Continued commitment and action will be required on the part of governments, international financial institutions, private companies and financial markets, and civil society organizations. The UN system, with the Security Council at its core, has a particular role in this endeavor, as this volume seeks to underscore. The Informal Working Group on the Political Economy of Armed Conflict, initiated by Secretary-General Kofi Annan and under the able direction of the UN Department for Political Affairs, represents an important step in mainstreaming the economic dimension into UN strategic planning and programming in the areas of peace and development. We commend the Secretary-General for his personal engagement to see this important work move forward. By identifying relevant policy challenges and opportunities for these various policy actors in the interim, we hope that this volume will make a modest contribution to improved conflict prevention and peacebuilding.

Many friends of the International Peace Academy were involved in the inception and design of the Economic Agendas in Civil Wars program, but Karen Ballentine, its fine program director, is the person most responsible for its success. Her incisive intellect, wide-ranging interests, and formidable network of multilateral and private-sector practitioners, scholars, and experts have been critical not only to this volume but to every phase of the project. Heiko Nitzschke, a valued colleague now with the German Foreign Service, with whom I have had the pleasure of writing on these issues myself, made a very significant contribution to this volume, not just organizationally but also conceptually. I am deeply grateful to them both.

Such an endeavor would not have been possible without the foresight and dedication of the funders who have supported the Economic Agendas in Civil Wars Program throughout its highly successful and productive three years of existence. We at the International Peace Academy extend our deepest appreciation to the Canadian Department of Foreign Affairs, the Canadian International Development Agency, the Department for International Development of the United Kingdom, the government of Norway, the government of Sweden, the government of Switzerland, the

International Development Research Centre, the Rockefeller Foundation, and the United Nations Foundation.

Donors providing "core" untied funding to IPA play a critical role in support of IPA's institutional and intellectual capacity building. They are particularly crucial in allowing us to develop new ideas and to get new projects (such as the EACW Program and its successor program on the nexus between security and development policies in international relations) off the ground and available for funding by others. Individual IPA board members, the governments of Denmark, Norway, Sweden, and Switzerland, the Ford Foundation, the William and Flora Hewlett Foundation, and the Rockefeller Foundation stand out in this regard. We are deeply grateful to them. We are also grateful to Lynne Rienner and her colleagues for their professionalism and forbearance in seeing our various publications through the publication process.

David M. Malone
Past President, International Peace Academy

Acknowledgments

A volume of this scope could not have been undertaken without extensive contributions from many valued colleagues and friends. First and foremost we would like to thank the contributing authors for their professionalism, patience, and good humor. It has been a most inspiring and educational experience for us to work with them in shaping the chapters that follow. Numerous reviewers provided excellent comments that were greatly valued by us all. To them, warmest thanks. We are also grateful to David M. Malone and Neclâ Tschirgi, at the time president and vice president respectively of the International Peace Academy, who were instrumental in developing and supporting the Economic Agendas in Civil Wars Program over the course of its three years. Our deepest appreciation goes to our colleagues Jake Sherman and Kaysie Studdard for their intellectual input and dedication in the development of this volume, as well as for their tireless efforts in attending to the mundane administrative details so essential to the program's success.

As the Economic Agendas in Civil Wars Program comes to a close, we extend special thanks to the chairs of our four working groups, Andrew Mack of the University of British Columbia, Ambassador Colin Keating of New Zealand, Virginia Gamba of SaferAfrica, and Leiv Lunde of the Econ Institute, who helped shape and extend the program's research priorities and policy development. Warm thanks are also due to Mark Taylor and Christian Ruge of Norway's FAFO Institute for their intellectual and institutional collaboration in pushing forward the legal dimensions of the global conflict trade and for their continued collegiality. We also wish to acknowledge the critical role of Ambassador Michael Small of Canada in driving early work on this set of issues at IPA and elsewhere during the years

1998–2000. Of course, as in any endeavor of this scope and duration, there have been numerous other individuals in governments, international organizations, academia, civil society, and the private sector whose encouragement, expert knowledge, and constructive criticism were indispensable to the success of the Economic Agendas in Civil Wars Program. To thank them individually would fill numerous pages. You know who you are. Many thanks.

We would also like to acknowledge our funders, who generously supported the Economic Agendas in Civil Wars Program both financially and intellectually. These include the governments of Canada, Norway, Sweden, Switzerland, and the United Kingdom, the United Nations Foundation and the United Nations Department of Political Affairs, the International Development Research Centre, and the Rockefeller Foundation. Ambassador Marjatta Rasi, permanent representative of Finland to the United Nations, and her colleagues kindly hosted our authors' meeting in New York. Linda Bloch of Riverside Travel ensured our authors' smooth travels. For their invaluable assistance in copyediting the manuscript, we want to thank Jason Cook and IPA's publications coordinator Clara Lee. Last but certainly not least, we also wish to thank Lynne Rienner and her excellent team for their patience in seeing this volume through to completion.

Karen Ballentine
Heiko Nitzschke

1

Introduction

Karen Ballentine
and Heiko Nitzschke

Since the mid-1990s, the increased commercialization of civil wars has gained unprecedented academic and policy attention. A large number of scholarly and policy studies have been produced that allow for a better understanding of the political economy of many contemporary conflicts, particularly those characterized by the predatory exploitation of lucrative natural resources and the pervasive criminalization of economic life.[1] What many of today's armed conflicts have in common, these studies show, is their increasing "self-financing nature."[2] As superpower patronage declined with the end of the Cold War, both rebel groups and governments in numerous conflict theaters have sought out alternative sources of revenue to sustain their military campaigns.[3]

Facilitated by economic globalization and financial market liberalization, many of the resulting war economies are centered on the exploitation of and trade in natural resources, such as oil, timber, precious minerals and gemstones, and narcotic crops.[4] The revenues generated through such "conflict trade" help to procure readily available weapons and military materiel, to hire mercenaries, to line the pockets of corrupt warlords and government officials, and to buy support of neighboring regimes. Numerous examples abound. During Cambodia's civil war, both the government and the Khmer Rouge sold gemstones and timber on Asian and European markets[5]; in Colombia, the guerrillas and paramilitaries have increasingly engaged in the production and trafficking of narcotics and in laundering their ill-gotten proceeds through elaborate quasi-criminal networks[6]; and Liberia's warlord-turned-president Charles Taylor controlled a large part of that country's trade in timber and smuggled diamonds to finance his violent rebellion and subsequent sponsorship of the Revolutionary United Front (RUF)

1

rebels in neighboring Sierra Leone.[7] Perhaps nowhere was the humanitarian price of conflict trade more evident than in Angola and the Democratic Republic of Congo (DRC), where the exploitation of diamonds, gold, and coltan enriched rival elites while exposing the civilian population to devastating poverty and enormous loss of life.[8]

This complicated reality of contemporary intrastate wars presents policymakers with a twofold challenge: to accurately assess the impact of resource predation and related financial flows on the dynamics of armed conflict and to develop and implement effective policy responses for conflict prevention, conflict resolution, and peacebuilding. Attention to the issue has led to numerous policy initiatives, which are the subject of this volume and are discussed in more detail in the ensuing chapters.

Among others, the governments of Canada, Norway, and the United Kingdom have championed policy development on relevant issues such as UN sanctions, corporate responsibility, and financial transparency in the extractive industries. The World Bank and its private sector arm, the International Financial Corporation (IFC), have stepped up their support of anticorruption efforts and of promoting transparent and accountable institutions for resource management, an example of which is the much-debated Chad-Cameroon oil pipeline project.[9] The UN Security Council has addressed the role of diamonds in fueling conflicts in West Africa through the imposition of diamond embargoes on warring factions in Sierra Leone, Angola, and Liberia. The Security Council has discussed the role of business entities in conflict prevention, peacekeeping, and peacebuilding, an issue that the UN Global Compact has also focused on in its multistakeholder dialogues.[10] Last but not least, advocacy organizations such as Global Witness and Partnership Africa Canada have brought the issue of war economies to the international agenda through, inter alia, their campaigns against "blood diamonds."[11] These nongovernmental organizations (NGOs) were also instrumental in the imposition of diamond sanctions against UNITA and the establishment of the so-called Kimberley Process for the certification of rough diamonds, a government, industry, and NGO initiative endorsed by the UN.[12]

Why Consider the Resource Dimensions of Civil Wars?

Throughout history, violent contests over natural resources have played a central role in warfare. Until recently, however, academic and policy attention to the economic dimensions of conflict was confined largely to interstate wars. With the ascendance of intrastate wars as the main type of armed conflict in the post–Cold War era, the focus has shifted. Sustained research on conflicts such as those in Sudan, Angola, Sierra Leone, and Cambodia has demonstrated that violence and armed intrastate conflicts often serve a range of political and economic functions for combatants, civilians, and external actors participating in the conflict and the war economy that sustains it.[13] This research has also gone far to identify the key linkages by which economic factors can promote or exacerbate violent conflict.

First, an abundance of lucrative natural resources can have detrimental effects on the socioeconomic and political stability of a country, creating permissive causes of violence and armed conflict. In fact, numerous qualitative and quantitative studies show that in resource-dependent countries, resource wealth is often associated with macroeconomic instability, rampant corruption, oppression of minorities or other groups at the hand of the ruling elite, and crippling poverty.[14] Among political scientists and economists, this phenomenon is known as the "paradox of plenty" or the "resource curse." While natural resources provide the bedrock for economic development and relative prosperity in countries such as Norway, Chile, and Botswana, in large parts of the world resource wealth does not benefit the majority of the population. To them, natural resources are a curse rather than a blessing.[15] This demonstrates the urgent need to foster the positive, productive role of natural resource exploitation for more equitable socioeconomic development and political stability through adequate policy responses aimed at export diversification and good governance, supported by complementary changes to the institutional frameworks of international aid, trade, and finance.[16]

Second, revenues generated from natural resource exploitation can significantly influence the character and the duration of conflicts.[17] Conflicts that have started as political rebellions, such as those in Colombia and Angola, can mutate over time as pecuniary considerations become as important to some combatants as political aspirations—or even more important. The types of natural resources a country is endowed with, their modes of exploitation, and the way related benefits accrue to conflict stakeholders can also influence the type of armed conflict it experiences. There are strong indications, for instance, that "unlootable resources" (oil, gas, and deep-shaft gems and minerals) tend to be associated with separatist conflicts such as those in Bougainville (Papua New Guinea), Aceh (Indonesia), and Sudan; by contrast, "lootable resources" (alluvial diamonds, narcotic crops, and timber) feature strongly in nonseparatist insurgencies, such as in Afghanistan, Angola, Colombia, Liberia, and Sierra Leone.[18] Furthermore, the ready availability of spoils of war in the form of lucrative and easily tradable natural resources in particular tends to complicate conflict termination and may pose important challenges for postconflict peacebuilding by creating "spoilers" with an interest in continuation of violence and instability.[19] Natural resource predation and criminal economic activities can also have strong regional linkages with cross-border trading networks, regional kin and ethnic groups, and supportive neighboring regimes, particularly where conflicts are embedded in regional conflict formations.[20] Properly understanding and addressing these complex economic dimensions of conflict may thus hold great promise for improving the international community's ability to prevent and resolve armed conflict and build lasting peace.

Third, there are nonnegligible moral, political, and even legal obligations for governments and companies in the developed world that arise from their commercial linkages with local war economies. While rarely acknowledged in official policy discourse, most of the natural resources fueling conflicts are destined for consumer markets (both licit and illicit) in the developed world. The majority of the oil and natural gas produced in the developing world fuels the economies of the developed world; the mineral coltan, which fueled much of the DRC war, is used in high-end electronics; the majority of the drugs produced in Colombia and Afghanistan are consumed in New York, Paris, London, and Moscow; and diamonds would be worthless were it not for their well-guarded status as a luxury item. Similarly, bank secrecy in the developed world continues to permit safe havens for stolen funds of unaccountable elites in the developing world and to facilitate money laundering by criminal networks. Policymakers, activists, and private-sector actors in the developed world thus have (or should have) a stake in positively influencing conflict dynamics through the numerous regulatory, legal, and market-based mechanisms at their disposal.

Taken together, these factors underline both the timeliness and the importance of current policy attention to the role of natural resources as a source of combatant self-financing. Indeed, the term *resource wars* has gained currency in scholarly work and policy discourse as a depiction of what to some observers represents a new type of insurgency.[21] Here, however, a word of caution is in order. Clearly, not all countries that suffer from armed conflict are rich in lucrative natural resources, nor are all resource-dependent economies prone to conflict. In conflicts in Sri Lanka, the Balkans, and Afghanistan, war economies have thrived instead on diaspora remittances, aid diversion, or contraband trade.[22] Furthermore, studies suggest that even where natural resource predation features strongly in conflict dynamics, it is seldom the sole or even main cause of conflicts.[23] Thus, while a political economy approach is a useful methodological framework for conflict analysis and policy development, it should not lead to "natural resource reductionism" that neglects other, still crucial political, security and social dimensions of armed intrastate conflict.[24]

Objectives and Design of the Book

Given the relative newness of economic factors in peace and security analysis, few systematic studies exist on the actual amenability of conflicts to economic regulation. Consequently, policy responses remain largely exploratory and ad hoc. Through its commissioned research and policy dialogues, the Economic Agendas in Civil Wars Program at the International Peace Academy has sought to fill this lacuna.[25]

The main objective of this volume is to assess and promote practical policy tools and strategies by which policymakers in governments, intergovernmental organizations, the private sector, and civil society, in both the developed and developing worlds, may more effectively address the economic dimensions of contemporary armed conflict. To that end, the volume first provides an overview of the complex linkages between natural resource wealth and armed intrastate conflicts and, based on these linkages, provides an overview of adequate policies and tools. The chapters in the second section analyze a range of policy responses to curtail and control the flow of resources and related finances to conflicts, as important mechanisms for conflict prevention and resolution. In the third section, the contributions detail different mechanisms to promote more responsible and transparent management of natural resources, both by companies engaged in resource extraction and by host governments in conflict-prone states. The fourth section comprises chapters that analyze the regulatory and legal frameworks that may be brought to bear upon the range of licit and illicit actors engaged in war economies as a means to establish accountability for human rights violations and to end impunity for those who profit from war. A concluding analysis with issues for further research and policy action is offered in the final section.

Natural Resources and Conflict: Issues and Policy Options

There are numerous ways in which the exploitation of and trade in lucrative natural resources and related financial interactions can have impacts on armed conflict. Early scholarly discourse on the economic causes of conflict centered on the *greed versus grievance* dichotomy in explaining the onset of armed rebellion.[26] According to the highly influential yet controversial "greed thesis," economic motivations and opportunities ("loot seeking") are more highly correlated with the onset of conflict than are ethnic, socioeconomic, or political grievances ("justice seeking"). By now, numerous academic and policy studies exist that allow for a more differentiated understanding of the complex political economy of armed conflict.[27] Based on a review of these studies, Macartan Humphreys in his overview (Chapter 2) discerns five modalities through which natural resources are linked with conflict:

- *rent seeking,* the political impact of the availability of large natural resource rents to ruling elites, often referred to as "the resource curse"

- *grievances,* primarily associated with the (mal)distribution of natural resource wealth and socioeconomic impacts of extractive operations
- *economic instability,* accruing from the distortions associated with a country's high dependence on natural resources
- *conflict financing,* the channels through which access to natural resource wealth affects the means for belligerents to continue fighting
- *peace spoiling,* by which natural resource wealth alters the incentives for peace

As Humphreys highlights, each of these modalities involves different sets of actors and incentives. Equally diverse is the range of possible policy responses he introduces, many of which are taken up in greater detail in the ensuing chapters.

Curtailing Conflict Trade and Finance

Much of the policy debate and action dealing with war economies thus far has focused on developing "control regimes" aimed at curtailing conflict trade and financial flows as sources of combatant self-financing.[28] The rationale for such global or regional control regimes is fairly straightforward: if conflicts thrive on licit or illicit trade in natural resources, then curtailing conflict trade may contribute to conflict resolution by weakening warring parties and shifting combatants' incentives from war to peace. The same logic holds for efforts aimed at attacking the financial lifelines of combatants, often by targeting white-collar and organized criminal activities though which this financing is channeled.

A range of initiatives, policy mechanisms, and regulatory instruments can directly or indirectly address the natural resource dimension of war economies.[29] Some were developed or adapted in direct response to armed conflict, such as UN targeted sanctions imposed through the 1990s and the Kimberley certification scheme for the trade in rough diamonds. Others, such as interdiction regimes against organized crime, money laundering, drug trafficking, and terrorist financing, are mainly reactions to threats posed by instability and conflict abroad to developed countries, yet they have indirect bearing on curtailing economic flows that sustain armed conflicts.

Perhaps the most robust policy instruments deployed to curtail resource flows to combatants are the targeted commodity and financial sanctions imposed by the UN Security Council on government elites and rebel groups in several conflicts. The jury is still out on the effectiveness of targeted sanctions as a tool for conflict resolution. Yet the creation of ad hoc, independent panels of experts to support the monitoring of the various sanctions regimes and to investigate illegal resource exploitation by the numerous parties to the DRC conflict was a particularly useful policy innovation.[30] The expert panel reports submitted to the Security Council have helped to improve understanding of the complex dynamics of "sanctions busting" and war economies more generally. Expert panels and their practice of "naming and shaming" sanctions busters have been an effective—if controversial—mechanism of "noncoercive diplomacy" in the arsenal of the Security Council. Whether this innovative policy mechanism will receive much-needed administrative strengthening and political support or fall victim to Security Council diplomacy and political trade-offs remains to be seen.

The work of the Angola and Sierra Leone expert panels was also instrumental in establishing the Kimberley Process Certification Scheme (KPCS) for rough diamonds, the first policy mechanism that deals in a detailed and comprehensive manner with a commodity that has been directly and heavily involved in fueling several African conflicts. The Kimberley Process, which came into effect in January 2003, grew out of commercial, political, and humanitarian concern over the destabilizing role of "conflict diamonds"—defined by the UN and the Kimberley Process as "rough diamonds used by rebel movements or their allies to finance conflict aimed at undermining legitimate governments."[31] In Chapter 3, Ian Smillie describes the emergence of this joint government, industry, and NGO initiative and discerns to what extent the KPCS may hold lessons for the regulation of other conflict commodities. Despite its shortcomings regarding, inter alia, independent monitoring and compliance monitoring, the Kimberley regime is a promising initiative. According to Smillie, it may help reduce the vast trade in "illegal diamonds" that has contributed to violent state collapse in numerous African countries. When supported by adequate capacity building in member states, the KPCS may thus become a key mechanism for conflict prevention in diamond-rich countries with weak governance structures.

Tracking the financial transactions involved in and proceeds from conflict trade offers another promising means of curtailing combatant self-financing. This regulatory dimension is the subject of Chapter 4 by Jonathan Winer, who offers practical suggestions to unify existing money-laundering regimes with efforts aimed at controlling the trade in conflict goods. Thus far, policy initiatives to establish financial transparency, such as the anti–money-laundering and anticorruption efforts of the Financial Action Task Force against Money Laundering (FATF), have not specifically included a conflict dimension. Conversely, enhanced initiatives to improve security in the cross-border transit of goods, such as that by the World Customs Organization (WCO), have no provisions regarding trade in conflict commodities. As Winer details, positive synergy effects may be achieved through the establishment of documentation regimes applying both to financial institutions and to importers, exporters, transport companies, and customs authorities. These documentation regimes could be readily adapted and expanded to include a conflict dimension and could be integrated into a unified documentation system for both conflict goods and their financial traces.

The terrorist attacks of September 11, 2001, have provided an important impetus for increased financial market transparency as a means of curtailing terrorist finance. In addition, "failed states" have regained currency in policy circles and national security strategies as breeding grounds for terrorist groups.[32] Reports that Al-Qaida laundered money by buying diamonds in West Africa have demonstrated the possible links between terrorism, conflict trade, and violent state collapse.[33] Based on an analysis of the work and mandate of the UN Counter-Terrorism Committee (CTC), Sue Eckert in Chapter 5 identifies two ways in which the UN's counterterrorism efforts may be applicable to the trade in conflict commodities. Where direct linkages exist between terrorism and conflict trade, the international legal framework against terrorist finance may in theory be broadened to include an investigation of the nonmonetary bases of terrorist funding. While this is technically feasible, Eckert cautions that politically such a step may be overly ambitious at present. More promising, according to Eckert, are the lessons that can be learned from the CTC's innovative monitoring and reporting requirements and capacity-building provisions for strengthening UN sanctions regimes and other regulatory efforts such as the Kimberley certification regime.

The often symbiotic relationship between organized crime networks and combatant elites in today's conflicts presents policymakers with a serious dilemma. For some observers, contemporary rebel groups such as those in Colombia and Sierra Leone are comparable to criminal organizations.[34] Yet Phil Williams and John Picarelli argue in Chapter 6 that, as much as insurgency and criminality may overlap, they are not the same. A conceptual distinction can be made between organized crime as an *entity* and as an *activity*. Whereas criminal organizations employ violence in the sole pursuit of profit, both government elites and rebel groups may engage in "do it yourself" criminal activities at least in part to pursue political and military goals. This understanding must inform policy action to tackle the crime-conflict nexus throughout the conflict cycle. Here, the authors suggest that a new policy framework is required that blends traditional law enforcement approaches and diplomatic expertise to develop innovative and flexible policy responses for conflict prevention, conflict resolution, and peacebuilding.

While resource control and interdiction regimes are both timely and warranted policy responses to the commercialization and criminalization of conflict, as Williams and Picarelli explain, they share the same inherent limitations as other policies that rely exclusively on "supply-side" controls. In Chapter 7, Stephen Jackson highlights another crucial shortcoming of supply-side controls: their unintended but often consequential negative impact on civilians. Drawing on empirical studies from the DRC, he demonstrates that violent economies based on resource predation not only generate substantive economic benefits for rebel groups, corrupt government elites, and shadowy business interests but often also provide critical sources of survival for the civilian population. Devising appropriate regulatory policies that tackle those engaged in armed conflict for profit and power but protect those forced to participate in violent economies to sustain their livelihood is a daunting task. Jackson employs livelihood analysis to develop a taxonomy of assets and actors in violent economies. As a methodological tool, he argues, livelihood analysis can help the international community to avoid the unintended negative humanitarian impacts of targeted commodity sanctions and interdiction efforts, as well as improve demobilization, disarmament, and reintegration (DDR) efforts as crucial preconditions for building lasting peace.

Improving Corporate Responsibility and Resource Revenue Management

Few governments in conflict-prone or war-torn states have the technical know-how, financial capital, or market access required to extract and process their natural resource endowments. Rather, they rely on multinational energy and mining companies that, often as joint-venture partners with host-state state-owned companies, are the main agents in the exploitation, trade, and transport of lucrative resources. Where these multinational companies operate in unstable or conflict-prone regions, they may knowingly or unknowingly contribute to or exacerbate armed conflict.[35]

The most commonly cited linkage between extractive industries and conflict involves the negative impacts that company operations can have on local communities in unstable countries. These may include environmental pollution and social impacts, such as the physical and labor displacement of local populations, as well as human rights abuses committed by security firms hired by companies or provided by repressive host governments to protect their plant and personnel.[36] A second linkage between companies and conflict is found in the financial deals concluded between extractive industry companies and repressive and unaccountable host governments. While some of these financial transactions involve the payment of bribes— illegal in most national jurisdictions—the majority, in the form of royalty payments, taxes, and signature bonuses, are legal, albeit morally questionable, payments that have only an indirect relationship with actual conflict dynamics.[37] However, the immense revenues generated from resource exploitation have at times been used by governments for self-enrichment or off-the-books military expenditures that finance counterinsurgency forces and oppression of opposition or minority groups.[38]

Paying attention to the problematic role of companies in conflict settings should not in any way excuse host governments from their responsibility to ensure the transparent, efficient, and equitable management of their country's natural resources and the adequate provision of public goods and services to their populations. Policy responses aiming to ensure that resources are a blessing rather than a curse to developing countries thus need to target the problematic behavior of both extractive industry companies and host governments, thereby addressing also the "demand side" of the equation. As the next chapters highlight, a range of policy responses from NGOs, governments, the financial markets, and aid agencies are exploring ways to adopt existing market and regulatory mechanisms to enhance the incentives for responsible resource management.

Extractive industry companies by definition are bound to operate in regions where oil, gas, and lucrative minerals are found. Often these are regions of the developing world that experience political instability or even active combat. Based on field research in numerous such settings, Luc Zandvliet in Chapter 8 argues that companies can have a positive or a negative impact on local conflict dynamics, but they are never neutral. Routine operations and even well-intentioned community development and social investment programs may inadvertently exacerbate existing tensions between the company and local communities and within communities, as well as between communities and the central government. Issues of contention include siting decisions, hiring and remuneration practices, and compensation payments that neglect the needs and traditional mores of local communities. In such contexts, the company can become the proxy target of local dissatisfaction and resentment, particularly when the affected population is already economically marginalized and politically disenfranchised. According to Zandvliet, a careful stakeholder analysis and adequate understanding of the various conflictual relationships is the prerequisite for devising appropriate company strategies that could improve interaction with local stakeholders and thereby earn companies a "social license to operate" that protects their host communities as well as their own bottom line.

To date, the role of financial actors and institutions in promoting and rewarding conflict-sensitive business practices has remained relatively undeveloped. However, there are a number of public and private financial actors and agencies whose financial leverage could be better applied to creating incentives for extractive industry companies to ensure that their operations do not contribute to armed conflict. As Mark Mansley explains in Chapter 9, for both commercial and ethical reasons a growing number of institutional investors (such as pension and mutual funds) and private commercial banks require extractive industry companies they do business with to operate in adherence to established environmental, labor, and human rights standards. The mechanisms that the private financial market employs to that end include avoidance of certain companies and industries; socially responsible investment (SRI); shareholder activism; corporate governance; reporting and disclosure requirements; and mandatory social and environmental impact assessments. Given the increasing financial, reputational, and legal liability risks for companies operating in conflict zones, the private financial market has started to realize the relevance of conflict-sensitive business practices, as reflected in their support of anticorruption initiatives, the Equator Principles for environmental and social impact assessments, resource revenue transparency, and conflict prevention more generally. If such measures are adequately encouraged by governments and nongovernmental organizations, argues Mansley, the heretofore limited influence that private financial actors have had in this area can become more decisive.

In addition to private financial markets, important leverage over extractive industry companies can be exerted by public export credit agencies (ECAs). These agencies provide companies with government-backed export credits, investment guarantees, and project financing—support that is often indispensable for foreign investments and operations in the extractive industries. As Nicholas Hildyard notes in Chapter 10, ECAs provide companies operating abroad with a financial safeguard against political risks, including those arising from armed conflict. Yet despite the disastrous socioeconomic and political impacts of many ECA-backed extractive industry projects in unstable countries, ECAs have been highly resistant to change. Indeed, both individually and within the OECD Export Credit Group, ECAs have been reluctant to incorporate environmental standards and performance obligations—to say nothing of human rights codes or conflict-impact assessments—into their lending and financing decisions. As Hildyard argues, because ECAs continue to see their mandate as promoting the international commercial competitiveness of domestic companies and not socioeconomic development or conflict prevention in the host country, if they are to begin to play a positive role in encouraging conflict-sensitive business practices among their clients, deep-rooted reform is essential.

The need for financial transparency in extractive industries as a precondition for conflict prevention has been championed by the Publish What You Pay (PWYP) campaign. Launched in 2002 by an international coalition of nongovernmental organizations, now numbering over 200, the campaign urges governments to make it mandatory for companies in the extractive industries to disclose the payments they make to host governments in the developing world. As Gavin Hayman and Corene Crossin argue in Chapter 11, reliable information about natural resource revenues would provide inroads for civil society and donor agencies to hold governments accountable for their use of these revenues. In advocating mandatory disclosure requirements, the PWYP campaign differs fundamentally from the open-ended, consensus-based approach chosen by the UK government-sponsored Extractive Industry Transparency Initiative (EITI), a diplomatic initiative that relies on voluntary company and government participation. Whatever approach ultimately takes root, it is clear that revenue transparency has to be part of a wider strategy of reform in the extractive industry sector. Here, Hayman and Crossin call for further policy action by key actors such as export credit agencies, regional organizations, and donor organizations such as the World Bank and the International Monetary Fund (IMF) to strengthen the promotion and implementation of revenue transparency.

The role of foreign development aid, and more specifically aid conditionality, in conflict prevention, resolution, and peacebuilding is the subject of Chapter 12 by James K. Boyce. Based on an examination of the cases of Angola, Cambodia, and Afghanistan, he demonstrates how "peace conditionality" by bilateral and multilateral donors may put pressure on combatants that benefit from war economies. Conditionality can be applied to create incentives for the transparent and equitable distribution of resource wealth, which in turn can help to ease social tensions and prevent violent conflict. Where neighboring regimes are involved in conflict trade, aid conditionality may be applied to them as a means of ending their complicit activities and depriving combatants of crucial finances. In postconflict settings, conditionality may support the crucial task of rebuilding transparent and effective state institutions (including those for resource management), help induce potential spoilers to cooperate with peace processes, and support alternative livelihood provisions for civilians and former combatants. As Boyce acknowledges, peace conditionality provides no panacea. In fact, the availability of large revenues in natural resource–rich countries can severely undermine donor leverage over governments. Where applied in a concerted manner and in coordination with other mechanisms described in this volume, however, conditionality attached to foreign aid is an important policy mechanism for managing the resource dimensions of armed conflict.

Establishing Accountability, Ending Impunity

Scholarly and policy attention to the political economy of armed conflict has led to a growing convergence among corporate social responsibility, human rights, and conflict-management agendas. Important policy developments in the field of corporate social responsibility (CSR) seek to incorporate conflict-sensitive business strategies into siting and investment decisionmaking, deter corporate complicity in human rights abuses, and foster a positive role for business actors in conflict prevention.[39] Similarly, academics and practitioners in the peace and security community have shown increasing concern over the role of companies in fueling violent conflict, based on NGO investigations that highlight intricate linkages between extractive companies and businessmen and the brutal civil wars in Angola, Sierra Leone, and the DRC.[40] The role of business activities in zones of conflict has raised a number of complex and still unanswered questions of whether, how, and by whom these activities should be regulated.

Those seeking to establish effective regulation where commerce and conflict intersect are faced with a diverse range of actors engaged in conflict zones, ranging from large multinational companies that—at least in theory—prefer stable business environments to less scrupulous "rogue companies" and middlemen (such as arms traders, diamond smugglers, and private security firms) that deliberately seek to profit by conducting the often illicit and always predatory business of war. Furthermore, there is disagreement among policymakers, legal experts, and activists as to what activities are in fact legal or illegal. While some activities are legal, others clearly violate national or international law. Many, however, remain in a regulatory gray zone. The lack of normative consensus on these issues continues to impede the development of coherent and effective policy and regulatory responses.

A growing number of company, industry, and public policy initiatives are seeking, however, to address the resource dimensions of conflict and the regulation of business actors in particular. The emerging policy discourse on regulatory options typically centers on the voluntary-versus-mandatory dichotomy, with companies, industry organizations, and home governments stressing the importance of voluntary self-regulation while NGOs, activists, and legal experts argue for mandatory rules and hard laws. Pointing to the limits of such a dichotomy, Leiv Lunde and Mark Taylor in Chapter 13 analyze what they conceive as a continuum of regulatory efforts, including company and industry voluntary self-regulation, voluntary multistakeholder initiatives, public-private partnerships, policy implementation obligations, conditionality, and national and international law. Lunde and Taylor note that policymakers seeking to develop regulation in this complex issue area are confronted with what they call a "malign problem structure." This is a policy problem characterized by a heterogeneous set of actors with strong—albeit varying—incentives to evade regulation, competing and ill-defined regulatory jurisdictions and normative frameworks, and an asymmetrical distribution of the costs and benefits of regulation. To overcome these regulatory and policy dilemmas, a concerted effort is required that utilizes the complementary strengths of the entire range of regulatory mechanisms currently on offer.

One such regulatory mechanism, the OECD *Guidelines for Multinational Enterprises,* attracted public scrutiny in October 2002, when the DRC expert panel's widely publicized final report to the Security Council listed eighty-five companies with operations in the DRC as having violated this little-known set of recommendations for responsible business conduct. As the ensuing controversy made clear, there was no consensus among the OECD governments and listed companies as to the specific nature of the alleged violations, nor even whether the OECD guidelines were applicable to conflict contexts. In Chapter 14, Patricia Feeney and Thomas Kenny provide a detailed assessment of the actual and potential applicability of the *Guidelines* to the specific case of company activities in conflict zones. While the *Guidelines* make no explicit mention of conflict situations, several existing provisions that address bribery, human rights, and environmental protection may warrant the *Guidelines'* applicability to conflict settings. Most important, the *Guidelines* include a complaint mechanism that requires member governments to investigate and seek to resolve specific instances of problematic business activity that are brought to their attention by NGOs, labor organizations, and others. Based on an assessment of two cases of company conduct in Burma/Myanmar and the DRC, Feeney and Kenny offer recommendations for strengthening the *Guidelines* so that they can serve as a more effective tool for ensuring responsible business conduct in conflict zones.

As important as industry self-regulation and voluntary codes of responsible business conduct have been in altering the corporate culture and operational practices of companies doing business in conflict zones, they have yet to make a decisive impact on the ground. In his 2002 report on the protection of civilians in armed conflict, Secretary-General Kofi Annan deplored the continuing state of affairs in which "individuals and companies take advantage of, maintain, and even initiate armed conflicts in order to plunder destabilized countries to enrich themselves, with devastating consequences for civilian populations."[41] Given the current inadequacy of policy and diplomatic means to effectively deter conflict-promoting economic activities, or reduce the prevailing impunity that surrounds them, efforts to wrestle with these challenges have thus increasingly looked to international norms of humanitarian and human rights law and domestic legal mechanisms as possible remedies.[42]

As numerous reports by UN expert panels and NGOs describe in detail, a large number of criminal networks, rogue companies, state-owned and state-protected enterprises, and shadowy brokers and middlemen routinely collaborate with rebel groups and government elites in many conflict theaters in the illicit exploitation of natural resources, often in violation of

UN sanctions regimes. And they do so with impunity. Against this background, Pierre Kopp in Chapter 15 analyzes whether and how UN sanctions regimes could be strengthened by focusing on the political economy of law and interdiction. Thus far, the implementation of sanctions regimes suffers from the unclear legal scope of the obligations that UN sanctions impose on member states. The criminalization of sanctions busting under national law would be an important step toward strengthening sanctions regimes. Doing so, however, would require a degree of political will and commitment among governments that has thus far been lacking. As Kopp also observes, efforts to curtail sanctions busting have been compounded by a certain reluctance of relevant governments, both in the North and the South, to enforce sanctions and to systematically follow up on the UN expert panels' recommendations. The difficulty of establishing an evidentiary trail for legal prosecution of even well-known sanctions busters is a continuing challenge, which allows shadowy businessmen such as Victor Bout and Leonid Minin, the notorious "merchants of death" named and shamed in several UN expert panel reports, to continue their nefarious dealings in a range of conflict theaters. In addition to domestic legislation, then, more robust sanctions enforcement will require greater cooperation between national law-enforcement and intelligence agencies.

In the absence of effective international regulation, one emerging avenue for holding business actors accountable for their conduct abroad is the use of domestic courts.[43] Indeed, an increasing number of civil and criminal lawsuits are being brought against companies, particularly large multinational extractive corporations, for alleged violations of human rights and the laws of war or for their complicity in such acts committed by host-country joint-venture partners or hired security firms.[44] As Paul Hoffman recounts in Chapter 16, the U.S. Alien Tort Claims Act (ATCA) of 1789 has become the unlikely, if controversial, remedy of choice for those seeking to hold companies accountable for their activities overseas. In several pending cases, courts have ruled in favor of alien plaintiffs' rights, under ATCA, to bring suit against companies in U.S. courts for alleged violations of "the laws of nations." While several jurisdictional hurdles remain, and while no company has yet been convicted under ATCA, the mere prospect of civil liability has put companies, private financial institutions, and host-state governments on alert. At the same time, ATCA's popularity among human rights lawyers and advocates may yet be its own undoing, as the U.S. administration and industry organizations may seek to reform or repeal ATCA for commercial and geopolitical reasons. Whether ATCA will survive this onslaught remains to be seen.

Clearly, as a U.S. civil law statute, ATCA is only one part of a larger body of international human rights and humanitarian law that may be used to promote accountability of commercial actors engaged in war economies. The potential of developing international mechanisms for this purpose was underscored in 2003, when the chief prosecutor of the International Criminal Court announced his intention to conduct investigations into financial activities as part of his larger investigation of war crimes and crimes against humanity committed during the conflict in eastern DRC.[45] According to William Schabas in Chapter 17, efforts to hold war entrepreneurs accountable under international humanitarian law are hampered by the inadequacies of current legal norms and mechanisms to address private-sector actors and crimes of an inherently economic nature. Some case law exists on corporate complicity in war crimes and crimes against humanity,[46] and indictments of the ad hoc tribunals for the former Yugoslavia and Sierra Leone incorporate the notion of "joint criminal enterprise"; both of these may establish important precedents for further legal action. Given the shortcomings of existing international criminal law, Schabas argues, a legal regime focused on corporate accountability and responsibility with civil or administrative consequences may be a more viable option at this point. As fact-finding bodies that can identify misdeeds and attribute responsibility, truth and reconciliation commissions may also be useful forums to address the role of companies in specific conflicts, even if no punishment or sanctions are attached. By contrast, the adoption of a new international instrument would first require broad intergovernmental agreement on the general principles applicable to commercial activity during armed conflict, a precondition that is unlikely to be satisfied in today's international political climate.

Toward Peace, Development, and Justice

The self-financing nature of many contemporary civil wars has drawn attention to the connections among trade in natural resources, global financial flows, and armed conflict. The contributions to this volume identify both the opportunities and the challenges that lie ahead for those seeking to devise adequate policy responses. From a political economy perspective, the key objective is to make peace more profitable than war. Several implications emerge for policy and practice, which our concluding chapter examines in more detail.

First, all chapters underscore the intricate linkages between local war economies and global markets for commodities, arms, and finance. The creation of robust international regulatory frameworks aimed at curtailing resource flows to combatants or ending impunity for entrepreneurs of violence is thus a necessary and significant means to contribute to conflict mitigation. Numerous relevant policy, regulatory, market-based, and legal frameworks exist that can and should be strengthened and adapted to contribute to improved conflict prevention, conflict resolution, and peacebuilding. Yet the authors in this volume caution that such global or regional regulatory mechanisms will be insufficient on their own. Even the most robust policies to curtail resources and finances to combatant parties and their criminal allies may produce diminishing returns as new illicit activities and networks and means to evade regulation develop. As long as the structural factors of underdevelopment, state weakness, and horizontal inequalities remain, international control and interdiction regimes will continue to treat the symptoms rather than the causes of conflict and the war economies fueling them.

These shortcomings point to a second finding discussed in several chapters. Few policy issues highlight more clearly the intersect between security and development than contemporary war economies based on resource predation, shadow trade, and economic criminality.[47] There is a need for development and trade agencies to address the structural causes of conflict and the determinants of war economies, including endemic corruption, socioeconomic inequality, and international trade and lending policies that, wittingly or not, may reinforce them.[48] Particular attention needs to be paid to creating more effective, transparent, and equitable resource management as an integral part of good governance programs for conflict prevention and postconflict peacebuilding. Aid programs may also better support alternative livelihood provision to conflict dependents and former combatants as part of DDR programs as well as efforts for drug eradication. Last, technical assistance and capacity-building efforts are also crucial for improved implementation of the various control regimes described above, including the administrative and regulatory provisions of the Kimberley Process, improved border control, and financial oversight in the banking sector, as well as law enforcement. In sum, then, just as efforts to prevent and resolve conflict need to be made more "development sensitive," so too does development policy need to be consciously "conflict sensitive." The synergy effects among aid, trade, and security policy in the context of war economies in particular need to be more systematically analyzed and addressed.

Third, the chapters in this volume demonstrate the potential of the growing, diverse set of regulatory mechanisms aimed at improving business behavior in zones of conflict and establishing accountability for their operations and financial transactions. For mutual efforts to achieve coherent and effective policy outcomes, however, there is a need for more careful consideration of the different, often unexamined priorities and objectives reflected in the parallel agendas of corporate social responsibility, human rights, and conflict management.[49] Not only are there differences between traditional CSR agendas and the agendas of conflict prevention and human rights, but there are also less apparent differences between the promotion of human rights and the promotion of peace. Simply put, the former seeks to end human rights abuses (which admittedly often go hand in hand with conflict), while the latter seeks to end conflict. Understanding these differences is essential to developing meaningful policy responses to business activities that affect conflict dynamics. Given the highly divergent set of business actors engaged in war economies and their differing amenability to regulation, policy efforts will need to make use of the full spectrum of regulation, from voluntary initiatives to international law.

Finally, one cannot overemphasize the centrality of the UN system, both as an actor and as a norm-setting forum, for a more concerted policy approach to address the economic dimensions of conflict. Through its renewed efforts to improve sanctions regimes and to sponsor open debates on the role of business in conflict prevention, the Security Council has set the stage for further policy development. Through its case-by-case decisions on sanctions and conflict diamonds, the Security Council has helped to promote new global norms and expectations for economic actors. As of yet, however, this firm recognition of the relevance of this issue to the maintenance of international peace and security has not coalesced into a comprehensive, UN-wide strategy for addressing the economic dimensions of armed conflict. Efforts by the Global Compact to promote conflict-sensitive business practices directly in the private sector need to be complemented by the work of other UN agencies. Most urgently, there is a need for UN peace and development missions to give priority to combating war economies and their legacies, including the continued availability of lucrative resources, economic criminality, and smuggling activities that strengthen peace spoilers while impeding civilian well-being.[50] The need for support to weak states in the management of their natural resources was recognized also by the UN High-level Panel on Threats, Challenges, and Change, which recommended that "the United Nations should work with national authorities, international financial institutions, civil society organizations and the private sector to develop norms governing the management of natural resources for countries emerging from or at risk of conflict."[51] Aware of these challenges and responsibilities, UN Secretary-General Kofi Annan in 2003 established an interagency working group on the political economy of armed conflict, charged with developing and mainstreaming such an analysis in the organization's mandate and operations. As the Secretary-General rightly stated, "The time has come to translate ad hoc efforts into a more systematic approach."[52] We hope that this volume will make a contribution to that end.

Notes

1. Mats Berdal and David M. Malone, eds., *Greed and Grievance: Economic Agendas in Civil Wars* (Boulder: Lynne Rienner, 2000); Karen Ballentine and Jake

Sherman, eds., *The Political Economy of Armed Conflict: Beyond Greed and Grievance* (Boulder: Lynne Rienner, 2003).

2. Karen Ballentine and Jake Sherman, introduction to Ballentine and Sherman, *Political Economy of Armed Conflict*, p. 1.

3. François Jean and Jean-Christophe Rufin, eds., *Economies des guerres civiles* (Paris: Hachette, 1996); Mark Duffield, "Globalization and War Economies: Promoting Order or the Return of History?" *Fletcher Forum of World Affairs* 23, no 2 (1999): 21–38.

4. Mary Kaldor, *New and Old Wars: Organized Violence in a Global Era* (Stanford: Stanford University Press, 1999); Mark Duffield, *Global Governance and the New Wars: The Merging of Development and Security* (London: Zed Books, 2001). For a critical assessment of the "new wars" paradigm, see Mats Berdal, "How 'New' Are 'New Wars'? Global Economic Change and the Study of Civil War," *Global Governance* 9, no. 4 (2003): 477–502.

5. Philippe Le Billon, "The Political Ecology of Transition in Cambodia, 1989–1999: War, Peace, and Forest Exploitation," *Development and Change* 31 (2000): 785–805.

6. Alfredo Rangel, "Parasites and Predators: Guerillas and the Insurrection Economy of Colombia," *Journal of International Affairs* 53, no. 2 (2000): 577–601; Nazih Richani, *Systems of Violence: The Political Economy of War and Peace in Colombia* (Albany: SUNY Press, 2002).

7. Stephen Ellis, *The Mask of Anarchy: The Roots of Liberia's War* (New York: New York University Press, 1999); John L. Hirsch, *Sierra Leone: Diamonds and the Struggle for Democracy* (Boulder: Lynne Rienner, 2001); David Keen, *The Best of Enemies: Conflict and Collusion in Sierra Leone* (London: James Curry, 2005).

8. Jakkie Cilliers and Christian Dietrich, eds., *Angola's War Economy: The Role of Oil and Diamonds* (Pretoria: Institute of Security Studies, 2000); Global Witness, *Same Old Story: A Background Study on Natural Resources in the DRC* (London: Global Witness, 2004); Koen Vlassenroot and Timothy Raeymaekers, *Conflict and Social Transformation in Eastern DR Congo* (Ghent: University of Gent, Conflict Research Group, 2004); Pole Institute and International Alert, *Natural Resource Exploitation and Human Security in the Democratic Republic of Congo* (London: International Alert, 2004).

9. Ian Gary and Terry Lynn Karl, "The Chad-Cameroon Oil Experiment: Rhetoric and Reality," in *Bottom of the Barrel: Africa's Oil Boom and the Poor* (New York: Catholic Relief Services, 2003), pp. 60–76.

10. United Nations, "Role of Business in Conflict Prevention, Peacekeeping, and Post-conflict Reconstruction," S/PV/4943, April 15, 2004.

11. Global Witness, *A Rough Trade: The Role of Companies and Governments in the Angolan Conflict* (London: Global Witness, 1998); Ian Smillie, Lansana Gberie, and Ralph Hazleton, *The Heart of the Matter: Sierra Leone, Diamonds, and Human Security* (Ottawa: Partnership Africa Canada, 2000).

12. J. Andrew Grant and Ian Taylor, "Global Governance and Conflict Diamonds: The Kimberley Process and the Quest for Clean Gems," *Round Table* 93, no. 375 (2004): 385–401; for more information, see www.kimberleyprocess.com.

13. Mats Berdal and David Keen, "Violence and Economic Agendas in Civil Wars: Some Policy Implications," *Millennium: Journal of International Studies* 26, no. 3 (1997); David Keen, *The Economic Functions of Violence in Civil Wars,* Adelphi Paper no. 320 (Oxford: IISS/Oxford University Press, 1998); William

Reno, *Corruption and State Politics in Sierra Leone* (Oxford: Cambridge University Press, 1995).

14. Michael L. Ross, "Does Oil Hinder Democracy?" *World Politics* 53, no. 3 (2001): 325–361; Carlos Leite and Jens Weidmann, *Does Mother Nature Corrupt? Natural Resources, Corruption, and Economic Growth,* IMF Working Paper no. 99/85 (Washington, D.C.: International Monetary Fund, July 1999); William Ascher, *Why Governments Waste Natural Resources: Policy Failures in Developing Countries* (Baltimore: Johns Hopkins University Press, 1999); William Reno, *Warlord Politics and the African State* (Boulder: Lynne Rienner, 1998).

15. Terry Lynn Karl, *The Paradox of Plenty: Oil Booms and Petro-states* (Berkeley: University of California Press, 1997); Leslie Gelb et al., *Oil Windfalls: Blessing or Curse?* (Washington, D.C.: World Bank, 1988); Michael L. Ross, "The Political Economy of the Resource Curse," *World Politics* 51, no 2 (1999): 297–322; Jeffrey D. Sachs and Andrew M. Warner, "The Curse of Natural Resources," *European Economic Review* 45 (2001): 827–838.

16. Paul Collier et al., *Breaking the Conflict Trap: Civil War and Development Policy* (Washington, D.C.: World Bank, 2003); Ian Gary and Terry Lynne Karl, *Bottom of the Barrel: Africa's Oil and the Poor* (Washington, D.C: Catholic Relief Services, 2003); Michael L. Ross, *Extractive Sectors and the Poor* (Washington, D.C.: Oxfam America, 2001).

17. Karen Ballentine, "Beyond Greed and Grievance: Reconsidering the Economic Dynamics of Armed Conflict," in Ballentine and Sherman, *Political Economy of Armed Conflict,* pp. 259–283 (see note 1 above).

18. Philippe Le Billon, "The Political Ecology of War: Natural Resources and Armed Conflict," *Political Geography* 10, no. 5 (2001): 561–584; Michael L. Ross, "Oil, Drugs, and Diamonds: The Varying Roles of Natural Resources in Civil War," in Ballentine and Sherman, *Political Economy of Armed Conflict,* pp. 47–70 (see note 1 above); Michael L. Ross, "How Does Natural Resource Wealth Influence Civil War? Evidence from 13 Cases," *International Organization* 58, no. 1 (2004): 35–67; Richard Snyder, "Does Lootable Wealth Breed Disorder? A Political Economy of Extraction Framework," www.santafe.edu/files/gems/obstaclestopeace/snyder.pdf.

19. George Downs and Stephen J. Stedman, "Evaluation Issues in Peace Implementation," in Stephen J. Stedman, Donald Rothchild, and Elizabeth M. Cousens, eds., *Ending Civil Wars: The Implementation of Peace Agreements* (Boulder: Lynne Rienner, 2003), pp. 43–69; Michael Doyle and Nicholas Sambanis, "International Peacebuilding: A Theoretical and Quantitative Analysis," *American Political Science Review* 94, no. 4 (2000): 779–801.

20. Barnett R. Rubin, Andrea Armstrong, and Gloria R. Ntegeye, eds., *Regional Conflict Formation in the Great Lakes Region of Africa: Structure, Dynamics, and Challenges for Policy* (New York: Center on International Cooperation, 2001); Michael Pugh and Neil Cooper, with Jonathan Goodhand, *War Economies in a Regional Context: Challenges of Transformation* (Boulder: Lynne Rienner, 2004).

21. Michael Klare, *Resource Wars: The New Landscape of Global Conflict* (New York: Metropolitan Books, 2001); Michael Renner, *The Anatomy of Resource Wars,* Worldwatch Paper no. 162 (Washington, D.C.: Worldwatch Institute, 2002); Jakkie Cilliers, "Resource Wars: A New Type of Insurgency," in Cilliers and Dietrich, *Angola's War Economy,* pp. 1–19.

22. Ballentine and Sherman, *Political Economy of Armed Conflict*; Barnett Rubin, "The Political Economy of War and Peace in Afghanistan." *World*

Development 28, no. 10 (2000): 1789–1803; Peter Andreas, "The Clandestine Political Economy of War and Peace in Bosnia," *International Studies Quarterly* 48 (2004): 29–51; Michael Pugh, "Postwar Political Economy in Bosnia and Herzegovina: The Spoils of Peace," *Global Governance* 8, no. 4 (2002): 467–482.

23. See Ballentine and Sherman, *Political Economy of Armed Conflict*; João Gomes Porto, "Contemporary Conflict Analysis in Perspective," in Jeremy Lind and Kathryn Sturman, eds., *Scarcity and Surfeit: The Ecology of African Conflicts* (Pretoria: Institute of Security Studies, 2002), pp. 1–49; Jeffrey Herbst, "Economic Incentives, Natural Resources, and Conflict in Africa," *Journal of African Economies* 9, no. 3 (2000): 270–294; Wayne E. Nafziger and Juha Auvinen, *Economic Development, Inequality, and War: Humanitarian Emergencies in Developing Countries* (Houndmills, UK: Palgrave Macmillan, 2003).

24. Charles Cater, "The Political Economy of Conflict and UN Intervention: Rethinking the Critical Cases of Africa," in Ballentine and Sherman, *Political Economy of Armed Conflict*, pp. 19–45 (see note 1 above); Christopher Cramer, "*Homo Economicus* Goes to War: Methodological Individualism, Rational Choice, and the Political Economy of War," *World Development* 30, no. 11 (2002): 1845–1864.

25. For reports and publications by the Economic Agendas in Civil War Program, see www.ipacademy.org. Follow-up works include David M. Malone and Heiko Nitzschke, "Economic Agendas in Civil War: What We Know, What We Need to Know," UNU-WIDER Discussion Paper, 2005; Karen Ballentine and Heiko Nitzschke, "The Political Economy of Civil War and Conflict Transformation," in Martina Fischer and Beatrix Schmelzle, eds., *Transforming War Economics: Strategies and Dilemmas,* Berghof Center Handbook for Conflict Transformation (Berlin: Berghof Research Center for Constructive Conflict Management, 2005); Heiko Nitschke and Kaysie Studdard, "The Legacies of War Economics: Challenges and Options for Peacekeeping and Peacebuilding," *International Peacekeeping* 12, no. 2 (2005): 1–18. Other influential research and policy development projects include the World Bank's Economies of Violence Project and the Fafo Institute's Economies of Conflict: Private Sector Activities and Armed Conflict. For publications, see Ian Bannon and Paul Collier, eds., *Natural Resources and Violent Conflict: Options and Actions* (Washington, D.C.: World Bank, 2003); Leiv Lunde and Mark Taylor, with Anne Huser, *Commerce or Crime? Regulating Economies of Conflict* (Oslo: Fafo Institute, 2003), at www.fafo. no/nsp/ecocon.htm.

26. Paul Collier and Anke Hoeffler, *Greed and Grievance in Civil War,* Policy Research Working Paper no. 2355 (Washington, D.C.: World Bank, 2001); Berdal and Malone, *Greed and Grievance.*

27. See Porto, "Contemporary Conflict Analysis"; Herbst, *Economic Incentives*; Ballentine and Sherman, *Political Economy of Armed Conflict*; Tony Addison and S. Mansoob Murshed, eds., *Explaining Violent Conflict: Going beyond Greed versus Grievance,* special issue of *Journal of International Development* 15, no. 4 (May 2003); Eboe Hutchful and Kwesi Aning, "The Political Economy of Conflict," in Adekeye Adebajo and Ismael Rashid, eds., *West Africa's Security Challenges: Building Peace in a Troubled Region* (Boulder: Lynne Rienner, 2004), pp. 195–222; Nicholas Sambanis, "A Review of Recent Advances and Future Directions in the Literature on Civil War," *Defense and Peace Economics* 13 (2002): 215–243. For critiques of the quantitative research, see Michael L. Ross, "What Do We Know about Natural Resources and Civil War?" *Journal of Peace Research,* 41, no. 3 (2004): 337–356. James D. Fearon, "Primary Commodities

Exports and Civil Wars," April 12, 2004, www.stanford.edu/~jfearon/papers/sxpfinal.pdf.

28. Neil Cooper, "State Collapse as Business: The Role of Conflict Trade and the Emerging Control Agenda." *Development and Change* 33, no. 5 (2002): 935–955; Jake Sherman, *Policies and Practices for Regulating Resource Flows to Armed Conflict,* IPA Conference Report, Bellagio, Italy, May 21–23, 2002 (New York: International Peace Academy, 2002); Emmanuel Kwesi Aning, "Regulating Illicit Trade in Natural Resources: The Role of Regional Actors in West Africa," *Review of African Political Economy* 30, no. 95 (2003): 99–107; Bannon and Collier, *Natural Resources and Violent Conflict.*

29. See Philippe Le Billon, Jake Sherman, and Marcia Hartwell, "Policies and Practices for Regulating Resource Flows to Armed Conflicts," background paper for International Peace Academy conference, Bellagio, Italy, May 21–23, 2002, at www.ipacademy.org (completed programs).

30. See, among others, United Nations, *Report of the Panel of Experts on Violations of Security Council Sanctions against UNITA,* S/2000/203, March 10, 2000; *Report of the Panel of Experts Appointed Pursuant to Security Council Resolution 1306 (2000), Paragraph 19, in Relation to Sierra Leone,* S/2000/1195, December 20, 2000; *Report on the Panel of Experts on the Illegal Exploitation of Resources and Other Forms of Wealth of the Democratic Republic of Congo,* S/2001/357, April 12, 2001, and S/2002/1146, October 16, 2002.

31. United Nations, "Role of Diamonds in Fuelling Conflict," Security Council Resolution 1385, S/RES/1385, December 19, 2001; UN Security Council Resolution 1459, S/RES/1459, January 28, 2003.

32. Robert I. Rotberg, ed., *State Failure and State Weakness in a Time of Terror* (Cambridge, Mass.: World Peace Foundation, 2003); European Security Strategy, *A Secure Europe in a Better World* (Brussels: December 12, 2003).

33. Amelia Hill, "Bin Laden's $20m African 'Blood Diamond' Deals," *Observer,* October 20, 2002; Global Witness, *For a Few Dollars More: How Al Qaida Moved into the Diamond Trade* (London: Global Witness, 2003); Douglas Farah, *Blood from Stones: The Secret Financial Network of Terror* (New York: Broadway Books, 2004).

34. Paul Collier, "Rebellion as a Quasi-criminal Activity," *Journal of Conflict Resolution* 44, no. 6 (2000): 839–853; Hirsch, *Sierra Leone*; Rangel, "Parasites and Predators." As Williams and Picarelli discuss, such conclusions are hotly contested. See also Francisco Gutiérrez Sanin, *Criminal Rebels? A Discussion of War and Criminality from the Colombian Experience,* Crisis States Programme Working Paper no. 27 (London: London School of Economies, 2003).

35. Jake Sherman, *Private Sector Actors in Zones of Conflict: Research Challenges and Policy Responses,* IPA Workshop Report (New York: International Peace Academy, 2001).

36. Scott Pegg, "The Cost of Doing Business: Transnational Corporations and Violence in Nigeria," *Security Dialogue* 30, no. 4 (1999): 473–484; Jason Switzer, *Armed Conflict and Natural Resources: The Case of the Minerals Sector* (Geneva: International Institute for Environment and Development, 2001); Amnesty International, *Making a Killing: The Diamond Trade in Government-Controlled DRC* (London: Amnesty International, 2002).

37. Global Witness, *All the President's Men: The Devastating Story of Oil and Banking in Angola's Privatized War* (London: Global Witness, 2002); Global Witness, *Time for Transparency: Coming Clean on Oil, Mining, and Gas Revenues* (Washington, D.C.: Global Witness, 2004).

38. Rights and Accountability in Development, *Unanswered Questions: Companies, Conflict, and the Democratic Republic of Congo* (Oxford: Rights and Accountability in Development, 2004); Human Rights Watch, *Some Transparency, No Accountability: The Use of Oil Revenue in Angola and Its Impact on Human Rights* (Washington, D.C.: Human Rights Watch, 2004).

39. Jane Nelson, *The Business of Peace: The Private Sector as a Partner in Conflict Prevention and Resolution* (London: Business Leader Forum, 2000); Juliette Bennett, "Multinational Corporations, Social Responsibility, and Conflict," *Journal of International Affairs* 55, no. 2 (2002): 393–410; Jessica Banfield, Virginia Haufler, and Damian Lilly, *Transnational Corporations in Conflict Prone Zones: Public Policy Responses and a Framework for Action* (London: International Alert, 2003); Andreas Wenger and Daniel Möckli, *Conflict Prevention: The Untapped Potential of the Business Sector* (Boulder: Lynne Rienner, 2003).

40. Virginia Haufler, *Is There a Role for Business in Conflict Management?* in Chester Crocker, Fen Osler Hampson, and Pamela Aall, eds., *Turbulent Peace: The Challenges of Managing International Conflict* (Washington, D.C.: U.S. Institute of Peace, 2001), pp. 659–676; Damian Lilly and Philippe Le Billon, *Regulating Business in Zones of Conflict: A Synthesis of Strategies* (London: Overseas Development Institute, 2002); Philippe Le Billon, "Thriving on War: The Angolan Conflict and Private Business," *Review of African Political Economy*, no. 90 (2001): 629–652; Timothy Raemakers and Jeroen Cuvalier, *Contributing to the War Economy in the DRC: European Companies and the Coltan Trade* (Brussels: International Peace Information Service, 2002); Arvind Ganesan and Alex Vines, *Engine of War: Resources, Greed, and the Predatory State* (Washington, D.C.: Human Rights Watch, 2004).

41. United Nations, "Report of the Secretary-General to the Security Council on the Protection of Civilians in Armed Conflict," S/2002/1300, November 26, 2002, p. 14.

42. International Peace Academy and Fafo Institute, *Business and International Crimes: Assessing the Liability of Business Entities for Grave Violations of International Law* (Oslo: Fafo Institute, 2005); Andrew Clapham, "The Question of Jurisdiction under International Criminal Law over Legal Persons: Lessons from the Rome Conference on an International Criminal Court," in Menno T. Kamminga and Saman Zia-Zarifi, eds., *Liability of Multinational Corporations under International Law* (The Hague: Kluwer Law International, 2000), pp. 139–195; William A. Schabas, "Enforcing International Humanitarian Law: Catching the Accomplices," *International Review of the Red Cross* 83, no. 439 (2001): 439–459; Tom Farer, "Shaping Agendas in Civil Wars: Can International Criminal Law Help?" in Berdal and Malone, *Greed and Grievance*, pp. 205–232 (see note 1 above).

43. Halina Ward, "Securing Transnational Corporate Accountability through National Courts: Implications and Policy Options," *Hastings International Law Review* 24, no. 3 (2001): 451–474.

44. Most of these cases are being brought in U.S. courts; a list of them is available at www.ccr-ny.org/v2/legal/corporate_accountability/corporate_accountability.asp. A more extensive catalogue of legal actions throughout the world is available at www.business-humanrights.org/Categories/Lawlawsuits/Legalaccountability.

45. Office of the Prosecutor of the ICC, press release no. pids.009.2003-EN, July 16, 2003, pp. 3–4.

46. Anita Ramasastry, "Corporate Complicity from Nuremberg to Rangoon: An Examination of Forced Labor Cases and Their Impact on the Liability of

Multinational Corporations," *Berkeley Journal of International Law* 20, no. 1 (2002): 91–150.

47. Duffield, *Global Governance and the New Wars,* and Jonathan Goodhand, "Enduring Disorder and Persistent Poverty: A Review of the Linkages Between War and Chronic Poverty," *World Development* 31, no. 3 (2003): 629–646.

48. Innovative research by the Overseas Development Institute, for instance, has contributed to a better understanding of war economies and the political economy of humanitarian aid. See Philippe Le Billon, *The Political Economy of War: What Relief Agencies Need to Know,* Humanitarian Policy Network Paper no. 33 (London: Overseas Development Institute, 2000); Sarah Collinson, ed., *Power, Livelihoods, and Conflict: Case Studies in Political Economy Analysis for Humanitarian Action,* Humanitarian Policy Group Report no. 13 (London: Overseas Development Institute, 2003).

49. Karen Ballentine and Heiko Nitzschke, "Business and Armed Conflict: An Assessment of Issues and Options," *Die Friedens-Warte, Journal of International Peace and Organization* 79, nos. 1–2 (2004): 35–56.

50. Heiko Nitzschke, *Transforming War Economies: Challenges for Peacemaking and Peacebuilding,* Report of the 725th Wilton Park Conference in association with the International Peace Academy, October 27–29, 2003 (New York: International Peace Academy, 2003); Nitzschke and Studdard, *The Legacies of War Economies.*

51. United Nations, "A More Secure World: Our Shared Responsibility," Report of the High-level Panel on Threats, Challenges, and Change (New York: United Nations, 2004), p. 35.

52. United Nations, "Role of Business," p. 4.

2

Natural Resources and Armed Conflicts: Issues and Options

Macartan Humphreys

Most contemporary studies of international conflict, and many models of intrastate warfare, rely on a traditional image of a conflict as a contest between two well-defined, exogenous, and internally homogeneous sides. Whatever its value for the study of international disputes—where rally-round-the-flag effects often appear to quell disagreements within nations—this approach is inadequate for describing many contemporary civil wars, particularly those centered on natural resource wealth.[1] In particular, the failure to recognize the diversity of actors and incentives results in an overly narrow consideration of the options available to policymakers.

Research since the 1990s suggests that the presence of natural resources can have unifying or fragmenting effects on political allegiances and military structures, depending on the motivations of fighters and the types of resources.[2] This work has pushed researchers to look more carefully at how groups are constituted, what motivates them, and how these factors affect the onset, duration, and intensity of conflicts. This new work draws attention to a dizzying array of actors—government and rebel fighting units, themselves often fractured into multiple competing factions that fight against or alongside mercenary units, civil defense militias, government-sponsored paramilitary organizations, international peacekeepers (sometimes with agendas of their own), spillover factions from neighboring states, and criminal networks eager to get in on the action.[3] Through their role in funding conflicts, other international actors are implicated. Foreign sources of funding include sponsorship by foreign governments and corporations, remittances from emigrant populations, the capture of international aid and relief, and financing provided by transnational organized criminal groups.[4] Most prominently, international actors are implicated by the part they play in trade that finances the various parties to a conflict. While contemporary conflicts cannot be explained by "globalization," it is nonetheless the case that the density of international economic exchange has resulted in a wide set of global actors that are implicated in domestic conflicts.[5]

Alongside a recognition of the multiplicity of groups and the diversity of their interests comes a greater recognition that belligerents are economic as well as political actors. They are motivated in part by their economic conditions, the economic structures that shape their views, and the economic alternatives available to them.[6] Economic structures affect the degree to which governments engage with their population, the attitudes of citizens toward their state, the groups with which individuals identify themselves, and the ability of states to resolve disputes, either peaceably or through force. The choices fighters make during conflict are determined in part by the economic costs and benefits associated with different strategy options and by the structures of rewards and incentives in the group within which they fight.[7] Economic structures affect the aims of groups: in some cases, patterns of fighting suggest that groups collude to perpetuate conflict in order to allow for local monopolies on extraction, production, and trade.[8] Economic interests also affect the *levels* of violence employed against civilians.[9]

So too, economic costs and benefits shape incentives for peacemaking: the attractiveness of peace depends, in part, on the economic conditions that fighters enjoy during conflicts and the economic pressures that can be brought to bear on them to bring conflicts to an end. Ending conflict also depends on the economic provisions of settlements—on provisions for continued control over "conflict commodities" and for jobs and training—and on expectations of future punishment for economic activities undertaken during conflict.

Such a diversity of actors and incentives suggests that there are many points of entry for policy to alter the linkages between exploitation and trade in natural resources and armed conflict. In order to better identify policy opportunities, this chapter describes five modalities through which natural resources are linked with conflict. These include *rent seeking,* or the political impact of the availability of large natural resource rents to ruling elites, often referred to as the "resource curse"; *grievances,* primarily associated with the (mal)distribution of natural resource wealth and project-related impacts on local communities; *economic instability,* accruing from the distortions associated with a country's high dependence on natural resources; *conflict financing,* or the channels through which access to natural resource wealth affects the means for belligerents to continue fighting; and, related to this, *peace spoiling,* by which natural resource wealth alters the incentives for peace.[10] In describing each modality, I highlight the policy challenges involved and propose possible policy responses and mechanisms—many of which are addressed in subsequent chapters of this volume. The diversity of these modalities demonstrates that the problem of managing the security implications of economic activity is not limited to the international politics of interrupting illicit commodity trades and breaking up transnational criminal networks but also to the more mundane tasks of promoting conflict-sensitive business practices among multinationals and helping governments to manage large annual variations in resource revenues and to facilitate balanced growth in resource-dependent economies.

Natural Resources, Rent Seeking, and Conflict Risk

The existence of natural resource wealth results in the availability of rents that can be easily monopolized by national elites. This can lead to three distinct types of conflict risk.

First, concentrated resource wealth may induce rebels to use violence to gain control over the state in order to capture these rents. Arguably in Sierra Leone, the Republic of Congo, and Angola, the availability of natural resource rents in the form of income from diamonds and oil worsened conflict risk by increasing the "prize" value of capturing the state.[11] According to several accounts, the desire to control oil rents in Chad led to the assassination of President Ngarta Tombalbaye in 1975, the rise of Hissène Habré in the 1980s, and the coup against him by President Idress Deby in 1990—all of which occurred long before any oil was actually pumped.[12]

Second, even if elites do not monopolize rents, their usage of natural resource wealth may readily be perceived as corrupt. Natural resource wealth is commonly viewed as "unearned" and particularly easy to embezzle, especially where associated transactions are not conducted with transparency. For these reasons, and because populations often lack adequate information on how much revenue is generated from natural resources, natural resource income is commonly, and popularly, associated with corruption. The problems commonly associated with perceptions of corruption can be compounded in the case of natural resource extraction, when losers interpret the actions of elites as a sell-off of national patrimony. Widespread suspicion of corruption provides would-be rebels and coup makers with the legitimacy required to undertake actions against the state.[13]

Third, and paradoxically, states that have access to large sources of income from external sources often have weak governance structures.[14] When states rely on income taxation or corporate taxation for their revenues, they are compelled to respond to the demands of their citizens and to create institutions that engage their citizens. However, when they come to rely almost exclusively on "unearned income" such as revenues from natural resources, they may fail to develop these stronger institutional structures and, as a result, become more exposed to citizen alienation and even violent protest.[15] In extreme cases, such as Zaire (now the Democratic Republic of Congo) and Sierra Leone, reliance on these external sources of revenue likely accelerated state collapse.[16] Against this background, various policy options for managing the resource curse suggest themselves.

Transparency Initiatives by Governments and Corporations

Several initiatives have been developed to increase the transparency associated with payments from extractive industry corporations to governments in developing and conflict-prone countries. Leading initiatives include the Publish What You Pay campaign, promoted by Global Witness and the Open Society Institute, which lobbies for greater transparency in reporting "who gets what" from natural resource wealth.[17] More transparent budgetary processes would allow populations to see that political leaders do not receive private benefits from being in government and can reduce the financial incentives to take up arms to control the state. Such transparency removes the legitimacy of would-be coup makers by giving governments the ability to demonstrate that business dealings in the natural resource sector are in fact straight. Policy mechanisms to provide greater financial transparency are being designed and promoted, notably through the Extractive Industries Transparency Initiative initiated by the government of the United Kingdom in 2002. These mechanisms are beginning to be tested. The June 2004 Abuja Joint Declaration by the governments of Nigeria and São Tomé and Príncipe, for example, is a departure from common practice with a declaration of their willingness to publish production sharing contracts as well as all revenues received from oil corporations.[18] To date, however, this sort of transparency remains rare. Even in the case of the World Bank–sponsored Chad-Cameroon pipeline project, often described as a model of socially responsible revenue management, the details of the deal struck between the governments of Chad and Cameroon and the oil consortium are not publicly available.[19]

There is formidable opposition to transparency initiatives among host governments and corporations. A core aim in the discussion of improved practices of transparency should thus be to determine under what circumstances nondisclosure agreements work to their advantage or disadvantage. Certainly, as evidenced by Angola's draft oil legislation of August 2004, states are often eager to maintain secrecy.[20] And corporations can argue that they cannot effectively promote transparency if host governments are against it. So, alongside lobbying to promote transparency, a better understanding of why some states oppose transparency measures will likely help the development of strategies for greater openness in the industry. Hiding corrupt practices is one obvious motivation, but others may be as important. Plausibly, the revelation of poorly bargained deals in the past may weaken the hand of domestic negotiators in future rounds. However, the logic could work in the opposite direction: in sufficiently competitive markets, information on older profitable deals won by corporations could increase interest in future deals, to the benefit of oil-producing states.

Oversight Institutions

Another approach to greater transparency in the extractive industries is to improve institutions of financial oversight. This can be done by using citizen advisory councils, as recommended, for example, by the Open Society Institute[21] and as instituted in Chad as part of the World Bank–supported revenue management program. There are several open questions as to how such advisory councils should be designed and, indeed, whether they should be used at all. Important design questions include (1) how to determine council membership in such a way that the composition is genuinely representative of the population, (2) whether these councils should include international representatives as members, and (3) how the councils can be assured the political independence needed to take governments to task for inappropriate revenue management. Perhaps the most important design question concerns the powers that such institutions should have: whether they should be able to block budgetary processes *ex ante* or refer abuses to courts *ex post* and whether their mandate extends to the review of procedural or substantive issues. In assessing the utility of supplemental oversight bodies, a core consideration is whether they risk undermining normal institutions of governance by fulfilling functions normally undertaken by parliaments and courts.

Strengthening Interdependencies
Between States and Citizens

A third way of undercutting the pernicious effects of rent seeking is to strengthen the linkages between states and their citizens. One approach is to increase the level of popular involvement in financial and development planning. This could involve strengthening oversight of government planning through parliamentary commissions, public hearings, or national conferences. In general, a way of reaching consensus regarding the use of natural resource revenues is to tie natural resource expenditure to longer-term development planning, linking it with national poverty reduction strategies or with national strategies to achieve the UN Millennium Development Goals. The concept of citizen advisory councils, discussed above, can also be broadened, for example, by making budgets subject to referendum or by structuring electoral competition more explicitly around expenditure plans.

A second approach focuses on policies that help to diversify the state's revenue base. Prohibiting the use of resource revenues to fund particular government functions, such as defense, could provide incentives for states to maintain targets for income or commodity taxation, rather than relying exclusively on resource rents. To further reduce the incentives to rely on resource rents, donor governments could place restrictions on natural resource–backed loans by prohibiting liens or encumbrances on the use of future natural resource revenues. A final possibility for achieving a similar goal through nondistortionary taxation is to convert rents into income tax by distributing all natural resource revenue directly to citizens and then reclaiming a share of distributed revenues in tax.[22]

Direct Distribution of Resource Revenues

A new approach to managing resource wealth is to allow natural resource revenues to bypass government altogether. One approach is to distribute revenues directly to citizens, as has been done in Alaska in the form of the Alaska Permanent Fund.[23] This approach has political and economic implications. It reduces the "prize" value of the state, making it less attractive for violent capture or corrupt rent seeking. In principle, direct distribution could also help strengthen state institutions, as government revenues would depend on developing efficient tax-collection systems. The risk, however, is that if these tax alternatives are not available, direct distribution could result in starving well-intentioned states of resources that they could use to build their governance capacity.

Aside from the question of whether the approach actually strengthens government institutions, there is the difficult question of economic efficiency: in what circumstances will private expenditure decisions be more efficient than public ones? The choice of policy will likely depend on the extent to which governments are capable of managing revenues well. Xavier Sala-i-Martin and Arvind Subramanian suggest that in the case of Nigeria, whatever the difficulties associated with the distribution process itself, direct distribution would certainly lead to more efficient expenditure than that presently undertaken by the central government. It is likely, however, that the states that would benefit most from this option—those that are least likely to spend resource wealth well—are also the ones least likely to redistribute wealth widely.[24]

Grievances: (Mal)Distribution of Natural Resource Wealth and Disruptive Social Impacts

There are many ways that a country's natural resource wealth can induce political grievances that may ultimately turn violent. First, distribution of natural resource wealth is more likely to be perceived as unjust in those areas closest to the resource deposits, where populations are most directly affected. In Nigeria, for example, to legitimate their increasingly violent political struggles, communities in the oil-producing regions have pointed to the unjust distribution of revenues from resources exported from their regions. In Niger, insurgent groups in the north protested that the south benefited disproportionately from revenues gained from the uranium wealth generated in the north. In some cases, such as in Casamance (Senegal), Bougainville (Papua New Guinea), and southern Sudan, arguments about inequitable distribution of resource wealth may reinforce existing ethnic or communal secessionist movements.

Second, the extraction of natural resources can spark new grievances in producing regions due to perceived inequity in the distribution of extraction and transport-related jobs. Grievances may also arise from the production process itself, if it leads to forced migrations from a producing region or new inflows of migrants into the region. Where left unattended, such grievances can produce violence after operations start, as was the case, for example, in West Papua.[25]

Third, grievances also may be provoked by the ways that security is provided to extractive operations on the ground. These operations, typically situated in remote areas, are often highly vulnerable targets of insurgent attack or criminal theft. In the Niger Delta, as much as 10 percent of all oil production disappears due to theft of oil from pipelines.[26] In some cases, such as Sierra Leone, responses to such concerns have included the use by both extractive companies and governments of unaccountable security forces, some of which have been implicated in assaults on civilian communities, forced labor, and other human rights abuses. There are a number of policy options to help reduce such resource-related grievances. While these may be employed individually, a coordinated, multifaceted approach is likely to have greater positive impact.

Consultations

Too often decisions about natural resource operations remain the prerogative of companies and their partners in host governments, regardless of their broader societal impacts. An obvious way of reducing resource-related grievances is to strengthen the consultative processes whereby populations are involved in deciding whether and how resources are to be extracted, how revenues are to be spent, and what institutions should oversee the use of resource revenues. Here there are a variety of options available to governments and companies alike.

In Bolivia, a referendum was held to determine how to manage the country's natural gas resources. This produced a limited form of national deliberation: the referendum itself consisted of five relatively complex questions, and many saw it as a vote of confidence in the government. Despite divisions in the run-up to the referendum, this approach appears to have brought political calm to the issue of resource management.[27] São Tomé and Príncipe has undertaken a much deeper consultative process. In the summer of 2004, a national forum was held to discuss the economic future of the country. The forum involved printing up bulletins for every household with details of the government budget process, the structure of the oil industry, and the likely size and impacts of oil revenues. Then small meetings, open to all, were held throughout the country, at which community groups discussed expenditure priorities and appointed representatives to voice their position at the national level. These approaches are just being tested, and what is needed now is an evaluation of the extent to which sharing the problems of natural resource management broadly in fact reduces suspicions and frustrations.

For extractive industry companies, introducing routine consultations with local communities can help them to better anticipate and manage the risks associated with their day-to-day operations. These consultations can take the form of periodic informal meetings with local populations or more formal stakeholder arrangements that involve local populations in routine monitoring of company performance. In both instances, such engagement can, in principle, reduce mutual distrust, identify potential conflict points, and provide a channel by which local concerns can be effectively communicated. To date, however, there is a dearth of reliable evidence as to what sort of company engagement works and what does not. While some companies have undertaken selected case studies that have yielded some promising ideas, more systematic comparative study is needed to determine when and how these consultations produce the desired effects.[28]

Earmarking Revenues for Resource-Producing Regions

A second approach is to ensure a fairer distribution of revenues to the areas whose populations are most likely to feel aggrieved—the producing areas. The government of Chad, for example, has earmarked 4.5 percent of dividends and royalties from annual oil production for "decentralized communities" within the oil-producing region. Although it is still early to say how well this will work, there are deep suspicions in the south that these funds will not reach the official targets. Indeed, the fears are that these benefits will pass to northerners moving to the south, will be substituted for other funds, or may not be spent at all; after all, the law allocating the funds, passed in 1999, can be modified by decree every five years.[29] Nonetheless, if these transfers are made, and made visibly, they would likely go some way toward countering complaints that the oil industry is based on the theft of southern resources by the northern government.

Besides being used to alter perceptions, earmarking can be used to alter incentives. An initiative in Sierra Leone is striking in this regard: in the diamond-rich Kono area, once a hotspot in the Sierra Leone war, the Diamond Area Community Development Fund has been established to earmark official diamond revenues for producing areas. The aim is to encourage local opposition to illegal mining by giving residents a stake in the legal diamond industry.[30]

"Do No Harm": Reforming Corporate Practices

There is a fairly broad consensus that corporations working in natural resource–producing areas should observe high standards for the respect of human rights, environmental protection, and respectful treatment of local populations. There is less consensus, however, about what exactly these standards should be and how they should be enforced. A large array of guidelines exist, including the Global Compact's Ten Principles, the OECD *Guidelines for Multinational Enterprises,* the Extractive Industries Transparency Initiative Statement of Principles and Agreed Actions, and the United Nations Sub-commission on Human Rights' draft "Norms on the Responsibilities of Transnational Corporations and Other Business Enterprises with Regard to Human Rights." In addition, the Voluntary Principles on Security and Human Rights have been developed by the U.S. and UK governments, several companies, and nongovernmental organizations, specifically to address problems arising in the course of providing security to operations and personnel. The principles are a voluntary code of conduct by corporate and government actors to ensure that the security forces they hire conduct themselves responsibly.

These voluntary guidelines and principles carry no legal weight and typically are not accompanied by enforcement mechanisms.[31] A core question, then, is what impact, if any, these guidelines have had. There are possible positive learning effects, to be sure, but there are also causes for concern. The fact that adherence to these guidelines is voluntary may mean that the companies most likely to sign on would be those least likely to violate the principles in the first instance. Furthermore, to the extent that compliance reduces the competitiveness of firms, the net result may be an increase in market share to firms that do not aim to comply. Even among those that do join, in the absence of enforcement, companies can reap reputational benefit by claiming to comply with guidelines without, in fact, altering their practices.

A second approach to corporate reform is the use of more robust regulation by the corporations' home countries in order to govern activities by corporations in host countries. This is the principle behind the U.S. Foreign Corrupt Practices Act (1977), the OECD's Convention on Combating Bribery of Foreign Public Officials in International Business Transactions

(1997), and, more recently, the UK's Anti-terrorism, Crime, and Security Act (2001, section 109). It is also the impetus that is driving recent plaintiff litigation against corporate misconduct in the developing world under the U.S. Alien Tort Claims Act.[32]

The two approaches are not in principle mutually exclusive. One advantage of the binding regulation over the voluntary initiatives is that, as it can be undertaken by states unilaterally, it can be done more speedily. For the same reason, however, it has a limited effect on corporations based in states that have less activist public oversight of corporate behavior. Again, this could work to increase the market share of companies less concerned about corporate social responsibility, including conflict mitigation and human rights protection. In principle, this problem could be resolved through universal adoption of norms, accompanied by international institutions of enforcement, but the development of the needed international consensus in support of such institutions will be a slow and complicated process.

The question, then, is how best to combine the regulatory strength of the first approach with the multilateral reach of the other. Some answers to this question may follow from an analysis of the Kimberley Process, discussed below, which succeeds in combining a voluntary framework with regulatory reform in participating states.

"Do Good"

While "doing no harm" should be an evident priority for companies engaged in extractive industries, large-scale resource extraction projects offer numerous opportunities for corporations to actually improve the standards of living of citizens in producing regions, and more broadly. The oil consortium in Chad, it seems, missed an opportunity to greatly improve relations with local communities when it did not move to support the development of the energy sector in Chad. With enormous technical skills compared to those of the host country, the consortium quickly built electric generation capacity of 120 megawatts for its own needs—a capacity more than five times Chad's total capacity at the time.[33] A requirement that such infrastructure projects also take place in and for the benefit of producing regions may reduce real and perceived inequities. The fear, however, is that social projects may not achieve their aims: they may open up possibilities for local rent seeking and may not necessarily benefit all sides equitably, thereby creating secondary sources of protest.

The question, then, is whether and how corporations can use such projects to better develop their relations with local communities to the real economic and security benefit of the latter. As in the case of community consultations discussed above, the answer to this question can best be found, not by firms' writing up select case studies of success stories, but by their partnering with research groups to engage in systematic comparative research in order to identify the relative efficacy of different types of interventions.

Resource Dependence and Economic Instability

Beyond the perverse incentives it creates for individual and corporate behavior, natural resource abundance, and particularly a country's dependence on resource exports, can have broad implications for the structure of national economies. First, changes in the value of natural resources can weaken the manufacturing sector of an economy—an effect sometimes referred to as "Dutch Disease." If the manufacturing sector is itself more intensive in internal trade, then the collapse of manufacturing may prevent the economy from benefiting from the conflict-mitigating effects of trade.[34] Second, economies that are dependent on natural resources may be more vulnerable to terms of trade shocks. These could cause instability and dissatisfaction within groups that suffer from the shocks. Unless citizens understand the source of these shocks, instability and political dissatisfaction within groups that suffer can lead to high levels of dissatisfaction with, and even violent opposition to, government. In both cases, effective policy responses will require the generation of longer-term development plans and revenue management strategies that aim to mitigate these security risks.

Policies to Reduce the Impact of Price Fluctuations

Natural resource funds (such as oil funds) can be used to stabilize national natural resource income. If annual budget financing is based on the interest on accumulated savings, rather than on the revenue earnings of a given year, then annual variations in finances injected into the economy will be largely independent of year-to-year changes in commodity prices and production. Even if the share of annual revenues to be injected into the economy depends in part on estimates of the present value of future commodity earnings, these can be calculated by using moving averages of prices in order to reduce the impact of year-to-year price fluctuations. Beyond the stabilization of actual injections, steps can be taken to manage expectations. Notably, the measures that promote transparency, as described above, have the benefit of allowing citizens to identify the international sources of (and to allocate blame for) income variation.

Policies to Ease Sectoral Reallocations of Labor

There are predictable effects of new finds of natural resources on sectoral labor allocations. If resources are extracted, natural resource booms will pull labor into the extractive sector itself, or into sectors that service it. In Chad, for example, the development of the Doba oil fields was associated with an influx of migrants from the north to the south. Even if the extraction process is conducted in an enclave, Dutch Disease effects can lead to labor flows from traditional export sectors to the nontradable sectors—or to new spin-off growth sectors. This can lead to frustrations in traditional export sectors as producers see incomes collapse, to clashes in producing regions as new migrants enter, and to new inequalities as some groups benefit more easily from new wealth opportunities than others.

Responses to these problems include retraining to facilitate movements to new sectors, particularly among disadvantaged groups, and allocating a share of revenue earnings for credit for start-up companies or for communities wishing to undertake individual projects. Such policies will likely involve economic inefficiencies. A basic policy question, then, is how to determine when conflict risks are such that these inefficiencies are worth accepting.

Economic Diversification

Each of these problems is likely to be reduced by policies that promote greater diversification of exports. The key problem, however, is that economies that are rich in natural resource exports will, by virtue of that fact, not have a strong comparative advantage in other economic sectors, such as manufacturing. Contrary to the prevailing prescriptions of international financial institutions, diversification will likely require that countries *not* follow their comparative advantage. This, in turn, will likely require greater government involvement in the design of economic structures, possibly through the use of tax incentives or the establishment of free zones. An obvious strategy for governments seeking to reduce natural resource dependence is to link the extraction of resources to the development of associated industries—for example, developing shipping services in countries with offshore oil, promoting diamond-cutting and -polishing industries in diamond-producing countries, and constructing oil refineries in oil-rich states. In some instances, firms involved in the extraction of natural resources have considerable expertise in related industrial sectors; in these cases, host countries could include projects designed to tap this expertise and to diversify domestic economic structures, as a part of their negotiations with extractive industries.

Conflict Financing:
Natural Resource Wealth and War Making

Even if conflicts are started for other reasons, access to natural resource financing can sustain them. Financing keeps combatants alive and fighting, even in the absence of significant military victories by either side. The problem of protracted conflict may be particularly severe when both sides benefit from resources. The duration of the Angola conflict, for example, can be explained in part by the fact that both sides had access to natural resource financing to support their combatants.[35] For this reason, much energy, in both the research and policy communities, has focused on ways to cut financing to belligerents once a conflict begins. Several policy options exist.

Sanctions

To date sanctions have proved to be a blunt weapon of policy, with most attempts at coercion through sanctions ending in failure.[36] If armed groups finance their activity through trading in illegal commodities such as drugs or smuggling commodities such as arms or rough diamonds illegally, the existence of sanctions is likely to be irrelevant. There are several political economy reasons that sanctions may fail.[37] The ability to transship through neighboring states can severely reduce the impact of sanctions. Leaders can also turn sanctions to their advantage, both economically and politically, by maintaining control over increasingly scarce commodities. Hence, even when sanctions have real impacts, it is not just the intended targets that suffer.[38]

Sanctions policies have become more sophisticated, with the development of targeted commodity sanctions and with the freezing of assets or blocking particular individuals' freedom of movement.[39] However, because of their lack of comprehensiveness, targeted sanctions may lead to the exemption of particular commodities through successful lobbying by industries with economic interests in those commodities. Needed, then, is a reexamination of ways to improve the use of sanctions, taking account of these political economy aspects.

Certification Regimes

A second approach targets commodities more than the individuals that control their flows. In some cases, such as efforts to curtail the trade in illicit commodities like narcotics, the implementation problems are old ones. A more recent challenge has been to devise methods to regulate illicit trade in *legal* commodities that can fuel conflicts. The commodity trade for which the greatest advances have been made is the trade in diamonds, particularly through the Kimberley Process Certification Scheme. The Kimberley Process uses a certification scheme to regulate the international trade in rough diamonds, aimed at separating "conflict diamonds" from "prosperity diamonds." The process is a good example of a voluntary mechanism that works. Unlike the Global Compact, for example, participants in the Kimberley Process include states and regional economic integration organizations as well as companies and encompass key exporting, refining, and importing countries. They are relatively few in number and are focused on a well-defined issue area of broad common interest. The process is multilateral but makes use of the domestic institutional strength of its members: one innovation of the Kimberley Process is its requirement that participating states pass legislation to ensure that diamond shipments are free of conflict diamonds. The process has demonstrated a commitment to ensuring that the scheme is not abused by participants hoping to whitewash practices taking place in their countries: following evidence of the Republic of Congo's failure to enforce the provisions of the process, it was ejected from the process in 2004. Despite ongoing concerns about weaknesses in monitoring and enforcement mechanisms, the Kimberley scheme has created an inclusive international regime for the certification of rough diamonds. It has also opened the prospect that the model can be extended to other conflict commodities.

Punishment

While sanctions target belligerents during the course of a conflict, tools also exist to punish economic actors after a conflict ends. Special courts have been established for holding actors accountable for their roles in violent conflict and egregious human rights abuse in Rwanda, Yugoslavia, and Sierra Leone. But, as yet, indictments have not been directed at actors for their commercial activities. Even in Sierra Leone, where the prosecutor of the Special Court has interpreted the war as being driven by greed and where his role has been to indict "those that bear the greatest responsibility" for war crimes, "economic crimes" have not resulted in indictments. The prosecutor of the International Criminal Court has also indicated willingness to investigate business entities that fuel conflicts and has begun his first investigations in Ituri in the Democratic Republic of Congo, stating that investigating "the financial aspects of the atrocities allegedly committed in Ituri will be crucial to prevent future crimes."[40]

Key questions in this regard are whether *ex post* punishment is sufficient to serve as a deterrent in these contexts and how the existence of *ex post* punishments can be balanced with the need to provide belligerents with the economic and political security they need to bring conflicts to a close.

Peace Spoiling: The Impact of Natural Resource Wealth on Incentives for Peace

Conflicts are likely to endure if belligerents gain more during conflict than they would in times of peace.[41] One reason why parties to a conflict may not agree to peace arrangements—even those that leave everyone better off—is that wartime provides them opportunities to engage in activities that they would not be able to undertake during peacetime, either because the activities are illegal[42] or because a party's dominance in the industry depends on its ability to use violence. For natural resource–fueled conflicts, approaches to help bring such peace spoilers to the negotiation table include the following.

Ad Hoc Training and Investment

Providing alternative inducements for would-be spoilers and establishing bases for alternative livelihoods can make peace more attractive. Where conflicts were driven in part by natural resource predation, there may be especially strong arguments for the expansion of the public sector in order to provide alternative employment opportunities, even if such expansions otherwise entail efficiency costs. This may require timely aid increases in tandem with peace negotiations. Such strategies are being attempted with United Nations–led disarmament, demobilization, and reintegration (DDR) programs, such as those in Sierra Leone, Liberia, and Haiti. Such programs can be expected to be particularly important in areas experiencing resource conflicts. Survey results indicate, for example, that fighters in Sierra Leone saw the provision of training and job creation as among the most important items of peace negotiations and an important incentive for laying down arms. However, while most were happy with the training supplied by the UN, few have been successful in integrating into the work force. Unemployment has been the greatest source of frustration for these ex-fighters,[43] and, by some accounts, limited employment opportunities and possibilities of advancement for ex-combatants may yet undermine the security of the country.[44] As one ex-fighter put it, "DDR should keep to their promise if they don't want more problems in the country. The bad thing is, if there is a re-occurrence of war, you will find it very difficult to disarm the combatants because they will think that they are lying to them the second time."[45]

Integrating Development Planning and Conflict Resolution

Alternative livelihoods are a precondition for peace for many fighters, but the investments that are needed to create these livelihoods are unlikely to flow into conflict and postconflict settings because of the uncertainty and risks involved. One way out of this dilemma is to encourage and coordinate the participation of the private sector and development planners in peace processes. Doing so can increase the information that economic actors need in order to encourage investments that can support and enhance the viability of a peace agreement. Such a process may also serve to reassure belligerents that alternative economic futures are possible.

In all cases, providing material incentives for belligerents to resolve conflicts carries two concerns—one normative, one positive. The normative concern is that, in practice, such policies may be viewed as rewarding criminals, particularly where the greatest rewards are directed to the worst perpetrators of violence and associated human rights violations. The positive concern—which has not been well examined in empirical academic work— is that the strategy may induce "moral hazard," the risk that expectations of future rewards for demobilizing may perversely encourage participation in future conflicts.

Conclusion

In this overview I have identified many policy options available to governments, corporations, and the international community more broadly. These options involve ways of cutting finances, managing expenditures, and distributing income with a view to breaking the major linkages between natural resource wealth and conflict. The options are promising, but many come with costs. The task undertaken in the subsequent chapters of this volume is to evaluate the multiple options, argue ways in which they may be improved, and identify which options are appropriate in what contexts.

Let me close with a caution. In discussing the policy options available for outside actors to intervene in order to prevent or resolve violent conflicts, I have set aside the normative implications of these options. Alongside a discussion of *how* to intervene to produce sustainable peace, there is a need for a treatment of *when* to intervene and *whom* to support. In practice, different policy options will typically have asymmetric effects on different parties to a conflict: advocating policies that target particular forms of commodity financing and financial flows means taking sides, depending on who is benefiting from the commodities at any particular point. Yet the arguments for favoring one side over the other are rarely articulated.[46] Indeed, much of the policy discussion of the financing of civil wars is often grounded in an assumption that lucrative natural resource sectors function to the benefit of rebels only. In response, policy responses tend to focus on ways of cutting these finances. But the latent assumption that the rebels are the—or the only —"bad guys" sidesteps the thornier question of the legitimacy of armed struggle. This assumption poses three problems. First and most evident, in some instances the judgment may not be normatively consistent: a default position of opposing rebels may in fact serve simply to strengthen abusive states against populations with few options to express their grievances. Second, the likelihood of a military victory will depend not simply on the level of economic assets available to rebels but on the relative strength of the fighting groups. If rebel groups have the upper hand, then reducing their resources may make a decisive victory less likely.[47] Third, *perceptions* of the legitimacy of a struggle have pragmatic as well as moral implications. In particular, in cases where there is local support for the actions of rebel groups, as with Chechen rebels, the Viet Cong, and the Irish Republican Army, and where people with regular employment can serve as "part-time guerillas," rebellion may be cheap. Purely financial responses to conflict in such cases are likely to be inadequate.

The appropriate response to managing the resource dimensions of armed conflict will therefore depend on which side those undertaking intervention want to win or whom they want to benefit from a negotiated settlement. This is a political, not a technical, question. Successful policy coordination based on answers to the question requires the development of criteria to establish the neutrality of intervention or the development of criteria for choosing which side, if any, "we" hope will win. The current international norm is to support governments over rebels, no matter how abusive the former. But, as was made obvious by the 2003 U.S.-led invasion of Iraq, while there is sometimes a powerful constituency supporting forced regime change, there is no international normative or practical consensus guiding when and how such regime change is appropriate.

Notes

1. Mary Kaldor, *New and Old Wars: Organized Violence in a Global Era* (Cambridge, UK: Polity Press, 1999).

2. See Philippe Le Billon, "The Political Ecology of War: Natural Resources and Armed Conflict," *Political Geography* 20 (2001): 561–584; Michael L. Ross, "How Do Natural Resources Influence Civil War? Evidence from Thirteen Cases," *International Organization* 58, no. 1 (2004): 35–67.

3. François Jean and Jean Christophe Rufin, *Économie des guerres civiles* (Paris: Hachette, 1996); Kaldor, *New and Old Wars*; David Keen, "Incentives and Disincentives for Violence," in Mats Berdal and David M. Malone, eds., *Greed and Grievance: Economic Agendas in Civil Wars* (Boulder: Lynne Rienner, 2000), pp. 19–41; Karen Ballentine and Jake Sherman, eds., *The Political Economy of Armed Conflict: Beyond Greed and Grievance* (Boulder: Lynne Rienner, 2003).

4. John Arquilla and David Ronfeldt, *Networks and Netwars: The Future of Terror, Crime, and Militancy* (Santa Monica, Calif.: RAND Corporation, 2001).

5. Mark Duffield, *Global Governance and the New Wars: The Merging of Security and Development* (London: Zed Books, 2001).

6. David Keen, *The Economic Functions of Violence in Civil Wars*, Adelphi Paper no. 320 (Oxford: Oxford University Press, International Institute of Strategic Studies, 1998).

7. See, for example, Macartan Humphreys and Jeremy M. Weinstein. "Handling and Manhandling Civilians in Civil War," paper presented at the 100th meeting of the American Political Science Association, September 2004.

8. William Reno, *War, Debt, and the Role of Pretending in Uganda's International Relations*, Occasional Paper (Copenhagen: Center for African Studies, University of Copenhagen, 2000); Musifiky Mwanasali, "The View from Below," in Berdal and Malone, *Greed and Grievance*, pp. 137–153.

9. Jeremy M. Weinstein, "Resources and the Information Problem in Rebel Recruitment," unpubl., Center for Global Development (CGD), Stanford University, 2004, available at https://upload.mcgill.ca/rgchr/weinstein.pdf; Humphreys and Weinstein, "Handling and Manhandling Civilians."

10. Many of these linkages have been discussed elsewhere. See Le Billon, "Political Ecology of War"; Ross, "How Does Natural Resource Wealth Influence War?" and Macartan Humphreys, "Natural Resources, Conflict, and Conflict Resolution," working paper, Columbia University, New York, 2004.

11. James D. Fearon and David Laitin, "Ethnicity, Insurgency, and Civil War," *American Political Science Review* 97, no. 1 (2003): 75–91.

12. For more details and references, see François-Xavier Verschave, *Noir Silence* (Paris: Éditions des Arènes, 2000); Humphreys, "Natural Resources, Conflict, and Conflict Resolution."

13. Philippe Le Billon, "Buying Peace or Fuelling War: The Role of Corruption in Armed Conflicts," *Journal of International Development* 15, no. 4 (2003): 413–426.

14. There is an extensive literature on this aspect of the resource curse. See Michael Ross, "The Political Economy of the Resource Curse," *World Politics* 51, no. 2 (1999): 297–322. For a treatment of the case of oil, see Terry Lynn Karl, *The Paradox of Plenty: Oil Booms and Petro-States* (Berkeley: University of California Press, 1997).

15. See, for example, Mick Moore, "Political Underdevelopment," paper presented at the 10th Anniversary Conference of the Development Studies Institute, London School of Economics, September 7–8, 2000.

16. See, for example, William Reno, *Corruption and State Politics in Sierra Leone* (Cambridge: Cambridge University Press, 1995).

17. See Chapter 11 by Gavin Hayman and Corene Crossin.

18. IRIN News Services, "Obasanjo, Menezes Sign Pact to Publish Joint Oil Accounts," June 28, 2004.

19. Estimates of earnings by the governments for particular oil prices and quantities produced are available in documents made public by the World Bank at www.worldbank.org/afr/ccproj/project/pro_document.htm, but the formulas for calculating these earnings are not publicly available.

20. Republic of Angola, "Projecto de Lei Reguladora das Actividades Petroliferas," draft law, August 2004.

21. Svetlana Tsalik, *Caspian Oil Windfalls: Who Will Benefit?* (New York: Open Society Institute, 2003).

22. Martin E. Sandbu, "Taxable Resource Revenue Distributions: A Proposal for Alleviating the Natural Resource Curse," Center on Globalization and

Sustainable Development (CGSD) Working Paper no. 21 (New York: Columbia University, 2004).

23. Tsalik, *Caspian Oil Windfalls,* pp. 19–25.

24. Xavier Sala-i-Martin and Arvind Subramanian, "Addressing the Natural Resource Curse: An Illustration from Nigeria," Working Paper no. 9804 (Cambridge, Mass.: National Bureau of Economic Research, 2003).

25. Michael L. Ross, "Oil, Drugs, and Diamonds: The Varying Role of Natural Resources in Civil War," in Karen Ballentine and Jake Sherman, eds., *The Political Economy of Armed Conflict: Beyond Greed and Grievance* (Boulder: Lynne Rienner, 2003), pp. 47–72.

26. "Dynamics of Violence in the Niger Delta," BICC Project Brief (Bonn: Bonn International Center on Conversion, 2004).

27. Juan Forero, "After Years of Growth, Bolivia's Gas Industry Faces Hurdles," *New York Times,* July 29, 2004.

28. There is much scope, however, for firms and governments to partner with researchers to undertake randomized interventions in order to achieve more reliable findings. See, for example, Donald Rubin, "Estimating Causal Effects in Randomized and Non-randomized Experiments," *Journal of Educational Psychology* 66 (1974): 683–704; and Ann Oakley, Vicki Strange, Tami Toroyan, Meg Wiggins, Ian Roberts, and Judith Stephenson, "Using Random Allocation to Evaluate Social Interventions: Three Recent U.K. Examples," *Annals of the American Academy of Political and Social Science* 589, no. 1 (2003): 170–189.

29. Interviews with community leaders in southern Chad, April 2003.

30. See, for example, Search for Common Ground, "Encouraging Transparency: Diamond Area Community Development Fund," www.sfcg.org/programmes/sierra/sierra_encouraging.html (accessed September 20, 2004).

31. For further discussion of the limits of voluntary codes, see Chapter 11 by Gavin Hayman and Corene Crossin, Chapter 13 by Leiv Lunde and Mark Taylor, and Chapter 14 by Patricia Feeney and Tom Kenny. In response to corporate pressure, the Global Compact has taken a step that reduces incentives for compliance by helping to ensure that corporations that take part are protected from lawsuits should their practices be construed as failing to live up to the principles of the compact. "Bluewashed and Boilerplated," *Economist,* June 19, 2004.

32. See Chapter 16 by Paul Hoffman.

33. I thank Vijay Modi at Columbia University's School of Engineering for pointing this out to me. See also IRIN News Services, "Chad: Plenty of Oil to Export, but No Electricity," October 28, 2003.

34. This effect takes its name from the impact of the Netherlands' oil discoveries on the Dutch manufacturing sector. It occurs because a rise in the value of exportable natural resources may result in an expansion of that sector and of sectors that are not traded (such as construction) and in a corresponding contraction of the export-oriented manufacturing sector.

35. Philippe Le Billon, "Angola's Political Economy of War: The Role of Oil and Diamonds, 1975–2000," *African Affairs* 100 (2001): 55–80.

36. Hufbauer, Schott, and Elliot find that most uses of sanctions between World War I and 1990 were failures: Gary C. Hufbauer, Jeffrey J. Schott, and Kimberley Ann Elliot, *Economic Sanctions Reconsidered: History and Current Policy,* 2nd ed. (Washington, D.C.: Institute for International Economics, 1990). See also Andrew Mack and A. Khan, "The Efficacy of UN Sanctions," *Security Dialogue* 31, no. 2 (2000): 279–292.

37. See Chapter 15 by Pierre Kopp.

38. Thomas Weiss, "Sanctions as a Foreign Policy Tool: Weighing Humanitarian Impulses," *Journal of Peace Research* 36, no. 5 (September, 1999): 499–510; Mack and Khan, "Efficacy of UN Sanctions."

39. Development of these new "smart" sanctions has been promoted by the Swiss government through the Interlaken Process, which focused on financial sanctions; by the German government, whose project focused on arms embargoes and travel bans; and by the Swedish government's Stockholm Process on Strengthening the Implementation of UN Sanctions. See www.smartsanctions.se.

40. IRIN News Services, "DRC: International Criminal Court Launches First Investigation," July 28, 2004.

41. See Keen, "Incentives and Disincentives for Violence."

42. James Fearon, "Why Do Some Civil Wars Last So Much Longer Than Others?" working paper, Stanford University, 2002.

43. Macartan Humphreys and Jeremy Weinstein, "What the Fighters Say. A Survey of Ex-combatants in Sierra Leone, June–August 2003," CGSD Working Paper no. 20, Columbia University (New York), 2004.

44. Paul Richards, Steven Archibald, Khadija Bah, and James Vincent, "Where Have All the Young People Gone?" unpubl., November 2003.

45. Humphreys and Weinstein, "What the Fighters Say."

46. Jeffrey Herbst is a notable exception. See his "Economic Incentives, Natural Resources, and Conflict in Africa," *Journal of African Economies* 9, no. 3 (2000): 270–294.

47. For a fuller discussion of this point, see Ross, "Oil, Drugs, and Diamonds."

PART 1

Curtailing Conflict Trade and Finance

3

What Lessons from the Kimberley Process Certification Scheme?

Ian Smillie

On January 1, 2003, the Kimberley Process Certification Scheme (KPCS), an international certification system for rough diamonds, came into effect. It represents the first such system to deal in a detailed and, for its members, binding manner with a commodity that has been directly and heavily involved in fueling armed conflict. The purpose of the agreement, which grew from a campaign by several nongovernmental organizations (NGOs) and a three-year series of joint government, industry, and NGO meetings, now known as the Kimberley Process, was to halt the traffic in "conflict diamonds"—a multimillion-dollar trade in African diamonds used by rebel armies to pay for weapons and prosecute war.

The KPCS effectively covers the entire chain of production of the majority of the world's diamonds. It includes the largest diamond producers—Botswana, South Africa, Russia, Namibia, Canada, Australia—and the smallest. It includes countries where the primary diamond business is sorting and transshipment, such as Belgium and Switzerland, and countries where the primary business is cutting and polishing; nine diamonds out of every ten are turned from their rough state into polished gems in Israel, China, and India. The KPCS also includes countries where the primary interest in diamonds is the retail trade, such as Japan and the United States. And most important, it includes the three countries ravaged by wars paid for with diamonds—Angola, Sierra Leone, and the Democratic Republic of Congo (DRC).

Drawing on the example set by the Kimberley Process, a small academic and policy-oriented industry has begun to examine this promising yet unfinished and untested scheme, looking for lessons on the feasibility of certification regimes for other "conflict commodities," such as timber,

47

coltan, and oil. In December 2002, for example, shortly before the Kimberley scheme came into effect, the British NGO Global Witness presented a paper on commodity-tracking systems at a World Bank–sponsored workshop on the governance of natural resource revenues. Drawing lessons from the success or failure of a dozen different certification efforts, among them the Kimberley Process, Global Witness posited ten elements of a good, generic commodity-specific tracking regime.[1] In terms of the content of such a regime, five elements are considered necessary:

- *Common definitions and reporting requirements.* All participants must be on the same wavelength in order to ensure coordinated action and a basis for tracking and subsequent monitoring for compliance.
- *An effective reporting structure and an effective exchange of information.* Good national data must be rolled into a harmonized international database that is accessible to all participants.
- *Adequate commodity labeling and auditable chains of custody.*
- *Effective compliance and enforcement measures.* These include national and international monitoring and penalties aimed at promoting compliance.
- *A strategy for capacity building.* This should be aimed at assisting national authorities in states with weak infrastructures and/or different levels of responsibility.

In addition, Global Witness suggested five contextual elements to consider in the design of a commodity-specific tracking regime:

- *Specificity.* Each commodity will have unique characteristics in terms of its extraction, processing, transportation, and sale. Each commodity agreement is therefore likely to have different characteristics in this regard.
- *Supply dynamics.* The dynamics of supply will differ from country to country. Applicable legislation, land tenure, labor codes, costs, and the economics of legal versus illegal access will all play a role.
- *Demand dynamics.* The nature of the market will play a key role in the shape of a certification system. Its dispersion or concentration and the elasticity of demand will affect the nature of a potential certification system.
- *Political and institutional context.* An effective agreement needs to consider the political, economic, and social circumstances of the countries that will be party to an agreement. A commodity may represent 90 percent of the foreign exchange earnings of a producer country but a fraction of gross domestic product in a processing

country. The political and economic imperatives for effective tracking in such diversity will be very different.
* *Harmonization with existing law.* Any new control systems must
take into account existing national laws and regulations as well as
international agreements such as those by the World Trade
Organization (WTO).[2]

This chapter begins with a brief account of how "conflict diamonds"
became an issue on the international policy agenda and sketches the evolution of the Kimberley Process. The next section draws preliminary lessons
from the Kimberley agreement. Based on parallels with the campaign to
ban land mines, the focus will be on the more important and more immediate lessons learned from the Kimberley Process that concern the *motivation*
of participants to join it and with the *process* of reaching an eventual agreement. With reference to the elements of effective certification schemes
posited by Global Witness, the final section considers a few lessons from
the Kimberley Process that might be of use in dealing with other conflict
commodities.

Conflict Diamonds and the Kimberley Process

Setting the Agenda

The issue of conflict diamonds was first brought to the world's attention in
1998 by the advocacy efforts and research of Global Witness, which
demonstrated conclusively the connection between diamonds and war in
Angola; its findings were subsequently published in a report titled *A Rough
Trade*.[3] The National Union for the Total Independence of Angola
(UNITA), a rebel movement that had long before lost any moral or political
justification for its twenty-year war effort, including the Cold War rationale
needed for its U.S. backing, was funded almost exclusively through the sale
of rough diamonds. Global Witness reported that between 1992 and 1998,
UNITA controlled between 60 and 70 percent of Angola's diamond production, generating $3.7 billion to pay for its war effort.[4] Half a million
Angolans died in the civil war, while many more were displaced, their lives
ruined.

In June 1998 the UN Security Council expanded its existing sanctions
regime against UNITA to include a ban on any Angolan diamond imports
not accompanied by a certificate of origin issued by the Angolan government.[5] In May 1999, reacting in part to the apparent ineffectiveness of the
sanctions and to the Global Witness report, the Security Council Sanctions
Committee on Angola, chaired by Canada's UN ambassador, Robert Fowler,

fielded an expert panel to assess the effectiveness of the sanctions regime. Based on the investigations conducted by the expert panel, the Angola Sanctions Committee presented the Security Council with its final report—later known as the Fowler Report—in March 2000. Borrowing a practice used by advocacy NGOs, the report "named and shamed" not only companies and weapons dealers but also sitting heads of state—the presidents of Togo and Burkina Faso—as "sanctions busters" for their continued involvement in the trafficking of both diamonds and weapons.[6] In UN history, this step was unprecedented and caused some irritation among member states. However, it was to become the model for ensuing expert panel reports.

The Angola expert panel's report to the Security Council had been preceded by a parallel NGO report on the role of diamonds in fueling the civil war in Sierra Leone. In January 2000, Partnership Africa Canada released *The Heart of the Matter: Sierra Leone, Diamonds, and Human Security,* which detailed how Sierra Leone's Revolutionary United Front (RUF) was financing its armed campaign largely through the smuggling of diamonds to neighboring Liberia.[7] Charles Taylor, the Liberian warlord-turned-president who had financed the early stages of his own fight for power by smuggling Liberian timber through the port of Buchanan, backed the fledgling RUF, giving it a Liberian base, weapons, and—most important—an outlet for diamonds captured in Sierra Leone. The RUF trademark was grisly: its members chopped off the hands and feet of civilians, often small children. As a terror technique, this was extremely effective in clearing the country's alluvial diamond fields of local populations and artisanal miners, ensuring that the RUF and Taylor had effective control over a highly rewarding source of income to continue their fight.

The Heart of the Matter traced Sierra Leone's diamond industry from its decline into systemic corruption in the 1970s through 1999, by which time formal diamond mining had come to an almost complete halt. By then, there were few government-supervised diamond exports.[8] Across the border in Liberia, however, diamond exports were thriving. Between 1994 and 1999, more than $2 billion worth of diamonds were imported into Belgium from Liberia, although Liberia has almost no diamond production of its own. At the very best of times, legitimate diamond exports never surpassed $10 million a year.[9] Partnership Africa Canada's report exposed a diamond fraud of massive proportions. It accused the international diamond industry at large of complicity, and Belgian authorities in particular of closing their eyes to massive corruption, in part to protect Belgium's important diamond trade in Antwerp, already vulnerable to increasing competition from Israel and India. Following the example of sanctions in Angola, in July 2000 the UN Security Council passed Resolution 1306, banning the trade of any Sierra Leone rough diamonds not accompanied by a government-issued certificate of origin.[10]

The problems were not limited to Angola and Sierra Leone. Under President Mobutu Sese Seko, formal diamond production in Zaire, now the Democratic Republic of Congo (DRC), fell from 18 million carats in 1961 to one-third of that volume by the 1990s.[11] But informal production continued at high levels, controlled in large part by Mobutu and his cronies for their personal benefit. Miners, middlemen, and *diamantaires* devised a simple way to avoid Mobutu's rapacious appetite. They simply smuggled their product across the river to Brazzaville, the capital of the neighboring Republic of Congo. The ups and downs of Belgian diamond imports from Brazzaville are in fact a relatively good barometer of war and corruption in the DRC. In 1997, when the DRC was undergoing the chaotic transfer of power from Mobutu to Laurent Desiré Kabila, Belgium imported $454.6 million worth of diamonds from Brazzaville.[12] By 1999, however, when things had settled down and it looked as though Kabila might actually represent a new wind sweeping away the corruption and cronyism of the past, these numbers decreased to $14.4 million, with a parallel growth in imports from the DRC. By 2000, however, the new government was reverting to type, and the volume from Brazzaville soared to $116.6 million, almost doubling again in 2001 to $223.8 million.[13] The human cost of this level of corruption and of the war, funded largely by looted resources, that followed Kabila's takeover, was enormous. Following a nationwide mortality study, the New York–based International Rescue Committee estimated that between 1998 and 2002, 3.3 million more people had died than would have been the case had the war not occurred.[14]

The stories of these conflicts give a sense of the magnitude of the human cost of conflict diamonds and of why the motivation of various actors to do something about the problem was so strong. In all, some 3–4 million people died during the 1990s as a result of wars fueled in part, or in whole, by the illicit trade in diamonds. Tens of millions of people were displaced, and the economies of entire countries collapsed. The civil war in Sierra Leone destabilized the entire region, and the aftershocks are still being felt as far away as Côte d'Ivoire.[15] While the conflict in the DRC has formally ended, the peace is a fragile one, and the war will have ongoing repercussions that could last a generation.

At the same time, these conflicts also revealed how a largely unregulated global diamond industry had become badly infected by criminal behavior. Creating an effective control system would not be easy. As defined both by the UN and in the Kimberley Process, conflict diamonds are "rough diamonds used by rebel movements or their allies to finance conflict aimed at undermining legitimate governments."[16] In fact, however, they are only a subset of "illicit diamonds" stolen from mines and used to launder money or evade taxes. In recent years, illicit diamonds have represented an estimated 20 percent of the $7 billion annual trade in rough diamonds.[17]

Because channels with lengthy pedigrees for laundering and selling these stones already existed, rebel armies had no difficulty in moving captured diamonds to world markets and in generating steady revenues to finance their military campaigns.

The Kimberley Process

The Kimberley Process began early in 2000, when South Africa's minister for mines and energy affairs, Phumzile Mlambo-Ngcuka, took up the reports on conflict diamonds by Global Witness and Partnership Africa Canada. The issue had caught fire in South Africa, with De Beers chairman Nicky Oppenheimer and others condemning nonexistent NGO boycotts and lashing out at the growing number of media articles on the subject. In May 2000, Mlambo-Ngcuka called a meeting of interested parties to discuss the issue. Held in the old South African diamond-mining town of Kimberley, the meeting brought together for the first time diamond industry officials, senior government officials of a dozen countries, and NGO advocates. The meeting was more than a little inconclusive, save for the fact that governments and industry leaders now realized that the issue would not disappear of its own accord. A follow-up "working group" meeting was organized a month later in Luanda, Angola. Somewhat surprisingly, the final recommendations of this meeting outlined all of the elements that would be contained in the final agreement, ratified at the twelfth Kimberley Process meeting some twenty-nine months later:

- the creation of a new global system that would prohibit, worldwide, the importation of rough diamonds unless accompanied by a "forgery-proof certificate of legitimacy and/or origin"
- expulsion from the trade of anyone found to be dealing in conflict diamonds, with adequate provisions for punishment and forfeiture of the goods in question
- the creation by the diamond industry of a "chain of warranties"
- engagement on the issue by the United Nations, the Group of Eight (G8), the World Trade Organization, and relevant diamond industry meetings in order to promote the scheme's "earliest possible adoption and implementation"[18]

The Luanda meeting also called for "a centralized and standardized data base, incorporating information from producer countries . . . on diamond production, exports and imports, evaluating any substantial discrepancy in these figures and any reports of violations within the system, and exposing violators." It called for "transparency, disclosure, and oversight of all diamond operations," although it stopped short of saying precisely who might do this or what it might mean.[19]

At this stage in the process, the South African government envisaged a ministerial meeting to be held in Pretoria in September 2000, at which a full-fledged scheme would be ratified and implemented. Although the meeting did take place, it ratified nothing. Two more years of negotiations and ten more meetings would be required to get the Kimberley Process to adopt a final agreement, which it did at a ministerial meeting in Interlaken, Switzerland, in November 2002.

In essence, the Kimberley Process Certification Scheme, as it came into effect on January 1, 2003, rests on three core provisions:

- The governments of diamond-producing countries will guarantee that stones leaving their borders do not originate from rebel-controlled areas and will issue a tamper-proof certificate to this effect. This means that each country will create a "chain of custody" arrangement so that it can trace diamonds from the mine to the point of export.
- All rough diamonds moving between countries will be accompanied by a government certificate. Diamonds arriving at any customs posts around the world without such a certificate will be seized, with penalties meted out to the importer.
- The governments of countries that import rough diamonds will establish a system to track them until they reach a cutting and polishing factory or until they are reexported. This tracking system, which will be based on an industry-managed "chain of warranties" arrangement in some countries, will allow governments to certify that diamonds being reexported are not "conflict diamonds." This third stage is essential because many countries import and reexport rough diamonds and it is in these centers that some of the most flagrant laundering of conflict diamonds has taken place.

Preliminary Lessons from the Kimberley Process

The specific *content* of a successful commodity tracking system is undoubtedly important for its ultimate effectiveness. Given the youth of the KPCS, however, few definitive lessons can be drawn at this point as to its effectiveness in halting the flow in conflict diamonds or its relevance for other commodity-tracking regimes. The following sections will thus focus on the *motivation* for and the *process* of reaching the agreement. These factors, it is argued, are more important considerations in drawing lessons from the Kimberley Process at this stage in its evolution and may provide useful lessons for other efforts to establish certification regimes, discussed in the concluding section of this chapter.

But first, it is worth taking a brief detour to examine the process that led to another international monitoring arrangement, the 1997 international convention to ban land mines.[20] Despite differences in content, type of regulation, and key stakeholders, the anti–land mine campaign, like the Kimberley Process, had to deal with a complex and sensitive issue, involved governments and NGOs working together rather than as antagonists, and appeared to reach international consensus in a relatively short space of time.

The 1997 Agreement to Ban Land Mines

In 1992, several NGOs began to discuss the need to coordinate the many existing initiatives aimed at banning antipersonnel land mines. The following year they formalized the International Campaign to Ban Land Mines (ICBL). The ICBL defined itself as a flexible network of organizations that shared common objectives, calling for an international ban on the use, production, stockpiling, and transfer of antipersonnel land mines, increased international resources for humanitarian mine clearance, and the creation of a mine victim assistance program. In 1993 a campaign steering committee was established and dozens of new national campaigns were formed, with hundreds of organizations joining. In October 1996, Canadian foreign minister Lloyd Axworthy addressed an Ottawa strategy conference on land mines and proposed something dramatic and unexpected: he called on all the nations of the world to negotiate a treaty to ban land mines and asked them to return to Ottawa in fourteen months to sign it. That it actually happened is no small miracle—not least because the protagonists were charting completely new waters in reaching an international agreement. According to some participants, there were several reasons for the campaign's success:

- A wide range of diplomatic, public, political, and technological tools were used to generate public awareness and political will.
- There was an open-ended, dynamic, and continually expanding community of self-selected, like-minded states.
- There was an "intimate" partnership among governments, international organizations, and NGOs.
- A credible political process and a negotiating forum were established where discussions could take place.
- The legitimacy and credibility of the final instrument were ensured by its placement within a UN context for long-term custodianship.[21]

Essentially, the campaign followed a conscious two-track approach. On the one hand, a massive public campaign was undertaken, mainly by the growing number of NGO participants, to create public support and political will by framing the threat posed by antipersonnel mines not as a weapons issue but as a humanitarian issue. The shift was important, because it down-played complex political factors and explained the issue in terms more readily understood by the public and the media. On the other hand, a formal negotiating process was established to create a forum where an agreement could be debated and concluded. More than a dozen meetings were hosted by as many governments, in Asia, Africa, Europe, Australia, and Canada.

Motivation

The most important factor in the Kimberley Process was, and remains, the motivation of the various actors to start or join a negotiating process and sustain it over a period of two and a half years. Without strong motivation, key players will be missing from such a process or will take a halfhearted or even negative approach.

For the early participants, and many of those who joined the negotia-tions as they developed, the motivations were a mix of commercial and rep-utational interests and genuine humanitarian concern. This was evident even among some industry actors. Most notably, Martin Rapaport, a lead-ing diamond trader in New York and Israel, visited Sierra Leone in 2000 and broke ranks with those denying a connection between diamonds and war. In a widely circulated, emotive article titled "Guilt Trip," he argued that it was time for the industry to become engaged with the issue.[22]

Other industry participants joined the process primarily out of com-mercial interest. At least tacitly, the threat of a consumer diamond boycott was present from the beginning and remains a possibility today. Through their campaigns, Global Witness and Partnership Africa Canada put the dia-mond industry on notice. The giant De Beers conglomerate, which tradi-tionally controlled about 80 percent of the world's trade in rough diamonds, was singled out for special attention.[23] For De Beers, control over supply was key to sustaining the high price of diamonds in a world where more and more gem-quality finds were occurring.[24] As the industry's leader and putative guardian of both image and price, De Beers could see the potential damage in a consumer boycott and welcomed the South African govern-ment's initiative in arranging the first and then the subsequent Kimberley meetings.

As with the land mine campaign, some governments came to the table because of the enormity of the humanitarian crises to which diamonds were contributing. No less important, however, was the fact that a number of key governments had important commercial interests at stake. The government of South Africa was perhaps motivated more by concern for its own dia-mond industry than by the wars in other parts of the continent, but that con-cern would not have arisen at all had NGOs and the UN not raised the humanitarian and security issues in the first place. Similarly, other governments, such as those of Botswana and Namibia, participated in the early meetings because they were concerned about their diamond industry. Belgium, too, had a particular interest, given that more than 80 percent of all rough diamonds move through Antwerp, one of the world's largest diamond entrepôts. Other countries—most obviously Angola—joined because of both commercial and humanitarian concerns. Canada, also an early player, had emerging commercial diamond interests of its own, but in chairing the UN Security Council Sanctions Committee on Angola, it had also taken a lead in relating issues of human security to the use of commodities such as oil and diamonds to pay for weapons and war. None of these countries or their diamond industries had anything to say about conflict diamonds until the issue was exposed by NGOs. However, once this occurred, their commercial interests were a driving force behind their early participation in the Kimberley Process.

By the time the Kimberley agreement came into effect in January 2003, there was a positive rush among countries that had missed the negotiating meetings to join the Kimberley system, including several previously reluctant small producers and processing countries, like Lebanon, Brazil, Guyana, Indonesia, and Venezuela. For these latecomers, the commercial interests and the process itself were the main motivators. The reason is straightforward. Participation in the Kimberley Process is "voluntary," but participating countries have agreed that they will not trade with nonparticipants. If a country is not a member of the Kimberley Process, therefore, its diamonds cannot enter the international market legally. This is a voluntary system that is, in effect, compulsory. Simply put, the last twenty-five governments to join the process did so because they did not want to be left behind or find their industry cut out of the trade.

But whether players came to the table from a sense of outrage, guilt, humanitarianism, or commercial panic is not so important as the fact that they came and were willing to talk together with a sense of deep concern and purpose. Whatever the motivation, or mix of motivations, they were powerful enough to encourage the start of a negotiating process and to sustain it over a period of two and a half years.

Process

Was all this just a happy confluence of people, events, and interests, or were there direct causes and effects? Similar to the process that led to the land mine ban, a number of factors that shaped the Kimberley Process were crucial to the eventual conclusion of an agreement.

First, there was a governmental champion willing to organize meetings and chaperone the process. While there was no clarion call from a Lloyd Axworthy, the initiative of Phumzile Mlambo-Ngcuka was key, and the willingness of the government of South Africa to champion the cause and chair the process from the start was essential to its success. Mlambo-Ngcuka called the first Kimberley meeting before the release of the ground-breaking Fowler Report on Angola. She approached Global Witness direct-ly and asked for a meeting with Partnership Africa Canada in February 2000, a month before the UN expert panel report was issued. That South Africa found strong allies in Canada and Britain also helped. In its early days, the Kimberley Process floundered because of weak chairing of meet-ings—not to be confused with South Africa's leadership on the overall issue—and the same was true of its committee work. When that changed with the appointment of an effective chair, the propensity to argue until dawn began to change as well.

Second, the diamond industry's reaction to the NGO campaign changed early on from a position of denial to one of engagement. Following the first Kimberley meeting in May 2000, an important industry forum, the World Diamond Congress in Antwerp, discussed the issue at length in July 2000 and created the World Diamond Council to act as an interlocutor between the industry and NGOs and governments. The knowl-edge that the industry brought to the task of developing a cost-effective tracking system was another important input to the Kimberley Process. Nevertheless, it would take almost two and a half years for the industry to produce details of a "chain of warranties" for rough diamonds, first dis-cussed at the Luanda meeting in the summer of 2000. The two sticking points for the industry were whether the chain of warranties should be vol-untary or mandatory and whether it should be subject to independent audit. The final Kimberley agreement dealt with the questions in part by deferring the answers to the government of each participating country, making it responsible for managing the process within its own borders. Each country thus agreed to implement a compulsory chain of warranties of one sort or another, and each took responsibility for monitoring it.

Third, it is not difficult to trace the spark for the Kimberley Process to NGO activism. It is arguable that the Fowler Report would have been con-siderably less tough, especially on lax Belgian controls, had it not been for the earlier reports by Global Witness and Partnership Africa Canada. Furthermore, in parallel to the ongoing Kimberley Process, there was an effective NGO lobbying effort that included rigorous background research and a high-powered media effort, backed by petition drives and street demonstrations. The participation of major brand-name NGOs such as Oxfam, World Vision, and Amnesty International helped to raise the public profile of the issue and consequently created a credible threat of a con-sumer boycott for companies and governments. The NGOs were hesitant to launch a general boycott, however, as they recognized that the economies of developing countries such as Botswana and Namibia depend on their diamond industries, which are predominantly clean of conflict diamonds.

Fourth, the Kimberley Process received strong public support—both implicit and explicit—from international organizations, especially the UN. Investigations by the Security Council–established expert panels on Angola, Sierra Leone, Liberia, and the DRC provided increasingly damning proof of the effects of diamonds in fueling African wars and served to remind negotiators that—commercial and political concerns aside—they were dealing with an issue that had major human security implications. The expert panel reports also provided the diplomatic fuel needed to keep the issue alive at the UN. As a result, two unanimous UN General Assembly resolutions endorsed the Kimberley Process, followed by Security Council endorsement in January 2003.[25]

The conflict diamond issue was also addressed at two G8 meetings, in Osaka in 2000 and in Kananaskis in 2002, where the G8 leaders publicly supported the Kimberley Process. Furthermore, after more than a year of debate about the relevance of the issue to the WTO, a handful of countries, including Canada and Japan, asked for a WTO waiver at the end of 2002. Until then, the debate had alternated in tenor between the humanitarian imperative and concern that any restriction on trade would sooner or later meet a challenge at the WTO. A preliminary WTO green light was given in February 2003 on human security grounds. This required further agreement from the WTO's General Council, however. The General Council agreed, by consensus, in May of that year. In approving the Kimberley Process scheme, the WTO said that "while there is no reason to believe that a conflict between WTO rules and UN activities would have occurred . . . the waiver eliminates any such risk beyond doubt."[26]

Fifth, the Kimberley Process was by and large a consensual and inclusive process. Unlike the "intimate" partnership of the land mine campaign, the relationships among the four sectors in the Kimberley Process—industry, governments, NGOs, and international institutions—were sometimes testy. Many governments found the full and sometimes aggressive participation of NGOs in the Kimberley meetings difficult to manage. As the meetings proceeded, however, all participants developed a healthy respect for one another and managed to work creatively and mostly cordially through the process. The general feeling was that it was better to have everyone inside the tent, even if some brought their stones with them. Furthermore, the "space" in which the Kimberley Process played out was different from the formal diplomacy of the UN and other multilateral negotiating forums. Much of the debate took place at the Kimberley meetings themselves, but some took place at informal ad hoc gatherings as well, sometimes hosted by academic institutions attempting to explore the issues and the Kimberley Process for their own reasons. A meeting in Cambridge,

Massachusetts, for instance, organized by the World Peace Foundation in October 2001, brought together a small group of key government, industry, and NGO representatives to discuss the Kimberley Process. This was of academic interest to the foundation, but it also provided a useful opportunity to discuss and at least partially resolve a number of outstanding issues before an approaching Kimberley meeting. The Conflict Diamonds in Africa meeting two years later, organized in Washington, D.C., by the Centre for Strategic and International Studies, provided similar opportunities.[27]

Sixth, adequate time was allowed for the negotiations to develop a critical mass and for most governments to come to terms with the legal and policy implications of an agreement for themselves and their diamond industries. The steady pacing of the process also helped to "educate" decisionmakers of two kinds. The first set of decisionmakers were consumers, who became better informed through media and NGO efforts as time passed. By the middle of 2002, every major television news magazine from London to Tokyo had run stories on conflict diamonds. Major stories, usually based on NGO research, had appeared in *Esquire, Vanity Fair, Time, Newsweek,* and other popular magazines and featured regularly in the *Financial Times,* the *New York Times,* and the *International Herald Tribune,* as well as in major newspapers and industry publications in Belgium, Israel, and South Africa. The second group of decisionmakers were government officials, both those who attended the Kimberley process meetings and those whom these officials had to convince upon returning to their capitals. At early meetings, delegates from countries as diverse as Russia, China, and Japan stalled and blocked debate, asking repeatedly, for example, why NGOs should be allowed to attend and participate. Over time this changed, as countries began to see and value the way the process was unfolding.

Last, in working toward the agreement, governments and the industry were mindful of the costs that the certification scheme and its implementation would entail. Several governments argued against the establishment of what they viewed as a costly and potentially authoritarian secretariat, while industry representatives warned against a system that would add costs to a trade in which, they claimed, profit margins were very low. While NGOs argued that an extra dollar on a $500 diamond ring would not drive consumers away, many of the regulatory costs would inevitably be borne by governments rather than consumers. In fact, the costs of the process and its implementation have actually been dispersed among governments. South Africa bore the organizational expenses of the first twelve Kimberley meetings, and host countries paid for the direct costs. Those who chair the working groups on statistics (Canada), monitoring (European Commission), and other issues bear the cost of these groups. Belgium has borne the cost of studying many of the technical details. Each country pays for its own implementation of the process within its borders. Yet while governments were willing to meet these costs and to spend as much as $50,000 to send delegations to each of a dozen Kimberley meetings, the idea of contributing a tenth of this to a common pool for ongoing running costs has remained problematic. There remains no pooled commitment from any source to the core costs of running the system.

Content: Missing Pieces

When the Kimberley Process certification system finally came into effect in January 2003, it lacked two of the elements identified as "necessary" by Global Witness. The first was a comprehensive system for the gathering and analysis of diamond production and trading statistics. This provision was first mooted at the Luanda meeting in June 2000. It was debated at various meetings thereafter and was finally agreed upon at a meeting in Ottawa in March 2002. That the system agreed upon still remained unimplemented two years later was largely the result of intransigence and bureaucratic ineptitude in dealing with the issue at Kimberley meetings. Russia argued that diamonds were a "strategic mineral," the production and trade details of which were protected by law from public scrutiny. In a similar vein, Israel argued that where one company had a monopoly arrangement—as had been the case with different Israeli companies in Angola and the DRC—its trade statistics should be protected as a matter of commercial confidentiality.

Agreement on a process for gathering, analyzing, and disseminating statistics was finally reached, however, in April 2003, when a simple, concrete proposal and the money to manage it were put forward by the government of Canada. Conceptual problems evaporated when a practical system, developed by statisticians, was proposed. Practical problems persisted, however, and many governments remained unable or unwilling to provide the agreed statistics a full year after the KPCS had been inaugurated. Without a comprehensive database on the production and trade of rough diamonds, the KPCS will be unable to identify anomalies or do even the most rudimentary tracking of diamond flows.

The second missing element in the final agreement, however, is more serious. No consensus was reached at the various Kimberley meetings on how monitoring of compliance with the agreement was to be ensured. The NGOs involved in the Kimberley Process had argued from the outset that any agreement would require regular independent monitoring. This was fiercely resisted by many governments, notably Russia, China, and Israel, which saw, variously, a potential NGO swarming, a commercial conspiracy, or an effort to breach national sovereignty. The real reason for resistance, however, may well have been a continued unwillingness to fully confront the endemic corruption within the diamond industry.

The NGO participants had agreed not to make the monitoring issue a deal breaker in concluding an agreement but said that they would continue to push the issue as the agreement went into effect. A minor breakthrough was achieved at a Kimberley Process meeting in October 2003, held after an emergency review mission to the Central African Republic in June, following a coup in the country and an uproar in the domestic diamond trade. A more general peer review process was established, which would see missions composed of government, industry, and NGO representatives visiting countries that *volunteer* for a review of their diamond industry. This, NGOs argue, falls well short of the universal mechanism needed in an industry so tainted with illicit behavior, but it is perhaps a start, one that NGOs can supplement with their own ongoing research and investigations.

There were other anomalies. Some countries without diamond industries, and countries that had never attended a Kimberley Process meeting, sent in membership applications that were readily accepted in the first weeks of 2003. One of the most questionable applicants was North Korea, but there were others. The Republic of Congo, a laundry facility for billions of dollars worth of stolen gems from the DRC and elsewhere, was admitted without question. And Burkina Faso, a country with no diamonds whatsoever, whose president, Blaise Compaoré, had been named in the Fowler Report as a facilitator in laundering Angolan conflict diamonds, was also admitted without question.

In principle, membership is open to any country that is willing and able to comply with the Kimberley Process's minimum standards. These include the development of a system to track the internal movement of rough diamonds, to vouch for their bona fides on export through the issuance of a standardized certificate with specific security features, to refuse entry for rough diamonds not accompanied by the certificate of another country, and to institute penalties for transgressors. Although dozens of countries said they were willing and able to do these things, by January 2003 very few had demonstrated that this was actually the case.

Two steps in the right direction were taken at the first postlaunch Kimberley Process meeting in April 2003. A credentials committee (euphemistically called a "participation committee") was struck, and it was agreed that countries without tamper-proof certificates and appropriate Kimberley-related legislation would be drummed out of the club. In this way, membership would no longer be automatic but would be tied to verifiable entry criteria. As a result, twenty-four of the sixty-three candidate countries were dropped from the membership list on July 31—including Burkina Faso and North Korea.[28]

A further "necessary element," capacity building, is certainly required for the Kimberley Process to be effective. The process itself has contained elements of capacity building. Belgium's Diamond High Council helped several countries—Sierra Leone, Angola, and Guinea—to develop pilot certification systems, which came to serve as the models for the Kimberley certificate. Canada has set money aside to assist in the development of a statistical database, while U.S. legislation in support of the Kimberley scheme contains specific provision for technical assistance to countries that need it.[29] It is not yet clear whether the volume or the quality of this proposed assistance will be appropriate or adequate.

Problems aside, in the first months of 2003 it was becoming clear the Kimberley Process was already having an effect. Seizures of diamonds without adequate Kimberley certification took place in India, Switzerland, and Canada. In one of the countries most plagued by war, Sierra Leone, there were very encouraging developments, which can be seen as an important indicator of what the wider Kimberley system might accomplish. In 1999, Sierra Leone officially exported only $1.5 million worth of rough diamonds. By 2000, exports increased to $11 million. The following year official exports reached $26 million, in 2002 they totaled $42 million, and in 2003 they reached $76 million.[30] The importance of this formalization and legitimization of the diamond trade cannot be overstated for a country emerging from a brutal ten-year conflict. It should be a sign of hope and encouragement for others, and for the diamond industry as a whole, which itself is more likely to prosper from well-regulated "development diamonds" than from those with secrecy and blood in their pedigree.

Conclusion:
Diamond Certification—Role Model or Special Case?

It is worth returning once more to the question of the lessons for other commodities that can be drawn from the Kimberley Process. This chapter began with a generic list of ten elements of a good commodity-tracking system, of which five are said to be "essential": common definition and reporting requirements; an effective reporting structure and an effective exchange of information; adequate labeling and auditable chains of custody; enforcement measures, including national and international monitoring, with penalties to promote compliance; and capacity building for those in the system that need it.

In its basics, the Kimberley system is fairly simple. Governments of all participating countries have agreed to certify that rough diamonds leaving their borders are clean. Importing countries have agreed to reject any diamonds that are not accompanied by such a certificate. If the process is effectively implemented and enforced, countries that are not part of the

Kimberley Process Certification Scheme will not be permitted to sell their diamonds legally anywhere in the world.

When one is thinking about how the Kimberley system might be applied to other problematic commodities, the level of substantiation required by governments to back their certificates and the level of international monitoring required to ensure international compliance are, in a sense, only detail. Theoretically, the same sort of agreement is possible with any commodity that may be traded illegally or that may be used to fuel conflict—timber, oil, coltan, tobacco, coffee—if sufficient *motivation* for engaging in a discussion about regulation exists and if the *process* used in reaching an agreement is effective. As I have argued in this chapter, what is interesting about the KPCS so far is not the fact that it entails, however imperfectly, four of the five "necessary elements" but *how* and *why* the four were achieved and whether or not the missing one—adequate monitoring and enforceable penalties—can be achieved in the future. That, ultimately, will be the test of whether the system is actually working to halt the trade in conflict diamonds and to prevent its recurrence in the future.

For some, the Kimberley Process heralds a bright new way of conceiving and dealing with the issues of greed, grievance, and commodity regulation. For contrarians, always quick to the fore whenever "Eureka!" is heard in the land, there is not much to be learned here, given the specifics of diamonds. Some have argued that the creation of a diamond certification scheme was easy because diamonds, as luxury goods, are particularly susceptible to boycott and can attract a lot of media attention and because the market is controlled by a cartel. Consequently, the NGO campaign was a no-brainer and a diamond regulation agreement was inevitable once De Beers caught the scent of boycott and bought into the idea.

Against this background, it is worth reconsidering the five "contextual elements" that may influence the feasibility of a commodity-specific tracking regime—the specifics of the commodity itself, dynamics of supply, dynamics of demand, the political and institutional context of the commodity, and the need for harmonization with existing law. With the exception of the last point, these are as obvious in the case of diamonds as they would be in regulating fishing for the Patagonian toothfish. The question is whether diamonds are unique in the annals of regulatory systems or if there are any lessons that can be applied to other commodities that fuel conflict.

As the chapter has highlighted, the physical nature of diamonds does not seem to be a critical factor. In fact, many *diamantaires* themselves still maintain that diamonds cannot be controlled—they are like water: once you have mixed one glass with another, you can never separate them. That is why the Kimberley Process focused on *systems* for monitoring the trade rather than on attempts to mark and trace every diamond. In the end, devising a system for tracking millions and millions of tiny stones did not present major technical obstacles, once industry specialists devoted some attention to it. If this can be done for diamonds, it can be done for other commodities.

Diamonds fueled the wars in Angola and Sierra Leone for a decade or more before the media became interested. Even after conflict diamonds became a hot issue, industry and government support was initially not a given. Reaching an agreement was far from easy in the case of an industry defined by poor governance in some of the producing countries, a lack of governance in the diamond industry as a whole, and an absence of any concern for producers in the regulation of diamonds by the governments of countries where they are cut, polished, and consumed. Only two years of high-energy NGO lobbying convinced the industry and enough governments that the issue was, after all, worthy of their attention.

The issue here is not the nature of the commodity but the structure of the industry. Certainly, a special feature of the diamond industry is the control exercised by one company, De Beers, as well as the "narrow funnel" of the diamond entrepôt in Antwerp. Because De Beers, the Belgian government, and the Antwerp industry took the matter seriously almost from the outset, much of the rest of the industry fell into line, convinced that they had to participate actively and meaningfully. Other industries, such as timber or oil, do not have the equivalents of De Beers and Antwerp—no obvious narrow funnel. The challenge would be to locate similar choke points where business might be vulnerable to pressure.

Industry cartel or not, *governments* were crucial to the process. The Russian government had to be involved in Kimberley, as did the governments of Belgium, the United States, Venezuela, Sri Lanka, Mauritius, and Namibia. An agreement might have been difficult or impossible without industry support, but the massive industry turnaround at the World Diamond Congress of 2000 came only after the industry had actively assessed the playing field at the first two Kimberley meetings and saw that governments were prepared to take action. While the motivation for many governments may have related to military, human, or economic security, for the industry the primary motivation was always commercial. The extent to which a harmony among different motivations exists in discussions on other troubled commodities will undoubtedly determine whether, as well as how well and how fast, negotiations evolve.

Ultimately, then, the "advantage" in diamonds was not so much their physical characteristics or the market structure as the political will generated around their regulation. The real question about diamonds, and any other conflict-related commodity, is whether they are associated with a problem that governments and the industry in question *want* to solve. Peace agreements were concluded in Angola, Sierra Leone, and the DRC in 2002 and 2003. Technically, with rebel movements having dissipated, there was no longer any such thing as "conflict diamonds," at least not as defined by UN resolutions. Within the diamond industry, there was renewed grumbling about the need for certification. Interestingly, by 2004 it was industry leaders such as De Beers, the Diamond High Council in Antwerp, and the World Diamond Council, along with the governments that had committed the most to the process—South Africa, Canada, the European Commission—that now began to take up some of the positions espoused by NGOs and once deemed radical or impossible. It was generally agreed that the Kimberley Process was important not just as a curative measure—to end the trade in conflict diamonds—but as a preventive measure to ensure that such a trade is never again possible.

Notes

1. Global Witness, "Tracking Systems: A Global Witness Perspective." Workshop on the Governance of Natural Resources and Revenues, World Bank, Paris, December 9–10, 2002. Apart from the Kimberley Process, the report analyzes the Convention on Migratory Species, the Stockholm Convention on Persistent Organic Pollutants, the ivory ban, and efforts to label and control traffic in tropical hardwood. The report was subsequently published as Corene Crossin, Gavin Hayman, and Simon Taylor, "Where Did It Come From? Commodity Tracking Systems," in Ian Bannon and Paul Collier, eds., *Natural Resources and Violent Conflict: Options and Actions* (Washington, D.C.: World Bank, 2003), pp. 97–160.

2. Global Witness, "Tracking Systems," pp. 5–6.

3. Global Witness, *A Rough Trade: The Role of Diamond Companies and Governments in the Angolan Conflict* (London: Global Witness, 1998). A second report followed in 2000, detailing how an international certification system could be applied to conflict diamonds. See Global Witness, *Conflict Diamonds: Possibilities for Identification, Certification, and Control of Diamonds* (London: Global Witness, 2000).

4. Global Witness, *Rough Trade*, p. 2. See also Jakkie Cilliers and Christian Dietrich, eds., *Angola's War Economy: The Role of Oil and Diamonds* (Pretoria: Institute for Security Studies, 2000).

5. See UN Security Council Resolution 1173, S/RES/1173, June 12, 1998.

6. *Report of the Panel of Experts on Violations of Security Council Sanctions against UNITA*, S/2000/203, March 10, 2000.

7. Ian Smillie, Lansana Gberie, and Ralph Hazelton, *The Heart of the Matter: Sierra Leone, Diamonds, and Human Security* (Ottawa: Partnership Africa Canada, January 2000). See also John L. Hirsch, *Sierra Leone: Diamonds and the Struggle for Democracy* (Boulder: Lynne Rienner, 2001).

8. For a discussion of the corruption of Sierra Leone's diamond sector, see William Reno, *Corruption and the State in Sierra Leone* (Cambridge: Cambridge University Press 1995).

9. Smillie, Gberie, and Hazelton, *Heart of the Matter*, p. 46.

10. UN Security Council Resolution 1306, adopted by the Security Council at its 4168th meeting, S/RES/1306, July 5, 2000.

11. Christian Dietrich, *Hard Currency: The Criminalized Diamond Economy*

of the Democratic Republic of the Congo and Its Neighbours (Ottawa: Partnership Africa Canada, 2002), p. 7.

12. Ibid., p. 16.

13. Figures compiled from various reports of the Diamond High Council, Antwerp, and the *Diamond Intelligence Briefs,* Tel Aviv.

14. International Rescue Committee (IRC), *Mortality in the Democratic Republic of Congo: Results from a Nationwide Survey* (New York: IRC, April 2003).

15. On the regional conflict dimension of diamond smuggling in Sierra Leone, see Michael Pugh and Neil Cooper with Jonathan Goodhand, *War Economies in a Regional Context: Challenges of Transformation* (Boulder: Lynne Rienner, 2004), pp. 91–142.

16. See United Nations, "The Role of Diamonds in Fuelling Conflict: Breaking the Link between the Illicit Transaction of Rough Diamonds and Armed Conflict as a Contribution to Prevention and Settlement of Conflicts," resolutions adopted by the General Assembly, A/RES/55/56, January 29, 2001, and A/RES/56/263, April 9, 2002. On the Kimberley Process, see www.kimberleyprocess.com/background.asp.

17. Ian Smillie, *The Kimberley Process: The Case for Proper Monitoring* (Ottawa: Partnership Africa Canada, 2002), pp. 8–10.

18. "Recommendations of the Luanda Working Group Meeting," unpubl., June 13–14, 2000.

19. Ibid.

20. Convention on the Prohibition of the Use, Stockpiling, Production, and Transfer of Anti-personnel Mines and on Their Destruction; see www.icbl.org.

21. Mark Gwozdecky and Jill Sinclair, "Landmines and Human Security," in Rob McRae and Don Hubert, eds., *Human Security and the New Diplomacy: Protecting People, Promoting Peace* (Montreal: McGill-Queen's University Press, 2001), pp. 28-41.

22. Martin Rapaport, "Guilt Trip," *Rapaport Diamond Report* 23, no. 1 (April 7, 2000).

23. The figure has dropped to approximately 60 percent in recent years.

24. In addition to diamonds from its own mines in southern Africa, De Beers bought diamonds on the "open market" and maintained offices in Guinea, the DRC, and elsewhere. In its annual reports in the mid-1990s, it had boasted of its ability to keep obtaining diamonds from Angola despite the war. See De Beers, annual reports, 1991, 1992, 1995, 1996, available at www.debeersgroups.com.

25. United Nations, "Role of Diamonds in Fuelling Conflict"; UN Security Council Resolution 1385, S/RES/1385, December 19, 2001; UN Security Council Resolution 1459, S/RES/1459, January 28, 2003.

26. "WTO Green Light for Kimberley," in *Other Facets* (Ottawa: Partnership Africa Canada, September 2003); "WTO Goods Council Approves Kimberley Process Waiver," *Bridges Weekly Trade News Digest* 7, no. 7 (February 27, 2003).

27. For a report that grew out of the World Peace Foundation–sponsored meeting of October 19–20, 2001, see Ingrid J. Tamm, *Diamonds in Peace and War: Severing the Conflict-Diamond Connection,* World Peace Foundation Report no. 30 (Cambridge, Mass.: Carr Centre for Human Rights Policy, 2002).

28. As of November 7, 2003, the Kimberley Process included forty-six participating states: Angola, Armenia, Australia, Belarus, Botswana, Brazil, Bulgaria, Canada, the Central African Republic, People's Republic of China, Democratic Republic of Congo, the Republic of Congo, Côte d'Ivoire, Croatia, the European

Union (including its member states), Ghana, Guinea, Guyana, Hungary, India, Israel, Japan, the Republic of Korea, Laos, Lebanon, Lesotho, Malaysia, Mauritius, Namibia, Poland, Romania, the Russian Federation, Sierra Leone, Slovenia, South Africa, Sri Lanka, Switzerland, Tanzania, Thailand, Togo, Ukraine, the United Arab Emirates, the United States, Venezuela, Vietnam, and Zimbabwe. See www.kimberleyprocess.com/background.asp.

29. U.S. Congress, Clean Diamond Trade Act, S. 760 and H.R. 1415, April 10, 2003.

30. Statistics provided by the Government Gold and Diamond Office, Freetown, Sierra Leone.

4

Tracking Conflict Commodities and Financing

Jonathan M. Winer

Illicit trade in natural resources has become a principal source of revenue for armed conflict and terrorism, while depriving the states from which these resources originate of potential revenues. In response, there has been increasing interest among the United Nations and other international organizations, national governments, the private sector, and civil society in the use of commodity-tracking systems, such as rough diamond certification under the Kimberley Process, as a mechanism to curtail resource flows to combatants.[1]

To date, these efforts have largely focused on tracking the movements of the physical commodity. Tracking the financial transactions involved in and the proceeds generated from illicit trade offers another, and potentially significant, means of curtailing illicit trade, ameliorating its negative consequences, and discouraging impunity for those engaged in war economies.[2] In the wake of the globalization of markets, access to the international financial sector has become a necessary condition for financing many of today's resource-related conflicts. Typically, electronic funds replace local currency-based transactions as goods move farther away from the zone of conflict toward the final consumers. Existing financial transparency initiatives, including anticorruption and anti–money-laundering regulatory regimes, have not explicitly addressed financial transactions involving the illicit trade in natural resources, let alone conflict commodities, except those involving narcotic drugs.

However, beginning with the Financial Action Task Force on Money Laundering (FATF) created in 1989, these initiatives have established heightened standards of care for commercial banks and similar financial institutions, requiring them to know both the identity of their customers and, to a considerable—though still in practice variable—extent, the sources of the funds moving through their institutions. Financial regulators have developed standard criteria, known as *red flags*, indicating suspicious transactions deemed likely to involve the proceeds of narcotics, corruption, fraud, or other illegal activity. Banks, brokers, and other commercial financial institutions connected to the global payments system are required to monitor the financial transactions they process, to apply red flags to any suspicious transactions, and to report these to appropriate authorities.

As part of the increased international policy attention toward regulating the trade in conflict goods, the world's financial regulators could create and require the financial institutions that they regulate to apply a set of red flags to conflict commodities. After using red flags to identify transactions deemed at high risk of involving either the proceeds of illicit transactions in natural resources generally or, more specifically, the proceeds of conflict commodities, commercial financial institutions could be required to report such transactions to regulators and law enforcement agencies, which could then take appropriate regulatory and criminal enforcement action.

At the same time, initiatives undertaken by the World Customs Organization (WCO) to improve the security of goods in cross-border transit, arising in part out of counterterrorism efforts, provide processes that could be adapted to address the trade in conflict commodities. Generally, these initiatives require greater documentation and marking of all goods that cross borders. The documentation and marking now being developed are designed to help governments both to discourage terrorists from hiding weapons of mass destruction—such as radioactive material or biological pathogens—in goods in transit and to enable them to trace such goods back to their source should something go amiss with a shipment. Their focus to date has been on enhancing the integrity of physical goods in transit. Additional documentation and marking requirements could be applied to shipments of raw materials, such as oil, timber, tanzanite, coltan, and even diamonds, so as to track the provenance of, location of, and controls upon such goods from extraction to destination.

These respective documentation regimes—one financial and applying to banks and other commercial financial institutions, the other physical and applying to importers, exporters, transportation firms, and customs authorities—could in turn be integrated to create a unified documentation system for both the goods and the funds used to pay for them. These regulatory measures could be combined with positive incentives for compliance by commercial financial institutions (for the financial regulations) and by global import, export, and transportation companies (for the customs-related regulations).

This chapter examines the mechanisms and the institutional and technical requirements for developing and implementing a tracking system for the financial dimensions of illicit resources and, in turn, linking it to a tracking system for the physical movements of illicit resources. I find that existing regimes covering cross-border activities of both money and goods could readily be adapted to identify and track transactions involving either illicit transactions in natural resources or conflict commodities. Likewise, I argue that technical limitations do not today prevent governments, regulators, and the private sector from distinguishing between licit and illicit commodity transactions. Rather, the principal limitations are the insufficient harmonization of norms in the relevant provisions for financial and transportation infrastructure documentation regarding conflict commodities that are subject to international sanction. Here, there is a need for policy action. Governments would need to decide to integrate conflict commodity regulation into regimes that are already being asked to prevent drug trafficking and money laundering, the financing of terrorism, and various forms of smuggling and fraud. New regulatory efforts affecting both financial and commodity transactions, driven by the United States since the September 11, 2001, terrorist attacks, have demonstrated that substantial enhancements to existing mechanisms can be developed and implemented rapidly when the stakes are recognized to be sufficiently high.

On the financial services side, applicable regimes could be facilitated by the development of red flags for identifying the proceeds of conflict commodities, as well as through the creation of an incentive-based approach for the private sector. On the customs side, counterterrorist security initiatives have already provided the foundations of a *white list*, under which companies that have agreed to adopt high standards to protect against their involvement in sanctioned commodities would receive preferential treatment from governments and international bodies, such as speedier processing of transactions or priority in obtaining government contracts compared to companies that have not agreed to adopt these standards. Current efforts could be made more effective by requiring additional documentation regarding the financial transaction counterpart to the goods in cross-border transit. Red flags should also be developed for use in customs documentation.

Definitions

There is not as yet consensus as to what is denoted by *conflict commodities*. Much of the writing on the topic tends to focus on the activities of rebel groups, unsanctioned by governments.[3] By contrast, this chapter defines them as commodities that are sold by any participant in a conflict to generate resources that can be used for political or military purposes in connection with the conflict and on which taxes have not been paid. The failure to pay taxes is a key element of the definition, as with this element the sellers of such commodities are engaged in illicit activity, regardless of their official status. Notably, this definition is broader than that of the UN for "conflict diamonds," which are defined as "rough diamonds which are used by rebel movements to finance their military activities."[4]

Within this chapter, *conflict commodities* include those commodities that are moved across national borders to sustain persons (whether official, rebel, or paramilitary) involved in a civil war, border war, or guerrilla or paramilitary movement, particularly in a region in which such conflict is taking place. Conflict commodities include commodities that are the products of illicit resource extraction but could also include secondary smuggled goods being used by actors in a conflict. Examples of the latter are the diamonds and gold purchased lawfully in open markets by Al-Qaida and then used to fund terrorist activities.[5] For regulatory and enforcement purposes, "conflict commodities" are a subset of a larger phenomenon, which is the extraction of and trade in natural resources or the smuggling of manufactured goods in violation of the laws of at least one of the countries in which the goods move.

Illicit resource extraction is defined as the production and sale of natural resources from a country by means that avoid the payment of taxes to the national government in the country from which the resources were extracted or by means carried out in violation of resolutions issued by the United Nations. This definition is intended to include the embezzlement of funds paid by companies to government officials but not paid into the national treasury. *Smuggling* involves the same activity for manufactured goods.

Thus when taxes are properly paid on resources extracted at market prices for goods not subject to UN sanctions or in violation of domestic laws, the transaction is deemed "licit." All of the situations in which these conditions are not met would be deemed "illicit." The broad term *illicit,* when applied to "goods," ties the exploitation of diamonds, timber, oil, and gas to what are ordinarily treated as very different phenomena, such as narcotics trafficking and arms trafficking. In all cases, the common denominator is the fact that taxes are not paid on the sale of the goods and the state is denied any benefit from the extraction or sale of the goods. Because conflict commodities, illicit resource extraction, and smuggling all involve the sale of goods in violation of customs laws, there may be potential to attack them simultaneously through modifying existing documentation requirements for goods in transit across borders and for cross-border payments for such goods.

Cross-Border Gaps

Conflict commodities are almost invariably cross-border commodities, moving across borders through the same infrastructure that provides for the licit movement of goods, people, funds, and information. Increased use of the infrastructure of legitimate cross-border trade to move narcotics and weapons, smuggle persons, and transport the proceeds of crime from one country to another in violation of applicable national legal and regulatory barriers[6] is an unintended consequence of reductions in trade barriers and border controls, sometimes referred to as the "dark side of globalization."[7] With government jurisdictions bound to the physical border of a country by traditional notions of sovereignty, no single authority is responsible for regulating cross-border activity or enforcing legal regimes applying to cross-border activity.

To redress this "governance gap," there have been a growing number of international initiatives targeting terrorism, international crime, drug trafficking, intellectual property theft, smuggling of people, and kleptocratic corruption. These include embargoes; certification programs; disclosure regimes; anticorruption, drug-trafficking, money-laundering, and terrorist standards; private-sector "seal" initiatives; and "name and shame" exercises.[8] Although these regimes have had some successes arising out of a growing agreement on global regulatory and enforcement norms, they have been only moderately effective, given the great gaps still apparent in governmental capacities to operate across borders.

First, few governments have enforcement capacities beyond their borders, apart from the information-gathering activities of their diplomats and intelligence agencies. In much of the world, and particularly in unstable and conflict-prone countries, governments even struggle to meet their obligations to engage in regulation and enforce laws on activities that are purely domestic. Common impediments to effective regulation and law enforcement include low salaries, poor training, too few personnel, and endemic corruption. In countries experiencing these limitations, transborder regulation and enforcement may be far from practical. Strained governments may not be able to afford airfare (or even carfare) to transport their officials to where the evidence may be, let alone maintain liaison relationships on a regional or global basis to respond to the kind of cross-border illicit activity involved in most transactions that fuel conflict.

The second constraint is technical. Currently, there is no system that integrates and harmonizes information systems among governments in a comprehensive fashion. Information exchange remains largely bilateral, ad hoc, and sectoral. Failure to share information on suspected criminal activities, "sanctions busters," and transnational organized crime among intelligence agencies, diplomats, regulators, and law enforcement agencies is the global norm, not the exception.

The third constraint is jurisdictional. There is no consensus as to the extent to which a government has the right to treat as domestic activity transactions that occur in whole or in part in foreign jurisdictions and that are undertaken by persons who may never have been in the country that is the target and victim of illicit behavior. Countries' enforcement of one another's claims of jurisdiction remains very limited in the absence of interstate agreements such as those on mutual legal assistance now in place by directive within the European Union (EU). When it comes to extradition, for example, most countries still require that an act constitute a crime in both jurisdictions ("dual criminality") and yet may refuse to deliver their own nationals up for trial.[9] The right of one country to demand information from another country, even when that information is essential to the enforcement of laws of the first country, is equally uncertain and susceptible to a host of idiosyncratic local barriers.

The lack of a common solution to these problems has broad negative consequences. Whether a government is trying to control or keep track of licit or illicit arms, licensed pharmaceuticals, illegal drugs, precursor chemicals, taxable income, goods subject to tariff, or conflict commodities, the ability to follow evidentiary trails is essential to both regulation and enforcement of domestic laws. When goods or money crosses a border, government inspectors in the countries of origin, transit, and destination need a common mechanism to follow evidentiary trails and to make inspections both efficient and effective. Together with harmonized rules that cross borders, there is a need for a common regulatory and enforcement infrastructure in which governments are joined by private-sector entities whose resources are already directed at cross-border activity. Currently this is accomplished in a fragmentary fashion by a number of diverse organizations.[10]

Overall, the difficulty in tracking and curtailing the trade in conflict commodities may be seen as a subset of the larger limitations in tracking illicit transactions in natural resources or smuggling activities generally and the financial transactions that accompany them. However, identical infrastructures are used to move both licit and illicit goods and money. Hence a system is needed that can identify the licit as well as the illicit. The question, then, is whether existing structures could be adapted to provide more complete and reliable information on goods and money crossing borders and whether synergies exist for integrating databases that historically have been separate.

There are two major forms of tracking systems in place that implicitly cover transborder movements of illicit commodities. The first is financial, the second physical. Both require public-private partnerships in enforcement in order to function properly. Both have already established robust and comprehensive documentation regimes, though they have yet to be effectively used on conflict commodities. To date, each form of tracking has largely ignored the existence of the other. Potential synergies between the two forms of documentary trails have yet to be exploited, let alone applied to conflict commodities or illicit transactions in natural resources.

Enhancing each documentation system to focus on conflict commodities or illicit transactions in natural resources more broadly and integrating elements of the two systems could help shrink the capacity, technical, and jurisdictional gaps that limit efforts to deal with cross-border illicit activity, including that involved in conflict commodities.

The First Trail: Financial

Given the speed at which electronic money moves across borders today, it is not surprising that regulatory measures to harmonize financial transparency standards on a global basis have accelerated rapidly in a relatively brief period.[11] The first of many complementary initiatives began with the inclusion of commitments to fight the laundering of drug money in the 1988 UN Convention to Combat Illicit and Psychotropic Drugs and the creation of the FATF by the Group of Seven (G7) in 1989.[12] Initiatives since have included the project undertaken by the Organization for Economic Cooperation and Development (OECD) against harmful tax competition in 1998,[13] the G7's creation of the Financial Stability Forum on February 22, 1999,[14] the 2000 UN Convention against Transnational Organized Crime,[15] the Council of Europe's GRECO program to assess and implement corruption prevention and prosecution mechanisms,[16] and the creation of various regional bodies to engage in mutual assessment of anti–money-laundering vulnerabilities and enforcement capacities as a means to greater financial transparency.[17] Further, there have been related but separate initiatives to promote financial transparency undertaken by the International Monetary Fund (IMF), the World Bank, and important sectoral self-regulatory organizations, such as the Basel Group of Bank Supervisors, which revised standards for assessing risk to bank capital,[18] the International Organization of Securities Commissions (IOSCO),[19] and the Offshore Group of Bank Supervisors.[20] Finally, a coalition of commercial financial institutions, known as the Wolfsberg Group, established its own set of transparency standards, initially aimed in 2000 at preventing its banks and brokerage firms from being used to hide the proceeds of corruption and extended in late 2001 to prevent the financing of terrorism.[21]

The initiatives all exhibit common elements, including the need to know one's customers to ensure that they are not engaged in illicit activity; the need for commercial financial institutions to share information pertaining to illicit activity with regulators, law enforcement agencies, and when needed, one another; the need for capability to trace funds; and the need of each country to assist all others in enforcing violations of their domestic laws. Principles initially used to combat drug trafficking were later extended to include all serious financial crimes and, more recently, the financing of terrorism and corruption. This broadening was based on a mutual recognition that a beggar-thy-neighbor approach to tax violations threatened to beggar all.

None of these financial transparency initiatives, however, have directly addressed the need to curtail the flow of funds generated through the exploitation of natural resources in zones of conflict, even though many aspects of these activities fall within the boundaries of standards and regulations designed to address money laundering, the financing of terrorism, and corruption. Existing standards have not directly identified the steps that a financial institution might take in handling what may be the proceeds of sales of timber, oil and gas, diamonds, coltan, tanzanite, or similar commodities used by warring factions to fund their armed campaigns. The closest the current standards have come to dealing with these issues is the requirement that commercial financial institutions eschew the proceeds of corruption and that such institutions respect, on a global basis, UN sanctions such as those set forth in Resolution 1373 against specially designated terrorists.[22] While both standards have existed in principle for a long time, their enforcement is very recent and remains incomplete.

Access to the global financial services infrastructure is a critical element in sustaining resource-related conflict. These services offer a speedy and secure channel for the transportation and investment of funds generated by the exploitation of resources by parties to conflict whose control of those resources is often very insecure. The power to control resource wealth is essential to combatants' ability to remain in power and sustain war making. While this may be the most important asset a combatant may possess, it is also one that opposing factions can most easily capture. Thus, in conditions of conflict, the ability to strip assets quickly and convert them into money stored safely and securely is a critical element in retaining political and military advantage. At the same time, those capturing the resources are also more likely in times of conflict than at other times to be in a position to evade any domestic constraints on the sale of their assets. The pervasive problem of limited domestic regulatory and enforcement capacity is exacerbated in war-torn countries. For this reason, it falls upon other actors to enforce the limited framework of global norms created to identify and limit transactions involving the proceeds of the illicit and conflict-promoting economic activity.

The increasing integration of national financial payment and clearing systems into a global financial infrastructure has made it possible for changes in financial regulatory systems to be contemplated, mandated, and enforced at a global level. This is well demonstrated by the twin "name and shame" exercises initiated in 1999 by the FATF and the OECD. In these exercises, member countries of the FATF and OECD agreed as a group to impose sanctions on countries with lax financial regulatory systems that were viewed as a threat to the integrity of the global payments system and domestic financial regulatory and tax regimes. The jurisdictions deemed to be lax were warned that they would face the loss of market access to the major financial centers if they did not harmonize their standards for financial transparency with the requirements levied by the members of those organizations. Both the FATF and the OECD developed lists of jurisdictions deemed noncompliant with their standards. In each case, targeted jurisdictions complained bitterly that this approach did not respect their sovereignty. However, in almost every case, those threatened with "blacklisting" hastened to adopt comprehensive domestic legislation that, at least on paper, complied with the required norms.[23]

Each of the existing international initiatives governing money laundering and financial transparency is founded on the FATF Forty Recommendations, which remain the core principles governing most national anti–money-laundering and financial transparency regulations and enforcement. Established in 1990, the Forty Recommendations were revised in 1996 and again in 2003 and are designed to be of universal application.[24] Although the recommendations are not legally binding, the FATF member states have agreed to sanction any other state, member or not, that fails to come into substantial compliance with them. The recommendations cover the criminal justice system and law enforcement, the financial system and its regulation, and international cooperation. From its inception, the FATF undertook a process of mutual assessment to review compliance with the recommendations. This process was supplemented in 1999 by the "name and shame" exercise, which innovatively threatened sanctions to nonmember jurisdictions for failure to live up to the recommendations established by member jurisdictions.[25] The FATF had the ability to do this because its membership included the major financial-center countries of Europe, North and South America, and Asia, which together had the leverage to impose weighty sanctions. The credibility of the initiative was further strengthened by the fact that the process was driven by neutral, technocratic analysis rather than politics, with decisions on the recommended targets of sanctions taken largely by career civil service bureaucrats rather than by more politicized senior policymakers. While the Forty Recommendations are nonbinding, the threat of loss of market access made universal compliance—at least on paper—compulsory. Indeed, as of 2001, the FATF had been sufficiently successful that the IMF and World Bank agreed to take on the responsibilities of further assessing jurisdictions for their compliance with the FATF's standards, together with technical assistance to help them meet these standards. In return, the FATF agreed with both institutions, as well as with countries in need of assistance in meeting its standards, to defer, for the present, further application of sanctions to nonconforming jurisdictions.

At bottom, the FATF Forty Recommendations require identification of the beneficial owners of funds for two purposes: first, to enable the identification of illicit funds at the time a money launderer, criminal, or terrorist financier seeks to introduce them into the financial system, and second, to enable the tracing of funds linked to crime or terrorism back to their source or forward to their destination. Several of the recommendations are sectoral and focused on the laundering of drug money, reflecting the origin of the recommendations at a time when money laundering was defined solely as a drug-related offense. Most of them, however, are applicable to all forms of illicit funds and therefore could be made applicable to funds generated from illicit transactions involving conflict commodities. Particularly in their current form as a result of the 2003 updates, which made the recommendations more stringent and comprehensive, they could readily be turned into a regime that *directly* addresses conflict commodities as a subset of illicit commodities (see Table 4.1).

The analysis provided in Table 4.1 suggests that a request to develop guidance and interpretative notes regarding the financial transactions for conflict commodities, made by the UN, other international organizations, FATF member states, and perhaps also by IMF or World Bank member states, could have a substantial impact. The essential elements of such a scheme would include providing a precise definition of conflict commodities, developing a mechanism by which UN sanctions applicable to a particular commodity would be communicated to the FATF for the development of red flags and guidance, articulation of specific red flags for each commodity and area of conflict, and a method to alert the FATF to the need to update existing guidance to reflect the cessation of conflict or other geopolitical changes. Other elements would include development by the IMF and World Bank, in collaboration with the FATF and other interested governments and governmental institutions, of training and conflict commodity–oriented systems and software.

For some conflict commodities, agreement on red flags for heightening scrutiny and reporting suspicious activity to governments might be relatively easy. For example, the criteria for flagging a transaction as potentially relating to conflict diamonds could comprise whether or not the transaction appears to involve the purchase or sale of diamonds, whether or not the source or entity purchasing or selling the diamonds is based in an arena previously identified as having handled the proceeds of conflict diamonds, and whether or not the beneficial owner of the funds being transacted is anonymous or nontransparent or otherwise cannot be traced to a legitimate source. A criterion for flagging a transaction as potentially relating to stolen or undeclared commodities such as timber, oil, or gas could be whether or not the transaction appears to be designed to disguise ownership and/or avoid taxes in the country from which the commodity has been extracted.

Recommendation (as excerpted)	Analysis	Potential Impact
Recommendation 1: Countries should apply the crime of money laundering to all serious offenses, with a view to including the widest range of predicate offenses.	Although handling the proceeds of corruption is now a predicate offense in most countries, which is required under the FATF recommendations, laundering the proceeds of conflict commodities is only implicitly criminalized, to the extent that the proceeds are deemed illicit.	The FATF, through issuing an interpretative note to this recommendation, could specify that the laundering of particular forms of conflict commodities is included within its scope. Were such commentary to be issued, jurisdictions either could interpret their "all crimes" criminal offense to apply to trade in conflict commodities or could add such an offense to a list of specific predicate offenses, facilitating identification, investigation, and prosecution of any laundering of the proceeds of conflict commodities.
Recommendation 2: Countries should ensure that criminal liability (and where possible civil or administrative liability) apply to legal persons (such as corporations).	When a financial transaction involving commodities is deemed illicit because the commodities (and thus the proceeds) have been tainted by corruption, fraud, theft, sanctions violations, or any other violation of law in countries with jurisdiction over the commodities or funds, liability under this principle could adhere not only to individuals involved with the transaction but to any businesses involved with the transaction. Potentially, such liability could extend to importers as well as exporters and to commercial financial institutions as well as methods of transport, to the extent that any of those businesses knowingly handled the illicit conflict commodities or the proceeds of such commodities.	To date, this recommendation and its precursor have not focused on conflict commodities, in part because the documentation requirements for such commodities—and for the funds relating to such commodities—have been too scanty to generate much evidence for regulators or investigators. Were such documentation to be thickened, this recommendation would provide the basis for substantial incentives for corporations to eschew involvement with such commodities so as to avoid the risk of liability.

(continues)

Table 4.1 continued

Recommendation (as excerpted)	Analysis	Potential Impact
Recommendation 3: Countries should adopt measures to enable them to confiscate laundered property, proceeds from money laundering and from predicate offenses, and the instrumentalities used to commit the offenses.	This recommendation authorizes confiscation of the instrumentalities of laundering and of the instrumentalities by which predicate offenses have been created. Applied to conflict commodities, it would authorize countries to confiscate the commodities themselves as well as the mechanisms that have transported them, such as boats and airplanes.	Applying this recommendation to confiscate conflict commodities, boats, and airplanes would create powerful economic disincentives to trafficking in conflict commodities designated as illicit. Again, an interpretative note by the FATF explicitly urging this interpretation could facilitate further action by countries adopting the FATF's recommendations.
Recommendation 6: Financial institutions should, in relation to politically exposed persons, take reasonable measure to establish the source of wealth and source of funds.	This recommendation is intended to combat the laundering of the proceeds of corruption. However, in the absence of further action to define conflict commodities and to deem them illicit, it is not clear that this recommendation would currently be applied to require financial institutions to treat as improper wealth and sources of funds generated from conflict commodities.	Again, an interpretative note by the FATF specifying particular forms of conflict commodities as illicit and encouraging countries to require due diligence for them would make it more difficult for senior political and governmental officials to place proceeds received from conflict commodities into financial institutions subject to regulation under the FATF recommendations.

(continues)

Table 4.1 continued

Recommendation (as excerpted)	Analysis	Potential Impact
Recommendation 12: Customer due diligence and record-keeping requirements should be applied to designated nonfinancial businesses and professions, including dealers in precious metals and dealers in precious stones.	This recommendation could readily be applied to require special due diligence of dealers in precious metals and dealers in precious stones to demonstrate that they are not dealing in conflict commodities such as conflict diamonds, coltan, or tanzanite.	An interpretative note could specify particular types of metals and stones that are subject to international controls, such as the diamonds subject to the Kimberley Process, and require countries to demand that businesses carry out due diligence to ensure that they are not handling such goods, at risk of loss of license, confiscation, and other sanctions, including criminal penalties. Here, the regulatory oversight of these otherwise minimally regulated businesses could have a profound deterrent effect, especially given the central role of consumer markets in the European Union and North America as purchasers of these goods.
Recommendation 16: Require dealers in precious metals and dealers in precious stones to report suspicious transactions when they engage in any large cash transaction with a customer.	This new FATF recommendation has obvious applicability to conflict commodities. Once precious metals and precious stones have been identified as illicit, dealers in these commodities would be required to report efforts to launder them, making investigation, prosecution, and confiscation possible.	Sanctioning of jewelers or precious metal dealers for failing to report suspicious transactions involving conflict commodities in their countries could have an immense deterrent effect on the smuggling of such commodities. Again, an FATF interpretative note could facilitate early implementation of this approach.

(continues)

Table 4.1 continued

Recommendation (as excerpted)	Analysis	Potential Impact
Recommendation 21: Financial institutions should give special attention to business relations and transactions with persons, including companies and financial institutions, from countries which do not or insufficiently apply the FATF Recommendations. Whenever these transactions have no apparent economic or visible lawful purpose, their background and purpose should, as far as possible, be examined, the findings established in writing and be available to help supervisors, auditors, and law enforcement agencies.	An FATF interpretative note could ask member states to promulgate regulations or guidelines to focus the financial institutions they regulate on giving heightened scrutiny to transactions involving jurisdictions in which conflict commodities are being routinely laundered. Often, these are states whose financial services sectors are profiting from war in neighboring areas of conflict. Application of the recommendation to this problem would be facilitated if nongovernmental organizations and international bodies, such as the UN, were to identify to the FATF particular jurisdictions where commercial financial institutions appeared to be handling the proceeds of conflict commodities.	Existing FATF efforts to "name and shame" have had a substantial impact in forcing jurisdictions to adopt global standards on anti–money-laundering efforts, at threat of loss of market access. Were the UN to ask the FATF to take on this form of "name and shame," jurisdictions whose commercial financial institutions are systematically profiting from conflict commodities could see those institutions face limits on access to major financial centers. In other jurisdictions, asset seizures and asset forfeitures of the proceeds of conflict commodities that are subject to international sanctions might also be facilitated as a result of the heightened scrutiny applied to financial transactions from those jurisdictions.

More detailed systems of red flags would require what the FATF terms "typology studies," in which experts from different jurisdictions convene and share experiences regarding prior cases involving a particular form of money laundering. Salient characteristics of the mechanism under study are identified, and the typological exercise becomes the basis for developing diagnostic criteria or red flags.

This approach is not a panacea. Numerous transactions could be disguised as being financially licit at their source, making subsequent identification of the proceeds as illicit difficult. However, regimes change, corrupt officials become subject to investigation, and illicit transactions can come to light over time. Where FATF standards have not led to the identification of the proceeds of conflict commodities prior to their introduction into the global payments system, they may still be helpful in permitting the tracking of these proceeds later. For tracking after the fact to be most effective, financial documentation alone may not be enough. Instead, documents relating to the underlying commodity may be needed as a means of comparing declared financial transactions with declared physical goods moving across borders and of comparing both with the actual goods in transit.

The Second Trail: Documenting Goods in Transit

This section undertakes a preliminary analysis of how a customs-based regime focused on documenting the cross-border movement of goods could parallel the above described financial tracking system through a similar system undertaken by the World Customs Organization (WCO).

To date, the principal control mechanism applied to any conflict commodity is that established by the Kimberley Process Certification Scheme (KPCS) to curtail the trade in conflict diamonds. While innovative and symbolically important, the KPCS has been criticized for being incomplete. Its certification and documentation process is voluntary, self-regulating, and focused on a sole commodity. It is policed by industry members. Regulators and law enforcement play only a secondary role in implementing the KPCS, through the ability of customs officials to seize obviously nonconforming diamonds at borders.[26] Rather than constituting a complementary system of private- and public-sector enforcement, implementation relies almost entirely on private-sector efforts.

Concomitant with the KPCS have been the continuing efforts of the WCO to standardize international norms for export and import regulation and controls. These efforts accelerated substantially following the September 11, 2001, terrorist attacks, enabling the WCO to move forward with an ongoing initiative to create uniform documentary records for cross-border trade, regardless of where it takes place, as a means of both managing terrorism risks and enforcing existing export control agreements and programs.[27] The initiative includes the creation of the WCO's Unique Consignment Reference (UCR) number system as well as a model approach for storing and organizing customs data to create harmonized and integrated controls on goods moving across borders.

The UCR system is intended to become a reference-number mechanism for customs use throughout the world. A UCR number is the equivalent of a bar code applied as early as possible to track all international movements of goods for which customs control is required and then used as an "access key" for audit, consignment tracking, and information reconciliation.[28] By requiring every good moving in international trade to have a unique number attached to it, the UCR system would create a mechanism to monitor and track the identity and movement of goods by region, by country, by type of good, by seller, by buyer, by shipper, or by any other broadly useful characteristic.

Endorsed by the Customs Cooperation Council of the WCO on June 30, 2001, the UCR system remains in its infancy. Relying solely on the incentive of expedited processing to encourage use of the system, the WCO anticipates that it will be implemented initially by individual customs agencies on a voluntary basis, country by country and business by business. Later, use of the UCR system could be made obligatory at export.[29] The UCR system is conceived to be simultaneously a law enforcement and a trade facilitation tool, as well as a mechanism to provide enforcement agencies from different countries with the ability to share information regarding cross-border shipments. Potentially, it provides an information system for tracking physical goods from place to place that is at least as complete as the existing information system used by commercial financial institutions to track transactions from bank to bank. By helping provide accountability over legitimate trade, it would further highlight and isolate illegitimate trade. In creating accountability, it would also allow governments to track and punish those seeking to make illicit trade look lawful.

To date, there has been no discussion of using the UCR system in connection with conflict commodities. However, such use could be made were an international organization, such as the UN, to document particular cases in which conflict commodities were a problem and then ask the WCO to develop appropriate red flags that customs agencies could integrate into their procedures for monitoring UCR numbers.

A second, potentially useful mechanism for identifying and tracking the movement of conflict commodities and enforcing any regime prohibiting them is the new Container Security Initiative (CSI) launched by U.S. Customs in January 2002 to prevent global containerized cargo from being exploited by terrorists. This initiative is designed to enhance the security of sea cargo containers, some 200 million of which move among the world's major seaports annually. The CSI consists of several elements: using intelligence and automated information to identify and target high-risk customers; prescreening high-risk containers at the port of departure, rather than upon their arrival at U.S. ports, using advanced detection technology; and using smarter, tamper-proof containers.[30]

To date, the focus of the CSI has been to uncover contraband that might be hidden in containers. Its potential use in connection with conflict commodities would come in the investigative phase, when such commodities have already been identified as being in transit and are targeted for tracking. Thus it is a secondary logistical mechanism that could be integrated with the UCR system to track and confiscate conflict commodities.

Were such a system implemented, it might work as follows. Conflict commodities that have been subject to sanction by the UN would not be allowed to enter the stream of commerce using an authentic UCR number, given that the point of origin of the goods would be labeled. The UCR system could potentially be applied to goods moving across national borders not only in containers and barrels but in briefcases and envelopes: all that is required is the international political will to mandate the use of UCR numbers for all commercial shipments of all types of goods across borders. When the activities of particular firms have been found to be suspect, their use of the UCR system would be prohibited, and any effort at further evasion would necessarily involve falsification of UCR documentation. Once a customs agency detects improper UCR documentation, other UCR documentation with the same characteristics could then be traced and matched to containers, and the ports participating in the CSI could treat this information as a red flag to apply to any containers relating to the persons, entities, or goods covered by the suspect UCR documentation. Because private-sector businesses would be required to use a UCR number to import goods to any of the most developed countries, the impact of the tracking system on the limited capacity of less-developed countries would be relatively minimized. Moreover, the less-developed countries could agree that a program to take advantage of the UCR system at their ports to improve monitoring and tracking could help both to increase security and to provide greater tax revenues associated with imports and exports. Their agreement could be leveraged by World Bank financing and technical assistance upon implementation.

Because both the UCR system and the CSI are recent initiatives, their combined use to track and curtail conflict commodities will likely be subject to a number of unforeseen or currently unaddressed technical factors, including appropriate methods that would allow the various customs authorities to store and exchange information. For this reason, it would be premature to assess the best mechanism by which the two initiatives might be linked and used as means of implementing red flag procedures applicable to conflict commodities. Still, some options are possible. To begin the process, WCO member states or the UN could ask the Customs Cooperation Council to consider the applicability of these initiatives to conflict commodities and to report back recommendations for action.[31]

At the same time, WCO member states or the UN might suggest to the Customs Cooperation Council that standard documentation for goods in transit, including those subject to the UCR system, include more information regarding the particular financial institution providing trade or other financial services for the flow of funds that corresponds to a given transaction. This information, when added to certificates of origin, might facilitate further tracking of any entities or individuals involved in efforts to circumvent international sanctions applicable to conflict commodities.

Merging Tracking Systems into a Common Mechanism

This chapter has traced the evolution of two separate universal systems for record keeping and tracking, one financial, the other physical. Gateways to enable movement of information from one government to another are recent on the financial side and are only now emerging on the physical side. A common information system for financial regulators was created in 1995 through the establishment of an informal network of financial intelligence units (the Egmont Group)[32] and had limited implementation prior to the terrorist attacks on September 11, 2001. The WCO has yet to establish a common database and information system, although the UCR system could readily evolve into one.

Even if the systems were fully implemented, they would still suffer from inherent limitations. Financial transactions are ordinarily "real" in financial terms, in that electronic impulses do move recorded digits from one account to another in the course of a transaction. However, the relationship of those electronic impulses to underlying economic realities—such as the transfer of ownership of goods for which payment has been made—may not be readily ascertainable from the documents associated with the financial transaction. These documents may refer to physical goods that do not exist, that exist in different quantities, or that are owned by persons other than the declared owners. Similarly, the actual financial transactions involved in shipments of goods may also be difficult to determine from the documentation associated with the goods themselves. While governments may be concerned that the goods be correctly valued in order to determine the correct tax due under the applicable tariff, documentation regarding the financial transactions associated with the goods is not part of what customs officials typically see.

The information system of the Egmont Group and the information system that may be developed in connection with the new UCR system could potentially be matched in cases involving suspicious transactions. Today, a request for information on a suspicious financial transaction moves from financial intelligence unit to financial intelligence unit of the respective counties through the Egmont Group process. A similar request involving an apparently improper shipment of goods could move from customs agency to customs agency. Cross-sectoral sharing of information, by contrast, is ad hoc, infrequent, and not governed by common sets of procedures or norms.

Improved sharing of information between financial regulators and customs agencies could be facilitated by the inclusion of financial information on customs documentation, such as the name of any bank or other commercial financial institutions involved in the financial portion of a cross-border transaction. In practice, parties to the transaction would have to provide the information to government representatives for official purposes. The provision of this information could be compelled by national authorities through the adoption of a common international norm, as a required element of all shipping documents. The creation of a system for information sharing could be undertaken through an agreement between the Egmont Group and the WCO, for example, developed at the request of the UN or member states. It could include the addition of basic financial transaction information to the UCR system or the creation of software to facilitate information matching from separate databases reflecting different elements (financial, physical) of the same underlying transactions.

Such a unified tracking regime would benefit the enforcement of all existing anti–money-laundering, terrorist finance, and customs regimes, as it would facilitate the tracking of both the funds and the goods involved in smuggling narcotics, weapons, and precursor materials used for weapons of mass destruction, as well as sanctions busting in any form, including that involving conflict commodities, especially where red flags have been developed to identify particular illicit commodities and funds. At the same time, a unified tracking regime could also form the basis for a new blacklisting or naming-and-shaming instrument to target countries, firms, and individuals that do not adhere to the now globalized monitoring and tracking standards. The regime, in short, could be applied to target either those who violate bans on the trade of conflict commodities or the proceeds of illicit resource exploitation, including buyers, sellers, consigners, financiers, and profiteers alike.

Incentive-Based Programs

Since the September 11, 2001, terrorist attacks, customs agencies around the world have increasingly accepted a movement toward incentive-based systems in which exporters and transportation companies seeking preferential treatment for their shipments have agreed to adopt enhanced security controls, including both improved documentation and physical security measures. Under this approach, the U.S. government has, for example, adopted "white lists" for ports, transportation firms, and particular exporters that meet specific requirements.[33] Given the huge commercial advantage of moving goods quickly, the private sector's implementation of standards generated by governments has been extraordinarily rapid.

The incentives-based approach of the U.S. Customs' Container Security Initiative has already had substantial impact, rapidly compelling ports in many countries to adopt "best practices" in container security as a condition for speedy entry to the U.S. market. To date, in dealing with transnational financial services, the major international organizations focused on financial transparency, the FATF and the OECD, have adopted an approach that is purely punitive in nature. These initiatives have relied on a process of naming and shaming that targets poorly regulated jurisdictions, identified as unfair tax competitors, as well as noncooperative countries, deemed to be resisting compliance with money-laundering initiatives. The FATF has actually imposed sanctions on a number of states, while the OECD has merely had to warn that it would do so to secure changes in the domestic legislation of offending jurisdictions. These initiatives have threatened offenders with possible loss of market access. The result has been that the legal and regulatory regimes in these jurisdictions are changing to more closely resemble those of the United States and Europe, even in such historically nontransparent areas as the Middle East and in such historically nontransparent sectors as alternative remittance houses. But the actual practices of many of these countries have not changed, largely due to the capacity problems described above.

Here, the work of the Wolfsberg Group, whose membership includes a number of the largest international private-sector banks, provides a possible model for action. The Wolfsberg Group has identified a set of standards for its member institutions to apply to all of their businesses as well as their activities throughout the world.[34] Thus, where a country with limited capacity is unable to enforce money-laundering and transparency laws within its own jurisdiction, members of the Wolfsberg Group have committed to assist them in building enforcement capacity as a matter of internal compliance with their own policies and procedures. The Wolfsberg Group commitments are still new and untested, so public evidence as to how this model has worked in reality is not yet available.

To enhance similar approaches, governments could work with the private sector to develop "seal initiatives," whereby private-sector entities agree to apply certain standards on a global basis to ensure that documents are created to cover all elements of an activity, that the documents are retained and shared with governments for regulatory and enforcement purposes, and that "dirty business" will be turned away. Seal initiatives could in turn lead to financial white lists, whereby those participating in the seal program are rewarded with business. Were the World Bank, the United States, and the EU, for example, to agree to place their deposits only in banks adhering to the Wolfsberg Group's standards, those standards would become a global norm at near lightning speed. Shareholders would demand the standards. Managers would insist on them. Compliance departments would become a corporation's profit center, rather than a drain on resources.

Conclusion

Economic globalization has been made possible, in part, by the increasing harmonization and networking of transportation systems and financial information afforded by technical progress in computerization and telecommunications. Governance, however, has not kept pace with globalization. Even in the most robust jurisdictions, the exercise of purely domestic sovereignty by government regulators cannot in and of itself effectively respond to cross-border problems. Conflict commodities can be viewed as one example of a cross-border problem requiring cross-border solutions. Emerging global norms for financial transparency, regulation, supervision, and enforcement have yet to be adapted to focus on conflict commodities, but as this chapter has indicated, they could readily be made to do so. Measures undertaken to track the movement of goods across borders could be expanded to directly address the trade in conflict commodities through the development of a red flag process that could be matched against documentation. Further synergies might be possible if the data collected under the requirements of financial and customs documentation could be linked. Should policymakers choose to undertake more effective tracking, the FATF and the WCO offer appropriate mechanisms to undertake the initial exploration of such synergies.

Notes

1. For a comparison of different certification schemes, see Corene Crossin, Gavin Hayman, and Simon Taylor, "Where Did It Come From? Commodity Tracking Systems," in Ian Bannon and Paul Collier, eds., *Natural Resources and Violent Conflict: Options and Actions* (Washington, D.C.: World Bank, 2003), pp. 97–160. The Kimberley Process involves more than sixty-five governments, the diamond industry, and civil society and has been establishing minimum acceptable international standards for national certification schemes relating to trade in rough diamonds. See also Chapter 3 by Ian Smillie in this volume.

2. See Jonathan M. Winer, *Illicit Finance and Global Conflict*, Fafo Report no. 380 (Oslo: Fafo Institute, 2002); and Jonathan M. Winer and Trifin J. Roule, "The Finance of Illicit Resource Extraction," in Bannon and Collier, *Natural Resources and Violent Conflict*, pp. 161–214.

3. See, for example, Philippe Le Billon, "Getting It Done: Instruments of Enforcement," in Bannon and Collier, *Natural Resources and Violent Conflict*, pp. 215–286.

4. United Nations, "The Role of Diamonds in Fuelling Conflict: Breaking the Link Between the Illicit Transaction of Rough Diamonds and Armed Conflict as a Contribution to Prevention and Settlement of Conflicts," resolution adopted by the General Assembly, A/RES/55/56, January 29, 2001.

5. See, for example, Global Witness, *For a Few Dollars More: How Al Qaida Moved into the Diamond Trade* (London: Global Witness, 2003); Douglas Farah, "Report Says Africans Harbored Al Qaida: Terror Assets Hidden in Gem-Buying Spree," *Washington Post*, December 29, 2002, p. A1.

6. See, for example, Sue Williams, "The Globalization of the Drug Trade," *Sources*, no. 111 (April 4, 1999): pp. 4–5, available at www.unesco.org/most/sourdren.pdf; and Mark Findlay, *The Globalisation of Crime: Understanding Transnational Relationships in Context* (London: Cambridge University Press, 1999).

7. See, for example, Lawrence Summers, "International Financial Crises: Causes, Preventions, and Cures," *American Economic Review* 90 no. 2 (2000): 1–16; and Robert E. Litan, "Economics: Global Finance," in P. J. Simmons and Chantal de Jonge Oudraat, eds., *Managing Global Issues: Lessons Learned* (Washington, D.C.: Brookings Institution, 2001), pp. 196–233.

8. See Winer and Roule, "Finance of Illicit Resource Extraction."

9. For a discussion of the traditional approach to dual criminality and its effect on international cooperation, see Steven Lubert and Jan Stern Reed, "Extradition of Nazis from the United States to Israel: A Survey of Issues in Transnational Criminal Law," *Stanford Journal of International Law* 23 (1986): 20. For a discussion of the historic principle of dual criminality and an expression of concerns about its erosion, see Susie Alegre (legal officer for EU Criminal Justice at the British Section of the International Commission of Jurists), "EU Cooperation in Criminal Matters: A Critical Assessment of the European Arrest Warrant," lecture in the International Seminar for Experts, Justice and Home Affairs: Toward the Full Implementation of the Amsterdam Treaty, organized by the Cicero Foundation in Paris in the series Great Debates, February 14–15, 2002, available at www.cicero-foundation.org/lectures/p4alegre.htm.

10. These include Interpol, the WCO, the Egmont Group, the FATF, and, in terms of norm setting in some areas, the UN and regional organizations. In Europe these organizations include EUROPOL and EUROJUST for policing and prosecutorial cooperation and the Schengen Group for immigration and asylum; in southern Africa, the law enforcement and regulatory components of the Southern African Development Community (SADEC); and in the Caribbean, the same components of Caribbean Community (CARICOM).

11. See, generally, International Institute for Strategic Studies, "Transnational Control of Money-Laundering," in *Strategic Survey, 2001/2002* (Oxford: Oxford University Press, 2002).

12. The member jurisdictions of the FATF currently include Argentina, Australia, Austria, Belgium, Brazil, Canada, Denmark, Finland, France, Germany, Greece, Hong Kong (China), Iceland, Ireland, Italy, Japan, Luxembourg, Mexico,

the Netherlands, New Zealand, Norway, Portugal, Singapore, Spain, Sweden, Switzerland, Turkey, the United Kingdom, and the United States, together with the European Commission and the Gulf Cooperation Council. In turn, the FATF has associated regional organizations whose members collectively include more than half the members of the United Nations.

13. Organization for Economic Cooperation and Development (OECD), *Harmful Tax Competition: An Emerging Global Issue* (Paris: OECD, 1998).

14. The Financial Stability Forum was convened in April 1999 to promote international financial stability through information exchange and international cooperation in financial supervision and surveillance. It brings together national authorities responsible for financial stability in major international financial centers, international financial institutions, sector-specific international groupings of regulators and supervisors, and committees of central bank experts. See www.fsforum.org/home/home.html.

15. United Nations Convention against Transnational Organized Crime, UN General Assembly Resolution 55/25, A/Res/55/25, January 8, 2001, available at www.undcp.org/pdf/crime/a_res_55/res5525e.pdf.

16. GRECO is responsible, in particular, for monitoring observance of the "Guiding Principles for the Fight against Corruption" and implementation of the international legal instruments adopted in pursuit of the Programme of Action against Corruption. So far three such instruments have been adopted, the Criminal Law Convention on Corruption (ETS no. 173), opened for signature on January 27, 1999; the Civil Law Convention on Corruption (ETS no. 174), adopted in September 1999 and opened for signature on November 4, 1999; and Recommendation R 10, on codes of conduct for public officials, adopted on May 11, 2000.

17. These include the Caribbean Financial Action Task Force (1990), the Asian-Pacific Group on Money Laundering (1997), the Financial Action Task Force on Money Laundering in South America (2000), and the Eastern and Southern Africa Anti–Money Laundering Group (1999). Regional initiatives also include conventions of the Organization of American States against money laundering (December 1995, amended October 1998), the European Union's two money-laundering directives (1991 and 2001), and to some extent the work undertaken by the Basel Committee of Bank Supervisors in its initiative (2000–2003) to revise standards for the treatment of bank capital, which would include certain provisions pertaining to risks associated with nontransparency.

18. "The New Basel Capital Accord: An Explanatory Note," Secretariat of the Basel Committee on Banking Supervision, January 2001, available at www.bis.org/publ/bcbsca01.pdf.

19. IOSCO's current membership includes the securities regulators and enforcement agencies of approximately sixty countries.

20. "Supervision of Cross-Border Banking," report prepared by members of the Basel Committee on Banking Supervision and the Offshore Group of Banking, October 1996.

21. The Wolfsberg Group consists of the following leading international banks: ABN Amro N.V., Banco Santander Central Hispano S.A., Bank of Tokyo-Mitsubishi Ltd., Barclays Bank, Citigroup, Credit Suisse Group, Deutsche Bank A.G., Goldman Sachs, HSBC, J.P. Morgan Chase, Société Générale, and UBS A.G. See www.wolfsberg-principles.com.

22. See also Chapter 5 by Sue Eckert in this volume.

23. The FATF has engaged in a major initiative to identify noncooperative countries and territories (NCCTs) in the fight against money laundering, to seek out

critical weaknesses in anti–money-laundering systems which serve as obstacles to international cooperation, and to ensure that all financial centers adopt and implement measures for the prevention, detection, and punishment of money laundering according to internationally recognized standards. In June 2000, fifteen jurisdictions (Bahamas, Cayman Islands, Cook Islands, Dominica, Israel, Lebanon, Liechtenstein, Marshall Islands, Nauru, Niue, Panama, Philippines, Russia, St. Kitts and Nevis, and St. Vincent and the Grenadines) were named as having critical deficiencies in their anti–money-laundering systems. In June 2001 the FATF updated the list of NCCTs, eliminating four countries (Bahamas, Cayman Islands, Liechtenstein, and Panama) and adding six (Egypt, Guatemala, Hungary, Indonesia, Myanmar, and Nigeria). In September 2001 two more countries were added to the list (Grenada and Ukraine); in June 2002 four more were removed (Hungary, Israel, Lebanon, and St. Kitts and Nevis). As of March 31, 2003, only four of the original fifteen countries remained on the list (Cook Islands, Nauru, the Philippines, and St. Vincent). In early 2003, both Nauru and the Philippines passed corrective legislation that amounted to complete capitulation to international standards, at least on paper.

24. The FATF Forty Recommendations are available at www1.oecd.org/fatf/40recs_en.htm.

25. "Report on Non Cooperative Countries and Territories," Financial Action Task Force, February 14, 2000, available at www.fatf-gafi.org/pdfncct_en.pdf.

26. This view appears to be widespread among nongovernmental organizations. See, for example, Canadian Centre for Foreign Policy Development's "Conflict Diamonds: The African Connection," available at www.ecommons.net/ccfpd-africa/main.phtml?section=vancouver&show=conflict; Washington Office on Africa, "Kimberley Process on Diamonds Inaugurated," *Washington Notes on Africa* 28, no. 3 (2002/2003), available at www.woaafrica.org/Diamonds9.htm. This view is also expressed by the U.S. General Accounting Office in its report to the U.S. Congress, "Significant Challenges Remain in Deterring Trade in Conflict Diamonds," February 13, 2002.

27. Major export control agreements and programs listed by the WCO include the Wassenaar Arrangement on Export Controls for Conventional Arms and Dual-Use Goods and Technologies; the Nuclear Nonproliferation Treaty (NPT) and Comprehensive Nuclear Test-Ban Treaty; the Missile Technology Control Regime (MTCR); the Chemical Weapons Convention; UN conventions on narcotics and transnational organized crime, including money-laundering provisions; the Biological Weapons Convention; UN Security Council resolutions on sanctions; the Convention on International Trade in Endangered Species of Wild Fauna and Flora (CITES); intellectual property rights treaties; the Convention on Facilitation of International Maritime Traffic; the Container Security Initiative; and the International Civil Aviation Organization's Facilitation (FAL) Convention (annex 9 of the Chicago Convention).

28. "The WCO Unique Consignment Reference (UCR) Number," WCO Fact Sheet (Brussels: World Customs Organization), available at www.wcoomd.org/ie/en/Topics_Issues/FacilitationCustomsProcedures/unique%20consignement.pdf. The WCO has designed the UCR numbering system around a simple code that uses up to thirty-five alphanumeric characters. The first character identifies the year; the next two characters identify the country. The remaining thirty-two contain an officially recognized national company identifier and a sequential and unique reference number applied internally by the issuer, to make the consignment reference unique.

29. "WCO Unique Consignment Reference (UCR) Number."

30. As of May 2004, countries with ports participating in CSI included Belgium, Canada, France, Germany, Hong Kong, Italy, Japan, Malaysia, Singapore, Sweden, and the United Kingdom. Ports in China, South Korea, Spain, Sri Lanka, and Thailand were in the process of complying with the requirements of CSI in order to enter the program. The United States describes the program as being in support of "cooperative G-8 action on transport security." See "Container Security Initiative Guards America, Global Commerce from Terrorist Threat," U.S. Customs Fact Sheet, March 12, 2003, available at www.customs.gov.

31. The United States has undertaken a third customs-related initiative called the Customs Trade Partnership against Terrorism (C-TPAT), under which U.S. Customs works closely with importers, carriers, brokers, warehouse operators, and manufacturers to ensure the integrity of their security practices and thus the integrity of their goods throughout the supply chain. C-TPAT is focused on security rather than enforcement but might also be relevant to facilitating the tracking of conflict commodities by increasing accountability of ownership of goods from point of origin to the end of the commodity chain.

32. See www.egmontgroup.org/about_egmont.pdf.

33. See, for example, the U.S. Container Security Initiative developed by the U.S. Department of Customs and now administered by the U.S. Department of Homeland Security Immigration and Customs Service; summary available at www.customs.ustreas.gov/xp/cgov/enforcement/international_activities/csi/csi_in_brief.xml.

34. See www.wolfsberg-principles.com.

5

Lessons from the UN's Counterterrorism Efforts

Sue E. Eckert

The terrorist attacks of September 11, 2001, moved the international community to embrace the issue of terrorism with renewed intensity. Within weeks the UN Security Council unanimously adopted Resolutions 1368 and 1373, containing comprehensive authority and binding obligations for all member states to take specific action to counter terrorism.[1] The requirement for member states to deny support for terrorists, including preventing the financing of terrorist acts, was unprecedented. It has set into motion a "new paradigm" for the international community's effort to combat terrorism that has resulted in substantive changes in the legal and administrative mechanisms of many countries.[2] Moreover, the body established to oversee implementation of Resolution 1373, the Counter-Terrorism Committee (CTC), developed innovative working methods and capacity-building efforts that may provide some useful lessons for improving UN sanctions regimes, as well as other attempts to address the trade in conflict goods.

The connection between the exploitation of natural resources and armed conflict has become a subject of significant analytical and policy attention, due largely to the increasing role that trade in lucrative commodities played in many civil wars of the 1990s.[3] Likewise, the relationship of armed conflict to terrorism has also gained greater prominence since the events of September 11. The Policy Working Group on the United Nations and Terrorism, established at the behest of the Secretary-General in October 2001, explicitly addressed this issue, noting that while efforts to prevent armed conflict are not primarily antiterrorist, they can serve to decrease the likelihood of terrorist acts by "narrowing the space in which terrorists operate."[4] Preventative action, especially measures to strengthen the national capacity of member states to stem conflict, can assist in efforts to deter terrorism. Similarly, some of the practices developed to combat terrorism can be adapted to enhance governments' abilities to address other related forms of conflict. Changes in the legal and administrative capacity of member states for counterterrorism purposes also can be beneficial to states wrestling with civil conflict. While not identical, these approaches can be complementary and mutually reinforcing.

To date, the UN's counterterrorism initiative has not focused specifically on the illicit exploitation of natural resources or the trade in conflict commodities, but linkages between the two have been alleged with increasing frequency in the media, by nongovernmental organizations (NGOs), and by UN expert panels. This chapter examines the experience to date of the UN's counterterrorism initiative under Resolution 1373 and assesses its potential applicability to the task of curtailing conflict commodities. A review of the structure and process of the CTC and a preliminary evaluation of its effectiveness in promoting more efficient counterterrorist practices among member states is followed by a consideration of two issues: first, the applicability of the innovative working methods of the CTC to the problem of conflict commodities more generally, and second, the options available for effecting this application in practice. While the CTC's mandate does not restrict it from investigating and taking action against the nonmonetary bases of terrorist funding, this analysis finds that an expansion of CTC activities to the terrorism-conflict commodities nexus, however useful, is neither likely nor desirable in the near term. Instead, this analysis suggests that other efforts to control the illicit exploitation and trade of resources in conflict zones, such as UN sanctions on commodities or commodity certification schemes, could be strengthened by incorporating some of the innovations developed by the CTC, in particular its monitoring, reporting, and capacity-building policies. In addition, creating greater linkages among these related efforts would be beneficial. Given the political will to do so, it is conceivable that in the longer term, the issue of conflict commodities could be addressed directly within a comprehensive international counterterrorism and conflict-resolution strategy.

Resolution 1373 and the Counter-Terrorism Committee

Security Council Resolution 1373

On September 28, 2001, acting under chapter VII of the UN Charter, the Security Council unanimously adopted Resolution 1373, calling upon all states to work together urgently to prevent and suppress terrorist acts.[5] It established a comprehensive set of requirements for all states to undertake to combat international terrorism. Under the binding resolution, all states must prevent and suppress the financing of terrorism (including by freezing terrorist assets), refrain from providing any form of support to terrorists, and deny safe haven to those who finance, plan, support, and commit such acts.

Beyond the mandatory provisions, Resolution 1373 also called upon states to intensify and accelerate the sharing of information on related issues; cooperate to prevent and suppress terrorist acts and take actions against perpetrators; become parties to relevant international conventions and protocols, including the International Convention for the Suppression of the Financing of Terrorism of December 9, 1999; and implement Security Council Resolutions 1269 (1999) and 1368 (2001) regarding strengthened international cooperation to combat terrorism. Of particular note, paragraph 6 of Resolution 1373 established the CTC to monitor the resolution's implementation through, among other things, mandatory reports from states on actions taken to that end.

While the issue of natural resources was not addressed explicitly in Resolution 1373, the Security Council noted the close connection between terrorism and "the related issues of transnational organized crime, illicit drugs, money-laundering, illegal arms-trafficking, and the illegal move-ment of nuclear, chemical, biological and other potentially deadly materi-als," emphasizing the need to enhance coordination of regulatory efforts on all levels.[6] In the Secretary-General's address to a Security Council meet-ing on counterterrorism in January 2002, he further underscored the linkage of counterterrorism efforts with other activities of the UN, "particularly on organized crime and the illicit traffic in weapons, drugs and other com-modities such as diamonds."[7]

In its entirety, Resolution 1373 is quite remarkable for the breadth and wide-ranging nature of the obligations imposed on member states. "For the first time, it imposed measures not against a State, its leaders, nationals or commodities, but against acts of terrorism throughout the world and the ter-rorists themselves."[8] According to one official, it is "undoubtedly one of the most comprehensive and far-reaching resolutions adopted in the history of the Security Council"[9] and is an unprecedented statement of the interna-tional community's political will to restrict terrorist financing in a manner that previously was unimaginable.

The Counter-Terrorism Committee

CTC structure and process. The CTC comprises the fifteen members of the Security Council and was chaired for the first eighteen months by Jeremy Greenstock, Permanent Representative of the United Kingdom; on April 5, 2003, the Permanent Representative of Spain, Inocencio Arias, assumed chairmanship of the CTC.[10] The committee has three vice chairs, each of whom chairs a subcommittee that reviews reports submitted by member states.[11]

From the beginning, the CTC signaled a unique approach to its task. The breadth and scope of its mandate, as well as its innovative working methods, distinguish it from other Security Council subsidiary organs such as sanctions committees. Indeed, while the CTC drew on the experience of previous sanctioning efforts, it has rejected any characterization as a sanctions committee. According to Greenstock, "The CTC is not a law-enforcement mechanism. Nor is it even a political instrument for bearing down on those who are politically less willing. It's a monitoring and analytical Committee, which will report facts to the Security Council, and then discussions and debates can continue in the Security Council."[12] It offers advice and guidance to governments on furthering the implementation of the resolution on the basis of self-assessments submitted by each state.

The CTC adopted principles at the outset that have become hallmarks of its work—cooperation, transparency, and equal treatment of member states.[13] A comprehensive website was created, and a directory of contact points within each member state was posted. Work programs for ninety-day periods were developed, and experts hired, initially in the areas of counterterrorism legislation and financial controls. To facilitate member states' preparation of mandatory reports on national actions taken to implement Resolution 1373, detailed guidance was developed.[14] This established an important threshold for substantive reporting and helped to serve as the basis for dialogue with states regarding follow-up actions to ensure implementation.

The detailed nature and specificity of information required of states has been a distinctive feature of the CTC. States must elaborate upon the legislative and executive measures they have in place, have taken, or contemplate to give effect to the resolution, as well as other efforts in related areas, with subsequent reports focusing on specific follow-up questions from the CTC.[15] The amount of detailed information on national practices to implement the requirements, especially regarding the legal basis and administrative mechanisms to control financial flows, is unprecedented. With nearly all reports translated and posted on the CTC website, the committee has amassed a wealth of information that provides both a benchmark of progress in improving counterterrorism policies and a source of policy models for member states. Indeed, by the end of 2001 when the first reports were due, the CTC had received 117 reports from member states, allowing the chairman to note the "excellent cooperation with the vast majority of Member States."[16] By May 12, 2003, the 191st report—from São Tomé and Príncipe—was received by the CTC, marking universal compliance of initial reporting by all UN member states.[17]

The process for evaluating each state's report is also novel. Each report is reviewed and analyzed by a team of independent experts. Based on the Forty Recommendations of the Financial Action Task Force on Money Laundering and the Eight Special Recommendations on Terrorist Financing,[18] and in consultation with other international institutions, the experts established criteria against which to assess each state's actions. These criteria focused on two questions: (1) Is there a need for follow-up for compliance with Resolution 1373, especially regarding legislation and terrorist financing? (2) Does the member state require assistance? Identification of weaknesses in the capacity of states to comply is important, since the CTC is responsible for assisting states to improve their implementation of all aspects of the resolution.[19] While questions from the CTC and advice to states are generally confidential as they relate to how states fill gaps in implementation, member states' reports and unclassified responses are circulated as Security Council documents and posted on the CTC website. In keeping with the objective of transparency, the CTC regularly produced discussion papers during the first eighteen months on issues associated with procedures for review of reports and guidance for states.[20]

Technical assistance. As the CTC began its review of reports, the lack of capacity within many states to implement Resolution 1373 became readily apparent. Implementation across states varies considerably, with many having little or no experience with counterterrorism efforts and some even lacking the most basic ability to prepare the required reports.[21] As of March 2003, more than 100 countries were identified as needing assistance, through either requests of the CTC or bilateral or multilateral overtures,[22] with the number rising by the end of August to 159.[23] The areas of greatest identified need were in legislative drafting of antiterrorism law and banking and financial law and regulations, especially regarding the financing of terrorism.

To assist governments in accessing information on best practices and potential assistance programs, the CTC developed a comprehensive Directory of Counter-Terrorism Information and Sources of Assistance, accessible online. The Technical Assistance Team was formed to raise awareness regarding the need for and sources of counterterrorism assistance, with Ambassador Curtis Ward appointed to head the program and to liaise with international and regional organizations. An assistance action plan was developed to facilitate self-help through resources such as the online directory, encourage donors to respond to assistance needs, and strengthen the capacity of regional and sectoral organizations to assist states. While the CTC itself does not provide technical assistance, it facilitates the flow of information between states with needs and potential providers, as well as promotes coherence between assistance activity and implementation gaps identified by the CTC.[24] With a growing realization among member states of the need for changes to implement Resolution 1373, identifying areas for technical assistance has become a major role of the CTC.

A key technical assistance tool is the regularly updated Matrix of Assistance Requests, which records the assistance needs of states and how such needs are being met. To better coordinate technical assistance efforts, on March 6, 2003, the CTC convened a special meeting of representatives of more than fifty international, regional, and subregional organizations. While each organization has its own mandate, this unique meeting helped to improve communications among groups regarding best practices relevant to the implementation of Resolution 1373, to eliminate duplication of effort and overlapping activities through increased cooperation and sharing of information, and to encourage regional organizations to develop counterterrorism action plans.[25] The CTC prepared a particularly informative index of the efforts of the international, regional, and subregional organizations with counterterrorism activities.[26] Follow-up meetings to coordinate technical assistance efforts have been regularized—one in October 2003, hosted by the Organization of American States in Washington, D.C., another in March 2004, organized by the Organization for Security and Cooperation in Europe in Vienna, and another to be hosted by the League of Arab States.[27] Further underscoring the critical need for assistance to countries with insufficient capacity to fight terrorism, the Group of Eight (G8) announced an action plan at the June 2003 Evian Summit. The stated purpose of the newly created Counter-Terrorism Action Group (CTAG) was to "support the CTC" in building political will and coordinating capacity-building assistance.[28]

Assessment of the CTC.[29] According to Sir Jeremy Greenstock, Resolution 1373 has resulted in "the beginnings of a global network to tackle terrorism," with the CTC being the "central catalytic body."[30] While it is too early to determine how effective the UN's counterterrorism efforts will be in the long run, there are positive indications that substantive changes have enhanced the legal and administrative mechanisms of many countries to combat terrorism.

In characterizing the initial cooperation and global support for the work of the CTC, the chairman noted that "the vast majority of governments throughout the world have begun to respond to the challenge laid down in Resolution 1373 to prevent and suppress terrorism. In almost every case, parliaments have begun to consider or adopt new laws. Governments have reviewed the strength of their institutions to fight terrorism, and in some cases, have already strengthened it."[31]

One indicator of progress is the number of states that have become parties to the international conventions on terrorism.[32] In September 2001, only two states were parties to all twelve conventions and protocols on combating terrorism. By 2004, that number had increased to more than fifty-seven.[33] In particular, widespread adoption of the International Convention for the Suppression of the Financing of Terrorism of December 9, 1999, led to the entry-into-force of the convention on April 10, 2002.[34] Broader adoption of these instruments by member states helps to strengthen the emerging international counterterrorism regime.

Another measure of progress relates to the international organizations addressing terrorist financing. The Financial Action Task Force on Money Laundering (FATF) adopted the Eight Special Recommendations on Terrorist Financing on October 31, 2001,[35] and has led a global self-assessment exercise to compare national practices against FATF standards. The FATF reports that more than eighty countries and jurisdictions have adopted, or are in the process of adopting, new legislation, regulations, or procedures to strengthen their ability to prevent terrorists from using their financial systems, including full or partial compliance of almost all thirty-three FATF members.[36] Moreover, the anti–money-laundering and counterterrorist financing recommendations established by the FATF have been adopted by the World Bank and International Monetary Fund as part of their institutionalized assessment of countries.[37] Additionally, as a result of the CTC, there is much greater coordination of the capacity-building assistance provided by the range of international, regional, and subregional organizations.

The reports submitted by member states to the CTC remain the primary indicators of changes resulting from the UN's counterterrorism initiative. The unprecedented 100 percent reporting compliance can be cited as a success in and of itself, as noted earlier.[38] However, even the CTC has recognized that its work in the next phase can no longer be measured by statistics but by depth of analysis, since the complexity of issues addressed in implementation will necessarily increase.

A review of the reports indicates that the CTC's greatest impact has been in three main areas: the adoption of national legislation, the formation of domestic institutions to address terrorist financing, and the identification of the technical assistance needs of states. The vast majority of states have put into place or proposed new legal instruments to criminalize the collection and/or provision of terrorist funds, as well as to freeze suspect assets.[39] Organizations such as the African Union attribute renewed momentum to harmonize and strengthen efforts to combat terrorism on a regional basis to Resolution 1373 and report the adoption of new banking and financial measures.[40]

In particular, the effect of the CTC can be seen in the evolution of states' views regarding the adequacy of anti–money-laundering legislation. Initially most states relied on such legislation to address Resolution 1373's requirement to prohibit the financing of terrorism. It was only after dialogue with the CTC that states came to understand that necessary legislation should not only cover money laundering but also specifically criminalize the provision or collection of terrorist funds and permit the freezing of terrorist finances. With regard to the freezing of assets, however, less information is available. Although numerous countries have issued orders to freeze terrorist assets, most of the reported $140 million of frozen funds were located in the United States, Switzerland, Pakistan, and Saudi Arabia.[41]

The Resolution 1373 reports also indicate an enhancement of the administrative capacity of numerous states to deal with terrorist financing. New procedures have been adopted, lead agencies and central contact points have been identified, and new financial intelligence units or intragovernmental mechanisms to address terrorism issues have been formed by many member states. In Kuwait, for example, an interagency committee was established in 2002 under the chairmanship of the finance ministry to combat terrorist financing activities and money laundering. Many states indicate new or enhanced reporting requirements on banks and financial institutions, especially mandatory reporting of suspicious transactions.

Despite progress on the legal and institutional fronts, important weaknesses remain in states' abilities to stem terrorist funding through charities and alternative remittance systems. Based on reports to the CTC and the Committee Established Pursuant to Resolution 1267 Concerning the Taliban and Associated Entities (1267 Committee), most states have taken only limited action to regulate informal money transfer systems such as *hawalas*, other than registration or reporting requirements, with a few states denying their existence entirely by declaring them illegal.[42] Likewise, there is little information in country reports regarding the specific enforcement measures they have taken, although subsequent reports to the 1267 Committee provide somewhat more detailed information regarding investigative efforts. It is important to note, however, that the small number of enforcement actions may be attributable partly to the fact that until recently many states lacked even the basic legal infrastructure to address terrorist financing or relied on inadequate anti–money-laundering authorities.

Taken together, these indicators suggest that the UN's counterterrorism initiative has resulted in substantive changes in the ability of numerous countries to combat terrorism. Changing national practices of the magnitude required by Resolution 1373, however, is a significant undertaking that will take time. Material progress in building capacity may be slow at times, but the very existence of the CTC is in fact an important accomplishment. The challenge will be sustaining the momentum and international political will necessary for the CTC to ultimately succeed.

A potential problem with the CTC's approach to date concerns the risk of "cosmetic compliance" and an overreliance on reporting without meaningful monitoring and enforcement. While much has been accomplished through reporting and dialogue between member states and the CTC, good intentions are not enough; new measures must be implemented and enforced by states. To address a perceived reporting fatigue and waning of momentum in late 2003, the chairman of the CTC proposed to the Security Council a revitalization plan to address "serious problems" encountered at both the state and the CTC levels with implementation of Resolution 1373.[43] The Security Council adopted the plan in Resolution 1535 of March 26, 2004, which creates a new Counter-Terrorism Executive Directorate.[44] According to Chairman Arias, the goal is to make the CTC operative and empower the executive director with the clout to monitor implementation and to identify which countries are willfully not complying with Resolution 1373.[45]

The true test for the long-term success of the UN's counterterrorism initiative will be the Security Council's response when states are found to be noncompliant with the provisions of Resolution 1373—due to lack not of capacity but of will. When such a decision is made (which is not likely to come about until technical assistance efforts have run their course), the Security Council will need to act decisively, including possibly imposing secondary sanctions against states, to maintain the credibility of the process. In the meantime, events such as the March 11, 2004, Madrid bombings, which underscored the continuing threat that terrorism represents to all member states, help to sustain the political will to propel the international counterterrorism effort forward.

Applicability of UN Counterterrorism Efforts to Illicit Exploitation of Natural Resources in Conflict Zones

Based on the UN's counterterrorism efforts to date, there are two primary ways in which the experience may be applied to efforts to control the illicit exploitation of natural resources and trade in conflict commodities that have fueled a number of contemporary armed conflicts. The first is to apply the provisions of Resolution 1373 to conflict commodities directly, based on linkages between these resources and terrorist groups. The second is to apply the general lessons of Resolution 1373 and workings of the CTC to UN commodity, financial, and arms embargoes and commodity certification schemes such as the Kimberley Process, whose primary objective is to curtail the trade in rough diamonds from financing armed conflicts.

Utilizing Counterterrorism
Instruments to Address Conflict Commodities

As noted previously, linkages between terrorism, transnational organized crime, money laundering, and trafficking in illegal drugs, arms, and nuclear, chemical, biological, and other potentially deadly materials were explicitly recognized in Resolution 1373.[46] Terrorism and criminology experts have written of the terrorist-criminal nexus, in which these types of criminality at times utilize similar methods to raise and move funds.[47] Whether through trafficking in drugs or in contraband, transactions involving high-value goods such as precious gems or other lucrative natural resources, or even trade diversion, terrorist groups have proven opportunistic in financing themselves. When governments clamp down on one type of activity, such groups have proven adept at replacing lost proceeds with revenues from other activities, leading to a balloon effect.[48] Such phenomena underscore the interrelationship between these issues, as well as the necessity of a multifaceted approach to effectively address these challenges.

Reports of alleged use of natural resource revenues to fund terrorist operations have existed for years. Prior to September 11, 2001, press articles appeared regarding a secret Belgian military report asserting a relationship between certain diamond merchants and rebels of the National Union for the Total Independence of Angola (UNITA), as well as Hezbollah and Amal.[49] Following the September 11 attacks, however, greater attention was focused on the trade in rough diamonds and other commodities in West Africa as means of financing terrorist activities, primarily based on one source that appeared in late 2001 linking the terrorist network of Osama bin Laden with transactions involving illicit diamonds from Sierra Leone and Liberia.[50] Reportedly, a "$20 million diamond-buying spree" resulted from U.S. actions in 1998 to freeze Al-Qaida's assets following the attacks on the U.S. embassies in Kenya and Tanzania, purportedly leading to a wholesale effort to convert assets into untraceable commodities such as diamonds and tanzanite in the months prior to September 11.[51]

Some NGOs have also drawn attention to the alleged use of diamonds, gold, and tanzanite to generate revenues and launder assets of Al-Qaida.[52] In April 2003, Global Witness released a report asserting Al-Qaida's involvement in the rough diamond trade in West Africa since the 1990s, first as a moneymaking venture and then as a means of safekeeping its assets outside the formal banking sector. In addition, the 1267 Monitoring Group in its report to the Security Council referenced allegations of Al-Qaida's transfer of assets into gold and diamonds months before September 11 but indicated that it was unable to obtain additional information on such transactions.[53]

Notwithstanding these reports, little public information is available regarding the veracity of their allegations, perhaps in part due to intelligence issues involved. Many legitimate questions remain regarding the relative importance of the illicit exploitation of natural resources as a systematic means of financing terrorist operations, as opposed to being just one of a variety of opportunistic ways in which terrorists may possibly raise and transfer assets.

Should the member states desire to use it, Resolution 1373 and the CTC provide a vehicle to address the financing of terrorism using natural resources. As noted previously, the breadth of Resolution 1373 in requiring states to act to address terrorism is unprecedented. The prohibition on financing terrorist acts included a freeze not only of funds (traditionally defined as those held by banks or financial institutions) but also of "other financial assets or economic resources" of terrorists, which is broader than the requirements of previous sanctions resolutions and even the International Convention for the Suppression of the Financing of Terrorism.[54] While these terms are not defined in Resolution 1373, the expansive scope allows implementing agencies to give wide interpretation to *funds* and *economic resources*, which the European Commission did in broadening its definition of funds to encompass property in a manner similar to U.S. implementation.[55] Under such a definition, therefore, Resolution 1373 could be read to prohibit financing through conflict commodities utilized by terrorists, as well as traditional forms of financial assets.

Although Resolution 1373 does not limit the form of assets and therefore is broad enough to encompass the illicit trade in lucrative natural resources that may be exploited by terrorist groups, the CTC has not, to date, defined its work to include monitoring such trade. Rather it has been left for governments or relevant sanctions committees such as the 1267 Committee to identify the linkages of nonfinancial assets to terrorists or their supporters. Once identified, such assets would then be subject to freezing or seizure. As noted in the second report of the 1267 Monitoring Group, few member states have addressed the need for restrictions to control the movement of gold, diamonds, and other precious commodities, and only a very few states currently appear to have the authority to block assets other than bank accounts or other financial instruments.[56]

That national reports and the CTC's follow-up questions relate solely to freezing of financial assets may also be due, perhaps in larger part, to the fact that many states still lack basic legal authority and practice in freezing financial assets. While mechanisms to freeze financial assets have been developed and are available, there is very little experience in dealing with nonfinancial assets beyond property. The CTC's first priority, therefore, has been to build capacity to implement fundamental measures, defined as legislative and executive machinery aimed at controlling financial flows, which as noted above is a significant undertaking. While other aspects of the resolution are being addressed on a case-by-case basis, most are to be tackled only in later stages of the CTC's work.[57] No effort has yet been made by the CTC with respect to addressing the potential use of illicit commodity flows by terrorist groups. The likelihood of applying the UN's counterterrorism initiative in such a manner is discussed below.

Potential and Limitations of Expanding the CTC

As noted previously, the CTC has not yet directly addressed the issue of the illicit trade in natural resources and conflict commodities, even though Resolution 1373 is broad enough to encompass these activities. This self-limitation appears to be voluntary and practical at this point, reflecting both the complexity of the conflict commodity issues and the still-nascent character of policy responses.

In the case of financial assets, regulated intermediaries in the form of banks and financial institutions handle transactions and have the ability, pursuant to appropriate legal authority, to freeze accounts and stop payments. The control of natural resources, however, raises a host of questions to which there are few satisfactory answers. Due in part to the illicit nature of the trade in conflict commodities and also to the way that shadow activities often blur the boundaries between illicit and legal business transactions, difficulties abound in locating assets other than bank accounts. Furthermore, identification of ownership, restrictions on modes of transportation, and, ultimately, effective enforcement measures are especially vexing challenges, particularly for commodities whose provenance may be difficult to identify, that are easily lootable by a large number of actors, and that, as in the case of precious gems, are easily transported.

The primary mechanism established to address one of the more visible natural resources fueling conflicts—diamonds—is the Kimberley Process Certification Scheme (KPCS). Initial UN sanctions on rough diamonds were unsuccessful, largely because there was no systematic way of tracking rough diamonds internationally. The KPCS is intended to address this problem but is still in a very early stage.[58] Expanding the CTC's mandate to include conflict commodities would logically entail a more direct relationship between the efforts of the CTC and the Kimberley Process. Yet doing so could place too great a burden on the certification system when fundamental issues such as effective monitoring have yet to be tackled. In addition, the costs of establishing a capability within the CTC—both human and technical—to address the range of conflict commodities would be considerable, even if the political will to undertake more concerted measures did exist. In short, the challenge of ensuring implementation of the financial requirements of Resolution 1373 would be multiplied to such a point as to be overwhelming if applied broadly to natural resources.

Furthermore, it is likely that efforts to extend the CTC's mandate to conflict commodities would be met with resistance in the Security Council. Industrialized countries might view such a proposal as a distraction from an exclusive focus on terrorism, while developing countries endowed with natural resources would likely chafe at new requirements falling disproportionately on them. Almost by definition, the states most affected by armed conflict and the conflict trade are those with the least capacity to implement Resolution 1373 or those that have little motivation to cooperate with enhanced international control of their precious revenue-producing resources. Several of the countries whose natural resources would be affected are already subject to intensive technical assistance efforts to create basic elements of governmental control; they currently have neither the legal framework nor the national capacity to respond to new requirements focused on resources.

Does Resolution 1373 provide a viable means through which to address illicit trade in diamonds and other natural resources? For the time being, the answer is no. The CTC's progress is attributable in large part to its single-minded focus on terrorism, with the terrorist attacks of September 11 serving as the catalyst to coalesce international will to respond. Any change to that mission, no matter how worthy the objective, is likely to dilute the effort and lessen its effectiveness. Moreover, the CTC has neither the resources nor the capacity at this point to broaden its scope to address conflict commodities directly. Beyond being ill-advised from a substantive standpoint, changing the focus of Resolution 1373 in such a way would face substantial political challenges. Given current priorities and constraints, for the foreseeable future it seems most unlikely that there would be the necessary consensus to move the CTC in the direction of addressing conflict commodities and the illicit exploitation of natural resources in conflict zones.

This does not mean that the CTC cannot or should not address the issue in the future. In fact, the CTC work program clearly envisions "increased monitoring of transactions involving highly valuable objects (precious metals and gems) or sensitive materiel (weapons, dangerous materials)."[59] The Counter-Terrorism Executive Directorate, created by Resolution 1535 to "revitalize" the CTC, could evolve to assume some of these tasks. Countries' greater compliance with Resolution 1373 in restricting terrorist assets globally could make it even more attractive for terrorist organizations to hold assets in diamonds, gold, and other commodities. If evidence were to emerge that terrorist groups are systematically utilizing nonfinancial assets such as diamonds, member states would likely be more amenable to expanding the CTC's mandate in this area. The December 2003 report of the 1267 Monitoring Group, for example, specifically acknowledges that no states gave any indication of having frozen any tangible assets and notes that "very few States appear to have the authority to block assets other than bank accounts or other financial instruments."[60] For this reason, it is important that alleged links between illicit diamonds or other resources and terrorist organizations be analyzed and a more systematic understanding pursued regarding the potential of commodities to finance terrorist activities. Further study of the topic would be particularly helpful to the CTC as it evaluates its future course in the months and years ahead.

Lessons from the CTC for Parallel UN Efforts

Several innovations of the CTC have already proven instructive for current sanctioning initiatives and offer useful lessons for efforts to control illicit and destabilizing commodity flows.[61] In the case of sanctions against the Taliban and members of the Al-Qaida organization (monitored by the so-called 1267 Committee, named after Resolution 1267),[62] the Security Council has drawn upon many of the procedural changes resulting from the CTC experience. An important relationship exits between the 1267 Committee and the counterterrorism effort, as the CTC relies on the 1267 Committee to develop and maintain the list of targets against whom the counterterrorism measures apply.[63] Resolution 1455 of January 17, 2003, modeled on the CTC experience, called for a detailed work program and guidelines for operations; development of guidance for member states as to the format and content of reports, including specification to an unprecedented degree of detailed information to be contained in member state reports; monitoring and assessment of member state compliance by outside experts; and regular reporting to the Council.[64] The resolution also stressed the need for improved coordination and increased exchange of information between the 1267 Committee and the CTC.[65] Moreover, Resolution 1526, adopted by the Security Council on January 30, 2004, to improve the implementation of sanctions against the Taliban and Al-Qaida organization, incorporated further enhancements based directly on experience with implementation of Resolution 1373, such as broadening the requirement to freeze "economic resources" in addition to funds and charging the committee with the task of assessing member states' implementation of Resolution 1267 and informing the Security Council of states failing to report to the committee.[66]

Other sanctions committees on Liberia (Resolution 1521 [2003]) and the Democratic Republic of Congo (Resolution 1533 [2004]) have also adopted features derived from the 1373 experience—related to member states' reporting and enhanced monitoring of implementation by the committee through the use of experts—but progress in applying lessons has been haphazard at best. A more systematic understanding of successful methods utilized by committees of the Security Council to ensure compliance with the council's mandates should be undertaken; the consistent application of lessons learned and best practices could help ensure more effective implementation of Security Council measures in the future.

Generally, the lessons from the UN's counterterrorism effort can be divided into three categories—political will, institutional and process-related characteristics of the CTC, and elements necessary for successful capacity-building initiatives—all of which are relevant for parallel UN and other multilateral efforts to control conflict commodities.

Political will. The importance of political will to the progress of the counterterrorism initiative cannot be overstated. Prior to Resolution 1373, targeted financial sanctions had been shown to be technically feasible, yet the biggest challenges to effective action were the absence of international political will and the lack of implementing capacity within states.[67] Resolution 1373 and the CTC were products of the unique circumstances of September 11, which resulted in a rare demonstration of international consensus and political will. The CTC became the mechanism to translate that will and commitment into concrete changes within member states. Because of the extraordinary circumstances, the CTC was able to sidestep traditionally divisive issues that had impeded progress previously—such as the definition of terrorism and listing of targets—to focus on national-level implementation. Periodic high-level ministerial meetings of the Security Council, subsequent resolutions such as 1377, 1456, and 1535, as well as statements of the president of the Security Council, have been important in helping to maintain a focus on implementation and sustaining the political will to keep the counterterrorism effort moving forward. Effectiveness and long-term success of an initiative is thus directly related to the priority the Security Council attaches to the issue.

Innovative working methods. As described above, the CTC distinguished itself from previous UN sanctions efforts through novel working methods that have become the hallmark of the committee. Three distinctive characteristics have been particularly important.

First, the CTC operated to an unprecedented degree in an open and transparent manner, publishing guidelines and procedures for the conduct of its work, maintaining an informative website on its activities (with member state reports and background documents posted), and regularly communicating through briefings of the Security Council, interested member states, and the press by the chairman, as well as public speeches to promote understanding and visibility of the committee's efforts.

Second, the CTC established robust reporting requirements and provided member states with specific guidance as to the type of information to be submitted in national reports. As a result of the dialogue between states and the CTC, an unprecedented amount of information has been generated on measures taken by member states to implement Resolution 1373—an important prerequisite for evaluation of states' compliance.[68] Additionally, the 1267 Committee has underscored the importance of detailed identifying information regarding targeted entities in order to improve enforcement efforts.[69]

Third, an important feature of the CTC, building on the experience of recent sanctions committees, is the exceptional degree of reliance on experts. Previously, outside experts were utilized primarily as part of expert panels or monitoring groups.[70] In the case of the CTC, however, experts hired by the committee developed the initial criteria for member state reporting and, since then, have been employed on a rotating basis to conduct ongoing assessments of implementation. The role of outside experts as part of the dialogue with member states to improve implementation constitutes one of the most significant reforms in monitoring member states' compliance with Security Council mandates.

Traditionally, UN sanctions efforts have lacked the degree of transparency and information sharing that has characterized the CTC. On more than one occasion, this shortcoming has complicated the efforts of the Security Council to promote sanctions compliance among member states. Since the primary task of the sanctions committees and their affiliated expert panels is to report on sanctions implementation to the Security Council, less effort has been made to ensure public understanding of both the purposes of a specific set of sanctions and the way they are being applied. As the task of public information sharing rests with committee chairs, the degree of transparency and information sharing has depended on the personal capacities of the chair and the resources that his or her national government can bring to bear.[71] In cases where these conditions have obtained, such as the sanctions against UNITA under Canada's chairmanship and the Liberia Sanctions Committee headed by Singapore, the result was an unprecedented degree of transparency and dissemination of information. This development has been particularly welcomed by nongovernmental organizations, which can use such information to help hold states accountable.

Perhaps most important, the information accumulated by one committee or expert panel is often not readily available to others, even where actors and issues are crosscutting. Again, ad hoc innovations on the part of individual committees have sought to fill this gap. Still, there is no regular and systematic information sharing and dissemination equivalent to the efforts of the CTC. While the sanctions committees are beginning to adopt some of the practices pioneered by the CTC, they could all benefit by the creation of a consolidated, comprehensive database of mandates, reports, and compliance evaluations, available to all sanctions bodies and member states.

Sanctioning efforts of the UN could also benefit from the model of member states' reporting developed by the CTC, and as noted above, several already have. Traditionally, both the quantity and the quality of reports submitted by states to UN sanctions committees have been poor. Failure to report is common, while many reports are pro forma exercises typically consisting of no more than one sentence indicating that states "have taken all necessary steps to comply with the requirements of the resolution." Establishing clear, consistent, and explicit guidelines for reporting by member states could significantly improve sanctions implementation and provide an avenue for ensuring that the recommendations of experts are acted upon. Not least, more detailed reporting could enhance the accumulated knowledge of sanctions-busting methods and actors, particularly concerning resource predation, where systematic and reliable information is difficult to obtain. As a starting point, the CTC and the 1267 Committee could require member states to include information in their reports regarding relevant links between terrorists and natural resources. In addition, the language "funds, financial assets, or *economic resources*" could be defined explicitly to include diamonds, gold, and other natural resources belonging to terrorists that are to be frozen and clarify that all transactions in such commodities are prohibited under Resolution 1373.

Sanctions committees of the UN could also benefit from the lessons of the CTC regarding greater use of experts, not just as part of monitoring groups but as part of in-house capacity to work with member states to enhance compliance. The recommendations of financial law and practice and customs experts hired by the CTC have been important in helping to improve member states' compliance with Resolution 1373. Especially with conflict commodities, where specialized expertise and differentiated approaches are required based on the type of resource—diamonds, oil, transportation, arms, and so forth—the UN needs to enhance its ability to utilize qualified individuals on a contract basis. The sanctions branch of the UN Secretariat has established a roster of experts, who are most often used for monitoring groups as opposed to working for sanctions committees. A more systematic identification and expanded use of experts, as well as provision of adequate resources for hiring experts on an as-needed contractual basis, could assist UN committees in working with states to improve implementation efforts.

Capacity-building efforts. Historically, many observers of UN sanctions have focused on the *lack of political will* of member states as a primary impediment to successful implementation of Security Council mandates. Only limited attention, primarily from academics, has focused on the inability of states to comply with sanctions due to *lack of capacity*.[72] The CTC has been unique in its explicit recognition of and focus on the lack of capacity of many member states to comply with such measures, even when the political will exists.

While experience with building member state capacity to combat terrorism is still at an early stage, lessons derived from efforts to date include the importance of three elements. First, the sine qua non for states to address issues of terrorist financing or resource flows to conflict zones is the requisite legal basis to act. One of the lessons of the CTC, and of financial sanctions previously, is that most countries lack the legal and administrative infrastructure to give standing to decisions of the Security Council in domestic law. It is therefore critical that the Security Council establish binding obligations on states to act through adoption of a chapter VII resolution and that a national legal framework is put into place to implement council decisions. Model legislation to give effect to Security Council decisions promoted through the technical assistance program of the CTC is directly applicable to initiatives focused on regulation of the illicit exploitation of natural resources. International efforts aimed at combating terrorism or controlling resources related to armed conflict will be only as strong as the weakest states' ability to implement the measures.

Second, beyond the legal basis, states must strengthen their national machinery to carry out UN resolutions through administrative capacity building. The same measures that enhance a state's ability to deter terrorism can also assist in addressing other forms of conflict or natural resource control. Basic institutional mechanisms and training in areas such as immigration, border control, customs, financial monitoring, police and intelligence, and law enforcement have important benefits across the range of issues, including the monitoring and interdiction of illicit commodity flows.

Third, perhaps the biggest problem in building capacity is the lack of adequate resources and coordination of technical assistance efforts. To be effective, training, tools, and equipment must be provided commensurate with the task, which is a substantial undertaking. A key test of the CTC's technical assistance initiative is whether it merely coordinates existing programs or facilitates the infusion of *new* resources for countries' counterterrorism measures. The CTC's technical assistance team encourages donors to develop new programs and resources for counterterrorism needs, but some aid recipients remain concerned that donors will redeploy existing foreign assistance funds, thereby sacrificing the provision of basic human needs to the counterterrorism effort.[73] Enhanced resources—both financial and human—will be necessary for capacity building to succeed over time. The newly revitalized CTC Executive Directorate or the G8 Counter-Terrorism Action Group may provide useful means to garner additional resources for capacity-building initiatives.

Likewise, new requirements on member states to reduce trade in conflict commodities will be successful only if adequate technical and financial assistance are provided to states to implement appropriate regulatory and developmental frameworks, including sustained support to develop the various mechanisms needed to monitor and enforce them. Many of the commodities implicated in conflict, such as precious gems, timber, oil, and natural gas, present different challenges for regulation that require specialized expertise in devising appropriate methods and approaches. This can impose additional burdens, especially on fragile or war-torn states that are heavily dependent on their natural resource endowments—that is, those with the least capacity and means to undertake meaningful regulation.

The Way Ahead:
Counterterrorism and Illicit Resource Flows

This chapter has suggested two ways in which the UN's counterterrorism efforts are applicable to managing the illicit exploitation and trade in natural resources that have supported armed conflict: (1) expanding the mandate of the Counter-Terrorism Committee to address directly the illegal exploitation of natural resources and (2) applying the innovative working methods of the CTC to parallel efforts to address the problem of conflict commodities more generally and providing greater linkage among related efforts.

As the CTC still has much to do in the priority areas specifically addressed by Resolution 1373, for now the conflict commodities issues are best addressed by existing mechanisms of the Security Council—sanctions committees, expert or monitoring panels, and commodity-specific initiatives such as the Kimberley Process. Rather than to create new requirements that add to the already challenging mandate of the CTC, a better near-term alternative is to utilize the lessons of the CTC to strengthen existing efforts to build member states' legal and administrative capacity to fulfill Security Council mandates.

In particular, incorporating the CTC's experience in reporting, monitoring, and use of experts to assess member states' compliance can help to strengthen UN sanctions—the primary tool of the international community to address commodities such as diamonds and timber. Likewise, the CTC's efforts to enhance transparency are instructive, as there is clearly a need for more information regarding the illicit exploitation of natural resources, as discussed in other chapters in this book. More information regarding natural resources and the role they play in sustaining conflicts, as well as greater analysis within specific commodity sectors regarding the technical details of effective tracking and control, are important in furthering the issue.

Moreover, the CTC's experience in monitoring implementation can help inform the Kimberley Process Certification Scheme to curtail trade in conflict diamonds and possibly other less developed schemes such as for conflict timber. With certification and enforcement initiatives at such a preliminary phase, greater horizontal linkages and dialogue among the related policy instruments of sanctions, monitoring, and commodity certification initiatives would be helpful. Enhanced communications and coordination between the various efforts would be a useful first step.

As has been discussed previously, one of the most critical aspects of enhancing the international community's ability to effectively combat terrorism is increasing the capacity within member states to implement Resolution 1373 on a national level. As states change their legal and administrative infrastructure to counter terrorism, residual benefits accrue across a range of issues, including the monitoring and interdiction of conflict commodities. Legal and institutional improvements in border controls, customs, immigration, police and intelligence cooperation, and law enforcement will ultimately strengthen the ability of member states to implement other UN requirements that may emerge, including those addressing natural resources. In this regard, the externalities of capacity-building initiatives provide important opportunities to address the responsible and effective management of natural resource exploitation.

The overarching question, then, is whether creating a new international regime to address conflict commodities or strengthening and linking current initiatives of the Security Council and related efforts provides the optimal means for addressing the resource dimensions of armed conflict. For reasons elaborated here and elsewhere, renewed focus on strengthening initiatives such as commodity sanctions, monitoring efforts, and certification schemes, while creating greater horizontal linkages between complementary efforts, is likely to be more fruitful in the near term than attempting to construct a new overarching framework to address the issues associated with natural resources or even to reorient the work of the CTC.

As with most international initiatives, it boils down to a question of political will. Prior to September 11, 2001, the will to make sanctions against terrorist financing effective was virtually nonexistent and generally considered unlikely to evolve. After the attacks of that day, however, everything changed, and the international community committed itself to combating terrorism, including restricting terrorist financing. Absent a compelling, globally transformative event, however, the task of building the political will among member states to systematically address illicit trade in natural resources is bound to be slower and more difficult, given the complexity of the interests and activities involved and their multiple jurisdictional character. Improved understanding of the resource dimension of intrastate conflict, as well as the identification of lessons learned and best practices, however, can help prompt member states to act.

Notes

This chapter is based on the ongoing research of the Targeting Terrorist Finances project at the Watson Institute. Other members of the research team include Thomas Biersteker, Peter Romaniuk, and Aaron Halegua, and their many contributions in the collaborative effort are gratefully acknowledged. For more information on the project, see www.watsoninstitute.org.

1. For a copy of Resolution 1373, adopted on September 28, 2001, as well as the comprehensive range of documents and reports related to the work of the Counter-Terrorism Committee, see www.un.org/docs/sc/committees/1373. In addition to Resolution 1373, on September 12, 2001, the Security Council adopted Resolution 1368, which recognized any act of international terrorism as a threat to international peace and security, thereby establishing a legal basis for action. Resolution 1377, passed on November 12, 2001, underscored the obligation of states to deny financial and other forms of support and safe haven to terrorists and invited the CTC to explore ways to assist states in the legal and regulatory implementation of Resolution 1373.

2. Curtis A. Ward, "Building Capacity to Combat International Terrorism: The Role of the United Nations Security Council," *Journal of Conflict and Security Law* 8, no. 2 (2003): 289.

3. See the policy research of the International Peace Academy's Economic Agendas in Civil Wars project, available at www.ipacademy.org/programs/programs.htm.

4. "Report of the Policy Working Group on the United Nations and Terrorism," S/2002/875, August 6, 2002, transmittal letter from the Secretary-General to the General Assembly and the Security Council.

5. UN doc. S/RES/1373, 2001.

6. Ibid., para. 4.

7. Kofi Annan, January 12, 2002, available at www.un.org/docs/sc/committees/1373/sgjan.htm.

8. "Report of the Policy Working Group," p. 9.

9. Ward, "Building Capacity to Combat International Terrorism," p. 298.

10. As is often the case, the chair of the committee can make a significant difference in the effectiveness of the effort. See Peter Wallensteen, Carina Staibano, and Mikael Eriksson, eds., *Making Targeted Sanctions Effective: Guidelines for the Implementation of UN Policy Options* (Uppsala: Uppsala University Press, 2004), pp. 18–19, available at www.smartsanctions.org. Ambassador Greenstock has been widely commended for his leadership role in devising the work plan of the CTC and driving the counterterrorism effort forward. For the Security Council's accolades for Greenstock at the time of his last briefing of the council, April 4, 2003, see Sir Jeremy Greenstock, "Statement to the Security Council," S/PV.4734, April 4, 2003, available at www.un.org/Depts/dhl/resguide/scact2003.htm.

11. Initially the permanent representatives of Colombia, Mauritius, and the Russian Federation served as the vice-chairs. As of January 8, 2003, the vice-chairmen at the CTC were the permanent representatives of Angola, Mexico, and the Russian Federation.

12. Jeremy Greenstock, press conference, October 19, 2001, transcript.

13. Most CTC documents, including reports from member states, are posted on the CTC's website: www.un.org/docs/sc/committees/1373. However, if states request confidentiality, they are entitled to submit a confidential annex to their report that is circulated to CTC members only. Further, if in the course of verifying a state's implementation of Resolution 1373 information emerges that is deemed too

sensitive to share with CTC members, the CTC may ask independent experts to pursue the issue with the concerned state, who would then orally brief the CTC without disclosing the substance of the answers. See Jeremy Greenstock, "Summary of Briefing for Interested UN Delegations," November 26, 2001, available at www.un.org/docs/sc/committees/1373/26novsum.htm.

14. Note by the chairman, "Guidance for the Submission of Reports Pursuant to Paragraph 6 of Security Council Resolution 1373 (2001)," SCA/20/02(2), October 18, 2001, available at www.un.org/docs/sc/committees/1373/sca2001(2).htm.

15. Ibid., p. 1. In addition to submitting reports, member state representatives may be called before the CTC to clarify key points and respond to questions of the committee and its experts.

16. Greenstock, "Statement to the Security Council."

17. "Report of São Tomé and Príncipe to the Counter-Terrorism Committee," S/2003/568, May 2, 2003, available at http://ods-dds-ny.un.org/doc/UNDOC/GEN/N03/375/21/PDF/N0337521.pdf.

18. See documents of the Financial Action Task Force on Money Laundering, available at http://www1.oecd.org/fatf. See also Chapter 4 by Jonathan Winer in this volume.

19. Resolution 1377, adopted by the Security Council on November 12, 2001, recognized the lack of capacity of some states for implementing the requirements of Resolution 1373. The council called on all states to take urgent action to fully implement Resolution 1373 and to assist each other in doing so. States were invited to indicate areas in which assistance was needed, and the CTC was directed to explore ways to assist states, including through international, regional, and subregional organizations and the use of model legislation and assistance programs in technical, legal, financial, or other regulatory areas. See UN doc. S/RES/1377 (2001).

20. For example, see "Discussion Paper: Focusing the Second Review of Reports," July 24, 2002; "Discussion Paper: Assistance—Next Steps," October 21, 2002; "Discussion Paper: CTC—Stage B," November 22, 2002; and a note dated November 11, 2002, from CTC expert Jeremy Wainwright on the requirements of Resolution 1373 with regard to freezing of financial assets, available at www.un.org/docs/sc/committees/1373.

21. At the time of Sir Jeremy Greenstock's final briefing to the Security Council on April 4, 2003, three states were reported as having not submitted even a preliminary report: São Tomé and Príncipe, Swaziland, and Vanuatu, in part due to lack of resources to prepare such a document. The CTC undertook measures to help these and other states that had fallen behind in submitting reports.

22. See "Matrix of Requests for Assistance and Responses," February 28, 2003, prepared by the Counter-Terrorism Technical Assistance Program for the Special CTC Meeting with Representatives of International, Regional, and Subregional Organizations that took place at the UN on March 6, 2003.

23. Ward, "Building Capacity to Combat International Terrorism," p. 302.

24. "Discussion Paper: Assistance—Next Steps."

25. "UN Security Council Steps Up Global Co-operation against Terrorism," report of the March 6, 2003, Special Meeting of the Counter-Terrorism Committee, available at www.un.org/docs/sc/committees/1373/specialmtoutcome.htm. The meeting was called following the ministerial meeting of the Security Council on January 20, 2003, which set objectives for counterterrorism activity in the declaration adopted by Resolution 1456 (S/RES/1456 [2003]).

26. See letter dated February 26, 2003, from Jeremy Greenstock to the Security Council transmitting the summary of the activities of all relevant international, regional, and subregional organizations in the area of counterterrorism (S/AC.40/2003/SM.1/2).

27. The ongoing nature of coordination among international, regional, and subregional organizations dealing with terrorism is particularly noteworthy, as it represents an unprecedented effort to eliminate duplication and enhance the effectiveness of technical assistance efforts, including development of the Matrix of Joint Activities as an overall picture of assistance programs. See Vienna Declaration, adopted March 12, 2004, available at www.osce.org/documents/sg/2004/03/2278_en.pdf.

28. "Building International Political Will and Capacity to Combat Terrorism: A G-8 Action Plan," available at www.g8.fr/evian/extras/499.html.

29. This section draws upon the work of the Targeting Terrorist Finances project at the Watson Institute, in particular the team's analysis of reports submitted by member states to the CTC and 1267 Sanctions Committee.

30. Greenstock, "Statement to the Security Council."

31. Jeremy Greenstock, "Statement to the High-level Meeting of the Security Council on Combating Terrorism," S/PV.4688, January 20, 2003.

32. For a list of UN conventions on terrorism and the status of signatories, see www.untreaty.un.org/english/terrorism.asp.

33. See "Fight against Terrorism Would Be Long with No Short Cuts, Counter-Terrorism Committee Chairman Tells Security Council," press release, SC/7823, July 23, 2003, available at www.un.org/news/press/docs/2003/sc7823.doc.htm. Statement made by Ms. Susan Moore on Agenda Item 148: Means to Eliminate International Terrorism, October 19, 2004. Available at www.un.int/usa/04_199.htm.

34. As of March 2004, the International Convention for the Suppression of the Financing of Terrorism had 132 signatories and 112 parties.

35. See www.fatf-gafi.org/TerFinance_en.htm.

36. S/AC.40/2003/SM.1/2, p. 80.

37. Reports on observance of standards and codes now include an analysis of the effectiveness of anti–money-laundering and counterterrorist financing measures adopted and recommendations for enhancements of national practices. For a list of the International Monetary Fund's "Reports on the Observance of Standards and Codes," see www.imf.org/external/np/rosc/rosc.asp?sort=date.

38. As of January 2004, 461 reports had been received, including first reports from 191 member states and 5 others; 158 second reports from member states and 2 others; 100 third reports from member states; and 5 fourth reports. See letter dated January 12, 2004, from the chairman of the CTC to the president of the Security Council, S/220/32.

39. For example, Antigua and Barbuda passed the Prevention of Terrorism Act 18 in December 2001 to prohibit the financing of terrorist organizations and provision of financial services to them. As a result of interaction with the CTC, noted shortcomings in the law, such as failure to criminalize the willful collection and provision of funds intended to finance terrorist acts, were to be corrected in new legislation. Likewise in Mauritius, the Prevention of Terrorism Act of 2002, as well as new anti–money-laundering legislation, was enacted but was to undergo subsequent refining to overcome problems noted by the CTC. Even countries with advanced financial and legal systems such as Austria have modified their legal regimes to address terrorist financing, relying in part on European Union legislation

implementing Resolution 1373 to incorporate changes into national law. See reports submitted pursuant to Resolution 1373 by Antigua and Barbuda (S/2002/600, S2003/521), Mauritius (S/2001/1286, S/2002/880), Austria (S/2001/1242, S/2002/969, S/2003/276), and Kuwait (S/2002/1221, S/2002/886), available at www.un.org/docs/sc/committees/1373/submitted_reports.html; and report S/AC.37/2003/(1455)/31, submitted by Kuwait pursuant to Resolution 1455, available at www.un.org/Docs/sc/committees/1267/1455reportsEng.htm.

40. "UN Security Council Steps Up Global Co-operation," p. 14.

41. The precise amount of terrorist assets frozen is difficult to determine. As of August 2003 the White House reported that "some 167 countries have issued orders freezing terrorist assets," with the U.S. blocking $34.4 million and other countries blocking $77.9 million. See "Financial Actions in the War on Terrorism," available at www.whitehouse.gov/response/financialresponse.html. The 1267 Monitoring Committee reported that "some 149 countries have issued freezing orders and more than $125 million in terrorist-related financial assets have been frozen." As of early 2004, U.S. government sources cited nearly $140 million of frozen assets. For a list of assets frozen as reported by member states, see "Second Report of the Monitoring Group Established Pursuant to Resolution 1363 (2001) and Extended by Resolutions 1390 (2002) and 1455 (2003) on Sanctions against Al-Qaida, the Taliban, and Individuals and Entities Associated with Them," S/2003/1070, app. 3, p. 56, available at www.un.org/Docs/sc/committees/1267/1267SelectedEng.htm.

42. Only a few states reference measures to deal with charities, which traditionally have been a significant source of funds for terrorist organizations such as Al-Qaida. Prior to September 11, there was little regulation of charities or oversight of their disbursements, and while some states have begun to take steps to address questionable charitable contributions, there continues to be little focus on the problem and reticence to act against charities (ibid., p. 15).

43. See "Report by the Chair of the Counter-Terrorism Committee on Problems Encountered in the Implementation of Security Council Resolution 1373 (2001)," S/2004/70, January 26, 2004, available at www.un.org/docs/sc/committees/1373/reports_chair.html; and "Letter dated 19 February 2004 from the Chairman of the Security Council Committee Established Pursuant to Resolution 1373 (2001) Concerning Counter-Terrorism Addressed to the President of the Security Council," S/2004/124, available at www.un.org/docs/sc/committees/1373.

44. See S/RES/1535 (2004), available at http://ods-dds-ny.un.org/UNDOC/GEN/NO4/286/41/PDF/NO428641.pdf?OpenElement.

45. "Security Council Sets Up UN Counter-Terrorism Executive Directorate to Fight Scourge," UN News Service, March 26, 2004, available at http://un.org/apps/news/printnews.asp?nid+10217.

46. S/RES/1373 (2001), para. 4. Other activities such as drug trafficking, arms sales, and charitable donations are frequently used and likely represent more significant means of financing terrorist operations but are not addressed here. This section focuses primarily on the natural resource of diamonds, since the diamond trade has received the most attention, has generated the most revenue, and has the most advanced international regime—the Kimberley Process—associated with it.

47. See Chapter 6 by Williams and Picarelli in this volume.

48. At a workshop at the Watson Institute in October 2003, Financial and Transnational Dynamics of Terrorism, jointly sponsored by the Kennedy School of Government, Rohan Gunaratna, author of *Inside Al Qaida: Global Networks of*

Terror, discussed Al-Qaida's shift from raising funds from charities toward fraud and illegal activities.

49. Agence France Presse, "Belgium Diamond Traders Dealing with Angolan Rebels," April 23, 2001.

50. Douglas Farah, "Al Qaida Cash Tied to Diamond Trade," *Washington Post,* November 2, 2001. See also Douglas Farah, *Blood from Stones: The Secret Financial Network of Terror* (New York: Broadway Books, 2004).

51. Douglas Farah, "Report Says Africans Harbored Al Qaida Terror Assets Hidden in Gem-Buying Spree," *Washington Post,* December 29, 2002, A1. Karen de Young and Douglas Farah, "Infighting Slows Hunt for Hidden Al Qaida Assets: Funds Put into Untraceable Commodities," *Washington Post,* June 18, 2002, A1, A10; Robert Block and Daniel Pearl, "Underground Trade: Much Smuggled Gem Called Tanzanite Helps Bin Laden Supporters," *Wall Street Journal,* November 16, 2001, A1.

52. Global Witness, "For a Few Dollars More: How Al Qaida Moved into the Diamond Trade," April 2003, available at www.globalwitness.org/reports/show.php/en.00041.html. For information regarding an established link between Sierra Leone's diamond trade and well-known Lebanese terrorists, see Lansana Gberie, *War and Peace in Sierra Leone: Diamonds, Corruption, and the Lebanese Connection,* Diamonds and Human Security Project Occasional Paper no. 6 (Ottawa: Partnership Africa Canada, 2002).

53. "Report of the Monitoring Group Established Pursuant to Security Council Resolution 1363 (2001) and Extended by Resolution 1390 (2002)," S/2002/541, May 2002, and "Second Report of the Monitoring Group Established Pursuant to Security Council Resolution 1363 (2001) and Extended by Resolution 1390 (2002)," S/2002/1050, August 2002, p. 14, available at www.un.org/Docs/sc/committees/1267/1267Selected.

54. S/RES/1373 (2001), para. 1(c).

55. Historically, the United States and European Union have implemented asset freezes differently, with the United States including property as assets. Over time the European Union has broadened the scope of its financial controls and in implementing Resolution 1373 requires the freezing of funds, "including funds derived or generated from property." See Council Common Position of December 27, 2001, on combating terrorism (2001/930/CFSP), in *Official Journal of the European Communities,* available at www.ecre.org/eu_developments/terrorism/terrorpos.pdf.

56. "Second Report of the Monitoring Group," p. 74.

57. The CTC initially divided its work into stages, roughly corresponding to different aspects of national activity aimed at enhancing counterterrorism capacity. Stage A entails the state's having in place legislation covering all aspects of Resolution 1373 and effective machinery for preventing and suppressing terrorist financing. Stage B focuses on strengthening executive machinery to implement the resolution. Finally, Stage C anticipates moving beyond legislative and administrative structures to engage in a dialogue with states on cooperation at bilateral, regional, and international levels to address links between terrorism and other threats to security such as arms trafficking, drugs, organized crime, money laundering, and illegal movement of chemical, biological, and nuclear weapons. See letter dated February 26, 2003, from Jeremy Greenstock to the Security Council, transmitting a summary of activities of all relevant international, regional, and subregional organizations in the area of counterterrorism (S/AC.40/2003/SM.1/2).

58. See Chapter 3 by Ian Smillie in this volume for a detailed discussion of the

Kimberley Process. It is important to recognize the limitations of the Kimberley Process and its voluntary nature in those countries choosing to participate. In this regard, it substantially differs from the counterterrorism initiative pursuant to Resolution 1373, which states are legally obligated to implement. Many associated with the Kimberley Process remain concerned for the success of the certification scheme without effective monitoring. Although the Kimberley Process was launched on January 1, 2003, the formal list of fifty-four participating countries was published on July 31, 2003, because many countries failed to pass the necessary legislation and put into place certificate programs with appropriate security features. See Nicol Degli Innocenti, "Strong Support for 'Conflict Diamond' Curbs," *Financial Times,* August 1, 2003.

59. "Report by the Chair of the Counter-Terrorism Committee on the Problems Encountered in the Implementation of Security Council Resolution 1373 (2001)."

60. "Second Report of the Monitoring Group," p. 13.

61. The lessons described here focus on the CTC but in fact reflect the cumulative experience with sanctions since the 1990s.

62. See Resolution 1267 (1999) and, subsequently, Resolutions 1333 (2000), 1390 (2002), 1455 (2003), and 1526 (2004).

63. For a detailed comparison of the mandates and operations of the two committees, see "Distinctions between Security Council Committees Dealing with Terrorism (1267 and Counter-Terrorism Committee)," press release, SC/7827, July 28, 2003, available at www.un.org/News/Press/docs/2003/sc7827.doc.htm.

64. The most detailed questions of states regarding compliance were developed as a result of the CTC experiences and are reflected in the guidance issued by the 1267 Committee following adoption of Resolution 1455. See "Guidance for Reports Required of All States Pursuant to Paragraphs 6 and 12 of Resolution 1455 (2003)," available at www.un.org/Docs/sc/committees/1267/guidanc_en.pdf.

65. As of July 29, 2003, sixty-four reports had been received, prompting the chairman of the committee to characterize the overall response in submitting reports as "disappointing." See "Some Recent Success Achieved against Al Qaida, but Recent Attacks Underscore Challenges Ahead in Fight against Terrorism, Security Council Told," press release, SC/7830, July 29, 2003, available at www.un.org/News/Press/docs/2003/sc7830.htm.

66. See www.un.org/News/Press/docs/2004/sc7995.doc.htm.

67. For information regarding targeted financial sanctions, see *Targeted Financial Sanctions: A Manual for Design and Implementation (Contributions from the Interlaken Process),* prepared by the Swiss Confederation in cooperation with the UN Secretariat and the Watson Institute for International Studies at Brown University, 2001, available at www.watsoninstitute.org. In addition, see Sue E. Eckert, "Targeted Financial Sanctions: Lessons from the Interlaken Process," paper prepared for the International Peace Academy's Conference on Adapting and Improving Existing International Policies and Practices, Bellagio, Italy, May 23–25, 2002.

68. Thus far the CTC has used "naming and shaming" as a device to get states to maintain their reporting timetable. The chairman has regularly named states that are late in reporting to the CTC, and the lists have been made public.

69. The report of the 1267 Monitoring Group (S/2003/669) noted the importance of an up-to-date, complete list of targets and the need for specific identifying data associated with names on the list.

70. On the importance of expert panels, see Wallensteen, Staibano, and Eriksson, *Making Targeted Sanctions Effective.*

71. Ibid.

72. See Vera Gowlland-Debbas, "The Review of the Security Council by Member States," in Vera Gowlland-Debbas, ed., *National Implementation of United Nations Sanctions: A Comparative Study* (Leiden: Martinus Nijhoff, 2004), pp. 63–76.

73. CTC staff have reported that some countries in need of assistance have hesitated to seek help for fear that funds would be diverted from development assistance.

6

Combating Organized
Crime in Armed Conflict

Phil Williams and John T. Picarelli

The dynamics of armed conflicts since the end of the Cold War have intersected with the rise of organized crime in ways that pose new challenges to the international community. As of yet, however, there has been no convergence of strategies or coordination of approaches that fully reflects the importance of organized crime activities in intrastate and ethnic conflicts, terrorism, and the actions of rogue states. In effect, the international community is still operating on Westphalian principles even though in many parts of the world the Westphalian state no longer exists other than as a formality.

This chapter seeks to develop a set of policy recommendations to address the range of organized criminal activities associated with fueling or profiting from armed conflict. To that end, the first section briefly discusses the changing context of armed conflict in the post–Cold War era. The second section establishes some important conceptual distinctions that facilitate understanding of the ways in which organized crime can not only precipitate and fuel conflict but also complicate its resolution and its aftermath. The third section elucidates more fully the ways that organized crime enterprises and criminal activities impinge on the outbreak of wars, the course of hostilities, and the aftermath of conflict and offers policy prescriptions designed to address the relationship between organized crime and conflict in these three stages.

The Changing Context of Armed Conflict

During the second half of the twentieth century, intrastate war became the prominent type of warfare. Unfortunately, too many observers explained these "civil wars" in terms of global geopolitics, rather than identifying them for what they were—independent and often autonomous conflicts that had their roots in the struggles of modern state building that both preceded and outlasted the imposition of the superpower template. Divergence between state and nation encouraged irredentism and secessionism; the retention of state structures claiming but not possessing legitimate authority provoked rebellion and insurgency; and the tendency arose to see the state as the prize of politics rather than as something that disciplines and moderates political competition. State weakness became even more salient during the 1990s as the long-term process of state making seemed to move into reverse.[1]

This had important implications for the growth of transnational organized crime. Indeed, it is no coincidence that the era of the qualified state—in which more and more states are weak, fragmented, decaying, collapsing, or imploding—is also the era of transnational organized crime, which is exploiting weaknesses in state structures as well as the new opportunities provided by globalization. Weak states provide highly congenial environments in which organized crime can flourish. When a state collapses into an orgy of violence, organized crime often either is present at the point of collapse or enters soon afterward to exploit the attendant opportunities. Although organized crime is best understood as a symptom rather than a cause of the disorder in world politics, it is also an exacerbating factor that helps both to precipitate and to perpetuate conflicts.

In the context of weak states, there has been a criminalization of warfare in terms of causation, course, and consequences. Disputes over both legal and illegal resources and markets are sometimes an immediate cause of intrastate war, sparking the fuel provided by historical hatreds, ethnic tensions, and tribal rivalries. Often this is linked to the exploitation of state resources by members of the dominant elite for their own profit, a process that contributes to a loss of legitimacy and resources, which in turn contributes to the implosion of the state.[2] In terms of the course of the war, once again transnational linkages, black-market economic activities, and organized criminal activities help to fund belligerents and enable them to sustain the conflict even (and perhaps especially) in the face of international isolation and embargoes. As Mark Duffield has noted, "In the case of the new wars, market deregulation has deepened all forms of parallel and transborder trade and allowed warring parties to forge local-global networks and shadow economies as a means of asset realization and self-provisioning. . . . Instead of conventional armies, the new wars typically oppose and ally the transborder resource networks of state incumbents, social groups, diasporas, strongmen, and so on."[3] Postwar recovery and regeneration have also been complicated by the activities of organized crime—in particular by the desire of the erstwhile belligerents to exploit criminal connections and criminal know-how developed during the war for both political and financial gain in the postconflict environment.[4] In all, the criminalization of warfare has had a major impact on the capacity of the international community to manage regional and local conflicts and engage in successful peacemaking and peacekeeping.

Organized Crime and Conflict: The Relationship

Concepts and Distinctions

Organized crime can be understood as both an entity and an activity. While many observers fail to make this distinction, it is enormously useful to understanding the different ways that organized crime feeds into conflict. In particular, it allows analysis to identify the role of transnational criminal enterprises, on the one side, and the local warlords, ethnic groups, governments, and terrorist organizations, on the other, that have appropriated what is, in effect, a "do-it-yourself" (DIY) form of organized crime. To recognize that much organized crime activity related to conflict situations is not directly carried out by transnational criminal enterprises, however, is not to minimize the role of these professional criminals.

Organized crime as entity can be understood as an organization, whether networked or hierarchical, that systematically adopts criminal activities in pursuit of profit as its ultimate objective. Organized crime groups are Clausewitzian: criminal activity is a continuation of business by criminal means. Criminal enterprises are pragmatic rather than ideological. While they can have a political dimension, sometimes creating what Roy Godson terms a "political-criminal nexus,"[5] their political activities are almost invariably intended to protect the illegal enterprise. Similarly, although often ruthless, they tend to use violence selectively to eliminate rivals and to remove threats or obstacles. Organized crime's use of contract killings is a carefully chosen strategy that is linked to the desire for financial gain. Anyone who threatens that gain is a legitimate target as far as criminal enterprises are concerned. Such enterprises can be domestic or transnational in scope, the latter when a significant part of their activities crosses borders. Usually, transnational criminal enterprises operate from a home base in one state but use other states as transshipment, service, or host (or market) sites for their activities.

Organized crime can also be understood as a methodology or a set of activities undertaken by other actors or entities to generate funds as means to other ends. In the case of ethnic factions, terrorist organizations, insurgent groups, and some governments that adopt organized crime methods to fund their political agendas, the ultimate ends are political. The defining characteristic is not the activity so much as the purpose, which remains distinct from that of criminal enterprises.[6]

This distinction between criminal enterprises and organized crime as method has important implications. It suggests that any entity can use organized crime as a means of generating resources to assist the pursuit of its political agenda, whether the aim of that agenda is to obtain control or remain in control of a country, to inflict harm on one's enemies through terrorism, or to engage in ethnic cleansing. This notion has not yet been integrated into policy, largely because of the failure to differentiate various forms of transnational threat. Unfortunately, this conceptual lacuna compromises both good analysis and effective policymaking.

There is an important wrinkle in all this, however. The distinction between political entities and profit-oriented criminal enterprises is a helpful starting point but captures only part of a more complex reality. In several regions, hybrid forms of organization have emerged that clearly combine an explicit political agenda and quest for power with a desire to make profits through illegal activities. Indeed, this dual dynamic is evident in many weak or collapsing states or states embroiled in armed conflict. The Tajik civil war from 1992 to 1997, for example, was partly an extension of old clan rivalries and traditional power struggles, partly a religious and ideological conflict, and partly a struggle for control of opium and heroin trafficking. In effect, drug-trafficking routes and markets helped to sustain the conflict through resource generation and intensified the conflict through enhancing the value of the spoils for the victor.[7]

In cases such as this, the major players are hybrid organizations, part criminal enterprise, part terrorist group, part mercenary, and part political faction. The most well-developed of these hybrid organizations are warlords, who typically engage in both criminal activities (including drug trafficking and extortion of traders who transit the territories under their control) and insurgent or military activities, while also providing a modicum of order in areas under their control. In Somalia and Kenya, for example, local warlords take enormous steps to maintain their control over khat, a drug whose use has become increasingly evident since the late 1990s in Europe.[8]

Organized Crime and the Outbreak of Conflict

There are several ways in which organized crime can contribute to the outbreak of conflict. Criminal enterprises (and indeed the criminalization process more generally) are not invariably negative in their impact on political stability.[9] In the short run, participation in informal and illegal economies can act as both a safety net and a safety valve for dispossessed populations, providing sources of employment and subsistence that are simply not available in the licit economy, thereby enhancing stability. In some countries in Central Asia during the 1990s, for example, opium became the dominant currency, facilitating a degree of commercial activity that would otherwise have been impossible. Short-term stability, however, is often purchased at the expense of long-term stability, especially where competition develops for control of drug-cultivation areas and drug-trafficking routes. Such competition, if combined with other sources of conflict, can move the state toward a "tipping point" where conflict becomes inevitable.[10]

Similar problems arise where the state itself is criminalized—a process that, as Jean-François Bayart notes, has characterized much of Africa.[11] There are several components of this process, all of which tend toward the outbreak of violence within the state. The first is elite corruption and rent seeking—activities that undermine government legitimacy, deprive the state of badly needed resources, obscure the distinction between leadership and ownership, and transform the state from being above politics into the prize of political competition. According to William Reno, the problem is not simply corruption or rent seeking but "corruption [that] is combined with a form of rule that is hostile to well-functioning state institutions and the rule of law. Such misrule often provokes substantial domestic criticism."[12] To placate dissent, leaders engage in further corruption, depleting state assets through ever-widening patronage.[13] While effective at building power bases, patronage undermines a state's capacity to provide services to the wider population, thereby further eroding political legitimacy. Another source of conflict is the creation of what Reno terms "shadow states," in which "rulers increasingly resort to manipulation of markets to manage their clients. . . . The ruler increasingly operates like a racketeer, selling exemption from prosecution or using his control over the state to help his business partners."[14] A third is the connection with international clients, both licit businesses and criminal enterprises, that seek preferential access to local markets (often for weapons) or to export commodities—a process that increases the value of political power, making it an even more attractive prize for armed contestation. When the state becomes the prize, with the spoils to be distributed by the dominant elite, ethnic group, or tribe,[15] politics becomes a zero-sum game, a form of exclusion in which compromise has no place, rules have no followers, and military power replaces political legitimacy as the only political currency.

These dynamics—especially when they are superimposed on existing divisions and disparities—help to explain both why some states fail and why failure often results in civil war or rebellion. It also suggests that the polarization between political scientists who emphasize "grievance" and economists who emphasize "greed" as a cause of rebellion or civil conflict is somewhat overstated. In countries based on "the politics of the belly,"[16] grievance can be economic as much as political. It is possible, therefore, to agree with Paul Collier's conclusion that dependence upon primary commodity exports, which are attractive targets for extortion by rebel organizations, provides opportunities for rebellion that would otherwise not be available, without ignoring, however, the role of grievance.[17]

In the kind of system described by Reno, grievance is likely to be widespread—based either on exclusion from the spoils of patronage or on dissatisfaction with the level of rewards being reaped within the system. Often this exclusion is based on tribal or ethnic identity and so exacerbates traditional divisions and rivalries. The predatory state engages in behavior that intensifies socioeconomic inequality, simultaneously depriving it of any legal or moral authority to contain the process of contestation and providing enormous incentives for the excluded or dissatisfied to use armed force to achieve control. In this connection, the crucial point about lucrative natural resource endowments is that they provide both an incentive to go to war (because controlling them is so lucrative) and the wherewithal to fight once even partial control has been achieved.

In addition to the internal dynamic linking crime and conflict, there are often transnational linkages between the domestic elites and transnational business or criminal networks that can help those who want to acquire control of state resources to become militarily competitive—especially if they already have something to trade for weapons. The trade in rough diamonds in the late 1990s suggests that prior to the outbreak of hostilities, and sometimes during them, business connections can be as important as connections to transnational criminal enterprises. When businesses are concerned only about access to natural resources and take a neutral view of control and ownership of resources, they play into the hands of warring factions—and behave in ways very similar to transnational criminal enterprises. Many diamonds, for example, have been smuggled into the global diamond market not only by outright criminals but also by ostensibly legitimate diamond merchants, who relied on the connivance of an industry reluctant to provide transparency, adequate regulation, or oversight of supply. Under some circumstances these transnational linkages might even provide another tipping point on the road to hostilities. The rebels in Sierra Leone, for example, would not have been able to procure weapons and matériel without linkages to transnational diamond and arms trafficking networks.[18] For the most part, though, the issue of resource generation is less important than the issue of control (which, as suggested above, is sometimes a catalyst) when it comes to the outbreak of conflicts.

Organized Crime and the Course of Conflict

Once conflict has broken out, resource generation takes on central importance, becoming part of "a vicious circle in which war has become a business, and business is used to wage war."[19] The resources that can be acquired through expanding territorial control fuel these conflicts by providing the wherewithal to continue fighting. War itself becomes "a source of accumulation: it enables the collection of international aid—diplomatic, military or humanitarian; it enables the seizure of the resources of the modern economy; and it enables the adaptation to the growing criminalization of the economy."[20]

The illicit trade in rough diamonds has been particularly important. So-called conflict diamonds "have helped finance, train and equip the Revolutionary United Front in Sierra Leone, have helped fund the [former] dictatorial regime in Liberia, perpetuated the conflict in the Democratic Republic of the Congo, financed UNITA rebels in Angola to the sum of US$3.7 billion, and have helped finance political instability and repression in Zimbabwe."[21] Here again, there are important distinctions between the roles of transnational criminal enterprises and do-it-yourself organized crime during hostilities.

Transnational criminal enterprises. It would be wrong to overstate the role of transnational organized crime in precipitating conflict. However, once conflict has broken out, there is a natural convergence of interest between the factions that control natural resource endowments such as diamonds or illicit industries such as narcotics and transnational criminal enterprises that can provide the needed access to global consumer markets. As R. Thomas Naylor has observed, "Any insurgency using the international black market to finance its activities inevitably forms mutually profitable and likely quite durable relations with international criminal groups."[22] Much the same is true for rogue governments.

In some cases, of course, conflict can complicate transnational criminal activities. The old Balkan drug-trafficking route, for example, was disrupted during the 1990s by the ethnic conflicts in the former Yugoslavia. One response was the development of alternative routes both north and south of the conflict zone. Another was greater reliance on Albanian criminals to transport drugs through the region, a development that allowed Albanian criminal organizations to push Turkish groups out of the heroin market in some Western European countries. Although some criminal enterprises prefer a stable, predictable, and peaceful environment for their activities and find armed conflicts an inhibition, for others conflict clearly offers lucrative opportunities.

Criminal enterprises typically provide two kinds of service for those in war zones—the supplying of goods to the conflict area (often armaments, which are especially important if there is an arms embargo) and the transportation, distribution, and marketing of products such as narcotics, timber, precious gems, and minerals from conflict zones. The role of arms supplier has become increasingly important to criminal enterprises. The geopolitical upheaval of the early 1990s reduced dependence on heavy arms and ended supply channels dominated by the two superpowers, while the emergence of weak and collapsing states and the growth of ethnic conflicts provided an unprecedented demand for light weapons.[23] Together these developments lead to what has aptly been described as the "commercialization of civil war,"[24] by providing opportunities for transnational criminal enterprises to become major players in the new arms trade. The existence of large stockpiles of weapons deposited in Cold War proxies, combined with what Naylor termed the "Warsaw Pact yard sale," meant that criminal enterprises could expand their repertoire of activities, and diversify into the arms business. This was particularly true in the former Soviet Union, where the rise of criminal enterprises was juxtaposed with a military establishment that had become a virtual cesspool of corruption and crime. It is hardly surprising, therefore, that Viktor Bout, a Russian from Tajikistan, and Leonid Minin, from the Ukraine, emerged as two of the leading suppliers of illicit arms to conflicts in Africa and elsewhere.

Transnational criminal enterprises often also become couriers or customers for drugs produced in weak or collapsing states or for natural resources illicitly exploited by armed factions. In the case of diamonds, some of the companies involved are ostensibly legitimate but very opaque. The Victoria Group, for example, is a front company, probably representing the interests of a network of Lebanese diamond merchants, that has linked members of the Ugandan military in the Democratic Republic of Congo (DRC) with the diamond markets in Antwerp.[25] Not only did this arrangement bring conflict diamonds to Europe, but it also gave members of the Ugandan military a vested interest in the perpetuation of conflict and turmoil in the DRC. Indeed, because of the local-transnational linkages, "the maintenance of insecurity has become a primary source of enrichment" for key figures in the Ugandan military.[26] Links to conflict zones in the DRC have also been established by Russian criminals, who, allegedly with the connivance of the government of Kazakhstan, have increasingly monopolized the Congolese coltan trade.[27]

In some cases, barter arrangements conflate the two distinct roles of supplier and customer. Barter arrangements have considerable merit in that they require little up-front financing yet allow the belligerents to continue fighting, while offering the criminals considerable opportunity for profit making. A notable example involves the Revolutionary Armed Forces of Colombia (FARC), which in the late 1990s swapped drugs for arms supplied by Russian criminal enterprises.[28] There are also instances of barter in the DRC conflict. Arms dealers Viktor Bout and Sanjivan Ruprah, who obtained diamond concessions in the DRC, were almost certainly involved in direct arms deals, through the swapping of diamonds and coltan, with various Congolese factions.[29]

In other cases, of course, the warring parties simply sell the products to criminal or legitimate enterprises, then use the funds obtained to procure arms through separate, often illicit, transactions. The Taliban, for instance, taxed the production and trafficking of drugs in Afghanistan. Indeed, most of the warlords and factions in Afghanistan (including the Northern Alliance) were involved in some way in the drug industry. Connections of this kind are particularly critical where the local actors lack the financial or organizational capacity to supply the commodities directly to the consumer markets. Yet it is also important not to exaggerate something that is largely ad hoc and a matter of mutual convenience.

Do-it-yourself organized crime. One reason the notion of a nexus between transnational criminal enterprises and other malevolent nonstate or even state actors is sometimes less important than assumed is that insurgents, ethnic factions, and terrorists often choose to meet their own financial needs through illicit economic activity. One journalist has described this phenomenon as "fighters-turned-felons."[30] Crucially, however, they are still fighters—the felonies simply allow them to continue fighting. One of the best examples of DIY organized crime was in Kosovo, where the Kosovo Liberation Army (KLA) funded its conflict with the Milosevic regime largely from the proceeds of smuggling heroin and undocumented migrants.[31]

The extent to which DIY organized crime is embraced by those involved in contemporary intrastate conflict varies considerably. While it is possible for the central leaders of a political organization to make a strategic decision to engage in criminal activities for funding, more often the decision lies at the level of the constituent units (whether fronts, cells, or factions) of the organization. The result is a divergence within the overall organization, with some units embracing criminality and other units rejecting it due to concerns that criminalization and commercialization will compromise or dilute their political objectives. This tendency toward fragmentation has been particularly evident among loosely connected network structures that force lower-level leaders to be entrepreneurial in raising funds (and selecting operations).[32] For example, some cells within the Irish Republican Army frequently raised funds through narcotics trafficking, even though its central command and other cells were decidedly against the practice. Similarly, within the FARC in Colombia, there are significant differences among the more than seventy fronts or units that are engaging in conflict with both government forces and the paramilitaries. Some embrace narco-trafficking, some simply tax the traffickers, and others want nothing to do with the narco-business.

These tensions are not surprising and can be explained in terms of a distinction made by Steven Metz between spiritual insurgency and commercial insurgency. According to Metz, spiritual insurgency is "the descendant of the cold war-era revolutionary insurgency" and is driven by "problems of modernization, especially anomie, the search for meaning, and the pursuit of justice." Commercial insurgency, in contrast, is "driven less by the desire for justice than wealth."[33] Although Metz suggested that on occasion these two forms will be married, it is now clear that the marriage, in Colombia at least, is an uneasy one. The internal debate within the FARC on the extent to which it should be involved in the drug-trafficking business is reflected in external assessments about the nature of the FARC. Noting the FARC's status as one of Colombia's most significant drug-trafficking organizations, it is possible to contend that while the FARC started as an ideological insurgency, it has morphed into a commercial insurgency, more concerned with making money through the drug trade than with achieving its political agenda. Also plausible, though, are claims that the political goals remain predominant and that involvement in drug trafficking and other criminal activities remains no more than means to obtain political ends.[34]

Whatever the precise balance between the spiritual and commercial goals of the FARC, it is clear that the organization has made a lot of money from DIY organized crime, predominantly in the drug business but also through extortion and kidnapping.[35] Not surprisingly, the FARC also became connected to transnational criminal enterprises involved in the drug business, including the "Tijuana Cartel" and a Brazilian drug-trafficking organization led by Luis Fernando Da Costa. In most cases, however, FARC members have sought to obtain arms for drugs, a pattern that suggests that the cause itself remains important despite the commercialization of the insurgency. It is clear that involvement in drugs and crime has enabled the FARC to pursue its struggle against the Colombian government and the paramilitaries with greater vigor and more resources than would otherwise have been available.

The drug connection appears to be equally important to the right-wing paramilitaries opposed to the FARC. In September 2002, for example, the U.S. government indicted Carlos Castaño and several leaders of the United Self-Defense Forces of Colombia (AUC), a major paramilitary organization, for trafficking over seventeen tons of cocaine into the United States and Europe from 1997 onward.[36] The AUC was also involved in major cocaine-for-arms deals, one of which involved $25 million worth of arms and was thwarted by the United States in November 2002.[37]

In short, DIY organized crime often fuels contemporary armed conflicts. Drugs have helped to perpetuate conflict in Colombia in the same way that diamonds have perpetuated armed conflicts in Africa. The linkages of both the FARC and the AUC to the narcotics trade continue to fund the struggle and negate or at the very least complicate prospects for peace. When the belligerents in contemporary armed conflict are able to fund themselves through DIY organized crime, this delays both their physical exhaustion and the depletion of their resources, thereby enabling them to continue pursuing their goals through violence. As long as funds are available for combatants to continue armed struggle, the prospects for a peaceful resolution are more remote.

Insurgents are not the only ones who resort to organized criminal activities for funding. There have also been instances of governments' using criminality to stay in power. A case in point is Serbia under Slobodan Milosevic. Although involvement in crime and corruption was natural for those who made careers in the communist system, international pressure and the imposition of sanctions on Serbia after the outbreak of war exacerbated this tendency. As a state under siege, Serbia under Milosevic survived through the underground economy and circumvented sanctions by tacit cooperation with other actors and stakeholders in the region, especially in Macedonia. The main beneficiaries of sanctions were businesses and individuals linked to Milosevic's Socialist Party of Serbia and to the United Yugoslav Party of the Left (headed by Milosevic's wife, Mirjana Markovic). Other key members of the ruling elite were able to exploit their official positions and benefit from Milosevic's tendency to reward political supporters with government monopolies. In effect, key figures in the regime had taken over the business of organized crime—they were not only its beneficiaries but also its leaders and organizers. This did not mean an end to links to more traditional criminal enterprises. On the contrary, the Milosevic regime had close links with criminal enterprises in Serbia and strong connections with particular individuals such as Zeljko "Arkan" Kaznatovic.[38] Ultimately, though, these were secondary to—and instrumental for—the regime's own criminal activities.

Do-it-yourself organized crime often has a systematic transnational dimension, especially if the combatant parties can draw on one or more sympathetic diaspora communities around the globe. Diasporas are often at least as nationalistic as their brethren in the origin state and thus readily provide support for ethnic and nationalist struggles in the homeland. Diasporas and émigré communities, however, are also often home to transnational criminal organizations that exploit the vulnerability of newly arrived migrants.[39] Perhaps the best-documented example of how these two factors merge is found in the role of Tamil communities overseas in financing the military and political struggle carried out by the Liberation Tigers of Tamil Eelam (LTTE) in Sri Lanka. The LTTE reportedly established cells in as many as thirty-eight countries to obtain support from Tamil communities through either voluntary contributions or intimidation and extortion.[40] Further, the LTTE cells engaged in DIY organized crime activities that extended well beyond the Tamil community, with narcotics and alien smuggling being major activities.[41]

Organized Crime as Spoiler in Postconflict Contexts

During the middle and late 1990s, as the international community was faced with a rash of stalled or failing peace processes, increased attention was paid to the phenomenon of peace spoilers.[42] The concept of a spoiler or spoilers can be extended into postconflict state building, where the notion of "greedy spoilers" takes on rather different connotations. Organized crime groups and other players engaging in DIY organized crime often have an interest in retaining a profitable status quo and will continue to resist buying in fully to the peace settlement. This does not mean that organized crime will spoil the peace by precipitating an immediate reversion to hostilities; it does mean, though, that organized crime contributes significantly to the development and maintenance of an environment in which postconflict reconstruction is problematic. Entrenched corruption, the continued use of coercion and violence to protect criminal activities and enterprises, and the cultivation of close relationships between criminal enterprises and political elites make it difficult to establish the rule of law and to create an effective and functioning state, let alone liberal democratic governance.

The situation in Bosnia provides a particularly graphic example.[43] A U.S. General Accounting Office report issued in 2000 contended that organized crime was undermining the implementation of the Dayton peace agreement and the extensive aid programs seeking to rebuild government institutions. The report noted that "crime and corruption continue to pervade Bosnia's political, judicial, and economic systems."[44] The head of the Bosnia mission of the Organization for Security and Cooperation in Europe (OSCE) was even more outspoken, claiming that it was "no exaggeration to suggest that the emerging relationship between extremist politicians, the remnants of the old security services, and organized crime in this country represents the single greatest obstacle to democratic reform, economic investment, and membership in Euro-Atlantic institutions."[45] Strong evidence points to nationalist political parties' using corruption and organized crime to fund their political campaigns and maintain their positions of power. Wartime experience established expertise in smuggling and other illegal activities and also created trust networks and alliances between the state and criminal operators that proved difficult to disrupt or dismantle. As a report by the U.S. Institute of Peace noted:

> Extremist political forces linked with security/intelligence agencies and organized criminal enterprises have carved out autonomous structures of power in the Balkans that have instigated conflict and profited ruthlessly from it. These power structures have been maintained via informal networks that allow them to operate with impunity from prosecution, suborn elected politicians, extort profit from entrepreneurs, and manipulate the

media. These political-criminal networks have the motivation and means, through coercion and politically motivated violence, to obstruct the transformation to self-sustaining peace.[46]

The Dayton peace agreement itself perpetuated some of these problems by creating a diffused governing structure that does not control sources of authority, thereby providing multiple opportunities for rent seeking, and by establishing interentity boundaries within Bosnia, thereby creating opportunities for evading law enforcement by simply crossing from one entity to another. The interentity boundaries also provide an additional source and impetus for black market activity. The international community failed to install police forces within the peacekeeping operation or provide them with the authority to combat criminal activity once they arrived.[47] Moreover, the introduction of peacekeeping forces as well as a large presence of the international donor community created a large market for commercial sex—and the trafficking of women through and to Bosnia has increased enormously since the end of hostilities. As well as tainting the international community, this has provided another source of criminal income to those who continue to resist long-term state building.

The dynamics in Bosnia have repeated themselves in Kosovo, Liberia, Afghanistan, and the DRC. Criminal clusters have risen to prominence and, in most cases, control both territory and particular economic sectors. In some instances, of course, it is necessary to distinguish between those stakeholders who want actively to sabotage the peace process and those who prefer to ensure that it evolves in ways that are politically desirable and financially rewarding. Sometimes, former rebels become "legitimate" actors but leave behind neither their old habits nor their old connections—both of which act as insurance against failure in the political realm. The KLA in Kosovo, for example, has supposedly been transformed into a constructive force for peace, yet many of those who made up its membership continue to be involved in both criminal activities and the fomenting of political instability. In fact,

> rogue ex-KLA fighters and some Kosovo Protection Corps (KPC) members acting autonomously are widely suspected of having been catalysts in the insurrections that erupted in southern Serbia in 2000 and in Macedonia in early 2001. They have proven adept at exploiting grievances among ethnic Albanian populations in the region to fuel inter-ethnic conflict, and there are continuing reports of involvement by ex-KLA in trafficking in drugs, arms, and other contraband, a particular risk with those forced out of the KPC.[48]

The intertwining of political groups and organized crime has proven very difficult to disrupt. It has also been very lucrative, in effect extending war profiteering into the subsequent peace and creating powerful vested interests in preventing long-term peace processes from moving beyond stabilization to effective state building. Organized crime activities provide flows of revenue to the major ethnic groups, enabling them to continue to pursue their divisive agendas. Corruption and the relationship with organized crime provide political parties with the resources that are essential to maintaining power. As a result, the authorities have little or no incentive to attack their organized crime partners. And when they do, organized crime is well poised to strike back—as was evident with the assassination of reformist prime minister Zoran Djindjic in Serbia. In short, the relationships that warring factions develop with organized crime during war (through either organizational links or the adoption of DIY organized crime) are enduring and pernicious. Consequently, the international community must develop effective strategies to attack these linkages, making such strategies a central component of peace missions.

Attacking the Crime-Conflict Nexus

The international response to transnational organized crime evolved significantly during the 1990s through several different international organizations and agencies, including the United Nations secretariat in the UN Office on Drugs and Crime (UNODC), the Group of Eight (G-8), Interpol, Europol, and bilateral activities.[49] Impressive as these individual initiatives were, however, they suffered from a lack of integration, inadequate implementation and observance by states of norms they had formally accepted, and—especially significant to the present discussion—a failure to make explicit the crucial linkages between crime and conflict. Further, no innovative policy linkages came from those with the responsibility for dealing with conflict.

The international community's approaches to conflict management are based on a diplomatic paradigm that had some prospect for working in a traditional Westphalian system with both effective states and a high degree of consensus among them. However, traditional diplomacy has little or no prospect of being effective in confronting the rise of transnational and non-state networked actors that are impervious to the traditional dictates of interstate relations and far more interested in profit than peace or stability; the pervasiveness of informal economies and illegal markets that are transnational in nature and outside state control; and the symbiotic linkages between some state structures and criminal organizations, which can encourage states to defect (tacitly or overtly) from multilateral efforts to establish modalities of global governance. The responses to organized crime, on the one side, and to conflict management, conflict resolution, and peacekeeping, on the other, have been separate from one another, a form of intellectual and policy stovepiping that has been both insidious and pervasive.

The emergence of criminalized warfare requires profound changes in the response of the international community; it requires both a new intellectual paradigm and a new policy framework.[50] The new dynamics of armed conflicts suggest the need for a novel approach that blends traditional diplomatic expertise with law enforcement, develops conflict resolution strategies based on creating positive incentive structures and avoiding perverse incentives, and integrates peacemaking and peacekeeping activities with efforts to develop the rule of law, to contain organized criminal activities, and to inhibit the development of—or dismantle—parallel power structures. At the same time, there are important dilemmas that require difficult and delicate trade-offs. Efforts at conflict resolution and conflict management, as well as subsequent attempts to maintain peace and stability, have to break the nexus between crime and conflict, even if this means permitting one in return for the abandonment of the other. It is also important to go beyond policy advocacy and to recognize the kinds of problems that might arise at the level of implementation, as efforts are made to amalgamate or separate (depending on the circumstances and what one is trying to achieve) diplomatic and law enforcement activities.

Combating the crime-conflict nexus requires innovative and flexible policy responses. A number of strategies are available that might help to mitigate the pernicious role of both criminal enterprises and DIY organized crime throughout the conflict cycle. At the same time, these strategies needs to be tailored to the specific kinds of challenges posed by criminal enterprises whose involvement in conflict is opportunistic and DIY organized crime where the crime is motivated by the broader political struggle. When a regime is engaging in organized crime to fund its military ambitions and activities as well as enrich the political elite, sanctions need to be directed against the leading members of the elite (and not against the country as such); when criminal enterprises are involved, the focus needs to be on altering the profit-to-risk ratio by a combination of measures designed to reduce the available opportunities while increasing the risks attendant on exploiting these opportunities. In other words, there is no one-size-fits-all strategy. Instead, it is necessary to devise a particular set of measures appropriate to the peculiar circumstances of each conflict. It is also necessary to develop what might be termed a *cumulative approach*. Just as prewar dynamics extend into conflict and postconflict situations, so must some prewar measures of prevention be integrated not only into efforts to halt hostilities once they are under way but also into peace enforcement operations and state-building efforts after the formal resolution of conflict.

Measures to Reduce the
Opportunity for Criminalized Conflict

The role of organized crime in the outbreak of conflicts has implications for both structural prevention and early warning.

Structural prevention. Reducing the scope for criminal enterprises or for would-be insurgents, rebels, factions, or even government members who use criminal methods to fund their political-military agendas requires a more concerted effort to regulate the flow of arms, commodities, and finance to countries with weak governance and law enforcement. As suggested above, the flow of arms can sometimes precipitate a move from political tension to violence. Consequently, better mechanisms need to be established to interdict illicit arms trafficking to potential conflict zones. In part, this is a matter of giving efforts to combat trafficking a much higher priority than is currently the case. Unfortunately, few governments have adequate regulatory capacity or political will to control the illicit arms trade: most of them are far more interested in promoting arms sales than in restricting arms trafficking. And for developing and transitional states, even illicit activities provide at least some infusion of funds into the economy, often becoming a substitute for foreign direct investment.

Although it will not be easy to persuade governments to act more vigorously against arms trafficking, some things can be done relatively easily. These include, first, better regulation of pilots who fly into potential and actual war zones, including removal of their licenses for infractions—and international acceptance of these revocations; second, the establishment of more effective monitoring mechanisms to make diversion of weaponry from official end-users both more difficult and more transparent when it occurs; and third, more stringent law enforcement pursuit and prosecution of those who engage in such diversions, particularly the brokers who play a key role in the trafficking business and typically put together specific supplies of weaponry.

More generally, it is essential to engage in systematic efforts to take the commerce out of conflict as such and not simply out of the crime-conflict nexus. As suggested above, the crime-conflict nexus is more often a nexus of roles (the warrior-criminal) than a nexus of relationships between belligerents and criminal enterprises.[51] Nevertheless, at least some of the activities that have traditionally been used against organized crime enterprises are also useful against potential belligerents who are turning to criminal activities to augment their war chest. Structural prevention requires efforts to regulate commodity flows and enhance border controls in ways that make trafficking of illicit goods more difficult. It is also essential to reduce the scope for corruption in extractive industries and to enhance financial transparency domestically in states at risk, as well as at the regional and global levels. The difficulty, of course, is that this requires the creation of good governance in circumstances where the root causes of conflict stem from inadequate, corrupt, ineffective, exploitative, or illegitimate governance. Nevertheless, initiatives by the international community to establish global standards with local application are steps in the right direction. They recognize, at least implicitly, that the problem is not so much the links between potential belligerents and criminal enterprises as the links between the would-be warrior-criminal and legitimate businesses. Particularly important in this connection is the Extractive Industries Transparency Initiative (EITI), sponsored by the United Kingdom, which focuses on payment and revenue transparency in the oil, gas, and mining industries. Although the EITI was endorsed by the World Bank Group in May 2004, much remains to be done to ensure effective implementation. The difficulty is that the compact is voluntary and that those regimes that most need to sign up are the least likely to do so.[52] Warrior-criminal regimes will continue to shun transparency. Nevertheless, the gradual acceptance of global standards in this area, along with the eventual extension of the initiative to other industries associated with criminalized conflict, such as logging, would make it easier to identify the holdouts as high-risk countries. Moreover, if greater transparency in the extractive industries is accompanied by greater corporate responsibility and accountability at the international level, then corporations engaged in these industries might be somewhat more leery of relationships with potential (or actual) warrior-criminals. Although transparency and accountability will not be achieved easily, particularly if they jeopardize corporate earnings, businesses are concerned about reputational harm.

In this connection, the nongovernmental organization (NGO) community can be critical not only in monitoring efforts that extend beyond early warning to the identification of war-related economic activities and financial connections but also in its capacity to put issues on the national and international agenda—as Global Witness so dramatically did with conflict diamonds. Pressure by NGOs to put real teeth into multilateral regulatory efforts such as the Kimberley Process so that it is possible to distinguish between "legitimate" commodities and their conflict-related brethren that come through the black market is also potentially valuable.[53] Only with such pressure and subsequent detailed oversight will it be possible to reduce the prospects for connivance by licit businesses that is essential to war profiteering and, indeed, to the effective functioning of many black or gray markets. It has to be acknowledged, however, that the prospects remain uncertain at best. Going after the warrior-criminal will be no easier than going after criminal enterprises.

Early warning. If structural preventive efforts are unlikely to have a major impact, developing a new and appropriate set of early warning indicators for conflicts becomes even more urgent. Although significant efforts have already been made to develop warning indicators of impending armed conflict in the developing world, the analysis here suggests that these indicators be expanded. The incorporation of indicators reflecting the dynamics of struggles over the control of natural resources and the distribution of their revenues could significantly augment the international community's capacity to anticipate the outbreak of armed conflict. Specific warning indicators would include not only obvious candidates such as political, ethnic, and religious divisions in the populace, low levels of governance, a low position on the human development index, a high level of corruption, and a high level of economic dependence on extractive commodities but also competition for control over licit commodities and natural resources, similar competition for control of illicit commodities and markets, the purchase of weapons from known arms traffickers, the development of smuggling routes and relationships for both entry and exit, the development of a "shadow state," the emergence of warlords, and the use of the state as a sanctuary for criminal enterprises or terrorist organizations.

Indicators themselves, of course, are of little use unless they are carefully monitored. While governments and international organizations have the primary responsibility for monitoring indicators of potential conflict, the kind of expertise developed by NGOs such as Global Witness and the International Peace Information Service, based in Belgium, could provide an important supplementary capability. In addition, an early warning network could incorporate academic and research institutions with relevant expertise. The Small Arms Project in Geneva, for example, has developed a capacity to monitor arms flows and could identify anomalous or unusual movements of small arms and light weapons that might presage a buildup to hostilities.

When early warning is achieved through a mixture of NGO and academic activity on the one side and government efforts on the other, this can be fed into national ministries of foreign affairs as well as international and regional organizations such as the UN, the OSCE, the African Union, and the Economic Community of West African States (ECOWAS). In these circumstances, opportunities for preventive diplomacy need to be strengthened by the rapid deployment of mediation and monitoring teams of representatives from global and regional organizations. These teams should include not only traditional diplomats but also law enforcement representatives able to highlight the illicit transactions that are a key component of the move to war. The more knowledge that is available about such activities, the more credible the threat to disrupt them and impose smart sanctions targeting acquisitive elites.

Although such measures may enhance the capacity for preventive diplomacy, past experience suggests that there are clear limits to what can be achieved by enhanced prevention efforts. Consequently, efforts to break the crime-conflict nexus will often have to be continued into the hostilities phase.

Measures to Reduce Criminality During Conflict

To date, the imposition of sanctions and embargoes has been the most prominent approach employed by the international community to mitigate the flow of commodities, arms, and finance to conflict zones. Too often, however, these regimes have failed to include effective implementation strategies that take into account the role of nonstate actors and the development of local-transnational networks of beneficiaries of the war economies. They have been oblivious to the dynamics of supply and demand and to the growing importance of "sovereignty free actors"[54] who participate in what has been appropriately described as "international 'network war,' a global shadow economy which is increasingly monopolized by individual military actors and their commercial allies."[55] By creating shortages and price increases, embargoes simply encouraged new entrants to the market, many of whom were already experienced in various forms of trafficking and had developed considerable skill in circumventing rules and regulations, whether through corruption and bribery or skillful concealment practices. In effect, sanctions and embargoes undertaken to mitigate or resolve conflict have had the perverse effect of contributing to the growth of a "serious crime community" in which criminal enterprises and entrepreneurs specialize in serving as the illicit bridge between conflict zones on one side and suppliers and consumers on the other.[56]

To be sure, attacking or disrupting the resource bases, financial assets, and criminal connections of warring factions is an important component of a comprehensive approach to conflict termination. For targeted sanctions to be effective, however, greater attention must be paid to strengthened enforcement, and greater anticipation of evasion strategies needs to be built into their design. This requires several innovations, including efforts to incorporate international and national law enforcement agencies in support of regulatory regimes for sanctions that are much more carefully targeted than in past conflicts. There are several components of such an approach.

First, it is necessary to use sanctions and embargoes much more discriminately and with a new emphasis on minimizing prospects for circumvention. Where neither the will nor the capacity for effective enforcement can be summoned, the UN Security Council should resist the temptation of imposing sanctions; doing so only increases criminal evasion while having a negligible effect on conflict dynamics. Given the myriad difficulties of enforcing arms and commodity embargoes, preference might be given to freezing the finances and assets of targeted actors, as these measures are generally easier to implement. Targeting the fortunes of members of the Milosevic family and their political and criminal cronies, for example, was far more effective than the sanctions on Serbia, which succeeded only in providing lucrative monopolies for government elites, undermining the middle class, and enfeebling the opposition to Milosevic.

Second, embargoes on weapons need to be enforced more vigorously and in ways that increase the potential costs and risks and thereby make sanctions busting far less attractive. One way of achieving this is through undercover-buyer sting operations that enable those governments imposing sanctions to identify, inhibit, or interdict potential supplies to the belligerents or rogue regimes by criminal organizations, black-market arms dealers, or unscrupulous governments. Such operations introduce risk and make the market far less attractive than would otherwise be the case. There is no guarantee that deterrence strategies of this kind will work—where the payoffs are attractive, the increased risks may well be deemed worth taking. Nevertheless, it is important to transform sanctions busting from a low-risk to a high-risk activity. All this will be easier, of course, where governments have already taken steps to regulate arms brokers and pilots as part of the broader approach to conflict prevention discussed above.

The overtly criminal facets of the crime-conflict nexus can be attacked using undercover operations and other strategies traditionally employed against organized crime, such as asset freezing and seizing. In cases where efforts are made to cut off the funds of warring factions in conflict zones, success will depend largely on the capacity to identify the sources of their funds (often criminal activities) and then disrupt criminal networks that are trafficking in commodities or bartering guns for drugs. Going after the money can be an effective tool against criminal networks (particularly when combined with attacks on the organizational structures and the leadership). Arms traffickers should be subject to seizures not just of the arms themselves but of the means of conveyance as well as the firms they own. When combined with undercover operations and the imposition of harsher jail penalties, asset seizure and forfeiture measures can help both to take the profit out of the arms business and to make it a dangerous profession. Since illegal profit is the raison d'être of criminal organizations, if the profit is removed then they have no reason to be in business. And if criminal organizations know that they will be particularly high-priority targets if they become involved in conflict zones, this too might alter their calculations.

There is, of course, the issue of how all this is done. No single international organization or international police agency has the authority or ability to do all that is envisaged in providing law enforcement support for regulatory regimes. To extend the UN's responsibilities into law enforcement investigations would be to stretch its resources and credibility too thinly. Interpol has a more appropriate set of responsibilities but is primarily an information-sharing body rather than a more ambitious global law enforcement agency. Similarly, Europol has very specific geographic limits on its mandate; although it has responsibility for combating arms trafficking in or through the European Union (EU) region, its writ does not extend to areas of instability outside the EU that are the most likely targets for sanctions and embargoes.

With no international organization or agency particularly well suited to this task, a new cooperative initiative is crucial. Given that the United States has already taken on a leadership role in responding to transnational organized crime and terrorist financing, it would be well suited to lead such an initiative. Alternatively, the G-8 could take on this responsibility, perhaps by setting up a committee that extends the work of the Expert Group on Transnational Organized Crime into the crime-conflict nexus. There are several advantages to this becoming a special responsibility of the G-8. The G-8 countries could use their intelligence agencies, which have feet planted in both the diplomatic and law enforcement worlds, to help to integrate law enforcement and diplomatic considerations—something that is difficult because the government agencies involved have very different targets and constituencies—both nationally and internationally. Tripartite task forces in G-8 nations, involving intelligence agents, law enforcement personnel, and diplomats, could be set up to monitor compliance with sanctions and embargoes, to identify efforts to circumvent or sabotage the regime, and to track down and impose penalties on the transgressors. In addition, a G-8 focus could provide opportunities for ad hoc cooperation in bringing key criminal figures such as Viktor Bout to justice. Although wanted by Belgium, Bout has been able to act with impunity in Russia, claiming that he is a legitimate businessman. High-level political agreement at the G-8 to tackle the crime-conflict nexus would make jurisdiction hopping much more difficult for Bout and other criminals who have violated international sanctions.

Whatever the institutional arrangements, it is essential to increase functional cooperation in the law enforcement arena. This requires the creation of multilateral law-enforcement task forces and networks that exhibit the same flexibility as criminal networks and efforts to build capacity and establish effective criminal justice and law enforcement systems in developing and transitional states. Multilateral approaches of this kind could be further strengthened by integrating into existing training programs, such as those in the Federal Bureau of Investigation's International Law Enforcement Academy in Budapest, the kind of expertise developed by the U.S. Office of Foreign Asset Control, and the Financial Crimes

Enforcement Network. These programs are important in building trust and establishing interagency contacts, both of which are essential to the creation of informal law enforcement networks. Extending their focus would contribute to building multinational capacity to target conflict-related criminal and financial networks.

This would be a useful supplement to law enforcement mechanisms that enable authorities to attack criminal enterprises and trafficking activities in general. These include the U.S. Racketeer Influenced and Corrupt Organizations–type laws that allow attacks on criminal organizations or associations, asset seizure and forfeiture laws that target ill-gotten profits, and development of the knowledge and skills required to conduct effective undercover operations, whether sting operations, infiltration, or the use of controlled deliveries. The creation of capabilities for electronic surveillance is a necessary complement to such initiatives. Such actions are expensive, but they could be paid for, in part, by forfeited criminal assets.

Alongside strengthened interdiction regimes, there are more radical alternatives that might be considered to combat the crime-conflict nexus— and that do have some precedents. These include explicit trade-offs or even decoupling strategies in which organized crime or drug trafficking is accepted if this facilitates an end to or reduction of conflict. This is in stark contrast to the approaches enunciated above, which typically seek either to reduce the ability to generate resources through criminal activities or to increase the risk of using DIY organized crime. Where insurgency, warlordism, civil war, or terrorism is supported by involvement in the cultivation and trafficking of drugs, measures that encourage a coalescing of interest and identity between those whose primary interest is profit and those who seek profit for a political cause are counterproductive. When it became clear in Peru, for example, that counterinsurgency forces were only after Shining Path and not attempting to eradicate the coca plantations on which peasants depended for their livelihood, political support from the peasants for Shining Path evaporated.

The situation in Colombia is rather different, as there many peasants and traffickers migrated to areas that were under the control of the FARC so that they could cultivate narcotics crops without interference from the Colombian government. The other problem, as suggested above, is that the FARC has become an important player in the drug-trafficking business in its own right. Moreover, the symbiosis of the insurgents and the drug traffickers has become so well established that trade-off strategies will prove particularly difficult. At the same time, treating insurgents and drug-trafficking organizations in Colombia as if they always have identical interests could become a self-fulfilling prophecy.

A variant of the trade-off or decoupling strategy is to take actions that separate the political and financial agendas in ways that encourage belligerents to transform themselves into "merely" criminal enterprises. Separating the agendas is not an easy task and is likely to be extremely controversial. Yet a model for such an approach can be found in a very unlikely place—Burma/Myanmar. Conflict in Burma/Myanmar was characterized by a complex nexus between ethnic conflict and separatism on the one side and involvement in drug trafficking on the other. For example, Khun Sa's Shan United Army funded its military and political campaigns through the proceeds of drug cultivation and drug trafficking, as did other ethnic factions demanding autonomy.[57] While drug trafficking initially perpetuated the civil strife in Burma/Myanmar, during the 1990s it facilitated a lessening of the conflict. The government succeeded in separating the political and the criminal agendas by negotiating "cease-fire agreements with most of the drug-trafficking groups . . . offering them limited autonomy and development assistance in exchange for ending their insurgencies" and in effect permitting them to remain in the drug business.[58] The U.S. government suggested that the "cease-fire agreements have had the practical effect of condoning money laundering, as the government encouraged these groups to invest in legitimate businesses as an alternative to trafficking."[59] There is much to this. Allowing these groups to invest in the economy gives them a stake in the system, gives the government greater control over their actions, and reduces the prospects for further conflict. Today, Burma/Myanmar's major entrepreneurs, such as Lo Hsing Han and Khun Sa, once major figures in the drug-trafficking business, own hotels, casinos, and multiple businesses. Indeed, the de facto legitimization of the trafficking business has brought a semblance of peace and stability to Burma/Myanmar, ending conflicts that otherwise could have proved intractable. This does not make the regime any more palatable—and it could be argued that such an approach has perpetuated the military control of power. Nevertheless, it has helped to reduce armed conflict in the country

There are obvious moral dilemmas and serious political trade-offs involved in approaches that privilege conflict reduction over crime reduction. Yet in a world in which multiple forms of criminality tend to intensify, exacerbate, and perpetuate conflicts, such alternatives may be worth considering. The world is not one of moral absolutes, and in some cases, where criminal activities such as drug trafficking can be decoupled from conflict and used to provide incentives to reduce or end hostilities and subsequently to maintain stability, this might be acceptable.

Arguably, there are elements of this approach by the international community in post–Taliban Afghanistan. Although the emphasis is on long-term nation and state building, people have to eat and survive in the short term. It is hardly surprising, therefore, that opium cultivation and trafficking have increased enormously since the overthrow of the Taliban regime. As the U.S. State Department's 2002 International Narcotics Control Strategy

Report (INCSR) noted, "Afghan farmers continued to cultivate poppy as a risk-avoidance response to continuing drought conditions and lack of credit, farm inputs, and markets for other agricultural products. Afghanistan returned to its former position as the world's largest producer of illicit opium. Also contributing to the increase was the chaotic situation in Afghanistan following the fall of the Taliban in late 2001, and the limited enforcement reach of the new government."[60] Moreover, although the report noted that President Hamid Karzai had issued a decree banning cultivation, production, processing, illicit trafficking, and abuse of narcotic drugs, it recognized that this had very limited impact given the new government's limited authority outside Kabul. The report explicitly acknowledged that dealing with Afghanistan's drug production is a long-term challenge. The concomitant of this is a tacit—and perhaps deniable—acknowledgment that in a country where warlordism is still rife, and where the United States and the international community are supporting the central government in Kabul, short-term efforts to combat the drug trade could have a significant destabilizing effect and further undermine the (already limited) legitimacy of the new regime. The dilemma is that unless tacit understandings to enhance short-term stability are parlayed into a long-term consensus, drug cultivation and trafficking will continue to provide the resource base for alternative centers of power. Ultimately, this will make it more difficult for the government in Kabul to establish real authority and legitimacy over the rest of the country. In this case, a permissive approach to criminality, expedient as it currently appears, could contain the seeds of its own destruction. As the INCSR noted, therefore, there are limits to law enforcement efforts where capacity is lacking and demand is profound; the only real long-term solution is a massive alternative development program.[61] The concomitant is that more often than not, tacit acceptance will need to be abandoned in favor of a more aggressive approach to organized crime in postconflict situations.

Measures to Combat Postconflict Criminality

As suggested above, many of the criminal dynamics and linkages that facilitate wartime profiteering endure into the postconflict peace, inhibiting efforts at the creation and maintenance of a legitimate state. If the "greedy spoiler" problem is to be dealt with, therefore, peace enforcement operations need to directly address the legacies of war economies and the criminal networks that were key components of these economies.

First, peace missions need to be trained and equipped to deal with organized crime. Specialist law enforcement units from outside need to be integrated into peace enforcement operations, with specific responsibility to attack and disband the criminal networks that threaten peace implementation. Obviously these units will need to integrate law enforcement personnel with local knowledge. Not only will such personnel contribute a detailed knowledge of the local networks, but they will also provide the core of the professional indigenous police force that needs to be developed for the longer term. Care has to be taken to ensure the loyalty of the local recruits, and they should undergo a very stringent vetting. These law enforcement units, with support from intelligence analysts, would need to map political-criminal connections and then take steps to disrupt them.

Second, there needs to be close cooperation between the military forces and these law enforcement units. A useful model for this has been provided by the British. As one study noted,

In their Balkans peace missions, the British military has repeatedly demonstrated the effectiveness of a mode of operation that is rooted in principles of counterinsurgency as applied in Northern Ireland. This emphasizes cohesive action with civilian counterparts, especially law enforcement; cultivating support and eliciting intelligence from the local population; and intelligence-led operations to manage and, when appropriate, arrest those who oppose peace through violent means.[62]

In the longer term, external law enforcement units need to be gradually phased out and replaced by a local, highly professionalized police force that has "trusted individuals to staff it, adequate and thorough training, the provision of a coercive capability, and most importantly . . . authority."[63] This process has to be strictly supervised, with a gradual transfer of power and responsibility from the external units to the indigenous police. There also needs to be continued oversight of the new force to prevent any abuses.

A similar process needs to be undertaken at the judicial level, with external judges being brought in to undertake politically sensitive trials and provide training and support until the local judiciary is strong, independent, and neutral and can itself exhibit both responsibility and effectiveness. Such a strategy has had some success in the UN peace operation in Kosovo, where "UNMIK incorporated international judges and prosecutors into the local courts. They are regularly asked by their local colleagues to assume sensitive cases because of a well-founded fear of reprisals against themselves or their families."[64] While this is an important short-term measure, it needs to be accompanied by an exit strategy that includes plans for transition to an indigenous, self-sufficient judiciary.

This emphasis on criminal law enforcement needs to be part of a broader approach that seeks to develop both the rule of law and a vibrant civil society. "For the rule of law to take root will require a comprehensive approach to building capacity, developing effective safeguards to ensure public accountability, and forging an enduring partnership between local institutions and the international community."[65] It will also require close cooperation between the NGO community and law enforcement at the local level that, in effect, mirrors the cooperation required at the international level both prior to and during hostilities. The elimination of the structures of war profiteering in a peacemaking context is only the first step in what is a lengthy and extremely formidable undertaking. Yet unless this is successful, the prospects for long-term recovery and the prevention of a recurrence of conflict will be significantly reduced.

Conclusion

It is worth emphasizing two additional observations—the need for flexibility and the need for humility in terms of what can be achieved. In developing and implementing the kinds of recommendations outlined above, it is necessary to consider the ways in which the UN and other international and regional actors engaged in conflict resolution can be most effective. It is also necessary to consider current "best practices" as well as to identify what needs to be changed in order to achieve maximum effectiveness. While appropriate lessons can be drawn from past experiences of conflict in areas such as the Balkans, Africa, and Central Asia, each conflict has its own distinct dynamic that must be recognized by those who are trying to bring it to an end, as well as by those who are trying to ensure that it does not flare up once more either in the short or the long term.

In the final analysis, it is also important to acknowledge that no strategy for combating the crime-conflict nexus is likely to be entirely satisfactory. Still, in a world where the dialectic between the forces of disorder and the impulse for governance is one of the defining characteristics, finding imaginative, if unorthodox, combinations of approaches is essential if the disorder is not to become overwhelming.

Notes

1. State weakness can stem from several causes, including long-term secular decline, the collapse of authoritarianism and the complexities of transitional politics and economics, and the failure to establish, let alone maintain, legitimacy. See, for example, Robert I. Rotberg, ed., *State Failures and State Weakness in a Time of Terror* (Cambridge, Mass.: World Peace Foundation, 2003).

2. For a more comprehensive examination of the causes of strong, failing, and failed states, see ibid.

3. Mark Duffield, *Global Governance and the New Wars: The Merging of Development and Security* (London: Zed Books, 2001), p. 14.

4. See Michael Pugh and Neil Cooper, with Jonathan Goodhand, *War Economies in a Regional Context: Challenges of Transformation* (Boulder: Lynne Rienner, 2004); and Heiko Nitzschke, *Transforming War Economies: Challenges*

for Peacemaking and Peacebuilding, report of the 725th Wilton Park Conference in association with the International Peace Academy, October 27–29, 2003 (New York: International Peace Academy, 2003).

5. See Roy Godson, "Transnational Crime, Corruption and Security," in Michael E. Brown, ed., *Grave New World: Security Challenges in the Twenty-first Century* (Washington, D.C.: Georgetown University Press, 2003), pp. 259–278.

6. For more on the similarities and differences between organized crime and terrorism, see John T. Picarelli and Louise Shelley, "Methods, Not Motives: Implications of the Convergence of International Organized Crime and Terrorism," *Police Practice and Research* 3, no. 4 (2002): 305–318.

7. Sergey Gretsky, "Civil War in Tajikistan: Causes, Developments, and Prospects for Peace," in Roald Sagdeev and Susan Eisenhower, eds., *Central Asia: Conflict, Resolution, and Change* (Washington, D.C.: Eisenhower Institute, 1995).

8. "The World Geopolitics of Drugs," *Crime, Law, and Social Change* 36, nos. 1–2 (September 2001): 242.

9. For a fuller elaboration of this argument, see Phil Williams, "Criminalization and Stability in Central Asia and South Caucasus," in Olya Oliker and Thomas Szayna, eds., *Faultlines of Conflict in Central Asia and the South Caucasus: Implications for the U.S. Army* (Santa Monica, Calif.: RAND, 2003), pp. 71–107.

10. On the general notion of a tipping point, see Malcolm Gladwell, *The Tipping Point: How Little Things Can Make a Big Difference* (Boston: Little, Brown, 2000).

11. Jean-François Bayart, Stephen Ellis, and Beatrice Hibou, *The Criminalization of the State in Africa* (Bloomington: Indiana University Press, 1999).

12. William Reno, "Warfare in Collapsed States and Special Problems of Conflict Resolution," available at www.igd.org.za/pub/g-dialogue/Special_feature/Collapsed_States.htm.

13. Ibid.

14. Ibid. See also William Reno, "Shadow States and the Political Economy of Civil War," in Mats Berdal and David M. Malone, eds., *Greed and Grievance: Economic Agendas in Civil Wars* (Boulder: Lynne Rienner, 2000), pp. 43–68.

15. Obi N. I. Ebbe, "The Political-Criminal Nexus: The Nigerian Case," *Trends in Organized Crime* 4, no. 3 (Spring 1999): 29–59.

16. Jean-François Bayart, *The State in Africa: The Politics of the Belly* (New York: Longman, 1993).

17. According to Paul Collier and Anke Hoeffler's earlier account as well as the accounts of other economists, "loot-seeking" is a primary cause of war and one that, in the words of H. I. Grossman, quoted in Collier and Hoeffler's work, renders rebels "indistinguishable from bandits or pirates." Paul Collier and Anke Hoeffler, *Greed and Grievance in Civil War* (Washington, D.C.: World Bank, October 21, 2001), p. 2. See also Paul Collier, "Doing Well out of War," in Berdal and Malone, *Greed and Grievance,* pp. 91–111.

18. Ian Smillie, Lansana Gberie, and Ralph Hazleton, *The Heart of the Matter: Sierra Leone, Diamonds, and Human Security* (Ottawa: Partnership Africa Canada, 2000).

19. Tim Raeymaekers, *Network War: An Introduction to Congo's Privatized War Economy* (Brussels: International Peace Information Service, October 2002), available at www.totse.com/en/politics/the_world_beyond_the_usa/167160.html.

20. Preface to the English edition of Bayart, *State in Africa,* pp. xiii–xiv.

21. Global Witness, *Resources, Conflict, and Corruption* (London: Global Witness, 2002), p. 10.

22. R. Thomas Naylor, "The Insurgent Economy: Black Market Operations of Guerrilla Organizations," *Crime, Law, and Social Change* 20, no. 1 (1993): 23.

23. Barry Buzan and Eric Herring, *The Arms Dynamic in World Politics* (Boulder: Lynne Rienner, 1998).

24. Jean-Paul Azam, Paul Collier, and Anke Hoeffler, "International Policies on Civil Conflict: An Economic Perspective," working paper, World Bank, Washington, D.C., December 14, 2001.

25. Raeymaekers, *Network War.*

26. Ibid.

27. Ibid.

28. As Bruce Bagley notes, "In the late 1990s Russian vessels docked repeatedly at the Caribbean port of Turbo in northern Colombia to offload shipments of Russian AK-47 assault rifles and rocket propelled grenades for the FARC guerrillas and, possibly, for right-wing paramilitary bands, in exchange for cocaine." Bruce Bagley, "Globalization and Transnational Organized Crime: The Russian Mafia in Latin America and the Caribbean," February 2002, available at www.mamacoca. org/feb2002/art_bagley_globalization_organized_crime_en.html.

29. Indeed, Bout's activities revealed the "strong connection that exists between occupying armies, minerals businesses and the regional proliferation of arms. While he has been supplying most of the warring parties with military equipment, his close relations to regional commodity traders has assured him of his involvement in the exploitation of precious resources such as coltan and diamonds. In turn, the trade in these resources has provided the military actors with their necessary cash flows to secure their power" (Bagley, "Globalization and Transnational Organized Crime").

30. Charles Hanley, "Increasingly, Guerrillas Financed by Drugs," *Toronto Star,* December 29, 1994, p. A19.

31. Written testimony of Ralf Mutschke, assistant director, Criminal Intelligence Directorate, International Criminal Police Organization, Interpol General Secretariat, before a hearing of the Committee on the Judiciary Subcommittee on Crime, December 13, 2000, "The Threat Posed by the Convergence of Organized Crime, Drugs Trafficking, and Terrorism," available at www.house.gov/judiciary/muts1213.htm. See also Alexandros Yannis, "Kosovo: The Political Economy of Conflict and Peacebuilding," in Karen Ballentine and Jake Sherman, eds., *The Political Economy of Armed Conflict: Beyond Greed and Grievance* (Boulder: Lynne Rienner, 2003), pp. 167–195.

32. John Arquilla and David Ronfeldt, eds., *Networks and Netwars: The Future of Terror, Crime, and Militancy* (Santa Monica, Calif.: RAND, 2001).

33. Steven Metz, *The Future of Insurgency,* December 1993. This provocative, useful, and prescient analysis is available at www.carlisle.army.mil/ssi/pubs/1993/insurg/insurg.pdf.

34. Alexandra Guáqueta, "The Colombian Conflict: Political and Economic Dimensions," in Ballentine and Sherman, *Political Economy of Armed Conflict,* pp. 73–106.

35. This paragraph draws heavily on an excellent research paper by Erin Wick that was done for the Capstone Seminar on Transnational Organized Crime (spring 2003) in the Graduate School of Public and International Affairs, University of Pittsburgh. We are grateful to Wick for also bringing the paper by Metz (note 33) to our attention.

36. "Attorney General and DEA Director Announce Indictments in AUC Drug Trafficking Case," Drug Enforcement Administration news release, September 24, 2002.

37. "Colombian Terrorists Arrested in Cocaine-for-Weapons Deal," Drug Enforcement Administration news release, November 6, 2002.

38. Peter Muench, "Milosevic Clan Involved in Organized Crime," *Sueddeutsche Zeitung* (Internet version, in German), October 17, 2000.

39. See, for example, James Finckenauer and Elin Waring, *Russian Mafia in America: Immigration, Culture, and Crime* (Boston: Northeastern University Press, 1998).

40. This section draws on an unpublished paper by Jason Collins, University of Pittsburgh, April 2000, and on Mackenzie Institute, *Funding Terror: The Liberation Tigers of Tamil Eelam and Their Criminal Activities in Canada and the Western World* (Toronto: Mackenzie Institute, 1996).

41. Don Pathan, "Tamil Tiger Foothold Shows Security Flaws," *Nation*, March 31, 2000; "Sri Lanka Seen as Important Drug Conduit," Colombo, Sri Lanka, United Press International, March 10, 2000. See also Rohan Gunaratna, "Sri Lanka: Feeding the Tamil Tigers," in Ballentine and Sherman, *Political Economy of Armed Conflict*, pp. 197–223.

42. For an analysis of the spoiler issue, see Stephen J. Stedman, "Spoiler Problems in Peace Processes," *International Security* 22, no. 2 (1997): 5–53. Also useful is Marie-Joëlle Zahar, "Reframing the Spoiler Debate," in John Darby and Roger MacGinty, eds., *Contemporary Peacemaking: Conflict, Violence, and Peace Processes* (Houndmills, UK: Palgrave, 2003), pp. 114-124.

43. Michael Pugh, "Postwar Political Economy in Bosnia and Herzegovina: The Spoils of Peace," *Global Governance* 8, no. 4 (2002): 467–482.

44. U.S. General Accounting Office (GAO), "Bosnia Peace Operation: Crime and Corruption Threaten Successful Implementation of the Dayton Peace Agreement," report to congressional requesters, Washington, D.C., July 2000. See www.gao.gov/new.items/ns00219t.pdf.

45. Robert Barry, speech at Sarajevo University, October 20, 1999, quoted in European Stability Initiative (ESI), *Reshaping International Priorities in Bosnia and Herzegovina, Part Two: International Power in Bosnia* (Berlin: ESI, 2000), p. 40. Available at www.esiweb.org/pdf/esi_document_id_P.pdf.

46. U.S. Institute of Peace, *The Balkans: Rule of Law or Lawless Rule?* special report, 2002, available at www.usip.org/pubs/specialreports/sr97.html.

47. Annika Hansen, *From Congo to Kosovo: Civilian Police in Peace Operations* (New York: Oxford University Press, 2002).

48. U.S. Institute of Peace, *Balkans*.

49. The United Nations secretariat in the UNODC in Vienna was particularly prominent and organized and managed a series of initiatives from the World Ministerial Conference on Organized Transnational Crime, held in Naples in November 1994, to the signing of the UN Convention against Transnational Organized Crime in Palermo in December 2000. The Palermo Convention helped to establish a set of norms and to provide guidance for governments in their efforts to combat organized crime. The G-8 did something similar with its development of forty recommendations to combat organized crime, while its Financial Action Task Force sought to combat money laundering by developing a set of requirements for its member states that included financial reporting mechanisms and the creation of financial intelligence units. At the same time, efforts were made to revitalize Interpol, which has an important but limited role in sharing of information among

its member states. For its part, the European Union created Europol, which also has important information-sharing and coordinating roles in criminal investigations in the European Union. Bilateral and multilateral efforts to combat crime were also facilitated by the extension of mutual legal assistance treaties (facilitating information exchanges in criminal cases) and extradition treaties.

50. The postinternationalist paradigm that James Rosenau has designed is intellectually closest to this notion. See, for example, James Rosenau, *Turbulence in World Politics* (Princeton, N.J.: Princeton University Press, 1989).

51. We are grateful to Margaret Beare, director of the Nathanson Center, Yorke University, Toronto, for this distinction.

52. See also Chapter 11 by Gavin Hayman and Corene Crossin in this volume.

53. Global Witness, *Conflict Diamonds: Possibilities for the Identification, Certification, and Control of Diamonds* (London: Global Witness, 2000).

54. Rosenau, *Turbulence in World Politics.*

55. Raeymaekers, *Network War.* See also Mark Duffield, "War as a Network Enterprise: The New Security Terrain and Its Implications," *Cultural Values* 6, no. 1 (2002): 153–166.

56. Alan A. Block, *Masters of Paradise* (New Brunswick, N.J.: Transaction, 1991). No one illustrates these serious crime figures better than Viktor Anatolevic Bout. A highly successful criminal entrepreneur, born in Tajikistan and with experience in the KGB, Bout has consistently flouted and circumvented embargoes on conflict zones. He succeeded by moving his base from Belgium to the United Arab Emirates, where he could operate with impunity, and by developing a dynamic, fluid, and opaque portfolio of companies with obscure registration, making his activities particularly difficult to identify, let alone stop. He has been connected to arms supplies to Hutu rebels in the Congo in 1996 and to rebel groups in Sierra Leone. See, for example, "German Daily Calls Diamond Trade Tajikistan Mafia's 'Global Business,'" *Sueddeutsche Zeitung* (Internet version, in German), January 31, 2001; and "Illegal Arms Trafficking: United Nations Expert Discusses Sudden Interest in Arms Dealer Viktor Bout," *Vremya MN,* March 5, 2002, available at www.corruptionlist.com/archive/March%202002/Corruption%20List%20Vol.%202 %20No.%2011.htm.

57. See Alfred W. McCoy, *The Politics of Heroin in Southeast Asia* (New York: Harper and Row, 1972).

58. Bureau for International Narcotics and Law Enforcement Affairs, U.S. Department of State, *International Narcotics Control Strategy Report, 1999* (Washington, D.C.: Author, 2000); see also Jake Sherman, "Burma/Myanmar: Lessons from the Cease-Fires," in Ballentine and Sherman, *Political Economy of Armed Conflict,* pp. 225–255.

59. Bureau for International Narcotics and Law Enforcement Affairs, *International Narcotics Control Strategy Report, 1999.*

60. Bureau for International Narcotics and Law Enforcement Affairs, U.S. Department of State, *International Narcotics Control Strategy Report, 2002* (Washington, D.C.,: Author, 2003), available at www.state.gov.

61. Ibid.

62. U.S. Institute of Peace, *Balkans.*

63. Transnational Crime and Corruption Center (TraCCC), *Transnational Crime and Peacekeeping: Comparative Perspectives,* conference report (Washington, D.C.: TraCCC, 2002), p. 48.

64. U.S. Institute of Peace, *Balkans.*

65. Ibid.

7

Protecting Livelihoods in Violent Economies

Stephen Jackson

If, as David Keen suggests, "war has increasingly become the continuation of economics by other means," its varying impacts on individual livelihoods are still not comprehensively understood.[1] Violence destroys many assets on which economic life is based, and it redistributes and mutates others. It destroys property but also alters its ownership; it despoils but also provides the cover for organized, even industrialized expropriation of profit. As it erases preexisting social solidarities, it also forges new ones within rebel movements or opportunistic economic networks enticed by the spoils of war.

A number of related implications follow. First, armed violence, particularly in regions rich in lucrative natural resources, is not, as too often characterized, mere chaotic predation but possesses a (dys)functional order and systemic logic of its own. Second, despite popular prejudices, not all participants in violent economies are greedy rebels or predatory warlords. Many ordinary people become dependent on violent economies. Nor are there always easy distinctions between "conflict entrepreneurs" who control violent economies, "conflict opportunists" who exploit subordinate positions in these economies, and "conflict dependents" at the bottom who subsist precariously within them (an important set of categories refined later in this chapter). Third, so-called war economies often build upon and intensify preexisting relations of economic violence that characterize periods nominally at "peace,"[2] thereby generating explosive compounds of both "greed" and "grievance" dynamics.[3] Hence, I prefer the more encompassing term *violent economies*. Fourth, and most fundamental to this chapter, many contemporary policies for tackling the resource dimensions of armed conflict risk unintended negative consequences when they pay insufficient attention both to the damage they may inflict on the most vulnerable and to the perverse incentives they may offer for further rent seeking by conflict elites. Improving these policies requires a better analysis of their impact upon livelihoods already under great pressure from violence.

In this chapter I therefore argue for close attention to how livelihoods are made within violence, who makes them, with what assets, and with what relation to and degree of control over the flow of violence. To make this argument, I first briefly describe the standard "sustainable livelihoods model" derived from rural development economics. Second, I draw from my research in the eastern Democratic Republic of Congo (DRC) as well as from research on other cases to illustrate how this model can be adapted to capture the complexity, instability, continuity, and changeability of violent economies. I argue that policymakers must pay close attention to three related dimensions: violent transformations in relationships to available economic assets; the emergence of a variety of economic actors with widely different degrees of control over or dependence on violent economies; and the scale and dynamics of the violent economy overall. In the final section, I first employ livelihoods analysis to identify the unintended consequences of some contemporary approaches to managing the resource dimensions of conflicts, which aim at curtailing resource flows as a means of conflict mitigation and resolution. I then offer some recommendations for complementary measures that seek to protect the most vulnerable but avoid offering further impetus to the economic predation by the most powerful.[4]

The Sustainable Livelihoods Model

> *That's the difference between crime and business. For business you gotta have capital. Sometimes I think it's the only difference.*
> —Raymond Chandler, *The Long Good-Bye*

The commonsense term *livelihood* has acquired a technical definition among rural development specialists, who argue that failures of rural development arise from poor understanding of the multidimensionality of rural poverty and the economic importance of nonagricultural activities. Sustainable livelihoods analysis seeks to assess how,

> in different contexts, sustainable livelihoods are achieved through access to a range of livelihood resources (natural, economic, human and social capitals) which are combined in the pursuit of different livelihood strate-

gies (agricultural intensification/extensification, livelihood diversification and migration). Central to the framework is the analysis of the range of formal and informal organizational and institutional factors that influence sustainable livelihood outcomes.[5]

Livelihoods analysis thus starts with an assessment of people's access to and control over key assets put to strategic, productive use. Six categories of assets are posited. *Human assets* concern individual levels of education, skill, experience, and health and the collective ability to deploy and control one's own and others' labor. *Natural assets* include land, water, crops, forests, animals (for draft or for food, skins, and other products), and mineral resources (such as gold, rough diamonds, and tantalum). *Financial assets* comprise cash, savings, convertible assets such as material and intellectual property, access to credit, remittances, and foreign investment. *Physical assets* include all forms of productive infrastructure, such as mills, dairies, markets, roads, airports, office space, warehousing, factories, machinery, fuel, and energy. *Social assets* concern "horizontal" relationships among actors that reinforce livelihood strategies, such as kinship, ethnicity, religious affinity, and professional networks. Finally, *political assets* are "vertical" relationships, such as membership in political parties, connectedness to judicial or customary spheres of legal influence, and so on. Each set of assets may in principle factor into the livelihood strategies pursued by individuals or groups.

Livelihoods analysis next considers the external trends and shocks that can have impact on relationships to these assets. Trends are ongoing local, regional, or global alterations in macroeconomic context, such as devaluations, demographic pressures, or advances in technology. Shocks concern acute changes, whether environmental or human in origin. Additional points for analysis include how customary norms, policies, the legal climate, political administration, and institutions, both formal and informal, circumscribe livelihood possibilities.[6]

Livelihoods amid Economic Violence

When sustainable livelihoods analysis is joined with a political economy approach, contexts of economic violence can be better illuminated.[7] I suggest a three-step schema of analysis as an essential prerequisite for a more careful design of policy instruments to combat the resource dimension of conflict. First, attention must be paid to how violence deforms prevailing relationships to economic *assets*. Second, economic *actors* must be disaggregated by their economic motivations, their relative degree of influence over the course of economic violence, and the nature of the benefits they derive from participating in it. Third, due weight must also be given to the *scale and dynamics* of the highly unstable and unpredictable nature of violent economies.

Violent Transformations
in Relationships to Economic Assets

Human assets. Violence takes a heavy toll on conventional human assets. As a direct or indirect result of warfare, a vicious circle emerges between food insecurity and diminished individual capacity for labor. Educational infrastructure is destroyed, and entire cohorts completely skip schooling, which wipes out future opportunities and engenders smoldering frustration. Displacement and deskilling produce pools of reserve youth cheaply recruited to economic violence by rumors of easy opportunity. Fighters gain skill in predatory tactics of survival and create "new egalitarian forms of social organization with violence as the main mode of discourse, . . . leading to a shift of influence to the advantage of this generation."[8] Through the skills it bestows and the new networks and alliances it creates, militia life can become a pernicious human and social "asset" of its own.

When postconflict demobilization threatens to deprive combatants of their only livelihood, migrating to other conflicts may become an attractive alternative. Thus, previous experience in West Africa has heightened concerns over a possible "negative domino effect" of peace in Liberia, whereby poorly demobilized and reintegrated combatants may choose to seek out new opportunities in a pan–West African market still hungry for fighters.[9]

Natural assets. The statistical correlation between lucrative natural resource endowments and endemic violence (one instance of the "resource curse") makes natural resources an obvious focus for livelihoods analysis. Through violence, natural resources can be looted, stripped, smuggled, and violently "taxed." Which mode of accumulation predominates depends on the scale and organization of actors and the "lootability" of resources.[10] "Lootable" resources, such as alluvial gems and minerals, timber, and narcotic cash crops, such as poppies and coca, are highly labor intensive and, because barriers to entry are extremely low, can be capitalized upon at numerous links in the commodity chain. Where violence has eliminated traditional agricultural livelihood options, peasant populations may be drawn into dependence on the exploitation of lootable resources for survival, with ambiguous implications for welfare. For example, the tantalum economy in eastern DRC enriched many ordinary people as well as powerful actors, but at the expense of the environment, formal economic development, and other segments of the peasant population. As successive reports of the UN Expert Panel on Illegal Exploitation of Natural Resources and Other Forms of Wealth in the Democratic Republic of Congo have made clear, armed factions either crack down on artisanal exploitation or control lucrative purchasing, processing, and forward shipment.[11] In the latter case, ordinary workers who have come to depend on illicit resource exploitation for survival may ally with those more powerful than them against international efforts to curtail illicit extraction.

"Nonlootable" resources, such as petroleum or deep-shaft minerals, have different impacts on livelihoods in violent economies. Extracting these resources demands industrial techniques of exploitation requiring high levels of investment and organization. On the whole, the main benefits accrue to those who can supply these factors—that is, governments and multinational companies.[12] To the limited extent that rebel groups are able to obstruct or extort from nonlootable resource extraction, modest benefits may be derived for them and for other local constituents. While nonlootable resource extraction offers fewer welfare benefits in violent economies, it can have profoundly devastating impacts on livelihoods in cases, such as Sudan, where securing access to resource deposits involves the violent physical displacement of civilian communities.[13]

Bound up in the postcolonial politics of "customary authority" and "ethnic citizenship," land rights are also profoundly altered by violence.[14] While only some conflicts begin in arguments over customary authority, almost all end up challenging it. Violent displacement and ensuing land or property disputes may fuel long-standing quarrels over "autochthony," intercommunal grievance expressed through the language of indigenous land rights. Violent conflict also alters land use patterns. As a result of a decade of violence, eastern Congo's vast pastures have been emptied of hundreds of thousands of cattle. Some areas remain empty, guarded for their landlords by armed militias. The "autochthon" population has taken back other areas and begun cultivating them, with unpredictable consequences when the landlords eventually return. Other areas of arable land have been lost to mineral grabs by private militias, Rwandan and Ugandan combatants, and quasi-independent producers "licensed" by local chiefs.[15] In previously productive areas, prices of staples quadrupled as agricultural land was abandoned or turned over to the exploitation of tantalum, tin, gold, and other minerals.[16] The result was a massive legacy of food insecurity.[17]

Financial assets.   Violence destroys some financial assets and shifts control of others to the powerful. In the DRC, wage income, already long crippled, collapsed during the war. State salaries have gone unpaid for years, while formal mining has been "liberalized," stripped and abandoned in favor of artisanal opportunism. "Fending for oneself"—a Congolese euphemism embracing both survival by one's wits and graft—is no longer a means to supplement meager salaries; it is often the only way people can obtain income. Eroding economic margins locked brittle survival livelihoods into vertical dependency on those controlling violence. The latter years of war saw peasants' financial reserves so completely eroded that local produce markets shifted from morning to evening to give people enough daytime to scratch together money for basic commodities.[18] Currency collapse and capital flight accelerated the already rampant dollarization and hyperinflation in both urban and rural areas of the DRC. The demise of the formal banking sector closely tied economic destinies to transborder sources of foreign exchange at inflated rates of interest, rendering accumulation and investment in productive capacity all but impossible, again adding to the tendency to strip assets. Meanwhile, bottlenecks in the supply of currency and credit provided additional openings for revenue generation. The fragility of these livelihoods, however, meant that external shocks—such as the 2001 collapse in the world price of tantalum ore (coltan)—facilitated the encroaching monopolization of remaining productive sectors by dominant elites intent on crowding out competitors.[19]

Physical assets. As conflict progresses, any physical infrastructure that is not destroyed outright continually degrades. Roads remain unrepaired and highly insecure, arterial waterways and railways are abandoned, and border crossings are heavily policed, permeable only by those with money and influence. All of this increases the premium on seizing and maintaining control of what little of the physical infrastructure still functions. Combatant factions compete to capture valued physical sites to generate rents through "visas," "customs duties," and "license fees" on individuals and goods transiting internally,[20] erecting "internal borders."[21] All of these activities constitute new barriers to commercial entry and thus new "gatekeeping" livelihoods. This competition escalates as the factions themselves splinter and the territory they dominate becomes smaller and smaller. No wonder that infrastructural bottlenecks such as airstrips, border gates, and ports become such fought-over tactical economic targets.

Social assets. In the conventional livelihoods models, social assets are viewed as benign forms of social capital.[22] However, social capital also has its dark side, facilitating violent domination of particular economic sectors.[23] From West African "brotherhood" crime syndicates to ethnic-group domination of trade sectors in eastern Congo, social capital interacts ambiguously with violence.[24] Ethnicity can become the basis for mutual insurance against the economic effects of violence but may also drive the violence itself. Elites and warlords often play on communal grievances for profit. For example, since 2000, leaders (and their international backers) on both sides of the extremely violent divide in Ituri, in northeastern Congo, have culpably stoked interethnic resentment to win control over mineral deposits.[25] However, analysts are often too quick to attribute the origins of identity-based violence to elite manipulation, underplaying the preexistence of grievances at the grassroots. What becomes important for analysis is the transformation of difference into grievance. If dense, overlapping social relations constitute benign (depreciating?) capital in democratic societies as Robert Putnam suggests,[26] in conditions of violent conflict these relations harden, flatten, and simplify. Webs of identity turn binary under violence: "in" or "out," "indigenous" or "foreigner," "us" or "them." Military leaders are not alone in leveraging such horizontal distinctions: at the village level, ordinary people instrumentalize them in squabbles over property, while at the provincial level, they propel fights for authority and advantage.

Political assets. Perhaps the most potent of all assets in the pursuit of conflict livelihoods are political. The lowercase *p* is emphasized. According to Paul Collier, today's rebellions and civil conflicts are seldom ideological *sensu stricto.*[27] Yet this should not be confused with an absence of politics. Parlaying vertical connectedness to those in positions of authority—whether new or old, contingent or deeply established—into economic opportunity pays dividends for entrepreneurs, opportunists, and dependents alike. What the Congolese call "trampolining"—springing from one position of advantage to another—critically depends on connectedness to power. Clinging to the coattails of rebel movements delivers protection as well as access to income-generating opportunities. Equally, while customary authority's power tends to be eroding, chiefs can usually deliver some protection and access to profit. An in with the local chief was necessary in the early stages of the Congolese tantalum boom if one was to purchase rights to dig.

The value of political assets is visible in continuing attempts to counterfeit them. Proliferating militia factions in the DRC and elsewhere—nine or so Rassemblements Congolais pour la Démocratie (RCDs) at one point, and as many Mayi-Mayi groupings—are not just products of the fragmentation generated by violent competition over control of valuable mineral resources. They also reflect a wager among aspiring winners that the inclusive logic of peace means that everyone with guns and a letterhead will have some claim to a place at the negotiating table and, hence, a place within a government of national unity.[28]

Regional, national, and local assets. A final and vital point on assets concerns the variety of levels at which they intersect with violent economies and at which they must be analyzed. Many relevant assets, such as control of land use and internal transportation links, are primarily local phenomena. However, generating revenue from lucrative commodities requires access to larger markets and financial flows. Networks of kinship, ethnicity, and political patronage that cut across international borders facilitate these flows. Indeed, such regional and international networks have been critical to sustaining the conflict trade that has fueled conflicts in the DRC and elsewhere, thus radically undermining the relevance of borders of "failing states." Too much analysis underpinning international intervention still privileges the state and national territory as the appropriate levels for analysis. Livelihoods analysis cannot afford the same error.

Disaggregating Violent
Economies and the Actors Within Them

Several analysts have proposed schemata by which to distinguish different facets of violent economies. Philippe Le Billon has proposed a tripartite distinction among "the war economy," "the collateral economic impacts of war," and "economic strategies of war."[29] Pursuing a related line, Jonathan Goodhand disaggregates the "combat," "shadow," and "coping" economies.[30] Goodhand notes that the coping economy may exist wholly or partially within the shadow economy. Perhaps what needs to be added explicitly here, though, is that while the combat economy is by definition explicitly violent, the shadow and even the coping economies may entail great violence too. Different conflicts, emerging at different times, in contrasting contexts, and with varying asset bases, exhibit differing mixes of these economies. Both Le Billon and Goodhand also note that the analytical distinctions they erect are often blurred by realities on the ground (an aspect strongly shared by the schema I will propose). Though alarmingly durable overall, violent economies are inherently unstable and prone to sudden shifts.

The foregoing analyses of economic assets and conflict economies permit a clearer picture of what kinds of actors gain and lose from violence. Adapting various existing schemata concerning actors, I distinguish three broad groups by their degree of control over violence.[31]

Conflict entrepreneurs. These are predatory elites who direct, deploy, or influence military strategy in order to maximize personal profit, forcefully colonizing key productive assets. Too frequently their predation is actually facilitated by the inexact application of interventions designed to control their activities. While often lumped together, conflict entrepreneurs can be taxonomized along a continuum between those with predominantly political or economic ends:

LOOTERS. At the economic extreme, looters have extremely short time horizons to maximize the opportunities violence offers them. Under a smokescreen of seemingly chaotic conflict that they or others generate through deliberate manipulation of local resentments (thus preempting challenge from customary authorities), they raid or strip natural resources and physical assets (such as plants and infrastructures, factories, equipment, and buildings). Constantly threatened by new contenders, they are perennially nervous and generate a highly unstable climate. Looters may organize along political or social lines as armed factions or ethnic militias, but they may also spontaneously coalesce and disperse to exploit fleeting opportunities. Looters, by definition, do not require financial assets such as banking systems or lines of credit and have no incentive to invest in securing them.[32]

ORGANIZED CRIMINALS. These actors require neither popular support nor the smokescreen of volatility that looters require. Organized criminal enterprises create time and space for profit by neutralizing customary authority in resource-rich districts, whether by payoffs, threats, or eliminating local leaders altogether. In parts of the DRC where military presence was light, for example, buying off local chiefs was a common strategy during the early stages of the "tantalum fever," further damaging the already weakened credibility of the institution of chieftaincy and thus adding a further impediment to political recovery.[33] Because of the sustained nature of their activities, organized criminal enterprises do depend on securing reliable access to physical and financial assets such as international markets, road, rail, or aviation networks, intermediary commercial actors, and a steady supply of cash. Organizationally sophisticated, they rely on sociocultural or political-military networks like the "elite networks" in eastern DRC, which feature collaboration between Rwandan and Ugandan militaries and local militia proxies.[34]

MILITARY MANAGERS. Military managers are often locally based commanders who engage in the semi-industrialized conversion of human and physical assets in areas under their control. They demand relatively large labor forces, conscripted or corvée, local or imported. Military managers and their units may splinter from within more organized fighting forces. As control depends on the loyalty of armed elements who share in the spoils, their radius is thus usually localized. Alongside military commanders, this group may include businessmen who forge alliances with paramilitaries, collectively employing militia acronyms as a "flag of convenience" and protection, as was the case in eastern DRC with the ever-proliferating RCD and Mayi-Mayi factions. Embedded in or directly wedded to organized violence, these actors have less need to draw on social assets to gain influence. Moreover, they can usually call on the logistical apparatus of their military partners to protect and transport their produce.

POLITICAL ENTREPRENEURS. Some actors who exploit violent economies do so with longer-term, primarily political goals. Interested in building durable power bases, they forge alliances with military managers in order to provide a ready flow of resources to realize their power ambitions, or they construct ethnic coalitions around preexisting economic grievances. Their political careers hinge on brokering unstable relationships among potentially competing economic actors, harnessing resources produced to underwrite continued military control of base areas, purchasing the acquiescence of customary authorities, and preserving their subordinates' economic rewards.

Conflict opportunists. All four varieties of conflict entrepreneurs exert strong control over how violence develops. They also usually enter the conflict with capital and experience. Conflict opportunists, by contrast, occupy an exploitative niche within economic violence. While they do not control its overall course, they nonetheless profit, often through the use of force, from the possibilities that violence throws up. As such, their actions are a paradox—part of the problem and a somewhat understandable response to it. Conflict opportunists include the middlemen who broker minerals from deposits worked by factions or traders who leverage differences in supply and purchasing power across markets effectively severed by conflict. Conflict opportunists include middlewomen too: many women currency traders and smugglers of the kind celebrated in accounts of Zaire's "second economy" morphed into conflict opportunists during the mineral free-for-all of the Congo's war.[35]

Opportunists may also include customary authorities—chiefs able to use their control over land and local taxation to extract revenue from a position of relative power but overall subordination to the violence. Additional conflict opportunists include the "local defense initiatives" that sprang up during various phases of Congo's conflicts claiming to provide community policing; many of these defense groups mutated into protection rackets. Locally, such predation blurs with petty crime, looting, and raiding. While almost all armed theft has been blamed on militia movements (the Mayi Mayi or the Interahamwe) even if the assailants were very few, many of the Congo's ethnic militias originated in earlier "self-defense" mobilizations.

Conflict opportunists occupy precarious niches in the economic ecology of conflict. Their livelihoods are highly vulnerable to local vagaries and external shocks. When the world price of tantalum ore crashed tenfold in 2001, hundreds of Congolese middlemen and middlewomen were driven out of business. Those really in control—the military commanders of the Ugandan and Rwandan forces, the Congolese RCD rebels—used the opportunity to eliminate a costly link in the commodity chain and further consolidate their control.[36] The vulnerability of conflict opportunists can be understood as a function of their relatively brittle relationship to productive assets. Their political and social connectedness to power is likely weak and personalistic—enough to have gained them a small niche but not enough to guarantee its endurance. Access to necessary financial and physical assets—such as credit, licenses, and customs approvals—likely depends on the same fragile connections. In sum, conflict opportunists are not exclusively drawn from the ranks of the most powerful. Members of the Congolese lower-middle classes—former teachers, unemployed government workers—were forced to seek livelihoods in minerals brokering to survive, borrowed heavily from friends and family, and went to the wall after the tantalum price crash.[37]

Conflict dependents. The broadest category of actors consists of those at the lowest levels, whose fragile survival livelihoods have become intimately bound up in economic violence and are easily damaged by incautious international responses. In January 2003, the UN Office for the Coordination of Humanitarian Affairs (OCHA) estimated that there were 2.7 million internally displaced persons in the DRC.[38] Most had been dislodged from rural areas into small provincial towns, their land seized or simply rendered too insecure to cultivate, themselves the targets of politically, ethnically, or economically motivated violence. Once displaced, they were forced to devise whatever survival livelihoods they could. For those who remained behind, productive plots located at an insecure distance from the homestead meant only tiny plots of nearby land continued to be worked. Insecurity severed their access to market centers and crippled demand/supply links, causing rural incomes to evaporate and urban prices to soar.[39] Traditional nonagricultural incomes vanished. State salaries went unpaid for years, factories were abandoned and pillaged, markets were depressed, and supply was severed. As the UN quietly understated in 2003, "Humanitarian needs in [Congo] continued to be of massive scale, while funding levels were low in comparison to these great needs."[40] Absent aid, the war-affected naturally seek other modes of survival.[41]

One can distinguish between several conflict-dependent survival livelihoods that emerged in the DRC. First, the booming, informalized mineral sector provided a key source of survival livelihoods. International advocacy has focused on the enormous fortunes being made by political, economic, and military elites exploiting the country's abundant gold, diamonds, tantalum, tin, and timber. Though accurate, this criticism is incomplete, neglecting the fact that many survival livelihoods for average Congolese have depended on the same resources. While military actors controlled the purchasing, refining, and transport of these commodities, in many areas of North Kivu province (eastern DRC) actual tantalum mining was accomplished individually and by hand.[42] Incomes of just a few dollars a day scratching ore from fields and riverbeds made a vital difference to the survival of some peasant families. Though mining and selling of natural resources had "liberalized" during "peace" under President Mobutu Sese Seko,[43] a total free-for-all ensued during the war that allowed some diggers to claw their way up to become entry-level traders. The tantalum boom had a number of positive if short-term effects. It reduced some unemployment among the displaced, provided incentives to demobilize youth militias, or prevented new ones from mobilizing.[44] In some areas, tantalum exploitation became seasonal—something to turn to in agriculturally unproductive months. While North Kivu's people lamented tantalum's clear connection to the war, many also felt it was the only viable economic alternative after the total destruction of the region's cattle. Though it has never been clear how many people directly benefited from tantalum, they certainly numbered in the multiple thousands. Moreover, spin-off economic activities that surrounded mineral extraction—food and small provisions supply, brewing and *shebeen* operations, prostitution, drug running—also offered important welfare benefits that have to be weighed against their other evidently negative social consequences.

Second, not all transborder trade in Central Africa relates to "conflict commodities" such as drugs or diamonds, even during conflict.[45] Eastern Congo was the historical terminus of lengthy informal trade routes extending back through Uganda and Tanzania to the Gulf states and the Far East, dominated by particular trader ethnicities, and along which, for decades or longer, have flowed supplies of small consumer goods.[46] Conflict did not interrupt these routes, but it certainly altered their dimensions and their control. The booming mineral economy caused dollars to flow and, in certain quarters, caused the demand for luxury goods to explode. The effective suspension of meaningful customs controls made trade routes more accessible in one sense. But their violent capture by armed groups drove out older players unconnected to new centers of power and influence, generating further resentment.

Survival livelihoods of a third variety are clustered around the internal borders that conflict creates. As factions proliferated through quarrels over natural resources, Congolese territory balkanized. For every front line, checkpoint, or no-man's-land that interrupted formal trade, livelihood possibilities emerged around the informal running of arms, cash, minerals, food, drink, fuel, and petty goods. A fourth cluster of livelihoods concerned subsistence agricultural production on land emptied by violence. At the start of the 1990s, just 512 families controlled 58 percent of available land in the Masisi region.[47] With the advent of war, the destruction of these vast cattle ranches in eastern Congo temporarily freed up land for agriculture, providing survival livelihoods to displaced and local populations alike. As landlords returned in 2002, however, a new round of expulsions began, leaving the displaced vulnerable once more.[48]

Finally, direct participation in armed violence itself can be a survival livelihood strategy. As an influential report by Congo's POLE Institute mordantly relates, "The AK-47 doesn't only mean physical and psychological security but also economic security."[49] Whatever the motives or priorities of their leaders, for many of the rank-and-file soldiers fighting was just another occupation. According to one soldier from the Katanga region, "I was fighting for Kabila and was captured in an action, imprisoned for four days, and then I started fighting for the RCD instead. . . . I just wanted to get back to work."[50] Continuous raids by military and militias against rural villages spread terror throughout eastern Congo, but they were often motivated less by political or military imperatives of commanders than by hungry soldiers in search of food.

The schema of "entrepreneurs," "opportunists," and "dependents" requires a further caveat. These terms might be taken to imply an ethics of intervention that I do not intend: namely that one should care not at all about the fates of conflict entrepreneurs, only a little about those of conflict opportunists, and a good deal about those of dependents. There would be a number of problems with such an ethics. First, while clearly engaged in destructive and often criminal behavior, conflict entrepreneurs may also provide certain kinds of "public goods" otherwise notably absent—privatized forms of security, rejuvenated markets and infrastructures, and greater-than-normal incomes to certain kinds of small producers.[51] Conflict entrepreneurs may sometimes, therefore, acquire a certain popular legitimacy that should be neither overestimated nor discounted. Meanwhile, the distinction between opportunist and dependent is, as already argued, unstable and not correlated in a straightforward fashion with degree of violence employed. Which should be more or less ethically acceptable, a currency trader opportunist who profits from providing a ready supply of cash dollars to a conflict diamond–smuggling operation or a conflict-dependent peasant who uses his AK-47 to put food on the table for his family? Attention needs to be paid, then, to how motives and incentives operate at different levels of violent economies—local, provincial, national, regional—and the scale of actors' violence at each of these levels.

Scale and Dynamics of Violent Economies and Their Livelihood Impacts

Gauging the scale of violent economies is important if we are to design effective policies against them. It is particularly crucial to know the number of ordinary people whose survival livelihoods have become dependent on violence, and the degree of that dependence, since this clarifies the potential negative welfare consequences of policies simply designed to interrupt trade in conflict commodities.

Hard numbers on conflict dependents in DRC have been difficult to obtain, given prevailing insecurity.[52] More often one must simply infer from the vast scale of economic activity. In Liberia, $300–500 million worth of diamonds and gold, $53 million of timber, and $27 million of rubber were exported through the war economy in 1995 alone.[53] Profits from the tantalum trade in the DRC's war economy were running at $17 million a month at the height of the boom.[54] Such massive levels of profit, where extraction is artisanal, not industrial, demand large numbers of laborers with sieves and shovels. Forced labor is a factor in some production, but tens of thousands of unemployed young men relied on digging for minerals to make their way. In both the DRC and Sierra Leone, a common system was for diggers to amass two piles of ore, with what was refined in one accruing to military profit, the other to their own.[55] A qualitative indicator of how widespread civilian participation was in artisanal mineral extraction is the commonly held view among miners that digging is "like farming" and thus a prevalent and normal occupation. Miners in some areas of the DRC have described tantalum extraction as having become a "seasonal" activity alternating with agriculture.[56]

If large numbers of survival livelihoods may become dependent upon violent economies, it is important to emphasize how fast-changing such economies actually are. Today's opportunist is tomorrow's dependent, and vice versa. Too frequently, "greed and grievance" analyses of conflict flatten analysis temporally when in reality violent economies are highly dynamic and unstable, characterized by "a constantly shifting pattern of conflict and collaboration" in response to endemic uncertainty.[57] This uncertainty forces all actors in violent economies to makes guesses about the future based on a calculus of risk versus opportunity. Economic "warlords" are too frequently imagined as Olympian deities with perfect control over violence and predictive powers. But like everyone else, they rely on their best guesses, hedging constantly against an unpredictable future. The same prevailing uncertainty forces the poor, meanwhile, into a Faustian bargain in which the pursuit of short-term security places them in dependent relationships with the powerful and violent that work diametrically against longer-term prospects for a sustained improvement in their lot.[58] The adaptability of entrepreneurs, opportunists, and dependents alike accounts for a number of the unforeseen consequences of present policy tools, as described below.

Finally, a general principle seems to be that the longer violent economies are allowed to persist, the more individual livelihoods they suck into their vortex. The pattern that Fuad Khuri notes for civil war in Lebanon is sadly typical:

As the war gained momentum, and the bases of economic production deteriorated, more workers, laborers and salaried personnel were drawn into the battlefield either through deliberate recruitment or on a voluntary basis. Given this influx of civilians into the fighting groups, the mechanisms of control within the fighting organizations began to collapse. This collapse created a state of lawlessness that, in turn, encouraged more civilians to take up arms.[59]

Even conflicts that do not begin with explicitly economic motivations rapidly "economize."[60] If outright military victory does not occur on schedule—as was the case in the DRC—internal political rivalries rapidly combine with the temptations of extraordinary profits to precipitate proliferating, and often violent, splits within rebel movements. In a reversal of the economic principle of economies of scale, the smaller the productive territories with lootable resources that these splinter groups control, the greater the intensity of their economic violence and their predation on ordinary civilians. One effect of such predation, naturally, is the destruction of livelihoods that constitute alternatives to dependence in the conflict economy. As these processes accelerate, economic horizons are squeezed, residual economic confidence and trust erode, uncertainty spirals outward, and violent economies tend ever more toward the short term.[61] Unfortunately, short-termism usually affects the will for international intervention in the postconflict arena too.

Livelihoods Analysis for Tackling the Resource Dimension of Conflict

Paying attention to assets, actors, and the scale and dynamics of violent economies raises implications for policies aimed at tackling the resource dimensions of conflict. Naturally, many implications are context specific, but some general conclusions are possible. Overall, livelihoods analysis urges that policy measures to contain and deter conflict entrepreneurs and (to a lesser extent) opportunists from using violence to secure economic objectives take into account the wide array of perverse effects of intervention on the political economy of violence. To mitigate such effects, policy interventions should also include remedial measures to preserve productive assets (of all kinds, not merely physical), protect dependents (by weaning them away from conflict-dependent livelihoods rather than abruptly severing them through ill-designed measures), and encourage economic actors to move away from techniques of violence.

Livelihood Impacts of Targeted Sanctions and Interdictions

When it comes to preventing the violent capture and exploitation of key natural resources amid conflict, the limited array of conventional international responses has tended to focus on "supply-side" measures, such as sanctions and control regimes. Alongside the commonly identified political and humanitarian shortcomings of sanctions—that they may strengthen the regimes or movements they attempt to undercut, weaken civil institutions, fuel social antagonisms, and exacerbate humanitarian suffering[62]—livelihoods analysis exposes several economic ones. Such measures risk creating perverse incentives that may intensify the economic activity they seek to curtail, displacing rather than disincentivizing production, widening the gap between rich and poor, and sometimes furthering economic violence. Other kinds of control regimes—licensing and certification mechanisms and crop-eradication and interdiction schemes—may have economically similar effects.

Perverse incentives. By formalizing the illegality of flows produced through economic violence, sanctions and control regimes may drive them, and the actors associated with them, further into the shadows of economic life. This can, in turn, place a higher premium on the use of violence to obscure them from view. The incomplete and porous application of sanctions or other control regimes may serve only to increase incentives for exploitation. By squeezing but not suppressing supply, they elevate producer prices. The sanctions imposed on Sierra Leonean diamonds nine years after the start of war, for example, permitted an exemption if a domestic certification scheme was introduced. Such a scheme "duly occurred in October 2000": while supposedly tamper proof, certification in fact accomplished comparatively little to halt illicit flows.[63] Though it appears to have increased legal exports, and thereby official revenues, "a substantial proportion of 'illicit' diamonds continued to be smuggled out of the country directly or laundered into the system," and there is "no evidence that illegal exports have declined appreciably."[64] A requirement that the dollar value of all official diamond exports be deposited in the national banking system simply added to the incentives for traders to circumvent the official system.[65] In essence, sanction and control regimes can offer new openings for rent seeking in violent economies.

Geographic displacement. Porous borders, basic and portable production technologies, and ready reserves of labor combine to make relocation a low-cost response for conflict entrepreneurs reacting to control regimes. Again in Sierra Leone, rather than curtailing the flow of conflict diamonds, the domestic diamond certification scheme displaced and reversed the direction of diamond flows—from Sierra Leonean diamonds laundered through Liberia to Liberian-held diamonds laundered through Sierra Leone's official certification system.[66] In Latin America, evidence suggests that Plan Colombia, designed to decrease coca production, caused much production simply to migrate to other countries. These displacement effects underline the inherent limitations of policies that continue unquestioningly to take states and national territories as their proper fields of intervention when both are radically problematized by ongoing conflict.

The political economy of virtually every contemporary "interstate" conflict is, in fact, regional and global in its reach. As early as the colonial era in West Africa, opportunities for gray commerce in diamonds and other commodities "were created by differences in fiscal, legal, and import regulations adopted in French and British colonies. In other words, regional actors were able to exploit the shadow spaces created not only by physical borders, but also by the differential economic and regulatory practices of the colonial power."[67] These differences were modified but substantively continued into postcolonial times and are exacerbated today by the imposition of different kinds of customs, sanctions, and control regimes, each of varying efficacy. The differences in the regulatory effects of such interventions between neighboring states exert strong economic incentives for cross-border shadow trade and displacement effects. In short, where regional economies of violence have emerged, solutions country by country not only are likely to fail on their own terms but are also likely to add to the difficulties. In the short term, regional coordination of all nationally focused efforts to combat economic violence is essential in order to avoid perverse outcomes. In the longer term, the resolution to economic violence may be found in establishing new common trade areas or strengthening ones currently moribund.

Sectoral displacement. A further displacement effect of sanctions and control regimes may occur within countries but across commodities. As international momentum for an embargo on "conflict tantalum" from the DRC gained momentum in 2000–2001, some traders whom I interviewed suggested they would seek to adapt by shifting to gold or tin instead. In the event, the sudden 2001 fall in the world price of tantalum had much the same effect as commodity-specific sanctions.[68] In Liberia, after the imposition of UN sanctions on diamond exports, armed factions switched to the illicit timber trade and to exploitation of the country's importance as a "flag of convenience" state for international shipping to generate million-dollar revenues to fund arms purchases.[69]

Hurting those you mean to help. While conflict entrepreneurs and opportunists who profit from conflict commodities tend to be mobile and able to adapt creatively to changing regulations, the unskilled laborers who come to depend on producing these commodities as a survival livelihood cannot so easily displace. Suddenly deprived once more of a living, they may turn to cruder economic violence—looting, plunder, kidnapping—to survive or prosper. The easy migration of drug production around different Andean countries in response to the "war on drugs" can leave peasant populations with "very few cash crops [that] offer such economic advantages to poor peasants."[70] From a political economy perspective, the effect of sanctions and control regimes is often to drive a further wedge between rich and poor, between particular identity groups, and between conflict entrepreneurs and opportunists/dependents, fueling inflation and crippling ordinary standards of living.[71]

A second potential area of damage to conflict dependents can occur when controls are applied to financial flows to zones of conflict. Clearly, such flows raise concerns about money laundering and other forms of internationalized crime. However, remittances from diaspora populations abroad are a major source of survival livelihoods for conflict-affected people around the world. In Somaliland, for example, they are estimated to amount to some $500 million annually, four times the value of livestock exports there.[72] In the context of a collapsed formal banking system, these remittances are forced to pass through a variety of more informal mechanisms—such as the "indigenous bank" Dahabshiil in Somaliland or the Hawalla system in Afghanistan—which can become targets of international proscription, with deleterious results.

Further violence?   Perversely, attempts to constrict "conflict trade" via control regimes may even, under certain circumstances, push conflict dependents to consider (or reconsider) violence. In eastern DRC, there is anecdotal evidence that during the tantalum boom the employment attractions of tantalum extraction limited youth mobilization in rebel movements and militias.[73] Conversely, in Sierra Leone it has been reported that former combatants, highly dissatisfied with the reintegration component of disarmament, demobilization, and reintegration (DDR) and facing bleak prospects in the formal economy, returned to "mining the diamond fields of Kono with little prospect of striking it rich."[74] In some cases, officially demobilized combatants who had returned to alluvial mining in Sierra Leone formed a pool of recruits later hired as mercenaries in neighboring Guinea and Liberia.[75] Finally, in Afghanistan, it has been argued that fencing in and criminalizing illegal trade via, say, the closure of the border between Afghanistan and Pakistan "would likely create the conditions for a social explosion in several regions of Pakistan, as cross-border trade is central to the coping and survival strategies of border communities."[76]

In sum, sanctions and control regimes risk hurting those whose livelihoods are already precariously dependent, while leaving mostly unscathed their intended targets. As we have seen, the scale of conflict-dependent livelihoods varies from context to context; so, therefore, does the impact of sanctions and control regimes upon them.

Recommendations for Complementary, Remedial Measures

Reassessing control regimes. From the previous discussion, an obvious but still strangely radical recommendation follows. Where there is a low probability of effective enforcement—whether because of the portability of the commodity, the logistical difficulty of the terrain in question, or the likely absence of international political follow-through—sanctions should not be applied. Under such conditions, not only are there negative welfare impacts, but there are also serious chances of adding to, rather than reducing, criminality and violence. A second, more minimal recommendation also follows. Where sanctions have been applied, the UN expert panels frequently established to monitor compliance with sanctions resolutions should also be mandated to monitor the welfare impacts (not just the conventionally humanitarian but also broader socioeconomic and political consequences) of those sanctions on dependent livelihoods. Third, if sanctions are to be applied, they must be based on a recognition of the regional nature of violent economies and thus on a recognition of the need for regionwide regulatory approaches and assessments of welfare impacts. Finally, their negative welfare effects should be softened by simultaneous complementary measures such as increased aid to restart basic agriculture and the economy.

Preserving and restoring productive assets. In wartime, it might be thought that little can be done to preserve or restore productive assets. However, experience suggests that some modest possibilities exist for intervention during conflict to prevent further distortions in already distorted economic life. More, certainly, can and must be done to shore up *human assets* through the provision of education during conflict, whether through measures to protect existing educational infrastructure and provide cash or food support to teachers during conflict or to provide education to internally displaced persons and refugee populations in camps.[77]

Interventions to preserve *physical assets* could focus on eliminating the internal borders that spring up during conflict between territories held by competing factions. Reopening such bottlenecks can have immediate ameliorative effects on livelihood opportunities. One international nongovernmental organization worked continuously with local partners throughout the DRC war to rehabilitate roads in eastern DRC. A socioeconomic evaluation of this work later determined that after one main road was reopened, food prices in local markets returned 30–50 percent toward normal.[78] Rampant hyperinflation in eastern DRC had been one factor in destroying agricultural livelihoods and driving young men in particular into violence.[79] Reconnecting communities through shared physical assets (such as roads or markets) thus can have significant effect.

With regard to financial assets, as noted above, policymakers may do great damage to ordinary people's survival by cracking down on international financial flows through local remittance banks. It would be far better to seek to create the kind of incentives that can encourage the businesspeople involved to make the transition from informal activity into the formal, legal banking sector. Experience in Somalia suggests that even amid continuing violence, important steps in this regard can be achieved. In December 2003, the UN Development Programme organized a conference to discuss ways to improve transparency and performance, bringing together representatives of the major remittance "banks" in Somalia and remittance-sector regulators from major Western countries. The conference launched the Somali Financial Services Association, an initiative of self-regulation across the remittance banks. It also recommended ways to strengthen and encourage formalization of the remittance banks themselves, by enhancing their knowledge of compliance regulations in major countries where remittances originate and supporting measures to increase openness, accountability, and transparency of management structures.[80]

Protecting dependents and their livelihoods. What remedial measures can be taken to protect the interests of the broad mass of conflict dependents prior to, during, and in the immediate aftermath of conflict? One implication is that creating and bolstering durable economic livelihoods should be seen as an integral component of conflict prevention strategies, in order to limit the emergence of conflict-dependent livelihoods. When conflict is incipient, there is a particular challenge of identifying what—if any—operational measures can be taken to preempt any collateral economic damage that might leave populations (and particularly youth) with little alternative to adopting conflict livelihoods. These may include measures to protect economic assets fundamental to existing youth livelihoods or to protect economically marginal populations.

While it is beyond the scope of this chapter to fully consider the complexities of trying to protect economic livelihoods during open conflict, suffice it to say that in many contexts of prolonged or chronic conflict, alongside the urgent need for lifesaving humanitarian relief, there emerge opportunities for practical interventions in support of ordinary people's subsistence strategies. These can include cattle vaccination programs, agricultural support (tools, fertilizer, and seed), credit schemes or food aid used as market interventions to support the price of livestock,[81] and interventions to alleviate "internal borders," such as roadblocks or shattered infrastructures, that have severed economic communities from one another. Most valuable of all, aid agencies can explore the possibility of procuring food relief locally, rather than from international donation. Even as war engulfs certain parts of a country, other parts can sometimes produce surplus food, which can be purchased to the benefit of both.

For the postconflict environment, the most important recommendation is that economic restart not be left until after all the political components of a peace deal have been consolidated. All too frequently the donor community hangs back to see whether a deal is likely to stick. A second set of postconflict recommendations concerns how to begin detoxifying the informal economy. Burgeoning in crisis-prone parts of the world under the impact of structural adjustment and liberalization of economic policies, the informal economy swells further during conflict as formal employment becomes a thing of the past. More and more livelihoods come to depend, often violently, on the informal economy. But while violent economies entail great destruction and huge suffering, under certain circumstances violent economies also provide welfare benefits. Writes Mark Duffield: "The transborder networks associated with organized violence have stimulated enterprise across large tracts of the South. This is not the activity of greedy elites, but the economy of everyday life. Ambivalence resides in the ability of such interconnected networks to support organized violence in one locality while providing employment and the means of life in another."[82] The energies of the informal economy therefore need to be harnessed, not eradicated, by those seeking to build peace. In the postconflict environment, the immediate challenge is how to preserve informal economies' welfare functions while diminishing their vulnerability to violent capture. Subsequently, one must then search for strategies to slowly transform informal economies into more formal ones, without sapping their vital energies.

This calls for careful balance in policy design. On the one hand, experience suggests that hyperliberalization (such as of landownership and mineral exploitation in Zaire in the 1980s) paves the way for predatory and criminal accumulation, which in turn contributes to the onset of conflict.[83] On the other hand, there has been an unwelcome tendency to stigmatize all informal activity as leading to criminal forms of commodity trade, when in fact much of it relates to trade in low-quality consumer products.[84] There is a danger that in postconflict reconstruction, efforts to rein in activity considered criminal will target the low-hanging fruit of ordinary informal activity with a long-established history rather than the harder-to-reach levels of illegal exploitation practiced by conflict entrepreneurs.

What might a balanced approach look like? One concrete example concerns the mining code promulgated in the postconflict DRC. Rather than trying to turn back the clock to a centralized, state-controlled mining industry, the code recognized that the mining sector had been fundamentally transformed by the war and that many ordinary people now had a stake (literally) in it. The new code, accordingly, set out what its framers hoped would be a decentralized system in which licensing would be devolved to local authorities rather than remaining at the center, license fees would be kept modest, and critically, tax receipts from the mining industry would be divided among national, provincial, and local levels. The aim, then, is to preserve a relatively open system that is nonetheless immune to violent control—to harness the economic energies unlocked within violent economies but, through a limited degree of regulation, draw the violence out.

Livelihoods provision and DDR.   As this chapter has highlighted, in many contexts even combatants may become dependent on the livelihoods provided through violent economies. From this perspective, the challenge of disarmament, demobilization, and reintegration is as much an economic as a politicomilitary one. After most conflicts, a formal political peace (if it comes at all) arrives far earlier than a resumption of normal economic life (if it ever existed). The demobilization of combatants therefore risks leaving them without livelihoods. Dangerously, this can occur at the same time that sanctions or other strictures against conflict commodities start to bite, depriving former combatants of their last livelihood option beyond fighting again. In this fashion, former combatants are quickly turned into "peace spoilers," either of their own conflicts or spilling across borders as mercenaries in neighboring ones. Unfortunately, DDR programs all too frequently fail to prioritize the livelihood needs of former combatants, with the reintegration component almost always the poor relation.[85] This was initially the case, for example, in Sierra Leone, where "the UN integration program experienced a substantial shortfall in funding from donors," since donors were much more attracted to the high visibility of weapons burnings than they were to funding training schemes and housing.[86] In general,

> DDR programmes have a tendency to be implemented in isolation from the overall reconstruction and development efforts and without taking into serious account the socio-economic context of the countries. This is partly due to the timing of DDR programmes that often start before serious economic inputs are provided, based upon the assumption that there needs to be some level of local security before development projects can commence.[87]

First, therefore, reintegration requires a clear connection to the rapid provision of alternative livelihood possibilities for demobilized fighters, through quick-impact projects followed by longer-term training schemes consonant with emerging new national economic priorities, all underpinned by campaigns of reeducation and public information. Sierra Leonean reintegration efforts have been reconceived broadly along these lines.[88] Second, analysis of the vortex of economic violence provides one explanation for why, at the lowest rungs of a command-and-control structure, the distinction between formal combatants and those adopting violence as a survival strategy (militias, bandit groupings) tends to evaporate as conflict progresses. Often DDR programs are conceived too narrowly, targeting only those within the ranks of formal armies and omitting those other actors who have been drawn into economic violence, leaving them as a potential destabilizing influence for the future. To be truly successful, DDR programs will often need to aim at fighters beyond those officially under the command of signatories to peace deals.

Third, given that economic assets and actors in violent economies usually flow across porous borders, livelihoods analysis urges that DDR be conceived with a regional perspective to stand any chance of success. The strong risk that former combatants starved of economic opportunities at home may spill over into neighboring conflicts within regional conflict complexes is one reason; the regional nature of many assets underpinning conflict livelihoods is another. But regional approaches to DDR are scarce. The present Greater Great Lakes Regional Strategy for Demobilization and Reintegration (conceived at the end of 2001 and known as the MDRP) is a pioneer in this regard.[89] The strategy envisages that an MDRP secretariat be specifically charged with "deepening the understanding of cross-border and cross-sectoral DDR issues," fostering "regional technical knowledge sharing, capacity building and joint analysis," and advising on the conduct of "cross-border information and sensitization campaigns to [apprise] combatant groups of the options being developed."[90] However, progress in the DRC within the framework of the MDRP was initially stalled until a reasonably stable national peace could be put in place. Though a peace deal has since been concluded, political and operational challenges continue. The latter, in particular, provide lessons for regional approaches elsewhere. How can one keep the multiplicity of stakeholders (multilaterals, bilaterals, governments, belligerent parties) working together within a regional platform when their short-term interests are likely to diverge? How can a necessarily large-scale, regional framework be kept sufficiently flexible to be alert to fast-changing dynamics on the ground, so as to seize opportunities to reintegrate into civilian life those who may "incidentally be willing or allowed to do so"?[91] In conflicts like the DRC's, characterized by fragmented fighting forces clustered around strategic centers and key economic assets, decisions to lay down arms are, alas, seldom governed by formal cease-fires; DDR must therefore be pursued opportunistically.

Fourth, the different elements of DDR programs cannot be expected to work in strict sequence.[92] Even after a peace agreement is concluded, the underlying processes of economic violence may continue to suck in more actors, as has been the case in parts of eastern DRC. Trying to disarm all fighters at once may thus be akin to trying to shoot at a moving target; delaying vital demobilization and reintegration components until the completion of disarmament may be most unrealistic. It may be better to begin demobilizing and reintegrating smaller numbers in ways that deliver meaningful livelihoods based on integrated strategies of economic support, reeducation and retooling, and banking; small successes will have larger signaling effects to other, more obdurate fighters.

Livelihoods and the rule of law. In longer-term postconflict contexts, diminishing the violence that has come to contaminate economic life depends on reaffirming the rule of law as it pertains to livelihoods and profit. To date, many efforts to promote the rule of law have been approached as essentially a technology transfer of Western expertise in the writing of constitutions and the restructuring of the justice sector[93] and tend to concentrate on criminal rather than commercial law. Because of the upsurge in awareness of economic violence, however, reform efforts are starting to focus on, for example, customs authorities and fiscal police services. However, such reforms are "not merely technical exercises; modernizing laws, rebuilding courts, enhancing the skills of police and prosecutors are necessary but not sufficient to build the rule of law. . . . [The] public's instinct after . . . years of repression is to distrust the police and the courts. Changing this attitude will take time."[94]

Where disobedience of laws designed to restrict economic activity in resource-rich contexts has become a survival reflex, why, in principle, should dependent populations view postconflict efforts to promote the rule of law as any different from previous elite attempts to use the law against them? Slowly "reformalizing" the informal activity that increases under conditions of violence requires patience, "selling in" (via public information campaigns, for example), and stage-managing the demonstration effects of new initiatives to the broad public. The latter can include careful initiatives to promote greater transparency in political and economic governance—particularly at levels where these come into contact with the ordinary individual. In postconflict reconstruction, donors can push for greater transparency as a means to reduce corruption, rent seeking, and the vulnerability of economic assets to seizure and of ordinary people to economic dependency. Similarly, the postconflict moment may be the very one in which property rights questions—including but not limited to land rights—may be most fruitfully addressed (precisely because conflict has thrown them open to question in the first place).

Conclusion

It might be called the first law of political economy: every action (and every policy initiative in reaction) has its economic winners and losers. The impacts of policy tools aimed at interrupting the link between economics and violence need to be assessed for the effects they will have on individual livelihoods. Perversely, if designed without due attention to the mutations that conflict engenders in different kinds of assets, the diverse kinds of actors who can capitalize on violence, and the scale and dynamics of such economic violence, they risk further hurt to the already vulnerable and further advantage to the already powerful.

Notes

Much of the Congolese material presented here was originally published as my case study in the final report of the Overseas Development Institute's Political Economies of War and Livelihoods project. See Stephen Jackson, "Fortunes of War: The Coltan Trade in the Kivus," in Sarah Collinson, ed., *Power, Livelihoods, and Conflict: Case Studies in Political Economy Analysis for Humanitarian Action,* ODI Humanitarian Policy Group Report no. 13 (London: Overseas Development Institute, 2003). Thanks for comments and insight are due to Laura Frost, Elizabeth Cousens, Karen Ballentine, Kaysie Studdard, Heiko Nitzschke, an extremely insightful anonymous reviewer, and other contributors to this volume.

1. David Keen, *The Economic Functions of Violence in Civil Wars,* Adelphi Paper no. 320 (Oxford: Oxford University Press, 1998), p. 11.

2. David Keen, "War and Peace: What's the Difference?" in Adekeye Adebajo and Chandra Lekha Sriram, eds., *Managing Armed Conflicts in the Twenty-first Century* (London: Frank Cass, 2001), pp. 1–22.

3. Mats Berdal and David M. Malone, eds., *Greed and Grievance: Economic Agendas in Civil Wars* (Boulder: Lynne Rienner, 2000); Stephen Jackson, "Nos richesses sont pillées: Economies de guerre et rumeurs de crime dans les Kivus, République Démocratique du Congo," *Politique Africaine* no. 84 (December 2001): 117–135.

4. Two caveats are warranted. First, the problem of obtaining accurate data on violent economies, and the livelihoods within them, is far from negligible and allows for only tentative findings. Second, although this analysis draws where possible from the literature on other conflicts, the reader should naturally remain cautious about conclusions based predominantly on the single case of the DRC.

5. Ian Scoones, *Sustainable Rural Livelihoods: A Framework for Analysis,* IDS Working Paper no. 72 (Brighton: Institute for Development Studies, 1998), p. 1.

6. Diana Carney, *Approaches to Sustainable Livelihoods for the Rural Poor,* ODI Poverty Briefing (London: Overseas Development Institute, 1999), available at www.odi.org.uk/publications/briefing/pov2.html.

7. Sarah Collinson, ed., *Power, Livelihoods, and Conflict: Case Studies in Political Economy Analysis for Humanitarian Action,* ODI Humanitarian Policy Group Report no. 13 (London: Overseas Development Institute, 2003).

8. Frank van Acker and Koen Vlassenroot, "Youth and Conflict in Kivu: 'Komona Clair,'" *Journal of Humanitarian Assistance,* July 21, 2000, available at www.jha.ac/greatlakes/b004.htm.

9. Personal communication, senior UN Secretariat official, fall 2003.

10. Philippe Le Billon, "The Political Ecology of War: Natural Resources and

Armed Conflicts," *Political Geography* 20, no. 5 (2001): 569. See also Michael Ross, "Oil, Drugs, and Diamonds: The Varying Role of Natural Resources in Civil War," in Karen Ballentine and Jake Sherman, eds., *The Political Economy of Armed Conflict: Beyond Greed and Grievance* (Boulder: Lynne Rienner, 2003), pp. 47–70.

11. See, in particular, United Nations Security Council, "Report of the UN Panel of Experts on the Illegal Exploitation of Natural Resources and Other Forms of Wealth of the Democratic Republic of the Congo," S/2001/357, April 12, 2001.

12. Ross, "Oil, Drugs, and Diamonds," p. 56.

13. Human Rights Watch, *Sudan, Oil, and Human Rights* (New York: Human Rights Watch, 2003), p. 115.

14. Mahmoud Mamdani, *When Victims Become Killers: Colonialism, Nativism, and the Genocide in Rwanda* (Princeton, N.J.: Princeton University Press, 2001).

15. Jackson, "Nos richesses sont pillées," p. 124.

16. Jackson, "Fortunes of War," pp. 30–32. Direct food entitlements, a reliable indicator of subsistence agriculture, declined by 11 percent for cassava between 1998 and 2000. Calculated from Food and Agriculture Organization figures cited in Emizet Kisangani, "Legacies of the War Economy: Challenges for Postconflict Reconstruction," in Michael Nest, with François Grignon and Emizet Kisangani, *The Democratic Republic of Congo: Economic Dimensions of War and Peace* (Boulder: Lynne Rienner, forthcoming).

17. Pole Institute, *The Coltan Phenomenon: How a Rare Mineral Has Changed the Life of the Population of War-Torn North Kivu Province in the Democratic Republic of Congo* (Goma, DRC: Pole Institute, 2002). Available at www.pole-institute.org/site_web/coltanglais.pdf.

18. Stephen Jackson, "War Making: Uncertainty, Improvisation, and Involution in the Kivu Provinces, DR Congo, 1997–2002," Ph.D. diss., Princeton University, 2003, p. 130.

19. Stephen Jackson, "Making a Killing: Criminality and Coping in the Kivu War Economy," *Review of African Political Economy* 29, nos. 93–94 (2002): 517–536.

20. For much of the war, for instance, North Kivu province in eastern DRC was severed north to south and controlled by competing splinter groups of the rebel Rassemblement Congolais pour la Démocratie (RCD) movement, who exacted levies on commercial and other movements under these various guises.

21. Achille Mbembe, "At the Edge of the World: Boundaries, Territoriality, and Sovereignty in Africa," in Arjun Appadurai, ed., *Globalization* (Durham, N.C.: Duke University Press, 2001), pp. 22–51.

22. See Robert D. Putnam, "The Prosperous Community: Social Capital and Public Life," *American Prospect* 4, no. 13 (1993): 35–42.

23. As Putnam himself has more recently footnoted: see Robert Putnam, *Bowling Alone: The Collapse and Revival of American Community* (New York: Simon and Schuster, 2000), pp. 350–363. For fuller discussions of this point, see Jean-François Bayart, Stephen Ellis, and Béatrice Hibou, *The Criminalization of the State in Africa* (Oxford: James Currey, 1999), pp. 32–48; and René Lemarchand's incisive paper "Ethnic Violence, Public Policies, and Social Capital in North Kivu: Putnam Revisited," presented to the Conference on Social Capital, Center for Development Studies, University of Antwerp, 1999, which assesses the strengths and weaknesses of social capital theories for explaining violence in the Great Lakes.

24. Bayart, Ellis, and Hibou, *Criminalization of the State,* p. 23; Mukohya

Vwakyanakazi, "Import and Export in the Second Economy in North Kivu," in Janet MacGaffey, ed., *The Real Economy of Zaire: The Contribution of Smuggling and Other Unofficial Activities to National Wealth* (Philadelphia: University of Pennsylvania Press, 1991), pp. 43–71; Jackson, "War Making," p. 35.

25. United Nations Security Council, *Final Report of the Panel of Experts on the Illegal Exploitation of Natural Resources and Other Forms of Wealth of the Democratic Republic of Congo,* S/2002/1146, October 16, 2002, paras. 118–123.

26. Putnam, "The Prosperous Community."

27. Paul Collier, "Doing Well out of War: An Economic Perspective," in Berdal and Malone, *Greed and Grievance* (see note 3), pp. 91–111.

28. Stephen Jackson and François Grignon, *The Kivus: Forgotten Crucible of the Congo Conflict,* ICG Report no. 56 (Brussels: International Crisis Group, 2003), p. 12.

29. Within the first, in a vicious circle, economic resources sustain armed conflict, and conflict facilitates exploitation of those same resources. Profit is extracted via violence, while part of that profit then underwrites continued violence. The second concerns unintended but direct consequences of conflict on economic life, such as currency collapse. The third concerns deliberately deployed economic weapons such as blockades and scorched-earth tactics to disempower enemy factions or populations. Philippe Le Billon, *The Political Economy of War: What Relief Agencies Need to Know,* Humanitarian Practice Network Paper no. 33 (London: Overseas Development Institute, 2000), p. 1.

30. Combat economies concern "the capture of control over production and economic resources to sustain a conflict" and "economic strategies aimed at the disempowerment of specific groups"; shadow economies involve "economic activities that are conducted outside state-regulated frameworks"; coping economies comprise "activities undertaken by population groups that are using their asset-base to more or less maintain basic living standards or survive by using a dwindling asset-base to maintain minimum or below-minimum living standards." Michael Pugh and Neil Cooper, with Jonathan Goodhand, *War Economies in a Regional Context: Challenges for Transformation* (Boulder: Lynne Rienner, 2004), pp. 8–9.

31. It combines ideas culled from Le Billon, Pugh, Cooper, and Goodhand and is particularly influenced by an incisive, as yet unpublished case study of violent economics in eastern DRC by Charles Petrie.

32. Between November 1998 and April 1999, Rwandan forces and their RCD allies looted 3,000 tons of tin and 1,500 tons of tantalum ore from the warehouses of Sociéré Minière et Industrielle du Kivu (SOMINKI), the former state mining concern. In the same period, soldiers of Ugandan major general James Kazini made off with large quantities of stockpiled tropical timber from the companies Amexbois and La Forestière. Some of the profits from these activities financed the military pursuit of political ends; much, however, lined elite pockets. See UN Security Council, "Report of the UN Panel of Experts on the Illegal Exploitation," S/2001/357, paras. 33–34.

33. Jackson, "Making a Killing," p. 532.

34. UN Security Council, *Final Report of the UN Panel of Experts on the Illegal Exploitation,* S/2002/1146, para. 12.

35. Janet MacGaffey, "Evading Male Control: Women in the Second Economy in Zaire," in Sharon B. Stichter and Jane L. Parpart, eds., *Patriarchy and Class* (Boulder: Westview, 1998), pp. 161–176.

36. Jackson, "Making a Killing," pp. 529–531.

37. Ibid., p. 530.

38. UN Office for the Coordination of Humanitarian Affairs (OCHA), "UN Inter-agency Mission Visits the DR Congo to Look into Internal Displacement Challenges," February 21, 2003, available at the IRIN website, www.reliefweb.int.

39. Jackson, "Fortunes of War," pp. 30–32.

40. OCHA, "Consolidated Inter-agency Appeal for the Democratic Republic of the Congo 2003: Mid-year Review" (New York: OCHA, 2003), p. 4.

41. Demographic projections suggest many survival strategies failed—3.3 million people are estimated to have died in five years of war, and only an estimated 1.6 percent of these deaths resulted from direct violence, the rest stemming from mass displacement and livelihood disruption. See International Rescue Committee, *Mortality in the Democratic Republic of Congo: Results from a Nationwide Survey Conducted September-November 2002* (Bukavu, DRC: International Rescue Committee, 2003), pp. 6, 13.

42. In other areas, the military operated large mines, with coerced labor.

43. Vwakyanakazi, "Import and Export in the Second Economy," pp. 55–58.

44. POLE Institute, *Coltan Phenomenon.*

45. Kate Meagher, "A Back Door to Globalisation? Structural Adjustment, Globalisation, and Transborder Trade in West Africa," *Review of African Political Economy* 30, no. 95 (2003): 66.

46. Vwakyanakazi, "Import and Export in the Second Economy," p. 49.

47. Koen Vlassenroot, "Household Food Economy Assessment: Consultancy Visit to North and South Kivu on the Issue of Land Access (18 September–1 October 1999)," Save the Children Fund, Goma, DRC, 1999.

48. Save the Children Fund, "Update of the Household Economy Analysis of the Rural Population of the Plateaux Zone, Masisi, North Kivu, Democratic Republic of Congo," Goma, DRC, 2003.

49. POLE Institute, *Coltan Phenomenon.*

50. Jackson, "War Making," p. 84.

51. See, in particular, Mark Duffield, "War as a Network Enterprise: The New Security Terrain and Its Implications," *Cultural Values* 6, no. 1 (2002): 160; and Jonathan Goodhand, "From Holy War to Opium War? A Case Study of the Opium Economy in North Eastern Afghanistan," *Disasters* 24, no. 2 (2000): 87–102.

52. Estimates are available from some other conflicts—between 3 and 4 million Afghans, or about 20 percent of the population, were dependent on poppy for their livelihood by the late 1990s. See Jonathan Goodhand, "Frontiers and Wars: A Study of the Opium Economy in Afghanistan," unpubl., 2003. But even here there is no exactness. More recent UN estimates put the figure at 1.7 million rural people, or about 7 percent of the total population of Afghanistan. See UN Office on Drugs and Crime (UNODC), *Afghanistan: Opium Survey 2003* (Vienna: UNODC, 2003), p. 8.

53. Pugh and Cooper, *War Economies in a Regional Context,* p. 104.

54. Jackson, "Making a Killing," p. 527.

55. Pugh and Cooper, *War Economies in a Regional Context,* p. 105.

56. Jackson, "War Making," p. 152. Similarly, the International Crisis Group has found that mining in parts of Sierra Leone is "more like 'farming' that involves tens of thousands of persons and is virtually impossible to control." See International Crisis Group, *Sierra Leone: Managing Uncertainty,* ICG Africa Report no. 35 (Brussels: International Crisis Group, 2001), p. 4.

57. Pugh and Cooper, *War Economies in a Regional Context,* p. 100.

58. Geoff Wood, "Staying Secure, Staying Poor: The 'Faustian Bargain,'" *World Development* 31, no. 3 (2003): 455.

59. Fuad I. Khuri, "The Social Dynamics of the 1975–1977 War in Lebanon," *Armed Forces and Society* 3 (1981): 383–408.
60. Jackson, "Making a Killing," p. 528.
61. Jackson, "War Making," p. 245.
62. Tim Niblock, *"Pariah States" and Sanctions in the Middle East: Iraq, Libya, Sudan* (Boulder: Lynne Rienner, 2001), p. 213.
63. Pugh and Cooper, *War Economies in a Regional Context,* pp. 118–120.
64. International Crisis Group, *Sierra Leone: The State of Security and Governance,* ICG Africa Report no. 67 (Brussels: International Crisis Group, 2003), p. 26.
65. Pugh and Cooper, *War Economies in a Regional Context,* p. 120.
66. United Nations Security Council, *Report of the Panel of Experts Appointed pursuant to Security Council Resolution 1343 (2001), Paragraph 19, concerning Liberia,* S/2001/1015, October 26, 2001.
67. Pugh and Cooper, *War Economies in a Regional Context,* p. 101.
68. Jackson, "Fortunes of War," p. 34.
69. Pugh and Cooper, *War Economies in a Regional Context,* p. 107.
70. Nazih Richani, *Systems of Violence: The Political Economy of War and Peace in Colombia* (Albany: State University of New York Press, 2002), p. 97.
71. Niblock, *"Pariah States,"* p. 219.
72. Ismail I. Ahmed, "Remittances and Their Economic Impact in Post-war Somaliland," *Disasters* 24, no. 4 (2000): 380–389.
73. POLE Institute, *Coltan Phenomenon.*
74. International Crisis Group, *Sierra Leone,* p. 16.
75. Mark Malan et. al., *Sierra Leone: Building the Road to Recovery,* ISS Monograph no. 80 (Pretoria: Institute for Security Studies, 2003), p. 92.
76. Pugh and Cooper, *War Economies in a Regional Context,* p. 71.
77. See, for example, the work of the Inter-agency Network on Education in Emergencies, www.ineesite.org; and Margaret Sinclair, *Planning Education in and after Emergencies,* Fundamentals of Educational Planning no. 73 (Geneva: UNESCO and International Institute for Educational Planning, 2002), available at http://unesdoc.unesco.org/images/0012/001293/129356e.pdf.
78. S. K. Endanda, *Evaluation socio-economique des travaux de réhabilitation de la route Sake-Mweso-Kanyabayonga, réalisés par agro action allemande* (Goma, DRC: Université Libre des Pays des Grands Lacs, 2001), p. 32.
79. Jackson, "Fortunes of War," pp. 30–33.
80. UN Development Programme, *Conference on the Somali Remittance Sector: Understanding the Somali Remittance Sector and the Regulations That Govern It,* final conference report, London, December 3–4, 2003.
81. Le Billon, *Political Economy of War,* p. 25.
82. Duffield, "War as a Network Enterprise," p. 60.
83. Jean-Pierre Nzeza Kabuzex-Kongo, "Du Zaïre au Congo: La question agraire au Nord-Kivu," *Afrique Politique: Entre Transitions et Conflits,* 1999, pp. 201–211.
84. Meagher, "Back Door to Globalisation?" p. 66.
85. Lotta Hagman and Zoe Nielsen, *A Framework for Lasting Disarmament, Demobilization, and Reintegration of Former Combatants in Crisis Situations* (New York: International Peace Academy, 2002), p. 9.
86. Pugh and Cooper, *War Economies in a Regional Context,* p. 122.
87. Irma Specht, "Jobs for Rebels and Soldiers," in Eugenia Date-Bah, ed., *Jobs after War: A Critical Challenge in the Peace and Reconstruction Puzzle* (Geneva: International Labour Office, 2003), p. 94.

88. Here reintegration programs have mainly focused on economic and social reintegration, reintegration for child soldiers, and special programs for the disabled and for women. Their aim has been to help ex-combatants become productive members of their communities; to provide them with marketable skills and access to microenterprise schemes; and to support social acceptance through information dissemination measures, social reconciliation, and sensitization processes. They have also sought to support sensitization by public education on the role of ex-combatants in a post-conflict society (Malan et al., *Sierra Leone,* p. 4)1.

89. Specifically, the study argues that given the cross-border factors that underlie the conflicts in the region, a solely country-focused approach to resolving conflict and planning DDR activities is likely to be inadequate. As the continuation of conflicts in any given country's territory depends on the actions of neighboring governments as well as of armed groups that ignore state boundaries, a long-term strategy to restore security in the region needs to addresses the linkages. World Bank, *Greater Great Lakes Regional Strategy for Demobilization and Reintegration,* report no. 23869-AFR (Washington, D.C.: World Bank, 2002), p. 6. For more information on MDRP, see www.mdrp.org.

90. Ibid., pp. 44–45.

91. Emeric Rogier, "Rebuilding the Democratic Republic of Congo: Which Role for the Donor Community?" seminar proceedings, Netherlands Institute of International Relations (Clingendael), Conflict Research Unit, June 6, 2003, p. 6.

92. Hagman and Nielsen, *Framework for Lasting Disarmament.* See also Heiko Nitzschke, "Transforming War Economies: Challenges for Peacemaking and Peacebuilding" (report of the 725th Wilton Park Conference, in association with the International Peace Academy, Wiston House, Sussex, October 27–29, 2003), International Peace Academy, New York, 2003, pp. 8–9.

93. Jamal Benomar, "Rule of Law Technical Assistance in Haiti: Lessons Learned," paper presented at the World Bank conference Empowerment, Security, and Opportunity through Law and Justice, St. Petersburg, Russia, July 8–12, 2001, p. 11.

94. Bill O'Neill, "Rebuilding the Rule of Law in Iraq: Ten Tips from Recent Experience," briefing paper, Henry L. Stimson Center, Washington, D.C., 2003, p. 2.

PART 2

Improving Corporate Responsibility and Resource Management

8

Assessing Company Behavior in Conflict Environments: A Field Perspective

Luc Zandvliet

More and more frequently, companies in the extractive industries are operating in areas characterized by profound instability and often open conflict. Unlike other industries, the extractive industries, by definition, deplete resource deposits on an ongoing basis and will go wherever untapped resource endowments are located. As most deposits of natural resources in relatively safe and politically stable countries have already been explored or exploited, companies increasingly find themselves operating in zones of conflict. These "conflict environments" can vary in terms of the level of violence: from "cold" conflict, such as in some parts of Indonesia, to occasional tribal warfare, such as in Papua New Guinea, to violent intergroup clashes, such as in Nigeria, to full-scale internal wars, such as in the Democratic Republic of Congo, Sudan, Colombia, and Nepal.

Research has shown that the resources that attract these multinational companies, whether oil, gold, diamonds, or timber, are the same resources over which many of today's conflicts are fought.[1] Hence the increased salience of the role of extractive industry companies in these conflicts, sometimes even in "fueling conflict," has become a subject of increased academic, policy, and advocacy debate.[2] Much of this debate centers on the adequacy of policy and regulatory mechanisms to control business transactions with combatants, to establish financial transparency in business deals, and to avoid their complicity in human rights violations committed by security forces or repressive regimes.[3]

In order to bring content to these debates, this chapter focuses on how companies' day-to-day operational activities, including local hiring policies, interactions with local communities, and exit strategies, can have unintended negative consequences on the conflict environment in which they operate. In so doing, this analysis proceeds from a field perspective, assessing the actual dynamics of company operations, policies, and assumptions of how business "should be done," based on research and consultations conducted by the Corporate Engagement Project in Colombia, Nigeria, Cameroon, Mozambique, Indonesia, Burma/Myanmar, Papua New Guinea, and Nepal.[4]

Companies generally seek to avoid becoming involved in conflict and to delink their own activities from the external environment in which they operate. Often field managers assume that "the conflict is not our conflict" and that their operations, whether mining gold, harvesting timber, or extracting oil, are neutral activities, occurring alongside but separate from local conflict. To the extent that conflict dynamics are recognized in business strategies and operations, they are viewed through the prism of traditional "political risk," as factors that may affect company operations and profits and as an "unavoidable consequence" of doing business in zones of conflict. The impact that company operations can have on conflict dynamics is too often neglected. Experience makes it clear, however, that companies inevitably become a part of the local context in which they operate. And when a particular context involves conflict, the company becomes a part of that conflict. Company activities may have positive or negative impacts on conflict dynamics, whether inadvertent or not. They are never neutral.

Against this background, the chapter begins with a brief analysis of the problems that conflict settings can pose for companies as well as the various ways in which company practices and policies, in turn, affect conflict dynamics. Focusing in particular on company-community relations, the chapter then takes a closer look at the origins of corporate policies and practices, as well as key aspects of corporate culture, including assumptions about how business "should be done," a mind-set of control, and the effect of implicit and explicit corporate reward structures. Unpacking these elements reveals expanded options for better company practices aimed at reducing conflict, which will be taken up in the penultimate section.

Identifying Potentially Conflicting Relationships

Historically, companies had to deal only with local groups knocking on their gates in protest. Since the early 1990s, catalyzed by companies' association with oppressive regimes in countries such as Indonesia, Sierra Leone, and Myanmar, extractive industry companies operating in zones of conflict have faced mounting public pressure and high-profile lawsuits at home to reform their conduct. International advocacy groups and concerned shareholders are relentlessly alerting companies to be more conscientious of their responsibility to conduct their operations in ways that do not worsen conflict. Faced with reputational and opportunity costs caused by boycotts or divestment campaigns as well as high management and security costs at field sites, companies themselves increasingly realize the business case for adopting better practices. Increasingly, to be profitable and competitive, the definition of success now includes an ability to manage "soft" issues such as maintaining constructive relations with local stakeholders and to ensure that corporate activities do not inadvertently feed into conflict. Experiences in Bougainville in Papua New Guinea and the Ogoni land in southern Nigeria show that when these issues are not handled adequately, it can become impossible to operate at all. In these cases, the nontechnical aspects of operations, traditionally considered as add-on activities rather than as essential to the profitability of the business, became critical factors in business failure.

Clearly, neither companies nor industries are monolithic. The degree to which the management of these "soft" issues is critical for conducting business varies across different sectors of industry, the types of companies within a given sector, the types of resources being extracted, the types of companies active in different phases of a project, and even across different departments within a single company. In order to identify the ways these differences can feed into conflict, let's note four key relationships in the conflict environment that can affect—and be affected by—companies' operations.

First and most obvious is the relationship *between corporations and the communities* where operations take place. Local communities are directly affected by a company's operations, through such factors as infrastructure development, the influx of workers, and possible environmental pollution. Experience shows that the consent of local populations has become essential to the viability of corporate operations. Cases of assault on company staff, sabotage, and seizure of company property in countries such as Indonesia, Nigeria, Peru, and Colombia, for example, have made clear that without a "local social license to operate," the ability to begin or continue company operations may be severely jeopardized.[5]

The degree to which company-community relations are affected by company operations varies among the mining, petroleum, and logging sectors. Historically, mining has had larger community impacts. These operations tend to employ a larger work force than the oil industry and create booming mining towns during mine development that become ghost towns after mine closure. Mining also tends to cause greater physical disruption of the land through open pits and the construction of new roads. For this reason, the mining industry has taken a lead over the petroleum industry in seeking to address the social, environmental, and human rights challenges it faces. Evidence of this mining-sector engagement is seen in such initiatives as the Mining, Minerals, and Sustainable Development Project.[6] In contrast to both mining and oil companies, whose operating horizon is usually long term, logging companies typically operate in one location only for a period of several months before moving to another area. As a result, they see less of a need to establish constructive long-term relationships with local communities and generally prefer to seek short-term solutions to the problems that may attend their operations.

Impacts on company-community relations can also depend on the phase of a given extraction project. In the initial phase of a project, exploration and construction are usually undertaken by contractors who are driven to finalize a project "on budget and on time." The short-term nature of their work, as well as their focus on achieving quantitative targets, can lead to behavior that creates problems between the community and the company. When the main operating company arrives, staff often confront the need to deal with unrealistic expectations, unfulfilled promises, and even communal conflicts created by the contractor before the community "allows" it to commence activities. Particular departments within a company, for instance those responsible for exploration, seismic surveying, and drilling, can cause the same negative dynamic when they conduct short-term technical work and then do not properly hand over relevant community information, including promises made and issues unresolved, to the department that continues the work—typically the operations department.

A second set of potentially conflictual relationships, equally important for corporate operations, concerns *intergroup or intercommunal conflicts* in the area of operation. Often predating company engagement, these sociocultural tensions may be inadvertently exacerbated by corporate operations. A worsening of relations among local adversaries frequently turns back on the corporation itself. For instance, in areas where unemployment is very high, local communities generally insist they provide labor to the company. When they see that "outsiders" obtain jobs that local residents believe they themselves should get, the "outsiders" may be chased away or even physically attacked. The company itself may be directly confronted with demonstrations, blockades, or other pressures to change its hiring practices.

Third, *corporations can become the proxy targets for grievances* held by local groups against the government. These grievances typically center on the national government's control over the revenues generated by extractive operations and the lack of revenues flowing back to communities where resources are located.[7] Local communities often feel that they do not benefit sufficiently from the exploitation of "their" resources while government leaders are using revenues for private benefit or to purchase arms, sometimes used to suppress local discontent. For marginalized communities, sabotaging company assets is often perceived as their best or only option to attract government attention and obtain necessary public services. This was the case in Papua New Guinea, where one community in a remote location chopped down a power line essential to mining operations in order to attract government attention. The ploy was successful. While the community later apologized to the company, its action led to joint efforts of the government and the company to redress local grievances. The community now has its own police post and a new school.[8]

Finally, *tensions between the company and government authorities,* while rarely violent, may diminish a company's ability to operate. Tensions can arise when companies, pressured by their shareholders or advocacy groups, challenge the government for failing to tackle corruption, for not investing in community development in the company's area of operation, or for government policies regarding human rights. In trying to balance home-country public expectations with host-government demands, companies often find themselves caught between a rock and a hard place. In countries such as Indonesia, for example, it is often difficult for companies to avoid the use of state security forces to protect company assets. In some cases, government partners may make this a condition of doing business. In others, local security forces may resort to threat or extortion to ensure that their staff are hired. The sometimes brutal behavior of these forces, however, can create more problems for the company than they solve. Not only can it foster more grievances among local communities, but it can also directly affect company security. In Indonesia, an FBI investigation linked the murder of Freeport McMoRan staff to the very Indonesian army unit that had been hired to protect company employees.[9] Obviously, such events can lead to strained relationships between companies and governments.

These relations and their potential for contributing to conflict are dynamic. Often they overlap and feed into each other. A conflict in the Niger Delta in Nigeria, for instance, originated with disputes between local communities and the central government over the share of oil revenues being returned to the community. Increasingly, however, oil companies were used as proxy targets by local communities to express grievances to the faraway, otherwise unreachable government in Abuja. Over time, then, the conflict has gained its own dynamic, poising local communities against the oil companies operating in the Niger Delta region, notably Shell, which have been accused of inadequately compensating communities for oil spills, for using government police forces known for their poor human rights record, and for not sufficiently asserting their political leverage with the Nigerian government to prevent the hanging of activists who were opposed to oil company practices. In response, the oil companies claim that they have been instrumental in ensuring that 13 percent of oil revenues in Nigeria now flow from the federal level to the oil-producing states. However, addressing this long-standing issue has not resulted in a reduction of violence and tension between the companies and the communities in the area of operation.[10]

How Corporate Norms Can Exacerbate Conflict

Clearly, business operations need not have a negative impact on conflict. With an adequate understanding of the context in which they are operating, companies can redesign their operations to reduce unintended impacts. A critical step in determining how companies can avoid feeding into conflict is diagnosing how things go wrong. Too often seemingly neutral or even well-intentioned activities, such as compensation for land property, hiring practices, engagement with local authorities, and the implementation of community projects, may end in negative impacts. The patterns by which negative impacts occur across contexts and company types are becoming clearer through comparative analysis of corporate field practices. Once these patterns are identified and recognized, they are predictable. If predictable, they may also be preventable.

Field research has identified several corporate norms common to many companies that shape company behavior across a range of local contexts and that exacerbate conflict dynamics. These include assumptions about the context of conflict, assumptions of how business should be conducted vis-à-vis local authorities and communities, a control-oriented mind-set, and the effect of internal and external corporate reward structures.

Corporate Assumptions About the Conflict Environment

Corporate activities are based on assumptions about the context of conflict and how business should be conducted. Generally, these assumptions are not verified with the stakeholders whom the policies influence. Erroneous assumptions about the complexity of conflict feed a sense of powerlessness about managers' ability to make a difference and often lead to daily decisions that increase conflict.

"Conflicts are too complex for the company to fully understand." Managers often feel overwhelmed by the complexity of the local conflict dynamics. This leads to two beliefs: first, that a detailed context analysis can never be achieved, so there is no point in aspiring to it; and second, that it is also too difficult to analyze how one's own operations interact with the conflict. Consequently, companies aim to implement seemingly "neutral" policies with regard to ethnic or other subgroup conflict. But as the following examples show, these "neutral" choices can have negative impacts.

In an attempt to maintain hiring policies that avoid favoritism, companies often announce that hiring decisions are based on merit alone. Within many conflict areas, however, one issue underlying conflict is a historical disadvantaging of some groups by others. Systems of exclusion, racism, prejudice, and privilege will have meant that some groups have greater access than others to the advanced education for "merit" hiring. Even well-intended hiring practices can thus unintentionally reinforce historical inequities in a society and exacerbate intergroup tensions and divisions. In countries such as Papua New Guinea, Cameroon, and Nigeria, this has led to serious tensions between local communities, whose members are employed mostly as unskilled laborers working as guards and drivers, and outsiders hired for skilled, well-paid positions.

Similar effects can occur through choices about whom a company interacts with as a community representative. An obvious choice for company managers is to favor those "representatives" who come to their offices, speak their language, and know local laws and customs. Experience shows, however, that these individuals are typically elites of the host community, who often do not represent the surrounding communities in any legitimate way and may be positioning themselves for personal gain. In Indonesia, such "elites" were ultimately forced out of the community when they were perceived to be enriching themselves at the expense of other villagers.[11] In Nigeria, the traditional leadership in the Niger Delta has lost its authority over youngsters, who feel that their elders have been corrupted.[12] Some traditional leaders have been murdered for the same reason. In some of these cases, violent demonstrations have been staged against companies to protest against perceived cronyism and corruption.

Corporate Assumptions About "How Business Should Be Done" in Unstable Contexts

Many corporate policies originate in assumptions that communities are excessively demanding and constitute a risk factor to company operations. This leads companies to adopt a standoffish, reactive approach to dealing with communities, which can increase conflict.

"The local government is corrupt; you cannot work with it." When dealing with local authorities, companies often feel trapped in a dilemma. On the one hand, companies need government support for obtaining permits, a system of law and order, and the provision of social services. On the other hand, companies seek to minimize engagement with government authorities whom they perceive to be corrupt or incompetent.

The failure to recognize the existing capacities of local authorities, however weak, as an opportunity to improve governance, often leads companies to substitute for government services. This is typically the case in the area of infrastructure development: most companies invest in the construction of roads, power lines, water sources, schools, and clinics in their areas of operation. Although some of these investments are required for their own operations, companies typically tout them as significant contributions to local welfare. To some degree this is accurate, given that local government is often unable or unwilling to provide these services. Yet by building clinics or schools and branding them with their corporate logos, companies may end up emphasizing the inadequacies of local government, directly undermining existing or potential government and civil servant capacities, and further feeding into antigovernment sentiments. Not only do companies thus inadvertently reinforce citizens' distrust of government and thereby undermine government legitimacy, but they may also find themselves trapped as the de facto government and be subjected to ever-increasing demands by local communities to provide social services.

"Maintaining relationships with stakeholders is difficult and complex." Because many managers emphasize the difficulty of maintaining positive relations with local stakeholders, most companies delegate responsibility for community relations to "experts" in a specialized department. While maintaining a dedicated department indicates a positive commitment to the importance of community relations, this separation between operational and community relations departments can create a "silo mentality" among managers. In such cases, well-intended and potentially effective community relations programs designed by dedicated departments can be undermined by insensitivity to community concerns on the part of operational managers, who may be unaware of how their policies and activities affect local conflict dynamics.

To some degree, community relations departments can compensate for negative impacts such as oil spills or increased traffic with community investment projects, such as the construction of community buildings or soccer fields. But as long as the root causes of such negative impacts are not addressed, or as long as the operational management is perceived as "arrogant" or "exploitative," the company will get little credit from the community for these projects.

Furthermore, many companies assume that "the community" begins and ends outside the company gate. They tend to forget that community members base their views of the company primarily on the information they get from their neighbors and family members who work for the company. Internal policies or work conditions perceived as degrading can thus feed into grievances in the community. Nongovernmental organizations in Nigeria, for example, explain that kidnapping of senior oil company staff by members of the local communities often occurs based on information from local employees who felt "exploited" by the company.[13]

"Communities pose a risk to our operations." Companies often consider community engagement as part of a strategy to mitigate risk for company operations. This strategy creates a staff mind-set that the community as a "risk factor" should be kept at a distance and contacts should be minimal. This strategy widens the distance between the company and the local community and may increase tensions between them. In Indonesia, for example, a mining company introduced a housing policy that encouraged its staff to move to the company compound instead of renting rooms in the local village. Several years later, local communities blocked access to the site for several months to protest perceived environmental damages caused by the company. In hindsight, company managers acknowledge that if staff had still resided among local communities and maintained routine social relationships, the demonstrations would likely not have happened.[14]

"Engagement should be on an as-needed basis only." Executives often fear that increased interactions with local communities will lead to a stream of insatiable and costly demands. Thus companies engage with local communities only when absolutely necessary. As a result, engagement is typically reactive rather than proactive. Experience from Colombia, Cameroon, Nigeria, and Nepal, however, shows that when companies engage communities or undertake community projects only in reaction to threats of violence or work obstruction, communities often conclude that they can achieve their goals only through violence and obstruction. By rewarding violent behavior or threats with social investment projects to "pacify" a community, companies reward negative rather than positive behavior. By responding only to triggers, companies ensure that such triggers happen.

"Community relations programs are sufficient to reduce conflict." Because companies tend to see conflict within and between surrounding communities as unrelated to their daily operations, when violence affects the company, managers usually categorize the problem as externally induced. While extensive community relations or social investment projects are often undertaken in a genuine effort to mitigate risk and reduce conflict, few companies question how their own activities may have contributed to the problem. However, these conventional risk-mitigation strategies are not fail-safe. Indeed, they can often increase conflict.

This happens because companies usually design their community relations projects in response to only the most visible and apparent threats. For instance, they might establish a project in the village that they identify as being most affected by the company's presence and that they therefore perceive to be the highest risk factor to the company. What most corporate managers do not see is that these rewarded communities are part of the wider context of conflict and may have their own rivalries with neighboring communities. Failure to think through the full social ramifications of even well-intended initiatives can thus backfire on a company. Other communities may feel left out and direct their grievances toward the company or try to obtain "their share" through violent means, either from the company or from other groups in the neighboring community.[15] One community in Papua New Guinea, for example, warned a neighboring community that received the most corporate benefits that "it will be pay-back time" after the company leaves.[16]

"For every problem, there is a monetary solution." Companies have a tendency to bring all interactions with communities down to an issue of financial remuneration, believing that there are financial incentives for everything. This tendency feeds directly into competition among recipient groups, as they vie for ownership of land for which the company will pay or for employment and subcontracting opportunities. In addition, when relations between a company and local communities are based predominantly on financial transactions, communities may come to view the company as nothing more than an endless source of cash, thereby reinforcing a "compensation culture." Community members may take advantage of the company's compensation policy for damage done to land or property by intentionally causing such damage. As happened in Nigeria, they may sabotage oil pipelines in order to receive compensation for environmental damage or to obtain a contract for repairing the pipeline. When the company pays, destructive behavior is reinforced.

Importantly, the introduction of large sums of cash into the communities through compensation payments, contracting, or employment can also be a contributing element to conflict. In addition, where cash is spent on short-term consumption, alcohol, and luxury items instead of sustainable income-generating tools, cash compensation can leave people more vulnerable than before, without either their land or the cash.[17] When communities have little experience in dealing with cash, particularly with large amounts, cash compensation may also upset traditional power structures and relationships between groups.[18] In many traditional societies, hierarchy is still based on wisdom and age. When cash is introduced into such communities, it may change how prestige and political importance are gained—from a traditional system involving demonstrated community responsibility to a cash-based system involving buying loyalties and, in some cases, hiring private police forces. Young men, who in traditional structures would not pass these social benchmarks, now become able to exert influence based on wealth acquired by compensation payments.

*　　*　　*

Overall, companies do not sufficiently appreciate that the manner in which they handle their day-to-day core activities (the "how") is at least as important as their actual community projects (the "what") in influencing community perceptions. Discussions with local communities reveal that if a company does not simultaneously address the intangible aspects of its relationship with local stakeholders, community relations efforts are, at best, only partially effective. In fact, communities stress that they value "neighborliness," including respect and inclusion in those decisionmaking processes that affect them.

The Corporate Mind-Set of Staying in Control

A corporate culture that emphasizes control is a pervasive feature of operational managers. This has been reinforced by trends in the extractive industries to concentrate on increasing control over the technical process of exploring and processing resources. Engineers, prevalent in extractive industries, explain that the mind-set of the technical department—often the pride of the company—is geared toward a diligent analysis to break down the technical process into small steps.[19] This analysis makes it possible to increase predictability, mitigate risk, and increase control. While these qualities are key to the technical success of the company, when it comes to interactions with local stakeholders, this mind-set hampers the establishment of productive, balanced relationships.

"When negotiating, keep your cards to yourself." Many companies treat stakeholder negotiations as means to achieve a specific position, rather than as an open process aimed at meeting mutual needs. Companies are interested in making negotiations quick, stakeholder representation narrow, and agendas fixed. Consequently, the parameters for stakeholder negotiations are often specifically defined in order to keep as much control over the process and the outcome as possible: negotiation should address only core operational activities; negotiations should be limited to those actors who are either potentially the most obstructive or the most influential to convince community members to support the company; negotiation should be approached with a fixed agenda for achieving set goals; and to obtain the best negotiation results, it is wise to be sparse with information.

As a result of these parameters, company negotiators tend to overlook the importance of the process, the sources of community concern, and even the existence of conflicting views within the company itself. In Papua New Guinea, a company negotiated vigorously with local landowners over compensation. After the settlement was finalized, as a gesture of goodwill, the company decided to pay more compensation than was agreed upon. Already disgruntled by the bullish way in which the company had acted during the negotiations, the landowners interpreted this gesture as a signal that they must have negotiated poorly and had achieved a suboptimal result, so they demanded more negotiations. The following week, a staff member was briefly kidnapped to signal what would happen if the negotiations were not reopened.

"Maintain control of exit strategies." The issue of control also surfaces in regard to operational policies, including developing exit strategies. There has been a great deal of debate around this issue, and companies, especially in the mining industry, increasingly recognize the value of a well-designed plan for departure.[20] Some companies now insist upon developing an exit plan even before a new project commences. Still, companies rarely work with communities to communicate or adapt their plans. Many companies fear that discussing an exit plan with communities well in advance will increase the risk of theft or looting of company assets. However, when communities have limited information and no clarity about what will happen once a company's operations are complete, they tend to focus on gaining short-term benefits and press for increasing demands while the company is still there.

Overall, companies equate "staying in control" with keeping the community at a distance and sharing information sparingly. According to community representatives in several countries, the standoffish approach taken by companies tends to only reinforce confrontational negotiations, as the door for negotiations is so often closed. They also maintain that greater provision of information through continued dialogue would enable them to control their own extremists, whose unreasonable positions only undermine progress and divert energy. This opinion suggests that sharing control of the negotiating process with communities may in fact lead to more productive relationships and less conflict.

Explicit and Implicit Corporate Reward Structures

The manner in which a company explicitly or implicitly values or rewards certain staff behaviors can also be an underlying factor that affects the local conflict environment.

The conflict-inducing effects of quantitative reward structures. Most companies base their systems for rewarding staff performance on quantitative indicators, including production measures, such as barrels of oil or annual percentage increases in production, or development projects, such as numbers of schools or hospitals constructed. Reward systems based on output, however, generally do not include criteria for evaluating how quantitative goals were reached or how community relations were affected in the process. Rarely do companies base employees' rewards on company impacts on the quality of life and measures of sustainability among affected communities, as they view these factors as more difficult to measure. The quantitative approach often means that managers focused on "meeting the numbers" are inadvertently undermining the work of their own colleagues in the community relations department. Even within the community relations department, an emphasis on outputs may lure managers into designing community relations efforts that focus on addressing short-term symptoms of company-community tensions rather than the underlying causes.

The impact of such internal policies on the local conflict environment is exemplified by a case in which a local manager's performance was measured only by his ability to minimize costs relative to returns for his production unit. This manager made a number of decisions with regard to hiring and firing of local staff that exacerbated existing tensions in the community over economic disparities and neglected communities' needs, ultimately resulting in the kidnapping of several staff members. Yet the response of the company's headquarters was to pay the ransoms. Not only did this episode not reflect negatively on the company's assessment of the manager's performance, but it was dismissed as "the cost of doing business" in conflict zones. Had the manager had an incentive to take the community impact of his unit into account, he likely would have made different decisions, consciously undertaking to reform contentious hiring practices, reduce the risk to company staff, and obviate the cost, both to the company and to the community, of extortion through kidnapping.

Department budgets determine influence. The formal and informal reward systems of most corporations emphasize size. Individuals are more important if they manage big budgets or big departments. This structural emphasis can perversely reinforce a tendency for security and community relations departments to play up security and community relations problems to receive larger budgets. In other words, the bigger the problem, the bigger the budget needed to address it. When salary levels are linked to financial responsibility, staff members are not encouraged to solve problems; rather, they may stand to benefit from perpetuating conflicts on a local level in order to justify an increase of their budgets.

*   *   *

In sum, most managers are not consciously aware of the aspects of corporate culture or their own "mental maps" used to make their decisions.

Making these norms explicit is valuable in two ways. First, companies can trace back to the root causes of some of their problematic practices. Second, if company-community conflict can be traced back to corporate policies and practices, it indicates that companies have a much higher degree of control over the conflict dynamics than they generally assume, and thus they have proactive options to address the potential sources of conflict more effectively.

Toward Better Corporate Practices of Conflict Management

For companies, developing better practices for working in conflict areas starts with acknowledging that company operations do have an impact on the environment in which they work and that a company, by definition, will never be perceived as playing a neutral role in the conflict dynamics. Long-term corporate success and profits may well depend on their ability to have a net positive impact on conflict, rather than simply to avoid having a negative impact. In addition, companies need to acknowledge that their daily operational interactions with communities are equally important as, if not more important than, any community relations project in establishing the terms by which local stakeholders assess the benefits of company operations for their community.

The Importance of Local Context Analysis

Companies are starting to acknowledge the value of a better local context analysis. They realize that traditional political risk assessments focused largely on macroeconomic and political developments are of limited value to plant managers dealing with day-to-day realities of local operations. Some companies, for instance, have hired cultural anthropologists to identify intergroup divisions that could become social pressure points during the company's project development.

A context analysis can provide the company with ideas about opportunities for reducing conflict by giving explicit attention to issues such as historic claims to lands designated for compensation, appropriate channels of communication, options for nonmonetary compensation, the identification of legitimate community representatives, intercommunal relations among local stakeholders, the availability and viability of traditional conflict resolution mechanisms, and identification of possible winners and losers from company activities.

In all societies, some factors—such as ethnicity or wealth—divide people and subgroups from each other, while others, such as trade, infrastructure, and intermarriage, connect them. Whether knowingly or unknowingly, the company's polices and operations can support either dividers or connectors, with either negative or positive impacts. When dividers are fueled or connectors undermined, societies fragment, sometimes to the point of violent conflict. When, on the other hand, companies focus on shared interests and common objectives between groups, they can assist these groups in overcoming difference and create incentives to work together to address common problems. Companies may find it helpful to analyze the context in which they work though such a connectors and dividers perspective.[21] Identifying and understanding existing dividers and connectors and how company operations interact with them should be a central part of the design of company policies. With the help of a skilled third-party mediator, for example, an oil company in Nigeria successfully negotiated with some communities an arrangement by which the company would ensure that maximum benefits flowed to the communities (including jobs, contracts, and community projects), provided that these communities halted their violent practices toward each other and toward the company.[22]

Context analysis may thus provide better insights into the various ways that potentially conflictual relationships stemming from the interaction of company operations and community dynamics may be mitigated. Clearly, each of these relationships will require a specific strategy from the company that includes an approach for dealing with underlying sources of conflict.

Options to Address Tensions
Between the Company and the Community

In order to minimize the negative impacts on local communities that are often associated with inflows of large amounts of cash, companies are increasingly focused on nonfinancial forms of compensation. One company in Peru, for instance, compensated land for land, in addition to paying part of the compensation in cash, an arrangement that proved satisfactory to the farmers involved. In Papua New Guinea, another company agreed with the landowners' collective to pay part of the compensation into a trust fund, which the company helped establish. Overseen by a professional fund manager, this trust fund generates a sustainable income stream for local stakeholders. Furthermore, several companies now provide guidance and support to local community members on how to best invest their money, to prevent former landowners from losing both their land and compensation money in short succession. To address the problem of sabotage for compensation, oil companies in Nigeria established impartial and independent investigation teams (including government officials and environmental specialists) to determine the cause of oil spills. In the case of sabotage, no compensation is paid.

In order to gain better awareness of community perceptions of the company, some managers have initiated a practice of holding regular, sometimes informal meetings with community members, such as lunches with local elders, to listen to their opinions about the company's behavior. Mining companies in Peru organize periodic information evenings, which are open to everyone and focus on informal information exchange. Importantly, it is acknowledged that no decisions are made during these meetings, so as not to bypass or undermine the official representation structure. Providing such a venue for interaction about the company's contracting policies, complaint procedures, and future plans or exit strategies helps to ensure that the company is seen as accessible and that local stakeholders do not have to resort to violence to attract attention.

To reduce mutual distrust, a company in Burma/Myanmar organized "open days" for members of the local communities. One positive outcome was that the communities expressed surprise at the large number of national staff working on site, refuting their assumption that the company was composed solely of foreigners. In like fashion, some companies in Papua New Guinea encourage their foreign staff to take part in local festivals and to attend wedding ceremonies and other community celebrations in order to counter the perception that communities pose a risk to the company.

Some companies in Tanzania, Peru, and Indonesia have developed official communication protocols that are triggered in case of a complaint. Other companies have developed complaint and monitoring procedures in cooperation with communities themselves. One oil company operating in Indonesia, for example, encourages villagers to monitor daily activities during seismic surveys in an area containing fishing grounds. In case of a perceived accident, the villagers can contact the company's environmental expert, and, together with an independent navy official, all stakeholders take water samples immediately. The samples are sent to a laboratory of the villagers' choice as well as to the company's laboratory to determine if the complaint is justified.

In order to address the likely negative impacts of traditional corporate reward systems, some companies integrate performance benchmarks on relations with local stakeholders, which affect the rewards earned not only by the community relations staff but by all staff. In Nigeria, for example, one oil company provides a bonus to each employee when good external relations are maintained or improved. This bonus system, based on incident reports and verbal feedback from the community, makes stakeholder relations a shared responsibility of all staff. Other companies give public rewards through "employee of the week" notifications to individuals who make a valuable contribution to community relations.

In order to increase ownership of community relations among all departments, one company in Indonesia works in cross-departmental teams to provide information directly to local villages about future activities such as drilling and seismic surveys. For many technicians, these are their first visits to local villages and the first time they are confronted by local concerns. Similarly, some companies insist that employees attend consultations with local communities, or they require every senior manager to spend two nights per year in the villages surrounding his or her plant.

Options to Address Tensions Between Groups

As a way of reducing local perceptions of discriminatory hiring practices, some companies publicly announce their vacancies for both skilled and unskilled positions through bulletin boards at the company gate or in local villages. Even though local villagers are unlikely to qualify for all positions, experience in countries such as Nepal and Mozambique suggests that if people are aware of the hiring criteria, they are more likely to accept whoever is hired—even "outsiders."

Some companies build on shared interests between conflicting groups in order to reduce intergroup conflict. In Sri Lanka, for example, a company that was seeking bids for staff transportation knew of fierce competition between two groups to gain the contract. Both groups own buses that do not meet the company's safety standards. While it would be a logical step for the company to hire an outside contractor (potentially alienating both groups), it instead encourages the competing groups to agree to sell their old buses, pool their resources, and buy a safe fleet. If they do so, the company has agreed to give the contract jointly to these groups.

Community programs can serve as connectors between different groups in a region of operations. To use them more effectively, companies can focus on the shared interests of more broadly defined groups, rather than just those of the most affected village. In Papua New Guinea, the beneficiaries of one company's engagement were limited to one locale in a small valley. When the company heard that villages outside this valley had grown jealous and had threatened villages within the valley, it decided to undertake a much broader sustainable development focus as part of its exit strategy. Instead of a "valley action plan," the company is designing a "regional development plan" to emphasize the joint interests and interdependence of the people in the entire area.

Particularly in regions where there are competing sources of social status and political authority, companies may encounter difficulties in distinguishing legitimate from self-selected community representatives. One way of doing so is for companies to observe representatives in their social milieu. Several companies have developed policies to meet with communities in villages, rather than at company headquarters. Communities value the fact that a company pays respect to villagers by visiting them in their environment. By doing so, company officials gain a clearer understanding of social and political dynamics within the community.

Options to Address Tensions
Between the Community and the Government

As discussed above, a primary source of community-government conflict is over the distribution of resource revenues, typically in favor of the company and government. One gold-mining company in Papua New Guinea addressed local complaints about the lack of revenues flowing back to the area by negotiating a tax credit scheme with the government. Under this scheme, the company used part of the taxes it would otherwise have paid to the central government to implement infrastructure projects that were already planned by the regional government. This approach ensures government buy-in and aids sustainability, for example, by ensuring that schools being constructed will have adequate staffing provided by the authorities. To improve the legitimacy and capacity of the government in the eyes of the local population, the same company now ensures a prominent role for local authorities in the planning process and, more symbolically, during the opening ceremonies of such infrastructure projects.

In other efforts to encourage the government to respond more effectively to community needs, one gold-mining company operating in Peru has undertaken to serve as a facilitator between local communities and government representatives in discussing the provision of services to the community. The company requests that the parties meet and provides a venue for the meetings. Villagers claim that without the company's encouragement the government would not have participated in this process.

Options to Address Tensions
Between the Company and the Authorities

Rather than assuming that "all" government officials are corrupt or ineffective, companies increasingly realize that no organization is monolithic and that within all governments there are committed and able civil servants who want to perform their jobs competently. In many instances, civil servants seek to distance themselves from politicians. They, too, are frustrated by a lack of sufficient resources and the politicization of decisions. These individuals offer opportunities for collaboration between companies and authorities. Even in contexts of violent conflict, many administrators still hold a formal or informal position to negotiate between conflicting groups or to calm community sentiments. On one occasion in Indonesia, for instance, the legitimacy provided to one official by recognition by the company gave this person the credibility to better negotiate cease-fires between conflicting local groups.

Ensuring the security of staff and operations remains one of the most difficult challenges facing companies in unstable areas. Despite sometimes daunting constraints, there are measures available to companies to enhance security, combat vigilantism, and increase civilian trust in the police. One company in Papua New Guinea trained local police forces to be better disciplined and provided them with housing and offices. Now the people in the area have sufficient confidence in the police to bring their cases to them. As a result, crime rates in the company's region are lower than the national average. In addition, since the training, the local police are better equipped to resolve tensions before they get out of control. In the past, the company called upon the police only once local tensions had already escalated to unrest, and then it was blamed for its sometimes heavy-handed response.

Some companies enter into discussions with national governments about how company revenues will be spent, as a way of influencing them to undertake responsible fiscal management. Companies increasingly address such issues prior to deciding to invest, which is when their leverage over national government decisions is largest. Especially in extractive industry projects that receive funding from the World Bank's International Finance Corporation (IFC), such as the Chad-Cameroon pipeline or the Baku-Tbilisi-Ceyhan pipeline in the Caucasus, the establishment of transparent revenue-sharing mechanisms has become part of loan agreements. While this is important at least on the normative level, some of these mechanisms are still experimental, and there are ongoing debates on how to ensure transparency.[23] Yet further developments on this front may also make it easier for projects without IFC involvement to insist on such mechanisms in other countries.

The Way Forward

The examples described in this chapter represent only a few of the efforts undertaken by managers of extractive industry companies operating in zones of conflict to mitigate their own impact on conflict dynamics. Though necessary, they are obviously not sufficient to resolve the macro-level dimensions of conflict, especially where conflicts are long-standing, involve corrupt and repressive regimes, or are complicated by ethnosecessionist aspirations. While companies often have more options and capacity for proactive conflict management than is commonly recognized, they do not have the influence, the expertise, or the legitimacy to appreciably alter these larger conflict dynamics.

Companies are not, and do not seek to be, peace agencies. Nor should they be regarded as such. However, they do have the capacity and the responsibility to mitigate the negative, conflict-inducing aspects of their own operations in weakly governed or war-torn communities, particularly at the local level, where companies have the greatest control over their impacts and where they have the strongest business case for contributing to a developing and peaceful environment. Understanding the patterns by which these negative impacts typically occur can point toward the range of available practical options that may be pursued both to avoid worsening social tensions in areas of operation and to promote the incremental development of just social and political structures. Naturally, it is not up to companies to manage the politics of a host country; it is up to the people themselves to determine their own future. Still, the challenge for the company is to play, and to be seen as playing, a positive and constructive role in the country.

There remain many lessons to be learned and new approaches that can—and must—be tried. Overall, however, it is important for companies to recognize that the particular type of conflict management policy employed is often less consequential to outcomes than *how* that policy is implemented. If there is no prior analysis of how these policy choices can interact with conflict dynamics in the broader society, then building schools and clinics, working with local leaders, and promoting local economic activities may do little to mitigate—and may even provoke—conflict. On the other hand, when designed to take account of the wider social and political context, even routine business decisions can help to (re)integrate divided groups, encourage intergroup cooperation and interdependence, promote reliable and trusted authorities, and otherwise contribute to broader social and political stability.

There is no standard manual for companies operating in a context of violent conflict. Different stakeholders have different, and continually evolving, definitions and expectations of responsible corporate behavior. However, each of the contexts examined reveals a variety of options available to companies interested in addressing the challenges of conflict management. Through discussions with the relevant stakeholders, interested parties can agree on common benchmarks and explore the alternatives available to a company to work toward arrangements that allow operations to continue while also satisfying the needs and concerns of the key stakeholders, especially those people most directly affected by corporate operations. Some companies are already anticipating how their current activities will hold up against societal expectations of the year 2020. Their vision may point the way forward.

Notes

I would like to thank Kristin C. Doughty, who worked on an earlier version of this chapter in her capacity as project associate of the Corporate Engagement Project.

1. See Michael T. Klare, *Resource Wars: The New Landscape of Global Conflict* (New York: Henry Holt, 2001); Michael Renner, *The Anatomy of Resource Wars,* Worldwatch Paper no. 162 (Washington, D.C.: Worldwatch Institute, 2002); Mats Berdal and David M. Malone, eds., *Greed and Grievance: Economic Agendas in Civil Wars* (Boulder: Lynne Rienner, 2000); and Karen Ballentine and Jake Sherman, eds., *The Political Economy of Armed Conflict: Beyond Greed and Grievance* (Boulder: Lynne Rienner, 2003).

2. See, for example, Philip Swanson, *Fuelling Conflicts: The Oil Industry and Armed Conflict,* Fafo Report no. 378 (Oslo: Fafo Institute, 2002); Christian Aid, *Fuelling Poverty: Oil, War, and Corruption* (London: Christian Aid, 2003); Global Witness, *Logs of War: The Timber Trade and Armed Conflict,* Fafo Report no. 379 (Oslo: Fafo Institute, 2002).

3. Jason Switzer, *Armed Conflict and Natural Resources: The Case of the Minerals Sector* (London: International Institute for Environment and Development, 2001); Jane Nelson, *The Business of Peace: The Private Sector as a Partner in Conflict Resolution* (London: International Alert and Prince of Wales Business Leaders Forum, 2000); Jake Sherman, *Options for Promoting Corporate Responsibility in Conflict Zones: Perspectives from the Private Sector,* IPA Conference Report (New York: International Peace Academy, 2002).

4. To assist companies in developing effective conflict-mitigating practices, the Corporate Engagement Project (CEP) works with them in a focused, inductive effort to identify common patterns from experience and to identify practical solutions. In field visits, a small team of experts (typically one expert in the local context and one CEP representative with extensive international experience) visits a company site for two weeks, and holds formal and informal interviews with local, national, and international stakeholders including company staff, contractors, local communities, opposition groups, service and advocacy nongovernmental organizations, and religious and political leaders. The CEP teams focus on learning about the ways that corporate operations affect, and are affected by, conflicts. These discussions enable the CEP team to factually analyze which aspects of corporate policies have either a positive or a negative impact on the conflict environment in which the company operates. In a two-year period, the CEP has developed twelve field-based case studies in regions including Cameroon, Colombia, Indonesia, Mozambique, Burma/Myanmar, Nepal, Nigeria, and Papua New Guinea. Across contexts, this analysis allows for the development of practical management options to ensure that corporate activities do not unintentionally exacerbate or feed into conflict. The validity of these options is further tested and refined in periodic workshops with representatives of participating companies. Two cautions bear mentioning. First, the CEP works with companies with a demonstrated willingness to examine and change operations, which influences the type of corporate experiences to which the project has access. Second, while the CEP has gathered rich data thus far, many more cases and company experiences are still being collected and analyzed. Therefore, the findings discussed in this chapter represent interim lessons, not final conclusions. In some cases, they raise additional questions and dilemmas that warrant further exploration.

5. See, for example, Juan Forero, "Pipeline Goes 'Boom!' Local Economies Go Bust," *New York Times,* August 16, 2001, p. 4; and Michael Peel, "Nigerian Women Win Changes from Big Oil," *Christian Science Monitor,* December 8, 2001.

6. The Mining, Minerals, and Sustainable Development Project was an independent, two-year project (2000–2002) of research and consultation seeking to understand how the mining and minerals sector can contribute to the global transition to sustainable development on the global, national, regional, and local levels.

For the project's findings, see MMSD Final Report, *Breaking New Ground: Mining, Minerals, and Sustainable Development* (London: Earthscan, 2002), available at www.iied.org/mmsd.

7. See, for example, Jeffrey Herbst, *The Politics of Revenue Sharing in Resource-Dependent States,* UNU/WIDER Discussion Paper no. 2001/43 (Helsinki: UNU/WIDER, 2001); Anthony J. Regan, "The Bougainville Conflict: Political and Economic Agendas," in Ballentine and Sherman, *Political Economy of Armed Conflict,* pp. 133–166 (see note 1); and Rotimi T. Suberu, *Federalism and Ethnic Conflict in Nigeria* (Washington, D.C.: U.S. Institute of Peace Press, 2001).

8. Personal interview with the mine's manager during a Corporate Engagement Project consultation, January 5, 2003, at Harvard University, Cambridge.

9. Simon Elegant, "Murder at the Mine," *Time,* February 17, 2003.

10. See Luc Zandvliet and Ibiba Don Pedro, *Oil Company Policies in the Niger Delta,* Corporate Engagement Project (Cambridge, Mass.: Collaborative for Development Action, 2002), available at www.cdainc.com/cep/publications/reports/Visit03Nigeria.pdf.

11. Luc Zandvliet and Sonny Sukada, "Report on Unocal's Oil and Gas Operations in Kalimantan," unpubl., 2003.

12. Zandvliet and Don Pedro, *Oil Company Policies in the Niger Delta,* p. 4.

13. Personal communication, Port Harcourt, Nigeria, March 2002.

14. Personal communication, Balikpapan, Indonesia, March 2003.

15. Mary B. Anderson and Luc Zandvliet, *Corporate Options for Breaking Cycles of Conflict,* Corporate Engagement Project (Cambridge, Mass.: Collaborative for Development Action, 2001), available at www.cdainc.com/cep/publications/articles/CorporateOptions.php.

16. Mary B. Anderson, Doug Fraser, and Luc Zandvliet, *Porgera Joint Venture (PJV) Gold Mining Operation,* Corporate Engagement Project (Cambridge, Mass.: Collaborative for Development Action, 2001), available at www.cdainc.com/cep/publications/reports/Visit01PNG.pdf.

17. Ibid., pp. 8, 10.

18. David Reyes and Luc Zandvliet, *A Look at the Operational Activities of Logging Companies in Cameroon,* Corporate Engagement Project Case Study (Cambridge, Mass.: Collaborative for Development Action, 2002), pp. 12–14; Anderson, Fraser, and Zandvliet, *Porgera Joint Venture,* pp. 16–19.

19. See also Gary MacDonald and Timothy McLaughlin, "Extracting Conflict," in Rory Sullivan, ed., *Business and Human Rights: Dilemmas and Solutions* (Sheffield, U.K.: Greenleaf, 2003), pp. 232–242.

20. See, for example, Cochilco (Chilean Copper Commission), *Research on Mine Closure Policy,* Mines, Minerals, and Sustainable Development Project Report no. 44, January 2002, available at www.iied.org/mmsd/mmsd_pdfs/044_cochilco.pdf.

21. For a fuller discussion of dividers and connectors, see Mary B. Anderson, *Do No Harm: How Aid Can Support Peace—or War* (Boulder: Lynne Rienner, 1999).

22. Personal interview with Akachukwu Nwankpo, Port Harcourt, Nigeria, August 7, 2003.

23. See Chapters 10 and 11 in this volume.

9

Private Financial Actors and Corporate Responsibility in Conflict Zones

Mark Mansley

The role of extractive industry companies in conflict-prone or war-torn countries has come to the forefront of the international policy debate on corporate social responsibility (CSR), business and human rights, and the political economy of armed conflict. Research shows that at times these private-sector actors may knowingly or unknowingly contribute to or exacerbate armed conflict through their routine business operations.[1] Driven by nongovernmental organizations (NGOs), governments, the United Nations, and to some degree companies themselves, there has been a proliferation of voluntary initiatives aimed at minimizing the negative consequences of companies' activities. Yet the persistence of resource-based conflicts has required expansion of the search for effective remedies. In particular, there is growing interest in the potential role of private financial institutions in using their leverage to create incentives for extractive industry companies in the private sector to ensure that their operations do not contribute to armed conflict.[2]

Various actors in the international private financial market can exert considerable influence on companies in a range of ways. Institutional investors, such as pension funds and life insurance companies, own significant proportions of company shares and can thus greatly influence the governance and management of companies; investment banks help companies to access capital and are influential in determining their cost of capital (and share price), partly through analysis of their prospects and risks; and commercial banks help to shape trade and investment by transnational corporations in unstable or conflict-prone countries and, through the provision of project finance, have a pivotal role in financing the infrastructure required for resource exploitation.

This chapter examines the ways in which private financial institutions currently encourage and at times even require the companies they invest in or lend to, to address conflict prevention and mitigation in their policies and practices. Much of this is based on existing or evolving corporate regulatory mechanisms that shape market forces through, inter alia, investment decisions, disclosure requirements, and lending conditionality, predominantly in the fields of social and environmental responsibility.

The focus of the chapter, discussed in the first section, is on the investment community, specifically on institutional investors. A consideration of investor motivations for taking action on conflict-related issues is followed by a discussion of their options for action. Based on this, the chapter identifies the limitations to their activity, particularly in the context of armed conflict, and then considers options for policymakers that could enhance the effectiveness of investors in contributing to conflict prevention and mitigation. The second part of the chapter deals with the international private-sector commercial banking industry and its role in armed conflict. While the direct role of banks as companies in their own right, as well as in providing financial services to combatants, is briefly touched upon, this section focuses on banks' provision of project finance for extractive industry projects and specifically on how conflict issues may shape lending decisions. Some issues for further research and policy action are offered in the concluding section.

Institutional Investors

Publicly held corporations do not operate in a vacuum. To varying degrees, they are held accountable to their shareholders, for whose benefit company directors are usually required to operate. Although their powers vary from country to country, shareholders typically have the authority to appoint the directors, support takeovers, mergers, and acquisitions, and approve capital restructuring. Importantly, they often implicitly approve incentive structures and reward management. Thus, shareholders are in a position to influence the way companies operate in conflict situations.

The following discussion focuses primarily on long-term institutional investors, such as pension funds, life insurance companies, mutual funds, and investment foundations. While individual investors and other actors in the investment arena, such as analysts, investment banks, and credit rating agencies, do play important roles, it is the institutional investors (broadly defined) that have taken a lead in addressing issues relevant to business operations in zones of armed conflict and who are the most dominant and influential forces in the investment sector.[3] Collectively, institutional investors hold a significant proportion of the shares of most publicly listed extractive industry companies and thus have significant influence over their conduct.

Investor Motivation

Fundamental to understanding the role that investors might play in influencing company behavior in conflict zones is the reasons investors might wish to get involved. While most investors are motivated by financial calculations, there is a growing pool of investors (ethical or socially responsible investors) who are also motivated by ethical considerations and considerations of the wider social responsibilities that attend corporate activity. And there is an emerging group of investors (universal investors) who seek to understand social and environmental considerations in the context of long-term financial and economic performance. Each category of investors will have a different set of concerns and motives for supporting conflict-sensitive corporate practices.

Financial investors. For most investors, particularly fiduciary investors, such as pension funds and insurance companies, maximizing investment returns at an acceptable level of risk is paramount. For these investors any argument about corporate conflict sensitivity must center on the "business case," that is, on the potential financial impacts in terms of return and risk for the company as a whole and for shareholder interests. While involvement in conflict zones can offer companies considerable access to cheap assets and opportunities for fast profits, there are a number of reasons that investors may look less favorably on investing in extractive companies operating in high-risk or war-torn countries.[4]

First, armed conflict dramatically increases security and commercial risks for extractive industry companies. Sabotage and attacks on company assets and personnel can significantly disrupt operations and increase costs of and delays in production. Measures to manage these risks, such as enhanced security and insurance, will involve increased costs. Security threats to company staff will also often adversely affect employee motivation and recruitment.

Second, political unrest and armed conflict bring high political risks for extractive industry companies with fixed assets and long-term operating horizons. These include risks of confiscation and expropriation, especially pertinent during wartime and after changes in government.

Third, extractive industry companies in these contexts may face the risk of regulatory or legal intervention. Company involvement in corruption, for example, can lead to temporary or permanent exclusion from the World Bank's lists of acceptable contractors or even to prosecution under national jurisdiction. In particular, an increasing number of litigations have been brought against extractive industry companies operating in repressive regimes and zones of armed conflict,[5] leading to an increased sensitivity within the investment community to consider litigation risk in their investment analysis.

Last, companies face reputation risks from their involvement in conflict. Reputation damage can affect a company not just in the conflict zone but more generally in its home country and other areas of operation. Assessing and valuing reputation is complex. Clearly, reputation is most significant for consumer-oriented companies—those with a significant retail presence or important brands. With a limited consumer presence, reputation among consumers is less of a concern for most companies involved in primary commodity production. But reputation more generally can still be significant for such companies. A damaged reputation can affect employee motivation across the organization and may particularly harm recruitment, compromising a company's ability to attract the best talent (for example, protesters have specifically targeted graduate recruitment events). Reputation can affect relationships with other governments as politicians become wary of becoming associated with tainted companies and this may affect the ability to develop business in other countries. Most significant, a damaged reputation may make other companies reluctant to do business with the company, if their reputation could be damaged by the connection. A growing number of companies are developing supply-chain policies, making them likely to avoid doing business with commodity suppliers with a poor reputation. And as a result of all these pressures, managing reputation risks can be very expensive in terms of management time, diverting focus from other business activities.

From a financial perspective, then, institutional investors have considerable interest in where and how companies they invest in operate. And even if the immediate business case is not apparent to purely financial investors, they may still recognize the importance of good corporate governance generally and may thus be willing to push companies for better management of high-risk activities, as discussed below.

Ethical and socially responsible investors. There is a significant group of investors who explicitly consider ethical and moral issues in addition to purely financial issues in their investment strategies—this is often referred to as "socially responsible investment" (SRI). They include various religious investors, both those investing a congregation's own funds (e.g., various church funds) and those providing products for their followers (e.g., Islamic investment products based on *sharia* law). In addition, there are substantial investments of charities and foundations seeking to ensure that their endowments are managed in accordance with their values. Finally, members of the general public are attracted to "ethical" investment funds, where their money is invested by professional fund managers according to ethical policies that typically screen companies for certain activities or poor policies and practice (see below). The size of the ethical and responsible investment market is substantial—$2.7 trillion globally according to one estimate,[6] and as much as 10 percent of the investment assets under professional management in the United States according to the Social Investment Forum, a Washington-based membership organization of socially responsible investors.[7]

Traditionally, a key issue for these investors has been the promotion of peace and the avoidance of conflict. Many socially responsible investors, for example, avoid investing in armament manufacturers. Increasingly, they are also concerned with limiting human rights abuses and may avoid investing in companies that do business with "oppressive regimes." For example, an important impetus for SRI in the 1980s came from a desire to avoid Western companies operating in the South Africa during the apartheid regime. As will be elaborated below, socially responsible investors are also increasingly involved in corporate governance and engagement with companies.

The divide between socially responsible investing and "mainstream" financial investing has been diminishing as more companies take SRI on board. For example, Insight Investment, the asset management arm of the HBOS group (established through the merger of Halifax and the Bank of Scotland) with over $100 billion under management and traditionally a "mainstream" investor, recognizes that shareholders have substantial powers over companies and thus moral responsibility for what companies do in their name. They exercise that responsibility by providing support and encouragement to companies to comply with global business principles as well as holding companies accountable for their compliance (primarily through a process of "engagement"; see below). HBOS explicitly consults conventions such as the Universal Declaration of Human Rights, the OECD *Guidelines for Multinational Enterprises,* and the International Labour Organization's Tripartite Declaration of Principles to provide authoritative ethical standards to assess the companies in which they invest.[8]

Universal investors. The concept of the "universal investor" is a new view of investment that provides a basis for long-term financial investors to consider social, environmental, and ethical issues in terms of holistic development—thereby providing a bridge between financially focused investment and socially responsible investment and a broader basis for looking at corporate activities in the area of conflict prevention.[9] Developed by academics and independent experts, the argument for the universal investor is that large institutions invest across a wide array of different market sectors and in a growing number of regions. In terms of the investor's fundamental

objective of long-term financial success, the returns on any single investment activity are less significant than the overall impact of that investment
on the growth and success of the economy as a whole. A number of observations follow from this. First, the universal investor is unlikely to approve
of companies that externalize costs. Typically, such costs will fall on society as a whole and so will add to public expenditures that reduce economic
efficiency and slow growth overall, offsetting the benefits and risks to the
company itself. Second, the universal investor can be justified in intervening in political debate, with care, as a long-term, neutral participant seeking
long-term sustainable growth (as well as monitoring the political activities
of investee companies to ensure they are compatible with that goal, rather
than serving only narrow self-interest). Third, the universal investor may
even be prepared to consider broader "quality of life" arguments rather than
looking at narrow financial success when setting its objectives. As armed
conflicts directly harm quality of life, undermine long-term growth, and
potentially create major risks for investors and beneficiaries, the universal
investor has adequate justification to consider explicitly how it can use its
actions and investment decisions to support conflict prevention.

Although the concept of the universal investor is new and far from
widely accepted, a number of major fund managers are considering the
concept and including some of the ideas in their policy statements. For
examples, Hermes, a fund manager that manages and is owned by the BT
pension fund (one of Britain's biggest, formerly British Telecom), launched
its Hermes Principles in 2002. These set its expectations for how companies should be run in the long-term interest of shareholders. A central principle is that "companies should behave ethically and have regard for the
environment and society as a whole." The principles include this statement:
"As a long-term diversified investor, we oppose companies behaving in a
way which knowingly passes costs on to other companies or to the taxpayer, and as such is socially or environmentally unacceptable, or unethical. It
makes no sense if business success is achieved by creating other costs
('externalizing costs') which the beneficial owners of companies will ultimately pay for."[10]

Options for Institutional Investor Leverage

Avoidance. The traditional approach of many ethical investors and SRI
funds has been to avoid investing in companies whose activities or products
they find unacceptable. Armaments have traditionally been one of the key
targets of such exclusions. A more recent innovation in investment exclusion policy is the "worst in class" exclusions used by some Scandinavian
funds, where companies found to be in breach of specific UN conventions
are excluded from the funds' investment portfolio. The Seventh Swedish

Pension Fund (AP7), a state organized pension fund,[11] for instance, has adopted a minimum ethical standard for its portfolio selections, which involves avoiding companies that, in the view of the fund, do not comply acceptably with the requirements of those international conventions to which Sweden is a signatory.[12] A similar policy has been adopted by the National Pension Fund for Municipal Employees (KLP), a Norwegian life insurance and pension manager with around $15 billion under management, whereby KLP applies a minimum ethical standard to all financial investments that excludes companies identified by UN reports to be in violation of human rights, labor rights, and environmental conventions.[13] As a result of these policies, both groups have excluded a small number of companies (thirty-nine for AP7, twenty-two for KLP). These include a number of extractive industry companies for conflict-related issues, such as Chevron Texaco, for alleged human rights abuses committed by the company's security services in Nigeria, and Unocal and TotalFinaElf, for reported cases of forced labor and forced relocation in connection with the companies' pipeline construction project in Burma/Myanmar.[14] Potentially, this approach to exclusion provides a coherent global framework for integrating human rights and conflict-related issues into investment decisions. However, there are practical issues concerning consistency and rigor in implementing these policies, with some critics arguing that the worst corporations are not always those identified for exclusion from investment.

More generally, while avoidance policies may be logical from the perspective of the responsible investor who does not wish to be involved with companies considered objectionable, the impact of avoidance strategies on the market as a whole is often fairly minimal. However, there are some exceptions. First, if avoidance reaches critical mass, as, for instance, with the boycott of companies operating in apartheid South Africa, then it can directly affect how companies behave, at times even causing companies to pull out or apply the so-called Sullivan Principles. Second, if an objectionable activity is only a small part of a company's overall business, the company may prefer to end that activity so as to increase its investor base. Finally, if avoidance is based to some extent on financial criteria, such as the risks posed to shareholder value, then it may send a broader signal to the marketplace about the value of the company, which could lead to a downgrading of its share price or negatively affect its ratings.

Corporate governance and investor engagement. Corporate governance is the system by which business corporations are directed and controlled, including the distribution of rights and responsibilities among the board, the managers, shareholders, and other stakeholders. The issue has gained prominence since the collapse of Enron and other corporate failures have highlighted the importance of transparency and good corporate governance to ensure than companies are well run and accountable to shareholders and society.[15]

While much corporate governance activity focuses on the structure of the board and on activities such as auditing, industry observers and activists have expanded the concept to encompass concerns about the social and environmental impacts of company decisions.[16] Typically, governance on social and environmental activities involves shareholders' asking companies to adopt appropriate policies and to make appropriate disclosures about the company's impacts and management processes. One example of this is the *Disclosure Guidelines on Socially Responsible Investment* issued by the Association of British Insurers (ABI).[17] These voluntary guidelines call on all companies listed on stock exchanges in the United Kingdom to identify and assess the significant social and environmental risks to the company and to disclose policies and procedures to manage such risks. The guidelines were developed taking account of the OECD *Guidelines for Multinational Enterprises*. They have been adopted, explicitly or implicitly, by many UK institutions. They make no explicit mention of conflict, however.

The ABI guidelines build on the so-called Turnbull Report, issued by the Institute of Chartered Accountants of England and Wales in 1999, which recommends that companies listed on the London Stock Exchange establish internal control systems to assess and adequately manage risks and to make these risk strategies public. The report explicitly mentions reputational risks that a company may incur when investing in or operating in a country with a poor human rights record. It does not take a position, however, on whether a company should avoid operations or divest in such settings.[18]

In the United States, an important initiative related to corporate governance and disclosure is that of the Interfaith Center on Corporate Responsibility (ICCR), a grouping of religious investors. One key project of the ICCR has been to develop a set of "Principles for Global Corporate Responsibility," which the ICCR sees as a model for corporate behavior.[19] These principles are specifically relevant with regard to extractive industry companies in zones of conflict. Not only do they explicitly mention additional demands for company disclosure in such settings, but they also include benchmarks for action to be taken by extractive resource companies related to the provision and hiring of security forces (see Box 9.1).

An increasingly important aspect of the corporate governance agenda is that it empowers investors to "engage" with companies based on compliance with principles covering corporate social and environmental responsibility. The process of engagement involves investors'—either individually or collectively—meeting with senior management and expressing their concerns. While an informal process, it can lead to more formal action such as shareholder resolutions and voting decisions, discussed below.

Box 9.1   Principles for Global Corporate Responsibility: Benchmarks for Measuring Business Performance

INTRODUCTION
Reporting Framework
- Additional demands for disclosure impinge on companies operating in zones of conflict.

THE GLOBAL REALITY
Political and Economic Influences

10.   All human activity, including business development and expansion, impacts on the natural environment, the community, and future generations. There are over-riding considerations which ethically constrain this activity in respect of:
- zones of conflict.
- inappropriate exportation of military equipment.

THE WIDER COMMUNITY
Section 1.2. National Communities

1.2.B.2   The company by policy and by practice does not commit or engage in activity which leads to the abuse and violation of internationally recognized human rights standards, nor does it assist in abuses and violations committed by others, be they government authorities, paramilitary organisations, armed gangs or other non-state actors.

1.2.B.3   The company adopts a security policy that protects human rights and is consistent with international standards of law enforcement. (UN Basic Principles on the use of Force and Firearms by Law Enforcement Officials and the UN Code of Conduct for Law Enforcement Officials)

Section 1.4. Indigenous Communities: Principles

1.4.P.2   The company where it operates in post-conflict and/or oppressive situations seeks to implement existing policies of reconciliation where they are in place.

Section 1.5. Resource Extraction

1.5.P.2   The company is careful to control its exploitation, management and extraction of natural resources, especially non-renewable resources, in countries where environmental laws and regulations are inadequate or are improperly enforced, or where there is protracted internal or regional conflict to which the government is a party.

(continues)

Box 9.1   continued

1.5.P.5   Where the company is engaged in the extraction of natural resources in zones of conflict it does not engage governmental or militia forces to provide security but conducts its own independent security operation.

1.5.P.6   The company, if it is unable to provide proper security for its workforce in zones of conflict does not enter into an engagement to conduct such extractive business or if already engaged, it withdraws from such locations.

1.5.C.4   In instances where the extraction of resources either violates human rights or where the extraction can only be carried forward with the aid of military intervention in zones of conflict, the company does not proceed with the work programme.

1.5.C.6   The company does not contract with or collaborate with governmental military authorities or with local militias to facilitate the extraction of natural resources.

1.5.B.5   The company, as a minimum, adheres to the Voluntary Principles on Security and Human Rights to ensure respect for human rights and fundamental freedoms in their security operations.

1.5.B.6   The company has in place policies that prohibit it from accepting protection from governmental military forces or from local militias.

Source: www.bench-marks.org

Engagement is particularly popular among investors in the United Kingdom, where a disproportionate number of extractive industry companies are listed. An example of successful engagement activity was the formation of the Institutional Investor's Group on Burma/Myanmar.[20] This investor initiative, partly prompted by NGOs, was undertaken to promote engagement with the management of the UK company Premier Oil over its operations in Myanmar. This engagement appears to have been influential in persuading Premier Oil to restructure itself and divest from the country in 2002.[21] Importantly, the investor group has continued its engagement work with the Malaysian company Petronas, which bought Premier Oil's Burmese assets, as well as other companies involved in the country—though UK investors are likely to be far less significant investors in Petronas than they were in Premier.

Shareholder resolutions and activism. Moving beyond engagement, investors can actively challenge a company's management by filing special resolutions on specific issues at a company's annual meeting. Shareholder resolutions are typically filed by socially responsibly investors. Organizations such as the ICCR, mentioned earlier, play a prominent role in assisting in the filing of shareholder resolutions in support of shareholder action on social and environmental issues. Sometimes activist groups may buy shares and file resolutions themselves, although mainstream investors have been increasingly willing to become involved in proposing such resolutions. For example, several large pension funds for state employees, such as CalPers (the California Public Employees' Retirement System), have helped file resolutions on social and environmental issues. In the United States, filing resolutions is often used as a tactic to get companies to discuss an issue with shareholders, something that is less necessary in the smaller UK financial community, where management is usually more accessible. While shareholder resolutions rarely gain direct majority support, they are an effective means of signaling issues of shareholder concern to the directors and the management.

There have been several instances of shareholder resolutions that have urged companies to adopt conflict-sensitive policies. Resolutions are often framed in terms of either reporting to shareholders on a specific issue or asking the company to adopt a set of principles. For example, in the 2003 proxy season in the United States, eleven companies, including ExxonMobil, faced the prospect of shareholder resolutions asking them to develop global business policies based on international human rights principles such as the UN Declaration of Human Rights and the International Labour Organization's Declaration on Fundamental Principles and Rights at Work. These resolutions are indicative of investors' concern and, at a minimum, force management to consider the issues and explain to shareholders why they think the resolutions are unjustified.[22]

In the United States, the MacBride Principles, which focus on avoiding discrimination in employment on religious or ethnic grounds in Northern Ireland and aim to help reduce the grievances that fueled that conflict,[23] have been used as a basis for shareholder resolutions. While the extent to which the principles contributed to peace in Northern Ireland is unclear, this experience shows that investors are prepared to call for companies to take actions to reduce the pressures that lead to conflict. Indeed, several components of the MacBride Principles could be adapted to other conflict situations.

In another case, a shareholder resolution was filed in 1997 at Shell Transport and Trading in the United Kingdom concerning its environmental and human rights policies, with specific reference to operations in Nigeria.

The resolution gained the support of shareholders owning 10.5 percent of the votes cast (and abstentions by 6.5 percent)—a significant level for such a resolution. More important, the company implemented most of the resolution's recommendations in the months after the resolution.[24] Similarly, in 2002 two Canadian funds, Real Assets Investment Management and Meritas Mutual Funds, submitted a shareholder resolution with the Canadian energy company Enbridge, calling on the company to adopt measures to avoid becoming complicit in human rights violations committed in relation with the company's operations in Colombia. Enbridge shortly afterward adopted the Voluntary Principles on Security and Human Rights, a set of standards agreed upon by several governments, companies, and NGOs in 2000.[25]

A seminal case of shareholder action, particularly relevant in terms of its links to conflict, is that of the Task Force on Churches and Corporate Responsibility in the case of Talisman Oil and the conflict in Sudan. As growing evidence of serious human rights abuse by the Sudanese military against civilian communities emerged, shareholders became increasingly concerned about Talisman's role. While Talisman was a minority stakeholder in the Greater Nile Consortium, its partnership with and financing of the Sudanese government, as well as allegations that it allowed government security forces use of its infrastructure to conduct raids against civilians, led to the creation in 2000 of the shareholder task force and its filing of a resolution with Talisman seeking assurance that company revenues were not supporting the conflict. The resolution gained 27 percent support at the company's annual meeting in May 2000, the highest support ever for such a resolution in Canada. It also gained the support of two large public employee pension funds in New York, as well as broader public backing. Together, these actions led Talisman to undertake reporting on social responsibility and ultimately to divest from Sudan in 2003.[26]

Supporting research and policy initiatives. Another approach that investors can take to address company conduct in conflict-affected countries is to sponsor research or support policy initiatives that address responsible corporate conduct. Research backed by investors can inform debate, highlight risks, develop analytical frameworks to evaluate companies, and offer practical recommendations. Findings can also be distributed to the media to raise awareness among investors and generate further support. An example, from a different area, is the work that the Universities Superannuation Scheme in the United Kingdom has supported on climate change and institutional investment, which has helped give credibility to investors considering the implications of climate change and enabled the formation of an investor initiative on the subject.[27]

Institutional investors can also lend substantial credibility to policy or business initiatives that seek to address the issue of companies in conflict zones. By far the most relevant example of this sort of initiative occurred in June 2003, when a large group of international institutional investors, representing over $3 trillion in assets, publicly supported the Extractive Industries Transparency Initiative (EITI), an initiative started by the UK government in response to the Publish What You Pay campaign launched by a consortium of NGOs the previous year.[28] The EITI has the objective of increasing transparency over payments and revenues in the extractives sector in countries heavily dependent on these resources. The investors, led by ISIS Asset Management and including such large mainstream investors as Fidelity Investments and Merrill Lynch Investment Managers, made a clear business case for their support of the EITI. In their official statement, they acknowledged that

> it is in the interest of the companies in which we invest to operate in a business environment that is characterized by stability, transparency and respect for the rule of law. . . . We are concerned that extractive companies are particularly exposed to the risks posed by operating in these environments. Companies that make legitimate, but undisclosed, payments to governments may be accused of contributing to the conditions under which corruption can thrive. This is a significant business risk, making companies vulnerable to accusations of complicity in corrupt behavior, impairing their local and global "license to operate," rendering them vulnerable to local conflict and insecurity, and possibly compromising their long-term commercial prospects in these markets.[29]

By calling on the companies they invest in to adopt the principles of the EITI, this group of investors has undoubtedly been useful in strengthening the credibility and efficacy of the EITI, while increasing the incentives for extractive industry companies to endorse the initiative.

Limits to Investor Action

As the above discussion makes clear, shareholders are increasingly prepared to press companies to behave in a more socially responsible manner, both generally and in the area of conflict prevention. Despite considerable progress, however, there are some significant limitations to the effectiveness of shareholder action.

First, not all legal jurisdictions and financial systems support activities such as the filing of resolutions or the intervention of shareholders. The use of shareholder resolutions varies from country to country, reflecting both company regulation in the country and the structure of investment institutions. Shareholder resolutions on social and environmental issues are common in the United States, occasional in the United Kingdom, and relatively uncommon in continental Europe and Asia—partly because such resolutions are the embodiment of the "shareholder model" of capitalism particular to the Anglo-Saxon world.

Second, key to any investor action is the availability of reliable information about company behavior as well as the conflict context. Here, inadequate company disclosure remains a significant impediment. Often shareholders are required to rely on NGOs, whose information on corporate conduct may be biased, contradictory, or incomplete. Information problems are compounded by the fact that conflict issues are only one part of a large number of issues that investors have to consider, so the time and effort that they can spend assessing a particular company operation in a conflict situation is necessarily limited. In many cases, information asymmetries leave investors at a distinct disadvantage, while allowing companies space to deny allegations of wrongdoing or claim that all activities are being properly monitored when the reality is very different.

Third, there is a considerable and ever-growing number of international frameworks for corporate conduct in conflict, such as the nine principles of the UN Global Compact, the OECD *Guidelines for Multinational Enterprises,* the International Labour Organization's Declaration on Fundamental Principles and Rights at Work, the Voluntary Principles on Security and Human Rights, and the United Nations Sub-Commission on Human Rights Norms on the Responsibilities of Transnational Corporations and Other Business Enterprises with Regard to Human Rights. Amid this proliferation of standards, there is widespread debate and confusion about which frameworks are appropriate and authoritative. Likewise, while industry organizations, NGOs, and the UN Global Compact have made progress in developing tools for companies to use in assessing conflict risks, including the impact that companies may have on conflict dynamics, these risk metrics and other diagnostic tools have yet to be fully tried and tested.[30]

Fourth, even where shareholder action succeeds in advocating divestment from zones of conflict, the overall impact on conflict amelioration may be negligible. As in the case of Talisman, which sold its Sudanese assets to India's National Oil Company, listed companies may sell their operations to companies less amenable to shareholder or public pressure, while the problematic investment activity continues unabated.

Last, investor action rarely succeeds in isolation. Pressures from NGOs, governments, and consumer groups are also important in getting companies to change. Again in the case of Talisman, shareholder action was only one part of a broader front of NGO advocacy, official inquiries by the Canadian government (in the form of the so-called 1999 Harker Report on Human Security in the Sudan, which inter alia looked into the alleged complicity of Talisman in human rights abuses committed by the Sudanese government), and the threat of legislative action in the U.S. Congress (a bill was passed in the House of Representatives in 2001 proposing that oil companies operating in Sudan be barred from listing their stocks on U.S. stock exchanges). While shareholder campaigns may seldom effect change on their own, their activism in favor of improved corporate conduct can prevent management from using "shareholder concerns" as an argument against change, while helping to catalyze broader support.

Overall, more effective shareholder efforts to address questionable corporate conduct in conflict situations will require greater transparency and analysis. Developing clearer guidelines for companies operating or considering operating in conflicts in the frameworks mentioned above would give these actions greater coherence and legitimacy. This would provide investors with a tool for assessing company performance and a set of good practices that companies can adopt. There is also scope for improved efforts to educate investors on the nature of companies' involvement in conflict situations and the potential negative impacts of that involvement, including financial risks as well as the risks posed to the affected communities.

Improving Effectiveness: The Role of Regulators and Policymakers

There are several opportunities for regulators and policymakers to encourage and enable investors to actively supervise company conduct in the interests of human rights and conflict prevention. These opportunities are typically nonprescriptive in that they do not tell companies or investors how to act (although they may use compulsory disclosure as a tool for changing behavior), but they aim to make it more possible for investors to address matters such as conflict in their dealings with companies.

Listing rules. Official disclosure ("listing") requirements specify in detail the information that companies are required to provide to investors in order to obtain a listing on a stock exchange. In theory, companies should provide investors with all the information they need to make an accurate assessment of the company. In practice, the provision of information is often limited to financial matters and by the company directors' view of what is "material to" the company. Regulators, such as the Securities and Exchange Commission in the United States and the Financial Services Authority in the United Kingdom, could require greater company disclosure particularly of nonfinancial issues, such as whether a company undertakes conflict impact assessments of its proposed or ongoing activities. At present, however, regulators appear reluctant to consider such issues, particularly in the absence of clear demand from investors, and also because national regulators often have concerns about maintaining their competitiveness as a financial center, which could be harmed by too-onerous requirements.[31]

Official disclosure requirements may be a particularly effective tool for putting pressure on smaller extractive industry companies, given that access to a stock exchange is especially important to their credibility and capital base. Broadening disclosure requirements would also require investment banks to consider issues such as conflict, as they are responsible for bringing companies to the stock exchange and for advising them on the particulars of disclosure requirements. As increasing amounts of investment are managed on an indexed basis—with all listed companies included in the index (allowing for size)—listing requirements have become an essential determinant of investor decisionmaking.

Specific listing requirements usually apply to extractive resource companies.[32] At present, these focus on the technical estimation of reserves. There is a strong case for arguing that disclosure should also include socioeconomic and environmental factors relevant to the exploitability of these reserves—for example, whether the title to the reserves is in dispute or whether local conflicts might make resource extraction problematic. The fact that specific rules exist for minerals companies makes changing listing requirements for such companies both relatively straightforward and fundamentally justifiable. Moreover, as argued by the proponents of the Publish What You Pay campaign, making listing requirements mandatory would help extractive industry companies and host governments to overcome the "collective action problem" that individual companies face when acting unilaterally to promote financial transparency.[33]

Shareholder rights. For investors to act as engaged and responsible shareholders, they need to have appropriate powers. Typical shareholder powers include the ability to vote their shares easily, to propose resolutions at low cost, to attend annual general meetings, and to question the board of directors. Shareholder rights are determined by company law and/or stock exchange or securities regulations (rules regarding shareholder rights form an additional element of listing requirements in some jurisdictions). In some countries, such as the United States, the rules are well established and enable shareholder activism, but in many they are not (for example, launching shareholder resolutions in Canada is generally difficult—Talisman was an exception). To address this, governments should introduce clear and balanced rules for investors and companies on how to lodge resolutions (in terms of time scales, the level of support required, and what is allowable text), and they should be upheld by regulators or by arbitration (rather than by the courts—shareholders are very unlikely to want to use legal action merely to place a resolution).

Supporting socially responsible investment. Importantly, government enactment of relevant legislation or regulation can encourage investors to look beyond short-term financial factors to take account of broader social and environmental issues. For example, a regulation on pension disclosure in the United Kingdom requires pension funds to state their policy, if any, on social and environmental issues and investment.[34] Doing so has compelled pension fund managers to consider such issues and so sensitized them to the broader impacts of investment decisions. Similar regulations have been adopted by a number of other countries, including Australia, France, and Germany.[35] Thus far, such moves have been resisted by many institutional investors concerned that social and environmental issues are incompatible with a traditional understanding of "fiduciary" requirements as stated in trust law or charity law. Yet emerging practice shows that a more extensive definition of shareholder responsibility enables (and even requires) investors to consider broader, long-term issues in making their investment decisions.

Another approach governments can take is to provide financial and political support to organizations that promote socially responsible investment, such as the Association for Sustainable and Responsible Investment in Asia, a multistakeholder organization responsible for promoting SRI in Asia, formed in 2001.[36] Supporting the creation of these associations is particularly desirable in rapidly developing countries, where there is greater potential to develop financial markets according to best practices, and given that a growing number of extractive industry companies from these regions have operations in conflict situations elsewhere. The growth in privatization or partial privatization of state-owned resource companies in many developing countries, and the desire of many such companies to expand their operations overseas, means there is a need for adequate corporate governance structures and investors able to hold these companies to account.

Supporting the business case for conflict-sensitive practices. Ultimately, the key to making institutional investors take greater account of the role of company operations in conflict situations is to strengthen, and make more visible, the business case for investor action, emphasizing the increased risk and reduced return on investments in conflict-affected areas. As discussed elsewhere in this volume, there are a number of legal and policy mechanisms—including the OECD *Guidelines for Multinational Enterprises,* the Extractive Industry Transparency Initiative, and international conventions on bribery and corruption—that governments and international organizations could build upon to strengthen the balance of incentives to make responsible investment pay, while deterring poor performers.

Private-Sector Commercial Banking

In addition to institutional investors, private-sector commercial banks can play an important role in influencing extractive industry behavior in conflict zones. In order to adequately analyze their role, it is important first to distinguish the variety of ways that banks can be involved in conflict and the mechanisms they can apply alongside the provision of services and finance to other companies.

First, it is important to note that banks are both transnational corporations in their own right and financial institutions investing in or providing services and funding to other companies. Second, one can distinguish among domestic banks based in the country where conflict is an issue, multinational banks with substantial operations in the country, and international banks that have only limited operations in the country but provide some services and lending. In addition, offshore banks may play a significant role, either through correspondent relationships with domestic banks or through direct dealing with the ruling elite and others.

Last, banking involvement in conflict settings can be divided into a number of activities: the provision of foreign exchange and money transfer ("moving the money around"), the provision of deposit services ("looking after the money"), the provision of short-term secured finance, such as trade financing, and the provision of long-term capital, most importantly in the form of project finance.

It is beyond the scope of this chapter to discuss the important role of private-sector banking in conflict prevention generally, during conflict, or in postconflict reconstruction.[37] Similarly, the role of banks as companies and their role in "conflict finance," money laundering, and the proceeds of corrupt government deals are only briefly touched upon. Instead, the focus of this section will be on the role of international banks in supporting the extractive industry, particularly as providers of project financing.

Banks as Companies

As transnational corporations, private-sector banks are themselves subject to both the investor pressures discussed in the previous section and some of the policy mechanisms dealt with elsewhere in this volume. Many banks appear keen to be good corporate citizens and, as part of their CSR strategies, have developed guidelines and policies as well as regular CSR reports covering a range of social and environmental issues. Many international banks are well aware of the risks involved in operating in undemocratic or oppressive regimes. For example, local branches can be pressured to support dubious government projects or to provide banking services to the ruling elite for questionable purposes. Increasingly, some banks, such as the Cooperative Bank in the United Kingdom, are choosing not to invest in such regimes and use reports by Amnesty International and Human Rights Watch as the basis for determining what regimes violate human rights as set out by the Universal Declaration of Human Rights.[38] Similarly, Standard

Chartered, one of the most prominent international banks in developing countries, has adopted a statement on operations in oppressive regimes. Standard Chartered stresses the role of investment as a "positive influence for good" in the affected country and, ultimately, its contribution to the raising of living standards in general.[39] Rather than divestment, it has adopted a strategy of positive engagement through dialogue and the provision of training and employment.

A clear area of concern in conflict situations is the financing of arms sales. Here, a number of banks have adopted voluntary policies. Barclays Bank, for instance, has a policy on the defense sector that excludes financing trade in weapons of mass destruction, land mines, or torture equipment and assesses other arms transactions on a case-by-case basis.[40] Aside from this area, however, few banks have comprehensive policies to address the wider range of challenges and risks of operating in conflict situations. Indeed, "conflict" is an issue seldom addressed in their CSR reports. In all, these reports instead focus on a range of positive generic activities in areas such as community investment and charitable joint ventures, as well as equal opportunity and employee training.

Banks as Financial Institutions

As financial institutions, banks operate within a highly regulated framework of national laws and financial regulations, central banking supervision, and international frameworks such as those laid down by the Bank for International Settlements. During periods of conflict, many banking activities, such as long-term lending, will virtually cease. However, short-term lending may continue even in conflict zones, if suitable loan security is available. Other transactions, such as foreign exchange, money transfer, and deposit-taking activities, involve lower risk for the banks and can be particularly lucrative activities, particularly if conflict conditions have reduced competition and increased profitability. In addition, private-sector banks, and particularly offshore banks, play a major role in providing "conflict finance" to combatants by knowingly or unknowingly facilitating the laundering of proceeds from drugs and illegally exploited extractive resources, as well as by serving as repositories of stolen capital of corrupt government elites.[41] In the case of the conflict in the Democratic Republic of Congo (DRC), the final report of the UN Panel of Experts charged with investigating illegal exploitation of natural resources in the DRC identified five banks (Barclays Bank, B.B.L. (Belgium), Belgolaise, Fortis, and Standard Chartered Bank) in its list of businesses considered to be in violation of the OECD *Guidelines for Multinational Enterprises*.[42]

A discussion of the various policy mechanisms and conventions addressing issues of money laundering and terrorist finance is beyond the scope of this chapter. Suffice it to say that the international community has already developed and strengthened policy mechanisms and legislation on money laundering and terrorist finance, as well as the repatriation of stolen assets of the likes of Sani Abacha and Mobutu Sese Seko.[43]

Project Finance and Major Long-Term Lending

According to a survey conducted for the World Bank's Extractive Industries Review, a large number of private-sector banks and other financial institutes participate in financing the extractive industries, particularly the mining sector. Much of the project finance for upstream activities comes from large U.S. and European financial service firms, with significant participation from Canadian, Japanese, and Australian banks.[44]

Motivation. Private-sector banks are generally very cautious about where they invest and have strict risk-management controls, particularly when it comes to long-term lending activities, such as project finance. Given the high vulnerability of extractive industry projects to the various risks identified above, private-sector banks will typically look to political risk guarantees or the involvement of international financial institutions, such as multilateral development banks or export credit agencies, to lower their own exposure. In practice, private-sector banks are unlikely to provide long-term lending directly to companies for projects in conflict zones without the involvement of such public agencies. The rules and standards of those agencies are thus often critical to lending in such situations.[45]

Regarding banks' consideration of social and environmental issues in their lending practices, one survey suggests that motivation for doing so is mixed. Many of the larger banks still hold a traditional view of corporate-level environmental and social policies as "corporate philanthropy" or "public relations" activities. Others see them as a way for companies to gain a competitive edge in a market that increasingly values "green" companies. A number of banks, however, are starting to see them through the prism of risk reduction and mitigation.[46] Particularly in financing controversial projects, including those in the extractive industries, lending decisions of banks can be influenced by the reputational risks that such activities can create. Banks with large retail franchises are increasingly sensitive to issues that could upset their customers. For example, Citigroup faced criticism and even the threat of a shareholder resolution over its involvement in supporting the Three Gorges dam in China.[47]

Options for action. Banks that provide long-term project finance have a number of options to influence company behavior through their own internal lending rules or policies. First and foremost, banks will typically assess political and conflict risk and either factor it into interest rate pricing or avoid lending altogether. They may impose "covenants"—formal requirements on the conduct of the project—to protect their interests. They can also seek guarantees and other expressions of support from national governments, parent companies, and international organizations.

Partly in recognition of the reputation risks and in response to pressure from campaigning groups and other organizations, a group of international private-sector banks launched the Equator Principles in June 2003. This voluntary initiative, developed in close cooperation with the International Finance Corporation (IFC), established a framework for addressing the social and environmental issues surrounding lending to controversial projects. The principles are based on the range of World Bank and IFC guidelines for environmental and social impact assessment.[48]

Banks that have signed the Equator Principles promise to ensure that loans to projects with medium to high social or environmental impacts ("Category A" projects) are made only if an environmental assessment has been carried out.[49] This assessment should address a range of factors, including socioeconomic impacts, land acquisition and land use, and involuntary resettlement and other impacts on indigenous peoples and communities. Where appropriate, the borrower is required to prepare a management plan, laying out how these issues are to be dealt with. Significantly, the banks have agreed to include stipulations in their loan conditions to ensure that where the borrowing company fails to follow up its environmental and social management plans or otherwise fails to remedy associated problems, the banks can declare the loans in default. Thus the banks have effective leverage in both the project design and execution phases to insist upon borrower compliance with the standards established.

The Equator Principles mark a significant step forward in addressing the social and environmental issues surrounding lending to controversial projects. As a set of standards complementary to those of the World Bank and the International Monetary Fund, the Equator Principles essentially extend the remit of such guidelines to most major international infrastructure and extractive industry projects. However, for NGOs and social investors they mark only a first step, and there is concern about adequate enforcement, transparency, and review mechanisms.[50] Furthermore, the Equator Principles make no explicit mention of armed conflict. Clearly, there is scope to extend the principles in this direction, but this may require action by the World Bank as well as concerted support by the international community.

Some time will be needed to assess the effectiveness of the Equator Principles to improve corporate behavior. Their first major test came in early 2004 with the $3.6 billion Baku-Tbilisi-Ceyhan oil pipeline project. Because implementation of the project required resolution of sensitive environmental and social issues, banks categorized it as a Category A project.[51] In due course, it may become appropriate to consider whether there is a need for a broader regulatory approach to reinforce such actions, for example, by requiring greater disclosure by banks of the social and environmental aspects of project lending or, more powerfully, by creating mechanisms to give advantages to banks that use the Equator Principles, such as making capital adequacy requirements reflect whether social and environmental assessments have been carried out.

In addition to addressing social and environmental issues in their own lending practice, some banks provide support to emerging policy initiatives on issues related to armed conflict. One example is the UN Environmental Programme's Financial Institutions Initiative (UNEPFI), which was founded in 1992 to engage the financial sector in a dialogue on sustainable development.[52] In September 2003 UNEPFI organized a roundtable on financial institutions and armed conflict, which was attended by a number of banks and investors. This meeting was preceded by a high-level symposium hosted by the Hong Kong Shanghai Banking Corporation (HSBC) the year before.[53]

Conclusion

Working with private financial institutions presents considerable opportunity to leverage existing actions and to develop new, sustainable, and socially beneficial approaches to dealing with the challenges and perils of doing business in conflict zones. Clearly, working with investment institutions and private-sector banks is at best an indirect approach to addressing the natural resource dimension of conflict, particularly the role of companies in such settings. However, while rarely involved as principal actors, in many cases investors and banks are able to exert considerable influence over the companies and individuals directly involved in the extraction of and trade in natural resources, so often at the heart of armed conflict. While any actions, to be effective, should be well designed and sensitive to the needs of banks and investors, a more concerted effort to bring investors and banks into multistakeholder efforts will allow them to better contribute to conflict prevention and mitigation.

The decisionmaking dynamics of institutional investors and private-sector banks are fundamentally long term in nature, although short-term pressures undoubtedly play a part. Thus these institutions will generally view conflict as disruptive to their investment plans and will have an interest in avoiding and minimizing conflict risks. They are likely to be sympathetic to measures to preempt conflict, although any proposed measure will need to be in harmony with day-to-day business priorities. At present, both institutional investors and banks are aware of the risks of investing in conflict-torn settings and increasingly, too, of some of the ways that private economic activities can give rise to or exacerbate conflict. Banks routinely assess conflict risk as part of lending decisions, particularly when financing long-term projects. While traditional risk analysis—analysis focusing on the impact of conflict on profits—continues to dominate, a growing number of investors are taking into account the social and environmental policies and behavior of companies they invest in.

Thus far, most of these concerns remain in the realm of social and environmental responsibility and, increasingly, human rights. However, on occasion investors have taken action on corporate involvement in conflict situations, including engaging with company management and using shareholder resolutions on corporate involvement in conflict regions. Investors have also occasionally spoken in support of policy measures and other actions, including the Extractive Industries Transparency Initiative. Banks have developed a range of policies covering conflict-related transactions, particularly concerning arms sales but also on relevant activities such as bribery and corruption and on large-scale infrastructural projects that risk broad social and environmental impacts.

While not insignificant, the leverage power of the private financial market to improve responsible business conduct in vulnerable and conflict-affected areas is still limited. Maximizing its potential will require complementary policy and regulatory efforts that together make a clear business case for improved corporate behavior. For both banks and investors, there are key challenges to both accessing information on business activity with a conflict dimension and understanding what is effective in terms of conflict prevention. Support by NGOs and governments to promote a better understanding of the complex dynamics of doing business in conflict settings and of the impact of business on conflict dynamics would be a useful first step. Beyond this, officially sponsored information gathering on corporate activity in conflict zones would be a useful service, if the information is well researched and authenticated. Financial institutions already use many of the existing international protocols and principles supported by international organizations, including the World Bank Guidelines, the Equator Principles, the Global Compact, the OECD *Guidelines for Multinational Enterprises,* and the Global Reporting Initiative. Each of these could be usefully expanded to address its relevance and utility in conflict settings.

Governments, regulators, and institutional investors could work to encourage corporate social responsibility at financial institutions generally, as well as supporting the promotion of socially responsible investment and active corporate governance, particularly in developing regions where these are relatively new concepts and not well established. They can do this by supporting industry associations, by encouraging and highlighting good practice, and by appropriate regulation (for instance, to ensure that investors can practically propose shareholder resolutions). Such activities should be encouraged to address conflict explicitly as an issue when appropriate.

For banks and investors, making the dangers of involvement in conflict clearer, in terms of the risks to their investments, is an important step. Measures could include the ability to hold companies liable internationally for their involvement in breaches of human rights and the ability of properly democratic governments to challenge long-term resource exploitation agreements forged by corrupt predecessors.

Finally, if appropriate, more formal action could be taken by regulators. In the investment area, regulators could require extractive industry companies, as a condition for their admission to listing on stock exchanges, to provide socioeconomic and environmental analyses of reserves as well as purely technical estimates. In the banking area, existing money-laundering regimes could be extended to deal with transactions related to conflict situations. Capital adequacy and risk-management requirements could be modified to provide incentives to banks to conduct thorough assessments of conflict and other socioeconomic risks.

Notes

1. See, for example, John Mitchell, ed., *Companies in a World of Conflict* (London: Earthscan, 1998); and Jessica Banfield, Virginia Haufler, and Damien Lilly, *Transnational Corporations in Conflict Prone Zones: Public Policy Responses and a Framework for Action* (London: International Alert, 2003).

2. See Philippe Le Billon, "Getting It Done: Instruments of Enforcement," in Ian Bannon and Paul Collier, eds., *Natural Resources and Violent Conflict: Options and Actions* (Washington, D.C.: World Bank, 2003), pp. 263–267.

3. Investment rules and practice vary significantly from country to country, and a full survey is beyond the scope of this chapter. While the chapter endeavors to take an international perspective, it concentrates on the United States, as the largest investment market, and the United Kingdom, as a market particularly significant to investment in international extractive industry companies.

4. See, for example, Ashley Campbell, *The Private Sector and Conflict Prevention Mainstreaming: Risk Analysis and Conflict Impact Assessment Tools for Multinational Corporations* (Ottawa: Country Indicators for Foreign Policy, 2002) pp. 11–12; and John Bray, "Attracting Reputable Companies to Risky Environments: Petroleum and Mining Companies," in Bannon and Collier, *Natural Resources and Violent Conflict*, pp. 291–294 (see note 2).

5. See also Chapter 16 by Paul Hoffman in this volume.

6. Russell Sparkes, *Socially Responsible Investment: A Global Revolution* (London: John Wiley, 2002), p. 389.

7. Social Investment Forum (SIF), *2003 Report on Socially Responsible Investing Trends in the United States* (Washington, D.C.: SIF, December 2003), p. i, available at www.socialinvest.org/areas/research/trends/sri_trends_report_2003.pdf.

8. See www.insightinvestment.com/Corporate/responsibility/investor_responsibility_home.asp.

9. See James P. Hawley and Andrew T. Williams, *The Rise of Fiduciary Capitalism: How Institutional Investors Can Make Corporate America More Democratic* (Philadelphia: University of Pennsylvania Press, 2000); and Robert A. G. Monks, *The New Global Investors: How Shareholders Can Unlock Prosperity Worldwide* (Oxford: Capstone, 2001).

10. Principle 9 states: "Companies should manage effectively relationships with their employees, suppliers and customers and with others who have a legitimate interest in the company's activities." See "The Hermes Principles," Hermes Investment Management, 2002, available at www.hermes.co.uk/corporate-governance/PDFs/Hermes_Principles.pdf.

11. Note that a number of large pension funds are for public-sector workers and others and are sponsored and administered by public-sector bodies. However, they are held separately on behalf of specific individuals and ring-fenced from public finance, so they can be regarded as part of private finance for the purposes of this discussion.

12. See AP7, *2002 Annual Report,* pt. 1, available at www.ap7.se/pdf/Annual_report_2002_1.pdf.

13. See www.klp.no.

14. AP7, *2002 Annual Report,* pp. 19–20.

15. See, for example, Organization for Economic Cooperation and Development (OECD), *Behind the Corporate Veil: Using Corporate Entities for Illicit Purposes* (Paris: OECD, 2001).

16. See, for example, Michelle Leighton, Naomi Roht-Arriaza, and Lyuba Zarsky, *Beyond Good Deeds: Case Studies and a New Policy Agenda for Corporate Accountability* (Berkeley: California Global Corporate Accountability Project, 2002).

17. See www.abi.org.uk/Display/File/38/SRI_Guidelines.doc.

18. See Bray, "Attracting Reputable Companies to Risky Environments," p. 302; and Institute for Chartered Accountants in England and Wales (ICAEW), *Internal Control: Guidance for Directors on the Combined Code* (London: ICAEW, 1999); and ICAEW, *Implementing Turnbull: A Boardroom Briefing* (London: ICAEW, 1999).

19. The principles were originally developed by the ICCR together with the Ecumenical Council for Corporate Responsibility (ECCR) of the United Kingdom and the Taskforce on the Churches and Corporate Responsibility (TCCR) of Canada (now KAIROS-Canada), and now they also involve the participation of groups in the Southern Hemisphere.

20. See ISIS Asset Management, *Responsible Engagement Overlay,* Quarterly reo® Report, 3rd quarter 2002, p. 18, available at www.isisam.com.

21. Terry Macalister, "Premier Oil Gets out of Burma/Myanmar," *Guardian,* September 17, 2002.

22. The other companies were Alcoa, Colgate-Palmolive, Delphi Automotive Systems, Dillard Department Stores, Hasbro, Home Depot, Procter and Gamble, Stride Rite, Wal-Mart, and Visteon. See the ICCR's website, www.iccr.org.

23. The MacBride Principles include practical measures that recognize the need to go beyond a simple equal opportunity policy, such as affirmative action in training policies. In the 2003 proxy season five U.S. corporations faced resolutions asking them to adopt the MacBride Principles (Baker Hughes, Crane, Raytheon, TJX, and YUM! Brands). See www.iccr.org/products/proxy_book02/gca/macbride.htm.

24. For the text of the resolution, see www.pirc.co.uk/shell4.htm.

25. See www.socialinvestment.ca/News&Archives/news-302-Enbridge.htm. For the U.S.-UK Voluntary Principles, see www.state.gov/www/global/human_rights/001220_fsdrl_principles.html.

26. Prepared from reports and news releases from the Social Investment Organization of Canada; see www.socialinvestment.ca/news.htm, the TCCR's Talisman-Sudan project at www.web.net/~tccr/CorpResp/Talisman.htm, and the KAIROS website (successor organization to the TCCR), www.kairoscanada.org/english/programme/sudankit.htm.

27. See Mark Mansley and Andrew Dlugolecki, "Climate Change: A Risk Management Challenge for Institutional Investors," published and commissioned by the Universities Superannuation Scheme, London, 2001.

28. By February 2004, this group of institutional investors represented $6.9 trillion; see www.publishwhatyoupay.org/releases/british_release_022604.pdf. For more on the Publish What You Pay campaign and the EITI, see also Chapter 11 by Gavin Hayman and Corene Crossin in this volume.

29. See www.dfid.gov.uk/News/News/files/eiti_draft_report_investors.pdf.

30. See, for example, Campbell, *Private Sector and Conflict Prevention Mainstreaming*; International Alert, Centre on Environmental, Economic, and Social Policy, and International Institute for Sustainable Development, *Conflict Risk and Impact Assessment: Towards the Integration of Conflict Assessment and Prevention in Extractive Industry Practice,* Project Note, March 13, 2003, available at www.iisd.org/pdf/2003/natres_cria_project_brief.pdf; and UN Global Compact, *Global Compact Business Guide for Conflict Impact Assessment and Risk Management* (New York: Global Compact, 2002), available at www.unglobalcompact.org/Portal/Default.asp.

31. Listing requirements are determined primarily by national authorities, and there are some variations in disclosure requirements between countries, although there is also much commonality, particularly in broad principles. Increasingly, however, listing requirements are being coordinated by the International Organization of Securities Commissions (IOSCO), and recognition by the IOSCO of the need for broader disclosure requirements to include conflict and other nonfinancial aspects would be very effective in encouraging change. For a fuller discussion, see Mark Mansley, *Open Disclosure: Sustainability and the Listing Regime* (London: Claros Consulting, 2003).

32. See, for example, in the United States, the Securities Act Industry Guides published by the Securities and Exchange Commission, or in the United Kingdom, chapter 19 of the Listing Rules published by the Financial Services Authority.

33. See, for example, www.publishwhatyoupay.org/appeal; and Global Witness, *Time for Transparency: Coming Clean on Oil, Mining, and Gas Revenues* (London: Global Witness, 2004), p. 6.

34. The Occupational Pensions Schemes (Investment and Assignment, Forfeiture, Bankruptcy, etc., Amendment Regulations 1999; Statutory Instrument 1999, no. 1849).

35. See, for example, Annette Yunus, "How Responsible Is Socially Responsible Investment?" paper presented at the Workshop on Issues in Pension Reform, Sydney, March 4–5, 2002, pp. 10–15, available at www.pensions-policy.org/papers/sydney/SRI.doc.

36. See www.asria.org.

37. For more on these issues, see, for example, Tony Addison, Philippe Le Billon, and S. Mansoob Murshed, "Finance in Conflict and Reconstruction,"

Journal of International Development 13, no. 7 (2001): 951–964; and Tony Addison, *Conflict and Financial Reconstruction,* Finance and Development Briefing Papers, March 2002, available at www.devinit.org/findev/BriefNote.pdf.

38. See www.co-operativebank.co.uk/ethics/ethicalpolicy_policy_revised_human.html.

39. See www.standardchartered.com/global/csr/hr_or.html.

40. See www.personal.barclays.co.uk/BRC1/jsp/brccontrol?task=articlesocial&value=3675&site=pfs.

41. For a discussion, see, for example, Jonathan M. Winer, *Illicit Finance and Global Conflict,* Fafo Report no. 380 (Oslo: Fafo Institute, 2002); and Valpy FitzGerald, *Global Financial Information, Compliance Incentives, and Conflict Funding,* Queen Elizabeth House Working Paper no. 96 (Oxford: University of Oxford, 2003).

42. United Nations Security Council, *Final Report of the Panel of Experts on the Illegal Exploitation of Natural Resources and Other Forms of Wealth of the Democratic Republic of the Congo,* S/2002/1146, October 16, 2002, pp. 7–11. See also Rights and Accountability in Development (RAID), *Unanswered Questions: Companies, Conflict, and the Democratic Republic of Congo* (London: RAID, 2004), pp. 73–81, available at www.oecdwatch.org.

43. Jonathan M. Winer and Trifin J. Roule, "Follow the Money: The Finance of Illicit Resource Extraction," in Bannon and Collier, *Natural Resources and Violent Conflict,* pp. 161–214 (see note 2). See also Chapters 4 by Jonathan Winer and 5 by Sue Eckert in this volume.

44. Richard Everett and Andrew Gilboy, "Impact of the World Bank's Social and Environmental Policies on Extractive Companies and Financial Institutions," report submitted to the Extractive Industry Review Secretariat (Washington, D.C.: Associates for Global Change, 2003), p. 33, available at www.eireview.org/eir/eirhome.nsf/englishmainpage/about?Opendocument.

45. See also Chapter 10 by Nick Hildyard in this volume.

46. Everett and Gilboy, "Impact of the World Bank's Social and Environmental Policies," p. 45.

47. See, for example, the proposed resolution at www.trilliuminvest.com/pages/activism/activism_resdetail.asp?ResolutionID=14.

48. For details of IFC guidelines, see http://ifcln1.ifc.org/ifcext/enviro.nsf/Content/EnvironmentalGuidelines.

49. The full Equator Principles are available at www.equator-principles.com/principles.shtml.

50. See www.socialfunds.com/news/article.cgi/1140.html.

51. See www.equator-principles.com/btc.shtml.

52. See http://unepfi.net. See also UN Environmental Programme (UNEP), *Finance, Mining, and Sustainability: Exploring Sound Investment Decision Processes* (Paris: UNEP, 2002), available at www.mineralresourcesforum.org/workshops/finance_wp/docs_slides/financereport.pdf.

53. See UNEP, *Investing in Stability: Conflict Risk, Markets, and the Bottom-Line,* Background Paper (Geneva: UNEP Finance Initiative, 2003), available at www.unepfi.net. See also www.iisd.org/pdf/2003/natres_investing_stability.pdf.

10

Export Credit Agencies
and Corporate Conduct
in Conflict Zones

Nicholas Hildyard

Many companies operating overseas, including those in the extractive industry sector, routinely seek to reduce the financial risks of their operations, including the risks of project failure due to conflict, through the government-backed export credits and investment guarantees offered by public export credit agencies (ECAs). Set up by governments to assist companies in exporting capital and project-related goods and services, ECAs are public agencies that typically provide export finance in the form of government-backed loans, guarantees, and insurance to private corporations from their home country to do business abroad.

The oil, mining, and gas sectors—industries often associated with repressive regimes, political instability, and violent conflict—have long been major recipients of official export credit support. Extractive industry projects in countries prone to, experiencing, or emerging from armed conflict that have received such support include the Lihar gold and OK Tedi copper mines in Papua New Guinea, the Freeport McMoRan gold mine in Indonesia, the Chad-Cameroon pipeline project, and the Baku-Tbilisi-Ceyhan pipeline project in the Caspian region.[1] Without such export finance, many large-scale private-sector extractive and extractive-related infrastructure projects in developing countries would not attract investment or project finance from private financial markets—quite simply, the risks would be considered too high.[2] ECA involvement provides "comfort" to would-be private-sector investors in the form of an assurance that the project has the backing of institutions with sufficient political muscle to ensure that debts and contracts will be honored by the host country. As such, ECAs also have the broad potential to promote corporate responsibility among those companies that apply for ECA benefits and services, including those operating in zones of conflict.

This chapter begins with a brief description of the rationale of ECA support for companies investing in resource extraction, infrastructure, and related projects in developing countries and explains why the demand for ECA support has increased in recent decades. It then assesses the direct and indirect influence that ECAs can have on conflict dynamics through the political and financial support they provide to companies operating in areas of conflict or in repressive regimes. The second section reviews the deficiencies of ECAs' current screening and lending procedures as well as the Export Credit Working Group of the Organization for Economic Development and Cooperation (OECD) (the body where the rules for ECAs of OECD member states are negotiated) and national governments. Much of the discussion will be based on how ECAs currently address social and environmental issues, exemplified on a national level by the United Kingdom's ECA. The third section considers the reform agenda set out primarily by nongovernmental organizations (NGOs) in terms of the potential leverage that ECAs as well as the banking industry could bring to bear on companies to assess the impacts of their activities on conflict and to take measures aimed at reducing their conflict potential. Overall, the case made here is that ECAs require deep-rooted reform if they are to be a positive force for sustainable development, human rights, and conflict prevention. Indeed, there is an urgent need to reclaim them for their potential to contribute to the common good.[3]

Export Credit Agencies, Companies, and Armed Conflict

Numerous studies show that extractive industry operations often knowingly or unknowingly exacerbate or trigger violent conflict, particularly in countries where company operations are predicated on active collaboration with repressive regimes or become associated with widespread environmental damage, corruption, human rights abuse, and poor labor relations.[4] The resulting local grievances may escalate into strikes, factory occupations, consumer boycotts, civil disobedience, and even violent resistance that can flare up into active armed conflict.[5]

Containing Risks

Armed conflict carries the risk of degrading or even destroying a company's financial value. Managing that risk is "the business of business." Most companies are thus concerned with developing strategies to contain conflict-related risks. Despite the high financial costs that can result when their

operations become embroiled in conflict,[6] very few companies have policies that would commit them to taking an active role in ensuring that their
operations minimize the potential for conflict.[7] On the contrary, the accent
is principally on "managing conflict"—even at the cost of prolonging it by
actively collaborating with repressive regimes—rather than seeking to
address its root causes.[8]

Management strategies to deal with such risks tend to take many
forms, but historically they have been primarily aimed at achieving four
ends: fostering a policy environment favorable to the company's interests;
ensuring the backing of state power to enforce that policy environment;
using public relations to manage the public's perception of company-gener-
ated conflicts[9]; and parceling off as many of the financial risks as possible
in order to minimize the damage caused when a conflict can no longer be
managed. ECAs play a vital role in realizing this fourth prong of corporate
risk strategy. For companies operating in high-risk areas, including zones
of armed conflict, the option of obtaining medium- to long-term investment
or export credit insurance from the private financial market is often not
available.[10] Yet without such insurance, many commercial banks are
unwilling to loan debt finance, as the risks of project failure are too high.[11]

ECAs provide companies with an attractive option. Established with
the specific mission of promoting national exports, ECAs have the prime
purpose of protecting companies against the commercial and political risks
of operating abroad. Such "country risks" include political violence or outright war, nationalization and expropriation, a moratorium on external debt,
a break-off in trade relations, foreign exchange shortages, the risk that the
project will not be completed or is not commercially viable, insolvency of
the buying institution, a refusal by the buying institution to pay, or interference with the project by the importing government. ECAs are not only willing to take on many risks that the market is unwilling to bear; they are also
able to do so at premiums that are typically below those that private financial institutes would offer in such cases.[12] In addition, ECA credits and
investment insurance come with a bonus that the private sector cannot provide: the political backing of governments that companies can call upon to
enforce contracts and ensure that they get paid for services provided.

The system is simple. To obtain an export credit guarantee, for example, the exporter takes out insurance with an ECA, which undertakes to pay
the exporter for the exported goods and services should the importer default
on payment. The financial liabilities of ECAs as public entities are under-
written, in the final event, by national governments. In theory, taxpayers'
money is not at risk since ECAs are required to cover any losses they incur
from the premiums charged to companies for the services ECAs provide.[13]
For companies and the banks that finance them, the advantages are obvious. As *Euromoney* comments: "Bankers are always very secretive about

the precise structuring of their deals, but essentially the strategy is simple. The key is to get as high a return as possible, while palming the risk off on somebody else. That is why you should never listen when people tell you that export credit agencies are . . . dinosaurs. What could be nicer in times of turmoil than having the risk picked up by the taxpayer."[14]

While there are wide variations among the policies of national ECAs, they typically provide credits, insurance, and project finance. The services provided by the UK Export Credits Guarantee Department (ECGD) are indicative:

- *Buyer credits.* These allow a UK exporting company to be paid by a UK bank upon delivery of the goods or services to the country concerned. The ECGD guarantees the UK bank both full repayment of the loan made and a reasonable rate of return.
- *Supplier credits.* These allow a UK exporter to pass on payment risks to the UK bank involved and to get paid quickly and in full as soon as goods or services are delivered or services performed, rather than having to wait until the overseas buyer can raise the funds.
- *Lines of credit.* These allow UK exporters to set up finance packages with buyer institutions to finance a series of contracts for either goods or services. A line of credit is put in place before the contract is signed and is therefore quick, as well as being available for contracts that are worth as little as $32,000.
- *Overseas investment insurance.* This is primarily political risk insurance on equity or loan investments made by a UK company in an overseas business or on a bank loan made to an overseas company. These political risks include expropriation, war, restrictions on remittances, and in some cases breach of undertaking. According to the ECGD, one of the many advantages of this scheme is that if a political event were to interfere with a business in which a UK company had an investment, the support of the UK government for the project would mean that the matter would hopefully be resolved before the investor needed to make a claim. That is, diplomatic pressure would be brought to bear to ensure the smooth running of the company.
- *Project finance.* Typically, this covers large projects from which revenues are relied upon for repayment and for which the assets and contracts involved are used as security. The involvement of the ECGD often enables UK banks and businesses to find further financing from other sources. Such large projects requiring project finance typically take several years to complete and are expensive.[15]

In some cases, national ECAs supply both investment insurance and export credits. In others, the two forms of risk insurance are separated out between different institutions. In the United States, for example, the Export-Import Bank (Ex-Im Bank) provides export credits, while the Overseas Private Investment Corporation (OPIC) provides investment insurance. Likewise in Germany, Hermes supplies export credits while Kreditanstalt für Wiederaufbau (KfW) provides export insurance. Germany also uses PwC Deutsche Revision, an affiliate of the international accounting firm PricewaterhouseCoopers, to administer the federal government's Overseas Investment Insurance Guarantee Scheme jointly with Hermes.

The Increasing Importance of Export Credit Agencies

Worldwide, there are now some seventy-six ECAs in sixty-two countries; fifty-one of them are members of the Berne Union, the international trade association for export and investment insurance business.[16] ECAs are responsible for providing 80 percent of gross capital market financing from private sources for developing countries, as few companies will operate in those countries without ECA support.[17] Between 1995 and 2002, every major commitment over $20 million by a Western commercial bank to companies operating in or trading with poor countries had some form of official public guarantee.[18] Indeed, ECAs are now the largest source of public finance for private-sector projects in the world, currently underwriting 10 percent of global exports from large industrial countries.[19] In 2000, ECAs were providing a total of $500 billion in guarantees and insurance to companies operating in developing countries and issued $58.8 billion worth of new export credits that year alone.[20] This compares to a total of $60 billion given out globally in overseas development assistance that year and the $41 billion provided as loans by multilateral development banks (MDBs), such as the World Bank or the Asian Development Bank, in 2000.[21]

The focus of many ECAs over the past decades has been on sectors with concentrated wealth and resources—notably oil, mining, and gas.[22] Despite the poor record of the extractive industries in alleviating poverty, and growing concern about their deleterious impacts in conflict zones, support for the sector is increasing in many countries. In the United Kingdom, for example, ECA credits for power generation and energy projects rose from 42 percent in 1999–2000 to 47 percent in 2001–2002. In 2002, oil and gas projects constituted 13 percent of new business, and mining projects constituted 2 percent.[23] While hopeful of expanding its support for oil and gas—describing the prospects for major future business as "promising"[24]—the ECGD foresees future demand for its support in the sector as "likely to be stable."[25]

Two trends have combined to make ECAs the "comfort blanket" of choice for private-sector infrastructure developers, be they in the extractive sector or in other areas of the global economy. The first is the increasing privatization of infrastructure development, with the developers rather than governments raising the capital for construction primarily through equity or loans from private banks. In the 1960s and 1970s, the lead role in funding infrastructure development was primarily taken by MDBs, such as the World Bank, via concessionary loans to host governments that planned, commissioned, and financed the projects. Since the 1980s, however, there has been a shift away from state-led infrastructure development toward private-sector financing and ownership. The increasing privatization of infrastructure development has meant that construction and engineering companies have been forced to take on financial risks that, in government-sponsored projects, were previously borne by the state. In the absence of taxpayer support, these risks could potentially threaten shareholder profits and may make raising the necessary finance more difficult. Commercial banks, in particular, have proved extremely reluctant to back large-scale private-sector infrastructure projects without investment insurance from ECAs.[26]

The second trend is the adoption by other funding sources, such as the World Bank, of mandatory standards on environment and development. This makes them a less attractive source of financial support for infrastructure companies, which see their standards as time-consuming red tape that adds to project costs by delaying implementation.[27] Although the World Bank and several other MDBs have formed private-sector arms, notably the International Finance Corporation (IFC) and the Multilateral Investment Guarantee Agency (MIGA), which lend directly to the private sector rather than to governments,[28] the funds offered by them are relatively small and support is conditional upon projects' meeting World Bank environmental and social standards, ruling out (or making more difficult) support for a wide range of projects. By contrast, the services provided by national ECAs have, until recently, come with virtually no social and environmental conditions.[29] Tellingly, and most significant from the perspective of conflict prevention and mitigation, not a single ECA has any mandatory human rights standards, and many remain reluctant even to consider human rights in their lending decisions. Although the financial due diligence procedures undertaken by ECAs do consider the risk that conflict may pose to a project, the risks that the project poses for conflict are not routinely assessed.

ECA Lending and Armed Intrastate Conflict

ECAs can have both direct and indirect impacts on conflict dynamics. For instance, failed ECA-backed projects impose a particularly onerous debt burden on developing countries, given that export credit debt is charged at commercial rates of interest, not the lower rates incurred by bilateral or multilateral loans.[30] One-quarter of the $2.2 trillion debt owed by developing countries and one-half of all debt owed by developing countries to official creditors is owed to ECAs.[31] Inevitably, the debt burden incurred through ECA-supported projects acts to the detriment of poverty alleviation by reducing the scope for public investment in health care, education, and community development programs and adoption of environmentally sustainable technologies.[32] Yet with the notable exception of the United Kingdom's ECGD, few ECAs consider the debt sustainability impacts of the projects they support.

More directly, however, ECAs provide finance or insurance to private companies whose operations may fuel conflict or exacerbate existing tensions in the host country. In some cases, conflict may arise from the direct impacts of a project on the environment or the local economy. In others, the impacts are more diffuse, interacting with wider local, regional, and even international power imbalances and governance failures. Yet as briefly described below, there are numerous instances where conflict has been associated with ECA-backed projects, particularly in the defense, hydropower, and extractive industries. These brief descriptions demonstrate the many weaknesses of current ECA financing arrangements in ensuring that ECAs do not support companies whose activities have deleterious environmental, human rights, and security impacts. In so doing, however, the examples given also highlight both the need and the potential for change within ECAs in terms of the sectors, types of projects, and areas of trade they support, while suggesting which conditions they might attach to their support of overseas projects to promote responsible corporate conduct.

ECAs and the arms trade. ECAs play a major role in the global arms trade. UK support for the defense sector, for example, constituted 30 percent of the ECGD's business from 1997 to 2002,[33] while more than a third of the guarantees given by France's COFACE are for the arms industry.[34] An exception is the U.S. Ex-Im Bank, which does not support arms sales. Instead, guarantees for U.S. arms exports are provided through the Foreign Military Financing Program and the Defense Export Loan Guarantee Program.[35]

As Ann Feltham of Campaign Against Arms Trade points out, "Arms and weapons may not in themselves cause war, but they can certainly prolong one and make it bloodier. Nor do arms necessarily lead to human rights violations, but they can assist them."[36] Much depends on whom the arms are sold to and in what political context. It is thus of particular concern that the major clients for many ECA-backed arms deals have been regimes that are recognized to be repressive. For example, Britain's ECGD has backed arms sales to Iraq, Indonesia (which at the time was deploying death squads in East Timor), Saudi Arabia, and Turkey[37]—all countries with human rights records that have been subject to international criticism and, in the case of Turkey, condemnation by the Council of Europe.[38] Not only do these arms sales send a message of political approval for the recipient government—often extending the life of repressive regimes—but there is also well-documented evidence that arms backed by ECAs have been directly used to suppress dissent. In the case of Indonesia, for example, Hawk "trainer" jets sold by the UK-based BAe Systems to the Suharto regime were used to bomb villagers in East Timor, where the Indonesian armed forces were engaged in a brutal war to crush popular resistance to Indonesian rule.[39] British-made Hawks were also used in a 2003 Indonesian offensive against separatists in Aceh province.[40]

ECAs and corporate collusion with host-country security forces. Where ECA-backed investments or exports are destined for areas of ongoing armed conflict, they may perpetuate or exacerbate violence when a company's "license to operate" is dependent on collusion with local paramilitaries or government security forces. In Colombia, for example, both Japan's Export-Import Bank (JEXIM) and Italy's SACE provided ECA support for the Ocensa pipeline, built by a consortium led by UK oil multinational British Petroleum (BP) to carry oil from its Cusiana and Cupiaga fields in the eastern part of the country, an area ravaged by civil war.[41] The pipeline has been routinely sabotaged by guerrilla groups opposed to the extraction of oil by foreign companies. The response of the Colombian security services to such guerrilla attacks has been brutal, with villagers subject to major human rights abuses by the army in its attempts to secure the pipeline.[42] In 1995, for instance, when residents of the village of El Moro set up a roadblock to demand compensation for damages caused by BP's trucks, soldiers from the Sixteenth Brigade, an army unit specifically assigned to protect the pipeline, killed two of the protest leaders and threatened others.[43] Government human rights lawyers who investigated the killings reported that the army was "out of control."[44] According to some sources, BP pays the Colombian government a mandatory "war tax" of $1 per barrel to help finance army and police protection of its oil facilities and is reported to have paid an additional $2.2 million as part of a three-year collaborative agreement with the Colombian Ministry of Defense.[45]

Other ECA-backed projects in the oil, mining, and gas sectors that have similarly been associated with violence through the collusion of companies with oppressive security forces include a Freeport MacMoRan mine in Indonesia and the Chad-Cameroon oil pipeline. In the latter case, the collusion was entrenched in a specially negotiated contract—known as the Convention of Establishment—that overruled all national laws and gave the security forces charged with protecting the pipeline rights to enter people's property at any time.[46] Fears have also been expressed over the conflict-generating potential of similar contracts that have been negotiated for the BP-led Baku-Tbilisi-Ceyhan oil pipeline, which will take oil from the Caspian, via Azerbaijan, Georgia, and Turkey, to Western markets, passing close to eleven conflict zones.[47] The legal contracts for the pipeline,[48] for which funding is currently being sought from a range of ECAs, give the security forces controlling the project permission to take action in cases of "civil war, sabotage, vandalism, civil disturbance, terrorism, kidnapping, commercial extortion, organized crime or other destructive events."[49] The vagueness of a rubric like "civil disturbance" would be worrying enough in a country where human rights were respected. In Turkey, however, where the responsibility for security has been handed to the gendarmerie, a paramilitary force implicated in some of the very worst atrocities of the ongoing armed conflict between the Turkish state and the Kurdistan Workers Party, it is highly disturbing.[50] In Georgia, where the pipeline passes close to a number of regions of recent conflict, security is to be handled by 400 "antiterrorism" troops to be trained by the United States under a $75 million military aid program. Worryingly, BP and its copartners in the pipeline project are exempted under the contract from any liability for human rights abuses caused by the security forces protecting the pipeline.[51] In May 2003, Amnesty International charged that the contracts violate international law and called for the ECAs considering the project to reject support.[52]

ECA-backed projects and ethnic tensions. Growing inequalities between ethnic groups, often the result of deliberate political manipulation, can create local grievances, which may provide further scope for unscrupulous interests to foment "ethnic" violence as part of a wider strategy for gaining, or shoring up, political power.[53] Wittingly or unwittingly, ECAs may actively encourage "ethnic" violence by backing projects that advantage one ethnic group over another, for example through discriminatory labor-hiring practices or through permitting one group to obtain control over key livelihood resources. Here ECA-backed dam projects are illustrative. In the 1980s, Britain's ECGD and other ECAs backed a series of dams that were built on Sri Lanka's Mahaweli River. Officials within the Mahaweli Authority later admitted that, in league with militant Buddhist priests, they used the subsequent resettlement program to drive a wedge between minority communities of Tamil-speaking Hindus and Muslims by settling poverty-stricken households from the Sinhala-speaking Buddhist majority within and around minority communities.[54] Similarly, in Senegal, the ECA-backed Manantali dam project encouraged the political and economic elite of the Moors in Mauritania, who before had had little interest in agriculture, to appropriate river basin land in anticipation of making large profits from the development of medium- and large-scale irrigation schemes. Backed by the security forces, the Moors began to take over lands from the local inhabitants of the valley, forcibly expelling thousands of black Mauritanian nationals as "foreigners" and expropriating their land. Senegal, meanwhile, retaliated by expelling thousands of its minority Moorish population. At least 60,000 Senegalese and black Mauritanians were deported or fled from Mauritania, and twice that number of Moors left Senegal.[55]

ECAs and environmental degradation. The adverse impacts of many ECA-backed projects on the environment are well documented.[56] These impacts go beyond the immediate destruction caused by pollution or forest destruction; of equal importance are the wider ramifications of infrastructure investments on poorer people's access to and control over the environments that they rely on for their livelihoods.[57] Where fishing grounds, forests, streams, and agricultural land are fenced off for extractive or infrastructure-related projects or destroyed by their operations, a downward cycle of dispossession, poverty, and immiseration may be precipitated as people are forced to move in search of new livelihoods, often triggering violence between those forced to move and the communities where they attempt to settle. Violence may also result where affected communities legitimately attempt to resist the imposition of projects that would have adverse impact on their lives and livelihoods.[58]

Bribery in ECA-backed projects. Surveys and studies indicate that specific sectors, including infrastructure construction, extractive industries, and armament, are prone to corruption.[59] Such corruption not only fuels poverty (bribes can add an average of 20–30 percent to the cost of government procurement, diverting money that could be spent on education, health, and poverty eradication) but also seriously undermines the legitimacy of the government among its citizens.[60] However, ECAs typically see their primary role as supporting domestic business opportunities, whatever the cost, in the fierce world of export competition. Consequently, they have frequently closed their eyes to large-scale corruption on the part of the companies they support, as doing so allows them to stay competitive. In effect, ECAs have been underwriting the bribery carried out by their domestic companies—to a point where Transparency International has warned that ECA behavior is often "close to complicity with a criminal offence."[61]

Lagging on Corporate Social Responsibility: Assessing Current ECA Policies

Given the growth of initiatives among individual companies, industry associations, and various investors and commercial financial actors to promote corporate social responsibility, the failure of ECAs to adopt similar measures to adequately screen for negative social, environmental, and human rights impacts of the projects they finance in developing countries presents a stark lacuna. While the laxity of standards among ECAs has made them more attractive to companies seeking risk insurance and project finance guarantees, the growing importance of ECA financing means that ECAs are increasingly likely to fund precisely those types of extractive and related projects that pose the greatest risks for social well-being and security and where the need for effective standards is most crucial. The lacuna underscores the need for ECA reform and for governments in the developed world to take seriously their commitments to international peace and security and human rights by promoting such reform.

The OECD Export Credit Group: Crablike Progress

At the international level, the main forum for negotiations on ECA reform has been the OECD's Working Group on Export Credits and Credit Guarantees (known as the Export Credits Group [ECG]), a subgroup of the OECD trade directorate focusing on, and negotiating, policy issues relating to OECD member country ECAs. But the response of the ECG to socioeconomic and human rights concerns has been limited. First, the ECG requires no assessment of the human rights impacts of projects receiving ECA support. In fact, attempts by NGOs and some ECAs to include labor standard and human rights provisions in the OECD negotiations were steadfastly resisted and ultimately blocked by a number of OECD governments.[62] As a result, the ECG has restricted its discussions to reaching agreement on a minimum set of environmental standards.

Yet even on environmental protection, progress has been crablike—often moving sideways rather than forward. In 2003, after more than five years of deliberations, an agreement was reached by the twenty-six member countries of the ECG on the adoption of a common approach to environmental screening of projects.[63] The agreement, known as the "Common Approaches," makes no mention of human rights and does not address issues related to conflict, even tangentially. Moreover, in the two areas where it could have made a positive contribution to conflict prevention—by screening out projects that damage the environment and by opening up decisionmaking to greater public scrutiny—it fails to deliver. For example, the agreement does not require compliance with a single specified set of mandatory environmental standards, deferring rather to a broad list of varying "benchmark" standards that ECAs can elect to apply, or not, at will.[64] There is mention of the need to comply with "host country standards"[65]—in effect, an injunction that project developers not break local law. However, this provision is interpreted by some ECAs as encompassing only local technical standards relating to the environment rather than the entire body of local law. More troubling, the provision is conditional and discretionary, stating that projects "should comply" rather than "shall comply" with standards of the host country. An escape clause sanctions the approval of projects that do not meet international environmental standards, although ECAs must notify the ECG when this occurs.[66] Another shortcoming is that environmental impact assessments (EIAs) are only required for "Category A" projects that have a high potential impact on the environment.[67] There is no requirement for the EIA to be made available for public comment, although ECAs must report to the ECG if the EIA is not disclosed.[68] Likewise, there is no obligation to consult communities affected by ECA funding and no obligation to release details of the projects for which ECA support has been requested,[69] thus denying affected communities and other interested parties the opportunity to comment on possible adverse impacts, including the potential for generating conflict. More broadly, on the increasingly important issue of adopting mandatory environmental standards, the OECD has refused to move. Tellingly, of the twenty-six countries represented in the ECG, only the United States has binding environmental standards for its export credit and investment insurance agencies.[70]

ECA action on combating bribery has been equally inadequate. In December 2000, for example, the ECG issued the Action Statement on Bribery and Officially Supported Export Credits.[71] While the statement was a major step forward in recognizing the role of ECAs in financing economic activities that can abet corruption, its implementation has been at best patchy and arbitrary. Two years following the action statement, of the thirty ECAs that responded to an ECG survey, only four (Turkey, Greece, Hungary, and Poland) attested that they did not underwrite commissions—a notorious vehicle through which bribes are paid—as part of the export contract, while only six set any kind of limit on the amount of agents' commissions they would cover.[72] Yet as Dieter Frisch, former director-general for development at the European Union (EU), has put it, the practice of underwriting commissions "constitutes an indirect encouragement to bribe."[73] Likewise, nine ECAs—including agencies from Japan, Switzerland, the United Kingdom, and the United States—do not yet have an institutional requirement to deny indemnification to companies in instances where bribery has been proven in a legal case, while two-thirds of the ECAs that responded to the survey indicated that they would not do so even when there was sufficient evidence of bribery.[74] Indeed, the vast majority of ECAs have refused to blacklist companies convicted of bribery from receiving future support.[75] Significantly, only four ECAs have thus far taken any action, such as withholding support for a project or notifying law enforcement agencies, when confronted with suspicions or evidence of bribery or with convictions for bribery.[76] Other ECAs claim to have had no suspicion, sufficient evidence, or legal judgment concerning bribery—a claim that flies in the face of substantive evidence that companies are continuing to bribe their way into winning contracts.[77] It also suggests that Western governments are in fact deeply reluctant to take a stand on the actions and practices of their ECAs for fear of losing business for their country. This "collective action problem" was summed up by EU trade commissioner Pascal Lamy, who observed that "every time any of them move forward a millimeter, they stop to see if anyone else moved."[78]

Unilateral Action: Limited Reform

Several ECAs have gone beyond the "built-in" agenda of the ECG reform process. In the United Kingdom, the ECGD, for example, has explicitly stated that it will take account of labor standards[79] when considering applications for support and has introduced screening procedures that include an "impact questionnaire" on whether or not companies have a policy on human rights and the environment.[80] In the Netherlands, meanwhile, the foreign trade minister in 2001 introduced measures that require any company receiving support from its ECA to "take account of" the OECD *Guidelines for Multinational Enterprises*.[81] The move was vigorously opposed by the OECD's Business and Industry Advisory Committee (BIAC), the main industry group within the OECD, on the ground that this, in effect, transformed the *Guidelines* from a voluntary agreement into a compulsory one.[82] However, closer scrutiny of such reforms quickly reveals their limits. In the case of the Netherlands, for example, the Dutch ECA (NCM, recently renamed ATRADIUS-DSB) deems a company to be in compliance with the rules of the *Guidelines* if it is "aware" of their existence and if it declares that it is prepared to implement them according to its ability. Compliance with the *Guidelines* provisions is not required.[83] Likewise, in the United Kingdom, despite the inclusion of questions on human rights, the screening procedures appear to be little more than an information-gathering exercise. Beyond completing the questionnaire, no further action is required by the companies. Indeed, the ECGD explicitly states that the questionnaire is not intended to disqualify projects that fail to comply with the ECGD's stated aims and requirements but rather to identify those that need further scrutiny and improvement.[84] There are no questions at all on the implications of the project for conflict risk.

Moreover, the ECGD's approach to human rights is limited and runs the risk of failing to ensure that the ECGD meets its obligations under the UK Human Rights Act of 1998. For example, there is no requirement for affected communities to be consulted on, nor indeed informed about, the potential effects of a project unless it is deemed to be of high potential impact.[85] Yet the right of citizens to participate in the decisions that affect their lives and livelihood is at the heart not only of any credible conflict prevention strategy but also of the relevant provisions of the European Convention of Human Rights and other international human rights instruments. For this right to be respected, it is critical that citizens are informed in advance of such life-affecting decisions and have opportunities to challenge the outcome if their rights are violated. A prerequisite for compliance with this set of rights would appear to be the timely disclosure of all applications received by the ECGD and their outcomes.[86]

The ECGD's impact questionnaire also demonstrates an approach to human rights that is of limited use in ensuring that human rights abuses do not flow from ECA-supported projects, a key requirement if local and regional conflict is to be prevented. The questionnaire's primary aim appears to be to elicit information on threats to property rights (for example, whether land will be compulsorily acquired) and to labor rights and the rights of certain vulnerable groups.[87] While this is welcome, the questionnaire fails to elicit any information about the human rights context in which the project will take place. For example, it does not ask whether people are free to express their views without fear of retribution or whether the political culture encourages or permits freedom of expression, including dissent. Such questions are of fundamental importance if affected communities are to be properly consulted on projects and if their rights are to be meaningfully protected.

Even the ECGD's apparent commitment to World Bank environmental and social safeguard policies is hedged by caveats. Again, the wording is crucial. The ECGD states, for example, that it is "expected" that high-impact projects should comply with World Bank standards—but an "expectation" does not amount to a "requirement." Whether a particular standard is applied or not is ultimately at the discretion of the ECGD's minister.[88] Indeed, such is the ECGD's insistence on retaining its discretion that until May 2003 it even sought to allow scope for derogating from provisions outlawing child labor and forced labor under the UN's Convention on the Rights of the Child and the International Labour Organization's Conventions on the Abolition of Child Labour. Suggestively, the ECGD's April 2003 "guidance notes" for its impact analysis procedures stated that "there must be exceptional circumstances for ECGD to provide cover to projects which involve child labour."[89] Although the ECGD has now adopted a clear policy of not supporting such projects, other ECAs have balked at following suit, for fear that this would diminish the competitiveness of their exporters and hence, it is argued, jobs at home.[90]

The ECGD also argues that it cannot operate a debarment policy at present because its legal mandate requires it to consider all applications for support.[91] But the 1991 Export and Investment Guarantees Act gave the secretary of state for trade and industry, who is responsible for the ECGD, considerable flexibility, including the right, under section 3(1), to "make *any* arrangements which, in his opinion, are in the interests of the proper financial management of the ECGD portfolio, or any part of it" (emphasis added). Given that "proper financial management" should require the ECGD not to give cover to companies with a record of corruption or to projects that are likely to generate conflict, it should be perfectly possible for the secretary of state for trade and industry to institute a debarment policy at the ECGD. NGOs have argued that should such measures not be possible under the terms of the act, the act should be changed.[92]

The Need and Scope for Reform

Since the late 1990s, nongovernmental organizations have lobbied hard for governments to take action vis-à-vis their ECAs across the entire range of issues that underlie conflict—from project-specific impacts to the broader problems of ECA debt and corruption. Reform proposals were set out in the Jakarta Declaration, which calls for the adoption of mandatory environmental and human rights standards and an end to ECA support for unproductive expenditures such as arms sales.[93] These reforms could be undertaken in a variety of ways. First, ECAs might make support conditional on applicants' supplying full environmental, social, and conflict impact assessments, meeting international human rights norms, complying with World Bank safeguard policies, and providing proof of compliance with the OECD *Guidelines for Multinational Enterprises*. Given the large impacts of ECA-backed activities on conflict, ECAs should make it mandatory for all applications to be accompanied by a "conflict impact assessment," which would examine not only the likely impacts of conflict on the project but also the project's potential for triggering, exacerbating, or otherwise contributing to violent conflict. Wider action should also be taken by governments to address the deleterious impacts of past ECA loans on developing-country debt burdens and to put in place stronger measures to combat bribery in ECA-backed projects.

While the need and scope for reform of ECA practices to become more conflict-sensitive is great, efforts to bring about reform face a daunting challenge arising from the very raison d'être of ECAs. The aim of export credit is not to foster development in poorer countries; export credit and insurance is about developing the industries of the exporting country. Accordingly, export credit and insurance are designed for competitiveness purposes, not for socioeconomic development, environmental protection, or conflict prevention in the host country. Moreover, as with extractive companies themselves, the priority of remaining competitive vis-à-vis rivals may profoundly inhibit efforts to reform ECA practices.

Where ECAs have moved to embrace even limited reform, it has almost invariably been as a result of national public protest over a specific, egregious ECA-backed project, for example the proposed Ilisu Dam in Turkey or the Camisea gas pipeline project in Peru. Indeed, the entire OECD reform process was originally initiated by the United States in an attempt to level the playing field after its own Ex-Im Bank was forced to adopt mandatory environmental standards following a public outcry over Ex-Im's proposed involvement in China's Three Gorges dam. Pressure from the powerful U.S. environmental movement not only forced Ex-Im to reject the Three Gorges proposal but also persuaded the U.S. Congress to make the reauthorization of Ex-Im's budget conditional on the agency's adopting an environmental policy.[94]

In most other OECD countries, however, the avenue of using budget reauthorization procedures to require the adoption of broader security, welfare, and environmental standards is not generally available, although parliamentarians' support for reform has increasingly proved critical in placing pressure on governments to act.[95] Progress has therefore been more difficult to achieve, not least because of strong lobbying from national exporters and a reluctance of national trade ministries to allow development and human rights concerns to interfere with the promotion of national economic interests. Where ECA support for egregious environmental and social projects has been blocked, it is generally because the companies involved have been placed under sufficient pressure from NGOs and the public to withdraw their applications—thus sparing the ECAs themselves from the responsibility of having to decide the matter.[96] In this respect, a key pressure point has been the uncontained reputational risk that companies may incur through remaining in a controversial project—a risk that has been highlighted by campaigners through shareholder resolutions,[97] reports to fund managers,[98] and direct action protests.[99] In the United Kingdom, for example, the construction giant Balfour has stated that had it been aware in advance of the adverse publicity that would result from its involvement in the proposed Ilisu dam in Turkey, it would not have bid for the project.[100]

Indeed, within the business community there are signs that the outcry generated by advocacy NGOs over specific ECA-backed projects, coupled with the uncertainties over funding for other projects created by the ECAs' piecemeal approach to reform, has prompted several key corporate players to embrace the case for mandatory environmental standards. In 2003, for example, Chris Beale, head of Citigroup's project finance department, urged the OECD's ECG to embrace the Equator Principles, a set of environmental standards that have now been adopted by leading commercial banks for projects receiving project finance. Such a policy would set World Bank safeguard policies as a floor standard for all project finance projects with a total capital cost of $50 million or more—a threshold that would cover some 97 percent of all project finance deals covered by ECAs.[101]

Significantly, Beale told the ECG that what the banking community was seeking was one universal, clear-cut set of standards that would be applied uniformly to all ECA applications.[102] By contrast, he pointed out, the ad hoc benchmarking method embodied in the OECD Common Approaches fails to provide exporters with the clarity and predictability that they need for long-term planning—to the potential detriment of national economies and to the disadvantage of individual companies. While Beale was referring primarily to environmental and social standards, the benefits that would accrue from the adoption of clear-cut conflict prevention standards would be comparable. NGOs argue that ECAs, as public bodies, should go further than the Equator Principles. Nonetheless, the adoption of the Equator Principles by Denmark's ECA, Eksport Kredit Fonden (EKF), the first ECA worldwide to do so, is welcome.[103]

While the banking community has moved beyond in-house action to press for accompanying institutional reform of ECAs, the socially responsible investment (SRI) community remains largely restricted to pressing individual companies to put their houses in order.[104] Indeed, many in the SRI community argue that they have no mandate to press for change beyond the companies in which they hold shares.[105] Bringing institutional and other investors into the debate over ECA reform is vital, however, if governments are to be persuaded of the merits of the case. At a time when many key players in the OECD are under pressure from high unemployment— Germany being a prime example—the prospect of jobs' being shed because of lost export orders is a powerful deterrent to taking actions that would bring ECAs into the sustainable development era, including action on the conflict-generating potential of ECA-backed investments. Here the SRI community could play a significant role in drawing attention to the implications for shareholder value of companies' seeking to contain the risks of conflict simply by ensuring that they are insured. Unions, too, have an interest in ensuring that their members' jobs are secure. Chasing contracts regardless of their adverse societal impacts is unlikely to provide such security. On the contrary, there is a strong argument that the companies that will prove best placed to prosper in the long term are those that are already developing policies that embrace environmental and human rights concerns.

Conclusion

Given the critical role that ECAs play in underwriting overseas investment and exports, a strong case could be made that they could and should use their considerable influence to—at the very minimum—screen out conflict-promoting projects or institute new policies aimed at reducing the conflict potential of the company operations they support. As this chapter has demonstrated, however, when it comes to the activities of their ECAs, governments have been extremely reluctant to move beyond the rhetoric of reform to substantive action. Indeed, thus far reform has been piecemeal, disjointed, and entirely discretionary.

Whether governments respond to the increasing calls for their ECAs to adopt mandatory social impact standards—including screening for conflict impacts—will depend critically on the extent to which the many parties that have an interest in reform (from NGOs to investment bankers to fund managers and unions) can bring concerted pressure to bear. This is perhaps the one clear lesson that has emerged from the limited progress that has been made in reforming ECAs to date. It is also a lesson that should be borne in mind in any attempt to ensure that ECAs do not act as a force for future conflict.

Such collective pressure would send companies a powerful message that the strategy of containing risks by palming them off on the taxpayer is no longer acceptable. In the future, the risks themselves must be addressed if ECA support is to be approved. Moreover, the suggested reforms are no more than those necessary to bring ECA procedures and practice into line with the stated sustainable development and conflict prevention aims of the vast majority of governments, aims that include not only the protection of the environment but also commitments to eliminate poverty and reduce conflict.

Notes

I would like especially to thank Susan Hawley, with whom I have worked closely on monitoring the UK Export Credits Guarantee Department, for her insights and comments on this chapter.

1. For more information, see Will Marshall, "Australian Firms Plunder Papua New Guinea," October 27, 2003, available at www.minesandcommunities.org/Country/png3.htm; the website of the Mining Policy Institute, www.mpi.org.au/oktedi; Friends of the Earth Australia, "Walhi Demands a Halt to Freeport Mine Operations," October 11, 2003, available at www.foe.org.au/mr/mr_11_10_03.htm; the website of the Bankwatch Network, www.bankwatch.org/issues/oilclima/mainchad.html; and the website of the Baku Ceyhan Campaign, www.baku.org.uk. See also Bruce Rich, Korinna Horta, and Aaron Goldzimer, *Export Credit Agencies in Sub-Saharan Africa: Indebtedness for Extractive Industries, Corruption, and Conflict* (Washington, D.C.: Environmental Defense Fund, n.d.).

2. Although the oil majors have not commented specifically on the importance of ECA support for ensuring that projects are financed, the following statement is indicative of the importance they attach generally to funding from public international financial institutions: "In a number of projects the very existence of WBG (World Bank Group) financial participation may make a project happen that otherwise would not be realised. This is especially true for cross-border projects or

projects in countries that otherwise would have difficulties in attracting finance. The oil and gas industry sees WBG participation as decreasing risk by providing a de facto guarantee that projects will take place in an orderly manner with maximum support from the WBG and host governments." See Petter Nore, Donal O'Neill, Alan Grant, and David Moorecroft, "Reactions to EIR Report from Representatives of the Oil Industry," December 2003, p. 1.

3. Criticism of institutions involved in promoting trade and overseas investment (whether ECAs, multinational companies, the World Bank, or the World Trade Organization) is sometimes met with suspicion that it is motivated by a hostility toward trade itself. This is regrettable but, in my experience, commonplace. At the outset, it should therefore be stressed that, in critiquing the current practices of ECAs, it is not my intent to suggest that trade and investment are undesirable. As with ECAs, one key question needs to be addressed in assessing the social value of any trade and investment: In *whose* interest does it operate and for *whose* benefit?

4. Jane Nelson, *The Business of Peace: The Private Sector as a Partner in Conflict Prevention and Resolution* (London: International Alert, Council on Economic Priorities, and Prince of Wales Business Leaders Forum, 2000); Karen Ballentine and Jake Sherman, eds., *The Political Economy of Armed Conflict: Beyond Greed and Grievance* (Boulder: Lynne Rienner, 2003); Jessica Banfield, Virginia Haufler, and Damien Lilly, *Transnational Corporations in Conflict Prone Zones: Public Policy Responses and a Framework for Action* (London: International Alert, 2003).

5. For examples, see Tebtebba Foundation and Forest Peoples Programme, *Extracting Promises: Indigenous Peoples, Extractive Industries, and the World Bank* (Baguio City, Philipppines: Tebtebba Foundation, 2003); Extractive Industries Review, *Striking a Better Balance,* 2003, available at www.eireview.net; and World Commission on Dams, *Dams and Development: A New Framework for Decision-Making* (London: Earthscan, 2001).

6. Where conflict involves violence, a company's plant and machinery may be destroyed. Other financial costs may be incurred through the destruction of roads and other infrastructure on which the company relies to bring its goods to market. According to the *Economist,* oil firms operating in civil war–torn Algeria in the late 1990s were typically spending 8–9 percent of their budgets on security ("Business in Difficult Places," *Economist,* May 25, 2000). See also Nelson, *Business of Peace,* p. 22.

7. Nelson, *Business of Peace,* p. 30.

8. The long history of conflict over oil resources in the Ogoni Delta of Nigeria provides a case in point, with the oil companies relying for years on repression of critics as their principal strategy for containing opposition, as exemplified by the extrajudicial murder in 1995 of Ken Saro Wiwa and nine other critics of Shell's operations in the delta. For further information, see www.essentialaction.org/shell/issues.html.

9. See, for example, John Stauber and Sheldon Rampton, *Toxic Sludge Is Good for You: Lies, Damn Lies, and the Public Relations Industry* (London: Common Courage Press, 1995); and Judith Richter, *Engineering of Consent: Uncovering Corporate PR,* Corner House briefing no. 6, Dorset, UK, March 1998.

10. Private insurers tend to operate at the short-term end of the risk insurance market. The main private providers of political risk insurance are ACE Guaranty, American International Group, Sovereign Risk, and Zurich Emerging Market Solutions. The private sector has increasingly pulled back from what it perceives as risky deals. As Jon Marks, a contributor to *The Berne Union Yearbook 2003,* notes:

"Some providers have pulled out of political risk insurance altogether, while even some of the most committed have scaled down their operations and, for private insurers, reinsurance capacity has been cut back." See Jon Marks, "Supporting Trade in Difficult Times," in *The Berne Union Yearbook 2003* (London: Berne Union, 2003), p. 27, available at www.berneunion.org.uk. Alan Mackie, another contributor, concludes: "Only Export Credit Agencies can meet the demand for export credit insurance in difficult markets." See Alan Mackie, "Changing Face of Trade Insurance," in *Berne Union Yearbook 2003,* p. 48, available at www.berneunion.org.uk. The Berne Union, established in 1934, is also known as the International Union of Credit and Investment Insurers.

11. Jon Marks writes: "In a hostile economic climate, commercial banks are less willing to take on stand alone deals in most emerging markets . . . while both the capacity and tenors available in private political risk insurance markets has diminished" (Marks, "Supporting Trade in Difficult Times," p. 27).

12. The premiums charged by private providers are generally higher than those available from public ECAs. However, this is not always the case. In 2002, the rate charged by the UK Export Credits Guarantee Department for expropriation risks in China was 0.7 percent, while that offered by private insurances ranged between 0.4 and 1.0 percent. See *Berne Union Yearbook 2003,* p. 22 (see note 10). While the terms of loans supported by ECAs to developing countries are similar to commercial terms, ECAs generally provide cover for larger sums, longer periods, and higher-risk countries than the private sector is willing to consider.

13. In reality, however, premium charges have generally been low, and income from premiums has covered only a portion of the losses of ECAs. Between 1982 and 1997, for instance, ECAs that were members of the Berne Union received a total of $40.2 billion in premiums but paid out $153.6 billion in claims. They clawed back $70.9 billion through recoveries. See Saul Estrin, Stephen Powell, Pinar Bagci, Simeon Thornton, and Peter Goate, *The Economic Rationale for the Public Provision of Export Credit Insurance by ECGD: A Report for the Export Credit Guarantee Department* (London: National Economic Research Associates, 2000), app. D. In 2000 and 2001, ECAs received around $2 billion in premium income and paid out around $3 billion in claims (OECD, "2001 Cashflow Report from the Export Credit Group Members," available at www.oecd.org/pdf/M00038000/M00038847.pdf).

14. Rupert Wright, "Forfeiting for Fun and Profit," *Euromoney,* December 1997, pp. 140–141, cited in Aaron Goldzimer, "Globalization's Most Perverse Secret: The Role of Export Credit and Investment Insurance Agencies," paper presented at the Alternatives to Neoliberalism Conference, New Rules for Global Finance Coalition, May 23–24, 2002, available at www.new-rules.org/Docs/afterneolib/goldzimer.pdf. In a similar vein, referring to ECGD-backed arms deals to Iraq under the Saddam Hussein regime, Midland Bank executive Stephen Kock has stated: "You see, before we advance monies to a company, we always insist on any funds being covered by the [UK] Government's Export Credits Guarantee Department. . . . We can't lose. After 90 days, if the Iraqis haven't coughed up, the company gets paid instead by the British Government. Either way, we recover our loan, plus interest of course. It's beautiful." Quoted in "Killing Secrets, *ECGD: The Export Credit Guarantee Department,*" 1998, available at www.eca-watch.org.

15. Information taken from the ECGD website, www.ecgd.gov.uk. See also Susan Hawley, *Turning a Blind Eye: The UK ECGD and Corruption* (London: Corner House, 2003).

16. Newly established ECAs that have not yet qualified for Berne Union

membership—of which there are currently twenty-five—belong to a premembership training group called the Prague Club, all of whose members are presently Middle Eastern, Eastern European, or developing countries.

17. World Bank, *Global Development Finance 2002: Financing the Poorest Countries* (Washington, D.C.: World Bank, 2002), chap. 4, p. 108. World Bank figures do not include a breakdown of export credit support by country, nor are figures available specifically for ECA support to projects located in war zones or conflict-prone areas.

18. Ibid.

19. Between 1982 and 2001, ECAs supported $7.334 trillion worth of exports, primarily to developing countries, and $139 billion of foreign direct investment. See Vivian Brown, "Looking to the Future," in *Berne Union Yearbook 2003*, p. 5 (see note 10).

20. World Bank, *Global Development Finance 2002*, chap. 4, p. 107; OECD, "Officially Supported Export Credits: Levels of New Flows and Stocks," data from 1999 and 2000.

21. Figures from OECD DAC Statistics and U.S. Treasury note "Multilateral Development Banks," available at www.ustreas.gov/omdb/tab9.pdf.

22. According to ECA-Watch, ECAs support four times the amount of oil, gas, and mining projects as all multilateral development banks, such as the World Bank Group. Cited in Malaika Culverwell, Bernice Lee, and Izabella Koziell, "Towards an Improved Governance Agenda for the Extractive Sector," workshop report, Royal Institute of International Affairs, London, November 4, 2003, available at www.riia.org. However, given the secrecy of ECA projects, it is doubtful whether a reliable global figure for ECA support for extractive industry projects exists. For an analysis of the poor record of extractive industries in relieving poverty, see World Bank Group, Extractive Industries Review, *Striking a Better Balance*, 2003, available at www.eireview.net.

23. ECGD, *Annual Report 2001/2002* (London: ECGD, 2003), p. 8.

24. The ECGD also reports: "ECGD's oil and gas team is continuing to receive a significant level of enquiries as the demand for British expertise in the world's oil and gas sectors remains strong" (ibid. p. 17).

25. Export Guarantees Advisory Council, minutes of meeting held November 19, 2003, p. 4, available at www.ecgd.gov.uk/egac_minutes_19_november_2003.doc.

26. Although in the boom years of the early 1990s a significant number of project financiers (perhaps believing their own free-market propaganda) thought they could avoid investment insurance, primarily by using bond issues rather than bank loans to finance their projects, many have had their fingers badly burned, particularly in Southeast Asia. As Malcolm Stephens, a former chief executive of the UK ECGD, observes, "In the year or so up to the end of 1997, there had been growing euphoria both that political risks were a thing of the past and also that any kind of project could be structured as a project financing on a viable basis and that, for example, it did not matter if the project was on the Isle of Wight or [in] Chad. Others thought that it was irrelevant whether the project concerned raw materials which could be extracted and sold for foreign currency or drinking water for consumption by people who had no experience of paying anything for water, let alone the true economic cost" (Malcolm Stephens, "A New Challenge for Insurers," *Project Finance,* November 1998, p. 38).

27. In an oft-cited case, for instance, it took the International Finance Corporation, the private-sector arm of the World Bank, six years to agree a private-

sector loan for a power project on the Hub River in Pakistan. See Alan Spence and Kevin Godier, "Multilaterals and ECAs: Powerful Sources of Support" (Survey: International Project Finance), *Financial Times,* December 3, 1996.

28. The World Bank group offers investment insurance through its Multilateral Investment Guarantee Agency (MIGA), in addition to direct project funding through the IFC. A number of regional development banks, such as the Inter-American Development Bank, the Asian Development Bank, and the European Bank for Reconstruction and Development, also provide guarantees. These private-sector arms of the multilateral development banks are structured differently from ordinary companies or banks. Rather than having equity capital paid up by investors and possibly some debt as well, their equity capital is provided by member countries. This capital is "callable": rather than having paid the actual cash, the governments/shareholders promise to pay the amount if required. The guarantee behind the callable capital means that the risks incurred are ultimately borne by governments rather than the MDBs themselves. The involvement of MDBs in a private-sector project therefore acts to provide greater security to private-sector investors, considerably easing the leveraging of other funds. Although the loans provided by MDBs to the private sector are provided at "commercial rates"—in contrast to the concessionary, subsidized loans made to governments—the interest charged is typically lower than a private-sector bank would charge.

29. Nicholas Hildyard, "Snouts in the Trough: Export Credit Agencies, Corporate Welfare, and Policy Incoherence," Corner House Briefing no. 14, Dorset, UK, 1999, available at www.thecornerhouse.org.uk.

30. Multilateral debt is owed to institutions such as the World Bank and International Monetary Fund or to regional development banks like the African Development Bank or Asian Development Bank. Bilateral debt is government-to-government debt. Private debt is owed to commercial banks and other private creditors.

31. Horst Köhler, "Reforming the International Financial System," in *Berne Union Yearbook 2001* (London: Berne Union, 2001).

32. Some 95 percent of the debt owed to the UK government by developing countries is export credit debt. Between one-third and one-half of this debt consists of interest owed on original debts and penalties. Much of the debt now owed to the ECGD has been incurred because of a lack of hard currency to repay British companies, debt that the ECGD described as incurred as a result of political rather than commercial risk. Often overseas companies or governments have been able to repay British companies in local currency by depositing money into a local bank, only to run into the obstacle that the bank is unable to convert the local currency into sterling or U.S. dollars. Export credit agency activity can thus lead to a balance-of-payments crisis for the borrowing country and macroeconomic instability.

33. Ann Feltham, "The Case for Removing Arms from the ECGD's Portfolio," presentation to the NGO Seminar on Export Credit Reform, House of Commons, Dorset, UK, May 23, 2002, available at www.thecornerhouse.org.uk.

34. ECA-Watch, *Arms Trade,* available at www.ecawatch.org/problems/arms/index.html.

35. Feltham, "Case for Removing Arms."

36. Ann Feltham, "Wars and Conflict Create Refugees," in Corner House et al., *Listen to the Refugee's Story* (London: Corner House, 2003), p. 52.

37. Hildyard, *Snouts in the Trough.*

38. See, for example, Council of Europe, Committee of Ministers, Interim Resolution ResDH(2002)98, adopted July 10, 2002.

39. Richard Norton-Taylor, "FO Inquiry into Use of Hawk Jets by Jakarta," *Guardian*, July 3, 2002.

40. John Aglionby, "Indonesia Uses UK Hawks in Aceh Offensive," *Guardian*, May 20, 2003.

41. JEXIM, now incorporated into the newly formed Japanese Bank for International Cooperation, approved a direct loan of $121 million and an untied loan of $300 million to develop the Cusiana and Cupiagua oil fields. SACE backed $296 million worth of loans with a five-year guarantee. See Berne Declaration et al., *Race to the Bottom: Creating Risk, Generating Debt, and Guaranteeing Environmental Destruction*, 1999), p. 13, available at www.eca-watch.org/eca/race_bottom.pdf.

42. See, for example, Michael Gillard, "BP Hands Tarred in Pipeline War," *Guardian*, October 17, 1998.

43. James Marriott and Greg Muttitt, *Some Common Concerns: Imagining BP's Azerbaijan-Georgia-Turkey Pipeline Systems* (London: Platform et al., 2002).

44. Michael Gillard, Melissa Jones, Andy Rowell, and John Vidal, "BP in Colombia: A Tale of Death, Pollution, and Deforestation," *Guardian*, August 15, 1998, p. 4.

45. Platform et al., *Some Common Concerns*, p. 111. Personal comment from Melissa Jones to Platform, May 2002. Some sources put the payment much higher (at $54 million, including $11 million from BP), but these higher figures could not be corroborated.

46. See Forests and the European Union Resource Network (FERN), *The Law in Whose Hand? An Analysis of the COTCO Convention of Establishment* (Brussels: FERN, 1998), available at www.fern.org/pubs/archive/cotco.htm. Article 27.12 of Cameroon Oil Transportation Company (COTCO) states: "In case of emergency, and in particular in case of immediate danger for people or the environment, COTCO [subject to certain compensation requirements set out in Article 17] is allowed, *under its sole responsibility* to have *access to any private or public land, whatever its status or location,* for the purpose of investigating the causes of or remedying the emergency or the situation of danger, *without prior authorization, and with the possible assistance of the public or private emergency services*" (emphasis added).

47. All three of the countries through which BP's Baku-Tbilisi-Ceyhan pipeline would run have suffered civil wars in the recent past and tensions remain, which could well be reignited by the project. As currently planned, for example, the pipeline would pass within 15 kilometers of Nagorno-Karabakh, 35 kilometers of South Ossetia, and 110 kilometers of Chechnya. Within weeks of the World Bank and European Bank for Reconstruction and Development's approving support for the project, Eduard Shevardnadze, then president of Georgia, was overthrown in a popular revolution.

48. Under the agreements, Turkey, Azerbaijan, and Georgia exempt the pipeline consortium from all host-country laws, other than the countries' respective constitutions, that might affect the project. The three countries would be obliged to compensate the consortium if new laws were introduced that affected the "economic equilibrium" or profitability of the project.

49. Host Government Agreement (Turkey), art. 12.1, available at www.caspiandevelopmentandexport.com. For a critique of the agreement, see www.baku.org.uk.

50. The gendarmerie's record has been routinely criticized by the European

Court of Human Rights. In 2002, it was the subject of a resolution by the Council of Europe. See Council of Europe, Committee of Ministers, Interim Resolution ResDH(2002)98, adopted July 10, 2002.

51. Host Government Agreement (Turkey), para. 11.2: "The MEP Participants shall be liable to a third party (other than the State Authorities and any Project Participant) for Loss or Damage suffered by such third party as a result of the MEP Participants' breach of the standards of conduct set forth in the Project Agreements; provided, however, that the MEP Participants shall have no liability hereunder if and to the extent the Loss or Damage is caused by or arises from any breach of any Project Agreement and/or breach of duty by any State Authority."

52. Amnesty International, "Human Rights on the Line: The Baku-Tbilisi-Ceyhan Pipeline Project," May 2003, available at www.amnestu.org.uk/business/btc/report.

53. See, for example, Frances Stewart, "Horizontal Inequalities as a Source of Conflict," in Fen Osler Hampson and David M. Malone, eds., *From Reaction to Conflict Prevention: Opportunities for the UN System* (Boulder: Lynne Rienner, 2002), pp. 105–136.

54. See Malinga Herman Gunaratna, *For a Sovereign State* (Ratmalana, Sri Lanka: Sarvodaya Vishva Lekha, 1998), p. 13; Thayer Scudder, *Recent Experiences with River Basin Development in the Tropics and Subtropics* (Berkeley: California Institute of Technology, 1994). As Scudder notes: "Though contrary to project goals, which stipulated that ethnic and religiously distinct populations were not to be mixed and that minorities were to receive plots according to their proportionate representation within the national population, these actions were ignored by such donors as the United States Agency for International Development and the World Bank. Subsequently, massacres on both sides occurred, in some instances in the very communities where they had been predicted." Thayer Scudder, "Victims of Development Revisited: The Political Costs of River Basin Development," *Development Anthropology Network* 8, no. 1 (1990): 3.

55. Michael Horowitz, "Victims of Development," *Development Anthropology Network* 7, no. 2 (1989): 1–8; Scudder, "Victims of Development Revisited."

56. For examples, see ECA-Watch, *Race to the Bottom, Take II: An Assessment of Sustainable Development Achievements of ECA-Supported Projects Two Years after OECD Common Approaches Rev. 6* (Paris: ECA-Watch, 2003), available at www.ecawatch.org.

57. For discussion, see Simon Fairlie, Nicholas Hildyard, Larry Lohmann, and Sarah Sexton, "Reclaiming the Commons," paper presented to the annual conference of the Political Studies Association of the United Kingdom, 1995, available at www.thecornerhouse.org.uk/document/commons.html.

58. Aracruz Cellulose's ECA-backed pulp factory in Espirito Santo, Brazil, illustrates the problem. To feed the factory—the world's largest short-fiber pulp plant—vast areas of eucalyptus have been planted, destroying fertile agricultural land and polluting rivers and streams through pesticide use. Rural landlessness has increased as a direct result of the project, and local indigenous peoples have been denied their rights to lands now occupied by Aracruz. Moreover, the company's willingness to pay high prices for new land has undermined federal efforts to buy land for redistribution to the landless, since the agency responsible cannot compete with the sums offered by the company. In protest, families from the Landless Workers Movement have occupied estates that the company is seeking to buy—only to be expelled by court order. Nongovernmental organizations report that "the failure of the courts and government agencies to resolve the problem of rural landlessness, exacerbated by Aracruz's massive plantation expansion, is leading to height-

ened rural tensions and a volatile environment." FASE and Tove Selin (Finnish ECA Reform Campaign), "Brazil: Aracruz Cellulose," in ECA-Watch, *Race to the Bottom, Take II*, p. 19.

59. This section is drawn with permission from Hawley, *Turning a Blind Eye*. Data on corruption from Transparency International, "Transparency International Releases New Bribe Payers Index (BPI) 2002," press release, Berlin, May 12, 2002.

60. Nelson, *Business of Peace*, p. 41.

61. Dieter Frisch, *Expert Credit Insurance and the Fight against International Corruption*, Transparency International Working Paper no. 26 (Berlin: Transparency International, 1999).

62. Off-the-record author interviews conducted in November 2003. Both Turkey and the United States sought—successfully—to limit the OECD recommendation to environmental impacts. The United States also opposed broadening the provisions to cover "sustainable development." By contrast, the United Kingdom pushed for human rights to be included.

63. OECD, *Recommendation on Common Approaches on Environment and Officially Supported Export Credits* (Paris: OECD, 2003).

64. Ibid. Article 12.1 states that ECAs "should" undertake benchmarking and specifies a basket of applicable standards. However, article 12.3 permits ECAs to derogate from applying the benchmarked standards, provided they justify the decision. See also ECA-Watch, "Groups Blast Weak OECD Agreement on Environment," December 11, 2003, available at www.eca-watch.org.

65. See OECD, Working Party on Export Credits and Credit Guarantees, *Draft Recommendation on Common Approaches on Environment and Officially Supported Export Credits: Revision 6* (Paris: OECD, 2000), para 15.

66. "If a Member finds it necessary to apply standards below the international standards against which the project has been benchmarked, it shall report and justify the standards applied on an annual *ex-post* basis." See OECD, Working Party on Export Credits and Credit Guarantees, *Recommendation on Common Approaches*, para. 12.3.

67. "For a Category A project, Members should require an EIA. The applicant is responsible for providing such an EIA." See ibid., para 8.

68. "For Category A projects, seek to make environmental impact information publicly available (e.g. EIAs, summary thereof) at least 30 calendar days before a final commitment to grant official support. In the case where environmental impact information cannot, for exceptional reasons, be made public Members shall explain the circumstances and report these." See ibid., para 16.

69. Ibid. Paragraph 16 requires that ECAs should "seek to make environmental impact information publicly available," but this applies only for high-impact projects. Moreover, it is possible to derogate from this requirement.

70. See World Wildlife Fund, "WWF-UK's Submission to the ECGD Public Consultation on Case Impact Analysis," Surrey, UK, August 2002.

71. OECD, Working Party on Export Credits and Credit Guarantees, *Action Statement on Bribery and Officially Supported Export Credits*, Paris, December 2000, available at www.oecd.org/EN/about/0,EN-about-355-10-no-no-no-0,00.html. Members of the group agreed to do the following: "Inform applicants about the legal consequences of bribery in inter-national business transactions; *invite* applicants seeking export credit guarantees to declare that neither they nor anyone acting on their behalf has or will engage in bribery; refuse to approve credit, cover, or other support where there is *sufficient evidence* of bribery; and take appropriate action against a company whose bribery is *proved* after credit, cover, or other support has been provided, such as denying indemnification, requiring a refund of

sums provided, and referring evidence of such bribery to national investigatory authorities" (emphasis added).

72. OECD, Working Party on Export Credits and Credit Guarantees, *Responses to the 2002 Survey on Measures Taken to Combat Bribery in Officially Supported Export Credits,* Paris, available at www.oecd.org. The survey is a working document and is continually being updated. For a detailed analysis of the survey, see Kristine Drew, *Analysis of the Working Party on Export Credits and Credit Guarantees Responses to the 2002 Survey of Measures Taken to Combat Bribery in Officially Supported Export Credits: As of 3rd October 2003* (London: Public Services International Research Unit, 2003), available at www.psiru.org.

73. Frisch, *Expert Credit Insurance.*

74. OECD, Working Party on Export Credits and Credit Guarantees, *Responses to the 2002 Survey.*

75. As of 2005, South Africa and Germany were in the process of introducing such blacklisting. Several ECAs are able legally to debar companies, such as Ex-Im in the United States, but do not do so in practice. Others, such as the ECGD in the United Kingdom, claim that they are not able to do so legally.

76. OECD, Working Party on Export Credits and Credit Guarantees, *Responses to the 2002 Survey.*

77. See Hawley, *Turning a Blind Eye.*

78. High-Level Panel of the Trans-Atlantic Environmental Dialogue, Brussels, May 2000, quoted in ECA-Watch, "Export Credit Agencies Explained," available at www.eca-watch.org. This view is clearly reflected in a statement by the minister for trade, Richard Caborn, to the UK Parliament during a November 2000 House of Commons debate: "I understand and share the concern of business that the ECGD's policy and process for handling sensitive cases should not get ahead of other ECAs" (*Hansard,* November 2, 2000, House of Commons Debate, Column 267WH, Export Credits Guarantee Department).

79. The ECGD states: "The [Business Principles Unit] will check which of the six core UN Human Rights treaties and eight International Labour Organisation's fundamental conventions the host country has ratified in order to identify those with which the project should comply. Relevant information is taken from the latest FCO Human Rights Annual Report and from the ILO website." See ECGD, "ECGD's Case Impact Analysis Process," October 2003, para. 5.18, p. 7, available at www.ecgd.gov.uk.

80. The ECGD states: "Corporate environmental and social policies are becoming increasingly common and are a guide as to how companies view these issues. A comprehensive corporate policy may indicate the manner in which the environmental and/or social aspects of a project will be managed. Important elements of an environmental policy statement include commitments to comply with relevant environmental legislation, to consider and minimise environmental impacts, to train staff and raise awareness, and to pursue a policy of continuous improvement" (ibid., para. 5.19, p. 7).

81. OECD, *Recommendation on Common Approaches.*

82. Bruno Lamborghini, chair, BIAC Committee on International Investment and Multinational Enterprises, letter to Marinus Sikkel, chair, OECD Committee on International Investment and Multinational Enterprises (CIME), May 29, 2001. See also Chapter 14 by Patricia Feeney and Tom Kenny in this volume.

83. Personal communication with Wiert Wiertsema, Both Ends, the Netherlands, November 2003.

84. "The analysis of potential impacts has not impeded the processing of any application and we do not propose to change this." ECGD, "Public Consultation on

Case Impact Analysis," 2003, available at www.ecgd.gov.uk/consultation-doc210602.doc, p. 3.

85. Projects having "high potential impact" involve greenfield projects or major expansions in potentially damaging business sectors, or cases that involve resettlement or major environmental impacts as identified through the ECGD's screening questionnaire.

86. Kerim Yildiz and Nicholas Hildyard, "The ECGD and the Human Rights Act," presentation to the seminar Beyond Business Principles, House of Commons, May 23, 2002, available at www.thecornerhouse.org.uk.

87. ECGD, "Impact Questionnaire."

88. Information acquired under Chatham House Rules.

89. The UK government states that it will "give particular attention to core labour standards" when supporting investment abroad. The United Kingdom has ratified the UN's Convention on the Rights of the Child and the International Labour Organization's Conventions on the Abolition of Child Labour. It has also ratified the International Labour Organization's Convention Concerning the Abolition of Forced Labour. While the ECGD expects projects to conform to these conventions, until recently it nonetheless allowed for derogations. Its April 2003 "guidance notes" for its impact analysis procedures, for example, stated that "there must be exceptional circumstances for ECGD to provide cover to projects which involve child labour." In effect, while the ECGD was unlikely to support a project that used child labor, it was nonetheless willing to do so. A similar derogation applied to the International Labour Organization's Convention on Forced Labour, although the ECGD stated that "it is difficult to imagine circumstances in which the ECGD could provide cover to projects which involve forced labour." See ECGD, "A Summary of ECGD's Impact Analysis Procedures, Annex 1 Guidance Notes," April 2003.

90. Personal communication with delegate to the OECD's Working Party on Export Credits and Credit Guarantees, September 2003.

91. Select Committee on Trade and Industry, ECGD oral evidence, ECGD inquiry, House of Commons, May 11, 2003.

92. Corner House, *Evidence to Environmental Audit Committee's Inquiry on ECGD and Sustainable Development,* House of Commons, July 17, 2003, available at www.publications.parliament.uk/pa/cm200203/cmselect/cmenvaud/cmenvaud.htm.

93. The Jakarta Declaration is available at www.fern.org/pubs/ngostats/jakarta.htm.

94. Douglas Norlen and Andrea Durbin, "History of the Establishment of Environmental Policies at U.S. Bilateral Finance Institutions" (Washington, D.C.: Pacific Environment and Resources Center/Friends of the Earth U.S., 1999); author interview with Douglas Norlen, Washington, D.C., 1999.

95. In the United Kingdom, parliamentary scrutiny of the ECGD's proposed support for the Ilisu dam project in Turkey was key to the ECGD's adopting a project screening process and a set of business principles.

96. In the case of the Ilisu and Yusufeli dams in Turkey, for which ECGD support was requested, public pressure forced the contractors—Balfour Beatty and AMEC—to withdraw.

97. For an account of the shareholder campaign, see Kate Geary and Hannah Griffiths, "Organising a Shareholder Resolution: The Balfour Beatty Campaign," in Nicholas Hildyard and Mark Mansley, *A Campaigner's Guide to Lobbying Financial Markets* (London: Corner House, 2001), p. 91.

98. See, for example, Mark Mansley, "Building Tomorrow's Crisis? The Baku-

Tbilisi-Ceyhan Pipeline and BP: A Financial Analysis" (London: Claros Consulting, 2003), available at www.baku.org.uk.

99. Such actions include the occupying offices, leafleting employees, and picketing ECAs.

100. Comment made by Sir David John Weir, then chair of Balfour Beatty, at the company's annual general meeting, London, May 2001.

101. See www.equator-principles.com.

102. Address by Chris Beale to the Export Credits Group of the OECD, Paris, November 2003.

103. See www.equator-principles.com/documents/EKF.pdf.

104. See Chapter 9 by Mark Mansley in this volume.

105. Unattributable comment from SRI investor to me, 2003.

11

Revenue Transparency and the Publish What You Pay Campaign

Gavin Hayman and Corene Crossin

There is a growing literature linking the dependency of a country on primary extractive industries with unaccountable and corrupt state institutions, poverty, and conflict.[1] Stanford academic Terry Lynn Karl has described the way that natural resource wealth can create poverty as the "paradox of plenty."[2] This paradox of poverty in the midst of wealth partly exists because the political structures that accrete around resource "bonanza" economies seldom convert this wealth into long-term social development policies, especially where public institutions are relatively young. If a state has direct access to substantial rents from natural resources, typically from foreign investors, it is freed from the pressures for public accountability that emerge in a state dependent on broad-based domestic taxation. Instead of trying to appeal to a broad domestic constituency, ruling elites may focus on controlling resource rents. "Crony capitalism" soon develops, with government officials diverting resource revenues away from the public purse and into systems of patronage to line their own pockets, to fund internal security control, and sometimes to finance military adventurism. Domestic politics itself becomes a struggle between different constituencies for access to resource rents, mediated by a ruling elite that bases its patronage on communal, regional, or other factional considerations. This "rentier" model of state (mis)behavior is inherently unstable and vulnerable to dissolution into armed conflict, as competing groups may resort to violence.[3]

This depressing picture of political volatility and insecurity is evident in many resource-dependent developing countries today, including Algeria, Angola, Burma/Myanmar, Bolivia, Cambodia, Colombia, Congo-Brazzaville, the Democratic Republic of Congo, Equatorial Guinea, Guinea, Indonesia, Kazakhstan, Nauru, Nigeria, Papua New Guinea, the

Solomon Islands, Sudan, Turkmenistan, and Venezuela. These and other countries possess natural resource wealth that is starkly at odds with their woefully inadequate provision of basic public services and generally poor economic performance, and they are characterized in varying degrees by the rentier politics described above.

In suggesting mechanisms to more effectively address the linkages among natural resource exploitation, corruption, and armed conflict, this chapter focuses specifically on the problem that governments in resource-rich developing countries frequently do not publish any information on what they earn from natural resources, while multinational corporations do not publish what they pay to these governments for access to resources.[4] This opacity makes it much easier for officials to reap colossal personal rewards from resource extraction without fear of being held accountable for revenue mismanagement either by their own peoples or by the international community, which is often a major provider of development aid to such countries.

In simple terms, the greed and concealment of governments and, by extension, the multinational resource extraction companies they do business with may aggravate political and social grievances that can result in conflict. Sometimes there is an even more explicit link among natural resource revenues, lack of transparency, and conflict. In Sudan, for instance, oil revenues of $1 million per day helped to fund the government's war in the south in the 1990s.[5] In Congo-Brazzaville in 1997, the arms used by President Denis Sassou-Nguesso's private militia during a bitter four-month war against incumbent president Pascal Lissouba were paid for, in part, by money obtained by the sale of rights to Congo's future oil production.[6] Perhaps the starkest example of the links among resource wealth, lack of financial transparency, and armed conflict is Angola, where natural resources provided revenues to both sides of the bitter thirty-year civil war. The ruling elite used Angola's vast oil reserves for personal enrichment and set up elaborate oil-for-arms deals, which enabled government officials and their international business partners to profiteer directly from the war. This grand-scale corruption was facilitated by the opacity of the arrangements made between foreign oil companies and the government of Angola, which hampered effective scrutiny from the outside. At the same time, the rebel movement, the National Union for the Total Independence of Angola (UNITA), funded its war effort through revenues from diamonds.[7] The result was to perpetuate three decades of violence and despair.

While natural resource wealth cannot be said to be the *only* source of conflict in a given country, it is clear that the mismanagement of those resources can aggravate existing political, social, and other grievances and heighten the risk of conflict. Policies that increase the likelihood of revenues' being used to alleviate such grievances through spending on poverty reduction, health care, education, and other public services, rather than being squandered or misappropriated by state officials, may prevent the occurrence of conflict in resource-dependent developing countries. Such policies could also strengthen the process of postconflict recovery. In short, a necessary condition for the effective and accountable management of resources is financial transparency.

The Publish What You Pay Campaign

The Publish What You Pay (PWYP) campaign was officially launched in London in June 2002 by an international coalition of nongovernmental organizations (NGOs) amid this growing consensus that the lack of transparency in the extractive industry sector was a particularly malign governance issue and that voluntary initiatives from extractive companies to address the problem had all but failed. The campaign was bolstered by the support of international financier George Soros, who believes that raising the governance standards of corporations that are geared toward exploiting markets in the developing world would go a long way toward ameliorating the negative effects of globalization. Since the launch of the campaign, more than 200 NGOs around the world have become members—and the number continues to grow.[8]

The key message of the campaign is that extractive companies should publish all their payments to governments and public agencies in the countries where they do business and that host governments should publish their receipts of such payments. Disclosure by both companies and governments should allow citizens and other concerned parties to double-check the accuracy of the figures, so that they can begin the task of holding their governments to account for the way resource revenues are spent. Such disclosure is seen as part of a wider strategy for reform of the rules and institutions of natural resource extraction to make them more open and accountable and thereby to reduce the risk of resource mismanagement and its contribution to conflict. Once public information on revenues is available, it should be scrutinized by local civil society, aid donors, and other concerned parties. Although publication of revenue data by companies and governments will not in itself curb corruption, nor will it change the ethos of nontransparency overnight, it provides a foundation on which wider efforts at reform can be built. When the public does not know how much money is being paid to whom by whom and for what purpose, it is difficult to see how any anticorruption strategy can make progress in countries that rely on resource rents as their main economic driver.

The PWYP campaign is perhaps unusual among international initiatives that address the economic dimensions of conflict and white-collar crime. Rather than addressing money laundering, organized crime, smuggling, or other clearly illegal activities per se, the campaign is trying to target the basic financial interactions between companies and governments to aim for the disclosure of legitimate payments that may be illegitimately used.

Extractive Industries and Governments: Changing the Rules of the Game

Grand-scale corruption scandals uncovered in Africa and Central Asia demonstrated that revenue transparency is needed not only for the sake of developing countries but also for the good of the extractive industries themselves. Misuse of company funds by employees of the French oil company Elf Aquitaine during the 1980s and 1990s, for instance, resulted in the conviction of thirty former senior executives of the company (now merged into Total) in mid-November 2003.[9] The trial revealed that senior executives, unconstrained by any disclosure requirements in Africa and elsewhere, had over a period of many years paid vast sums in bribes to politicians in several African countries, including Angola. Those executives in charge of paying the bribes also enriched themselves at the company's expense (and were prosecuted for this embezzlement rather than for the bribery and corruption itself), including siphoning off commissions into secret bank accounts, buying multimillion-dollar properties and expensive jewelry, and embezzling money for divorce and alimony fees.[10]

Similarly, in Kazakhstan, the largest-ever foreign corruption investigation in U.S. legal history uncovered a major international corruption scandal that "defrauded the Government of Kazakhstan of funds to which it was entitled from oil transactions and defrauded the people of Kazakhstan of the right to the honest services of their elected and appointed officials."[11] As a result, over $1 billion of Kazakhstan's oil income paid by the U.S. oil company Mobil (now ExxonMobil) appears to have ended up offshore and out of sight under President Nursultan Nazarbayev's direct control in a secret fund in Switzerland.[12] Riggs Bank in Washington, D.C., was recently fined $25 million for its role in laundering revenues from, among others, an offshore and out-of-sight bank account run by Equatorial Guinea's dictatorial president Teodoro Obiang.[13] It is hard to imagine that corruption of these proportions would have been possible if companies had been obliged from the start to be transparent about their payments to governments.

Understanding the Rules of the Game

Mechanisms for achieving transparency have to be specifically geared to the complex business relationships between extractive companies and host governments. This requires an appropriate understanding of the financial and contractual arrangements that characterize the extractive industry sector.[14] For instance, payments that oil, mining, and gas companies make to host governments typically include royalty payments denominated as a percentage value of production; bonus payments made to governments on signing a contract ("signature bonuses"), on locating commercial mineral deposits, or on reaching certain production levels; and corporate income tax, paid on income after permitted deductions for operating, exploration, interest costs, and depreciation of assets. In addition, companies pay withholding tax on dividend payments, excise tax, customs duties, sales or value-added tax, and property taxes. In some countries, company payments to state agencies can take other forms, such as contributions to the expenses of public or paramilitary security forces that guard their facilities.

There are two main types of contractual arrangements through which extractive companies interact with governments. Most mining contracts, and many oil and gas contracts signed before the mid-1980s, are "concessionary agreements." Under such an agreement, companies are given the right to explore, develop, produce, transport, and market a commodity within a certain area for a specific amount of time. The company holds title to the resources produced, but production and sale from the concession area are subject to rentals, royalties, bonuses, and taxes. Concessionary agreements often take the form of a "joint venture," in which companies take up a percentage of an operating license for a given concession, pay proportionate development and operational costs, and, after the payment of taxes and royalties, receive any remaining profits in proportion to their shareholding. In such cases, requiring concession holders to disclose their payments to a government would provide a clear picture of a government's income from these types of concessions.

Most of the more recent oil and gas contracts, by contrast, leave the ownership of hydrocarbon and mineral reserves with the host government. The extractive company or companies bear all exploration costs and risks, as well as the development and production costs, in return for a stipulated share of the resulting oil or gas production. Most commonly these arrangements take the form of production sharing agreements (PSAs). In the oil industry, where PSAs are most important, contracting companies are entitled to recoup their costs from a share of the oil ("cost oil") extracted from a production area or "block." After payment of taxes and other charges, the remaining oil ("profit oil") is divided among the equity partners, usually including the state oil company of the host country, in proportion to the size of their shareholdings in the block. The theoretical advantage of a PSA over a joint venture, from a host government's point of view, is that the government gets its own share of the oil, which it can control and sell independently of the marketing networks of its private-sector partners. However, PSAs tend to be less transparent than concessionary agreements. Because the government is receiving revenues both directly (through signature bonuses, royalties, taxes, etc.) and indirectly (through the sale of its share of the oil), efforts to reach the disclosure of the complete income become more complicated.

Mechanisms for Corporate Disclosure

Because of the complexity of corporate-government agreements in the extractive industries, there is no one regulatory mechanism that would bring about revenue transparency from all the companies involved. The PWYP campaign advocates various control mechanisms, the list of which is expanding as the campaign's knowledge and experience grows. A revision of stock market listing rules and international accounting standards are two mechanisms that exemplify the current thinking of the campaign.

Stock exchange listing rules. In order to be listed and have their securities admitted to trading on financial markets, companies must publish a prospectus outlining their activities and regularly report on their financial records. The PWYP campaign proposes that, as a condition of listing on stock exchanges, extractive companies should be required by financial market regulators to disclose information about tax payments, royalty fees, revenue-sharing payments, and commercial transactions with government and public-sector entities on a country-by-country basis. This requirement would not necessitate a dramatic reform of current practices.

Most stock exchanges already require that risks to investors be clearly disclosed, and they have the power to require disclosure in the public interest. Although the legal provisions pertaining to disclosure in the public interest are often interpreted narrowly, the history of securities regulation shows that disclosure of corporate financial data has long been used to effect change in the way that corporations are managed and held accountable for their actions. The 1934 Securities Exchange Act, which created the U.S. Securities and Exchange Commission (SEC), for example, specifies that disclosure requirements for securities are subject to conditions, rules, and regulations that the SEC prescribes "as necessary or appropriate in the public interest or for the protection of investors."[15] In this light, it could reasonably be argued that the promotion of transparency and good governance in corrupt and conflict-prone countries where listed companies operate would be "appropriate" and in the public interest, not least given the costly effects of corruption scandals on domestic markets and taxpayer money in the companies' home countries.

To date there has been reluctance on the part of multinational companies to publicly support this form of regulation. An objection sometimes raised is that listings-based disclosure would not capture privately held companies or state-owned enterprises, particularly from those countries that may not value corporate social responsibility. This is a valid point but not an insuperable barrier to transparency. An important step toward overcoming this "collective action problem" would obviously be to apply changes to disclosure rules and reporting requirements across all major securities markets and jurisdictions, so that compliant companies cannot be undercut by less cooperative ones. Rather than forcing changes to company laws at the national level, listing rules and reporting requirements would then apply to multinationals quoted on securities markets beyond the jurisdiction in which they are incorporated.

Furthermore, privately held or state-owned companies that wish to engage in resource extraction on an international scale increasingly need to raise the large sums required for investment on the global equity or capital markets. Transparency conditions attached to loan financing from banks or the underwriting commitments from insurance companies, for instance, would further shrink the number of companies that remain outside the circle of mandatory transparency. Encouragingly, in June 2003, a group of private-sector investors controlling some $3 trillion in funds (by February 2004 the group represented $6.9 trillion) issued a public statement warning that lack of transparency could have negative reputational impacts on companies.[16] The investors, including CalPers (the largest pension fund in the United States), Merrill Lynch Investment Managers, ISIS Fund Management, and Fidelity Investments, state that

> legitimate, but undisclosed, payments to governments may be accused of contributing to the conditions under which corruption can thrive. This is a significant business risk, making companies vulnerable to accusations of complicity in corrupt behavior, impairing their local and global 'license to operate,' rendering them vulnerable to local conflict and insecurity, and possibly compromising their long-term commercial prospects in these markets.[17]

The group of investors is therefore actively encouraging the companies that they invest in to adopt transparent business practices.

There is a need for further creative thinking on other areas for policy intervention that could address the issue of potential competitive disadvantages of more progressive companies vis-à-vis less responsible companies that lack domestic pressure. In the interim, the changes to listing rules suggested by the PWYP campaign would apply to the overwhelming majority of significant players in the extractive industries, including such publicly traded oil supermajors as ExxonMobil, ChevronTexaco, British Petroleum (BP), Royal Dutch/Shell, and Total. When their potential competitors, such as PetroChina or Lukoil, seek to tap the world's major capital markets to compete more effectively with the world's major players, these changes will apply to them too.

International accounting standards. Another potential mechanism for disclosure of company payments to host governments consists of the International Accounting Standards (IAS), a set of reporting requirements for companies presently adopted by thirty states. All listed companies in the enlarged European Union (EU) and Australia will report under the IAS from 2005 onward. In addition, there are signs of convergence between the IAS and the Generally Accepted Accounting Principles (GAAP) applied in the United States, which have come under pressure for reform in the wake of the Enron scandal. Although there continues to be disagreement between supporters of the two sets of standards, much of the international financial community recognizes the value of a single, principles-based reporting standard like the IAS.

In the United Kingdom, accounting principles generally comply with the current incarnation of the IAS. Companies file their end-of-year accounts at the UK Registrar of Companies, according to UK Standard Accounting Principles. Declarations of tax payments are currently listed as "UK tax payments" and then "overseas taxation." In the United Kingdom, as elsewhere in Europe, the United States, and other developed jurisdictions, one can find out what tax a company has paid in that jurisdiction by simply requesting the information from their country's equivalent of the UK's Companies House. But if a UK-registered company operates in a number of different countries, the overseas tax payment data included in annual accounts are an amalgamation of separate information for all locations. Therefore, examination of the accounts of such companies would not reveal data on tax payments to individual countries like Angola. This problem is further compounded by the fact that better-regulated jurisdictions generally do not demand the same degree of detail in reporting of companies' overseas operations as they do for activities at home.

The campaign advocates that the reporting requirements of the IAS (and other standards such as the GAAP in the United States) be adjusted to include the disclosure of tax and other payments made by extractive industries, broken down not only per country but also, importantly, for all their countries of operation.

A significant shortcoming of this mechanism of disclosure is that the IAS is currently not a global accounting standard. The IAS requirements are generally not enforced by developing countries, and so this mechanism would not apply to extractive companies and related commercial entities based in these countries, such as Angola's state-owned oil company, Sonangol. Like the listings-based mechanism discussed above, the IAS option would be most effective if it were to apply to all extractive businesses irrespective of their domicile. Again, there is a need for lateral thinking about policy options on how to harmonize disclosure requirements across all jurisdictions. One option, once transparency requirements have been written into the IAS, would be to condition development aid on a government's incorporation of the IAS into domestic law.

The Need for Mandatory Disclosure

The intricacies of extractive companies' financial dealings with host governments are frequently concealed by confidentiality clauses in their contracts. These clauses are sometimes cited by companies as a reason that they are legally unable to disclose their payments to governments, and it is true that the latter may have no hesitation in using such clauses to muzzle companies that might otherwise be willing to publish their payments. This problem in fact demonstrates the need for mandatory and industrywide mechanisms advocated by the PWYP campaign, rather than voluntary disclosure by individual companies. The case of BP in Angola is instructive. In 2001, after twelve months of dialogue with the nongovernmental organization Global Witness about the role of extractive industries in encouraging transparency and good governance, BP publicly announced its intention to reveal its total net oil production by block and aggregate payments to Sonangol—both in respect to its PSA terms. BP also said it would publish total taxes and levies paid to the Angolan government. As a consequence of BP's announcement, Sonangol, in a letter copied to all other multinational oil companies in Angola, threatened to terminate BP's contract if it published the data.[18]

Although contractual confidentiality clauses may prevent companies from disclosing their payments voluntarily, they often contain an opt-out, which allows companies to make such disclosures if required by the laws or regulations of their home countries. The standard Deep Water Production Sharing Agreement in Angola, for example, states that "either Party may, without such approval [i.e., the approval of the national government or the state oil company], disclose such information . . . to the extent required by any applicable law, regulation or rule (including, without limitation, any regulation or rule of any regulatory agency, securities commission or securities exchange on which the securities of such Party or of any of such Party's affiliates are listed)."[19]

Clauses such as this are one reason the PWYP campaign champions mandatory measures that would eventually capture all extractive companies, rather than voluntary initiatives like that undertaken by BP. Following the mandatory route would mean that a company like BP, along with its competitors, would disclose all its payments to a government like Angola as a routine aspect of its compliance activities, not as a political or ethical statement. In such circumstances, the host government would have no contractual argument with which to retaliate. Although certain companies appear resolutely opposed to greater disclosure of financial information, public statements and private discussions suggest that others could accept the case for mandatory measures as long as they are enforced comprehensively, so that fair competition is preserved.

Disclosure by Governments

There is another strand to the PWYP campaign's activities that bears on the other side of the revenue equation, namely the receipt of payments by governments that are host to resource extraction operations. Some governments have decided to require transparency through domestic legislation. In 2003, the government of Nigeria, the most notable example, stated its intention to create laws that would require double disclosure of revenues in the oil sector, so that companies publish what they pay and state agencies (such as the finance ministry) publish information about what they receive.[20] Any discrepancies would then be investigated. The motivation for this stance appears to be that a group of reformers within the government, led by President Olusegun Obasanjo, are attempting to demonstrate to the world that Nigeria can tackle its huge and destabilizing problem with oil-related corruption.

Clearly, there are also some governments that have no interest in transparency because the ruling elites that dominate them are enriching themselves from oil and mining revenues, at the expense of other citizens. These governments may look for ways to signal their commitment to transparency, for example by signing up to international processes that promote it, while stalling any real action on the ground for as long as possible. Although these governments may make limited and cosmetic gestures to appease international sentiment, they are unlikely to volunteer to take action that constrains the freedom of corrupt officials to loot state assets. This is the major flaw with the voluntary approach to transparency, which, as will be discussed later, currently dominates the debate among donor governments.

If governments will not open their books, even when their own citizens want them to, then what levers can be brought to bear? One obvious lever is development aid conditionality. Revenue transparency could and should be made a condition of all loans by the World Bank, the International Monetary Fund (IMF), regional development banks, and all development assistance from bilateral donors, as well as of all funding or guarantees to private-sector extractive projects given by export credit agencies. The PWYP campaign is currently campaigning for the World Bank and IMF to mainstream revenue transparency requirements into all their operations in the more than fifty countries where, according to the World Bank's own measure, natural resources are economically significant.[21] There may be other economic and diplomatic pressures that could be brought to bear, for example the use of trade preferences and reduced tariff charges for countries that are perceived to be taking concrete steps to encourage fair and accurate revenue reporting and budgeting or conditional provision of economic assistance on the same basis.

Conditionality on development assistance and trade is controversial in much of the developing world because of its use in support of the geopolitical and commercial interests of Northern countries. Thus, in some developing countries, civil society organizations that on the one hand favor external support for domestic revenue transparency may for other reasons be bitterly opposed to the influence exerted on their governments by the World Bank, the IMF, and other international financial institutions. There is no inconsistency, however, in arguing that the role of these institutions in the developing world should be debated and challenged and at the same time arguing that where they do make loans or provide technical assistance, revenue transparency should be among the attached conditions. Lending conditionality is not flawless, but if it is to be used, promoting transparency must be among its main goals.[22]

Assuming that a government has consented to publish its receipts from natural resource exploitation, there are still some technical complexities that need to be overcome. An extractive company in a country like Nigeria or Indonesia, for instance, may be making dozens of payments to different state agencies, in more than one currency, and at national, regional, and local levels. Any transparency regime would need to create accounting systems for tracing and adding up all these receipts in such a way that they can be reconciled against the data published by companies or, in cases where the numbers do not add up, finding the source of the discrepancy. One possibility is that a third party, such as an international accounting firm, could take on responsibility for reconciling the data, while donors like the World Bank could help countries and their civil societies to build the technical and administrative capacity to perform this accounting themselves.

It is very important, however, that all this monitoring proceed on a basis of complete openness of revenue data, not along the lines of the "aggregated disclosure" currently touted as a model by some industry representatives and the World Bank. In the aggregated disclosure model, a third party such as the World Bank would collect revenue data on payments from companies in confidence and would publish only an aggregated figure of total payments by all companies operating in that country. There are two obvious problems with this model. The first is that it is only quasi-transparent; the data from each company are revealed not to the wider public but to an intermediary whose own objectivity may be controversial in the country concerned. In some developing countries, for example, the World Bank is not regarded as an honest broker because of its perceived association with the interests of Northern governments and multinational companies. Thus civil society, meaning the whole range of institutions and individuals in a given country that need to know how their natural resources are being managed, is cut out of a significant part of the monitoring process.

The second problem is that "aggregated disclosure" would undermine the principle that companies are individually responsible for their actions. Companies do not aggregate the data they publish about their financial operations in their home countries, so why should they do so in the developing countries where they operate? The proponents of aggregated disclosure are therefore touting an international double standard. The only obvious beneficiaries of aggregated disclosure would be oil and mining companies, which would thereby be relieved of the need to reveal the contract terms they have struck with different countries (which may vary considerably) or global tax minimization arrangements (which may be legal but are controversial). Although the thought of providing any information that may help developing countries in collective bargaining is an anathema to many large multinational companies, such concerns are unlikely to generate much sympathy elsewhere, given the desperate poverty of many countries in which these companies do business.

A Principle with Wider Implications

The mechanisms proposed by the PWYP campaign are closely tied to the notion that a country's natural resources are held in trust and managed by the host government for the benefit of ordinary citizens, who as the true owners have a right to enjoy the benefits derived from the exploitation of those resources. In fact, UN General Assembly Resolution 1803, concerning permanent sovereignty over natural resources, states that foreign investment agreements entered into by a state shall "strictly and conscientiously" respect the sovereignty of peoples over their natural resources and their right to development and shall be observed in good faith.[23] Opaque transactions between extractive industry companies and host governments fall short of complying with the "good faith" requirement in Resolution 1803. It is difficult to see how opaque business agreements that encourage bad stewardship of revenues can also be said to respect the right of people to development.

The policy reforms proposed by the PWYP campaign for resource revenue disclosure need not be viewed as contrary to state sovereignty doctrines, where these are interpreted in terms of government's custodial rights and responsibilities over resources belonging to the nation. Such disclosure requirements could also assist in assuaging industry and investor concerns over the need for socially responsible corporate practices. The campaign seeks to change the rules of natural resource extraction to sever the nexus among revenue opacity, corruption, poverty, and the propensity for violent conflict in resource-dependent countries. There is also a clear need for parity between the North and South. Extractive companies routinely publish their payments to governments in Europe, North America, and Australasia. Promulgating a lower standard in the South implies that citizens in the developing world are not entitled to the same standards of disclosure accepted in the North.

There have been encouraging indications that the principles advocated by the PWYP campaign will become part of a global government-led movement toward transparency in the extractive sector. Responding to the issues raised by the campaign, UK prime minister Tony Blair announced at the World Summit for Sustainable Development in September 2002 that his government would lead an initiative working toward the creation of an international framework for revenue disclosure. The result was the Extractive Industries Transparency Initiative (EITI).[24] A large number of international extractive companies and national governments are broadly supportive of the scheme, though many have raised questions over its details.

The EITI, the most significant response to date to the work of the PWYP campaign, has brought together representatives of governments, industry, and civil society. It has also broadened international dialogue beyond the issue of company disclosure to also consider how to promote the transparency of governments' revenue streams. A broad set of principles has been agreed upon that "underline the importance of transparency by governments and companies in the extractive industries," "the principle and practice of accountability by government to all citizens for the stewardship of revenue streams and public expenditure," and the need for double disclosure (by both companies and governments) to reconcile company figures with government accounts.[25] The EITI has demonstrated that transparent reporting of revenue flows is neither burdensome nor difficult, and it has identified a number of pilot countries willing to begin the process, including Nigeria, Azerbaijan, and Ghana. São Tomé and Príncipe, on the eve of significant oil exploration efforts, also indicated its interest in following the EITI approach.

Alongside the EITI, the June 2003 declaration of the Group of Eight (G-8) countries also supports revenue transparency in the extractive industries, along with a commitment to encourage governments and both private and state-owned companies to disclose their revenue flows and payments. The G-8 pledged to work with participating governments to achieve high standards of transparent public revenue management, extending to the processes for awarding contracts and concessions; to provide capacity-building support where needed; and to encourage the IMF and World Bank to give necessary technical support to this end.[26]

Policymakers sometimes confuse or simply conflate the PWYP campaign with the EITI, which makes it important to stress the differences in character and focus between the two. The former is an NGO campaign that emphasizes the role of companies in promoting transparency and argues that mandatory measures are needed to achieve its goal. The EITI, by contrast, is a framework for discussion and action that involves governments, companies, and civil society (including representatives of the PWYP campaign), which until now has emphasized a purely voluntary approach to publishing information. This voluntary approach is a major flaw, because it will inevitably mean much slower, if any, progress in those countries where ruling elites have the most to hide. Without strong international pressure, the leaders of countries like Angola have little reason to implement an initiative that would threaten their personal enrichment. Indeed, concerted international pressure was credited for the Angolan government's 2003 decision to publish a signature bonus received from ChevronTexaco.[27]

The attractiveness of the PWYP campaign, and one of the reasons for its success in catalyzing the debate on revenue transparency, is its simplicity. It merely asks extractive companies to do abroad what they are already obliged to do in their home countries. Yet it comes as no surprise that even this simple measure encounters many problems.

Opportunities and Limitations

The governance of a sovereign state comes with rights and responsibilities. Governments have a legitimate right to maintain law and order within their state's borders by using revenues derived from its resources. As highlighted in Resolution 1803, however, governments also have the responsibility to act conscientiously in the stewardship and management of these resources. Although the primary responsibility for good management of a state's natural resource revenues rests with its government, the PWYP campaign has focused predominantly on the corporations that do business with it. There are several reasons for this.

First, there are various levers that can be used to press a government to change the way it runs its country, but not all of them are effective all the time. Development assistance is one such lever, but it can be of limited use in countries with significant natural resources, as a government whose officials embezzle billions of dollars of resource rents can easily afford to refuse tens of millions of dollars in external aid. There are other problems with development assistance too. For example, donors often continue to provide generous aid to resource-dependent countries for short-term geopolitical reasons even when it is clear that massive resource revenues are being squandered by those countries' rulers in ways that contradict the aid's stated aims.

A second reason for the focus on companies is that the number of multinationals that actually pay revenues to governments in the developing world is quite small, given the massive capital costs and the technical sophistication of investments required in resource extraction. For a coalition of NGOs, it is easier to influence a small number of companies to adopt more progressive disclosure policies than to target a large number of governments, many of which are highly resistant to imposing greater accountability on themselves. Once companies have started declaring what they are paying to a particular government, it will become progressively harder for the latter to avoid disclosing what it is doing with the money.

Third, the PWYP campaign does not focus on companies purely as a lever for changing the behavior of governments. While the principal responsibility for action on transparency lies with governments, this responsibility does not end with them. All direct and indirect participants in the extractive industries, which include extractive companies and the home governments in the developed world that regulate their activities, have an obligation to act in good faith with respect to the sovereign owners of natural resources—the ordinary citizens of resource-rich countries. Clearly, the nature of this obligation needs to be further explored. Technically speaking, there is no direct international legal obligation owed to "the people," in relation to the exploitation of their natural resources, by entities without international legal personality, such as multinational companies. However, it is evident that natural resource extraction companies do not operate in a moral vacuum, nor is it in their own commercial interest for them to do so.

In fact, it is easy to argue for a "business case" for corporate transparency. There is little value to companies in having their legitimate payments to governments misappropriated and squandered, if this may lead to social divisiveness and instability that may eventually threaten their operations. As Shell and Chevron have experienced in Nigeria, the long-term reputational damage from dealings with a corrupt regime can be huge and can have direct impact on the bottom line. For instance, poverty, ethnic unrest, and resentment against oil companies boiled over in the Niger Delta region in March 2003, and the ensuing turmoil slashed Nigeria's oil output by more than 750,000 barrels per day—a loss of one-third of the total production of sub-Saharan Africa's biggest oil producer.[28] Because of the unrest, some oil tankers loading in Nigeria have even been required to take out war risk insurance.[29] Even in relatively peaceful poor countries, companies whose legitimate payments are squandered by host governments are vulnerable to accusations of complicity with corruption, which can damage their reputation locally and internationally.

Increasing awareness of the costs of being associated with "bad" or nontransparent business in developing countries is tied in with the growth in recent years of initiatives to promote corporate social responsibility more generally. Transparency is therefore in the interest of companies, both morally and commercially. The additional costs of being transparent are few, because companies already possess revenue data. It is simply a matter of publishing these data. Irresponsible companies will inevitably try to evade transparency requirements, perhaps by looking for ever-more complex or obscure routes through which to channel their payments to governments. But once the need for mandatory disclosure has been accepted by governments and industry, dealing with this problem becomes a question of closing off loopholes, just as in any other area of regulation.

The Need for Global Action

Collective action is key to the success of all the mechanisms advocated by the PWYP campaign to compel extractive companies to disclose their payments to host governments. In addition, these mechanisms would work best alongside multilateral efforts to compel governmental transparency. A systematic policy approach is needed to mainstream transparency as a tool for conflict prevention in resource-rich countries, supported by institutions such as the World Bank, the IMF, and export credit agencies.

The Role of the World Bank and the IMF

Despite widely documented links among resource dependence, corruption, and the prevalence of poverty and conflict, the issue of revenue transparency has still not received sufficient prominence in the policies and practices of the World Bank and the IMF. Both are frequently criticized for their failures in demonstrably committing to openness and accountability in all projects they are involved in. For instance, although the World Bank made disclosure and auditing of revenues from the Chad-Cameroon oil pipeline a condition for its support for the project, it failed to apply such conditionality to the signature bonuses paid by participating companies. In addition, the World Bank's showpiece disclosure agreement with the government of Chad will come up for renegotiation at the same time that the first significant revenues will be flowing back from the pipeline. Similarly, although an independent panel was set up to oversee the disbursement of revenues, the panel currently lacks the capacity to fulfill its mandate.[30] A 2002 World Bank and IMF review of their national poverty reduction strategies concluded that transparency within countries and international development partnerships is critical if efforts to reduce poverty are to succeed.[31] Yet both the IMF's "Oil Diagnostic" revenue-tracking exercise with the Angolan government and the IMF–World Bank audit of oil revenues in Congo-Brazzaville have lacked any commitment to publish publicly any results, and it is not clear how those results will be factored into a future assistance programs.[32]

Notwithstanding their weaknesses, the IMF and World Bank do have the capacity to effect positive change and encourage the publication of earnings by host governments and domestic companies. They can, for example, assist in the comparative analysis of data published, can provide technical support to host governments to accurately compile and publish earnings, and have the power to penalize governments that do not disclose relevant data. The Extractive Industries Review, a two-year multistakeholder consultation by the World Bank that completed its final report at the end of 2003, states that

> the WBG [World Bank Group] should vigorously pursue transparency at country and company level in all the resource-rich countries it works with. The WBG should partner with, for instance, the Extractive Industries Transparency Initiative and Publish What You Pay to promote revenue transparency in its client countries and should use its power as a convener to vigorously support existing efforts to build common action against corruption. WBG requirements need to be in line with these initiatives.[33]

The Role of Export Credit Agencies

Export credit agencies (ECAs) are another group of international financial players able to influence government monetary policy and fiscal transparency.[34] These are public agencies that provide government-backed loans, guarantees, credits, and insurance to private corporations from their home country to do business abroad, particularly in the financially and politically risky developing world. ECAs often back projects considered too risky by multilateral banks. They work to reduce the risk for their national companies wishing to invest overseas, and in this way ECA finance is a form of subsidy for companies from the ECA's home country by taxpayers of that country. Financing, either in terms of direct loans to participating companies or as a form of credit insurance to mitigate the risk of project payment default, is normally provided in return for the contractors' obtaining required equipment or some of the necessary workforce from the country that is providing the underwriting insurance. Leading agencies include COFACE in France, the Export-Import Bank (or the Ex-Im Bank) in the United States, Mediocredito Centrale SpA in Italy, and the

Export Credit Guarantee Department (ECGD) in the United Kingdom. These and other ECAs make up the world's biggest class of public international finance institutions, collectively exceeding the World Bank Group in the value of loans provided. They are also the primary sources of finance for oil, gas, and mining projects throughout the world. However, unlike the multilateral lending institutions, most ECAs are not required to consider the social and environmental impacts of the projects they support—nor do they have firm transparency standards. Current UK practice is illustrative of the need for transparency. In the case of the ECGD, projects covered by overseas investment insurance (OII) continue to be treated as "commercial-in-confidence." Between 1988 and 1996, the worldwide value of new export credit plans and guarantees increased fourfold, from $26 billion to $105 billion per year.[35] OII is issued mainly in developing and transitioning countries, where the problems of corruption and unproductive expenditure have a disproportionate impact. It is a concern, therefore, that this part of the ECGD's work remains secretive.

Against this background, the PWYP campaign argues that ECAs that extend support to extractive projects could require as a condition of support the disclosure of payments to the state by the investors in those projects. If taxpayers are to subsidize companies through ECAs, then public-interest criteria on social and environmental standards, including transparency, should be considered. Such conditionality would not affect state-owned oil or mining companies in host countries, however, except in cases where the state company is a partner in the particular investment sponsored by the ECA. Only then, in line with other partners, could it be required to publish its payments to the national treasury. There is no overarching international body that oversees the activities of ECAs, and so it will be difficult to implement coordinated, collective policy reform by all ECAs. Again, there is no simple method of ensuring collective action, and ultimately, whether reforms are implemented will depend on the leadership and commitment of the Northern governments allied with the world's largest ECAs.

The Role of Regional Organizations

There are other steps that can be taken at regional and global levels to enhance both corporate and government transparency. Multilateral initiatives and institutions like the New Partnership for African Development (NEPAD) and the Organization for Economic Cooperation and Development (OECD) could, for instance, encourage the adoption of best practices in revenue disclosure and insist that all companies registered in their member states disclose taxes paid to individual countries. NEPAD, in particular, could play an important role in influencing host governments in

Africa to provide their consent to the disclosure of information. Supported by the international donor community, NEPAD could also play a role in building the capacity of governments to negotiate fair deals with extractive companies according to strict standards of transparency. The OECD also could assist in ending "secret deals" by structuring clear rules for transparent financial relationships between multinational companies and host governments. The OECD Anti-bribery Convention may offer a useful platform. Similarly, the EU could extend its recognition of the importance of transparency in the proper functioning of capital markets to its development aid projects. The EU's Cotonou Agreement with African, Caribbean, and Pacific recipients of development assistance already recognizes that fighting corruption is a fundamental element of future development assistance, and there is scope to use EU funds earmarked for promoting transparency to pay for local capacity-building and revenue-monitoring projects.

Conclusion: Will Revenue Transparency Prevent Conflict?

If the problems and challenges raised above were resolved and mandatory disclosure requirements were put in place, what would be the effect of disclosure of revenues in conflict-prone, resource-rich countries? Transparency in revenue payments is not a panacea for problems of revenue mismanagement. Rather, it is a necessary first step for corporate and government accountability—you cannot manage what you cannot measure. The PWYP campaign does not suggest that extraction companies tell host governments how to spend their money but rather that they should publish information that will help ordinary citizens—perhaps with external assistance—to hold their own government accountable. The logic is simple. When greater accountability is achieved through transparency and revenues are redirected toward poverty alleviation and improved governance, the propensity for grand-scale corruption by government officials and violent conflict in resource-dependent poor countries is likely to be diminished.

In the 1930s, U.S. legal scholar and future Supreme Court justice Felix Frankfurter identified the power of public scrutiny to this end as he piloted the landmark Securities Act through Congress. He wrote,

> The Securities Act is strong insofar as publicity is potent; it is weak insofar as publicity is not enough. . . . The existence of bonuses, excessive commissions and salaries, of preferential lists and the like, may all be open secrets among the knowing, but the knowing are few. There is a shrinking quality to such transactions; to force the knowledge of them into the open is largely to restrain their happening. Many practices safely pursued in private lose their justification in public.[36]

A possible argument against the publication of what is paid to host governments is that disclosure could ignite conflict in already politically and socially unstable countries. That is, publication of data on what a government earns may further anger already marginalized peoples and lead to violent opposition to suspected government malfeasance. However, it is difficult to predict whether publication of payments or earnings from resource revenues will have this effect. Any potential adverse impact of publication could be mitigated by planning and by providing local civil society organizations with tools to accurately interpret data and manage the nationwide dissemination of information. Indeed, the way information on payments and earnings can be managed and used to lobby for greater government accountability will vary depending on the particular country involved.

This highlights the need for a comprehensive, long-term strategy for integrating transparency and accountability at all levels of the extractive sector—from multinational companies to governments and state-owned companies and their international financial supporters. What is most important, of course, is transparency on the side of governments, not only in what they receive but ultimately in what they spend and how they spend it. The reform of revenue management from the extractive sector is only a subset of larger public finance management issues. These are outside the reach of the campaign on resource revenue transparency at the moment, but getting companies to publish their payments and governments to publish their revenues is part of an enabling environment for such larger reform issues.

A balanced perspective is required. The range of reforms proposed by the PWYP campaign are not a magic solution to the poverty and conflict associated with the paradox of plenty. A great deal of additional thought and planning is needed to handle carefully the transition from secrecy to openness in weakly democratic or undemocratic countries that have suffered years of poor economic performance. In particular, a major challenge will be to devise methods of strengthening democratic institutions to provide a secure domestic environment for people to question their leaders and air grievances about the management of national resources. This will include putting in place workable procedures to bring corrupt officials to justice.

Ultimately, whether the regulations and policy reforms advocated by the PWYP campaign are adopted will depend on the commitment of the resource extraction sector, international organizations, governments in the developed world, and their counterparts in developing countries to bring transparency to the fore of poverty reduction and conflict prevention strategies. All stakeholders need to act in concert to institutionalize transparency, good governance, and accountability. Simple and logical adjustments to existing policies of company disclosure, international accounting standards, and legislation to require the disclosure of company payments to host governments will guarantee collective action, create a level playing field for all operators, and provide the extractive industries with a "social license to operate."

Much work remains to be done by a wide range of actors before transparency can be established at the center of the extractive industries. Nevertheless, considerable progress has been made since the inception of the PWYP campaign in 2002 and the subsequent work of the UK government and others. Strong leadership will be needed from governments in the developed world and industry to tackle the major problems of the status quo and ensure that natural resource revenues, instead of becoming a cause of massive injustice and human misery, are used to prevent conflict and alleviate poverty, to the ultimate benefit of all.

Notes

1. See, for example, Halvard Buhaug and Scott G. Gates, "The Geography of Civil War," *Journal of Peace Research* 39, no. 4 (2002): 417–433; Paul Collier and Anke Hoeffler, "On Economic Causes of Civil War," *Oxford Economic Papers* 50 (1998): 563–573; Paul Collier, Anke Hoeffler, and Mans Söderbom, "On the Duration of Civil War," paper presented at the Workshop on Civil Wars and Postconflict Transitions, University of California, Irvine, May 18–20, 2001; Indra De Soysa, "Paradise Is a Bazaar? Greed, Creed, and Governance in Civil War, 1989–99," *Journal of Peace Research* 39, no. 4 (2002): 395–416; Philippe Le Billon, "The Political Ecology of War: Natural Resources and Armed Conflicts," *Political Geography* 20 (2001): 561–584; Philip Swanson, *Fuelling Conflicts: The Oil Industry and Armed Conflict* (Oslo: Fafo Institute for Applied Social Science, 2002); and Michael Ross, "How Do Natural Resources Influence Civil War? Evidence from Thirteen Cases," unpubl., 2003.

2. Terry Lynn Karl, *The Paradox of Plenty: Oil Booms and Petro-States* (Berkeley: University of California Press, 1997).

3. Collier and Hoeffler, "On Economic Causes of Civil War"; and Paul Collier, "Doing Well out of War: An Economic Perspective," in Mats Berdal and David M. Malone, eds., *Greed and Grievance: Economic Agendas in Civil Wars* (Boulder: Lynne Rienner, 2000), pp. 91–111; Paul Collier and Anke Hoeffler, "Greed and Grievance in Civil War" (Washington, D.C.: World Bank Development Research Group, 2001.

4. This chapter draws on Global Witness, *Time for Transparency: Coming Clean of Oil, Mining, and Gas Revenues* (Washington, D.C.: Global Witness, 2004), as well as other reports published by Global Witness, which are available at www.globalwitness.org.

5. Christian Aid, *The Scorched Earth: Oil and War in Sudan* (London: Christian Aid, 2001), p. 18.

6. Global Witness, *Time for Transparency*, pp. 18–33.

7. Ibid., pp. 36–52; Global Witness, *A Rough Trade: The Role of Companies and Governments in the Angolan Conflict* (London: Global Witness, 1998); and

Global Witness, *All the President's Men: The Devastating Story of Oil and Banking in Angola's Privatised War* (London: Global Witness, 2002).

8. For more information, see www.publishwhatyoupay.org.

9. The total embezzled was estimated at around $370 million. "Elf: Une histoire française," *Le Monde,* November 13, 2003; "AFP Previews 'Massive' Government Corruption Trial Involving French Oil Company," Agence France Presse, March 14, 2003; "Trente condemnations, dont quinze peines de prison ferme, et sept relaxes," *Le Monde,* November 14, 2003.

10. "AFP Previews 'Massive' Government Corruption Trial"; "Le procès Elf en correctionnelle: 'Pour qui tous ces bijoux?' Alfred Sirven interrogé sur ses emplettes place Vendôme," *Liberation,* April 9, 2003.

11. The scheme was based around Kazakh president Nursultan Nazarbayev and oil minister Nurlan Balgimbayev's demand that international oil companies such as Chevron (now ChevronTexaco) and Mobil (now ExxonMobil) pay a series of unusual fees to middleman James Giffen on behalf of the Republic of Kazakhstan. This arrangement, the indictment alleges, helped Giffen to skim money from the deals and send some $78 million in kickbacks to President Nazarbayev and others through dozens of overseas bank accounts in Switzerland, Liechtenstein, and the British Virgin Islands. See *United States v. James H. Giffen* (U.S. District Court, Southern District of New York, 2003), indictment, p. 3.

12. Global Witness, *Time for Transparency,* p. 9.

13. Kathleen Day, "Record Fine Levied for Riggs Bank Violations," *Washington Post,* May 14, 2004, p. A1.

14. See, for example, Philip Swanson, Mai Olgard, and Leiv Lunde, "Who Gets the Money? Reporting Resource Revenues," in Ian Bannon and Paul Collier, eds., *Natural Resources and Violent Conflict: Issues and Actions* (Washington, D.C.: World Bank, 2003), pp. 43–96.

15. As per secs. 12–15 of the U.S. Securities Exchange Act.

16. "Investors' Statement on Transparency in the Extractives Sector," joint statement by ISIS Asset Management et al., June 17, 2003, revised February 2004.

17. Ibid.

18. Global Witness, *Time for Transparency,* p. 72.

19. Article 33(2) of the *Standard Deep Water Production Sharing Agreement with Angolan state oil company Sonangol,* on file with the authors.

20. Transparency International, "Nigeria Takes the Lead on Oil Transparency," press release, Berlin, November 7, 2003.

21. This figure is a conservative extension from that contained in the World Bank's 2002 report on the global mining industry to incorporate developing-country economies dependent on the oil and gas sector. World Bank analysts used a 6 percent cutoff point as an indicator that a sector is critically important to an economy.

22. See also Chapter 12 by James K. Boyce in this volume.

23. Art. 8 of UN General Assembly Resolution 1803, no. 17, December 14, 1963.

24. See UK Department of International Development, *Draft Report of the Extractive Industries Transparency Initiative (EITI) London Conference,* June 17, 2003, available at http://www.dfid.gov.uk.

25. See ibid., "Statement of Agreed Principles and Actions."

26. "Fighting Corruption and Improving Transparency: A G8 Declaration," June 2003.

27. Heather Timmons, "Angola Set to Disclose Payments from Big Oil," *New York Times,* May 13, 2004, sec. W, p. 1.

28. "Shell Nigeria Closures Continue," *BBC News,* March 24, 2003, available at www.bbc.co.ulc/1/h1/business/z8 80955.htm.

29. "Insurers Put Nigeria on War Risks List," *Energy Compass,* September 5, 2003; "Insurers Want War Premium," *Africa Intelligence,* September 17, 2003.

30. See, for example, "Chad Sees First Trickle of Cash from Pipeline," *Los Angeles Times,* December 26, 2003.

31. Joint IMF and WBG Development Committee, *Poverty Reduction Strategy Papers (PRSP): Progress in Implementation,* Report no. DC2002-0016 (Washington, D.C.: International Monetary Fund and World Bank Group, 2002).

32. A poorly edited summary of the Angola diagnostic, however, has now been released.

33. World Bank, *Striking a Better Balance,* final report of the Extractive Industries Review (Washington, D.C.: World Bank, 2003), 1:47.

34. See Chapter 10 by Nicholas Hildyard in this volume.

35. Nicholas Hildyard, "Snouts at the Trough: Export Credit Agencies, Corporate Welfare and Policy Incoherence," Corner House Briefing #14, Dorset: The Corner House, 1999, available at www.thecornerhouse.org.uk.

36. Felix Frankfurter, quoted in Global Witness, *Time for Transparency,* p. 83.

12

Development Assistance, Conditionality, and War Economies

James K. Boyce

Official development assistance (ODA) usually comes with strings attached. Multilateral and bilateral donors use conditionality to advance a variety of goals, some noble, others not so noble. Sometimes the conditions are spelled out in formal performance criteria, as in the economic policy targets in International Monetary Fund (IMF) loan agreements. Other times, the conditions are communicated informally in a process known as "policy dialogue." Whether formal or informal, conditionality makes access to assistance contingent on actions by the recipient. Foreign aid is seldom a blank check.

The objectives of conditionality typically do not include the prevention or resolution of armed conflict. The IMF and the World Bank primarily use conditionality to pursue short-term macroeconomic stabilization and longer-term structural adjustment. Bilateral donors often use conditionality for commercial purposes, as when aid is tied to purchases of goods and services from the donor country. They also may use it to advance geopolitical aims, as illustrated in the U.S. government's efforts to enlist support for the war in Iraq.[1] Donors have also attempted, albeit rather sporadically, to use conditionality to promote political reforms under the rubric of "good governance."[2]

These conditionalities may affect the likelihood of war or peace indirectly. Proponents of conventional macroeconomic conditionality sometimes claim, for example, that neoliberal policies serve the cause of peace by fostering economic growth. On the other hand, critics argue that these same policies not only often fail to promote growth but also exacerbate income disparities and, thus, social tensions.[3] At the same time, trade liberalization—a standard reform pressed by the international financial institutions—and the resulting loss of tariff revenues can squeeze the fiscal capacity of governments to fund peace-related programs.[4]

In principle, conditionality can also be harnessed directly to the objective of promoting peace. Where there is a risk of violent conflict, the aid "carrot" can be designed to provide incentives for steps to reduce social tensions. In war-torn societies, aid can serve as an inducement for conflict resolution. And where a negotiated settlement has been achieved, donors can use "peace conditionality" to encourage the implementation of peace accords and consolidation of peace.

In practice, such efforts have been the exception rather than the rule, and where attempted, the results have been mixed. Three constraints have contributed to this spotty record. First, domestic parties may not wield sufficient authority, or enjoy sufficient legitimacy, to strike and implement aid-for-peace bargains. Second, the amount of aid on offer may be inadequate to provide a compelling incentive for the adoption of peace promoting policies. And finally, donor governments and agencies themselves may not put peace at the top of their agendas, ahead of other geopolitical, commercial, and institutional objectives.

This chapter considers the scope for using development aid conditionality to promote peace in an especially challenging terrain: settings where natural resources—such as oil, minerals, timber, and illicit drugs—play an important role in both instigating and sustaining violent conflict. In such settings, donors can make aid conditional upon improved government policies for natural resource management. For example, they can insist that natural resources be exploited wisely and that the proceeds be used to fund equitable development rather than armed conflict. Yet large-scale natural resource revenues tend to undermine donor leverage, since this leverage depends on the magnitude of conditional aid relative to other funds available to the recipient. Moreover, because official development assistance is generally provided only to governments, donors have few opportunities to use conditionality to influence rebel groups that generate funds by exploiting natural resources. Nevertheless, there are times and places when and where conditionality can prove useful, particularly if it is applied in concert with other policy instruments discussed in this volume.

The chapter begins by briefly reviewing the relevance of aid conditionality for conflict prevention, conflict resolution, and peace implementation. This is followed by a discussion of some of the special challenges in applying conditionality in conflict settings where natural resources provide major income to combatants. Three case studies are presented to illustrate these dynamics: logging in Cambodia, the oil sector in Angola, and opium and customs revenues in Afghanistan. The chapter concludes with some observations on both the potential and the limits of applying development aid conditionality to address the conflict-resource nexus in what have come to be known as "war economies."

Peace Conditionality

The term *peace conditionality* was coined in a UN-sponsored study of economic policy in El Salvador in the mid-1990s.[5] The study recommended that in "postconflict" settings, following a negotiated peace accord, donors should tie reconstruction and development aid to concrete steps to implement the accord and consolidate the peace. In the case of El Salvador, the government's failure to implement key aspects of the 1992 peace accord—including the provision of adequate funds for high-priority peace programs, such as the land transfer program for former combatants and the creation of a national civilian police force—jeopardized the peace process.[6] Hence the study recommended that the international financial institutions (IFIs)—the World Bank, IMF, and Inter-American Development Bank—should apply peace conditionality to encourage the government to mobilize domestic resources to fulfill its commitments.

In a sense, the aid pledged at international donor conferences after the signing of a peace accord is conditional from its inception, in that the accord is necessary to unlock the pledges. Subsequent aid disbursements are inherently conditional, too, insofar as the resumption of violence would trigger suspension of aid and failure to make progress toward building peace would jeopardize future aid commitments. Peace conditionality moves beyond these all-or-nothing choices in which the aid tap is either "on" or "off." It seeks to calibrate the flow of support more closely to the peace process by tying specific aid agreements to specific steps to build peace.

Peace conditionality can be applied to reconstruction and development aid, but most observers agree that it should not be applied to humanitarian assistance, for both ethical and practical reasons. Ethically, it would be untenable to punish vulnerable people for the sins of their leaders. And practically, the leaders may not be terribly sensitive to humanitarian needs. Since conditionality usually involves specific aid agreements rather than across-the-board cutoffs, there is room for flexibility in deciding what types of aid will carry what conditions. A starting point for the application of conditionality is those types of aid that are most valued by political leaders and least crucial for the survival of at-risk populations.[7]

Aid officials sometimes disclaim responsibility for engaging with the political issues of war and peace. At the World Bank, for example, officials frequently invoke their mandate to make loans "with due attention to considerations of economy and efficiency and without regard to political or other non-economic influences or considerations."[8] Yet violent conflict is not only a political matter: it has profound economic implications, too. For this reason, in the case of El Salvador, an internal World Bank evaluation concluded that "if tax effort and the pattern of public expenditures have a direct bearing on post-conflict reconstruction, as they did in El Salvador, it is legitimate to include these parameters in the conditionality agenda."[9]

The application of peace conditionality to fiscal policy is not a great stretch for the IFIs, which have a long history of applying conditionality to issues such as budget deficit reduction and trade liberalization. In the fiscal arena, peace conditionality simply involves a reorientation of objectives toward the goal of building peace. In some cases, this may mean relaxing budget deficit targets to permit governments to finance high-priority peace programs. In others, it means paying more attention to the composition of public expenditures, the level of tax revenues, and the distributional impacts of expenditure and taxation.[10]

Donors occasionally have pushed the envelope further, applying peace conditionality in arenas beyond their usual concerns. At a donor conference on aid to Bosnia, a few months after the 1995 Dayton Peace Accord, European Commissioner Hans van den Broek and World Bank president James Wolfensohn declared: "Developments on the ground should be constantly reviewed to ensure that aid is conditional on the thorough implementation of the obligations undertaken by all parties, in particular, full cooperation with the international tribunal for the prosecution of war criminals."[11] In keeping with this stance—and spurred by U.S. legislation that instructed the U.S. representatives on IFI executive boards to oppose loans to countries or entities not cooperating with the International Criminal Tribunal for the former Yugoslavia—the World Bank and IMF held up loans to Croatia in 1997, until the Tudjman regime turned over ten indicted war crimes suspects to stand trial in The Hague.[12] This remarkable episode showed that where there is the will to apply peace conditionality, even for unconventional purposes, ways to do so can be found.

Peace conditionality can be applied at the local level, too. In its Open Cities program in Bosnia, for example, the UN High Commission for Refugees allocated reconstruction aid to municipalities that demonstrated a commitment to the right of refugees and internally displaced persons to return to their homes. The aim was to use aid to reward local authorities who sought to implement the Dayton Accord, penalize those who obstructed implementation, and encourage vacillators to get off the fence.[13]

Similarly, the U.S. Agency for International Development requires banks and loan recipients in its private-sector lending program in Bosnia to certify that none of their officers, directors, or principal shareholders have been indicted for war crimes by the Hague tribunal. The contrast between the congressionally mandated support for war crimes prosecutions in the Balkans and subsequent U.S. pressures on aid recipients around the world to exempt U.S. personnel from the jurisdiction of the International Criminal Court illustrates the plasticity of conditionality: its aims reflect the diverse, and not always consistent, objectives of donor governments.[14]

In addition to supporting "postconflict" peacebuilding, conditionality can be used in efforts to promote the resolution of ongoing conflicts and to prevent conflict from breaking out in the first place. The following discussion considers the scope for "peace conditionality" in this broader sense of the term as well. There is an important difference, however, between the situation following a peace accord and cases where violent conflict is actively under way or where there is a high risk of its breaking out. In "postconflict" settings, the peace accord furnishes a set of benchmarks that the warring parties have formally accepted, against which donors can judge performance. In preconflict or conflict settings, donors do not have ready-made criteria on which to base conditionality, so they must develop conflict-related benchmarks themselves.

Conditionality and the Resource-Conflict Nexus

When natural resources provide a motive or fuel for violent conflict, the use of aid conditionality for conflict prevention, conflict resolution, and peacebuilding faces special challenges. Three broad tasks can be distinguished: (1) the need to ensure that the benefits and costs of natural resource exploitation are distributed so as to ease social tensions rather than exacerbating them; (2) the need to ensure that revenues from natural resources are used for peaceful and productive purposes rather than being used to fund armed conflict; and (3) in support of the first two objectives, the need to promote accountability and transparency in natural resource management. In examining the scope for aid conditionality to help address these issues, it is useful to distinguish among countries that are at risk of conflict, actively engaged in conflict, and emerging from conflict.

Aid Before Conflict: Conditionality for Conflict Prevention

In countries at risk of violent conflict, the critical issue is how to prevent natural resource abundance from creating or exacerbating social tensions that could lead to civil war. This requires careful attention to how the benefits and the costs of resource exploitation are distributed across the population, in terms of both "vertical equity" between rich and poor and "horizontal equity" across ethnic, religious, and regional lines.[15] Natural resources are often concentrated in certain regions of a country, as in the case of oil in Nigeria or minerals in the Democratic Republic of Congo (DRC). If residents of these regions do not receive a fair share of the benefits of resource extraction yet are burdened with its environmental costs, resentments can fuel violence.[16] At the same time, if the other regions do not receive some share of the benefits, this too can give rise to tensions.

Aid conditionality can seek to ensure a transparent and equitable distribution of the benefits and costs of resource extraction. The scope for conditionality is greatest when aid is needed to finance public infrastructure, such as roads for access to the resources, or when private-sector firms are unwilling to invest without the guarantees and legitimacy provided by donor involvement, as in the case of the World Bank–supported Chad-Cameroon pipeline project. As this case illustrates, however, even when agreements are reached on the distribution and uses of resource revenues, the enforcement of these agreements can prove difficult.[17]

Aid During Conflict: Conditionality for Conflict Resolution

In wartime, a key issue is how to curtail the use of natural resource revenues to fund armed groups, including both government and rebel forces. The potential for conditionality to address this is limited, however, since during conflicts the volume of development aid relative to other resources tends to be small. Apart from humanitarian assistance, flows of aid are typically disrupted by hostilities. At the same time, conditions of war offer combatants greater opportunities to generate resources by seizing assets, including natural resources. Yet opportunities for conditionality can arise, especially in times of declining resource prices, as was the case in Angola in the late 1990s, discussed below.

Any donor leverage is mainly on the government side, since governments receive ODA while rebels typically do not. There may be some scope for conditionality in curtailing resources-for-arms deals by rebel forces too, when neighboring countries are involved in the trade, particularly if the governments of these countries value good relations with the donor community. As discussed below, in Cambodia, international pressures on the Thai government played an important role in curtailing timber revenues to the Khmer Rouge after the latter defected from the Cambodian peace accords. Similarly, the UN Panel of Experts on the Illegal Exploitation of Natural Resources and Other Forms of Wealth in the Democratic Republic of Congo called for reductions in budget support and stabilization lending to neighboring governments that host individuals, firms, and financial institutions involved in the illicit exploitation of the DRC's natural resources.[18]

Aid in "Postconflict" Settings: Conditionality for Peacebuilding

A negotiated peace accord can chart the transition from war to peace, but whether the country will reach this destination remains uncertain. The contests for power and wealth that precipitated war do not disappear with the signing of an accord, and the risks of renewed violence can remain high for many years.[19] At best, a peace accord marks the beginning of the peace-building process. At worst, it achieves only a temporary cease-fire.

In such settings, optimistically called "postconflict" transitions, conditionality can play a particularly important role. The large sums of aid pledged for postconflict reconstruction and development—often billions of dollars—give the donors considerable leverage. Conditionality can help to address all three natural resource management issues: distributional equity, the use of revenues for peaceful development rather than military purposes, and the promotion of greater transparency and accountability.

The case studies presented in the following sections illustrate both the potential and the limitations of aid conditionality in addressing the resource-conflict nexus. They also illustrate the slipperiness of the distinction between conflict and "postconflict" settings, as all three countries studied here, Cambodia, Angola, and Afghanistan, saw peace accords followed by renewed outbreaks of violence.

Cambodia: The "Logs of War"

Cambodia's natural resources—rubies, fish, rubber, and above all, timber—were an important source of funding for three main combatant groups, the Cambodian People's Party (CPP), the royalists, and the Khmer Rouge, that contended for power for two decades after the 1979 Vietnamese invasion installed the CPP in Phnom Penh. As external military aid to the opposing sides was withdrawn after the 1991 Paris peace agreement, the export of logs for guns and profit became particularly central to the dynamics of conflict and the financing of armed groups.

The scale of Cambodia's timber trade and the identities of its key players have been carefully documented over the years by Global Witness, a London-based nongovernmental organization (NGO) dedicated to investigating the links between natural resource exploitation and human rights abuses. In the mid-1990s, Global Witness reported on the tacit cooperation in logging operations between government authorities and the Khmer Rouge, which had repudiated the peace agreement and returned to war. These reports, and lobbying efforts based on them, prompted the aid donors to attempt to curb logging by both sides.

The logging operations of the Khmer Rouge were conducted in partnership with powerful elements in Thailand's military forces.[20] While the donors lacked direct leverage vis-à-vis the Khmer Rouge, they could bring pressure to bear on the Thai government to take steps to end the trade. After the U.S. Congress passed legislation that threatened to terminate military assistance to Thailand in 1996 and to terminate all assistance in 1997, and the IMF canceled part of a loan to Thailand, the Thai government moved to close the border and block further trade with the Khmer Rouge, steps that "significantly contributed to the demise of the Khmer Rouge movement."[21]

Aid donors also have attempted to curb nominally "illegal" logging activities on territories controlled by the Cambodian government, not only because logging revenues continue to finance quasi-autonomous military units and because deforestation imposes high human and environmental costs but also because the donors are understandably reluctant to provide budgetary support to the government while substantial forestry revenues remain off the books.

"Overall, the diversion of public resources has probably reached the same amount as actual budget revenue collections," IMF representative Hubert Neiss informed the donors' Consultative Group for Cambodia in July 1997. Neiss claimed that illegal logging was responsible for "well over $100 million" in lost revenues in the previous year and declared this to be "the single most critical issue in Cambodia."[22] The IMF had demonstrated its displeasure over the forestry issue by repeatedly delaying and freezing loan disbursements. Ultimately, loans were suspended altogether. Although this action was primarily in response to the Cambodian government's failure to meet the revenue targets specified in its loan agreement, Neiss made clear that IMF aid would be resumed only when the government took steps to halt illicit logging and bring legitimate logging revenues into the government budget.

Other donors offered verbal support to the IMF's concerns, but they did not follow suit by cutting aid. Their timidity can be explained, at least in part, by their desire to maintain cordial relations with the Cambodian government. After criticizing the government for human rights abuses, the Australian ambassador had become the target of a scurrilous rumor campaign in Phnom Penh; more important, Australian firms were cut out of business deals. The lesson was not lost on other members of the diplomatic community. "What is important for many of these ambassadors is to defend their few miserable contracts," a senior UN official in Cambodia complained. "It is as if they represent their companies rather than their countries."[23] In donor priorities, short-run commercial interests can loom larger than the long-run goal of building a durable peace.

In mid-1997, violent clashes broke out between the CPP and the royalists, and their coalition government collapsed. More aid cutoffs soon followed. Global Witness reported that this "coup d'état" was "primarily funded by logging revenue" and that, for the next two years, militias allied with the ruling party "were given carte blanche to log anywhere they chose and keep the money."[24]

After a Japanese-brokered agreement led to fresh elections in mid-1998 and a new coalition government, the donors pledged renewed aid to Cambodia in 1999. In response to continued donor pressures, the government launched a crackdown on illegal logging. But the crackdown primarily targeted "small loggers and unruly political clients, rather than key forest concessionaires."[25] In an unusual arrangement backed by the donors, the government contracted Global Witness to act as an independent forestry monitor, funded by the British government's Department for International Development. Despite repeated declarations of good intentions by the authorities—including an official suspension of all logging operations in late 2001—Global Witness reported in mid-2002 that illegal logging was "still taking place throughout Cambodia."[26]

Senior Cambodian leaders have been unhappy about these pressures for reform. At times, they have openly played the commercial-relations card in an effort to pit bilateral donors against each other. "Japan is taking a lead," a Cambodian commerce ministry official declared in 1999, while denouncing conditions on U.S. aid. "By the time the US shapes up, if a US company is bidding on a contract against a Japanese company, do you think the US will win? I don't think so."[27]

The efforts of aid donors to rein in the "logs of war" in Cambodia, through formal performance criteria in the case of the IMF and through informal policy dialogue in the case of bilateral agencies, have not been a resounding success. But neither have they been a complete failure. The IMF's leading role in this effort was made easier by the fact that the logging-revenue issue could be packaged as a matter of fiscal responsibility rather than as a political question. Yet the political ramifications are obvious, given the close interconnections between incomes from the timber trade and political power backed by arms. In the case of the Khmer Rouge, third-party conditionality helped to cut off their sales of timber to the Thai market. On the government side, progress has been slow, often frustratingly so. In April 2003, the Cambodian government terminated Global Witness's official role as independent monitor.[28] Yet without the restraining influence of international pressures, backed by formal and informal conditionality, the pillage of Cambodia's forests might have been even more rapacious.

Angola: Oil for Blood

Angola's natural resource revenues played a key role in sustaining the decades-long war between the ruling Movement for the Liberation of Angola (MPLA) and the National Union for the Total Independence of Angola (UNITA). The conflict, which began before Angola's independence from Portugal in 1975, reflected class and ethnic divisions, particularly between the Luanda-based *mestiço* elites who dominated the MPLA and the impoverished Ovimbundu of the central highlands, where UNITA found support.[29] The fighting continued—with brief interruptions by abortive peace accords—until the death of UNITA leader Jonas Savimbi in 2002. To fund the war, the MPLA relied on oil revenues along with backing from the

Soviet Union and Cuba; UNITA relied on diamond revenues along with backing from the United States and South Africa. With the end of the Cold War and the fall of South Africa's apartheid regime, support from these foreign sponsors dried up, making oil and diamond revenues all the more crucial. "The relative value of the controlled resources," a World Bank report observes, "largely explained the relative strength of the opposing armies."[30]

UNITA reportedly obtained at least $3.7 billion from diamond sales between 1992 and 1998. Oil revenues received by the MPLA government are estimated to have ranged from $1 billion to $3 billion per year in the 1990s, the exact amount being unknown since much of it escaped recording in the government's books.[31] Oil revenues take three main forms: (1) oil taxes, which reached about $3 billion per year in 2000 and 2001; (2) "signature bonuses," onetime payments by oil companies in return for development rights, which reportedly totaled $879 million in 1999; and (3) oil-backed loans, whereby the government in effect mortgages its future oil revenues, which reportedly amounted to $3.5 billion in 2000–2001.[32]

The rest of the Angolan economy is a shambles. "Over the last 35 years, economic activity collapsed in almost all sectors except oil and diamonds," the World Bank reports. "As a result, the non-mineral economy virtually disappeared as a contributor to national output and a source of foreign exchange."[33] For example, the production of coffee, Angola's principal export before the war, has plummeted from 400,000 to 2,000 tons per year.[34] The country's per capita income is less than half its preindependence level. The human toll of the conflict has also been huge: roughly 750,000 deaths, 445,000 refugees, and 4.1 million internally displaced persons in a total population of about 12 million.[35] In 2000 the Save the Children Fund called Angola "the worst place on earth to be a child."[36]

In addition to funding for arms purchases and payments to combatants, Angolan oil and diamond revenues allowed senior leaders to amass great personal wealth. Global Witness traced $1.1 billion, apparently derived from Angolan oil revenues, to a single bank account in the British Virgin Islands.[37] A March 2003 World Bank document provides this frank assessment:

> Since independence, the availability of oil and diamond revenues in a conflict environment has created tremendous opportunities for corruption. Privileged access to state contracts, regulatory agencies, foreign partnerships, elite health and education facilities, privatized state assets, and subsidized credit and foreign currency enriched a few at the expense of the many. It also resulted in a hugely inefficient allocation of resources; high levels of consumption; and a business climate characterized by favoritism, kickbacks, connected transactions, and other distortive and non-transparent practices. In addition, severe weaknesses in Angola's fiduciary framework have led to the occurrence of very large unexplained discrepancies

in the country's fiscal accounts, varying from 2 to 23 percent of GDP between 1997 and 2002. It has been estimated that total unexplained discrepancies in 2001 amounted to 10% of GDP, or more than $900 million.[38]

The international campaign against "conflict diamonds," and the 1998 expansion of the UN Security Council–mandated sanctions regime against UNITA to include a ban on their import, impeded UNITA's access to international markets and thereby reduced its ability to generate resources to sustain its armed campaign.[39] Other policy instruments are required, however, to address the issue of "conflict oil," which provided large revenues to the MPLA government. Aid conditionality is one such instrument, but it is not a terribly potent one since Angola's oil revenues greatly exceed the amount of aid on offer.

The World Bank began lending to Angola in 1991, after the signing of the Bicesse peace agreement, which broke down the following year. In 1995, after the new Lusaka agreement, an international donor conference for Angola was held in Brussels, yielding pledges of more than $1 billion in development assistance. "These funds were subsequently held back," the World Bank reports, "due to insufficient progress in the peace process and lack of a clear reform agenda."[40] In July 1995 the IMF began a Staff-Monitored Program (SMP), a move that could pave the way for IMF lending, but it was "seriously off-track" by the end of the year.[41]

To obtain financing from private-sector creditors, the Angolan government has relied on oil-backed loans, a practice that dates from the mid-1980s. The state oil company, Sonangol, set up offshore "escrow" accounts, into which income from oil shipments is deposited; oil-backed loans are repaid from these accounts, bypassing the Angolan financial system.[42] "Because of high interest rates, typically 2 percentage points above Libor [the London interbank offer rate], and safe repayment structures," the *Financial Times* reports, "the banks' appetites for these oil-backed loans are voracious."[43] The IMF estimates that oil-backed loans composed one-third of Angola's total debt at the end of 1999. The government has limited its debt-service payments to these private loans and some of its debts to multilateral creditors; new lending from bilateral and multilateral creditors is "virtually shut off" due to accumulated arrears of more than $4 billion.[44]

The world oil price slump in 1998–1999 made the Angolan government more receptive to donor pressures for reform, at least temporarily. The IMF launched a new SMP in April 2000, under which the government agreed to increase expenditures on education (from 4.8 percent of total spending in 1999 to 12.5 percent in 2000) and health (from 2.8 percent to 9.3 percent) and to hire an international auditing firm to undertake a "diagnostic study" of the oil sector.[45] Successful completion of these steps reportedly would have opened the door to a $75 million emergency loan from the IMF and to a rescheduling of external debts to bilateral creditors, permitting new borrowing on terms more favorable than those of the oil-backed private loans.[46]

The international accounting firm KPMG was awarded a $1.6 million contract to conduct the oil diagnostic study, funded jointly by the Angolan government and the World Bank. The aim of the study was simply to examine discrepancies between projected oil revenues and the revenues actually deposited in Angola's central bank over the eighteen-month period from mid-2000 to the end of 2001. KPMG's mandate did not extend to monitoring the actual use of revenues, nor to a retroactive accounting of oil revenues in the 1990s.[47] In these respects, the study represented only a small step toward greater transparency.

The Angolan government's willingness to accommodate the donors faded as oil prices rebounded. A 2002 IMF report, leaked to the press after its publication was blocked by the Angolan government, found that more than $900 million in oil revenues was missing from state coffers in 2001—roughly three times the total value of humanitarian aid to Angola—and that $4 billion had gone missing over the previous five years.[48]

Savimbi's death in February 2002 opened the way for the signing of a memorandum of understanding between the government and UNITA representatives two months later, in which both sides agreed to a cessation of hostilities. This agreement appears to have marked the end of the road for UNITA, but whether it will provide the basis of a lasting peace remains to be seen. Resources are desperately needed to address the needs of former combatants, internally displaced persons, and other vulnerable groups and to redress the historic disparities between the Luanda-based elite and the rest of the country, particularly the Ovimbundu in the central highlands. "If these disparities are not dealt with," a report by the International Crisis Group warns, "more organised and strident opposition may eventually coalesce, whether through UNITA or some other political group."[49]

With the end of the war, the government may be somewhat more inclined to undertake reforms, both to enhance its public image in advance of elections and to induce donors to convene an international conference to pledge aid for reconstruction and development. An agreement with the IMF on a reform program is widely seen as a precondition for significant reconstruction aid.[50] Reflecting this generalized though informal conditionality, a report by the UN Secretary-General to the Security Council observes that "a redirection of expenditures by the Government towards the social sectors will make it easier to advocate for complementary funding from the international donor community."[51]

More specific conditionalities have been set out in the World Bank's "transitional support strategy" (TSS) for Angola, initiated in March 2003.

The TSS seeks to promote greater transparency and efficiency in public resource management, to support the delivery of services to war-affected groups and vulnerable populations, and to prepare the ground for "pro-poor economic growth." The World Bank's strategy explicitly incorporates conditionality in support of this agenda:

> Further lending in outer years would be triggered by decisive progress against selected indicators, including satisfactory implementation of the demobilization program, completion of the oil sector diagnostic study, and a substantial reduction in extra-budgetary and quasi-fiscal outlays. Alternatively, in the event that conflict re-emerges or governance deteriorates, impeding service delivery and even modest economic reform, the Bank would continue to support AAA [analytical and advisory activities] but new lending would cease and a gradual disengagement would begin.[52]

Although the scope for aid conditionality in Angola has improved since the cessation of hostilities with UNITA, the leverage that donors can bring to bear on the government continues to be constrained by the availability of easy oil money. "The IMF is holding out carrots," explains one observer, while the "industry is holding out T-bone steaks."[53] If there is to be any realistic prospect of significant reform, complementary international actions are clearly needed. These include efforts to promote greater transparency on the part of oil companies doing business in Angola, such as the Publish What You Pay campaign launched by Global Witness and the Extractive Industries Transparency Initiative (EITI) sponsored by the UK government.[54] As always, however, the willingness of donors and investors to press for reforms is tempered by considerations of "commercial expediency."[55] Angola is now the seventh largest source of oil imports to the United States, and soon the country is expected to rival or surpass Nigeria as Africa's top oil exporter.[56] Profits from the country's oil are partitioned between domestic and international actors. It would be misleading simply to identify the former with the problem and the latter with the solution.

Afghanistan: Aid on the Margins of a War Economy

In Afghanistan, too, natural resource revenues have played an important role in financing armed conflict, particularly after the 1989 Soviet pullout.[57] The UN Office on Drugs and Crime (UNODC) reports that the opium trade has become "an integral part of Afghanistan's war economy, with opium going out of the country and arms coming in." The UNODC estimates that farmers and local traders earned about $180 million annually from opium in 1994–2000. Afghan traffickers, who buy opium in local bazaars and then export raw opium and processed opiates, received even larger incomes, estimated at a total of $720 million in 2000.[58] During its five-year war against the Taliban in the late 1990s, the Northern Alliance exported gemstones—emeralds, rubies, aquamarines, and lapis lazuli—mined in the slice of Afghan territory it controlled, and used the proceeds to buy "guns, ammunition, rocket launchers, and second-hand helicopters."[59] Meanwhile, millions of acres of Afghanistan's forests were "stripped bare" to export timber to Pakistan.[60]

If we expand the definition of "natural resources" to include all wealth bestowed by virtue of location, then the customs revenue derived from Afghanistan's "transit trade"—the smuggling of goods overland from the Persian Gulf to South Asia—should also be counted. The profitability of this trade arises mainly from "policy-induced price differentials" among countries in the region, notably between duty-free Dubai and high-tariff Pakistan.[61] The transit trade was estimated at $2.5 billion per year in the late 1990s, with the Taliban deriving at least $75 million annually from informal duties.[62] Today, both customs revenues and opium profits appear to be substantially higher.

To date, the potential for aid conditionality as an instrument to curb these resource flows has been quite limited. Three key prerequisites for effective conditionality, as noted earlier, are (1) domestic parties who wield authority with enough legitimacy to serve as interlocutors for aid agreements, (2) a "carrot" of reconstruction and development aid that is big enough to provide an incentive to shift from the war economy to a new peace economy, and (3) an accompanying determination among international actors to assign priority to the goals of conflict resolution and peacebuilding. In Afghanistan, all three have been in short supply. Rather than being able to reduce the profit margins of the war economy, aid has operated at the margins of that economy. At best, it has helped to mitigate the human costs of conflict.

To some extent, the first prerequisite—the presence of a party with whom to negotiate—was met in the years of Taliban rule (1996–2001), although fighting persisted and the Taliban never controlled the entire country. But with its repressive internal policies, willingness to host foreign terrorist groups, and close ties to Pakistani intelligence agencies, the Taliban never won international recognition as the legitimate government of Afghanistan. The country's seat at the United Nations remained in the hands of the Northern Alliance. This choked off access to reconstruction and development aid; what foreign aid the country received was almost entirely humanitarian assistance.

During this period, tensions arose within the international community over whether aid should be used in an effort to modify Taliban policies. The "Six plus Two" group, consisting of government representatives from the six neighboring countries plus the United States and Russia, established under UN auspices in 1997, pressed for changes on the political front. The Afghan Support Group, an interdonor body also formed in 1997, was divided between those donors advocating a hard line—notably the United States and the United Kingdom—and others advocating greater engagement, such as the Scandinavians.[63] Similar divisions existed within the UN.

The "Strategic Framework for Afghanistan," adopted by the UN Secretariat in 1998, was intended as a pilot effort to foster greater "coherence" among the activities of UN agencies by attempting to reconcile political objectives with aid objectives. It would have been hard to choose a less promising terrain for such an initiative. The preponderance of humanitarian relief in aid to Afghanistan meant that many donors and NGOs considered it unethical to apply conditionality. Moreover, it was doubtful that threats to withhold humanitarian aid would have much impact on the Taliban, for whom the well-being of vulnerable populations did not seem to be an overriding concern. After much debate, the Strategic Framework adopted a compromise whereby "life-saving" aid was exempt from conditionality, while "life-sustaining" aid could be subject to conditionality, a tenuous distinction that prolonged the controversy rather than resolving it.[64]

In the end, the Strategic Framework was widely regarded as a failure. Conditionalities "did little to change the Taliban," one observer concluded, but they "undermined the effectiveness of the assistance programme."[65] In addition to the paucity of aid to which conditionality could be applied, reasons advanced for this failure include the business-as-usual mentality at the aid agencies, which led to the "triumph of project over plan and agency over agenda"[66]; the relatively large scale of other resource flows, including opium and transit trade revenues and financial aid the Taliban received from Saudi Arabia[67]; and the fact that the bulk of aid was channeled through UN agencies and NGOs that often were reluctant to apply conditionality, rather than being administered directly by the donors.[68]

Seeking a more substantial "carrot," Francesc Vendrell, the head of the UN Special Mission to Afghanistan (UNSMA), asked the World Bank to begin reconstruction planning for Afghanistan.[69] Several prominent experts on Afghanistan similarly argued, in a paper issued by the Swiss Peace Foundation in June 2001, that "conditional planning for reconstruction can function as an incentive for both Afghan and regional actors." They urged the UN, World Bank, and major donor governments to launch a "public diplomacy process" that would stake out the conditions for reconstruction assistance and suggested that aid money be placed in an escrow account pending an agreement.[70] Whether such moves could have borne fruit in the course of time remains an open question.

International pressures on the Taliban did score one eleventh-hour triumph. In mid-2000 the Taliban issued a decree banning poppy cultivation, in advance of the October planting season. The ban was remarkably effective, virtually eliminating the crop in provinces under Taliban control and causing great economic hardship for farmers who depended on it. The country's opium production plummeted from 3,300 tons in 2000 to 185 tons in 2001.[71] The Taliban's prime motive was probably not to attract aid but rather to bolster its campaign for official recognition at the UN.[72] The move was followed, however, by $43 million in additional emergency aid from the United States and by a pledge by U.S. secretary of state Colin Powell to explore ways to help farmers hit by the ban.[73]

The terrorist attacks in New York and Washington, D.C., on September 11, 2001, starkly exposed the inadequacy and perils of the policies pursued by the international community in Afghanistan in the previous two decades—policies that can be summed up as opportunistic support for armed groups in the 1980s and malign neglect in the 1990s. After the Taliban's refusal to hand over individuals implicated in the attacks, the U.S.-led coalition intervened militarily, paving the way for the interim Afghan administration and culminating in the election of Hamid Karzai in the country's first presidential election in 2004. Yet the international community has yet to break definitively with past policies. Once again, armed Afghan groups have been enlisted opportunistically, this time to fight Al-Qaida and Taliban forces. And despite pledges of aid for reconstruction and development, little has materialized, raising fears that Afghanistan will remain trapped in a war economy.[74]

In November 2001 the major parties to the Afghan conflict—apart from the Taliban—agreed at a conference in Bonn to establish an interim administration, to be followed by a new constitution and elections to form a new national government. Rather than a peace accord, the Bonn agreement represented "a power-sharing agreement brokered by the United States and the United Nations," one that "put control of the security forces in the hands of one political group in Kabul, marginalized the largest ethnic group in the country, and left local commanders and other 'warlords' to rule their districts with impunity."[75] In the absence of a central government with an effective monopoly of legitimate force and fiscal capacity, efforts to use aid conditionality for conflict resolution and peacebuilding in Afghanistan would have to involve bargains with local military commanders and with governments of neighboring countries that support rival Afghan factions.

So far, the needs of state building have been subordinated to short-term military objectives. In the first year after the Bonn agreement, 84 percent of international spending on Afghanistan went to the fight against Al-Qaida and the Taliban, 9 percent to humanitarian assistance, 4 percent to the International Security Assistance Force (ISAF) mandated by the UN Security Council to provide security in the capital, and only 3 percent to reconstruction.[76] Not only has the reconstruction aid "carrot" remained small, but it also has been heavily concentrated in Kabul and its environs, due not only to the urban bias of aid agencies but also to prevailing insecurity in the countryside. The "bubble economy" in the capital and the resulting exacerbation of rural/urban dichotomies threaten to replicate features of the prewar "rentier state" that helped to precipitate the Afghan conflict.[77]

The interim administration collected some $80 million in customs duties—its only significant source of domestic revenue—in 2002. In the same year, regional commanders are estimated to have collected more than $500 million in customs duties. In May 2003 the administration launched an effort to persuade the latter to remit revenues to the central government. President Karzai and Finance Minister Ashraf Ghani threatened to resign over this issue, a threat perhaps directed as much at the international community as at the regional warlords. U.S. deputy secretary of state Richard Armitage warned that the warlords would face "some rocky times" if they refused to comply. Initial efforts focused on Ismail Khan, who controls the country's most lucrative border post in Herat, and Rashid Dostum, who controls northern oil fields and Soviet-built fertilizer and electricity plants.[78]

Lacking the means of violence to force regional leaders to hand over the revenues, the central administration must rely on its "moral authority" to secure compliance.[79] Its moral clout is circumscribed, however, by its own failure to accomplish visible reconstruction and deliver government services. Observers compare the situation in Kabul unfavorably to the success with which Ismail Khan has rebuilt roads and bridges in Herat.

Revenues are needed to build state capacity, but state capacity is needed to gain revenues. In principle, foreign aid can help to provide a way out of this chicken-and-egg dilemma, providing external resources so that the government can demonstrate its capacity to deliver goods and services. In practice, however, the donors have channeled less than 20 percent of their aid through Afghanistan's new administration, preferring to manage the spending themselves or through subcontracts with NGOs.[80]

Meanwhile, opium production has rebounded. The UNODC estimates the total value of the 2002 crop at a record $2.5 billion.[81] This figure, equivalent to more than one-third of Afghanistan's gross domestic product, is probably an overestimate, since it was obtained by valuing the crop at the high price of the preceding year, but there is no doubt that the opium economy is again in full bloom. The U.S. and UK governments sought to use aid conditionality to curb the trade in spring 2002, delivering an ultimatum to the Karzai government "to cut off the drug trade" to start the flow of reconstruction and development aid. Given the administration's limited power, this had a predictably modest impact. The United States, United Kingdom, and World Bank earmarked $80 million to compensate poppy farmers for eradicated crops, but much of the money reportedly was pocketed by warlords who "fabricate reports of the crops destroyed" and have "a strong interest in seeing that the eradication program remains a job only partly done."[82]

In March 2003, at meetings of the Afghan Development Forum in Kabul and the Afghan High-Level Strategic Forum in Brussels, Finance Minister Ashraf Ghani sketched three possible future scenarios. The first, the creation of a stable and relatively prosperous Afghanistan, would require, he estimated, about $15–20 billion in international aid over the next five years. The second, in which the country would become "another failed development project" lurching from crisis to crisis, would cost about $7.5 billion in the same period, a level of annual expenditure roughly comparable to that in 2002. The third, in which Afghanistan would degenerate into a "narco-mafia state" run by criminal syndicates, would have the lowest short-term cost but the highest cost in the long run.[83]

By thus reminding the donors of their own incentives to provide aid, Ghani effectively stood the conditionality debate on its head. In Afghanistan, as elsewhere, the problem is not only for aid donors to induce recipients to put peace at the top of their agendas. It is also for aid recipients, and others committed to conflict prevention and peacebuilding, to persuade donor governments to do the same.

Conclusion

Conditionality is seldom popular. Recipients naturally would prefer aid without strings attached. Among aid donors, too, conditionality has fallen into disfavor in recent years. Several studies have questioned its efficacy in promoting conventional economic objectives such as budget deficit reduction and trade liberalization and have called for a shift from conditionality to "selectivity," the preferential allocation of aid to governments that demonstrate domestic "ownership" of the desired policies.[84] At the same time, there have been calls to retreat from extending conditionality to nontraditional issues. Citing IMF interest in poverty alleviation, for example, the Meltzer Commission, appointed by the U.S. Congress, warned in 2000 against "mission creep," and in response the IMF announced moves to "streamline" its conditionality.[85]

Whatever their merits, the selectivity and the back-to-basics movements are ill suited to addressing the challenges posed by violent conflict. To allocate aid only to "good performers," in the name of efficiency, would be to deny it to many of those countries most at risk of conflict. To await domestic ownership of policies that promote peace in a society torn by conflict may mean waiting a very long time. And simply to ignore the risks of violent conflict, in the name of sticking to the "core competencies" of donor agencies, is a recipe for wasting scarce aid resources, since war can destroy the best-laid economic plans.

Opportunities

Experiences in Cambodia, Angola, and Afghanistan suggest that aid donors can use conditionality to support peace, even where links between natural resource revenues and conflict make this task especially challenging. In such settings, conditionality is one tool by which the international community can seek to address several critical issues.

Management of natural resource revenues by governments. In places at risk of an outbreak or renewal of violent conflict, a key task is to ensure that the benefits and costs of natural resource exploitation are distributed so as to ease social tensions rather than exacerbate them. As we have seen, this could turn out to be a make-or-break issue in Angola and Afghanistan, where disparities between urban elites and rural populations could interact with ethnic divisions to reignite conflict. During conflicts, a key need is to curtail the use of resource revenues to finance war, although there is little scope for conditionality when conflict has blocked flows of aid other than humanitarian assistance. After the signing of a peace accord, a key task is to encourage governments to channel natural resource revenues into peace implementation. In these settings, conditionality can be used to encourage greater transparency and accountability in revenue management, as the IFIs have attempted to do in Cambodia and Angola. Indeed, it is hard to make a convincing case for unconditional aid to governments whose leaders keep substantial resource revenues off the books.

Containment of "spoilers." In many places, a key issue is how to deal with spoilers, leaders of government or rebel forces who oppose peace agreements and are willing to use violence to undermine them.[86] In some cases, conditionality can help to induce such individuals to cooperate with the peace process, a strategy that scored some success in Bosnia.[87] In other cases—particularly where the spoiler "sees power as indivisible, holds immutable preferences, and will take strategic advantage of any inducement"—the challenge is containment rather than cooperation.[88] Here, too, conditionality can play a role when spoilers rely on support from neighboring governments, as illustrated by the Thai government's curb on log exports by the Khmer Rouge.

Construction of alternative livelihoods. When the goal is not to redirect natural resource revenues but to reduce or eliminate them—as in the case of opium production—then a critical issue is the provision of alternative livelihoods. Again, there can be a role for conditionality, as when donors provide aid to farmers on the condition that they stop growing poppies—the obvious caveat being that the aid must actually reach the farmers, rather than being pocketed by local power brokers as appears to be the case in Afghanistan. Conditionality could also be used to encourage governments to create a favorable economic environment for alternative livelihoods—for example, by supporting remunerative prices for legitimate crops. The latter would require an about-face on the part of some donors, notably the IFIs, whose economic policy conditionalities often have precisely the opposite effect, requiring the lifting of trade barriers and removal of price supports to farmers in developing countries, even in the face of competition from subsidized producers in the industrialized countries.

Curtailment of private loans backed by future resource revenues. The role of oil-backed loans by private creditors in Angola poses the issue of how to handle debts that were contracted not to benefit the populace but rather to finance warfare and feather the nests of powerful leaders. It would be a sad irony if aid to postwar Angola were used to repay these debts. Yet given the fungibility of aid—the fact that external resources free up domestic resources for other purposes—the only way that donors can prevent this outcome would be to condition their aid on the repudiation of such debts. Selective debt repudiation would have a legal basis in the doctrine of "odious debt" in international law, particularly if done by a successor government to the regime that contracted the debts.[89] Again, support for such a policy would represent a marked departure from past donor policies. But it would have two salutary effects: in the short run, it would conserve natural resource revenues for reconstruction and development needs, and in the long run, it would serve as a warning to creditors that such loans are not risk free.

Challenges

At the same time, the cases discussed in this chapter illustrate the constraints on both the ability and the willingness of aid donors to use conditionality to promote peace. There are serious obstacles on both the recipient side and the donor side of the aid relationship.

Limited leverage. The extent of donor influence on the parties to a conflict depends on the volume of aid relative to other sources of income. Given the practical and ethical objections to conditionality on humanitarian aid, the relevant sort of aid is development and reconstruction assistance. In wartime, official development assistance is often minimal, so there is generally less scope for conditionality than in preconflict and postconflict settings. And since ODA goes to governments (or, with government permission, to NGOs), conditionality generally offers little scope for influencing antigovernment rebel groups, unless they receive support from neighboring governments to whom conditionality can be applied.

Lack of authorities with effective control. A further constraint is that aid recipients may lack sufficient power to implement the conditions. In Afghanistan, for example, donor threats to make reconstruction aid to the Karzai administration conditional on poppy eradication are not likely to have much impact in the field, where real authority is in the hands of autonomous regional commanders. More generally, as also illustrated in Afghanistan, state capacities in postconflict settings are often constrained by a lack of revenues, while revenue collection is in turn constrained by the lack of state capacities.

Competing priorities of donor governments. History makes it all too clear that peace is not invariably the highest priority of donor governments. They may espouse conflict prevention as "a flag of convenience" but pursue other aims in their deeds.[90] Thus conflict resolution in Afghanistan has taken a backseat to the "war on terror," much as it was subsumed by superpower rivalry during the Cold War. Commercial interests also can exert a powerful influence in donor decisionmaking, as noted in the Cambodian case. Worldwide, roughly half of all bilateral aid is tied to exports from the donor countries.[91] Conditionality is not welcomed by firms seeking to win contracts, particularly if other donors do not follow suit and thereby give their own firms a competitive edge. Similarly, when foreign firms are engaged in natural resource exploitation—as in the case of the oil industry in Angola—their short-term interests may lead them to oppose conditionality on the part of donor governments, even where this could help to foster a more stable environment for long-term investment.

Business as usual at the aid agencies. Within the aid agencies, a similar business-as-usual ethos can pose a further obstacle to conditionality. Individual aid officials typically are rewarded for making loans and disbursing grants, not for holding them up by seeking to impose tough conditions. In the annual budget cycles of donor governments, agencies that fail to "move the money" often find themselves penalized by reduced allocations in the following year. Conflict-related conditionality requires an overhaul of these bureaucratic incentive structures. The performance of both individuals and agencies must be judged not in terms of how much money they spend but rather in terms of how effectively their aid supports the goals of building and sustaining peace.

Given these constraints, it is evident that aid conditionality cannot offer a panacea for violent conflict. No matter how favorable the setting, and no matter how committed the aid donor, conditionality is not a magic "antibullet." Aid is at best one instrument in the international community's toolkit for promoting peace, and not always the most potent one.

The absence of conditionality, however, can undermine efforts to prevent or resolve conflict by other means. In the months before the 1994 Rwandan genocide, for example, the international community was pressing the government to implement the Arusha peace agreement, signed the previous year. Yet the donors failed to cut aid in response to mounting human rights abuses, leading the Steering Committee for the Joint Evaluation of Emergency Assistance to Rwanda to conclude that "donors collectively sent the message that their priorities lay elsewhere."[92]

The question is not whether donors will send a message with their aid but what that message will be. It is not tenable to pretend that economic performance and foreign aid can be divorced from questions of war and peace. Nor can aid donors disclaim responsibility for the impact of their actions—or inaction—on the dynamics of conflict. Although aid conditionality seldom will be sufficient to prevent violent conflicts, end wars, or guarantee the success of peacebuilding efforts, it may be a necessary element of broader international strategies to bring about a more peaceful world.

Notes

I wish to thank the editors and participants in the International Peace Academy's Economic Agendas in Civil War project for helpful discussions and suggestions. I am also grateful to Neil Cooper and Barnett Rubin for comments on an earlier draft of this chapter. The views expressed here are mine alone.

1. There is ample precedent. For example, in 1990 the United States retaliated for Yemen's vote against UN Security Council Resolution 678 authorizing force against Iraq by cutting off aid. See Tom Zeller, "How to Win Friends and Influence Small Countries," *New York Times,* March 16, 2003, p. 3-WK.

2. For discussion, see Gordon Crawford, "Foreign Aid and Political Conditionality: Issues of Effectiveness and Consistency," *Democratization* 4, no. 3 (1997): 69–108; and Martin Doornbos, "Good Governance: The Rise and Decline of a Policy Metaphor?" *Journal of Development Studies* 37, no. 6 (2001): 93–108.

3. For discussion, see Manuel Pastor and Michael E. Conroy, "Distributional Implications of Macroeconomic Policy: Theory and Applications to El Salvador," in James K. Boyce, ed., *Economic Policy for Building Peace: The Lessons of El Salvador* (Boulder: Lynne Rienner, 1996), pp. 155–176.

4. See James K. Boyce, *Investing in Peace: Aid and Conditionality after Civil Wars,* Adelphi Paper no. 351 (Oxford: Oxford University Press, 2002), chap. 3; and Barsha Khattry and J. Mohan Rao, "Fiscal Faux Pas? An Analysis of the Revenue Implications of Trade Liberalization," *World Development* 30, no. 8 (2002): 1431–1444.

5. James K. Boyce et al., *Adjustment toward Peace: Economic Policy and Post-war Reconstruction in El Salvador,* report prepared for the UN Development Programme, San Salvador, May 1995. A revised version of this study was published as James K. Boyce, ed., *Economic Policy for Building Peace: The Lessons of El Salvador* (Boulder: Lynne Rienner, 1996).

6. See Alvaro de Soto and Graciana del Castillo, "Obstacles to Peacebuilding," *Foreign Policy* no. 94 (1994): 69–83. Some observers attributed funding shortfalls to fiscal austerity measures demanded by IMF and World Bank conditionalities. See, for example, Robert C. Orr, "Building Peace in El Salvador: From Exception to Rule," in Elizabeth M. Cousens and Chetan Kumar, eds., *Peacebuilding as Politics: Cultivating Peace in Fragile Societies* (Boulder: Lynne Rienner, 2001), pp. 167–168. A careful analysis of policy formation in the early years of the Salvadoran peace process suggests, however, that the core problem was the unwillingness of the government to fund these programs rather than its inability to do so. See Elisabeth J. Wood, "The Peace Accords and Postwar Reconstruction," in Boyce, *Economic Policy for Building Peace,* pp. 73–105; and James K. Boyce, "External Resource Mobilization," in Boyce, *Economic Policy for Building Peace,* pp. 129–154.

7. For discussion, see Boyce, *Investing in Peace,* chap. 4.

8. International Bank for Reconstruction and Development, *Articles of Agreement,* art. III, sec. 5(b).

9. World Bank, *The World Bank's Experience with Post-conflict Reconstruction,* vol. 3, *El Salvador Case Study* (Washington, D.C.: World Bank, 1998), p. 51.

10. For discussion, see Boyce, *Investing in Peace,* chap. 3.

11. European Commission and World Bank, "Chairman's Conclusions of the Second Donors' Conference on the Reconstruction of Bosnia and Herzegovina," Brussels, April 13, 1996.

12. See Boyce, *Investing in Peace,* p. 10; and Guy Dinmore, "Croats Surrender to War Crimes Tribunal: Tudjman Bows to U.S. after Assurances on Trials," *Financial Times,* October 7, 1997.

13. See Boyce, *Investing in Peace,* p. 18. A ministerial meeting of the Peace Implementation Council endorsed this principle in May 1997, recommending that "assistance for housing and local infrastructure should be dependent on the acceptance of return" of refugees and displaced persons. *Political Declaration from Ministerial Meeting of the Steering Board of the Peace Implementation Council,* Sintra, Portugal, May 30, 1997, para. 46.

14. On the U.S. position on the International Criminal Court, see Geoffrey Bindman, "Washington and the International Court," *International Herald Tribune,* July 16, 2003.

15. See Frances Stewart, "Crisis Prevention: Tacking Horizontal Inequalities," *Oxford Development Studies* 28, no. 3 (2000): 245–262.

16. On Nigeria, see Human Rights Watch, "The Price of Oil: Corporate Responsibility and Human Rights Violations in Nigeria's Oil Producing Communities," January 1999, available at www.hrw.org/reports/1999/nigeria; and Jedrzej George Frynas, "Corporate and State Responses to Anti-oil Protests in the Niger Delta," *African Affairs* 100, no. 398 (2001): 27–54. On the DRC, see Léonce Ndikumana and Kisangani Emizet, "The Economics of Civil War: The Case of the Democratic Republic of Congo," Political Economy Research Institute Working Paper no. 63 (Amherst: University of Massachusetts 2003), available at http://www.umass.edu/peri/pdfs/WP63.pdf.

17. See Ian Gary and Terry Lynn Karl, *Bottom of the Barrel: Africa's Oil Boom and the Poor* (Baltimore: Catholic Relief Services, 2003), chap. 5, available at www.catholicrelief.org/africanoil.cfm; and Daphne Eviatar, "Striking It Poor: Oil as Curse," *New York Times,* June 7, 2003.

18. See United Nations Security Council, *Final Report of the Panel of Experts on the Illegal Exploitation of Natural Resources and Other Forms of Wealth of the Democratic Republic of Congo,* S/2002/1146, October 16, 2002. For a discussion of this and other examples of conditionality applied to third parties, see Philippe Le Billon, "Getting It Done: International Instruments of Enforcement," in Ian Bannon and Paul Collier, eds., *Natural Resources and Violent Conflict: Options and Actions* (Washington, D.C.: World Bank, 2003), pp. 215–286.

19. A World Bank study estimates that in the first five years after a peace accord, a country has a 44 percent chance of reverting to war. Paul Collier, Lani Elliott, Havard Hegre, Anke Hoeffler, Marta Reynal-Querol, and Nicholas Sambanis, *Breaking the Conflict Trap: Civil War and Development Policy* (New York: Oxford University Press, 2003).

20. See Global Witness, "Forests, Famine, and War: The Key to Cambodia's Future," March 1995, available at www.globalwitness.org/reports/show.php/en.00037.html; and Global Witness, "Thai–Khmer Rouge Links and the Illegal Trade in Cambodia's Timber," July 1995, available at www.globalwitness.org/reports/show.php/en.00036.html.

21. Le Billon, "Getting It Done," p. 251. See also Mats Berdal and David Keen, "Violence and Economic Agendas in Civil Wars: Some Policy Implications," *Millennium: Journal of International Studies* 26, no. 3 (1997): 795–818. Berdal and Keen report that Thai traders shifted their timber dealings to elements of the Cambodian government.

22. Statement by Hubert Neiss, IMF representative, Consultative Group Meeting, Paris, July 1–2, 1997, quoted in Boyce, *Investing in Peace,* p. 30. The full text of Neiss's remarks appears in the proceedings of the meeting published by the Council for the Development of Cambodia.

23. Personal interview by the author, Phnom Penh, November 1998.

24. Global Witness, "The Logs of War: The Timber Trade and Armed Conflict," March 2002, p. 20, available at www.globalwitness.org/reports/download.php/00044.

25. Philippe Le Billon, "The Political Ecology of Transition in Cambodia, 1989–1999: War, Peace, and Forest Exploitation," *Development and Change* 31, no. 4 (2000): 793.

26. See Global Witness, "Deforestation without Limits: How the Cambodian Government Failed to Tackle the Untouchables," July 2002, available at www.globalwitness.org/reports/show.php/en.00007.html.

27. Adam Piore, "Some in U.S. Say Prime Minister Was behind Cambodia Attack," *Boston Globe,* October 10, 1999, p. A35.

28. Global Witness, "Cambodian Government Terminates Independent Forest Monitoring," press release, April 22, 2002.

29. For discussion of ethnic divisions in Angola, see Linda Heywood, *Contested Power in Angola, 1840s to the Present* (Rochester, N.Y.: University of Rochester Press, 2000).

30. World Bank, "Transitional Support Strategy for the Republic of Angola," March 4, 2003, p. 4, available at www.worldbank.org/afr/ao/reports/2003_angola_tss.pdf. For more on the role of oil and diamonds in the Angola conflict, see Jakkie Cilliers and Christian Dietrich, eds., *Angola's War Economy: The Role of Oil and Diamonds* (Pretoria: Institute for Security Studies, 2000).

31. International Monetary Fund, "Angola: Statistical Annex," IMF Staff Country Report no. 99/25, April 1999, tab. 16, available at www.imf.org/external/pubs/ft/scr/1999/cr9925.pdf.

32. World Bank, "Transitional Support Strategy," p. 10; and Global Witness, "All the Presidents' Men," March 2000, p. 4, available at www.globalwitness.org/reports/show.php/en.00002.html.

33. World Bank, "Transitional Support Strategy," p. 9.

34. International Crisis Group, "Angola's Choice: Reform or Regress," April 7, 2003, p. 5, available at www.crisisweb.org/projects/showreport.cfm?reportid=935.

35. World Bank, "Transitional Support Strategy," p. 4.

36. Save the Children Fund, *War Brought Us Here: Protecting Children Displaced within Their Own Countries by Conflict* (London: Save the Children Fund, 2000).

37. Global Witness, "All the Presidents' Men," p. 22.

38. World Bank, "Transitional Support Strategy," pp. 6–7. See also Jedrzej George Frynas and Geoffrey Wood, "Oil and War in Angola," *Review of African Political Economy* 28, no. 90 (2001): 587–606; and Assis Malaquias, "Making War and Lots of Money: The Political Economy of Protracted Conflict in Angola," *Review of African Political Economy* 28, no. 90 (2001): 521–536.

39. Global Witness, "A Rough Trade: The Role of Companies and Governments in the Angolan Conflict," December 1998, p. 4, available at www.globalwitness.org/reports/show.php/en.00013.html. See also Chapter 3 by Ian Smillie in this volume.

40. World Bank, "Transitional Support Strategy," p. 17.

41. Ibid., p. 11.

42. Global Witness, "A Crude Awakening: The Role of the Oil and Banking Industries in Angola's Civil War and the Plunder of State Assets," December 1999, pp. 15–18, available at www.globalwitness.org/reports/show.php/en.00016.html.

43. Nicholas Shaxson, "Angola Secures Loan from Foreign Banks," *Financial Times,* March 23, 2001, p. 12. Thus Standard Chartered Bank, which assembled a $455 million oil-backed loan to Angola in March 2001, had a "huge oversubscription" from eager creditors.

44. International Monetary Fund, "Angola: Recent Economic Developments," August 2000, p. 15, available at www.imf.org/external/pubs/ft/scr/2000/cr00111.pdf.

45. International Monetary Fund, "Angola: Memorandum of Economic and Financial Policies," April 3, 2000, available at www.imf.org/external/np/loi/2000/ago/01/index.htm.

46. Global Witness, "Crude Awakening," p. 7; World Bank, "Transitional Support Strategy," p. 14.

47. For discussion, see Human Rights Watch, "The Oil Diagnostic in Angola: An Update," March 2001, available at www.hrw.org/backgrounder/africa/angola.

48. Justin Pearce, "IMF: Angola's Missing Millions," British Broadcasting Corporation, October 18, 2002, available at http://news.bbc.co.uk/1/hi/world/africa/2338669.stm. See also Henri E. Cauvin, "I.M.F. Skewers Corruption in Angola," *New York Times,* November 30, 2002.

49. International Crisis Group, "Angola's Choice," p. 1.

50. Ibid., p. 4.

51. UN Security Council, "Report of the Secretary-General to the Security Council on Angola," S/2002/834, July 26, 2002, p. 7, available at www.angola.org/referenc/reports/unrep072602.pdf.

52. World Bank, "Transitional Support Strategy," p. 2.

53. Quoted in Carola Hoyos and John Reed, "Angola Forced to Come Clean," *Financial Times,* October 2, 2003, p. 14.

54. Similarly, the World Bank's "Transitional Support Strategy" (p. 22) proposes a study on corporate responsibility "to sensitize oil companies to the importance of transparency and good governance with a view to reducing the collective action problem that currently discourages greater transparency by any individual company (if any one company attempts to implement more transparent policies, its competitive position may be compromised)." The importance of the latter issue was underscored in 2001, when the Angolan state oil company retaliated against British Petroleum's announcement that it would publicly disclose its payments by threatening to cancel its contract. See Global Witness, "All the Presidents' Men," pp. 41–42. For more on the Publish What You Pay campaign and the EITI, see Chapter 11 by Gavin Hayman and Corene Crossin in this volume.

55. International Crisis Group, "Angola's Choice," p. 13.

56. For discussion, see Jon Lee Anderson, "Letter from Angola: Oil and Blood," *New Yorker,* August 14, 2000.

57. External resources nevertheless continued to play an important role after the Soviet pullout. See Human Rights Watch, "Afghanistan: The Crisis of Impunity; The Role of Pakistan, Russia, and Iran in Fueling the Civil War," July 2001, available at www.hrw.org/reports/2001/afghan2.

58. UN Office on Drugs and Crime (UNODC), *The Opium Economy in Afghanistan: An International Problem* (New York: United Nations, 2003), pp. 8, 12, 67, available at www.reliefweb.int/library/documents/2003/unodc-afg-31jan.pdf.

59. James Kirkup, "Gemstones Finance Afghan Rebels," *International Herald Tribune,* November 14, 2001, p. 12.

60. Ahmed Rashid, *Taliban: Militant Islam, Oil, and Fundamentalism in Central Asia* (New Haven, Conn.: Yale University Press, 2000), p. 192. Despite a nominal ban on logging, timber exports from eastern Afghanistan continue: in September 2003 a road to Nangarhar province on the Pakistan border was "bumper-to-bumper with timber-laden 16-wheelers." Kathy Gannon, "Afghans See U.S.-Backed Warlords as Enemy," Associated Press, September 7, 2003.

61. Barnett Rubin, "The Political Economy of War and Peace in Afghanistan," *World Development* 28, no. 10 (2000): 1790.

62. Ibid., p. 1795; and UNODC, *Opium Economy,* p. 128, citing World Bank estimates.

63. Haneef Atmar and Jonathan Goodhand, "Coherence or Cooption? Politics, Aid, and Peacebuilding in Afghanistan," *Journal of Humanitarian Assistance,* July 30, 2001, p. 25, available at www.jha.ac/articles/a069.htm.

64. For discussion, see Konrad Von Brabant and Tony Killick, "The Use of Development Incentives and Disincentives in Influencing Conflict or Civil Violence: Afghanistan Case Study," paper prepared for the OECD Development Assistance Committee, Paris, March 1999; Mark Duffield, Patricia Gossman, and Nicholas Leader, "Review of the Strategic Framework for Afghanistan," paper commissioned by the Strategic Monitoring Unit, Afghanistan, October 2001; and Jonathan Goodhand, "Aiding Violence or Building Peace? The Role of International Aid in Afghanistan," *Third World Quarterly* 23, no. 5 (2002): 837–859.

65. Goodhand, "Aiding Violence or Building Peace?" p. 847.

66. Duffield, Gossman, and Leader, "Review of the Strategic Framework," p. 38.

67. Von Brabant and Killick, in "Use of Development Incentives and Disincentives" (para. 122), report that Saudi support amounted to $2 billion, compared to $300 million in other aid.

68. Von Brabant and Killick, "Use of Development Incentives and Disincentives," para. 168.

69. Barnett Rubin, Ashraf Ghani, William Maley, Ahmed Rashid, and Olivier Roy, "Afghanistan: Reconstruction and Peacebuilding in a Regional Framework" (Bern: Center for Peacebuilding [KOFF], Swiss Peace Foundation, 2001), p. 34, available at www.institute-for-afghan-studies.org/afghan%20conflict/analysis/1_2001.pdf.

70. Ibid., pp. 6, 41–42.

71. UNODC, *Opium Economy,* p. 28. Skeptics note that the ban did not apply to the activities of traders, whose stocks from the previous year's crop soared in value after the ban on new cultivation was imposed.

72. Barbara Crossette, "Taliban Open a Campaign to Gain Status at the U.N.," *New York Times,* September 21, 2000.

73. Barbara Crossette, "Taliban's Ban on Poppy a Success, U.S. Aides Say," *New York Times,* May 20, 2001.

74. See Barnett Rubin, Humayun Hamidzada, and Abby Stoddard, "Through the Fog of Peace Building: Evaluating the Reconstruction of Afghanistan" (New York: New York University, Center on International Cooperation, 2003), available at www.cic.nyu.edu/pdf/through%20the%20fog2.pdf.

75. Patricia Gossman, "Elusive Peace: Afghan Pointers for Iraq," *International Herald Tribune,* February 5, 2003.

76. CARE International, "Rebuilding Afghanistan: A Little Less Talk, a Lot More Action," CARE Policy Brief no. 8, Kabul, Afghanistan, October 1, 2002, available at www.reliefweb.int/library/documents/2002/care-afg-6dec.pdf. See also Rubin, Hamidzada, and Stoddard, "Through the Fog of Peace Building."

77. See Barnett Rubin, *The Fragmentation of Afghanistan: State Formation and Collapse in the International System* (New Haven, Conn.: Yale University Press, 1995).

78. See Carlotta Gall, "Kabul Announces Push to Gain Revenue and Combat Corruption," *New York Times,* May 24, 2003; and April Witt, "U.S. Official Reaffirms Pledge to Aid Afghans," *Washington Post,* May 10, 2003.

79. See Finance Minister Ashraf Ghani's remarks quoted in Vanessa Gezari, "Kabul Acts to Enforce Customs Deal," *Chicago Tribune,* May 25, 2003.

80. See Rubin, Hamidzada, and Stoddard, "Through the Fog of Peace Building."

81. UNODC, *Opium Economy,* p. 69.

82. John F. Burns, "Afghan Warlords Squeeze Profits from the War on Drugs, Critics Say," *New York Times,* May 5, 2002, p. 22.

83. Ghani's remarks are reported in Rubin, Hamidzada, and Stoddard, "Through the Fog of Peace Building," pp. 6–7.

84. See, for example, Christopher L. Gilbert, Andrew Powell, and David Vines, "Positioning the World Bank," in Christopher L. Gilbert and David Vines, eds., *The World Bank: Structures and Policies* (Cambridge: Cambridge University Press, 2000), pp. 39–86; and Paul Collier, "Conditionality, Dependence, and Coordination: Three Current Debates in Aid Policy," in Gilbert and Vines, *World Bank,* 299–324.

85. See International Financial Institution Advisory Commission (Meltzer Commission), *Report of the International Financial Institution Advisory*

Commission (Washington, D.C.: U.S. Department of the Treasury, 2000), pp. 39–40; and "IMF Seeks to Streamline and Focus Conditions for Lending to Member Countries," *IMF Survey,* September 2001, available at www.IMF.ORG/external/pubs/ft/survey/sup2001/index.htm 7.

86. Stephen John Stedman, "Spoiler Problems in Peace Processes," *International Security* 22, no. 2 (1997): 5–53.

87. For example, conditionality coupled with the threat of force prompted Serb Republic president Biljana Plavsic to break from the hard-line Bosnian Serb leadership in 1997, a move that was followed by the election of a pro-Dayton prime minister in the Serb Republic in 1998. See Jim Hoagland, "Success in Bosnia Awaits a Persistent Clinton," *International Herald Tribune,* August 21, 1997.

88. Stephen John Stedman, introduction to Stephen John Stedman, Donald Rothchild, and Elizabeth M. Cousens, eds., *Ending Civil Wars: The Implementation of Peace Agreements* (Boulder: Lynne Rienner, 2002), p. 12.

89. For discussion, see James K. Boyce and Léonce Ndikumana, "Africa's Debt: Who Owes Whom?" Political Economy Research Institute Working Paper no. 48 (Amherst: University of Massachusetts, 2002), available at www.umass.edu/peri/pdfs/wp48.pdf.

90. Barnett Rubin, *Blood on the Doorstep: The Politics of Preventive Action* (New York: Century Foundation Press, 2002), pp. 127, 130.

91. See "Gifts with Strings Attached," *Economist,* June 17, 2000.

92. Steering Committee for the Joint Evaluation of Emergency Assistance to Rwanda, *The International Response to Conflict and Genocide* (Copenhagen: Danish Foreign Ministry, 1996), p. 18. See also Peter Uvin, *Aiding Violence: The Development Enterprise in Rwanda* (West Hartford, Conn.: Kumarian Press, 1998), p. 237.

PART 3

Establishing Accountability, Ending Impunity

13

Regulating Business in Conflict Zones: Challenges and Options

Leiv Lunde and Mark Taylor

In the last century, technological developments both in economic production and in warfare have made access to and control of economic resources central to a state's strategic interests. At the same time, developments of international law have enshrined a state's right to self-defense, as well as a right to sovereign control over the exploitation of its natural resources, with the result that security policy and economic regulation continue to define much of the content of state sovereignty. Over the same period, states have developed equally legitimate and powerful international norms aimed at defining public goods in relation to, among others, trade in goods and services, labor markets, communications, the environment, armed conflict, and international peace and security, as well as human rights and crimes against humanity. Recently, the humanitarian impulse toward norm building has focused on the toll exacted in human suffering in many parts of the world, in part as a response to the protracted nature of contemporary conflicts.[1] As part of this movement, new attention is being paid to the effects on people when armed conflict meets unregulated markets.

Concerns over the so-called conflict trade and other conflict-promoting economic activities have to date manifested themselves in two main policy arenas: international peace and security and corporate social responsibility (CSR).[2] Since the end of the 1990s, the United Nations Security Council has been forced to grapple with the economic dimensions of intrastate wars, including the evasion of UN sanctions regimes, the trade in so-called conflict commodities such as diamonds and timber, the illicit exploitation of natural resources by combatant groups and their foreign sponsors, and terrorist financing. At the same time, the rise in fair trade certification regimes, a series of advocacy campaigns against child labor, corruption, and other economic issues at the intersection of development and human rights, and an increasing number of lawsuits against companies for their alleged complicity in human rights violations have forced companies and industry associations to deal with increasing demands to improve the ethical value of their products and services.

In a signal of the convergence between the economic dimensions of international peace and security and growing concerns about the impact of private-sector activities on human rights and development, a UN Security Council–mandated Panel of Experts, reporting in October 2002 on "The Illicit Exploitation in the Democratic Republic of Congo (DRC)," listed eighty-five companies as being in violation of the OECD *Guidelines for Multinational Enterprises.*[3] Yet the *Guidelines* say nothing about conflict and little about the kinds of human rights abuses being committed in the DRC.[4] By referring to the *Guidelines,* the UN Panel pointed not only to the worrying convergence of trade and armed conflict but also—perhaps inadvertently—to the stark inadequacy of policy and law in this regard. As subsequent chapters here explore, jurists and practitioners are struggling to identify the principles or norms to address this lacuna, so that the worst manifestations of economic activities in conflict zones may be brought under the rule of law, and to identify the right combination of policies and institutions for managing the economic aspects of armed conflict.[5]

The aim of this chapter is to provide some analytical clarity to the emerging policy framework and policy debates concerning ways to regulate economies of conflict, including which standards of behavior companies operating in conflict zones should be expected to uphold.[6] To that end, we start with a brief discussion of the limits of the "voluntary versus mandatory" dichotomy that thus far dominates the discourse on private-sector regulation. We then outline the malign problem structure of economies of conflict which makes regulation of conflict-related economic activity such a daunting yet necessary task for policymakers. By way of conclusion, we suggest some general principles for constructive policy formulation in response to private economic activity related to armed conflict.

Beyond the "Voluntary Versus Mandatory" Dichotomy

There is a rapidly growing global discourse on the relative merits of voluntary versus mandatory approaches to regulating economic activity where this activity entails wider social, environmental, or humanitarian consequences. This discourse became one of the main hallmarks of the World Summit on Sustainable Development in Johannesburg in 2002. There, business interests advocated the promotion of sustainable development through so-called self-regulation, that is, through voluntary agreements and partner-

ships with other stakeholders (governments, nongovernmental organizations [NGOs], and civil society groups), which they presented as an alternative to legal or government regulation. The opposite message came from
NGOs and certain government representatives. Without rejecting the merits
of voluntary action per se, they held that complementary, comprehensive,
and targeted external regulation is needed in order to ensure social and
environmental accountability for company performance.[7]

This "voluntary versus mandatory" dichotomy has prompted intense policy research and debate. There are reasons to caution, however, against an
approach that assumes voluntary and regulatory measures are somehow
mutually exclusive. In its report *Beyond Voluntarism,* the Geneva-based
International Council on Human Rights Policy expressed the view of many in
the human rights community by emphasizing that voluntary approaches to
regulating company behavior, while helpful, have been inadequate. The
report argued that more robust legal regulation is required to create an incentive structure for companies to change unacceptable behavior. In this sense,
Beyond Voluntarism argued, the two approaches are mutually supportive:

> Neither legal nor voluntary approaches should be a substitute for the
> other. Both are needed, and they can be complementary. Voluntary codes
> will make binding regulation more likely to succeed because they have
> started to build consensus—or at least understanding—around some core
> rights. Willing consent to such norms will be helpful when binding regula-
> tions are introduced in the future. As companies introduce new manage-
> ment practices to implement codes, they develop business expertise that
> will also be essential to successful implementation of binding regulations.
> Overall, however, we believe it is time to move beyond voluntarism—not
> in order to stop voluntary approaches but because a new international
> legal regime will become increasingly necessary. The future should hold a
> blend of voluntary and binding rules that together will ensure that compa-
> nies respect human rights and demonstrate that they do so.[8]

Rather than view the options for regulation as a contest between two
contrasting approaches, it is more useful to conceive of a policy continuum.
On such a continuum, purely voluntary company self-regulation is at one
end and coercive regulation, binding on companies and backed by legal
sanction, is at the other. Again, it would be a misconception to assume that,
in practice, all voluntary measures lack incentives for meaningful adherence or that the sanctions underpinning mandatory regulations are always
implemented or effective. The reality is more complex. The value of this
continuum is analytical: it allows an assessment of actual effectiveness
based on how specific "carrots and sticks" combine in specific company
and government policies, while remaining agnostic on the wider debate
over the relative merits of voluntarism vis-à-vis the legal regulation of
companies.

Mapping the Voluntary-Mandatory Continuum

Voluntary Self-Regulation

Voluntary measures can be described as initiatives by individual companies and industry associations that are adopted and implemented in the absence of external compliance measures. General policies for CSR or more specific codes of conduct concerning behavior in conflict settings are examples of what is sometimes called "self-regulation" at the individual company and industry levels.[9]

The Anti-corruption Task Force (ACTF) of the International Association of Oil and Gas Producers (OGP) is an example of purely voluntary action at industry level.[10] The Wolfsberg Principles, signed in October 2000 by eleven leading international banks, also belong here, as the principles represent a voluntary set of global anti–money-laundering guidelines. They were elaborated in cooperation with the international anti-corruption NGO Transparency International, which also played the role of facilitator.[11]

The category of self-regulation includes voluntary initiatives by companies and industry associations where corporate actors invite governments and/or NGOs into partnerships, with the primary motivation of managing a company's reputational risk. The Global Mining Initiative's Mining Minerals and Sustainable Development project (MMSD) is a relevant example, even though the main cooperating partner of the nine major international mining companies behind this initiative was a research institute (the International Institute of Environment and Development, IIED) and not governmental players.[12]

Increasing numbers of companies are adopting such codes, along with management systems to oversee their implementation across the company.[13] The security and human rights policy adopted by the Canadian firm Talisman Energy is but one of many examples of company responses to the problems posed by natural resource exploitation and armed conflict. Talisman's move was based on the company's experience in Sudan, where it struggled unsuccessfully to bridge the concerns of NGOs and shareholders about government-sponsored human rights abuses with the company's contractual dealings with the Sudanese government on issues of security. While Talisman ultimately divested from Sudan, the security policy that it developed as a result of its Sudan venture has been adopted as a company standard to guide Talisman activities worldwide.[14] Another sign of corporate voluntary action was the decision by the French oil company Total to engage an external research body (GoodCorporation) to develop a methodology for independently evaluating the extent to which the company is following its own ethical and security code of conduct. Total, and the formerly independent companies Elf and Fina with which Total merged, has been an important target of human rights campaigns, notably for its investment in Myanmar and its relations with a range of undemocratic African regimes.[15]

Beyond their potential direct impact on corporate behavior and human welfare, the main value of these "purely voluntary" initiatives lies in the explicit or implicit acceptance by those companies that embrace them of societal principles and norms that transcend the basic objective of profit maximization. The significance of industry-wide measures is that they extend throughout a sector standards that would otherwise be limited to individual firms, thus helping to level the playing field for the range of companies operating in that sector. As indicated by the work of the Wolfsberg group and the MMSD initiative, companies considering the adoption of such policies generally network with others facing similar challenges, often gaining experience from and contributing to public-private partnerships featuring more tangible regime-building elements. Insofar as they help to elaborate common rules of the game that are acceptable to companies, the development of company and industry-wide policies may be seen as a first tentative step in building the normative content of a broader regulatory regime.

Yet voluntarism is not without its problems. For companies, collective action and free-riding problems top the list. Companies that unilaterally adopt codes of conduct run the risk of increasing their own costs and losing their competitive edge vis-à-vis rivals, while at the same time doing the work of setting standards for an entire industry that their competitors may benefit from at little or no cost. These problems point to the need for common benchmarks against which to measure company performance and the need for credible monitoring mechanisms, neither of which exist under most voluntary regimes. In their absence, there is a strong sense among human rights, environmental, and other CSR advocates that pure voluntarism is not working.[16] Indeed, despite the plethora of voluntary codes, problematic conduct continues, indicating that when voluntary codes clash with significant commercial interests, the latter wins out. While disturbing to many, this pattern is entirely explicable. After all, companies are not moral entities.

Voluntary Multistakeholder Initiatives

Often originating from "multistakeholder dialogues," these initiatives are usually managed by national or international governmental bodies. Typically, a government sees its role in these initiatives primarily as a convener, facilitator, and motivator, rather than as actively pursuing specific policy ambitions or regulatory objectives with regard to company conduct. Examples in this category include the UN Global Compact, set up in 2000 by UN Secretary-General Kofi Annan to catalyze CSR action around a range of general, nonbinding principles of corporate behavior regarding the environment, labor practices, and human rights.[17] One of the Global Compact's multistakeholder dialogues has focused on the challenges for business in conflict zones. Since 2001, this dialogue has sought to promote conflict-sensitive business conduct by identifying and elaborating best practices in transparency, community development, and revenue sharing that might be embraced by businesses with operations or investment in countries experiencing armed conflict.[18] Similarly, in 2003, the UN Subcommission on Human Rights issued the Norms on the Responsibilities of Transnational Corporations and Other Business Enterprises for consideration by the UN Commission on Human Rights in 2004.[19] The UN Norms are a "soft law" instrument that seeks to clarify the content of human rights obligations for companies, based on already existing principles in international human rights law.[20] Their formulation involved extended consultations with representatives from a wide range of actors, including business, government, and civil society.[21]

The OECD *Guidelines for Multinational Enterprises* represent a voluntary framework for responsible business conduct applicable to companies from OECD countries as well as other adhering countries. The *Guidelines* were formulated and revised through a multipartner process of consultation, and their promotional mechanism, the National Contact Points (NCPs), relates to the tripartite partners of the OECD, principally governments, trade unions and business.[22] As Patrica Feeney and Tom Kenny highlight in their contribution to this volume (Chapter 14), observance of the *Guidelines* is voluntary for businesses. Adhering governments, however, are committed to promoting them among companies operating in or from their territories. NCPs, located in assigned OECD country ministries, are charged with making the guidelines known to national companies, labor unions, and NGOs and also with responding to "specific instance" complaints. The NCPs possess powers of facilitation and in this sense may have the potential to respond as an administrative mechanism analagous to commercial conciliation processes. The NCPs can make recommendations, but they have no authority to issue sanctions of any kind, although this does not constrain governments from doing so.

The Voluntary Principles on Security and Human Rights were established in late 2000 in cooperation between these two governments, a number of large oil and mining companies, and some human rights NGOs such as Amnesty International.[23] The principles are meant to guide companies in maintaining the safety and security of their operations within an operating framework that ensures respect for human rights and fundamental freedoms of populations affected by company operations. Work on the principles started against the backdrop of a mounting number of high-profile cases of human rights abuses linked by the media and advocates to extractive industry security operations.[24] The principles were undertaken with the intention of initiating a dynamic process in terms of both expanded company and government participation (Norway and the Netherlands joined in early 2003) and substance, implying continuous review by and among participating members to maintain relevance and promote efficacy.[25]

A general lesson from multipartner initiatives is that a growing number of companies view cooperation with governments in such ventures to be in their own interest. Indeed, the proliferation of these initiatives indicates that many companies are motivated to work with governments and other stakeholders to address their roles, both positive and negative, in the provision of global common goods. Although each of these mechanisms could in theory develop compliance measures, there is usually no "stick" involved. Still, companies find these initiatives sufficiently important to spend time and resources to participate in meetings, to undertake follow-up related to adherence requirements, and also to contribute to the actual development and refinement of the schemes. Companies thereby gain experience in the demanding business of effectively engaging in public-private partnerships and managing both reputational risk and regulatory developments. In addition, this category of initiatives contributes to wider norm-building efforts by creating ways for companies, governments, and NGOs to engage and to understand their different motivations and constraints.

An important limitation of the voluntary approach to improved company conduct is that it tends disproportionately to benefit large and well-endowed multinational companies. Medium and small companies typically do not have sufficient human and other resources to fully participate in such initiatives.[26] As global standards are being set by the larger companies, there is a risk that market access will, in effect, be closed off to middle-range and smaller companies, particularly those from the developing world.

Public-Private Partnerships

In public-private partnerships (PPPs), governmental bodies take on more active roles and have more specific policy objectives with regard to the behavior of companies. They also seek to induce improved company conduct through positive incentives, or "carrots," that appeal to the enlightened self-interest of companies. Often these carrots include direct financial incentives and/or tax exemptions for companies complying with specific policies.

Included in this category is the Chad-Cameroon Development and Pipeline Project. Important partners in this scheme are the governments of Chad and Cameroon, the World Bank and its private-sector affiliate, the

International Finance Corporation (IFC), a consortium of international oil companies led by ExxonMobil, and a range of civil society groups in Chad and Cameroon. One might add to this a large number of international NGOs that are monitoring project developments with a shifting combination of enthusiasm and skepticism. The overall aim of this cooperative venture has been to reduce the political risk of the project by stimulating responsible and socially beneficial management of future oil revenues by the government of Chad and ensuring that prospective revenues do not become the pretext for violent conflict between rival groups in Chad. The incentive structure for the different partners to the Chad-Cameroon project may shed light on the potential to build relevant regulatory regimes based on such a model. Oil companies have welcomed the World Bank–led social compact for the project, largely because they need the World Bank to offset an otherwise unacceptable political risk. For their part, the World Bank and the IFC regard a broad social compact involving civil society as a way to provide legitimacy to their further involvement in the petroleum sector and to respond to pressure from shareholder governments, particularly in the North, to take on such roles.[27] The World Bank's interest in facilitating a partnership between international oil companies and host governments is also based on a recognition that oil revenues undermine the motivation of even very poor governments to abide by World Bank and International Monetary Fund (IMF) advice and conditionality. For the government of Chad, the deep poverty of the country leaves few options in the face of a fait accompli by a consortium of strong international players. However, the weak bargaining position of Chad's government also indicates the limits to which this model may be applicable elsewhere. Countries such as Angola, Azerbaijan, and Indonesia, or a free Iraq for that matter, would not necessarily accept conditions on domestic revenue distribution from oil deals with foreign companies of the kind that Chad has accepted.

Another public-private partnership is the UK government–sponsored Extractive Industries Transparency Initiative (EITI). Launched in late 2002, the EITI aims to gather all the main stakeholders—including governments in the North and South, oil and mining companies, and NGOs—around the common cause of fostering transparency of revenues generated from extractive industries. An important aspect of the EITI is its conscious effort to resolve collective action problems. By stimulating the improvement of transparency globally, the initiative intends to reduce incentives for companies to free-ride and for host governments to employ divide-and-rule tactics in relation to companies seeking oil or mining concessions. The EITI was featured on the agenda of the Group of Eight (G-8) meeting in Evian, France, in June 2003 and has since commanded substantial attention from governments, multilateral institutions, extractive industries, and NGOs. Whether the EITI results in voluntary or mandatory measures for companies and affected governments—an issue that remains to be resolved—the policy objective of the British and other governments is to achieve tangible changes in both corporate behavior and the practices of host-country governments. While the EITI has yet to achieve this ambitious objective, it has succeeded in placing the problem of fiscal transparency of revenue from oil and mineral wealth firmly on the agenda of development and foreign ministries worldwide.[28] The capacity for effective follow-through remains a critical question. Just as small and medium-sized companies are challenged by the costs of implementing multistakeholder initiatives, the ability of a company's societal partners to participate meaningfully in PPPs is often inadequate. NGOs and some host governments regularly find themselves hard pressed to summon the resources needed for meaningful implementation. As with other company-based and industry-wide initiatives, the costs of carrying out systematic and comprehensive monitoring, so crucial to evaluating progress and effectiveness, is often prohibitive.

Policy Implementation Obligations

The OECD Financial Action Task Force on Money Laundering (FATF) exemplifies a hybrid approach—that is, embodying both "carrots and sticks"—to encourage states to create regulatory obligations for companies in domestic jurisdictions. The FATF requires states to implement a multilateral, common policy toward money laundering in order to avoid being blacklisted for poor regulatory performance. Unlike the OECD *Guidelines for Multinational Enterprises,* which obligate participating governments only to promote standards and to establish a nonbinding conciliation mechanism (the NCPs discussed above), the FATF "encourages" member countries to implement legislation that would oblige their companies to adhere to internationally authorized performance criteria by assessing countries against its revised Forty Recommendations concerning regulatory oversight of private financial institutions. Central to this incentive structure is a mutual self-assessment mechanism, a facility in which all members must participate, that was introduced to enhance peer pressure on nonperforming governments.[29] In addition to the pressure of peer review, the "stick" element includes a blacklist through which the FATF may "name and shame" countries—even nonmember states—that are in noncompliance with its recommendations. In this way, the FATF creates domestic legal obligations on companies via nonbinding international regulation.

Over time, the incremental success of the FATF has enabled it to accrue increased political backing from member states, as the fight against money laundering moved from the margins to the center of the international political stage, first as part of the "War on Drugs" and, more recently, within the "War on Terrorism."[30] In 2001, in an unprecedented move, the

FATF threatened a number of countries with sanctions, including the withholding of IMF and World Bank loans, if appropriate money-laundering legislation was not passed. In September 2002, the FATF approach was softened again with a temporary blacklist moratorium to allow a "carrot-based" initiative with the World Bank and IMF, including capacity-building efforts to improve legislation.[31]

Certification mechanisms to dissuade or encourage the purchase of a given good or commodity can be voluntary, mandatory, or somewhere in between in terms of the obligations they create for companies. As it now stands, the Kimberley Process Certification Scheme (KPCS) for rough diamonds is a political agreement among states—those engaged in the mining, trade, and processing of diamonds—NGOs, and diamond industry members, with the aim of establishing minimum common rules for rough diamond certification. Formally, the Kimberley scheme, which entered into force in January 2003, creates no legal obligations for companies. However, participating states agree to legislate and implement certification procedures, thus creating obligations for companies through binding domestic legislation. Companies or individuals shipping diamonds without proper certificates can have shipments seized and may be subject to criminal prosecution. Peer-review missions on member-state compliance are to be conducted with the consent of the participating country, but the multilateral participation criteria and compliance and enforcement mechanisms remain weak and reflect a basically voluntary approach. There is no explicit mention of exclusion procedures for non-complying participants, although two participating countries have been excluded to date.[32] Like the OECD *Guidelines,* the Kimberley regime does create some obligations for states. While state participation in Kimberley is voluntary, participating states agree not to trade rough diamonds with nonparticipating states, just as OECD states agree to promote the *Guidelines* for multinational corporations. Over time, continued political pressure by NGOs, media, and concerned governments has contributed to a tightening of the Kimberley regime. In this the KPCS is similar to the FATF: both have developed a multilateral political framework, implemented via the deployment of mixed incentives to create domestic legal obligations for private-sector actors doing business abroad. As Ian Smillie makes clear in Chapter 3, the threat to their industries of being excluded from the global diamond trade has provided a powerful incentive for nonparticipating states to join the Kimberley Process. This mix of carrot and stick has helped create an incentive structure that promotes a "race to the top" in terms of participation and the possibility that the KPCS can become a form of regulation that is both globally inclusive and nationally robust.

Economic Supervision and Conditionality

In the absence of effective domestic economic governance, public international institutions have played a significant—and often controversial—role in providing advice and assistance to the management of the fiscal and economic affairs of some states. In general, economic supervision by public international institutions aims to improve fiscal or other aspects of economic governance in countries experiencing transitions from conflict. In Bosnia, following the Dayton Agreement, international institutions such as the Office of the High Representative and the Peace Implementation Council, often in cooperation with international financial institutions, were deeply involved in the management or oversight of economic policy with a view to supporting implementation of the peace agreement.[33] The same has been true of UN transitional administrations, such as those in Kosovo and East Timor, as well as in other peacebuilding processes, as in Palestine after the Oslo accords. In each situation, the supervising institutions and their member states, very often the major donors to the reconstruction of the country, have worked with the domestic authorities to manage economic policy. The powers of the international actors have varied from case to case: from full executive authority—as in the case of Kosovo, East Timor, and, after a time, Bosnia—to different forms of conditionality, as in the case of post-Oslo Palestine.

Conditionality, as conventionally understood, relates to the formal linkage of specific conditions to the provision of loans from the World Bank and IMF for improved macroeconomic performance by developing or transition countries.[34] In reality, it is a wider phenomenon, implying explicit or implicit pressures that follow loans or grants from bilateral or multilateral aid organizations to recipient governments. Philippe Le Billon has identified a number of cases where conditionality has been applied by either the World Bank or IMF as an instrument of enforcement for curtailing the conflict trade. These include the delay of World Bank loans to Indonesia in 1999 due to concerns about illegal logging, U.S. and IMF pressure on Thailand in the late 1990s to end Thai economic support to the Khmer Rouge in Cambodia, the European Union's suspension of aid to Liberia to cut off resource flows from that country to the Revolutionary United Front (RUF) in Sierra Leone, and, finally, IMF efforts from 1999 onward to press Angola to undertake greater transparency in the management of the country's oil revenues.[35]

Conditionality is usually defined as a negative incentive or "stick" because it is predicated upon the threat of halting development and/or reconstruction aid to a given country. While conditionality relates mainly to governments, business interests may be affected by the withdrawal of development aid from nonperforming countries, particularly where export credit assistance is affected. The content, impact, and legitimacy of peace conditionality are large areas of research and debate.[36] It is worth noting that governments benefiting from or expecting large inflows of revenues from natural resource exploitation are far less likely to accept the terms implied by given conditionalities from bilateral or multilateral players. The larger the inflow of natural resource revenues, the weaker the motivation for countries like Angola and Kazakhstan to abide by conditionality, particularly with reference to transparency requirements. Because of these specific traits, the "agents of conditionality" depend on informal or formal cooperation with other stakeholders in order to achieve the goals sought by conditionality. In theory, this can take the form of cooperation between multilateral agencies, bilateral donors, and the main companies involved in resource extraction in a collective approach to ensuring compliance by the country in question. This kind of conditionality was a part of the policy mix employed in the case in the Chad-Cameroon project discussed above.

National and International Law

State legislation is the legal reference of first instance for business conduct, whether at home or abroad. In conflict zones, some activities of economic actors or the economic activities of political actors—such as property theft and smuggling—may be clearly illegal under the domestic laws of the country in which they occur. Often, however, there is little or no will or capacity to enforce these laws and to prosecute violators. Other business activities, such as obtaining a profit or an economic advantage from the exploitation of natural resources in a war zone, may appear morally unacceptable. However, in the absence of a law that specifically prohibits these activities from being used to finance conflict, they are not illegal. Particularly in conflict situations, there are typically no regulators, or at least none that have effect. In addition, the evolution of "shadow states" characterized by massive levels of corruption, the loss of control over territory to rebel factions or invading states, and simply the "fog of war" all undermine the application of the law, resulting in de facto domestic legal anarchy.[37]

In effect, then, economic activities in conflict zones, some of which may fuel or exacerbate hostilities, continue in a context of virtual impunity. Attempts to tackle the problem of impunity of economic actors in war economies through legal regulation must confront problems of jurisdiction and legal personality. Most legal regimes deal with violations committed within their jurisdiction. While some countries have laws on the books that permit universal or extraterritorial jurisdiction for some crimes, they are rarely invoked.[38] In most jurisdictions, natural persons (individuals) may be prosecuted for crimes, while legal persons (such as companies) rarely are. In some jurisdictions—for example, Canada and Norway—the penal code expresses jurisdiction over companies.[39] In general, however, companies rarely qualify for prosecution under the criminal laws of states, regardless of whether their activities have been identified as financing combatants or implicated in human rights violations or war crimes. While it would be possible to target individual company employees for prosecution for their commission of specific criminal acts in war, or for complicity in such acts, such charges are rarely, if ever, pursued. Indeed, it is not illegal for companies to do business in war zones or to profit from war zone trade and production.

A range of international instruments that deal with separate aspects of the economic dimensions of armed conflict do have some potential to bridge this regulatory gap. These include targeted UN sanctions, such as those imposed against rough diamonds traded by UNITA and the RUF, supported by the monitoring of the UN Expert Panels; the UN Convention against Transnational Organized Crime (2000); the Moratorium on the Exportation, Importation and Manufacture of Light Weapons (1998) by the Economic Organization of West African States (ECOWAS); the UN Convention for the Suppression of the Financing of Terrorism (1999); the OECD Convention on Combating Bribery of Foreign Public Officials (1997); the UN Convention against the Illicit Traffic in Narcotic Drugs and Psychotropic Substances (1988); as well as regional and domestic law-enforcement efforts in the area of drugs and crime control. However, these are directed against clearly criminal activities and, in relation to the economic activities of otherwise legitimate firms, do not directly target the economic activities that help sustain conflict.

The effectiveness of this patchwork of legal instruments is weakened by incomplete coverage and by difficulties in ensuring compliance. UN-authorized sanctions, while theoretically binding on all states, are unevenly implemented and cover very few conflict trade areas.[40] This is not to say that the effective targeting of economic resources cannot help to mitigate or end conflict. Sanctions on illegal logging in Cambodia are widely credited with facilitating the collapse of the Khmer Rouge.[41] Likewise, Serbian president Slobodan Milosevic was weakened and eventually overthrown after the funds he used to service his patronage networks were pursued and eventually put beyond his reach.[42] The end of the Angolan war was hastened in part by the effectiveness of UN sanctions in restricting UNITA's ability to market diamonds.[43] However, none of these sanctions efforts were successful on their own. More to the point here, none of them created effective liability for business entities that continued operating in these embargoed markets. The same is true even for those criminal and other shadow actors who engage in conflict trade for profit. Despite increased evidence of systematic sanctions violations, for example, there have been

few, if any, convictions of shadowy and criminal arms traffickers and diamond dealers known to be chronic "sanctions busters."[44]

In international humanitarian law, very few activities are defined as
economic crimes against humanity or economic war crimes per se; these
are largely limited to predatory crimes with economic dimensions, namely
enslavement and the property crimes of plunder, pillage, and spoliation.[45]
Similarly, international trade law is concerned primarily with lowering barriers to trade and does not address the problem of trade that is based on war
or conflict. International economic law, including both the rules of the
World Trade Organization and the bilateral investment agreements of
recent years, explicitly excludes from the scope of those treaties any trade
or investment relations considered of strategic interest by a state on the
grounds of national security.[46] In fact, most international trade and commercial service sectors are not regulated at the global level at all, let alone
regulated to control for their involvement in financing armed conflict. In
short, there is currently little by way of domestic or international law to
regulate the economic dimensions of armed conflict.

Taken together, the various points on the policy continuum range from
initiatives and campaigns that focus squarely on curtailing the financial
bases of war but are basically voluntary in nature, with weak if any
enforcement mechanisms, to binding laws or conventions with very general
aims that are only indirectly linked to the economic dimensions of armed
conflict. Arguably, these initiatives and conventions may represent the
emergence of an international moral and political norm under which economic activity that sustains or profits from armed conflict or human rights
abuse is deemed unacceptable.[47] It should be stressed, however, that there
is as yet little consensus as to the content of this emerging norm, as evidenced by the vocal resistance from industry representatives to the elaboration of the UN Sub-commission on Human Rights' Norms on the
Responsibilities of Transnational Corporations and Other Business
Enterprises.[48]

Economies of Conflict: A Malign Problem Structure

Governments, multilateral organizations, industry associations, and individual companies have yet to elaborate operational definitions of what
might constitute unacceptable business activities in war zones.[49] In addition, there is no natural policy home—no single, obvious national or international institution—where these problems might be routinely addressed.
This is due, in part, to the fact that the economic dimensions of armed conflict constitute a relatively new and politically immature post–Cold War
policy issue. It is also because the political problems associated with regu-

lation, as with the issue of climate change, are particularly malign, in the sense that there is much that stands in the way of developing a coherent and effective policy response.[50] Several key characteristics define the malign problem structure of economies of conflict: difficulties in establishing clear and causal links between economic and conflict activity; a large and complex set of heterogeneous actors with strong incentives to oppose or evade regulation; cost-benefit asymmetries, particularly the immediate and high costs to important actors versus the more diffuse and long-term social benefits; problems in assessing the legitimacy of given involvements in conflict; difficulties in targeting regulation in a manner that does no harm to civilians; and problems of policymaking among politically divided actors in the consensus-oriented decisionmaking system of the United Nations.

Difficulties in Establishing Clear and Causal Links Between Economic and Conflict Activity

Corporate and banking secrecy, the "fog of war," and the sheer volume of trade in goods and services make establishing clear causal links between specific economic and conflict activities a daunting analytical challenge. Nonetheless, such efforts have begun to bear fruit. Accumulated research indicates that economic factors play an important role in sustaining armed conflict, particularly civil wars.[51] It has been clearly established that the availability of money-laundering opportunities is central to financing civil and armed conflict and that revenues from oil production contribute to corruption, help keep unaccountable governments in power, and also fund war efforts.[52] These findings have, at least in part, informed the motivation behind the EITI. It has also been shown that proceeds from the extraction of and trade in natural resources such as oil and gas, diamonds, coltan, gold, and timber have provided financing to a range of combatant parties in numerous civil wars that have resulted in the deaths of millions of people. Sustained efforts by the UN and NGOs to differentiate conflict diamonds and timber from the legitimate trade in these commodities have created the basis for some of the tangible, if still fledgling, regulatory initiatives described above.

To date, these and related empirical findings that link economic activity and armed conflict provide *necessary*—but not, or not yet, *sufficient*—evidence upon which to build effective policy measures to deal with the problem. The main challenge is that most of the linkages are indirect and diffuse, crossing the normative lines between licit and illicit. Indeed, the bulk of natural resource production and financial transactions that sustain warring factions are ultimately dependent upon legitimate elements of today's liberalized global economic order. The oil industry is a case in point. Although explicit corruption can be documented in oil company dealings with particular governments, and although particular governments have been successful in keeping vast chunks of oil revenue outside the official domestic budget process, the overwhelming flow of resources from oil wells into government coffers in conflict areas around the world reflects legitimate business practice.[53] As regards conflict dynamics, this represents a major regulatory dilemma. The size of revenues adhering from business transactions of generally legitimate companies may have a much larger impact on conflict dynamics and inflict more harm on war-affected populations than those revenues generated by activities commonly accepted as shady or explicitly illegal. As noted at the outset, states continue to assert primacy in waging war and managing their economies, and in the present international system, both activities remain well within their sovereign rights as states. The main analytical challenge, then, is to develop perspectives and methods that will enable the design of policies that end impunity for illicit economic activities in zones of conflict, as well as address otherwise legitimate business conduct that has adverse effects on conflict dynamics.

Difficulties in Designing Targeted Regulations That Don't Harm Civilians

International sanctions policy has, for a number of years, undergone significant reform, not least because of the humanitarian impact of UN sanctions on Iraq. The effort to develop targeted sanctions, particularly commodity and arms embargoes and financial freezes, has transformed them from a blunt instrument that, in effect, penalized whole populations for the misbehavior of their leaders to a tool that seeks to interdict the financial and other resources of rogue elites.[54] These developments are laudable. However, implicit in the logic of targeting the economic activities that sustain conflict is the assumption that squeezing financial flows to belligerents will end their motivation to fight. This assumption is problematic on many accounts.

First, even if increased attention to economic motives behind conflict behavior is justified, any conflict has a complex web of causes and agents. Therefore, in cases where explicit economic motives are not the key driver, belligerents are likely to continue fighting even if funding is squeezed quite significantly. A squeeze at one point may also lead warring parties to look elsewhere for resources, which serves to underscore the need for a comprehensive approach to regulating the conflict trade. Policy analysis within the context of the International Peace Academy's project on Economic Agendas and Civil War indicates that where political cohesion or ideological commitment is high, armed groups—or key elites within them—may endure the higher costs of fighting and try to supplement them by seeking out other available sources of revenue. At least in the short term, the denial of resources to belligerents may lead to an intensification of violence and increased predation on civilian populations.[55] Increased predation is considered to have happened in the case of the partially successful UN sanctions against UNITA's diamond trade. Importantly, in many cases the illicit exploitation of natural resources benefits not only rogue elites but civilian livelihoods. As Stephen Jackson has detailed elsewhere in this volume (Chapter 7), international interventions to curtail conflict trade may directly undermine civilian welfare by depriving civilians of an ability to eke out a livelihood, whether by panning for alluvial diamonds, growing illicit narcotics, or engaging in the variety of related business activities that support armed conflict. Unless accompanied by determined efforts to provide alternative economic opportunities, interdictions can have a variety of unintended consequences, both for civilian welfare and for conflict dynamics.

Difficulties in Assessing Contested Legitimacy of Conflict Economies

Regulation is often enacted with the intent of choking off financial flows to parties waging war or preparing and conspiring to do so. At first glance, this seems an intuitively attractive and unproblematic goal. Unfortunately it is not. Both formal and informal rules of international politics and law acknowledge that armed conflict can be legitimate and justified.[56] This means that one or more parties to a given conflict may be viewed as fighting a "just war." As legitimacy in international politics is often in the eye of the beholder, efforts to smother the economic resources of parties involved in violent conflict will inevitably involve contests over claims to a just cause or normative principle. As some critics of UN sanctions have noted, in some cases targeting rebel groups' economic assets exclusively may risk supporting unsavory regimes and denying repressed groups legitimate recourse to self-defense. To date, regulation of the conflict trade has taken the form of intergovernmental measures, for instance, UN conventions or sanctions. This often leads to an obvious prostate bias at the expense of nonstate actors. Where outsiders aim to interdict economic flows in order to significantly alter the military balance in favor of a government, there is a risk that they may provoke, or support, state repression or even genocide. Who is to decide on the merits of attempts to block the resources of ethnically based insurgents fighting an ethnically based but undemocratic and potentially racist government? In cases where clearly democratic and legitimate governments are attacked by unscrupulous, unrepresentative insurgents or mere bandits, the case for financial sanctions against the latter is more easily justified. However, in most conflicts the reality is much more complex.

The development of arms export controls demonstrates that third-party governments make specific and often controversial judgments about the best way to stop a war as well as adjudicating competing claims of the justice of one belligerent's cause against another.[57] In Bosnia, for example, an arms embargo imposed on the parties to the conflict was widely criticized for having undermined the military capacity of Bosnia-Herzegovina to the benefit of Serbia, which had inherited much of the Yugoslav army's materiel. An alternative agnostic approach might be to implement uniform arms controls against all states and others involved in armed conflict. Quite apart from the challenges of implementation, such an approach would still be biased in favor of the status quo, regardless of whether the status quo favored dictators or democrats, friends or foes.

A Heterogeneous Set of Actors with Strong Incentives to Resist Regulation

The regulatory bits and pieces described above are what they are—bits and pieces—because of the complexity of the challenge in general and the diverse structure of relevant actors with strong incentives to resist regulation in particular. Here we present a proposed categorization of the main players likely to be affected by any proposed regulation.

Extractive industry companies. Most companies engaged in the extraction of oil, minerals, and other natural resources are legitimate businesses, ranging in size from some of the world's largest multinational corporations to medium-sized regional enterprises to national and local firms linked to particular extraction projects. Some are private, some state owned, and some publicly held; thus they possess different incentive structures and a varying amenability to regulation.

Banks and other financial institutions (including investment funds, pension funds, and hedge funds). Illicit financial dealings take place across the licit network of global financial services. Global, regional, national, and local institutions can be key players in making possible the purchase of arms and other key military items (mostly, but not exclusively, for states). Despite stepped-up efforts to stamp out the most conspicuous money-laundering practices, the international financial architecture continues to offer opportunities for illegitimate groups inside or outside government to hide and move funds needed to initiate or continue armed conflict.

Trading companies and brokers. In various guises, these middlemen facilitate all kinds of commercial deals (including barter) among parties engaged in war and between combatant parties and external economic agents. While many of these middlemen represent legitimate companies, a large number of them are gray- or black-market players seeking to enrich themselves from the shady business of war. Arms brokers and dodgy transportation companies are important parts of this sector.

Governmental institutions. This is a broad category that includes everything from bilateral development agencies and national export-promotion and investment-guarantee agencies through regional development banks to global multilaterals such as the UN and the Bretton Woods institutions. Export credit and lending agencies may be most closely associated with filling the coffers of governments engaged in civil and interstate wars, while aid fungibility means that even the most well-intentioned bilateral budget support program may indirectly serve to sustain military budgets.[58]

Regulation Inflicts Immediate Costs on Powerful Players

A common regulatory dilemma is that regulation can have immediate negative impacts on companies' bottom lines and even put some companies out of business, while the positive impacts, if measurable at all, may benefit only future generations. Problems arise partly because those at risk of being constrained by regulation and of bearing the brunt of its costs can point to significant uncertainties as to the beneficial impacts of regulation. Significant groups of players—such as industry associations—are politically strong, well organized, and in general strongly opposed to regulation. While some corporations themselves may voice moderate views on such questions, often the industry associations in which they participate advocate more conservative positions—a reflection of the tendency to appeal to the lowest common denominator in a particular industry. In addition, broader support for the longer-term perspectives required to advance comprehensive approaches to managing the economic dimensions of armed conflict can be easily undermined by interested constituencies or political leaders failing to stay the course.

Challenges in Finding Common Ground at Global Organizations

Much of the emerging discourse on regulating economic activities in conflict zones has focused on the UN system. This is primarily due to the organization's mandate in the area of international peace and security as manifested in the authority of the UN Security Council. The UN's less unique and more contested mandate in the economic and social areas also serves to identify it as a possible arena for collective policymaking. Already UN conventions and initiatives concerning small arms, transnational organized crime, and corruption have indirectly contributed to multilateral efforts to address the economic dimensions of armed conflict, particularly through Security Council sanctions committees and the monitoring of sanctions implementation by UN expert panels.

As is well known, however, the UN's identity as a consensus-oriented intergovernmental body is also a liability insofar as it creates serious limitations to the UN's capacity to act effectively. In dealing with the economic dimensions of armed conflict, this systemic weakness is compounded by further problems. First, quite a number of UN member governments are presently involved in armed conflicts and are thus not likely to accept the agnostic approach presented above with respect to complicity in and responsibility for curtailing economic activities that sustain hostilities.[59] Accordingly, it has been far easier for the UN to arrive at agreement on restrictions to the flow of diaspora remittances and on economic sanctions against nonstate armed groups than on actions that imply judgments about the complicity or responsibilities of particular governments in conflicts against insurgents. In short, the prostate bias of the UN is an abiding challenge to developing comprehensive and just regulatory mechanisms for managing economies of conflict within a UN framework.

Second, and related, the discourse on the conflict trade threatens to exacerbate the North-South divide that has paralyzed UN action in a number of other areas for decades. The notion that the search for pecuniary rewards (sometimes characterized as "greed") motivates conflict behavior in developing and transition countries, rather than legitimate national security or political grievances, can easily be interpreted as a new condescending strategy of Western nations that may give rise to new conditionality on aid, loans, and investments in the developing world.[60] One example of such sensitivities is the effort, backed mostly by developed countries, aimed at regulating money-laundering and tax havens, the bulk of which are in small developing nations. Countries facing allegations of providing havens have been known to use the traditional language of North-South confrontation to fend off attempts at regulation.[61]

Resistance to effective multilateral regulation, however, is not limited to states. The extractive industries, financial institutions, and a range of other private sector actors share comprehensive interfaces and common interests with home and host governments. As already noted, this implies intensive lobbying efforts against regulatory proposals that are considered negative to short-term commercial interests. More specifically, many of the economic actors identified as alleged accomplices in war economies by several NGO and expert panel investigations are based in powerful nations, some of which are permanent members of the Security Council. In some instances, notably in the case of Liberian timber, the economic interests of these powerful states have impeded UN efforts to mitigate the conflict trade. Still, it is the Security Council that has been the most responsive policy actor in seeking to grapple with the economic dimensions of conflict, particularly through the mechanisms of its sanctions committees. Despite the political limitations imposed by its members, it remains the case that no other international body has been as responsive on the question of the economic dimensions of international peace and security. However, to date, the nature of this responsiveness has been ad hoc, and it remains likely that the Security Council will resist pressure to legislate a more general form of regulation of the problem.

Conclusion

The policy issue of economic dimensions of armed conflict has developed quickly. Once the scope of the problem became clearer, policymakers responded, both by seeking to regulate some business practices, as in the case of diamond certification and extractive industry transparency, and in seeking to monitor and better understand the dynamics at work.[62] These efforts have been matched by a burgeoning policy research agenda which has made significant gains in knowledge, pointing increasingly toward the need to better understand the intersection of the economic, political, and social dimensions of armed conflicts.[63] Yet in 2003 and 2004, as the wars in Sierra Leone and Liberia moved into some form of transition to peace and as the Democratic Republic of Congo struggled to implement its peace agreement, the attention of policymakers threatened to move elsewhere.

This would be a serious mistake. None of the conditions that gave rise to these war economies have been remedied by sustained policy measures, whether domestic or international, voluntary or mandatory. As a result, the patterns of economic behavior that sustained those wars and undermined human security are still being played out in fragile and war-torn countries in Africa, Asia, and the Americas.[64] Because of the malign problem structure of the conflict trade, moving beyond crisis-based policy responses will not be easy. Complicating matters further is the fact that because the economic dimensions of armed conflict constitute a multifaceted policy problem that crosscuts political and institutional boundaries, it has as yet no logical institutional policy home. In the UN context, are conflict trade and conflict financing an issue for the Security Council or the Economic and Social Council? Should they be dealt with as a conflict prevention issue, a human rights issue, a development issue, or some combination of them? Is it an issue for the World Bank or the Organization for Security and Cooperation in Europe? In domestic terms, is it an issue for defense, justice, trade, foreign, or industry departments of government?

The practical problem of locating a proper policy home, or forum, through which to shape an international response to the issue is one of the most pressing questions on the policy agenda. To the extent that diplomacy seeks to develop an answer, efforts should be based on a clear understanding of the issues at stake. Ongoing initiatives across the policy continuum, from voluntary measures to legal regulation, from small arms to financing terrorism, collectively indicate the nascent emergence of an international moral and political norm prohibiting economic activities that sustain—and perhaps also profit from—armed conflict and grave human rights abuse. This norm is a natural development of the elaboration and extension of human rights principles throughout the twentieth century, which have steadily qualified what states can and cannot do in the exercise of national sovereignty and extended the protection and obligations of international law beyond the state to individuals and to companies.

Yet the policy responses to the economic dimensions of armed conflict tend to have not one but two overlapping but distinct objectives. One, a human rights objective, seeks to end the impunity of economic actors operating in conflict zones for activities that violate or assist in the violation of internationally accepted standards of behavior. The second, a conflict prevention objective, seeks to address the economic activities that apparently sustain wars and other threats to international peace and security. Both seek to change or remedy the behavior of economic actors operating in—or otherwise linked to—armed conflict. Both seek to end impunity for violations of international norms. And both impulses implicitly recognize that a variety of policy instruments are needed to create the incentive structure necessary for change.

By mapping the policy continuum on this issue, we have tried to suggest that no initiative that focuses on only one point on the continuum will be effective on its own. Voluntary measures will require legal regulation in order to level the playing field and increase the costs of noncompliance, while the effectiveness of legal regulation should be measured in terms of positive changes to company conduct and the beneficial impact for affected communities, rather than, say, by the numbers of companies that end up in court. An immediate challenge in this regard is to identify and prohibit unacceptable behavior and practices that occur where trade and conflict converge.[65] Ending the impunity of economic actors in conflict zones will require building a more coherent regulatory regime on the basis of good causal theory, existing legal principles, and mechanisms that create liability, not least through more reliable forms of monitoring. The effectiveness of these efforts will be dependent in no small measure on companies' realizing that there is a business case to be made for this kind of regulation, one that engages their own interest in overcoming collective action problems as well as in improving predictability in relation to the reputational and financial risks of doing business in conflict zones.

Notes

1. See Dan Smith, *Trends and Causes of Armed Conflict* (Berlin: Berghof Research Centre for Constructive Conflict Management, 2001).

2. Elsewhere we have defined conflict trade narrowly as "legally or illegally produced commodities traded on the legitimate, but highly unregulated, global markets to obtain financial resources, weapons and other materiel needed to sustain war": Leiv Lunde and Mark Taylor with Anne Huser, *Commerce or Crime? Regulating Economies of Conflict,* Fafo Report no. 434 (Oslo: Fafo Institute, 2003), p. 12.

3. United Nations Security Council, *Final Report of the Panel of Experts on the Illegal Exploitation of Natural Resources and Other Forms of Wealth of the Democratic Republic of the Congo,* S/2002/1146, October 16, 2002.

4. See Patricia Feeney and Tom Kenny, Chapter 14 in this volume.

5. Karen Ballentine and Heiko Nitzschke, "Business and Armed Conflict: An Assessment of Issues and Options," *Die Friedens-Warte: Journal of International Peace and Organization* 79, nos. 1–2 (2004): 35–56.

6. This chapter is based in part on Lunde, Taylor, and Huser, *Commerce or Crime?* (see note 2).

7. Daniel Graymore and Isabella D. Bunn, "A World Summit for Business Development? The Need for Corporate Accountability in the World Summit for Sustainable Development Agenda" (London: Christian Aid, 2002).

8. International Council on Human Rights Policy (ICHRP), *Beyond Voluntarism: Human Rights and the Developing International Legal Obligations of Companies* (Geneva: ICHRP, 2002), p. 9.

9. "Self-regulation" is often used to refer to voluntary measures and in this sense is something of a misnomer: in normal usage, *regulation* involves legal or administrative sanction and is not voluntary. Here we use *regulation* in the latter, non-voluntary sense of the term, and we use both *voluntary* and *self-regulation* more or less interchangeably.

10. See International Association of Oil and Gas Producers (OGP), *Combating Corruption: OGP Progress Report,* Report no. I.2I/334 (London: OGP, 2002).

11. See Jonathan M. Winer and Trifin J. Roule, "Follow the Money: The Finance of Illicit Resource Extraction," in Ian Bannon and Paul Collier, eds., *Natural Resources and Violent Conflict: Options and Actions* (Washington, D.C.: World Bank, 2003), pp. 186–189.

12. See Philippe Le Billon, "Getting It Done: Instruments of Enforcement," in Bannon and Collier, *Natural Resources and Violent Conflict,* pp. 258–259 (see note 11).

13. For a comprehensive list of these, see Gare Smith and Dan Feldman, *Company Codes of Conduct and International Standards: An Analytical Comparison* (Washington, D.C.: World Bank and International Finance Corporation, 2003).

14. Talisman Energy, "2002 Corporate Social Responsibility Report," Calgary, Alberta, Canada, March 2003, p. 8 (www.talisman-energy.com).

15. Total published its first CSR report in May 2003, available at www.total.com/csr2003/en/index.htm.

16. Arvind Ganesan and Alex Vines, *Engine of War: Resources, Greed, and the Predatory State* (Washington, D.C.: Human Rights Watch, 2004); and ICHRP, *Beyond Voluntarism.*

17. The voluntary nature of the Global Compact principles was reemphasized

after *Ethical Performance,* a CSR newsletter (April 2003 issue), had reported that the compact had decided to introduce a "disciplinary procedure." On its website, the Global Compact states that this is plainly wrong and holds that "as a voluntary initiative, the Global Compact has neither the mandate nor the resources to monitor company behaviour." See www.unglobalcompact.org.

18. See *Global Compact Business Guide for Conflict Impact Assessment and Risk Management* (New York: Global Compact, 2002).

19. See Amnesty International, *The Human Rights Norms for Business: Towards Legal Accountability* (London: Amnesty International, 2004).

20. *Soft law* can be defined several ways. We use it here to refer to rules or norms that are not enacted by legislation or government regulation nor created by contract.

21. Amnesty International, *Human Rights Norms for Business.*

22. The Business and Industry Advisory Committee (BIAC) and the Trade Union Advisory Committee (TUAC) are advisory bodies to the OECD. NGOs have been given a similar status.

23. U.S. Department of State, "Voluntary Principles on Security and Human Rights," Washington, D.C., February 20, 2001.

24. Amnesty International, *Human Rights and Business Matters,* Spring / Summer 2001; and U.S. Department of State, "Voluntary Principles on Security and Human Rights."

25. Bennett Freeman and Genoveva Hernández, "Managing Risk and Building Trust: The Challenge of Implementing the Voluntary Principles on Security and Human Rights," in Rory Sullivan, ed., *Business and Human Rights: Dilemmas and Solutions* (Sheffield, UK: Greenleaf, 2003).

26. Jake Sherman, *Options for Promoting Corporate Responsibility in Conflict Zones: Perspectives from the Private Sector,* report of the Working Group on the Role of Private Sector in Armed Conflict, Program on Economic Agendas in Civil War (New York: International Peace Academy, 2002).

27. An important motive of the 2001–2003 World Bank Extractive Industries Review is to explore to what extent there is general public/political support for continued World Bank Group lending to extractive industries worldwide. This was prompted by mounting questions surrounding its mandate to operate in these areas. This is an additional reason for the topicality of the World Bank's participation in the Chad-Cameroon project.

28. An example of company adherence to increasing demands for transparency is the 2002 CSR report of Canadian oil company Talisman (published in March 2003), which provides updated figures for fiscal contributions to host governments, including countries such as Sudan and Indonesia (p. 35; see www.talisman-energy.com).

29. See Fabrizio Pagani, "Peer Review, A Tool for Cooperation and Change: An Analysis of the OECD Working Method," OECD SG/LEG (2002)1, for an assessment of how peer review is increasingly used to beef up otherwise voluntary cooperation mechanisms. Availabe at www.oecd.org/dataoecd/33/161955285pdf.

30. Jonathan M. Winer, "Globalising Transparency: Implementing a Financial Sector White List," Fafo Policy Brief, May 2003 (www.fafo.no/piccr/ecocon).

31. Edward Allen and Alan Beattie, "Blacklist of 'Dirty Money' Havens Put on Temporary Hold," *Financial Times,* September 26, 2002.

32. Lebanon and Congo-Brazzaville have at different times been removed from the list of participants due to a failure to comply with the minimum requirements of the scheme.

33. Mark B. Taylor, "Public Sector Finance in Post-Conflict Situations," Report of the Peace Implementation Network Forum, FAFO AIS, Washington, D.C., April 1999.

34. James K. Boyce. *Investing in Peace: Aid and Conditionality after Civil Wars,* Adelphi Paper no. 351 (Oxford: Oxford University Press, 2002). See Chapter 12 by James Boyce in this volume.

35. Le Billon, *Getting It Done.*

36. See Chapter 12 by Boyce in this volume.

37. William Reno, "Shadow States and the Political Economy of Civil Wars," in Mats Berdal and David M. Malone, eds., *Greed and Grievance: Economic Agendas in Civil War* (Boulder: Lynne Rienner, 2000), pp. 43–65; see also Jean-François Bayart, Stephen Ellis, and Beatrice Hibou, *The Criminalization of the State in Africa* (Oxford: James Currey, 1999).

38. There are civil liability laws in some countries that permit suits to be filed for torts caused abroad, such as the U.S. Alien Tort Claims Act (ACTA). See Chapter 16 by Paul Hoffman in this volume.

39. Criminal Code of Canada, R.S. 1985, c. C-46, s.2; Norwegian General Civil Penal Code, chapter 3a, "Criminal Liability of Enterprises."

40. Le Billon, *Getting It Done.*

41. Global Witness, *The Logs of War,* Fafo Report no. 379 (Oslo: Fafo Institute, 2002) p. 18.

42. Jonathan Winer, *Globalizing Transparency: Implementing a Financial Sector White List,* Fafo Policy Brief no.705 (Oslo: Fafo Institute, 2003).

43. Although a failure for much of their existence, sanctions against UNITA improved dramatically under the stricter implementation monitoring ushered in by the UN Security Council sanctions committee. See David Cortright and George Lopez, *The Sanctions Decade: Assessing UN Strategies in the 1990s* (Boulder: Lynne Rienner, 2000).

44. Le Billon, *Getting It Done;* and Chapter 15 by Pierre Kopp in this volume.

45. GC Additional Protocol II article 4(2)(g); ICTY article 3 ("plunder of public or private property"); ICTR article 4(f); ICC article 8(2)(e)(v).

46. Article XXI(b)(iii) of General Agreement on Tariffs and Trade (GATT, 1994).

47. In 2003, there were indications that the legal gap concerning illicit exploitation in armed conflict may be closing: indictments issued in 2003 by the Special Court for Sierra Leone against Sam Bokarie and Charles Taylor both refer to a "joint criminal enterprise" to exploit the diamond resource. In addition, the ICC chief prosecutor indicated that, as part of his investigation into alleged war crimes and crimes against humanity committed in the Ituri region of the Democratic Republic of Congo (DRC), he was considering looking into the complicity of economic actors engaging in criminal transactions that have aided and abetted the perpetration of war crimes. The Office of the Prosecutor mentioned "money-laundering and other crimes committed outside the Democratic Republic of Congo which may be connected with the atrocities," adding that "various reports have pointed to links between the activities of some African, European and Middle Eastern companies and the atrocities taking place in the Democratic Republic of Congo. The alleged involvement of organized crime groups from Eastern Europe has also been mentioned. Their activities allegedly include gold mining, the illegal exploitation of oil, and the arms trade. There is general concern that the atrocities allegedly committed in the country may be fuelled by the exploitation of natural resources there and the arms trade, which are enabled through the international

banking system." See www.icc-cpi.int/library/newspoint/mediaalert/pids009_2003-en.pdf.

48. Amnesty International, "Confederation of British Industry Must Follow Rights Roadmap," letter to the editor, *Financial Times,* March 9, 2004; see also letter from the International Chamber of Commerce excerpted in ICHRP, *Beyond Voluntarism,* p. 8.

49. See, for example, Jake Sherman, *Private Sector Actors in Zones of Conflict: Research Challenges and Policy Responses,* Report of the Fafo's PICCR and the International Peace Academy project on Economic Agendas in Civil Wars (New York: International Peace Academy, 2001).

50. For a summary of various arguments around the politics of climate change, see Bill McKibben's useful review of a number of contributions in this area, "Crossing the Red Line," *New York Review of Books,* June 10, 2004, available at www.nybooks.com/articles/17179.

51. See, for example, Mark Taylor, *Conflict Trade: The Private Sector and Contemporary Wars* (London: Pluto, 2004); Karen Ballentine and Jake Sherman, eds., *The Political Economy of Armed Conflict: Beyond Greed and Grievance* (Boulder: Lynne Rienner, 2003).

52. Jonathan Winer, *Illicit Finance and Global Conflict,* Fafo Report no. 380 (Oslo: Fafo Institute, 2002).

53. For comprehensive Global Witness documentation and analysis of alleged international oil and financial company complicity in the bloody civil war in Angola, see Global Witness, *Fatal Attractions* (London: Global Witness, 1999); and Global Witness, *All the President's Men* (London: Global Witness, 2002). The complicity of oil (and by implication international oil) companies in fueling conflict in Sudan is probably more direct than in the case of Angola, although even there establishing a general case against a company like Talisman Energy and the Sudanese government has proved to be a challenge. For an analysis of oil's contribution to the civil war, see International Crisis Group, *God, Oil, and Country: Changing the Logic of War in Sudan* (Geneva: ICG, January 2002).

54. Cortright and Lopez, *Sanctions Decade.*

55. Ballentine and Sherman, eds., *Political Economy of Armed Conflict.*

56. Not least in self-defense. See Charter of the United Nations chap. 7, art. 51.

57. Arms export controls are a different, although clearly related, policy area that offers a relevant perspective on how to judge the legitimacy of wars and warring parties. In most OECD countries, legislation exists to control arms exports to countries in war or warlike situations. These can be fairly strict regulations that are consciously monitored by politicians and NGOs alike. In Norway, as in many other countries, exports of arms to Turkey—a fellow NATO country—are particularly controversial. Is Turkey at war with its ethnic Kurd minority? If so, is it legitimate self-defense or repression of the weak by the strong? The present political climate in Norway dictates an embargo on arms exports to the government in Ankara, even if Turkey's NATO membership makes this a controversial stand that implies diplomatic skirmishes between the two allied countries. To judge from an Oxfam briefing paper, UK legislation is more lenient than that of Norway. Existing UK policy is to not issue licenses for arms exports if "there is a clearly identifiable risk that the proposed export might be used aggressively against another country, or for internal repression or where it would undermine sustainable development." According to Oxfam, in the context over a debate on an arms export bill (2001–2002), this policy did not hinder UK arms exports to countries such as Angola, Burma/Myanmar, Colombia, Congo, Indonesia, Sri Lanka, and Sudan.

58. The fungibility issue became salient in the context of the 1998–2000 war between Ethiopia and Eritrea, in which donors disagreed sharply among themselves and with the respective governments as to what extent aid funds fueled the (universally considered futile) war efforts.

59. The resistance by large numbers of UN members to the concept (and assumed implications) of humanitarian intervention and human security present similar challenges.

60. For further discussion of this issue, see David Keen, *The Economic Functions of Violence in Civil Wars,* Adelphi Paper no. 320 (Oxford: Oxford University Press, 1998); and Michael Pugh and Neil Cooper with Jonathan Goodhand, *War Economies in a Regional Context: Challenges of Transformation* (Boulder: Lynne Rienner, 2004).

61. Helge Ole Bergesen and Leiv Lunde, *Dinosaurs or Dynamos? The United Nations and the World Bank at the Turn of the Century* (London: Earthscan Publications, 1999).

62. This was exemplified by UN Security Council practice with respect to Angola, Sierra Leone, and the DRC. See S/2000/1306, December 2000; S/2000/1225, December 21, 2000; and S/2002/1146, October 16, 2002.

63. Pugh, Cooper, and Goodhand, *War Economies in a Regional Context;* Ballentine and Sherman, eds., *Political Economy of Armed Conflict;* and Taylor, *Conflict Trade.*

64. See Ganesan and Vines, *Engine of War.* See, also Amnesty International, *On Whose Behalf? Human Rights and the Economic Reconstruction Process in Iraq* 2003, available at www.amnesty.org/library/index/engmde141282003; Caroll Rory, "Chocolate War Erupts in Ivory Coast," *Guardian,* May 14, 2004; "Beating the Drug Lords and Rebuilding a Country"(on reconstruction in Afghanistan), *Deutsche Welle,* March 31, 2004, Sam Zia-Zarifi, *Losing the Peace in Afghanistan,* Human Rights Watch, 2004, available at www.hrw.org/wr2K41/download/S.pdf; Juan Forero, "Colombia's Landed Gentry: Coca Lords and Other Bullies," *New York Times,* January 21, 2004.

65. In early 2004, the Fafo Institute for Applied International Studies (Fafo AIS) launched a project to define prohibited practices related to economies of conflict; see www.fafo.no/nsp/index.htm.

14

Conflict Management and the OECD *Guidelines for Multinational Enterprises*

Patricia Feeney and Tom Kenny

Powerful groups, businesses and individuals, using violent or non-violent means, can acquire a vested interest in sparking and perpetuating violent conflict. Just as it is important to limit the proliferation of weapons, exter-nal partners—public and private—need to help combat illicit trafficking, corrupt resource deals, rent seeking and the flow of economic resources that can stoke or be the aim of violent conflicts. This can be done through joint international actions including . . . the OECD Guidelines for Multinational Enterprises.[1]

In October 2002 the UN Panel of Experts on the Illegal Exploitation of Natural Resources and Other Forms of Wealth in the Democratic Republic of Congo published what was intended to be its final report.[2] Included as an annex was a list of eighty-five companies with business operations in the Democratic Republic of Congo (DRC), which the expert panel considered to be in violation of the *Guidelines for Multinational Enterprises* adopted by the Organization for Economic Cooperation and Development (OECD). The report not only "named and shamed" particular companies but also stated that "countries which are signatories to those Guidelines and other countries are morally obliged to ensure that their business enterprises adhere to and act on the Guidelines." Furthermore, it recalled that "home Governments have the obligation to ensure that enterprises in their jurisdic-tion do not abuse principles of conduct that they have adopted as a matter of law. They are complicit when they do not take remedial measures."[3]

The annex created controversy. Many of the companies claimed that their inclusion on the list was unwarranted. The prerogative of the DRC Expert Panel to apply the *Guidelines* was questioned. There was also confusion over what legal obligations, if any, would arise for adhering governments whose companies were listed in the annex. The controversy laid bare the widespread ignorance among companies, governments, and advocacy organizations of the existence, let alone the specific provisions, of the *Guidelines*. Most important, the "extracurricular" use of the *Guidelines* by the DRC Expert Panel placed them squarely on the agenda of those concerned with the role of extractive industry companies in zones of armed conflict. The degree to which this attention is warranted is a key concern of this chapter. Our aim is to analyze the promise and limits of the *Guidelines* as a set of principles of corporate conduct that may govern the practices of companies involved in the exploitation and trade of natural resources in zones of armed conflict.[4]

The chapter begins with a brief account of the content of the *Guidelines* to assess the extent to which a code drawn up with the norms of business conduct in mind are inherently suited to conflict situations or whether they can be made relevant by elaboration. The next section discusses the nature of the *Guidelines* and their advantages vis-à-vis other codes and initiatives for corporate conduct. Particular attention will be paid to elucidating the voluntary nature of the guidelines: their lack of legal force is at least partially offset by an implementation mechanism that obligates adhering governments to examine specific instances of questionable company conduct. Based on this discussion, the third section analyzes the implementation procedures of the *Guidelines,* the obstacles to their implementation, and the additional challenges that may be encountered when applying the *Guidelines* in conflict zones. Preliminary lessons will be drawn from the way in which the *Guidelines* have been applied to corporate conduct in Burma/Myanmar and the DRC. A number of policy-relevant formulations are offered in a final section, aimed at strengthening the operation of the *Guidelines* generally as well as in settings of armed conflict.

The Relevance of the OECD *Guidelines* to Corporate Conduct in Zones of Conflict

The *Guidelines* were adopted in 1976 as part of the OECD Declaration on International Investment and Multinational Enterprises. The declaration itself came into being in part as a response to disquiet over the involvement of U.S. multinationals in the 1973 overthrow of the democratically elected government of Salvador Allende in Chile. According to the preface of the *Guidelines,* "The common aim of the governments adhering to the *Guidelines* is to encourage the positive contributions that multinational enterprises can make to economic, environmental and social progress and to minimize the difficulties to which their various operations may give rise."[5] To that end, the various chapters of the *Guidelines* contain detailed recommendations on key aspects of multinational companies' operations, such as information disclosure, employment and industrial relations, competition, taxation, and the protection of the environment. In June 2000 the *Guidelines* were revised to ensure their continued relevance and effectiveness. Chapters on consumer interests and combating bribery were added alongside new provisions on the elimination of forced and child labor, human rights, and sustainable development. In addition, a revised commentary on the *Guidelines* was drafted by the Committee on International Investment and Multinational Enterprises (CIME), the body that oversees their implementation.[6]

Despite their origin, the *Guidelines* do not specifically address corporate conduct in conflict situations. Written to make recommendations on the norms of business conduct, they are silent on the questions of conflict finance, private security companies, and thresholds of violence or repression that may warrant divestment. However, they do address several issues, such as bribery, corruption, and environmental damage, that often go hand in hand with resource extraction activities in conflict-prone countries. In addition to these core provisions, there are bridges within the main text and the related commentary that allow the *Guidelines* to be interpreted and elaborated by reference to human rights, international labor standards, and other specified international instruments. This significantly increases the scope and relevance of the *Guidelines* to conflict situations.

Geographic Reach and Supranational Applicability of the OECD Guidelines

The *Guidelines* are one of the most geographically extensive sets of corporate codes of conduct in the world, having been adopted by the governments of all thirty OECD member countries and eight nonmembers.[7] This membership includes countries that, when taken together, are a major source of foreign direct investment and home to the majority of privately held multinational companies, including major extractive industry companies. Importantly, the *Guidelines* apply not only to companies operating in adhering countries but also to companies based in adhering countries operating in any other country.[8] In this way, their scope includes company operations in nonadhering countries, where most of today's conflicts take place. This effectively reduces the number of multinational companies that lie outside the scope of the *Guidelines* to those operating out of nonadhering countries. This means, however, that extractive companies—both privately held and state owned—headquartered in countries such as China, Malaysia, and Russia are not covered by the *Guidelines*. Undoubtedly this impedes their usefulness as a global standard, but the CIME is making serious efforts to encourage more countries outside of the OECD area to adhere to the *Guidelines*.

Furthermore, the recommendations of the *Guidelines* are addressed to both parent companies and local entities according to the actual distribution of responsibilities among them.[9] Companies should also encourage, where possible, suppliers and subcontractors to apply principles of corporate conduct compatible with the *Guidelines*.[10] Yet there has been considerable debate as to the extent to which a sourcing company can or should regulate its suppliers as distinct legal and economic entities.[11] The usual direction of application of the supply-chain provision is "upstream" among suppliers, but there is nothing to limit its application "downstream" toward the market. Such an interpretation is supported by the fact that this provision applies to "business partners" in general and is not limited to the supplier-subcontractor relationship. The commentary on the *Guidelines* recognizes that compatible conduct is sought with all entities with which companies enjoy a "working relationship," although established or direct business relationships are the main object of the recommendation.[12] It is further acknowledged that while there are practical limitations on the ability of a company to influence the conduct of business partners, companies having market power vis-à-vis their suppliers may be able to influence business partners' behavior even in the absence of investment giving rise to formal corporate control.

A closely related issue is the degree to which the *Guidelines* apply to the trading as opposed to the investment activities of companies. The CIME has issued a statement on this issue, noting that the *Guidelines* have been developed in the context of the Declaration on International Investment and that "their application rests on the presence of an investment nexus."[13] However, as the statement continues, "when considering the application of the Guidelines, flexibility is required. This is reflected in Recommendation II.10 and its commentary that deal with relations among suppliers and other business partners. These texts link the issue of scope to the practical ability of enterprises to influence the conduct of their business partners with whom they have an investment like relationship." Prior to the CIME's statement, the OECD's Working Party on the Declaration (WPD) instructed the OECD Secretariat to prepare a background paper on this issue, which asserts that the way in which the *Guidelines* are formulated—references to international human rights and International Labour Organization (ILO) standards, complementarity with private codes relevant to both trade and investment—militates against their narrow application to investment activities per se.[14] Moreover, the text of the *Guidelines* gives explicit recognition to the trading dimension of the activities of multinational enterprises whereby "their trade and investment activities contribute to the efficient use of capital, technology and human resources"[15] and to the promotion of sustainable development "when trade and investment are conducted in a context of open, competitive and appropriately regulated markets."[16] CIME acknowledges that "the fact that the OECD Declaration does not provide precise definitions of international investment . . . allows for flexibility of interpretation and adaptation to particular circumstances."[17] Hence the degree to which relationships in the supply chain constitute pure trade outside the scope of the *Guidelines,* or else constitute "investmentlike" activity, is to be decided on a case-by-case basis. Already this issue is being fiercely contested by nongovernmental organizations (NGOs) in those instances where national contact points (NCPs) are seeking to exclude cases from scrutiny—for example, on the coltan supply chain in the DRC—on the grounds that an investmentlike relationship does not exist.[18]

A final key issue concerns the relationship between the supranational applicability of the *Guidelines* and the domestic laws of host countries. The *Guidelines* are ambiguous as to whether a foreign company is expected to apply standards in the conduct of its business that go beyond host-country requirements. On the one hand, the *Guidelines* stipulate that "the entities of a multinational enterprise located in various countries are subject to the laws applicable in these countries."[19] This might suggest that companies need comply with only national laws of host countries. But this conclusion is based on a partial interpretation. According to the commentary text, the recommendations within the *Guidelines* should be seen not as a substitute for national law and practice but in supplementary terms, with the expectation that companies will adhere to them.[20] On this reading, companies would be required to comply with standards over and above those required by national laws. In fact, the *Guidelines* are premised on the recognition that multinationals face a variety of legal, social, and regulatory settings and that unscrupulous enterprises may exploit this circumstance for comparative advantage.[21] In a destabilized country where central government is weak—as exemplified by the continuing situation in the DRC—laws, conventions, and presidential decrees may be promulgated to legitimize the de facto demands of influential companies rather than acting as a robust regulatory framework. A provision in the *Guidelines* recommends that companies refrain from seeking or accepting legal or regulatory exemptions.[22]

Overall, requiring companies to adhere to supranational standards does not mean that they should disregard or contravene national law; rather, they should do more than simply meet domestic legal requirements when these are silent or fall short of the standards set forth in the *Guidelines*. After all, the raison d'être of the *Guidelines* is to create standards applicable across national boundaries to mirror the OECD's expectations for the operation of multinational companies. As will be discussed below, the fact that there are explicit references in the main text and commentary to international human rights and labor instruments itself strengthens an interpretation of the *Guidelines* that gives primacy to supranational standards.

Conflict-Relevant Provisions of the OECD Guidelines

Tied as they are to the geographic occurrence of natural resource wealth, extractive industries often operate in conflict settings that other branches of industry might choose to avoid. Even a cursory survey of their operations suggests a number of areas of conduct that may run counter to the recommendations entailed in the *Guidelines*. In conflict settings, where regulation is weak or nonexistent and competition for lucrative natural resources is intensified by the exigencies of war, the potential for bribery, corruption, environmental damage, and labor abuse is extremely high. The *Guidelines* add content in all these areas, albeit through somewhat generalized provisions and with significant caveats.

According to chapter VI of the *Guidelines,* on combating bribery, companies should not offer, promise, give, or demand bribes or other undue advantage to obtain or retain business; accounting and auditing practices should prevent the establishment of "off-the-books" or secret accounts; transparency is to be enhanced, inter alia, through public commitments against bribery and extortion; and companies should extend their anticorruption programs to subsidiaries and business partners.[23] The OECD's 2003 annual report on the *Guidelines* even has a special focus on the role of corporations in combating corruption.[24] Yet there are numerous cases where extractive companies have taken advantage of conflict and instability to exploit natural resources. According to Transparency International's account of corporate activities in the DRC, "Valuable mineral resources provided the incentive for international companies to deal with rebels, with revenues transferred into personal bank accounts that were used to purchase more arms to sustain the war."[25] In Angola, a country ravaged by a decades-long civil war, the lack of transparency in business deals over lucrative drilling rights for Angola's offshore oil fields has enabled substantial off-the-books revenues for the government.[26]

Even where bribery and corruption per se cannot be proven, chapter IX of the *Guidelines,* on competition, includes a general recommendation against any anticompetitive agreements and a specific recommendation against rigged bids, a practice that is not uncommon in conflict zones.[27] During the DRC conflict, for example, the DRC Expert Panel reported that

> the richest and most readily exploitable of the publicly owned mineral assets of the Democratic Republic of the Congo are being moved into joint ventures that are controlled by the [elite] network's private companies. These transactions, which are controlled through secret contracts and

off-shore private companies, amount to a multi-billion-dollar corporate theft of the country's mineral assets. . . . The elite network has been trying to legitimize such corporate theft and market these assets to legitimate international mining companies.[28]

Chapter V of the *Guidelines* states that enterprises should "take due account of the need to protect the environment, public health and safety, and generally to conduct their activities in a manner contributing to the wider goal of sustainable development." It contains detailed recommendations on, inter alia, environmental auditing and monitoring, employee education and training, public disclosure and consultation with affected communities, and the preparation of contingency plans to deal with accidents and serious incidents.[29] Yet reports abound of environmental damage caused by the operations of mining and oil companies, such as by Freeport McMoRan in Papua New Guinea, ExxonMobil in Chad and Cameroon, and Shell in Nigeria, whose activities have sparked or exacerbated local grievances and thus contributed to violent conflict.[30]

Last, the revised *Guidelines* do now make explicit reference to human rights and have extended their reference to key labor standards set by the ILO. These revisions have significantly increased the scope of the *Guidelines* and their relevance to conflict situations. Chapter II, on general policies, now contains an explicit, albeit broad, recognition that companies should "respect the human rights of those affected by their activities consistent with the host government's international obligations and commitments."[31] Furthermore, both the preface and the commentary refer to the international legal and policy framework in which business is conducted, including the Universal Declaration of Human Rights.[32] The fact that the human rights provision is not elaborated in the text proper gives leeway for bringing the content of international human rights instruments to bear on corporate conduct. The incorporation of a dedicated chapter on human rights under the *Guidelines* would help clarify expectations and make their application more concrete.

Clauses added to chapter IV, on employment and industrial relations, explicitly state that companies should contribute to the abolition of forced and child labor.[33] Again, these provisions are in contrast to the actual situation in several conflict zones. In Myanmar, for example, French and U.S. oil companies have allegedly benefited from the use of forced labor provided by the Burmese military in the construction of the Yadana pipeline project.[34] In the DRC, the DRC Expert Panel alleged that trading posts, or *comptoirs,* some with parent companies in OECD countries, had collaborated with the Rwandan Patriotic Army "to receive privileged access to coltan sites and captive labor."[35] In addition, there is evidence that the various parties of the DRC conflict—themselves business partners in a range of extractive industry companies—used child labor in the exploitation of gold, diamonds, and coltan in the territories under their control.[36] What is important in this context is that the commentary on the *Guidelines* does affirm that multinational corporations are subject not only to host-country but also to supranational levels of regulation.[37] Explicit reference is made to a corpus of ILO conventions and declarations whose more detailed provisions on labor rights should be consulted when one is interpreting the *Guidelines*.[38] Potentially at least, these provisions allow the conduct of the multinationals concerned to be examined directly and in greater depth.

In sum, the *Guidelines* have potential applicability to corporate conduct in conflict zones. The key question concerns what implications, if any, this applicability may have for those companies operating in zones of conflict whose operations may run counter to the recommendations of the *Guidelines*.

The Nature of the OECD *Guidelines:* Voluntary or Mandatory?

By adopting the *Guidelines,* adhering governments signal their commitment to make recommendations to guide the practices of multinational companies operating in or from their territories. The recommendations entailed in the *Guidelines* are addressed directly to companies. Their observance by the companies, however, is voluntary and not legally enforceable.[39] According to the commentary, the *Guidelines* fall within the realm of "self-regulation and other initiatives in a similar vein."[40] At the same time, the OECD has explicitly stated that "their non-binding nature . . . does not imply less commitment by adhering governments to encourage their observance."[41]

The voluntary nature of the *Guidelines* is at the heart of a number of paradoxes. A defining element of voluntarism is the ability to opt out. An obvious shortcoming of voluntarism is that individual companies may reject the *Guidelines,* either in toto or by seeking to limit their use in a particular situation. Yet it is the voluntary nature of the *Guidelines* that has led to their wide endorsement by governments and businesses. Moreover, when compared to other voluntary industry codes and initiatives, the *Guidelines* have certain characteristics that highlight their greater potential to effectively influence corporate behavior.

First, while adopted by OECD member governments, the *Guidelines* have also been endorsed by the OECD's Business and Industry Advisory Committee (BIAC), a corpus representing multinational companies, as well as by the corresponding Trade Union Advisory Committee (TUAC) and by NGOs (which were for the first time given some status in the process when the CIME invited their participation in the 1998–2000 review process of the *Guidelines*). This endorsement gives the *Guidelines* a high degree of legitimacy and ensures that they do, in fact, represent "shared expectations for business conduct."[42]

Second, because this is a government-adopted policy mechanism, individual governments have discretion in the ways that they promote adherence to the *Guidelines* by their respective home companies, most notably through national export credit agencies. This has opened the way for an increasingly fluid, although contested, boundary between voluntary and mandatory endorsement. In Finland, for example, the national export credit agency is required to call the *Guidelines* to the attention of applicants.[43] Some governments have made access to official export credits contingent upon proactive corporate action. French companies seeking such credit, for example, need to sign a letter to acknowledge their awareness of the *Guidelines*. In a controversial move, the Dutch government went even further, requiring companies to agree to abide by the *Guidelines* in order to receive export credits.[44] There is no compelling reason that governments should not have a prerogative to attach such conditions on what are, in fact, public subsidies for those companies that decide to apply for export credit. The BIAC, however, has publicly stated its resistance to what it views as "coerced compliance" with a voluntary instrument and "rejects any explicit or implicit linkage with the availability of export financing or similar instruments."[45] Those advocating linkage point out that companies are not compelled to apply for public subsidies and that governments, in providing them, have the prerogative of attaching conditions. This demonstrates the inherent tension that the *Guidelines,* like other voluntary mechanisms, face in terms of their implementation. On the one hand, more robust efforts of implementation risk alienating those businesses and, importantly, the BIAC, whose endorsement adds legitimacy to the *Guidelines*. On the other hand, if the *Guidelines* are perceived as ineffective and weak, they will be seen as a corporate veil and will lose any support they have gained among civil society.

The voluntary nature of the *Guidelines* has another important qualification. As government-adopted principles, they do not require an explicit endorsement by individual companies. Whether or not companies have individually endorsed the *Guidelines,* they may still find their operations under scrutiny. This points to the third, and unique, advantage of the *Guidelines* when compared to other voluntary codes, such as those embodied in the UN Global Compact.[46] As explained in more detail below, adhering governments are required to examine allegations of company misconduct. Thus they do not rely purely on self-reporting by companies. Through the national contact points (NCPs)—publicly accountable government officers appointed in each member state—the *Guidelines* include a mechanism that allows unions, NGOs, and others to request an examination and assessment of company behavior in specific instances. While the voluntary nature of the *Guidelines* might not allow for legally enforceable remedies or sanctions, it is no barrier to scrutiny. After all, there is no point in having a code unless someone is prepared to say whether or not a company is abiding by it. The key question is how this judgment is made—and what implications this might entail for companies.

Implementation of the OECD *Guidelines:* From Words to Action?

The *Guidelines* are implemented through a dual system of national contact points based in government ministries in each adhering country and the CIME, which oversees the process.[47] According to the *Procedural Guidance,* adopted at the 2000 review to facilitate implementation of the *Guidelines,* the role of NCPs is threefold. The first task of NCPs is to promote awareness of the *Guidelines* among businesses, employee organizations, NGOs, and the interested public by making them known and available in national languages. In promoting the *Guidelines,* NCPs have to respond to inquiries from interested parties, including other NCPs, companies, employee organizations, NGOs, the general public, and governments of nonadhering countries.[48] The importance of promoting awareness of the *Guidelines* as a means of implementation should not be underestimated. After all, their observance is likely to be greater when they are internalized by companies and become a proactive means by which appropriate conduct is developed.

Beyond these promotional and informational activities, the second task of NCPs is to implement the *Guidelines* in "specific instances."[49] Parties to a "specific instance" are listed as the business community, employee organizations, and "other parties," which could theoretically also include individuals. While couched in terms of a forum for discussion for the resolution of issues, this procedure functions in effect as a complaints mechanism open to trade unions, NGOs, and other interested parties. Once a "specific instance" is brought to the attention of an NCP, it makes a prima facie assessment of whether the issues raised warrant further investigation. An NCP may seek advice from business, employee representatives, NGOs, and relevant experts, consult with NCPs in other countries concerned, and seek the guidance of the CIME over matters of interpretation. In warranted cases, the NCP then offers its good offices to bring the parties together to resolve the issue. Provided the parties agree, the NCP then offers conciliation or mediation to deal with the issue. However, if the parties fail to reach agreement, the NCP releases a statement and makes recommendations on the implementation of the *Guidelines*. The examination procedure is confidential, and the NCP must protect sensitive business and other information. The results of the procedure are made public, but only after consultation with the parties and only "unless preserving confidentiality would be in the best interests of effective implementation of the *Guidelines*."[50] The third task of the NCPs is to report annually to the CIME on their activities, including those concerning implementation in "specific instances."

The main responsibilities of the CIME are to organize exchanges of views on the *Guidelines*, clarify and interpret them, and report to the OECD Council (the body with ultimate decisionmaking power at the OECD, made up of representatives from each member country) on all relevant matters.[51] The CIME has the power to consider a substantiated submission by an adhering country or an advisory body on whether an NCP is fulfilling its responsibilities in respect of "specific instances." Again, on the basis of a substantiated submission, it may issue clarification on whether or not an NCP has correctly interpreted the *Guidelines* in "specific instances." The CIME may then make recommendations to improve the functioning of NCPs but will not reach conclusions on the conduct of individual enterprises.[52]

Implementation Problems

According to the OECD's published figures, some sixty-four "specific instances" were filed with NCPs from June 2000, when the *Guidelines* were revised, to June 2003.[53] The CIME has also considered a number of issues concerning their application. Despite this relatively short track record of implementation, a preliminary assessment is warranted in terms of the potential of the *Guidelines* as a mechanism for affecting company behavior, both generally and in conflict zones. Several problems can be identified with what at the outset appears to be a relatively robust implementation mechanism. While these problems are generic, they are likely to become even more relevant when extractive industry corporations under scrutiny are operating in situations of conflict, where important geopolitical and commercial interests of governments are concerned. These shortcomings will be discussed in more detail below in the cases of corporate scrutiny in Burma/Myanmar and the DRC.

In assuming their responsibilities laid out in the *Guidelines*, NCPs are to take due account of the *Procedural Guidance* adopted at the 2000 review. This aims to further the objective of "functional equivalence" to ensure that all NCPs operate in accordance with the core criteria of "visibility, accessibility, transparency and accountability."[54] However, this guidance is minimal, and there are marked differences in both the organization and the operation of individual NCPs. A number of factors risk weakening the implementation of the *Guidelines* and open up loopholes in the complaints mechanism.

Heterogeneous composition. Institutional arrangements set out in the *Procedural Guidance* are flexible, allowing adhering countries to nominate an official, a government office, or a cooperative body to carry out the NCP function. Out of thirty-six established NCPs, nineteen are based in single government departments and six in multiple government departments.[55] Only nine NCPs follow the cooperative approach, with business and labor involvement.[56] The overriding majority of NCPs are based in economic or trade ministries.[57] While this may pragmatically reflect the raison d'être of the *Guidelines*—to govern trade and investment—it also raises the issue of whether those whose primary mandate is to promote private-sector development overseas can at the same time credibly undertake the role of an objective mediator or even a "watchdog." Contrary to the suggestions in the *Procedural Guidance,* NCP officials also tend to be middle-ranking or junior officers with little training in issues such as socioeconomic development, conflict prevention, or human rights. This is a particular problem for single-ministry NCPs. But even where the NCPs can draw on support from other ministries, in many cases they appear to lack both resources and the necessary status to give the cases submitted much priority attention within the governmental bureaucracy.

Absence of uniformity in procedures. There is little elaboration in the *Procedural Guidance* of warranting criteria for a case, nor of eligibility criteria beyond taking into account the identity of the party concerned, the issue of material substantiation, and whether consideration contributes "to the purposes and effectiveness of the *Guidelines*."[58] There are no stated requirements, for example, that interested parties must be directly affected. While this lack of defined rules appears to make the process open and flexible, local autonomy in determining eligibility is increased and may in fact result in the introduction of stricter criteria. A German NGO, for instance, was told by the NCP that it would have to produce a power of attorney before a case concerning the operations of a multinational enterprise in Indonesia could be submitted. In France, the NCP will not accept cases from NGOs unless they are channeled through a trade union.

In addition, the *Procedural Guidance* does not offer clearly specified time frames for dealing with "specific instances." While this is supposed to offer the advantage of flexibility in the dealings of the NCPs, it appears to result in inaction and foot dragging. It is difficult to accurately count the number of active, rejected, and closed "specific instances," because the OECD does not keep a central register of such cases. It is estimated by the TUAC that of the thirty-six cases raised by unions between 2000 and the end of 2003, seventeen had been closed, although the union body notes that "only a few of the cases have been successfully resolved or led to recommendations to companies. Five of the cases have been withdrawn or resolved in other ways than through the efforts of the responsible NCP."[59] Of fifteen cases submitted by NGOs, two have been resolved by the NCP's issuing an agreed statement, one has resulted in a recommendation from the NCP to the company concerned, and two others have been closed by the NCP because they were deemed to lack an investment link.[60] By mid-2002, the U.S. NCP alone had failed to conclude on five cases, some of which had been initiated over a year before. Such inaction has led the TUAC to seek a timetable for NCP action.

With regard to "specific instances" arising from corporate operations in conflict situations, an additional issue may ensue. The supporting documents explicitly recognize that it is vital to apply the *Guidelines* to business conduct in nonadhering countries,[61] many of which are in the developing world. Within the *Procedural Guidance,* there is an unequivocal expectation upon NCPs to examine "specific instances" in nonadhering countries and to develop an understanding of the situation. Yet it is precisely in these countries that implementation of the *Guidelines* is most problematic. Overall, NCPs have been reluctant to respond to cases of apparent company noncompliance in these settings. They will follow the implementation procedure only "where relevant and practicable."[62] Often this is due to resource constraints facing NCPs, an indication of the low political priority sometimes accorded to their work. In other cases, however, especially in respect of information on companies forwarded to them by the DRC Expert Panel, NCPs have demurred from follow-up, downplaying their investigative function or claiming that they cannot act in the absence of a complainant. Yet the OECD's own commentary on procedures makes clear that when issues arise in a nonadhering country, NCPs "may . . . be in a position to pursue enquiries and engage in other fact finding activities."[63] Indeed, there is nothing in the *Guidelines,* the *Procedural Guidance,* or the commentary that prevents NCPs from acting on their own initiative. There are precedents where NCPs have, to all intents and purposes, initiated the examination of specific instances in the absence of a formal complainant.[64]

Lack of transparency in NCP action.   While transparency is one of the core criteria by which NCPs must operate, and while NCP statements and recommendations on specific instances are to be made public, the caveat of "preserving confidentiality" has in reality come to dominate the process.[65] A distinction is made between the confidentiality of the implementation proceedings and the transparency of the result.[66] However, the results are not transparent: it is made clear that the NCP will both protect "sensitive business information"—without further elaborating on how such information is identified—and preserve confidentiality if this is in the best interests of effective implementation.[67] Most telling is the almost total absence of company names from published information. The identities of companies under examination are expunged from the annual reports. A Dutch NGO was reprimanded for issuing a press release announcing that it had filed a complaint. At a roundtable discussion on supply-chain issues at the 2002 NCP annual meeting, the BIAC and some NCPs objected to the naming of Dole, Del Monte, and Chiquita by Human Rights Watch, even though its concerns were already in the public domain and had been communicated to the companies involved.[68] The names of the companies were removed from the official proceedings.[69] In contrast, companies *are* named when disputes are resolved amicably.[70] While examples of constructive action should not be downplayed, neither should more controversial instances be suppressed in deference to corporate sensibilities.

Lack of visibility of the Guidelines. Despite the NCPs' explicit informational and promotional role, the *Guidelines* themselves—let alone the procedures for filing specific instances—are still not well known to companies, NGOs, and trade unions. Outside of the small world of the NCPs, the *Guidelines* have had little visibility, apart from the occasional, somewhat tokenistic expressions of endorsement at Group of Eight meetings. In February 2003, for example, the Belgian Senate's Great Lakes Commission of Inquiry, which exonerated all Belgian companies, individuals, and members of the government of charges of improper conduct in relation to the DRC, made much of the fact that the *Guidelines* were hardly known by most companies—adding that even when companies were aware of them, they were not regarded as "a priority principle."[71] This situation has undoubtedly changed with the controversy sparked by the DRC Expert Panel report, yet there still remains much to do.

Lack of intra-OECD cooperation by the CIME. In general, the OECD's multiple committees and working parties tend to operate in isolation from one another. The CIME is no exception, although since 2003 it began to undertake steps to coordinate its work with other OECD committees. The CIME cooperates most closely, at least at a secretariat level, with the Development Assistance Committee (DAC). The DAC Working Group on Conflict has advised the CIME about its work on the role of companies in situations of violent conflict and human rights abuses.[72] The CIME agreed at its March 2004 meeting to undertake a study intended to provide companies with terms of reference about investment activities in conflict zones and to give NCPs dealing with the DRC cases background analysis about companies investing or trading in "weak governance zones."[73] The work was to be coordinated with the DAC's Conflict, Peace, and

Development Cooperation Network and the DAC's Governance Network.

The OECD's Working Party on Export Credits and Credit Guarantees agreed in April 2003 to promote the *Guidelines* to its clients. Though hardly revolutionary, this should at least lead to greater cooperation with the CIME. The main way the CIME has tried to relate to the work of other OECD committees is through the organization of roundtables, yet it is unclear how successful this has been as a mainstreaming strategy. Worryingly, the CIME has blocked an initiative by the OECD's Environment Directorate to prepare a handbook on implementing the environmental chapter of the *Guidelines*. Another important omission from the CIME's work is the absence of formal dealings with the OECD's Financial Action Task Force on Money Laundering (FATF). If the *Guidelines* are to realize their potential as an effective corporate accountability tool for conflict situations, a much more integrated approach will be required so that the various initiatives of the OECD can be mutually reinforcing.

Burma/Myanmar: A Case of Best Practice?

An early test of the effectiveness of the implementation process of the *Guidelines* arose in the context of extractive industry operations in Burma/Myanmar, a country with an abysmal human rights record. In June 2000 the ILO took the unprecedented step of adopting a resolution that called upon its constituents (governments, employers, and trade unions) to review all links with Burma/Myanmar and cease any relations that might aid its military junta in the use of forced labor.[74] Against this background, the International Confederation of Free Trade Unions, through the TUAC, encouraged its members to take up the matter with their respective NCPs, and asked the CIME to consider the situation in Burma/Myanmar and the role played by foreign direct investment. How the NCPs and CIME in fact handled this issue provides some important lessons for other such cases.

In March 2001, French trade unions filed a specific instance with the French NCP about the conduct of the oil company TotalFinaElf, which they accused of participating in a joint venture with the Burmese military regime, knowing that forced labor was used for road building and maintenance and other infrastructure work connected to the joint venture's Yadana pipeline operation.[75] Making use of the procedural discretion described above, the French NCP sidestepped the implementation procedure for specific instances by opting instead for a generalized consultation with French companies with operations in Burma/Myanmar. This maneuver enabled the NCP to avoid having to find any of the French companies in breach of the *Guidelines*. Instead, the NCP's recommendations were of a general nature and called upon all companies "to do everything possible in order to avoid direct or indirect recourse to forced labor in the normal course of their operations, in their relations with sub-contractors or through future investments, particularly in zones with a strong military presence and in activities controlled by the military."[76]

The French NCP further inverted the specific instance procedure by arriving at general interpretations of the *Guidelines,* which, if they were to become the modus operandi in such cases, would reduce their scope in other conflict situations. In his recommendations, the French NCP noted that private-sector practices "cannot substitute for the enforcement of measures necessary for the suppression of forced labor by the Burmese government itself in conformity with the recommendations of the ILO, nor for actions by its Member States." In other words, despite the fact that the *Guidelines* are specifically aimed at corporate conduct, the office charged with their implementation retreated behind the bankrupt notion that forced labor is predominantly a matter of state responsibility.[77]

Recognizing the need for an authoritative interpretation, and to help avoid piecemeal or ad hoc national-level responses, the TUAC tabled a letter asking the CIME to discuss "how the *Guidelines* can be used to contribute to the elimination of forced labor in Burma/Myanmar."[78] This represented an opportunity for the CIME to use its overarching authority to issue a general interpretation of the *Guidelines* that could make them more pertinent to corporate conduct in conflict zones. However, the CIME likewise acted to neutralize the specificity of the *Guidelines* with regard to Burma/Myanmar as well as generally. While cautiously noting the important contribution that observance of the *Guidelines* by multinational companies might make to the elimination of all forms of forced or compulsory labor in Burma/Myanmar and elsewhere, the CIME shied away from issuing a clear warning that companies found to use or to benefit indirectly or directly from forced labor would be in breach of the *Guidelines.* The CIME did agree to work to complement an ILO investigation on the issue, but in many ways this represents an abdication of its responsibility.

As a promising step toward an authoritative interpretation of the *Guidelines,* however, the CIME instructed the OECD Secretariat to prepare a background paper on the problems and challenges that arise for multinational enterprises operating in societies troubled by internal conflict and widespread human rights abuses.[79] The resulting paper frankly acknowledges that extractive industries doing business in troubled countries may benefit from high natural resource rents and a margin of profit that can be used to offset the extra costs and risks of doing business.[80] It even concedes that "companies have provided billions of dollars in revenues to corrupt regimes and, by signing confidentiality agreements with them, have at times appeared to be 'silent partners' in wrong doing."[81] Yet the final conclusions are ambivalent. Stripped of concrete cases and mindful to avoid any definitive interpretation of the *Guidelines*, the paper offers no guidance to companies or adhering governments about what actions should be taken to avoid collusion or implicit support for repressive regimes in such an environment. It also leaves unresolved under which circumstances it would be appropriate to recommend that a firm withdraw from a country with a poor human rights record. The paper nevertheless did propose further discussion on the role of multinationals in conflict and human rights situations.[82] Unfortunately, this was ruled out by a majority of NCPs. There was little appetite for developing within the CIME a clarification of the relevant provisions of the instrument to situations of conflict or severe human rights abuses.

Ownership of the OECD Guidelines:
The Case of the DRC Expert Panel

The greatest impetus thus far to the application of the *Guidelines* to conflict situations has come from their citation by the DRC Expert Panel.[83] The listing of companies in the panel's report as violators of the *Guidelines* was both unprecedented and controversial, and it caused consternation among companies and governments alike. Many within the OECD were unhappy with the panel's extracurricular use of the *Guidelines*.[84] Companies lobbied their own governments and the UN Security Council to seek their removal from the list. Most denied all wrongdoing, others claimed ignorance of the content of the *Guidelines*, and many demanded the right to reply to the panel's allegations. The Security Council invited companies to send their reactions, which would be published.

Among the ranks of the cautious NCPs, the expert panel reports caused considerable disquiet. Wrong-footed because of their exclusion from the discussions that had taken place earlier between the DRC Expert Panel and OECD foreign ministries, the NCPs were at first uncertain how to proceed. They argued that they had no investigative powers, although this claim did not deter them from requesting the expert panel to provide them with documentation on the listed companies' behavior. Equally worrying has been the reluctance of the NCPs to fulfill their responsibility under the implementation procedures of the *Guidelines* to determine whether a breach has occurred.[85] Certain NCPs, for instance, have stressed that their role is to mediate and not to decide whether a company has breached the *Guidelines* in a particular instance.

The failure of the DRC Expert Panel to state explicitly which provisions of the *Guidelines* the companies had allegedly violated made it easy for the companies to reject the allegations, and some NCPs have claimed that the charges had no foundation. The Belgian government in particular was quick to question the legitimacy of the DRC Expert Panel's use of the

Guidelines. In a letter to the chair of the CIME, the Belgian representative to the OECD questioned the OECD's prerogatives, and their limits, in determining the status, use, and scope given to the *Guidelines* by a third party. She also sought clarification as to how it could be determined whether or not the *Guidelines* had been respected and whether this was the exclusive prerogative of the NCPs.[86]

Initially possessive of the *Guidelines* and put out by their appropriation by the DRC Expert Panel and by its lack of consultation, the CIME reacted defensively and criticized the panel for its lack of knowledge of the *Guidelines* and its procedures. Subsequently, however, the CIME did at last move to consider the substance of the allegations. Although the CIME expressed its willingness to cooperate with the DRC Expert Panel in clarifying the allegations made, communication between them was slow. Meanwhile, there were several indications that some NCPs and governments would like to extricate themselves and the companies from the embarrassment of the implementation procedures. In addition to calls for a reduction in the scope of the *Guidelines* to remove supply-chain cases and the investment nexus issue, there were suggestions for introducing a time limit, which could be used, for example, to justify the exclusion of companies that ceased importing coltan from the DRC only after the fall in world prices in 2001. These have seemed little more than ill-disguised attempts to short-circuit the implementation procedures and deter NGOs from presenting complaints.

As a result of the controversy created by the DRC Expert Panel's October 2002 report, in particular the UN Security Council's decision to allow companies "named and shamed" a right of reply, the Security Council extended the panel's mandate, but it was limited to reviewing existing and new information "in order to verify, reinforce and, where necessary, update the Panel's findings, and/or clear parties named in the Panel's previous reports, with a view to adjusting accordingly the lists attached to these reports."[87] The result was an addendum report containing replies from companies, published on June 20, 2003,[88] and a truly final report published by the panel on October 23, 2003.[89] In the end, most of the companies' names were removed from the panel's list of alleged offenders. Instead, companies were divided into five categories. Forty-two of the eighty-five companies originally listed as having breached the *Guidelines* were placed in Category I, indicating cases that had been "resolved." Category II addressed two companies that had reached a "provisional resolution" on matters of substance and had given commitments to the panel. Eleven companies were included in Category III, indicating cases where issues had been "referred to NCPs for updating or further investigation." Category IV identified twenty-nine cases of companies and individuals that either had been "referred to governments for further investigation" or had been the subject of requests from governments for further information. Finally, Category V contained those companies and parties, thirty-eight cases in all, that "did not react to the Panel's report."

The DRC Expert Panel's final classification has been criticized for being confusing and contradictory. For instance, there is no way of differentiating between those companies that were in violation of the *Guidelines* and those that were not, because the panel leaves unexplained the passage to Category I status. "The 'resolved' category includes many cases where it is not at all apparent that there has been any resolution, and the reasons for determining that a case has been 'resolved' are not transparent."[90] Dossiers on only eleven companies were forwarded by the DRC Expert Panel to NCPs in Belgium, Germany, and the United Kingdom for further investigation. The UK and Belgian NCPs were asked to monitor the conduct of two other companies listed in Category II. It is not satisfactory that certain companies were listed for further investigation when others were not even though their compliance with the *Guidelines* is equally, if not more, questionable. NGOs have recommended that the limited list of companies for further investigation by NCPs be extended.[91]

Despite all controversy, one indisputable positive outcome of the DRC Expert Panel's accusations that the *Guidelines* had been violated has been to increase their visibility. In a statement sent to the CIME, for example, an alliance of Congolese civil society organizations called on governments to ensure that companies adhere to the *Guidelines*.[92] In the companies' responses to the panel's report, published by the UN Security Council, almost all accepted the validity of the *Guidelines*, even when they were not registered in an adhering country.[93] This response may also force the CIME to reconsider its decision about the need to draw up some guidance for companies operating in conflict zones. Undoubtedly, the DRC Expert Panel's report also challenged the OECD to match its rhetoric with action. Furthermore, the reactions by companies and governments to the *Guidelines* suggests that they already have some potency. The reputational risk that a breach entails should in the future establish them as one of the instruments that can help curtail the economic underpinnings of conflict.

There are obviously dangers in extrapolating lessons from only two cases while implementation of the revised *Guidelines* is in its infancy. Yet the cases of Burma/Myanmar and the DRC highlight an important feature of the *Guidelines,* which can be both an advantage and a disadvantage when it comes to implementation. The *Guidelines* are a multilateral code, yet their implementation is governed by national institutions and, thus, national preoccupations. The multilateral standards advocated in the *Guidelines* change as they are viewed through the lens of each local NCP. This might be an advantage when it comes to more "progressive" adhering countries; as the cases of Burma/Myanmar and the DRC show, however, effective follow-up depends on the competence, capacity, and political will of individual NCPs and the adhering countries' governments to follow up and scrutinize their companies. Uneven local interpretation and application of the *Guidelines* gives rise to inconsistencies that, if left unchecked, might damage the normative legitimacy and public credibility of the *Guidelines*.

The future of the *Guidelines* as a credible code depends upon the quality and robustness of the CIME's interpretation. Even "functional equivalence" is unlikely in the context of low-level procedural guidance and the lack of clear guidance from the CIME. Potentially more unifying is the role of the CIME in both interpreting the *Guidelines* and clarifying the interpretations—although not the outcome of specific instances—reached by individual NCPs.

Recommendations: Strengthening the OECD *Guidelines* for Improved Multinational Conduct in Conflict Zones

The *Guidelines* promise much. They are a multilateral code governing business conduct that move beyond the multiplicity of firm-level standards and self-regulation. The *Guidelines* apply to all companies based in adhering countries wherever they operate in the world and extend to their supply chains. There is a low-cost and relatively accessible avenue for trade unions and NGOs to raise their concerns over specific instances of alleged corporate misconduct. The fact that the *Guidelines* offer a monitoring mechanism that brings company actions under government supervision may prove particularly important in the context of corporate conduct in situations of armed conflict.

Clearly, the *Guidelines* are no substitute for binding regulation, but they do represent the best existing mechanism to assess and scrutinize the conduct of multinational corporations. In circumstances of violent conflict, the *Guidelines* might even have certain advantages over more binding regulation. The imposition of economic sanctions or mandatory divestment may have some leverage against an authoritarian state like Burma/Myanmar, where power is centralized. But these policies are much less suited to war-torn but resource-rich countries like the DRC, where the withdrawal of multinationals is likely to create even more opportunities for unscrupulous traders, corrupt local administrations, and warring factions. In such settings, the *Guidelines* provide a framework for business conduct that encourages companies to think through the implications of their activities and take responsibility for outcomes. They may also provide potential cover for progressive companies to be more proactive in engaging local authorities on human rights and conflict issues.

There are even pragmatic benefits over legal action. The special instances process, at least in theory, should be swift, inexpensive, and open to many interested parties, with few administrative and procedural barriers. Legal representation is not necessary, and the weight of evidence required may be less exacting than the standard of evidence demanded by many home government jurisdictions to bring cases of corporate malfeasance to trial. While there are no legal sanctions or punishments attached to nonobservance of the recommendations, public scrutiny and reputational concern may be sufficient for more reputable corporations to change their behavior or seek solutions through dialogue with home governments, trade unions, or NGOs.

The *Guidelines* were not written specifically to deal with corporate behavior in conflict situations or the illegal exploitation of natural resources per se, but many of their provisions governing corporate conduct in general have a heightened relevancy in such situations. It is probable that, following the DRC Expert Panel's forwarding of dossiers on companies to NCPs, a growing number of specific instances will be submitted, as public interest in corporate activities in conflict zones grows. UK prime minister Tony Blair, for example, publicly supported the use of the *Guidelines* as a means of promoting responsible behavior among companies in conflict zones in Africa.[94]

For some, strengthening the *Guidelines* may ultimately require their revision to incorporate conflict-specific recommendations that would set a benchmarks for acceptable conduct, particularly because a variety of other voluntary codes now do so.[95] An interim step might be the inclusion of a separate human rights chapter in the *Guidelines*—a recommendation that was discussed prior to the 2000 revision but was resisted by the BIAC and several governments. A wholesale revision seems unlikely, at least in the short term. However, the above-mentioned study commissioned by the CIME may further elaborate on the application of the *Guidelines* if conducted with the necessary vigor.

While a revision of the *Guidelines* seems necessary in the long run, the potential of the text yet remains unexplored. There are sufficient provisions within the existing text, for example, to take companies to task over their conduct on specific matters of forced labor or complicity with human rights abuse. The scope for using the *Guidelines* to bring the content of international human rights instruments to bear on, for example, companies accused of collusion with internal security forces, is apparent, if untested. Similarly, general provisions specifying the application of the *Guidelines* to the supply chain allow the detailed content of ILO Convention 105 to be brought to bear not only on the producers, but also potentially on the multinational purchasers, of illegally produced commodities.[96] It would be a mistake to assume that the current *Guidelines* lack scope. Using the provision on respect for human rights, the preamble, and the commentary, the corpus of existing international standards can deliver content. Against this background, practical and immediate steps can be taken to deepen the applicability of the *Guidelines* to conflict situations, particularly by capitalizing on the opportunity given by their reference to human rights.

Governments

Clearly, the *Guidelines* are only one of the instruments available to governments if they are serious about grappling with the link between resource exploitation and conflict. To be effective, they need to be used in conjunction with other measures discussed in this volume. However, governments should renew their efforts to promote the *Guidelines* as a truly global standard relevant to the conduct of all companies in both adhering and nonadhering countries. For countries in transition from conflict, the *Guidelines* offer a model of how they might promote, identify, and enforce good corporate behavior. Postconflict governments should be encouraged to append the *Guidelines* when drawing up contracts with foreign investors.

An important step would be to bring the policies of export credit agencies into line with the objectives of the *Guidelines,* as recommended by the Belgian Commission of Inquiry in its investigation into alleged violations of the *Guidelines* by Belgian companies operating in the DRC.[97] Following the example set by the Dutch government, adhering governments could make public finance and export credit to extractive industry companies conditional on compliance with the *Guidelines*. The decision by the OECD's Working Party on Export Credits and Credit Guarantees to promote the *Guidelines* is a first—albeit timid—step in this direction.

Progress, however, will depend on government champions to drive implementation of the *Guidelines* forward. The failure of many governments to provide political direction and leadership in support of NCP investigations into the DRC Expert Panel's allegations of corporate misconduct in the DRC risks undermining the credibility of the implementation process. Governments adhering to the *Guidelines* made a commitment in their correspondence with the panel to ensure their proper use and application. Governments therefore have an obligation to launch thorough, prompt, and impartial investigations into not only those specific instances where the DRC Expert Panel has forwarded dossiers to NCPs but all specific instances where questions over compliance remain unanswered. Importantly, if government commitment to the *Guidelines* is to go beyond rhetoric, action is required to strengthen the role of NCPs.

National Contact Points

The way the *Guidelines* are implemented through NCPs in adhering countries is much more pedestrian than it appears at the outset. While the system has produced general recommendations to multinationals and even consensual action, it has also been characterized by NCPs' deference to corporate confidentiality and even inaction. To address the problem of tardiness, time limits might be specified for the handling of cases, unless special circumstances dictate otherwise. Furthermore, the ultimate aim of NCPs should be to issue recommendations on compliance.

Individual NCPs would benefit from capacity building and training on conflict issues. Workshops conducted by trained NCPs or a subgroup of the CIME in conflict or postconflict countries on the value of the *Guidelines* would help foster their use. The secrecy with which many NCPs operate has blocked the development of a more robust peer review mechanism, which might induce the most progressive NCPs to put pressure on the "slower" ones. But the DRC cases may bring about change given that the allegations against some companies have been made public by the DRC Expert Panel, allowing all NCPs (as well as civil society) to scrutinize how these specific instances are handled.

For the effectiveness of NCPs to be improved, it is essential that they be better integrated with other relevant government agencies and departments, including labor, international development, and foreign affairs, in particular their departments of human rights and conflict prevention. More systematic channels of communication with unions, businesses, and NGOs should also be developed. NCPs who at present have limited investigative capacity should be able to count on support from relevant foreign ministry or development assistance staff. Where resource constraints are an impediment to such investigations, NCPs should be given additional support by national governments to carry out this task. This applies in almost all adhering countries. Embassy staff in affected countries could play a supervisory or even investigative role in support of the NCPs. Thus far, NCPs have sat back and complained about a lack of documentation, while diplomats intrepid enough to act upon concerns about the behavior of their countries' entrepreneurs or businesses run the risk of being severely reprimanded.

NCPs should be self-executing. Rather than await a submission from an interested party, they should be required to initiate their own examination of situations pertaining to conflict or gross human rights violations. In order to avoid conflict of interest problems with NCPs, their offices should not be exclusively located in trade ministries, but rather shared across foreign, justice, and labor ministries. Some adhering countries already use a cooperative approach, with business and labor involvement in the NCP office. This model should be extended to include NGO participation and adopted in other countries. In order to raise the political profile of the *Guidelines,* a high-ranking official or independent expert should be appointed in each adhering country to coordinate the work of the NCP and to prepare a report on progress for consideration by national parliaments. The findings of NCPs should be subject to parliamentary scrutiny.

Committee on International
Investment and Multinational Enterprises

As the analysis above suggests, the CIME is a key actor in potential deepening and adaptation of the *Guidelines* to conflict situations. The *Guidelines* were never intended to deal with extreme conflict situations. This might explain the caution and reluctance of both the CIME and a number of NCPs to apply the *Guidelines* to conflict zones. One of the CIME's key roles should be to provide an authoritative interpretation of the *Guidelines*. It has shied away from precisely this elaboration, indicating its lack of political appetite for the task. To be sure, the CIME did take an important step in revisiting the question of the application of the *Guidelines* in conflict zones by convening several expert consultations on its study, "Conducting Business with Integrity in Weak Governance Zones" in late 2004, addressing, in particular, the case of the DRC. It also began to explore the potential of enhancing awareness of the OECD "integrity instruments" (e.g., the OECD Anti-Bribery Convention, Principles of Corporate Governance, and the *Guidelines*) and making them a risk management tool for companies operating in weak governance zones. However, to date, these reviews have had no palpable impact on the reluctance of NCPs to apply the *Guidelines* to companies operating in conflict zones.[98]

Ultimately, the CIME should prepare commentary on the application of the *Guidelines* in conflict situations and issue a clarification to companies about the use of the *Guidelines* in determining acceptable and unacceptable corporate conduct in conflict and postconflict situations. It should consider setting up a subgroup on conflict and the establishment of a roster of experts to advise on specific situations or to provide an annual review of activities.[99]

The CIME should also consider maintaining a list of conflict or post-conflict countries, with recommendations to companies about whether investment is compatible with observance of the *Guidelines*. The CIME should authorize the publication by the secretariat of a list of all specific instances, even those rejected, including details on their status and any outcome. The CIME has already agreed to pilot a confidential, electronic register of cases, but this does not meet adequate transparency standards. In the short term, the CIME should increase cooperation among its different specialized committees and working groups, which all have a role to play in conflict resolution—in particular the FATF, the DAC's Working Group on Conflict, and the OECD's Working Party on Export Credits and Credit Guarantees. This would enhance the complementarity among OECD's legal instruments, policies, and voluntary approaches.

In order to clarify the interpretation of the provision on human rights in the *Guidelines,* the CIME should incorporate the UN's Norms on the

Responsibilities of Transnational Corporations and Other Business Enterprises with regard to Human Rights into the commentary and, once the text is revised, into the *Guidelines* themselves. This would immediately strengthen companies' understanding of what is expected of them and reinforce the existing—if unelaborated—human rights provision.

Trade Unions and NGOs

Trade unions, the "traditional" initiators of complaints to NCPs, have availed themselves of this mechanism and filed the majority of labor-related specific instances. Among NGOs, however, the *Guidelines* have met with considerable suspicion. Until recently, NGOs have been reluctant to present cases concerning alleged corporate misconduct to the relevant NCPs. Many NGO leaders believe that simply for using the *Guidelines* and their implementation procedures, they may be accused of legitimizing an instrument that in their opinion is fundamentally flawed. With the Burma/Myanmar and DRC cases, this has somewhat changed as NGOs have become increasingly familiar with the content and procedural rules of the *Guidelines*.

To make the *Guidelines* more conflict relevant, trade unions and NGOs need to continue to file cases with NCPs to test the scope of the *Guidelines* on issues of human rights abuse and bribery, particularly in the context of armed conflict. Again, pressure groups need to test the political will of NCPs and the CIME by filing well-argued cases. A pragmatic strategy at the current time would be for interested parties to track the OECD's handling of the DRC case and to exert influence where possible.

Notes

1. Development Assistance Committee (DAC) of the Organization for Economic Cooperation and Development (OECD), "Ministerial Statement on Helping Prevent Violent Conflict: Orientations for External Partners," report of Paris meeting, April 2001.

2. United Nations Security Council, *Final Report of the Panel of Experts on the Illegal Exploitation of Natural Resources and Other Forms of Wealth in the Democratic Republic of the Congo*, S/2002/1146, October 16, 2002.

3. Ibid., paras. 177–178, p. 32.

4. In this chapter the terms *enterprise, company,* and *corporation* are used interchangeably. A precise legal definition of a "multinational enterprise" is not given in the *Guidelines*. See OECD, *The OECD Guidelines for Multinational Enterprises* (Paris: OECD, 2000), chap. I, "Concepts and Principles," para. 3.

5. Ibid., pref., para. 10.

6. OECD, *Commentary on the OECD Guidelines for Multinational Enterprises* (Paris: OECD, 2000). The CIME, comprising delegates from the OECD

member states, interprets and implements the 1976 Declaration and Decisions on International Investment and Multinational Enterprises.

7. The member countries of the OECD are Australia, Austria, Belgium, Canada, the Czech Republic, Denmark, Finland, France, Germany, Greece, Hungary, Iceland, Ireland, Italy, Japan, Korea, Luxembourg, Mexico, the Netherlands, New Zealand, Norway, Poland, Portugal, Slovak Republic, Spain, Sweden, Switzerland, Turkey, the United Kingdom, and the United States. The eight adhering nonmember countries are Argentina, Brazil, Chile, Estonia, Israel, Latvia, Lithuania, and Slovenia.

8. OECD, *Guidelines*, chap. I, "Concepts and Principles," para. 2.

9. Ibid., para. 3.

10. Ibid., chap. II, "General Policies," para. 10.

11. OECD, *OECD Guidelines for Multinational Enterprises: Focus on Responsible Supply Chain Management; Annual Report 2002* (Paris: OECD, 2002). See especially pt. II, "Roundtable on Corporate Responsibility: Supply Chains and the OECD *Guidelines for Multinational Enterprises.*"

12. OECD, *Commentary*, para. 10.

13. CIME statement on the scope of the *Guidelines*, reproduced in OECD, *OECD Guidelines for Multinational Enterprises: 2003 Annual Meeting of the National Contact Points*, Report by the Chair (Paris: OECD, 2003), p. 12, available at www.oecd.org/dataoecd/3/47/15941397.pdf.

14. Working Party on the Declaration, "Background Paper on the Scope of the Guidelines," I.3. This paper is reproduced in OECD, *OECD Guidelines for Multinational Enterprises: 2003 Annual Meeting of the National Contact Points*, pp. 25–28.

15. OECD, *Guidelines*, pref., para. 4.

16. Ibid., para. 5.

17. CIME statement on the scope of the *Guidelines* (see note 13).

18. Milieudefensie (Friends of the Earth Netherlands) and others filed a specific instance concerning the conduct of Chemie Pharmacie Holland (CPH) in the coltan supply chain in the DRC. Discussion centered on whether or not CPH's business in DRC constituted an "investment nexus," a requirement for the *Guidelines* to be deemed applicable. In February 2004, the Dutch NCP declared that this requirement was lacking and that the *Guidelines* did not apply. Several NGOs formally protested that the Dutch NCP relied on an "excessively narrow definition of 'investment nexus,' one that restricts the utility and the credibility of the *Guidelines*." See www.oecdwatch.org/docs/update%20cases.pdf. A detailed discussion of the role of NCPs in the implementation process of the *Guidelines* follows later in the chapter.) The German NCP refused to accept a case filed by Greenpeace Germany, concerning the impact on the environment of certain TotalFinaElf operations in Russia, on the grounds that there was no investment nexus. The filing NGO is considering seeking clarification on this issue. See SOMO, Centre for Research on Multinational Corporations, "Complaints under the OECD Guidelines: Specific Instances Brought by NGOs," March 2004 update, available at www.oecdwatch. org/docs/update%20cases%20March%202004.pdf; see also SOMO, "Table of Cases Raised by NGOs at National Contact Points," March 2004 update, available at www.oecdwatch.org/docs/table%20cases%20March%2004.pdf.

19. OECD, *Guidelines*, chap. I, "Concepts and Principles," para. 7. In the same paragraph, the obligations of states is specified: "Governments have the right to prescribe the conditions under which multinational enterprises operate within their jurisdictions," yet this right is qualified as "subject to international law."

20. Ibid., pref., para. 7. See also OECD, *Commentary,* "Commentary on General Policies," para. 2.

21. OECD, *Guidelines,* pref., para. 6.

22. Ibid., chap. II, "General Policies," para. 5.

23. Ibid., chap. VI, "Combating Bribery."

24. OECD, *OECD Guidelines for Multinational Enterprises: Enhancing the Role of Business in the Fight against Corruption; Annual Report 2003* (Paris: OECD, 2003).

25. Transparency International, *Global Corruption Report 2003* (Berlin: Transparency International, May 2003), p. 237.

26. Global Witness, *A Crude Awakening: The Role of the Oil and Banking Industries in Angola's Civil War and the Plundering of State Assets* (London: Global Witness, 1999); Global Witness, *All the President's Men: The Devastating Story of Oil and Banking in Angola's Privatized War* (London: Global Witness, 2002).

27. OECD, *Guidelines,* chap. IX, "Competition," preamble and para. 1(b).

28. United Nations, "Final Report," para. 36, p. 9.

29. OECD, *Guidelines,* chap. V, "Environment," introd. para.

30. See the case studies in International Right to Know Campaign, *International Right to Know: Empowering Communities through Corporate Transparency* (Washington, D.C.: International Right to Know Campaign, 2003), "Freeport McMoRan: Profit by Land Grab," pp. 17–18, and "ExxonMobil: Corporate Giant Ignores People and the Planet," pp. 19–20. On the Chad-Cameroon pipeline, see Center for Environment and Development et al., *Broken Promises: The Chad Cameroon Oil and Pipeline Project—Profit at Any Cost?* (Yaounde/Amsterdam: Center for Environment and Development/Friends of the Earth International, 2001). On Nigeria, see Human Rights Watch, *The Price of Oil: Corporate Responsibility and Human Rights Violations in Nigeria's Oil Producing Communities* (New York: Human Rights Watch, 1999).

31. OECD, *Guidelines,* chap. II, "General Policies," para. 2. The commentary on the revised *Guidelines* makes it clear that this respect for human rights applies not only to the dealings of companies with their employees but also to their relations with others affected by their activities. See OECD, *Commentary,* "Commentary on General Policies," para. 4.

32. See, respectively, OECD, *Guidelines,* pref., para. 8; and OECD, *Commentary,* "Commentary on General Policies," para. 4.

33. OECD, *Guidelines,* chap. IV, "Employment and Industrial Relations," paras. 1(b), 1(c).

34. Letter from the general secretary of the International Confederation of Free Trade Unions (ICFTU) to the Committee of Experts on the Application of Conventions and Recommendations, "Burma/Myanmar, Forced Labor Convention, 1930 (Convention no. 29)," Brussels, October 14, 2002; also accompanying app. 2, "Force [*sic*] Labor along the Offshore Gas Pipeline."

35. United Nations, "Final Report," para. 79, p. 16.

36. United Nations, "Report of the Panel of Experts on the Illegal Exploitation of Natural Resources and Other Forms of Wealth in the Democratic Republic of the Congo," S/2001/357, April 12, 2001, para. 69; Amnesty International, *Democratic Republic of the Congo: "Our Brothers Who Help Kill Us"; Economic Exploitation and Human Rights Abuses in the East* (London: Amnesty International, 2003).

37. OECD, *Commentary,* "Commentary on Employment and Industrial Relations," para. 19.

38. The commentary refers by name to, inter alia, ILO Convention 111, on

nondiscrimination; Conventions 29 and 105, on forced labor and its abolition; and Conventions 182 and 138, on the worst forms of child labor and minimum ages of employment. See OECD, *Commentary,* "Commentary on Employment and Industrial Relations," para. 20. The preface of the *Guidelines* itself recognizes the relevance of the 1998 ILO Declaration on Fundamental Principles and Rights at Work. See OECD, *Guidelines,* pref., para. 8.

39. OECD, *Guidelines,* chap. I, "Concepts and Principles," para. 1.

40. OECD, *Commentary,* "Commentary on General Policies," para. 11.

41. Organization for Economic Cooperation and Development, *Policy Brief: The OECD "Guidelines for Multinational Enterprises,"* available at www.oecd.org/document/45/0,2340,en_2649_201185_1903277_119696_1_1_1,00. html.

42. OECD, *Guidelines,* pref., para. 7.

43. In April 2003 all export credit agencies agreed to draw the *Guidelines* to the attention of applicants.

44. OECD, *Annual Report 2002,* tab. 1, p. 25.

45. BIAC, "Statement on OECD MNE Guidelines Linkages," Paris, September 12, 2001.

46. "The Global Compact is a voluntary corporate citizenship initiative. As such, the Global Compact is not a regulatory instrument—it does not 'police' or enforce the behavior or actions of companies." See United Nations, *Guide to the Global Compact: A Practical Understanding of the Vision and Nine Principles,* 2003, available at www.unglobalcompact.org.

47. OECD, *Commentary,* para. 4.

48. OECD, "Procedural Guidance. I. National Contact Points. B. Information and Promotion," in *Decision of the Council on the OECD Guidelines for Multinational Enterprises.* Paris, June 2000, p. 4.

49. Ibid., I, "National Contact Points," C, "Implementation in Specific Instances," p. 5.

50. Ibid., 4(B), p. 5.

51. OECD, *Implementation Procedures,* II, "The Committee on International Investment and Multinational Enterprises," 3, 4b.

52. OECD, *Procedural Guidance,* II, "Committee on International Investment and Multinational Enterprises," sec. 3(b)–(d). See also OECD, *Implementation Procedures,* para. 4.

53. OECD, *Annual Report 2003,* p. 17. The NCP annual reports in 2001 and 2002 record twenty-two and eight cases respectively. It is difficult to count the number of rejected, active, and closed specific instances because the OECD does not hold a central register of such cases. This makes it difficult to distinguish between new and existing cases. Certain specific instances are counted twice if they are subject to consideration by more than one NCP, although it is doubtful whether this is sufficient reason to account for the difference between the OECD totals and those counted by NGOs and trade unions. A study by Oxfam Netherlands (Novib) and SOMO cites thirty-one cases. See Milieu Defensie et al., *International NGO Training and Strategy Seminar on the OECD Guidelines for Multinationals: A Tool to Combat Violations of Environmental and Worker's Rights* (Amsterdam: Friends of the Earth/IRENE, 2003), pp. 32ff. The TUAC details seventeen closed and nineteen ongoing specific instances up to December 2003: see TUAC, *The OECD "Guidelines for Multinational Enterprises": TUAC Summary of Cases Raised with National Contact Points,* Paris, December 2003, available at www.tuac.org.

54. OECD, *Procedural Guidance,* I, "National Contact Points," preamble.

55. Some NCPs are based in a single department but have arrangements for consultation. This is the case, for example, in Austria, Switzerland, and the United States, where special *Guidelines* advisory groups have been created or existing groups used to encourage business, trade union, and NGO participation in implementation of the *Guidelines*. See OECD, *Annual Report 2001*.

56. Belgium, Chile, Denmark, Estonia, Finland, France, Luxembourg, Norway, and Sweden. Two—Finland and Chile—are quadripartite. OECD, *Annual Report 2002*, annex I.

57. Thirty NCPs are located in such ministries or in linked offices. OECD, *Annual Report 2002*, annex I.

58. OECD, *Commentary on the Implementation Procedures*, I, "Procedural Guidance for NCPs," "Implementation in Specific Instances," para. 14.

59. TUAC, *Working Paper on the OECD Guidelines for Multinational Enterprises*, reproduced in OECD, *Annual Report 2003*, p. 95. See also TUAC, *OECD "Guidelines": TUAC Summary of Cases*.

60. Of the remaining ten cases, one was deemed inadmissible, two have been dropped, and seven more are ongoing. The analysis of figures is from SOMO, Centre for Research on Multinational Corporations, "Complaints under the OECD Guidelines," Amsterdam, March 2004 update.

61. See OECD, *Implementation Procedures*, II, "The Committee on International Investment and Multinational Enterprises," 3. See also OECD, *Commentary on the Implementation Procedures*, para. 5.

62. OECD, *Procedural Guidance*, I, "National Contact Points," C, "Implementation in Specific Instances," para. 5.

63. OECD, *Commentary on the Implementation Procedures*, I, "Procedural Guidance for NCPs," para. 20.

64. The Finnish NCP, for example, at the request of a company listed by the DRC Expert Panel, examined the issues raised by the panel and made a report of its findings. Similar actions were taken by the UK and Austrian NCPs. The UK NCP found that the allegations made by the UN Panel of Experts on the Illicit Exploitation of Natural and Other Resources in the DRC that De Beers was operating in breach of the *Guidelines* were "unsubstantiated." See "NCP Statement on De Beers," April 26, 2004, available at www.dti.gov.uk. In a complaint against the conduct of H. C. Starck and A. Knight in mineral exploitation in the DRC, the Austrian NCP determined that there was no investment nexus and that the *Guidelines* did not apply. See OECDWatch Newsletter, March 2005, available at: http://www.oecdwatch.org/docs/newsletter%20E%202005%201.pdf.

65. OECD, *Procedural Guidance*, respectively, I, "National Contact Points," preamble, and C, "Implementation in Specific Instances," para. 4(b).

66. OECD, *Commentary on the Implementation Procedures*, I, "Procedural Guidance for NCPs," "Implementation in Specific Instances," 19.

67. OECD, *Procedural Guidance*, I, "National Contact Points," C, "Implementation in Specific Instances," paras. 4(a)–(b).

68. Human Rights Watch, *Tainted Harvest: Child Labor and Obstacles to Organizing on Ecuador's Banana Plantations* (New York: Human Rights Watch, 2002).

69. OECD, *Annual Report 2002*, pp. 101–ff.

70. As in the joint statement issued at the end of the Dutch NCP's examination of working conditions in Adidas's supply chain or when evictions from mine land in Zambia owned by First Quantum were averted following an intervention by the Canadian NCP. (The joint statement by the NCP, Adidas, and ICN is posted with

other documentation on the Netherlands NCP website, www.oesorichtlijnen.nl [accessed May 2003].)

71. Commission d'Enquête Parlementaire Chargée d'Enquêter sur l'Exploitation et le Commerce Légaux et Illégaux de Richesses Naturelles dans la Région des Grands Lacs au vu de la Situation Conflictuelle Actuelle et de l'Implication de la Belgique, Sénat de Belgique, Session de 2002–2003, February 20, 2003, *Constatations et Recommendations,* para. 2.11.

72. OECD, "Multinational Enterprises in Situations of Violent Conflict and Widespread Human Rights Abuse," Background Note (Paris: OECD, 2002). The paper was prepared by Kathryn Gordon and published under the authority of OECD's secretary-general.

73. The outline of the paper, to be titled "Conducting Business with Integrity in Weak Governance Zones: OECD Instruments and Examples from the Democratic Republic of Congo," was presented at an April 2004 meeting of the CIME.

74. ICFTU, Practical Contents of the 88th ILO Conference Resolution on Burma/Myanmar.

75. General secretary of the ICFTU, "Burma/Myanmar, Forced Labor Convention" (letter).

76. "Recommendations by the French Contact Point to Companies on the Issue of Forced Labor in Burma/Myanmar," March 28, 2002 (translation from the original French), in OECD, *Annual Meeting of the National Contact Points for the OECD "Guidelines for Multinational Enterprises": Overview and Summary of Information Contained in NCP Reports,* Doc. DAFFE/IME/NCP(2002), Paris, June 27, 2002, annex 5.

77. The French NCP also failed to examine in any depth the validity of TotalFinaElf's self-serving argument that the presence of multinational firms accelerates economic development and thereby improves the social conditions of workers, or its claim that "it is more and more difficult for multinational firms to implement changes in their operations in accordance with national, European, and international laws that are not always compatible." Ibid. and *Reports by the National Contact Points: Annual Meeting of the National Contact Points for the OECD "Guidelines for Multinational Enterprises,"* Doc. DAFFE/IME/NCP/RD(2002), Paris, June 14, 2002, annex 3.

78. "Letter from John Evans, General Secretary of TUAC, to Mr. Marinus W. Sikkel, CIME Chair," June 12, 2001, in OECD, *Annual Meeting of the National Contact Points for the OECD "Guidelines for Multinational Enterprises": TUAC Survey of the Functioning of National Contact Points,* Doc. DAFFE/IME/NCP/RD (2001), 2.

79. OECD, "Multinational Enterprises in Situations of Violent Conflict."

80. Ibid., para. 34.

81. Ibid., para. 59.

82. Ibid.

83. For a critique of the DRC Expert Panel's work, see Rights and Accountability in Development (RAID), *Unanswered Questions: Companies, Conflict, and the Democratic Republic of Congo* (Oxford: RAID, 2004), available at www.oecdwatch.org.

84. *OECD "Guidelines for Multinational Enterprises": 2003 Annual Meeting of the National Contact Points,* Report by the Chair, sec. V, p. 11; letter from the chair of CIME to the UN Secretary-General, January 23, 2003.

85. OECD, *Commentary on the Implementation Procedures,* I, "Procedural Guidance for NCPs," para. 18. For a fuller discussion of the problems, see RAID, *Unanswered Questions.*

86. Regine de Clerq, Permanent Representative of the Government of Belgium to the OECD, letter to M. Sikkel, chair of CIME, December 2, 2002.

87. UN Security Council Resolution 1457, S/RES/1457(2003), January 23, 2003, para. 9.

88. UN Doc. S/2002/1146/Add.1, June 20, 2003.

89. United Nations Security Council, *Final Report of the Panel of Experts on the Illegal Exploitation of Natural Resources and Other Forms of Wealth in the Democratic Republic of Congo,* S/2003/1027, October 23, 2003.

90. RAID, *Unanswered Questions,* p. 4.

91. Ibid., p. 5.

92. *Declaration by Civil Society of the Democratic Republic of Congo regarding the Illegal Exploitation of Natural Resources and Conflict in the Country,* Kinshasa, March 14, 2003.

93. UN Doc. S/2002/1146/Add.1.

94. Andrew Parker, "Blair Calls for Clampdown on Companies That Exploit Africa," *Financial Times,* February 7, 2002.

95. Craig Forcese, *Review of the "Guidelines for Multinational Enterprises,"* Submission to the Department of Foreign Affairs and International Trade on behalf of the Canadian Lawyers Association for International Human Rights, Ottawa, September 1999.

96. This potential has not been formally tested, although it is pertinent to note that the German government has vigorously attempted to restrict the scope of the supply-chain provision, arguing that such cases should only be considered when there is "an investment nexus."

97. Commission d'Enquête Parlementaire, *Constatations et Recommendations,* para. 2.

98. See OECDWatch Newsletter, March 2005, available at http://www.oecdwatch.org/docs/newsletter%20E%202005%201.pdf.

99. There is scope for seeking and considering expert advice under the *Guidelines.* See OECD, *Implementation Procedures,* "Procedural Guidance," II, "Committee on International Investment and Multinational Enterprises," para. 4.

15

Improving Sanctions Through Legal Means?

Pierre Kopp

The use of economic sanctions as a tool of international policy has had varied objectives. Unilateral sanctions, such as the comprehensive trade embargoes imposed by the United States against Cuba, are typically undertaken to further the goals of a country's foreign policy. Multilateral sanctions, such as those imposed by the United Nations Security Council under Chapter VII of the UN Charter, often share broader political ends, such as punishing a country for its policies or actions (Rhodesia in 1966, South Africa in 1977, Iraq in 1990, or Libya in 1992). Frequently, UN sanctions are initiated in order to hasten a political solution to armed intrastate conflict, as was the case in Angola, Sierra Leone, and Liberia. In fact, since the end of the Cold War, Security Council–imposed economic sanctions have become an increasingly important means of enforcing international peace and security.[1]

Faced with the dire humanitarian impacts caused by "traditional," comprehensive economic sanctions, such as those against Iraq in the 1990s, the UN Security Council has increasingly imposed sanctions of a more targeted nature in the form of commodity and arms embargoes, financial freezes, and travel bans against rebel groups and government elites, such as the National Union for the Total Independence of Angola (UNITA) in Angola, the Revolutionary United Front (RUF) in Sierra Leone, and the government of Charles Taylor in Liberia.[2] The imposition of these targeted economic sanctions was also a reaction to the increased self-financing of combatants, primarily through trade in valuable natural resources, such as rough diamonds or timber, as well as related financial transactions.[3] In such cases, the primary objective of the sanctions regimes is to curtail the resource flows deemed to fuel internal conflict. The objective, thus, is not only to apply pressure for a political solution but also to limit the capacity of the belligerents to do harm by depriving them of the resources to purchase or import the weapons and materiel necessary to pursue their military campaigns.[4]

While warranted as one means of conflict termination, the sanctions approach faces controversy over its usefulness and effectiveness. Some have suggested that efforts to limit the intensity of a conflict through sanctions may in fact increase its duration, thereby heightening the suffering of the affected population. Similarly, given the economic dependence of civilian populations on some of the targeted activities or goods, civilian suffering may further increase as a result of even targeted sanctions.[5] Further, by stigmatizing targeted belligerents, targeted sanctions may in fact aggravate conflict by making those targeted less inclined to negotiate a political solution to the conflict.[6]

For the purposes of this analysis, I take as a given the need for outside intervention into civil wars through targeted sanctions, and thus I discuss only the means of improving their effectiveness, measured in terms of minimizing civilian suffering while maximizing the intended deprivation of resources of the intended target groups. The methodology I employ is inspired by the field of law and economics, which examines the impact of laws and their methods of application on the behavior of particular actors. For the most part, the economic literature has focused on the effects of embargo-type sanctions on the economy of the target country.[7] Despite the increased number of sanctions imposed on nonstate actors, few systematic studies have been undertaken to assess the effectiveness of sanctions against nonstate armed groups, companies, and criminal networks, but accumulated empirical research has demonstrated that these actors continue to engage in the circumvention of UN sanctions.[8] This chapter seeks to help bridge this gap in research and policy. The first section of the chapter lays out the logic of sanctions busting. The second is devoted to a discussion of the current legal force of UN sanctions and what the contours of an effective law to control sanctions busting should be. The third part provides an examination of the difficulties of enforcing sanctions domestically. Finally, the chapter concludes by offering a few ideas for strengthening international efforts against sanctions busting.

The Logic of *Sanctions Busting*

Ultimately, the effectiveness of sanctions depends on the sanctioned target's ability to circumvent them.[9] As with every interdiction effort, moreover, the imposition of sanctions on commodities or arms immediately raises their value to those who own or control them, thereby increasing the economic incentive for them to engage in the evasion of sanctions (*sanctions busting*). No wonder, then, that UN sanctions are routinely violated by a host of actors. Such sanctions busting takes place in two directions: the illicit import of arms and other essential products to belligerents in a given country and the clandestine export of valuable resources from the country. Typically these transactions require the establishment of large-scale financial networks designed to keep them undetected.

Based on empirical research, one can identify three types of sanctions busters, each with somewhat differing incentive structures. The first type consists of transnational criminal organizations—arms and narcotics traffickers, diamond dealers, and shadowy businessmen who *specialize* in the business of war. Given that illegal or illicit economic activities are the raison d'être for this group of actors, their violation of sanctions regimes is pretty much *business as usual*. The degree to which their activities are affected by sanctions regimes depends on the degree to which these are enforced. As long as the actual profit is higher than the potential risk of detection and punishment, sanctions busting for them will be a lucrative activity. Dealing with this group of sanctions buster would thus seem to be a straightforward matter of enforcing existing domestic and international laws that proscribe smuggling, drug trafficking and unofficial arms running. As will be discussed below, however, prosecuting these actors is hampered by a variety of jurisdictional obstacles, as well as by the fact that criminal organizations and *rogue companies* routinely operate in high-risk, high value activities and are well adapted to evade any type of regulation.

The second group of actors affected by sanctions against combatants are legitimate companies that may, through their routine operations and business deals, find themselves in real or potential violation of the sanctions regimes imposed by the UN in a given context. Particularly in the competitive natural resource industries, trade, and transport, these companies may employ a number of intermediaries in order to avoid directly violating the sanctions and thereby avoid liability. These intermediaries, though legal, are often established precisely in order to allow companies to evade regulation in one national jurisdiction by exploiting the lack of regulation in another. Working across national jurisdictions, these smaller intermediaries are generally too elusive to constitute identifiable targets for effective enforcement. The activities of foreign subsidiaries typically cannot be controlled by a multinational's home government.[10] They thus provide an important channel through which sanctions compliance by otherwise legal entities can be undermined. Where technology and production capabilities can be easily diffused through the foreign subsidiaries of multinational firms in response to perceived embargo threats, sanctions are rendered ineffective.

Here, sanctions enforcement would require holding accountable companies that benefit from the activities of their foreign intermediaries. In many respects, these cases raise even more complex problems than do cases of the first type. First, any attempt by the international community at preventing this type of activity confronts the myriad problems associated with national sovereignty as well as with corporate structure.[11] Foreign companies are always regulated by a national set of laws, which makes almost impossible any direct action on company activities in the place of conflict.[12] Laws are also protective for those who circumvent them. In such situations either the home state lacks the will to press charges or—as is typically though not universally the case—national legislation does not allow (or facilitate) legal proceedings for crimes committed in a foreign country.[13]

The third group of sanctions busters includes those governments or government elites that may facilitate, as well as benefit from, sanctions busting. These actors can also be located beyond the borders of a targeted conflict. The Angola Monitoring Mechanism, for example, identified government officials in Burkina Faso, Togo, and the Democratic Republic of Congo (Zaire) as having facilitated illegal arms shipments to UNITA.[14] In such cases, it is impossible to use national law to prosecute the violators, as the state itself either participates in or tacitly condones the violations. Diplomatic and economic pressure may be applied to induce compliance by reluctant governments, for example in the form of secondary sanctions, as was the case with the Liberian government when it was seen as facilitating the smuggling of diamonds from RUF-controlled territories in Sierra Leone. The only possible *legal* recourse would be to press charges against members of these governments before an international criminal court. However, neither international law nor international courts yet have this capacity, and the emergence of a universal criminal justice system is a process whose outcome remains uncertain.

Strengthening the Legal Force of Sanctions

The majority of the resource flows that supply conflicts are valuable only if they can reach international markets. This is why the international community has aimed its efforts at suppressing the profit-seeking activities of civil war combatants and curtailing their trade routes and support networks, through targeted commodity embargoes, transport bans, and financial freezes. Minimizing the scope and profitability of wartime economic transactions, has, in some cases, cut off established supply routes and raised the transaction costs for targeted groups, thereby affecting their capacity to finance further hostilities.[15] Clearly, however, the fact that such transactions may be prohibited under UN sanctions is not sufficient to prevent them entirely. Thus, questions arise not only of the exact delimitation of the transactions to be proscribed but also of how to implement an effective mode of prohibition. Typically, the prohibition of certain activities or commodities under UN targeted sanctions will create incentives for combatants and their supporters to shift to alternative sources of revenue generation. To combat this, UN sanctions regimes need to be flexible and responsive to new developments. The latter problem consists in finding ways to deprive the combatants of the resource flows that fuel the conflict. Targeting rebel actors alone is not sufficient. Effective sanctions must also take into account the incentives and capacities of official governments, corporate decisionmakers, criminals, and traffickers, whose economic behavior promotes and profits from civil war.

The Uncertain Legal Status of UN Sanctions

Security Council resolutions adopted under Chapter VII are binding upon UN member states.[16] According to Nicolas Angelet, it is nonetheless difficult to determine the precise scope of the obligations that Security Council resolutions impose on UN member states.[17] It remains unclear, for instance, whether it is sufficient for states to adopt only those measures explicitly provided for in the relevant Security Council resolution or whether circumstances allow or require them to take additional measures, such as more robust monitoring, investigation, and prosecution of potential sanctions busters. More practically, many states lack adequate legal and enforcement machinery to ensure compliance with sanctions regimes. This is particularly true of countries in the developing world, which are often frontline states neighboring zones of conflict, but also obtains in many otherwise well-institutionalized legal systems.[18] Even where law enforcement capacity does exist, as it does in some national jurisdictions that are home to large multinationals, a lack of political will may impede effective implementation. Especially where the sanctioned activities implicate strategic resources or otherwise legitimate economic activities, home governments will be loath to restrict their own companies' activities abroad when they cannot be certain that other countries will do the same. Finally, existing Security Council resolutions do not directly criminalize the behavior of individuals, let alone corporate entities, acting in violation of the coercive measures they establish.[19] Doing so would require recourse to a sort of international criminal law that does not presently exist.

Toward International Criminal Law?

While the international criminal system is exploring ways to address this vacuum, the process faces numerous difficulties, such as the reluctance of many states to compromise their sovereignty. Indeed, the idea of an international criminal system combines two branches of law that are a priori incompatible. In classical law doctrine, international law and criminal law are mutually exclusive. They do not function at the same level: the one deals with states, the other with individuals. The former is a law of coordination of independent sovereignty, the latter an attribute that lies at the basis of independent sovereignty. The power to promulgate repressive laws and to enforce them on a given territory remains the privilege of the state. As long as this doctrine dominated international relations, an international criminal system was not possible for lack of a common criminal law, third parties to judge, and persons to be convicted. In such a model, the distinctions between violations of international law and other violations were clear. The former sanctioned actions undertaken in contact zones between sovereign actors—that is to say, chronologically: piracy on the high seas, slave trade, drug trafficking, airplane hijacking, terrorism, and environmental abuses. In other words, international law held jurisdiction only over crimes committed in international spaces, or in those where no internal sovereignty existed.[20]

However, newly created international criminal jurisdictions are competent to judge certain types of infractions, beyond the classical international law violations just enumerated, based on a new hybrid category involving both national and international spheres of law.[21] In theory, the violation of UN sanctions would fall precisely into this category because UN sanctions combine decisions taken on an international basis with nationally based enforcement. Ideally, some variety of a comprehensive universal legal regime would be the best means of enhancing both the authority and the capacity of the international community to penalize those whose economic activities serve to support and exploit armed conflict.

However, given present international circumstances, the likelihood that such a regime could be developed is very low. Because international law is primarily concerned with defining state responsibilities, its enforcement depends upon state capacity and will. As noted above, few states currently have the capacity, and fewer still the political will, to enforce Security Council resolutions under Chapter VII of the UN Charter. While there has been much progress in the development of the International Criminal Court (ICC), with broad jurisdiction to prosecute war crimes and grave violations of international humanitarian law,[22] its capacity to provide redress to economic exploitation of armed conflict is limited in several respects. First, sanctions busting is not criminalized under international law, nor are many of the other economic activities that fuel conflict. Second, while the ICC has signaled its intention to investigate economic actors deemed complicit in war crimes committed in the Ituri region of the Democratic Republic of Congo, it is likely that priority will be given, as with other criminal tribunals, to a narrow range of specific crimes and human rights violations committed by those deemed "to bear the greatest responsibility" for criminal acts.[23] Third, the application of international law to nonstate actors remains very problematic. The suggestion that the ICC statute extend to criminal liability of legal persons (such as corporations) was ultimately dropped by the drafters.[24] As such, criminal accountability does not apply to collective or legal entities but only to their individual members; prosecutions can proceed only against crimes committed by natural persons, a limitation that militates against efforts to hold business entities liable for sanctions busting.[25]

In sum, it is clear that violations of UN sanctions cannot lead to criminal prosecutions under a universal law, since such legal norms are only starting to emerge with the creation of the ICC and with the tentative promotion of the concept of universal jurisdiction by some states and jurists. National legal systems are very heterogeneous and do not equally facilitate the prosecution of sanctions violators and international law generally. At one extreme, Belgium has championed the idea and practice of universal jurisdiction.[26] A 1993 Belgian law gives the national legal system universal competence to pursue and punish persons presumed responsible for war crimes or crimes against humanity committed abroad, whatever their own nationality or that of their victims.[27] On the other hand, the vast majority of states refuse to move in this direction, preferring instead to rely on national jurisdiction, despite the fact that this approach continues to hinder legal actions they might take against nonnationals in their own jurisdictions as well as those taken against their nationals in other jurisdictions. The international legal system under which those engaging in conflict-promoting economic activities—even those activities that are, under national or international law, clearly deemed illegal—could be prosecuted thus remains very imperfect. The following review of actual attempts to enforce legal prosecution of cases of sanctions busting highlights several of the concrete problems that remain to be resolved.

From International
Sanctions to National Criminalization?

As indicated above, UN Security Council resolutions to impose targeted economic sanctions on actors in a conflict setting in order to prohibit the illicit import of weapons to belligerents or the illicit exploitation of natural resources have proved generally incapable of achieving these ends.[28] There are several reasons for this ineffectiveness: first, despite the obligatory nature of the sanctions imposed by the Security Council under Chapter VII, they do not necessarily result in a commitment by the member states to put them into practice, whether because of lack of will or lack of means; second, the implied threat of sanctions against countries that continue to trade with state or nonstate actors under UN sanctions does not necessarily criminalize the acts of individuals and companies engaged in such trade; third, as the cases below show, collecting the evidence necessary for legal action against arms brokers and smugglers of sanctioned commodities is extremely complicated and expensive. Certainly, the degree to which Security Council sanctions have been enforced has depended in large part on the will—or lack of will—of individual states to see them applied.

The Challenges of Busting Sanctions Busters

Private brokers and middlemen are essential players in moving weapons to and commodities from regimes, insurgents, or terrorist groups under international embargoes who otherwise have no legal means of purchasing arms. Brokers cover their tracks with complex financial transactions to thwart efforts to follow the money, bribes to ensure that customs inspectors and other officials avert their gaze from illicit cargo, and bogus documents, including *end-user certificates* that show a false destination for the arms. Once shipped, the goods are rerouted to their true destination.[29]

The difficulty in effectively prosecuting such brokers lies in the fact that existing Security Council resolutions do not themselves criminalize the behavior of individuals acting in violation of the measures they establish. Doing so would require that states prosecute these individuals under domestic law, which, assumes that national authorities are committed to sanctions enforcement and that the appropriate domestic enabling legislation exists. Yet even where these factors are given, successful prosecution poses the delicate problem of gathering the necessary elements for a legal action likely to meet with success. Efforts to prosecute two high-level weapons traffickers—Leonid Minin and Victor Bout, notorious for their role in supplying rebel groups from Liberia to Afghanistan as well as for their violations of UN sanctions—illustrates many of these difficulties.

Leonid Minin was born in Odessa, Ukraine, in 1947 and in the 1970s emigrated to Israel, where he established a global web of companies, many of them discreetly incorporated off shore. Minin's primary business was a Monaco-based company, Limad AG, which also has offices in Switzerland, China, and Russia. In addition to arms, his business interests included timber, chemicals, food, clothing, scrap metal, and oil. By the late 1990s, Minin had become a major broker of arms to Liberia, where Charles Taylor took power in 1997 following a seven-year civil war.[30] Initially Minin was arrested in Italy, by chance, for drug possession, a charge that kept him in jail for six months.[31] According to the arrest report, a prostitute led police to his disheveled hotel room after not being paid for her services. There the authorities discovered a shopping list of guns and stacks of weapons manuals, faxes discussing arms deals with Liberia and Côte d'Ivoire, forged end-user certificates, large amounts of cash, and polished diamonds worth nearly $500,000. This evidence was enough to charge Minin with illegal arms trafficking in violation of UN sanctions. If convicted, he faced twelve years in prison for international arms trafficking.

However, in September 2002 the Italian Supreme Court ruled that Minin could not be prosecuted, as the trafficked weapons in question neither originated in nor transited through Italy. The court stated it could not find any justifiable basis for his prosecution, "not even in the fact that the trafficking of arms has taken place in violation of an embargo established by a UN resolution," adding that it could not act against Minin as long as he did not "threaten the internal security" of the state. As a result, the charges against Minin for illicit arms trafficking were dropped.[32]

Victor Bout, a Russian citizen, began his career after the fall of the Soviet Union. A former soldier in the Soviet Army, he set up a network of air transit, initially in Angola, that enabled him to ship and sell surplus military equipment from the ex-Soviet army to the African continent, in particular to Sierra Leone. Reports of UN expert panels found him to be in violation of embargoes on Liberia, Sierra Leone, and Angola. He also developed business networks in Afghanistan, where he supplied both the Taliban and the Northern Alliance with weapons.[33] In late summer 2000, Richard Clarke, the U.S. National Security Council's counterterrorism director, asked his team to get a warrant for Bout's arrest.[34] Efforts to enforce this order encountered immediate difficulties, as the Russian government refused to cooperate. Realizing that the international options were limited, the United States turned to a diplomatic campaign to disrupt Bout and his assets. The strategy was to urge other nations where Bout had operations to file charges against him and shut him down. In return, the United States promised to back them up with the full force of its intelligence and diplomatic machinery.

First the U.S. government focused on South Africa, in an effort to catch Bout under that country's newly established antimercenary laws. However, it quickly became clear that they lacked sufficient evidence to make a case. The United Arab Emirates then seemed a more promising option. Here, the government of the United Kingdom wanted help with its own efforts: to publicly shame Bout and drive him from the Emirates. But Western diplomats discovered how difficult it was to stir the United Arab Emirates to action when its direct interests were not threatened. Bout had an influential partner in Sharjah, and the royal aide did not respond to attempts to interview him. Finally, in the immediate chaos that followed September 11, Bout and his partners moved out of the Emirates back to Russia, thereby evading efforts to bring him to prosecution.

Bout's U.S. pursuers then explored possibilities for procuring a warrant in the United States. Federal law-enforcement agencies uncovered evidence that Bout had interests in several U.S. cities. However, proving a criminal case would be difficult. In theory, the United States had stronger laws than most: the 1996 Arms Export Control Act mandated that all weapons brokers with U.S. operations register with the State Department. Under the act, munitions sales are allowed only to national governments or others specifically approved by the U.S. government.[35] American dealers who violate this law anywhere in the world can be prosecuted, as can foreign nationals who break the law while conducting their business within the United States. However, in order to charge Bout, the authorities would have to prove that he had operations in the United States and also find clear evidence of his crimes.

In 2000, San Air General Trading was established in Plano, Texas, a Dallas suburb. Bout's name does not appear on the corporate papers, but two of his Russian associates based in the United Arab Emirates were listed as directors. Federal agents pored over the company's phone records, discovering that callers from Plano were in frequent communication with Bout's enterprises abroad. But there was no evidence of wrongdoing. In the summer of 2000, Bout applied for a visa at the U.S. embassy in Abu Dhabi, listing the Plano corporation address as his destination. Ironically, Bout was on the embassy's watch list, and his visa application was refused.[36] Incredibly, an otherwise open opportunity to hold him accountable, including for committing crimes in the United States, such as violating anti-brokering laws, was missed.

After September 11, under U.S pressure, the Belgians moved against Bout. A federal prosecutor issued an arrest warrant, alleging that Bout headed a complex scheme to launder African weapons profits. Interpol followed with a worldwide alert. According to Belgian law-enforcement officials, the police investigation into Bout led to the discovery of massive flows of money coursing through two Bout-controlled firms. Several hundred million Belgian francs moved into bank accounts across Europe, funds that allegedly came from Angolan weapons profits. American officials had assumed that Bout would be in the Emirates if a warrant came down. Instead, he was in Moscow, where authorities declined to arrest him on the basis of an Interpol alert. Soon after, the Russian Federal Security Service issued a short notice claiming that there was no evidence that Bout had committed any illegal actions.[37]

Evidently, none of these efforts has impeded Bout's ability to engage in sanctions busting. More than for lack of evidence, Bout has been able to evade prosecution because of the considerable political protection he has enjoyed, and not only from Russian authorities. Indeed, in a stunning about-face, British Gulf, a company with links to Bout, was discovered to be providing air support to the U.S. military in Iraq in 2004, reputedly under sub-contracts with the U.S. Department of Defense. Even as Bout continues to be listed under a Security Council–mandated travel ban, U.S. authorities have been allegedly pressuring other governments to drop his name from the list.[38]

In the end, these two cases exemplify the difficulties of successfully mounting national criminal prosecutions of violations of internationally agreed violations. In the case of Minin, it was excesses characteristic of his personality that drove him behind bars, and that only for a short period. Both Minin and Bout continue to elude prosecution for sanctions busting due to an ongoing lack of cooperation within and between states. These cases demonstrate that traffickers at this level can be successfully prosecut-ed only where and when states decide to effectively cooperate.

Enforcing Sanctions by Sanctioning Enforcement

This brief discussion suggests a variety of options for modifying the mode of sanctions in order to make them more effective. When a repressive mechanism proves to be ineffective, there are generally four solutions available: harden the criminal policy; transfer to private agents the task of supervising behavior by subjecting them to criminal liability; rely on the voluntary actions of agents who do not wish to have their reputations sul-lied and are thus ready to adhere to improved standards of behavior; or decriminalize the activity altogether. Given our purpose of considering how to strengthen UN sanctions compliance, the option of decriminalization will not be considered here.

The first solution consists in hardening criminal enforcement. This entails, on the one hand, a modification of the law to address the existence of continuing loopholes and, on the other hand, enhancing penalties for the crimes as well as the means devoted to their detection. Since it has proved difficult to pursue arms traffickers and other sanctions busters by applying national laws, the Security Council should consider an alternative means to criminalize the violation of UN sanctions that would be consistent across national jurisdictions.

The Security Council has been reluctant to undertake efforts to make criminal liability for sanctions busting effective in domestic legal orders. Not a single Security Council sanctions resolution expressly obliges mem-ber states to take action against such an offense in their internal legal order.[39] In fact, the Security Council cannot decide for states whether to prevent or prohibit the activities concerned. It is the council itself that pro-hibits them. This formula does not expressly provide for territorial and per-sonal jurisdiction. In principle, this might be construed to mean that the Security Council's jurisdiction in the area of sanctions is universal in kind, which means that states must enforce the prohibition whether or not it has been violated on their territory or by their nationals.[40] In principle, then, the Security Council could enhance sanctions compliance by urging member states to adopt and implement the appropriate national criminal legislation. While this is not the current practice of Security Council sanctions resolutions, it would not be entirely unprecedented. The Security Council's action on counterterrorism, embodied in Resolution 1373, expressly requires that member states enact legislation to criminalize terrorist-financing activities. While this may prove to be an exception to the general rule, it underscores the potential for the Security Council to strengthen state obligations for sanctions enforcement.[41]

The second solution consists in delegating to private actors the responsibility of transforming their behavior by subjecting them to legal liability. The operative principle here is well known. It rests on a relation of agency, where an incentive system is put in place that compels the agent to adopt certain objectives. An apt example is the extension of criminal liability to companies by common law countries in an effort to fight against white-collar delinquency. The underlying principle is simple: since the state is not in a position to detect white-collar criminality, it is more cost effective to delegate this task to companies by threatening them with criminal liability for the crimes committed in their name, even without their being informed of it by their employees. In the field of UN sanctions, this track would consist in making the companies that produce, sell, or transport arms or other commodities in violation of UN sanctions criminally liable when the rules that govern these exchanges are contravened by their employees or subsidiaries, even when it is done without their knowledge. Given that many companies that supply weapons to or import commodities from markets in countries subject to UN sanctions repeatedly turn a blind eye to the original sources or the final destinations of their goods, it is likely that they would reorient their attitude if they were to incur legal liability for doing so.

This remedy, however, encounters two problems. First, establishing criminal liability for companies often has a perverse effect.[42] Do the companies have an improved incentive to better supervise their working procedures if, each time that they observe a violation of the law by an employee, they must declare it to the authorities and face legal prosecution? Second, it is doubtful that individual states would have the political will to introduce in their national law provisions that would "pierce the corporate veil" and weaken the operations and profitability of an export industry that is often economically vital to the country concerned.

There remains a final option, usually retained by the civil law—but not common law—countries that generally hesitate to resort to the criminal liability of third parties, whether companies or persons, when intentionality is not established.[43] This solution consists of using "soft law" measures to increase incentives for agents to comply voluntarily with UN sanctions regimes.[44] The soft law approach generally requires mobilizing private economic actors in order to obtain their cooperation in adopting policies that reduce the conflict-promoting aspects of their investments and operations in conflict zones.[45] It is then a question of building incentive schemes that are cost beneficial to encourage these private-sector actors to participate in the implementation of Security Council sanctions policies, as relayed by the national state.

The example of the fight against the laundering of drug money provides some lessons that are applicable to the repression of violations of international economic sanctions. The OECD Financial Action Task Force against Money Laundering (FATF), an assembly of member states, checks that member states translate its recommendations into their national legal codes. When a country refuses, it can be publicly censured by FATF, as Austria, Liechtenstein, Russia, Panama, and Nauru, among others, have been.[46] The annual publication of a blacklist of noncomplying jurisdictions has proven to be a powerful and effective incentive for countries to undertake legal and policy reforms to demonstrate their conformity with FATF provisions.

Indeed, the UN Security Council has already undertaken similar measures that aim to increase incentives for compliance among economic agents. Noting that the sanctions issued between 1992 and 1998 were violated with impunity, the council acknowledged that enforcing sanctions would require some form of monitoring to identify sanctions busters. In the case of UNITA in Angola, the Security Council, through its Sanctions Committee, established a panel of experts in May 1999 with a six-month mandate to collect relevant information. On March 10, 2000, the panel produced the pioneering *Final Report of the UN Panel of Experts on Violation of Security Council Sanctions against UNITA,* a report that explicitly "named and shamed" particular governments, companies, and individuals alleged to be in violation of UN-mandated sanctions. The practice of "naming and shaming" by this and subsequent UN expert panels increased pressure on some member states to uphold their legal obligation to implement UN sanctions. In some cases, this has produced improved compliance efforts. However, the overall impact of this mechanism in reducing the incidence of evasion of Security Council sanctions has been modest at best, in large part because of the domestic political concerns and legal loopholes discussed above, in part because companies have little incentive for self-regulation, particularly if they perceive that defection is high and that compliance hampers their relative competitiveness, especially against less scrupulous players. Still, there is scope for strengthening the incentives for country and company compliance with UN sanctions through a more consistent use of "naming and shaming" and by encouraging governments to devise positive inducements to reward compliance.

Conclusion

What becomes clear from the discussion above is that each of the solutions suggested here places the burden of responsibility for enforcing Security Council sanctions on different actors. To give Security Council resolutions the character of universal law supposes that the council is capable of imposing a collective will over that of the range of member states. To count on transformation of the national law of individual countries transfers the burden of improvement of mechanisms to the various states, an approach that is bound to further exacerbate existing national discrepancies. Obviously, determined sanctions busters will not fail to capitalize on the heterogeneity of these efforts and exploit the advantages offered by the weak links in the chain of enforcement over various national jurisdictions. Equally, public reprobation by independent panels of experts, even though these are mandated by the Security Council, lacks the full force of an authoritative and official judgment.

In the final analysis, if the UN Security Council is, indeed, seriously committed to addressing the problem of sanctions busting, particularly where these activities exacerbate and promote armed conflict and its associated undesirable and illegal impacts upon broader conflict and humanitarian dynamics, then it must address the current gaps in international law which this study has identified and by which member states, though obligated, remain unaccountable.

Notes

1. David Cortright and George A. Lopez, *The Sanctions Decade: Assessing UN Strategies in the 1990s* (Boulder: Lynne Rienner, 2000).

2. These have included commodity sanctions, arms embargoes, and travel bans. See UN Security Council resolutions concerning Angola, S/RES/864 (1993), S/RES/1173 (1998); and Sierra Leone, S/RES/1132 (1997), S/RES/1306 (2000).

3. See Mats Berdal and David Malone, eds., *Greed and Grievance: Economic Agendas in Civil Wars* (Boulder: Lynne Rienner, 2000); Karen Ballentine and Jake Sherman, eds., *The Political Economy of Armed Conflict: Beyond Greed and Grievance* (Boulder: Lynne Rienner, 2003).

4. Philippe Le Billon, "Getting It Done: Instruments of Enforcement," in Ian Bannon and Paul Collier, eds., *Natural Resources and Violent Conflict: Options and Actions* (Washington, D.C.: World Bank, 2003), pp. 215–286.

5. See also Chapter 7 by Stephen Jackson in this volume.

6. Pierre Kopp, "Embargo et criminalisation de l'economie," in François Jean and Jean-Christophe Rufin, eds., *Economie des guerres civiles* (Paris: Hachette, 1996), pp. 425–465.

7. Gary C. Hufbauer, Jeffrey J. Schott, and Kimberley Ann Elliot, *Economic Sanctions Reconsidered: History and Current Policy* (Washington D.C: Institute for

International Economics, 1985); J. M. Lindsay, "Trade Sanctions as Policy Instruments: A Re-examination," *International Studies Quarterly* 30 (1986): 153–173; Sofia Heine-Ellison, "The Impact and Effectiveness of Multilateral Economic Sanctions: A Comparative Study," *International Journal of Human Rights* 5, no. 1 (2001): 81–112; Thomas Weiss, David Cortright, George A. Lopez, and Larry Minear, eds., *Political Gain, Civilian Pain: Humanitarian Impacts of Economic Sanctions* (Lanham, Md.: Rowman and Littlefield, 1997).

    8. Reports of the various UN expert panels monitoring targeted sanctions in Angola, Sierra Leone, and Liberia have made an invaluable, if still preliminary, empirical contribution to understanding the impact of targeted sanctions on nonstate actors. See, among others, United Nations Security Council, *Report of the Panel of Experts on Violations of Security Council Sanctions against UNITA*, S/2000/203, March 10, 2000; *Report of the Panel of Experts Appointed Pursuant to Security Council Resolution 1306 (2000), Paragraph 19, in Relation to Sierra Leone*, S/2000/1195, December 20, 2000. Useful analytical assessments of the effectiveness of targeted sanctions more generally can be found in David Cortright and George A. Lopez, eds., *Smart Sanctions: Targeting Economic Statecraft* (Boston: Rowman and Littlefield, 2002); and David Cortright and George A. Lopez, *Sanctions and the Search for Security: Challenges for UN Action*, Project of the International Peace Academy (Boulder: Lynne Rienner, 2002).

    9. Hufbauer, Schott, and Elliot, *Economic Sanctions Reconsidered*; Lindsay, "Trade Sanctions as Policy Instruments"; Van Bergeaux, "Success and Failure of Economic Sanctions," *Kyklos* 42, no. 3 (1989): 385–404.

    10. A. Smith, *East-West Trade: Embargoes and Expectations*, Center for Economic Policy Research Discussion Paper 139 (London: Center for Economic Policy, 1986).

    11. Phillip I. Blumberg, "Accountability of Multinational Corporations: The Barriers Presented by Concepts of the Corporate Judicial Entity," *Hastings International and Comparative Law Review* 24, no. 3 (Spring 2001): 297–320.

    12. There are some important national exceptions to this, notably the U.S. Alien Tort Claims Act.

    13. Again, there are some important exceptions whereby national jurisdiction has some extraterritorial reach, notably the U.S. Alien Torts Claims Act. Under universal jurisdiction, a case has also been brought against TotalFinaElf in Belgium for alleged complicity in human rights violations in Burma/Myanmar. See Chapter 15 by Paul Hoffman in this book. "TotalFinaElf Faces Lawsuit by Myanmar Refugees over Government Human Rights Abuses," AFX News, May 8, 2002, available at www.business-humanrights.org.

    14. "Final Report of the Monitoring Mechanism on Angola Sanctions," S/2000/1225, December 21, 2000.

    15. Karen Ballentine, "Conclusion," in Ballentine and Sherman, eds., *Political Economy of Armed Conflict*.

    16. Steven R. Ratner, "The Security Council and International Law," in David M. Malone, ed., *The UN Security Council: From the Cold War to the Twenty-first Century* (Boulder: Lynne Rienner, 2004), pp. 591–605.

    17. In accordance with article 25 of the Charter, Security Council resolutions adopted under Chapter VII offer the possibility of enacting sanctions at a quasi-universal level. Security Council measures must be applied by UN members notwithstanding, for example, bilateral or other treaties guaranteeing free trade with the target of the sanctions. Security Council decisions concern imports from and exports to the target and even a broader scope. Nicolas Angelet, "Criminal Liability for the

Violation of United Nations Economic Sanctions," *European Journal of Crime, Criminal Law, and Criminal Justice* 7, no. 2 (1999): 89–102.

18. Vera Gowlland-Debbas, ed., *National Implementation of United Nations Sanctions: A Comparative Study* (Leiden: Martinus Nijhoff, 2004).

19. Angelet, "Criminal Liability."

20. A. Garapon, *Des crimes qu'on ne peut ni punir ni pardonner* (Paris: Odile Jacob, 2003).

21. International Law Association, Committee on International Human Rights Law and Practice, "Final Report on the Exercise of Universal Jurisdiction in Respect of Gross Human Rights Offenses," London, 2000.

22. The International Criminal Court provides a key possible venue for holding individuals responsible for "the most serious crimes of concern to the international community." The statute of the ICC explicitly asserts the responsibility of someone who "for the purpose of facilitating the commission of such a crime, aids, abets or otherwise assists in its commission or its attempted commission, including providing the means for its commission." See Lisa Misol, "Weapons and War Crimes: The Complicity of Arms Suppliers," *Human Rights and Armed Conflict, World Report 2004* (New York: Human Rights Watch, 2004), pp. 279–300.

23. Office of the Prosecutor of the ICC, press release no. pids.009.2003-EN, July 16, 2003, pp. 3–4. For example, the Sierra Leone Special Court has a mandate limited to prosecuting only those "most responsible" for crimes. Office of the Attorney General and Ministry of Justice, Special Court Task Force, *Statute for the Special Court*, January 16, 2002; and "The Special Court Agreement, 2002 Ratification Act, 2002," *Supplement to the Sierra Leone Gazette* 130, no. 2 (March 2, 2002), available at www.specialcourt.org.

24. Per Saland, "International Criminal Law Principles," in Roy S. K. Lee, ed., *The International Criminal Court: The Making of the Rome Statute* (The Hague: Kluwer Law International, 1999), pp. 189–216.

25. Garapon, *Crimes qu'on ne peut.*

26. For a broad survey of cases, see Chandra Lekha Sriram, "Contemporary Practice of Universal Jurisdiction: Disjointed and Disparate, Yet Developing," *International Journal of Human Rights* 6 (Fall 2002): 49–76.

27. Facing pressure from the United States and Israel after suits were announced against Ariel Sharon and members of the Bush administration, in 2003 Belgian legislators modified the 1993 law, adding a requirement that defendants be present in Belgium and an amendment making it possible to withdraw a case from the Belgian courts and send it to another country if that country incriminates genocide, crimes against humanity, and war crimes and can grant a fair trial to all parties concerned. See Luc Walleyn, "The Sabra and Shatila Massacre and Belgian Universal Jurisdiction," 2003, www.ssrc.org/programs/gsc/publications/ICA_memos/Panel3.Walleyn.doc.

28. Le Billon, "Getting It Done."

29. C. H. Anderton, "Economics of Arms Trade," in Keith Hartley and Todd Sandler, eds., *The Handbook of Defense Economics,* vol. 1 (Amsterdam: North-Holland, 1995); Brian Wood and Johan Peleman, *The Arms Fixers: Controlling the Brokers and Shipping Agents,* Research Report no. 99.3 (London: British American Security Information Service, 1999).

30. *Report of the Panel of Experts Appointed Pursuant to Security Council Resolution 1306 (2000), Paragraph 19, in Relation to Sierra Leone;* Global Witness, "The Usual Suspects," London, March 2003; International Consortium of

Investigative Journalists, "The Merchant of Death" (Washington, D.C.: Center for Public Integrity, 2002).

31. Peter Landesman, "Arms and the Man," *New York Times,* August 17, 2003.

32. Amnesty International, *Terror Trade Times,* issue 4, June 2003, available at www.amnesty.org/pages/ttt4-article_2-eng.

33. "Victor Bout Linked to Al Qaeda," *Los Angeles Times*, February 16, 2002; Landesman, "Arms and the Man."

34. Douglas Farrah. "Arrest Aids Pursuit of Weapons Network," *Washington Post,* February 26, 2002.

35. http://resource.lawlinks.com/Content/Legal_Research/US_code/Title_22/title_22_39.htm.

36. Landesman, "Arms and the Man."

37. Ibid.

38. United Nations, "Security Council Committee on Liberia Includes Additional Information on Travel Ban List," press release no. SC/8033, March 23, 2004. According to one report, Bout's name was indeed dropped from the United Kingdom's list of UN sanctions busters. See Mark Turner, "US Seeks to Protect Weapons Trafficker," *Financial Times,* May 16, 2004; Jean-Philippe Rémy, "The Trafficker Viktor Bout Lands US Aid for Services Rendered in Iraq," *Le Monde,* May 18, 2004, available at www.globalpolicy.org; James Daly, "Viktor Bout: From International Outlaw to Valued Partner," *Terrorism Monitor* 2, no. 20 (October 21, 2004), available at www.jamestownfoundation.org. Likewise, a recent search of Interpol no longer shows an outstanding warrant for Mr. Bout; see www.interpol.int.

39. Angelet, "Criminal Liability."

40. Ibid

41. See in particular article 1(b), www.un.org/docs/sc/committees/1373, September 28, 2001. In addition, on September 12, 2001, the Security Council adopted Resolution 1368, which recognized any act of international terrorism as a threat to international peace and security, thereby establishing a legal basis for action. Resolution 1377, passed on November 12, 2001, underscored the obligation of states to deny financial and other forms of support and safe haven to terrorists and invited the CTC to explore ways to assist states in the legal and regulatory implementation of Resolution 1373. Indeed, some commentators view 1373 as move by the Security Council away from soft law toward hard law. See Paul Szasz, "The Security Council Starts Legislating," *American Journal of International Law* 96 (April 2002): 901. See also Chapter 5 by Sue Eckert in this volume.

42. Jennifer Arlen, "The Potentially Perverse Effects of Corporate Criminal Liability," *Journal of Legal Studies* 23, no. 2 (1994): 833–868.

43. Pierre Kopp, *The Political Economy of Illegal Drugs* (London: Routledge, 2004).

44. The term *hard law* refers to legally binding obligations that are precise (or can be made precise through adjudication or detailed regulation) and that delegate authority for interpreting and implementing the law. "Soft law" begins once legal arrangements are attenuated along one or more of the dimensions of obligation, precision, and delegation. This softening can occur in varying degrees along each dimension and in different combinations across dimensions. I use the term *soft law* to distinguish this broad class of deviations both from "hard law" and, at the other extreme, from purely political arrangements from which legalization is largely absent. Kenneth W. Abbot and Duncan Snidal, "Hard Law and Soft Law in International Governance," *International Organization* 54, no. 3 (Summer 2000): 421–456.

45. Promising soft law initiatives of this sort—ones that seek to reduce the conflict-promoting effects of otherwise legal economic activities—include the Voluntary Principles on Security and Human Rights and the UK-sponsored Extractive Industry Transparency Initiative. See also Chapter 11 by Gavin Hayman and Corene Crossin in this volume.

46. Financial Action Task Force (FATF-XI), *Annual Report, 1999–2000,* June 22, 2000, pp. 20–22.

16

Corporate Accountability Under the U.S. Alien Tort Claims Act

Paul L. Hoffman

In 1992 the California-based oil giant Unocal entered into a joint venture project, with the French oil company Total and the military dictatorship in Burma/Myanmar, to build a natural gas pipeline from the Andaman Sea to market in Thailand. The route of the pipeline cut through several Karen villages in the Tennasserim region of Burma/Myanmar. Prior to undertaking the project, Unocal was advised on the risks involved in the investment by its security consultant, Control Risks Group. Noting the Burmese government's widespread human rights violations, particularly its use of forced labor, the consultant's report warned of the high political risks that the pipeline would create and advised that the profits of the project would have to be "unusually high" to justify these risks.[1] When Unocal proceeded with the joint venture, many of Control Risks' assessments came true. Thousands of villagers were forcibly removed from their land, forced to labor for the military as porters, and driven into exile in refugee camps on the Thai-Burma/Myanmar border. When villager complaints and wider publicity about these violations failed to alter the joint venture's practices, the villagers turned to public interest organizations like the Center for Constitutional Rights, Earthrights International, and the International Labor Rights Fund to vindicate their rights in a U.S. courtroom.

The plaintiffs in the proceedings against Unocal base their claims on the U.S. Alien Tort Claims Act (ATCA), a federal statute that dates back over 200 years. In its present-day use, the ATCA opens U.S. courtrooms to foreign victims of human rights violations committed abroad, giving them the possibility of civil redress. Since 1980, dozens of cases have been filed under the ATCA in U.S. courts against alleged human rights perpetrators. These cases, usually involving claims of torture, summary execution, disappearance, genocide, war crimes, or crimes against humanity, have become well established in U.S. jurisprudence.[2] Although the lower courts have uniformly upheld the availability of the ATCA as a basis to litigate at least some fundamental human rights claims,[3] in December 2003 the U.S. Supreme Court accepted review in *Sosa v. Alvarez-Machain,* a case in which the defendant and the Bush administration have argued that the ATCA is merely a jurisdictional statute and does not authorize U.S. courts to hear and decide human rights claims. In June 2004, the Supreme Court rejected these arguments and upheld the use of the ATCA in human rights cases. The significance of the Sosa decision is considered at the end of this chapter.

This chapter primarily addresses one recent development in the use of the ATCA: its application to multinational corporations alleged to be complicit in human rights violations committed by government authorities in connection with projects outside the United States.[4] Many of the accused corporations in these cases operate in conflict zones, often maintaining their ability to extract natural resources, such as copper or oil, by doing business with repressive regimes with dubious human rights records. These corporate human rights cases filed under the ATCA should be seen in the context of broader international efforts to regulate the behavior of corporate actors in repressive or war-torn countries and to eliminate what amounts to corporate impunity for the human rights violations that too often accompany their activities.[5] These cases have generated considerable public attention because of the financial stakes involved and because of the concerted response of corporations, challenging the use of the ATCA as a means to hold them accountable for complicity in human rights violations. Though it is difficult to establish a direct connection between the ATCA cases and the recent development of other international regulatory efforts, the litigation appears to have contributed to the growing debate about the need for international regulation of the activities of corporations in repressive states and zones of conflict.[6] Indeed, ATCA litigation may be seen as filling the prevailing accountability vacuum left by the absence of comprehensive international regulation and may yet serve as a catalyst for future reform efforts.

The chapter starts with a brief overview of the evolution of human rights litigation under the ATCA, specifically how the act became a tool for human rights litigation against corporations. It then discusses some of the most prominent issues to emerge from the corporate ATCA cases so far, focusing in particular on the above-mentioned *Unocal* case as the case furthest along in the judicial process. Based primarily on cases of alleged corporate complicity in human rights violations, the essential elements of an ATCA claim and some of the legal and procedural thresholds and obstacles are discussed. Whether ATCA-like litigation is possible in other countries is briefly considered as well. The chapter concludes with an examination of corporate efforts to dismantle the ATCA and the potential ramifications for international human rights litigation should these efforts succeed.

Evolution of the ATCA: Toward Corporate Accountability

The ATCA, enacted by the first U.S. Congress in 1789, provides that U.S. district courts shall have original jurisdiction over civil actions brought by "aliens" for "a tort only, committed in violation of the law of nations or a treaty of the United States."[7] Importantly, the ATCA addresses only *civil* liability. Thus, while ATCA plaintiffs may receive monetary compensation for their injuries or injunctive relief, the ATCA may not be used to impose criminal sanctions on human rights violators.[8] The starting point for the ATCA is an "alien" with a "tort" claim that involves a violation of the "law of nations." A U.S. citizen may not bring an ATCA claim.[9] The foreign plaintiff need not reside within the United States or have any contact with the United States before bringing an ATCA case.[10] Courts have had little difficulty with the requirement that an ATCA claim sound "in tort," because most egregious human rights violations (e.g., torture) take a tortious form. However, claims that would ordinarily be viewed as contractual in nature— for example, a claim for restitution of property—would not fall within the ATCA.[11] Foreign governments or their instrumentalities cannot be sued under the ATCA. Such suits must be brought under the Foreign Sovereign Immunities Act (FSIA).[12] Equally, the U.S. government cannot be sued under the ATCA.[13]

The ATCA applies to tort in violation of the "law of nations," now commonly called customary international law. Under the ATCA, an international law norm qualifies as customary international law when it is "specific, universal, and obligatory."[14] By now, it is well established that claims for torture, summary execution, disappearance, prolonged arbitrary detention, genocide, at least some war crimes (particularly violations of Common Article Three),[15] crimes against humanity, and slavery or slavery-like practices (such as forced labor) fall within the ATCA's ambit.[16] There is still controversy, however, about the applicability of the ATCA to some human rights violations. For example, there is conflicting case law as to whether the prohibition against cruel, inhuman, and degrading treatment is enforceable under the ATCA.[17] Moreover, uncertainty remains about the ATCA's scope with respect to the full range of humanitarian and human rights violations in conflict situations, including whether acts of pillage and plunder are actionable. Future cases will establish whether the courts will adopt a broader view of the range of norms actionable under the ATCA in this context.

Enacted in 1789, the ATCA lay dormant for most of its existence.

While there is little specific legislative history for the ATCA, historical analysis suggests that it was originally intended, at a minimum, to provide a forum and remedy for contemporary law-of-nations violations such as piracy, slave trading, and attacks on foreign diplomats.[18] The use of the ATCA to redress international human rights and humanitarian law violations began only in 1980, with the Second Circuit's landmark decision in the case of *Filártiga v. Peña-Irala*.[19] The *Filártiga* case arose out of the torture and murder of the seventeen-year-old son of a Paraguayan human and social rights activist in Asunción, Paraguay. The case was brought by Joelito Filártiga's father and sister when they found Joelito's murderer, Peña-Irala, the former inspector general of police in Asunción, living in the United States. Initially the case was dismissed based on the traditional view that international law or the "law of nations" did not apply to claims arising between citizens of the same country occurring within that country's territory.[20] On appeal, though, the Second Circuit found that courts examining ATCA claims were required to evaluate those claims based on the state of international law at the time of the events in question and not as of 1789.[21] The court recognized that jurisprudence in the Nuremberg trials and subsequent international human rights developments had altered the traditional international law landscape and made the ATCA applicable to such individual human rights claims. Aided by an *amicus curiae* (friend of the court) brief filed by the U.S. government, the court also found that the prohibition against torture had become part of customary international law by the time of Joelito's torture and murder and was enforceable under the ATCA.[22]

The *Filártiga* case inspired an increased and expanded use of the ATCA to redress international human rights violations in U.S. courts. This first generation of modern ATCA cases involved individual defendants, usually former foreign government officials, who were personally implicated in the commission of human rights violations or accused of having had command responsibility for such violations. The defendants have been served with process in the United States either because they were residing in the United States or because they were found within the United States during a visit.

A landmark case that paved the way for subsequent corporate litigation under the ATCA was *Kadic v. Karadzic* in 1995. In the context of overturning a district court's dismissal of claims made against Bosnian Serb leader Radovan Karadzic, the ruling of the Second Circuit expanded the contemporary reach of the ATCA to private parties for at least certain international human rights claims. The district court in *Kadic,* relying on pre-*Filártiga* views of international law, had based its dismissal on the grounds that Karadzic was a private person and could not be sued under the ATCA because international law classically had applied to only the modern sovereign state. In reversing this judgment, the Second Circuit found that certain international human rights and humanitarian law norms—such as those concerning genocide and war crimes, and possibly summary execution, rape, and other forms of torture committed in pursuit of these crimes—do apply to private (i.e., nonstate) actors under international law and therefore could be the basis of an ATCA claim.[23] The *Kadic* decision was also a strong reaffirmation of *Filártiga* and the view that courts hearing ATCA cases must examine the "law of nations" as it has evolved rather than as of the time ATCA was passed in 1789.

Among the later generation of ATCA cases, most involve defendants who are private persons or other "nonstate actors" rather than foreign state officials.[24] Suits charging corporate complicity in human rights violations are a logical extension of the Second Circuit's analysis in *Kadic,* allowing ATCA suits against nonstate actors for certain human rights and humanitarian law violations.[25] The first corporate accountability lawsuits under the ATCA, and the first involving the prosecution of a corporation as a legal entity, are the *Doe v. Unocal* and *Roe v. Unocal* cases, filed in 1996. The plaintiffs are Burmese villagers who lived near the route of the gas pipeline, planned to cut across the Tennasserim region, who allege that they were subjected to murder, forced labor, rape, and other forms of torture in connection with construction of the pipeline. The plaintiffs further allege that Unocal is liable for their damages because, inter alia, Unocal, together with its joint venture partners, Total and the Burmese state–owned Moattama Oil and Gas Enterprise (MOGE), hired the Burmese military to provide security and other logistical support for the pipeline, knowing that the military had a long record of violent human rights abuses.[26] In December 2004, the parties in the *Unocal* case reached a confidential settlement (resolving the pending cases) before the Court of Appeals had the chance to consider a number of important issues in the case after the Supreme Court's decision in *Sosa v. Alvarez-Machain.* Because of the confidentiality provisions of the settlement, very little can be said about the settlement terms other than that the settlement provided compensation for the plaintiffs and other resources for other persons affected by the pipeline project in the region. Thus, the issues discussed in this chapter will be resolved in the context of other pending cases, none of which was as far along in the legal process as the *Unocal* case.

The facts of the *Unocal* case are typical of this generation of ATCA cases, in which the corporation enters into a business arrangement with a repressive regime or its instrumentalities, in this case the MOGE, to facilitate natural resource extraction.[27] Similar suits have been filed arising out of human rights abuses in many other countries, including Nigeria, Sudan, Colombia, and Indonesia.[28]

Corporate Liability Under the ATCA:
Cases, Requirements, and Limitations

Among the ATCA cases involving corporations, one can distinguish between, on the one hand, claims based on corporations' direct involvement in destructive environmental practices, abusive sweatshop conditions in the garment industry, or the production of dangerous products and, on the other hand, claims based on allegations of corporate complicity in the actions of government officials or soldiers who actually commit the human rights violations. The latter category of cases is the more common, and the most frequent context concerns projects involving the extraction of natural resources in developing countries.

There are a number of legal and procedural requirements for ATCA cases to proceed. While some of these thresholds apply to all cases brought under the ATCA, some are especially relevant in the context of corporate cases.

ATCA Cases Alleging Direct Corporate Abuses

Several ATCA cases seek to hold corporations liable for environmental injuries that are a direct result of the corporate defendant's business operations.[29] In all of these cases, plaintiffs are trying to expand the definition of the "law of nations" beyond the most commonly recognized human rights crimes to apply to other developing international norms, especially concerning the environment. So far the courts have resisted these claims, either dismissing them on jurisdictional grounds or finding that the alleged harms do not violate "specific, universal, and obligatory" norms of international law.[30]

In the environmental cases, plaintiffs seek to collect damages for personal injuries caused by corporations that released harmful pollutants into the ground, air, and water of their communities. The earliest of these cases was *Aguinda v. Texaco,* in which Ecuadorian and Peruvian citizens attempted to recover for injuries suffered as a result of Texaco's alleged pollution of rainforests in Ecuador and Peru.[31] The case, although dismissed on *forum non conveniens* grounds, premised its judgment on the assumption that Ecuadorian courts must provide an adequate alternative forum for environmental tort actions, while also noting that any foreign judgment on the matter could be enforced against Texaco in the United States.[32] In *Flores v. Southern Peru Copper Corporation,* residents of Peru claimed that a mining company had polluted their environment, causing health problems such as lung disease.[33] The court dismissed the claim, stating that, under international law, each nation has a sovereign right to determine the appropriate balance between economic development and environmental protection within its borders and also that there is no universally accepted standard of environmental law.[34] In August 2003 the Second Circuit affirmed the dismissal of the *Flores* case.[35] Although adhering to *Filártiga* and *Kadic,* the Second Circuit rejected the plaintiff's reliance on general international human rights norms like the right to life in this context and found that there was insufficient evidence of a specific enough international consensus to allow these ATCA claims to proceed. If followed by other courts, the *Flores* decision appears to place nearly insuperable obstacles to environmental claims brought under the ATCA. The *Flores* opinion also demonstrates that the courts will set demanding standards for the proof of customary norms in ATCA cases. Indeed, beyond the fundamental human rights claims already recognized in ATCA cases, it seems likely that plaintiffs will have a heavy burden to convince courts to expand the scope of actionable human rights claims under the ATCA.[36]

Indirect Corporate Action

In the majority of corporate cases—and in those that are the central concern here—plaintiffs are asking courts to find the corporations liable for the actions of third parties, either government or private, because the corporations are alleged to have caused the plaintiffs' injuries in some way or are vicariously liable because of their structural connection (e.g., through a joint venture) to the project. In some of these cases, the corporations are entering areas of active hostilities, and because their activities may be perceived as enriching and empowering a repressive incumbent regime, their activities may become targets of protest or even attack by opposition groups. To protect their operations and personnel, the corporations typically respond by employing government-provided security or private security companies, which in turn commit human rights violations, often indiscriminately targeting civilians who play no part in any armed hostilities. For example, *Wiwa v. Royal Dutch Petroleum* arises out of the internationally condemned execution of Ken Saro-Wiwa and other leaders of the Movement for the Survival of the Ogoni People, who led protests against the environmental degradation of Ogoni lands by Shell and other multinational oil companies.[37] Plaintiffs, the survivors of the victims, alleged that Shell Nigeria recruited the police to violently suppress the opposition, using tactics including murder, false imprisonment, and torture, and then assisted the military in fixing the trial that led to the victims' execution.[38] Similarly, a cluster of cases involve allegations that U.S. corporations operating in Colombia, among them the mining company Drummond, have hired private paramilitary groups that in turn violently suppressed labor union activity.[39]

Meanwhile, the governments maintain a financial and military interest in controlling the natural resources, which many of them pursue through violent suppression of civilian populations. Corporations, in turn, are accused of facilitating government repression. In *Presbyterian Church of Sudan v. Talisman Energy Inc.,* for instance, plaintiffs allege that Talisman, a Canadian oil company, participated in the Sudanese government's war against the separatist movement in southern Sudan by constructing an oil pipeline in that region, knowing that the government was engaged in ethnic cleansing and enslavement of local populations in order to protect the pipeline.[40] Talisman is also alleged to have provided the government with logistical support for the war by supplying the Sudanese air force with fuel and granting it access to the company's airstrip. Similarly, in April 2003, Luis Alberto Galvis Mujica, a Colombian now in exile in the United States, announced the filing of a complaint in a federal court against Los Angeles–based Occidental Petroleum Corporation and its security contractors in Colombia for their role in a 1998 bombing raid of his village, Santo Domingo, that took the lives of eighteen civilians, including his mother, sister, and cousin. The Colombian air force dropped at least one cluster bomb on Santo Domingo, which is located not far from Occidental's oil pipeline. Plaintiffs allege that the air force was directed to Santo Domingo by Air Scan, a private U.S. security company hired by Occidental, and that the raid was planned in Occidental's Colombian facilities.

As highlighted in these instances, ATCA cases often arise in the context of armed conflict—a context that has a variety of legal ramifications, in terms of the available claims and defenses—and pose both legal and practical challenges for the litigants and the courts. As discussed below, the determination of when civil liability attaches to these activities is usually *the* central issue in corporate ATCA cases—how much knowledge and involvement in the violation must be shown to find a corporation legally responsible.

Corporate Complicity: Aiding and Abetting Standards Under the ATCA

Most plaintiffs disavow the argument that merely investing in or establishing operations in a country in which human rights violations are common will subject a corporation to ATCA liability. In most of the cases, the claims are rather that the corporation's activities contribute to *specific* human rights violations in connection with *specific* projects for which corporations should be held accountable. The federal courts have been called upon to apply international law and domestic standards of accomplice and vicarious liability.[41]

The *Unocal* case, as the corporate complicity case furthest along in the judicial process, provides a good illustration of these issues. While Unocal claims not to have actively pursued forced labor or participated directly in specific human rights violations, the courts have found that there was evidence that Unocal had extensive notice that such abuses would occur and were occurring in connection with the project and that Unocal received the benefits of those abuses. The judicial battleground has concerned whether Unocal's financial and other involvement in the project, given its knowledge of human rights violations and benefits, are sufficient to make it responsible to the human rights victims as an aider and abettor or otherwise.[42]

In support of their claims that Unocal aided and abetted the human rights violations they suffered, the plaintiffs relied upon international and domestic law authorities, including precedents from the military tribunals that prosecuted German industrialists for their complicity in Nazi acts of genocide and war crimes, to provide the substantive standards of corporate complicity.[43] In the *Flick* case, for example, owners of a steel and coal factory had been found liable for seeking and utilizing slave labor provided by the Nazi regime. However, some of the defendants in the Nazi cases successfully argued a necessity defense, with the court finding that they had no choice in using forced labor, since any resistance would likely have resulted in punishment at the hands of the Nazis. The court reached similar holdings in the *Krauch* and *Krupp* cases regarding forced labor. The district judge in *Doe v. Unocal* read the Nuremberg precedents to hold that the international legal standard for corporate complicity was something more than knowledge of and benefit from human rights violations. Accordingly, the court formulated a doctrine of complicity that required plaintiffs to demonstrate that Unocal *actively* sought to use forced labor or "actively participated" in the human rights abuses.[44] In essence, the district judge found that Unocal's passivity in the face of knowledge that human rights abuses were occurring in connection with the project did not give rise to liability. Unocal could accept the benefits of forced labor and other human rights violations so long as it did not want or intend them to occur.[45]

On appeal, the Court of Appeals reversed the District Court's ruling on *Doe v. Unocal,* although the three-judge panel rendered a split decision. Two judges (Harry Pregerson and A. Wallace Tashima) found that the Nazi industrialist cases were not directly applicable because the "active participation" was formulated in the context of a necessity defense.[46] Because Unocal could not credibly claim a necessity defense (as no Unocal executive or employee was forced to accept forced labor under threat of imprisonment or violence), the Ninth Circuit rejected the "active participation" standard formulated by the district court.[47]

These judges found that the appropriate international law standard for aiding and abetting was better articulated in the setting of international criminal tribunals such as the International Criminal Tribunals for the former Yugoslavia and Rwanda (ICTY and ICTR). The best discussion of that standard is contained in the ICTY's decision in *Prosecutor v. Furundzija,* in which a military officer was found responsible for assault and rape committed by soldiers under his command.[48] The *Unocal* majority found that the standard for the *actus reus,* or act, of aiding or abetting derived from this case should be "knowing practical assistance or encouragement that has a substantial effect on the perpetration of the crime."[49] The majority also found that the applicable international law standard for *mens rea,* or mental state, was not an intent to commit the offense but rather knowledge that the offense would occur.[50] Under this standard, summary judgment was found to be inappropriate because evidence existed in the record that the Burmese military had utilized forced labor and committed other human rights violations in connection with the construction of the pipeline, and because Unocal had employed the military for security purposes, had directed the military in its execution of its security duties, and had demonstrated that it had known about the human rights violations.[51] In making these findings, the court looked to the language of contracts between the Burmese government and the project, to documents showing that the joint venture partners had told the military where to build helipads and roads, to reports by Unocal consultants and nongovernmental organizations warning of human rights abuses by the government, and to the testimony of numerous witnesses.[52]

Though concurring in the reversal of summary judgment in *Doe,* Judge Stephen Reinhardt disagreed with the majority's reliance on international criminal law authorities as the source of third-party liability rules. Instead, Reinhardt was of the view that federal common law principles developed in the United States, utilized in other major legal systems, and expressed in international treaties governing maritime and space law should govern this issue.[53] Reinhardt found that plaintiffs could rely on federal common law principles of joint venture, agency, and reckless disregard.[54]

The conflict between these approaches may be more apparent than real, because courts have often consulted international norms in fashioning federal common law responses to disputes as to the rules necessary to litigate ATCA cases.[55] Judge Reinhardt's reluctance to utilize rapidly developing international criminal law norms in this context is difficult to understand, given his willingness to employ international standards in finding that other federal common law principles were applicable to plaintiffs' claims. It seems likely that the courts will fashion federal common law rules governing third-party liability issued in ATCA cases with reference to both international and domestic standards. Crucially, however, the *Unocal* majority's analysis of aiding and abetting under international law is the most extensive yet in the corporate ATCA cases and the only appellate decision setting forth the crucial complicity standard for private-actor ATCA liability.[56]

The December 2004 settlement in the *Unocal* case includes the dismissal of the appeal before the *en banc* panel can rule on this issue. In November 2004, U.S. District Judge John E. Sprizzo dismissed all of the cases filed against corporations alleged to have been complicit in apartheid crimes in South Africa and specifically rejected aiding and abetting liability under the ATCA.[57]

The Jus Cogens *Argument*

Although no court has yet accepted the argument, ATCA corporate defendants have contended that the "law of nations" within the meaning of the ATCA extends only to *jus cogens,* or peremptory international, norms. A *jus cogens* norm refers to "the set of rules of law whose authority is so strong that it can be imposed on all states. . . . All states are under obligation to respect these rules, no matter what the conditions are in a country, and whether or not they have signed any international conventions."[58] If the ATCA were limited to violations of *jus cogens* norms, the scope of ATCA cases could be sharply limited. In the short run, this requirement, if imposed, would likely freeze the substantive development of ATCA litigation. Although most of the norms recognized as actionable in existing ATCA case law would qualify as *jus cogens* norms, at a minimum, arguments over whether particular norms had reached that status would become a standard feature in ATCA litigation. An *en banc* panel of eleven judges in the Ninth Circuit refused to accept this narrow reading of the ATCA's domain in the *Alvarez* case by calling the proposition an "imported restriction" on the language of the statute.[59]

Corporate Structure Arguments: Piercing the Corporate Veil

At the heart of Unocal's defense in the pending cases, and certain to be an issue in most corporate ATCA cases, is the claim that the real corporate culprit, if any, is a foreign subsidiary based in the country of the project or another country wherein it would be practically impossible for plaintiffs to bring an action. In the *Doe v. Unocal* case there are several layers of corporate structure that Unocal claims insulate the California-based parents from liability for human rights violations suffered by plaintiffs in connection with the pipeline project. So far, these issues have not been the subject of published opinions in ATCA cases and are still being hotly contested in a number of pending cases. The main legal issue presented so far has been whether the corporate veil of these subsidiaries should be pierced on behalf of human rights plaintiffs. When a court pierces a corporate veil, it means that it disregards the formal corporate structure, which may have insulated a corporate parent from liability, based upon a finding that the formal corporate structure is a façade or sham and that it would be an injustice to recognize the corporate form. A lurking question is whether such issues should be litigated based on traditional corporate veil-piercing principles (e.g., undercapitalization, fraud, etc.) or whether the courts will recognize that there is a fundamental conflict between corporate efforts to acquire an immunity by creating corporate shields for this purpose and the need to ensure accountability for gross human rights violations. In January 2004 the state court judge in *Doe/Roe v. Unocal* refused to pierce the corporate veil of Unocal's subsidiaries, using traditional alter ego principles.[60]

State Action

Another issue that has arisen in corporate ATCA cases is the extent to which defendants may be said to be acting under color of official authority where international norms (e.g., the prohibition against torture) require a connection to government action. As noted above, many international norms (e.g., genocide, piracy, slaverylike practices) do not require state action. So far, courts confronting this issue in ATCA cases have used color of law jurisprudence developed under federal civil rights law,[61] by analogy, to find that private actors that perpetrate human rights abuses in cooperation with states or de facto states satisfy ATCA's state action requirement.[62] Under this standard, a private corporation will be found liable if it willfully acts together with state officials or with significant state aid.[63] In *Doe v. Unocal,* the district judge found that plaintiffs have to show that Unocal somehow "controlled" the military's commission of human rights violations in order to show state action.[64] Such a requirement would be nearly impossible to meet if accepted by the courts. The initial *Doe v. Unocal* panel avoided this issue by finding that Unocal would be liable for all human rights violations, including torture, if such violations occurred as part of a pattern and practice of forced labor, a violation not requiring that any state action be shown. The "control" cases relied upon by the district court in *Doe v. Unocal* arise in the very different domestic context of requests by private parties for police protection and in which officers are accused of misconduct. In *Doe v. Unocal,* the relationship between the military and the joint venture partners was not of this model.

Act of State Doctrine

The act of state doctrine has been raised as a defense in almost every ATCA case arising out of actions occurring outside the United States. The act of state doctrine is a judge-made doctrine providing that U.S. courts will not sit in judgment of the sovereign acts of another nation committed within their own territory.[65] The basis of the doctrine is international comity, a "courtesy" or respect one court shows to political entities of another nation-state, and the desire of the courts, based upon separation of powers concerns, to avoid making pronouncements that may embarrass the executive branch in its exercise of its foreign affairs powers. The courts have rejected the application of the act of state doctrine in ATCA cases mainly on the grounds that it should not be applied when the courts are being asked to enforce universally accepted international human rights norms. The only reported ATCA case in which the act of state doctrine was applied to dismiss a claim is *Roe v Unocal*,[66] in which the claims of a former soldier against Unocal for its complicity in forced labor were rejected because the court found that a government's ability to instruct its military personnel was unreviewable.

The political question doctrine is a similar judge-made prudential doctrine under which federal courts may refuse to hear cases otherwise properly before them, if the dispute requires the court to pass judgment on matters reserved for the political branches of government. This rarely invoked doctrine finds its roots both in separation of powers concerns and in concerns about judicial competence to resolve certain types of controversies. The U.S. Supreme Court has made it clear, though, that not every controversy touching on foreign relations is a "political" question.[67] Because of the limited scope of the political question doctrine, it has not been a serious impediment to ATCA cases so far. Judge Roger Robb relied upon the political question doctrine in his opinion concurring in the affirmance of the dismissal of the plaintiffs' claims in the *Tel Oren v. Libyan Arab Republic* case.[68] No ATCA case had been resolved based on this doctrine until March 2002, when a district court in Los Angeles dismissed, based on political question grounds, all claims against the Rio Tinto mining company in an ATCA case arising out of Papua New Guinea (PNG) because the case was said to interfere with U.S. efforts to achieve peace and stability in that country. However, the court dismissed the case only after insisting on the PNG government's written consent to the lawsuit's proceeding in PNG courts and the waiver of defenses to the litigation of the claims in PNG courts.[69] This decision is now on appeal in the Ninth Circuit.

Forum Non Conveniens *Doctrine*

ATCA cases involving foreign plaintiffs suing foreign defendants for harms occurring in a foreign country have the highest risk of being dismissed based on the *forum non conveniens* doctrine. A court applies a *forum non conveniens* analysis to decide whether there is an adequate alternative forum to try the matter in another jurisdiction or country and, if so, which forum will best serve public and private interests. In ATCA corporate cases, especially those against foreign corporations, *forum non conveniens* arguments and arguments that U.S. courts lack personal jurisdiction are likely to be standard fare. In *Doe v. Unocal,* for example, the French company Total was found not to be amenable to suit in a U.S. court, because the court found that its U.S. subsidiaries were not involved in the Burma/Myanmar project and there were insufficient contacts with California to allow Total to be sued there. In *Wiwa v. Royal Dutch Petroleum,* however, the Second Circuit found that a lawsuit could be brought against Shell, a British-Dutch company, in a New York court, given that the company was traded on the New York Stock Exchange and that Shell maintained an office in the city.[70] This ruling could prove especially important for future cases.

*   *   *

In sum, the case law to date indicates that a successful ATCA claim against a corporation for human rights violations has to pass several legal and procedural thresholds. First, the plaintiff must be a non-U.S. citizen, the subject of the case must be a tort, and the claim must be based on a violation of a specific customary international law. In addition, the plaintiff must overcome an array of procedural and substantive barriers to jurisdiction and liability, including the doctrines discussed above.[71] Some ATCA claims (e.g., torture) will require proof of an adequate connection to governmental action. Moreover, the standard for corporate complicity, direct or vicarious, is still unclear; however, it appears that aiding and abetting, conspiracy, joint venture, reckless disregard, and vicarious theories of liability are likely to be available in corporate complicity cases. The exact tests and scope of these theories will be determined in the first wave of corporate ATCA cases now percolating through the courts. It seems likely that this area of law will remain in a state of flux until a number of appellate opinions accumulate or the Supreme Court decides one of these cases.

Application of the TVPA and Other Statutory and Common Law Norms for Corporate Accountability

In addition to the ATCA, there are several other potential vehicles available to those seeking to hold corporations accountable for human rights violations. Congressional support for ATCA actions on behalf of human rights led to the passage in 1992 of the Torture Victims Protection Act (TVPA), which extended ATCA-like jurisdiction to U.S. citizen plaintiffs claiming torture or extrajudicial execution if committed under the color of foreign authority; the act also demonstrated legislative approval of the *Filártiga* line of cases.[72] The TVPA has been successfully applied to private actors, including corporations and their officials. Two district courts, each in the context of cases arising out of repression of union activities in Colombia, have decided this issue, finding that the TVPA was intended to encompass corporate complicity in torture or extrajudicial killings.[73] In both cases, the defendants attempted to argue that the use of the word *individual* in the TVPA's statutory language was meant to refer only to natural persons.[74] The courts rejected the argument based on a decision of the Supreme Court that found *individual* to be synonymous with the legal definition of "person" and thereby applicable to corporate entities.[75] Further, the courts found that there was no legislative history indicating any intent to exempt corporations from the reach of the statute.[76] These cases effectively reject the suggestion in an earlier case that the TVPA did not apply to corporations, though corporate defendants continue to make this argument.[77]

In addition to the TVPA, other statutes may operate to hold corporations civilly liable for human rights abuses. At the federal level, the Racketeer Influenced Corrupt Organizations Act (RICO) provides a civil remedy to persons injured by other persons or organizations that commit any action or threat—more than once and in a way that affects interstate commerce—involving murder, kidnapping, gambling, arson, robbery, bribery, extortion, dealing in an obscene matter, or dealing in a controlled substance. As well, an organization or person can be charged with violating RICO for conspiring to commit any of these acts. Plaintiffs bringing ATCA claims against corporations often also bring RICO claims, though it is unclear whether the courts will apply RICO in this context.[78]

At the state level, California's business and professional code provides civil remedies to persons injured by a corporation's use of unfair business practices in the context of a claim that a company falsely advertised its allegedly positive human rights record.[79] In *Doe v. Unocal,* a demurrer (motion to dismiss) to this claim in the state court action was overruled. Similarly, many ATCA plaintiffs also make claims based on state tort law, such as wrongful death and intentional and negligent infliction of emotional distress. The *Doe v. Unocal* state court action is the most advanced of these actions in that the first phase of the trial has been completed. Corporate defendants have argued that attempts to use state tort law to remedy human rights violations committed abroad are preempted by federal law. This argument was rejected in *Doe v. Unocal* but likely will be raised on appeal, as well as by defendants in other cases.[80] If the courts reject or limit the use of the ATCA in corporate cases, it is certain that many of these cases will instead be filed in state courts alleging state law claims.

Availability of ATCA-Like Remedies in Other Countries

An examination of the domestic corporate accountability regimes in the world is beyond the scope of this chapter.[81] Most states that actively participate in foreign business ventures with corporations have enacted regulatory legislation and are parties to international agreements for the purpose of regulating corporate activities within and outside their borders. However, there appear to be few available judicial remedies in most municipal law regimes for torts committed by business organizations or their agents outside their borders. Rather, most mechanisms for corporate accountability are limited to subjects other than human rights (e.g., taxation, transfer pricing, or competition).

Even without developing specific human rights legislation to regulate extraterritorial corporate conduct, some countries have applied existing municipal remedies in ways analogous to ATCA jurisprudence.[82] For example, in *Al-Adsani v. Government of Kuwait,* an English court entertained a civil lawsuit by a Kuwaiti citizen who had been tortured by Kuwaiti officials.[83] As in an ATCA case, the plaintiff sought civil damages. However, the case differed from an ATCA case in that it based its claims on the continuing mental anguish the plaintiff experienced while in England, rather than the injuries he had suffered abroad. Even so, the mental anguish claim in effect required litigation of, and damages based on, the victim's torture, which had occurred in Kuwait. In the event, however, the lawsuit was dismissed on immunity grounds despite arguments that immunity should not apply in the context of the violation of *jus cogens* norms like the prohibition against torture.[84]

Other states have also applied domestic tort law to the extraterritorial conduct of their corporations.[85] In Canada, an action was filed against Cambior, a mining company, based on environmental damages from the collapse of a dam in Guyana. Similar litigation reached settlement in Australia, based on a dam collapse in Papua New Guinea.[86] In England, a major suit was filed by South African miners who claimed that Cape, a UK-based mining company, was responsible for their contraction of asbestos-related illnesses.[87] In France, plaintiffs have begun to seek legal action against Total, Unocal's partner in the controversial Burmese oil project, following the dismissal of a case against Total in U.S. courts on jurisdictional grounds.[88] A criminal case against Total is also being pursued in Belgium.[89]

As with the ATCA, in all of these cases a number of legal restrictions, especially *forum non conveniens,* remain substantial hurdles to plaintiff recovery.[90] The Canadian courts ultimately dismissed the *Cambior* case based on the finding that Guyana was a superior forum.[91] The English courts eventually dismissed the *Al-Adsani* case on grounds of Kuwait's sovereign immunity. Other extraterritorial tort claims are discouraged because the legal system will not recognize a tort unless it would be recognized in the courts of the jurisdiction where it occurred.[92] Nevertheless, although there are relatively few international examples, the use of international law in domestic court appears to be on the rise, and it can be expected that future international litigation initiatives will occur.

The Specter of ATCA Repeal

Until the 1990s, the use of the ATCA to redress international human rights violations where perpetrators were found in the United States met with little objection except among a handful of academics and a few federal judges.[93] With the increasing number of corporate ATCA cases, however, and in the changed context of the U.S. "war on terror" following the terrorist attacks of September 11, 2001, companies, business lobbies, and the U.S. government have begun a concerted campaign to reform or repeal the ATCA. These efforts have proceeded along two tracks: (1) comprehensive legislative reform or repeal and (2) political interventions by the U.S. State Department to have particular cases dropped.

Legislative Reform or Repeal

In a widely reported meeting held just after the midterm U.S. elections in November 2002, a coalition of multinational companies came together to seek legislative "reform" of the ATCA.[94] This strategy may be seen as one part of the so-called tort reform movement, which seeks reform of class actions generally.[95] These efforts may also relate to prior efforts by the federal government to limit the authority of state and local governments to impose sanctions on companies within their jurisdictions that conduct business with repressive regimes, especially with the military dictatorship in Burma/Myanmar.[96]

This effort appears to be motivated by a belief among corporations and business groups that the Bush administration may be willing to support legislative efforts to obtain corporate immunity from human rights claims. There appears to be little merit to arguments that the ATCA should be reformed or repealed because the courts have been unwilling or unable to weed out insubstantial or frivolous claims or arguments that the courts have treated corporations unfairly in ATCA cases. Application of the ATCA in corporate complicity cases has not developed to the point where any firm conclusions can be made either way. Even so, there is no reason to believe that the courts would not reject insubstantial claims of corporate complicity. As the Second Circuit's decision in the *Flores* case demonstrates, the courts have been very reluctant to accept claims in ATCA cases that go beyond very well established international norms like prohibitions against torture, crimes against humanity, extrajudicial killings, and genocide. It is very likely that any insubstantial or frivolous claims would be handled easily by the judiciary using well-established procedures.

At the time of this writing, no legislative proposals to reform or repeal the ATCA have been introduced in either the House or the Senate. The Bush administration has made it clear in its arguments to the Supreme Court in the *Alvarez* case that it is seeking what amounts to a judicial repeal of the ATCA. However, the administration has made no legislative proposals to date. Thus it is premature to comment about what form such legislative proposals might take and what their chances of success might be. In the wake of the corporate scandals of 2002, most notably the Enron debacle, the corporate community may find it difficult to persuade Congress that it requires blanket immunity from alleged complicity in gross human rights violations. On the other hand, a wave of litigation brought against an array of corporations for their alleged complicity in apartheid in South Africa may be used as the poster child for such legislative efforts, in large part because of the vocal opposition to such suits by the South African government and business community.[97] In raising the specter of repeal, the U.S. business community may use the ATCA apartheid cases to assert that the ATCA as a human rights tool is overbroad, disrespects other countries' internal justice systems, and invites frivolous suits.[98] The existence of South Africa's Truth and Reconciliation Commission and the process of reconciliation it oversaw also raise issues distinct from most of the other ATCA cases now pending against corporations, because potential plaintiffs in South Africa have had a forum within the country that was developed specifically to address crimes arising from apartheid. To date there have been no substantive rulings in the South African cases.

Political Interventions

Apart from legislative repeal or "reform" efforts, in many of the pending corporate ATCA cases, corporate defendants have approached the executive branch of the U.S. government seeking letters from the State Department to advise the courts that foreign policy concerns should prevent a particular case from proceeding. The first, and so far only, successful use of this tactic occurred in the *Rio Tinto* case, wherein the State Department submitted a letter urging dismissal of the case and the district judge agreed to do on political question grounds.[99] In *Doe v. Unocal,* the district judge consulted the State Department on his own initiative at the motion-to-dismiss stage. The State Department issued a letter indicating that the case could proceed without impairing U.S. foreign policy. The State Department issued a similar letter at the end of December 2004 in *Mujica v. Occidental Petroleum*

Co. District Judge William Rea issued a tentative ruling in January 2005 suggesting that he was prepared to dismiss the action in deference to the State Department letter, but asked for additional briefing. As of this writing, Judge Rea had not issued a final ruling. In 2003 the State Department, citing Indonesia's crucial role as an ally in the "war against terror," issued a letter seeking the dismissal of another case pending in the D.C. Circuit against ExxonMobil for its complicity in human rights abuses in the Indonesian province of Aceh. At the time of this writing, the district judge had not ruled on the pending motion to dismiss in that action.

In addition to the State Department letters, the executive branch has revived its practice of weighing in on pending ATCA cases through the *amicus* process, wherein persons not party to the suit file a brief in the action because of strong interest in the subject matter. The Justice Department's *amicus* brief in the *Marcos* litigation, for example, sought to convince the court that the ATCA was merely a jurisdictional statute that required further congressional action before it could be used as the basis for lawsuits.[100] In *Kadic,* the Clinton administration returned to its *Filártiga* position and supported the application of the ATCA to the human rights and humanitarian violations alleged against Bosnian Serb leader Radovan Karadzic. Later, however, the Bush administration intervened in *Doe v. Unocal,* reversing the government's stance once again. In its argument to the Supreme Court in the *Alvarez* case, the Bush administration maintained that the ATCA is merely a jurisdictional statute without any contemporary relevance and that Congress must act to implement the ATCA before plaintiffs may bring international law claims in U.S. courts. It seems likely that corporations will continue to seek case-by-case immunity from the State Department via letters or the Justice Department via *amicus* briefs in these cases, though it is less clear whether the courts will automatically defer to the executive branch's views and render the ATCA an illusory promise.

If the ATCA is repealed, legislatively or judiciously, it will not end human rights litigation to hold corporations responsible for their actions. Litigation will continue to be used as an enforcement tool. The human rights movement has become more active in recognizing and protesting the abuse of corporate power in the contexts discussed here. An assault on the ATCA will serve only to intensify this scrutiny. No matter how the Supreme Court decides the *Alvarez* case, there will be further attempts to find a legislative solution. At the *Alvarez* argument on March 30, 2004, at least one justice (Sandra Day O'Connor) suggested that the issues before the court should be resolved by Congress.[101]

The state court action in *Doe v. Unocal* illustrates what would likely happen were the ATCA to be repealed. Corporations, especially U.S. corporations, will remain subject to legal action in state courts for the torts they commit or are complicit in abroad. Though corporations would argue that such actions are preempted by federal law, it seems unlikely that the Supreme Court would accept the argument that the ATCA has no contemporary meaning while at the same time accepting that the ATCA preempts all attempts by state legislatures and courts to hold corporations accountable for their complicity in serious human rights violations abroad. One of the obvious benefits of the ATCA is that it allows the application of uniform national standards by federal courts where violations of international law are at stake. Corporations should think twice before committing to the repeal of the ATCA, because they may like the state court litigation process even less.

Conclusion

Lawsuits brought under the ATCA and TVPA for corporate complicity in human rights violations offer an available and effective remedy to victims in circumstances where few such remedies are available. It is mainly the absence of equally effective remedies outside the United States that has led to a "wave" of litigation since the early 1990s. Clearly, a more effective international remedial system would be preferable to such litigation. It can only be hoped that ATCA litigation will inspire such global efforts. However, in the short term, the ATCA offers the only hope that victims of corporate complicity currently have for overcoming the impunity with which some multinational corporations operate, without regard to the human rights consequences of their actions.

Addendum

This chapter was completed before the Supreme Court's June 2004 decision in *Sosa v. Alvarez-Machain*.[102] In *Sosa,* although the Court denied *Alvarez's* particular claim, the Court ratified the *Filártiga* doctrine that the ATCA opens the doors of the federal courts to victims of violations of at least some widely accepted norms of international law.

In particular, the Court, over Justice Scalia's vehement dissent, endorsed the approach of dozens of federal courts—including the Ninth Circuit's analysis in *In re Estate of Marcos Human Rights Litigation,*[103] and the *Filártiga* decision that plaintiffs may pursue claims for violations of international norms that are "specific, universal, and obligatory."[104]

Justice Souter, joined by six justices, wrote the opinion for the Court accepting the government's view that the ATCA creates only jurisdiction and not a cause of action. However, for the Court this was not the end of analysis.

The Court recognized that the founders had intended to enforce the "law of nations" when the first Congress enacted the Alien Tort Claims Act in 1789. The Court was persuaded by the historical evidence that Congress did not believe it was necessary to enact separate implementing legislation before the federal courts could hear and decide such claims.

Having accepted that premise, the issue for the Court was translating this intent from the eighteenth-century world in which only a handful of "law of nations" violations were actionable.[105] "The reasonable inference is that the statute [the ATCA] was intended to have practical effect the moment it became law."[106] Although the Court determined that nothing in the intervening 215 years since the passage of the First Judiciary Act precluded federal courts from recognizing such common law claims, the Court decided that the federal courts should require such claims to "rest on a norm of international character accepted by the civilized world and defined with a specificity comparable to the features of the eighteenth century paradigms we have recognized."

The *Sosa* Court did not address corporate liability cases directly, nor did it address the existence or scope of vicarious or secondary theories of liability under the ATCA, leaving these issues to be litigated in the lower federal courts. The most direct reference to any of the corporate human rights cases is in footnote 21, in which Justice Souter refers to the letters submitted by the South African government and the U.S. State Department in the apartheid cases, suggesting that this case might be an appropriate one for "case specific" deference to the political branches. Given the Bush administration's opposition to the ATCA generally and to corporate complicity cases brought under the ATCA specifically, it seems likely that the State Department will issue many letters seeking "case specific deference" in ATCA cases and the courts will have to decide whether the executive branch is entitled to control the litigation of such claims in U.S. courts. As of this writing there are no appellate decisions examining this crucial issue.

Notes

I wish to thank Daniel Zaheer, Abigail Reyes, and Melanie Partrow for their contributions to this chapter, and Jennifer Green and William Aceves for their helpful comments.
    1. See *Doe v. Unocal,* 110 F. Supp. 2d 1294, 1295–1296 (2000).
    2. See, for example, *Filártiga v. Peña-Irala,* 630 F. 2d 876 (2d Cir. 1980); *Hilao v. Estate of Marcos,* 25 F. 3d 1467 (9th Cir. 1994), *cert. denied,* 513 U.S. 1226 (1995); *Abebe-Jira v. Negewo,* 72 F. 3d 844 (11th Cir. 1995), *cert. denied,* 519 U.S. 830 (1996); *Mehinovich v. Vukovic,* 198 F. Supp. 2d 1322 (N.D. Ga. 2002), a civil judgment entered against a Bosnian war criminal for war crimes and crimes against humanity.

3. See, for example, *Royal Dutch Petroleum Co. v. Wiwa,* 532 U.S. 941 (2001), denial of petition for certiorari; *Karadzic v. Kadic,* 518 U.S. 1005 (1996), same; *Estate of Marcos v. Hilao,* 513 U.S. 1126 (1995), same; *Tel-Oren v. Libyan Arab Republic,* 470 U.S. 1003 (1985), same.

4. This chapter will not address the large number of cases that have been filed seeking to redress human rights and other wrongs committed in the Holocaust. For a comprehensive overview of those cases, see Michael J. Bazyler, "Nuremberg in America: Litigating the Holocaust in U.S. Courts," *University of Richmond Law Review* 34, no.1 (2000): 1–283.

5. See United Nations, "Norms on the Responsibilities of Transnational Corporations and Other Business Enterprises with Regard to Human Rights," E/CN.4/Sub.2/2003/12/Rev.2 (2003), available at www1.umn.edu/humanrts/links/norms-Aug2003.html. The UN Subcommission on Human Rights approved theses norms on August 13, 2003. See also International Council on Human Rights Policy (ICHRP), *Beyond Voluntarism: Human Rights and the Developing International Legal Obligations of Companies* (Geneva: ICHRP, 2002), pp. 121–141.

6. See Jeff Gerth, "U.S. and Oil Companies Revised Effort on Disclosure," *New York Times,* September 19, 2003, p. W1.

7. The ATCA is codified at 28 U.S.C. sec. 1350. The "treaty" clause of the ATCA is seldom used in human rights cases, because the United States ratified very few human rights treaties before the 1990s, and when it did, it attached declarations that the treaties should be considered "non-self-executing."

8. For a discussion of U.S. laws relating to criminal prosecution of human rights offenders, see William Aceves and Paul Hoffman, "Pursuing Crimes against Humanity in the United States: The Need for a Comprehensive Regime," in Philippe Sands and Mark Lattimer, eds., *Justice for Crimes against Humanity: International Law after Pinochet* (Oxford: Hart, 2004), pp. 239–270.

9. U.S. citizens must either bring claims under the 1992 Torture Victims Protection Act (discussed later in the chapter) or seek to establish subject-matter jurisdiction under general federal question jurisdiction, 28 U.S.C. sec. 1331. These issues are beyond the scope of this chapter. See Beth Stephens and Michael Ratner, *International Human Rights Litigation in U.S. Courts* (Ardsley, N.Y.: Transnational, 1996), pp. 31–40, 130.

10. The residence of the alien plaintiffs or their lack of contacts may be relevant in a *forum non conveniens* analysis, discussed later in the chapter.

11. See, for example, *Iwanowa v. Ford Motor,* 67 F. Supp. 2d 424, 462, n. 44 (D.C. N.J. 1999), finding a claim for restitution by survivor of Nazi-era forced labor barred under the ATCA because the restitution claim sounds *in quantum meruit,* not tort, and seeks recovery for a breach of implied contract; *Moxon v. The Fanny,* 17 F. Cas. 942 (1793), ruling that ATCA was not available where plaintiff sought restitution of property, in this case slaves.

12. *Argentine Republic v. Amarada-Hess,* 488 U.S. 428 (1989). Foreign sovereigns can be sued in U.S. courts for human rights violations committed within the United States. See, for example, *Liu v. Republic of China,* 892 F. 2d 1419, 1424 (9th Cir. 1989); *Letelier v. Republic of Chile,* 748 F. 2d 790 (2d Cir. 1984). For an unusual case allowing FSIA jurisdiction for human rights violations committed in Argentina, see *Siderman v. Republic of Argentina,* 965 F. 2d 699 (9th Cir. 1992). In *Siderman,* immunity was denied primarily because Argentina was found to have waived its sovereign immunity by pursuing legal action against Siderman in the United States (ibid., at 720–723). The FSIA would apply to state-owned enterprises.

See, for example, *Callejo v. Bancomer, SA,* 764 F. 2d 1101 (5th Cir. 1985); 28 U.S.C. sec. 1603(b).

13. Whether individual U.S. officials can be sued under the ATCA is still an open question. In *Alvarez-Machain v. United States,* 331 F. 3d, at 631, the Ninth Circuit held that the United States could substitute itself as a defendant under the Westfall Act with respect to ATCA claims brought against individual U.S. officials claimed to have violated international human rights norms. Such substitution would lead to the dismissal of the ATCA claims because they are not cognizable as such under the Federal Tort Claims Act (FTCA). A plaintiff might still prevail on a tort theory under the FTCA, as was the case on appeal in *Alvarez.* See *Jama v. INS,* 22 F. Supp. 353 (D.N.J. 1998), for a different result. If the *Alvarez* view is followed, the ATCA would be unavailable for claims against federal officials but would still be available for claims against state and local officials. See *Martinez v. City of Los Angeles,* 141 F. 3d 1373 (9th Cir. 1998).

14. *Hilao v. Estate of Marcos,* 25 F. 3d 1467, 1475 (9th Cir. 1994). The formulation differs slightly in other circuits but appears to be the same substantive test. The Second Circuit requires a "well established, universally recognized" norm of international law for ATCA jurisdiction. *Filártiga,* 630 F. 2d, at 888.

15. Common Article Three of the Geneva Conventions of 1949 contains a list of prohibited conduct (e.g., murder, torture) that applies in all forms of armed conflict, including internal armed conflicts. The application of Common Article Three in ATCA cases is important because many of the cases arise out of armed conflicts that would not be characterized as international armed conflicts and thus other provisions of the Geneva Conventions may not apply.

16. *Presbyterian Church of Sudan v. Talisman Energy Inc.,* 244 F. Supp. 2d 289 (S.D. N.Y. 2003), slavery, genocide, extrajudicial killing, torture; *Kadic v. Karadzic,* 70 F. 3d 232, 244 (1995), genocide, war crimes, crimes against humanity; *Forti v. Suarez Mason,* 694 F. Supp. 707 (N.D. Cal. 1988) *[Forti II],* disappearance; *Forti v. Suarez Mason,* 672 F. Supp. 1531 (N.D. Cal. 1987) *[Forti I],* prolonged arbitrary detention, summary execution; *Filártiga,* 630 F. 2d, at 884, torture.

17. See *Forti II,* 694 F. Supp. 707, 709. But see *Abebe-Jira v. Negewo,* 72 F. 3d 844 (11th Cir. 1995). There are many other cases in which the courts have found that the particular allegations do not fall within established international human rights norms. See, for example, *Martinez v. City of Los Angeles,* 141 F. 3d 1373, 1384 (9th Cir. 1998), in which the plaintiff's claims were found not to be "arbitrary arrest or detention" as a matter of law.

18. For an extensive analysis of the historical underpinnings of the ATCA, see Kenneth C. Randall, "Federal Jurisdiction over International Law Claims: Inquiries into the Alien Tort Statute," *New York University Journal of International Law and Politics* 18, no. 1 (1985): 1–72; William S. Dodge, "The Historical Origins of the Alien Tort Statute: 'A Response to the Originists,'" *Hastings International and Comparative Law Review* 19, rev. 221 (1996): 221–258.

19. 630 F. 2d 876 (2d Cir. 1980). The literature about the *Filártiga* case and its progeny is vast. See, for example, Ralph Steinhardt and Anthony D'Amato, eds., *The Alien Tort Claims Act: An Analytical Anthology* (Ardsley, N.Y.: Transnational, 1999); and Stephens and Ratner, *International Human Rights Litigation in U.S. Courts.* Regular updates on ATCA litigation appear annually in the *International Civil Liberties Report* of the American Civil Liberties Union (ACLU), which may be found on the national ACLU website, www.aclu.org.

20. See *Filártiga,* 630 F. 2d, at 878.

21. Ibid., at 881.

22. Ibid., at 884–885. Significantly, the court relied on a series of international treaties that had not been ratified by the United States, as well as a variety of other evidence of the stated practice of nations and *opinio juris*. The U.S. government filed an amicus brief in which it informed the court that no nation took the position that torture was a permissible way to treat persons within its jurisdiction, notwithstanding the existence of torture in the world. Memorandum for the United States as Amicus Curiae, *Filártiga v. Peña-Irala,* 630 F. 2d 876 (2d Cir. 1980), reprinted in 19 I.L.M. 585 (1980).

23. *Kadic v. Karadzic,* 70 F. 3d 232, 241–244 (1995).

24. The corporate ATCA cases have generated considerable academic commentary. See, for example, Steven R. Ratner, "Corporations and Human Rights: A Theory of Legal Responsibility," *Yale Law Journal* 111, no. 3 (2001): 443–545; Anita Ramasastry, "Corporate Complicity: From Nuremberg to Rangoon; An Examination of Forced Labor Cases and Their Impact on the Liability of Multinational Corporations," *Berkeley Journal of International Law* 20, no. 1 (2002): 91–159.

25. Andrew Clapham, *Human Rights in the Private Sphere* (Oxford: Oxford University Press, 1998). In principle, there should be no difference between corporations and private individuals in terms of ATCA liability. In practice, one of the significant issues in the corporate ATCA cases has been whether parent corporations may be found liable for acts they claim are the responsibility of their foreign subsidiaries. These corporate structure issues are discussed later in the chapter.

26. *Doe v. Unocal,* 963 F. Supp. 880 (C.D. Cal. 1997); *National Coalition Gov't of Burma/Myanmar v. Unocal,* 176 F.R.D. 329 (C.D. Cal. 1997). Both the *Doe* and *Roe* cases were filed in federal court and made similar claims. In 2000 the *Doe* and *Roe* plaintiffs also filed complaints in California courts, raising similar state tort claims. The lawsuits are referred to as *Doe v. Unocal* herein.

27. Corporate ATCA cases have been filed in other situations too, including claims of historical injustice. Claims have been made against corporations that utilized forced labor during World War II. See, for example, *Iwanowa v. Ford Motor Co.,* 67 F. Supp. 2d 424 (D. N.J. 1999). Others involve banks that aided and abetted the Holocaust or apartheid either by facilitating the seizure of stolen assets or by financing the abusive practices. See, for example, *Badner v. Banque Paribas,* 114 F. Supp. 2d 117 (E.D. N.Y. 2000). Some of the complaints in the apartheid suits have pointed to computer and insurance companies that allegedly facilitated the South African apartheid regime's activities.

28. See *Galvis v. Occidental Petroleum* (filed in C.D. Cal. 2003), complaint posted at www.sdshh.com, Occidental in Colombia; *Presbyterian Church of Sudan v. Talisman Energy,* 2003 U.S. Dist. LEXIS 4083 (S.D. N.Y. 2003), Talisman in Sudan; *Bowoto v. Chevron,* Case no. C99-2506 (filed in N.D. Cal. 2002), complaint at www.earthrights.org/chevron/4thamendedcomplaint.doc, Chevron in Nigeria; *Doe v. Exxon Mobil Corp,* Case no. O1-CV-1357, complaint at www.laborrights. org/projects/corporate/exxon/exxoncomplaint.pdf, Exxon Mobil in Indonesia; *Wiwa v. Royal Dutch Petroleum,* 226 F. 3d 88 (2d Cir. 2000), Shell in Nigeria.

29. The corporate human rights cases contain what may be termed direct liability theories (e.g., aiding and abetting). The distinction here is between cases in which a corporation's employees directly commit the violations and cases in which the claim is that the corporation was complicit in human rights violations committed directly by government officers, employees, or soldiers.

30. See text accompanying notes 12–14.

31. 303 F. 3d 470 (2d Cir. 2002).

32. Proceedings on the plaintiffs' claims were considered in an Ecuadorian court in early 2004. Information about these proceedings is available from Amazon Watch (www.amazonwatch.org). The *forum non conveniens* doctrine is based on the idea that it would be more appropriate to have a certain case heard in another jurisdiction based on a consideration of relevant factors (e.g., access to evidence, convenience of witnesses, etc.).

33. 253 F. Supp. 510 (S.D. N.Y. 2002).

34. A similar result was reached in *Beanal v. Freeport-McMoran Inc.*, 197 F. 3d 161 (5th Cir. 1999).

35. 2003 U.S. App. LEXIS 18098 (2d Cir. 2003).

36. A new and perhaps developing use of the ATCA against corporate entities can be found in *Abdullahi v. Pfizer*, 2002 U.S. Dist. LEXIS 17436 (S.D. N.Y. 2002). There children in Nigeria claimed that Pfizer, a U.S. pharmaceutical corporation, failed to seek informed consent from their parents before including the children in a trial of a new drug that the company knew caused serious joint and liver damage. The plaintiffs also argued that the Nigerian government had participated in the harms by authorizing Pfizer to conduct the study. The court, although dismissing the case on *forum non conveniens* grounds, found that the involvement of the Nigerian government allowed the families to state a claim under the law of nations. *Abdullahi* may signify a new trend in ATCA cases in which courts will entertain product liability–like causes of actions.

37. 226 F. 3d 88 (2d Cir. 2000).

38. In *Bowoto v. Chevron,* similar claims are being made by residents of the Niger Delta against Chevron for its complicity in killings and other human rights violations committed by the Nigerian military against those protesting environmental degradation caused by Chevron's oil operations. On March 23, 2004, the district judge in Bowoto denied Chevron's motion for summary judgment and allowed plaintiffs to proceed on agency, aiding and abetting, and ratification theories.

39. *Villeda v. Del Monte,* filed before S.D. Fla., Case no. 01-3399. Complaint available at www.laborrights.org/projects/corporate/delmonte/DelCOMPFINAL. pdf. See also *Sinaltrainal v. Coca-Cola,* 256 F. Supp. 2d 1345 (S.D. Fla. 2003), allegations that Coke used paramilitaries to murder, torture, and detain union leaders; *Estate of Rodriguez v. Drummond Co.,* 256 F. Supp 2d 1250 (N.D. Ala. 2003), allegations that this Alabama mining company hired paramilitaries to torture, kidnap, and murder union leaders in Colombia.

40. 244 F. Supp. 2d 289, 308 (S.D. N.Y. 2003).

41. For a discussion of criminal and civil standards of liability, from direct participation to acceptance of benefits, for corporations complicit in human rights abuses, see ICHRP, *Beyond Voluntarism,* pp. 121–141. See also Ramasastry, "Corporate Complicity."

42. This question is also raised in an analysis of a potential liability of the South African diamond company De Beers under the ATCA for its trade in so-called conflict diamonds in West Africa. See Lucinda Saunders, "Rich and Rare Are the Gems They War: Holding De Beers Accountable for Trading Conflict Diamonds," *Fordham International Law Journal* 24, no. 4 (2001): 1402–1476.

43. Plaintiffs cited a number of treaties and other sources of positive law. See Statute of the International Criminal Tribunal for the Former Yugoslavia, S/RES/8271 993, reprinted in 32 I.L.M. 1192 (1993), at art. 7; Convention against Torture and Other Cruel, Inhuman, or Degrading Treatment or Punishment, G.A. Res. 39/46, 39 U.N. GAOR (No. 51) (1984), arts. 1, 4; Convention on Combating Bribery of Foreign Public Officials in International Business Transactions, reprinted

in 37 I.L.M. 1 (1998), art. 1(2); Supplementary Convention on the Abolition of Slavery, 266 U.N.T.S. 3 (1956), art. 6. Plaintiffs also relied on several international cases in support of their position on the standard of aiding and abetting liability. See *Prosecutor v. Furundzija,* Case no. IT-95-17/1/T, reprinted in 38 I.L.M. 817 (1999); *Prosecutor v. Delia,* Case no. IT-96-21 (November 17, 1998); *Prosecutor v. Akayesu,* Case no. ICTR-96-4-T (1998); *U.S. v. Krauch,* Eight Trials of War Criminals Before the Nuremberg Military Tribunals Under Control Council Law no. 10, 1081, 1169–1172 (1952); *U.S. v. Friederich Flick,* Six Trials of War Criminals before the Nuremberg Military Tribunals under Control Council Law no. 10, 1, 1216–1223 (1949); *in re Tesch,* 13 Int'l L. Rep. 250 (Br. Mil. Ct. 1946). In addition, the plaintiffs claimed that domestic tort principles of aiding and abetting liability were substantially similar to the international standards. See, for example, Restatement of Torts, sec. 876(b).

44. See *Doe I v. Unocal Corp.,* 110 F. Supp. 2d. 1294, 1308–1310 (2000).

45. Ibid., at 1310.

46. *Doe I v. Unocal Corp.,* 2002 U.S. App. LEXIS 19263 (2002) at *37 (hereinafter *Unocal Appeal*). However, the court found that Unocal's conduct did satisfy the "active participation" standard set out by the district court. Ibid., at *38 n. 22.

47. Ibid., at *37–38. The Ninth Circuit also noted that the evidence in the summary judgment record revealed disputed issues of fact precluding summary judgment even under the district court's standard. Ibid., at *38 n. 22.

48. *Unocal Appeal,* at *36 and *46 n. 26. This principle of command responsibility was also accepted as a source of liability under the ATCA in the *Marcos* cases. *Hilao v. Estate of Marcos,* 103 F. 3d 767, 777 (9th Cir. 1996). See also *Ford v. Garcia,* 289 F. 3d 1283, 1286 (11th Cir. 2002), cert. denied 123 S.Ct. 868 (2003), where the jury did not find command responsibility. A year later, a different jury found the defendants liable in a case raising similar claims in *Romogoza v. Garcia,* a case against the same Ford defendants. The judgment was reversed on other grounds in early 2005

49. *Unocal Appeal,* at *36 and *46 n. 26.

50. Ibid., at *48.

51. Ibid., at *49–56.

52. Ibid., at *11–21, 51–55.

53. Ibid., at *109.

54. Beyond the scope of this chapter, however, plaintiffs in the *Doe v. Unocal* case have brought an action in California state court asserting claims based on joint venture, agency, ratification, and other state law theories: *John Doe I v. Unocal Corp.,* Case no. BC 237980 (Cal. Sup. Ct.); *John Roe III v. Unocal Corp.,* Case no. BC 237679 (Cal. Sup. Ct.). Unocal's arguments that such claims are barred by federal preemption and the act of state doctrine and are unsupported in California law have been rejected so far in the state court litigation but will no doubt be asserted again in future state court cases, now that the *Unocal* case has been settled. A complaint raising state law claims has been filed in *Bowoto v. Chevron.*

55. The majority pointed out that there was no substantive distinction between the international law standard and the federal common law standard: *Unocal Appeal,* at *40 n. 32 ("The standard for aiding and abetting in international criminal law is similar to the standard for aiding and abetting in domestic tort law, making the choice between international and domestic law even less crucial"). The majority did not reach the plaintiff's claims of joint venture, agency, and so forth but did note that these theories might also be viable in the case: *Unocal Appeal,* at *49, n. 28

("We have done no more than declare that the decisions by these tribunals are one of the sources of international law, rather than the source of international law"). See Paul L. Hoffman and Daniel A. Zaheer, "The Rules of the Road: Federal Common Law and Aiding and Abetting Under the Alien Tort Claims Act," *Loyola International Comparative Law Review* 47 (2003).

56. In *Talisman* (see notes 18, 30), a district court looked to the same international judicial authorities to find that the assistance must be "direct and substantial," finding that precisely the same practical assistance and encouragement standard as in *Unocal* was the requisite *actus reus:* 244 F. Supp. 2d, at 321–325. Moreover, the court found the mental state to be "some knowledge that the assistance will facilitate the crime," where the knowledge may be "actual or constructive" (ibid.). In the *Wiwa* case the district court denied a motion to dismiss in an unpublished opinion that addresses these issues in a similar manner.

57. I argued on behalf of the *Doe* plaintiffs.

58. *In re South Africa Apartheid Litigation*, 346 F. Supp. 2d 538 (S.D.N.Y. 2004). These cases are likely to go up on appeal in 2005 and lead to a decision on many of the issues discussed in this chapter at some point in 2006. The Eleventh Circuit reached a contrary decision on aiding and abetting liability under the ATCA in a noncorporate context in *Cabello v. Fernandez-Larios*, 2005 U.S. App. Lexis 4216 (11th Cir. 2005).

59. This argument was made to the Supreme Court in March 2004 by the defendant in *Sosa v. Alvarez-Machain*.

60. In September 2004, the judge in the state actions ruled that the plaintiffs were entitled to a jury trial on their agency and joint venture theories of liability notwithstanding her previous ruling that the Unocal subsidiaries were not the alter egos of the parent corporations. The trial, originally scheduled for May 2005, will not take place because of the December 2004 settlement of the case.

61. 42 U.S.C. sec. 1983.

62. See, for example, *Kadic*, 70 F. 3d, at 245; *Wiwa v. Royal Dutch Petroleum Co.*, 226 F. 3d 88, 104 (2d Cir. 2000).

63. Ibid.; *Talisman*, 244 F. Supp 2d; *Doe v. Unocal*, 963 F. Supp. 880, 890–891 (C.D. Cal. 1997). In *Doe v. Unocal*, the district court imposed a requirement that the corporate actor must be able to "control" the state actor in order to find that the joint action requirement would be satisfied: *Doe v. Unocal*, 110 F. Supp. 2d 1294, 1307 (C.D. Cal. 2000). *Unocal Appeal*, at *56.

64. 110 F. Supp. 2d 1294, 1307 (C.D. Cir. 2000). The district court also found that defendants' actions were not the "proximate cause" of plaintiffs' injury (ibid.).

65. *Banco Nacional de Cuba v. Sabbatino*, 376 U.S. 398, 416 (1964).

66. *Roe v. Unocal*, 70 F. Supp. 2d 1073, 1076–1078 (C.D. Cal. 1999).

67. *Baker v. Carr*, 369 U.S. 186, 211 (1962).

68. *Tel-Oren v. Libyan Arab Republic*, 726 F. 2d 774, 823–827 (D.C. Cir. 1984), J. Robb concurring.

69. *Sarei v. Rio Tinto*, 221 F. Supp. 2d 1116, 1209 (C.D. Cal. 2002). The appeal was argued on September 8, 2003, and is awaiting decision.

70. Compare *Doe v. Unocal*, 248 F. 3d 915 (2001), with *Wiwa v. Royal Dutch Petroleum*, 226 F. 3d 88, 102 (2000).

71. This chapter cannot give a comprehensive account of all of the possible defenses. In addition to those discussed here, defendants in ATCA cases have raised, inter alia, the following defenses: (1) the particular plaintiffs lack standing to sue, (2) exhaustion of domestic remedies, (3) statute of limitations, (4) law of proxi-

mate cause, (5) absence of indispensable parties, usually a foreign sovereign, (6) foreign sovereign immunity, and (7) international comity.

72. See Pub. L. no. 102–256, 106 Stat. 73 (1992), codified at 28 U.S.C. sec. 1350 n (1994). See H.R. Rep. no. 102–367, at 4 (1991), reprinted in 1992 U.S.C.C.A.N. 84, 86 (noting that purposes of the TVPA are to codify and expand *Filártiga* and to dismiss separation of powers concerns).

73. *Sinaltrainal v. Coca-Cola,* 256 F. Supp. 2d 1345, 1358–1359 (S.D. Fla. 2003); *Estate of Rodriguez v. Drummond Co.,* 256 F. Supp. 2d 1250, 1257 (N.D. Ala. 2003).

74. See *Sinaltrainal v. Coca Cola.*

75. Ibid., citing *Clinton v. New York,* 524 U.S. 417, 428, n. 13 (1998).

76. Ibid.

77. See *Beanal v. Freeport-McMoran Inc.,* 969 F. Supp. 362, 382 (E.D. La. 1997).

78. Plaintiffs' RICO claims were dismissed in the *Doe v. Unocal* and *Wiwa* cases.

79. See Cal. Bus. & Prof. Code sec. 17200. Section 17200 has been found to apply to a corporation's false claims about its good human rights record. *Kasky v. Nike Corp. Inc.,* 27 Cal. 4th 939 (2002), *cert. denied as improvidently granted,* 123 S.Ct. 1554 (2003). In September 2003 it was reported that Nike settled this case for a payment of $1.5 million: Adam Liptak, "Nike Move Ends Case over Firm's Free Speech," *New York Times,* September 13, 2003, p. A8. Section 17200 claims of unfair business practices based on complicity in human rights violations have been made in the state court litigation in *Doe v. Unocal* and *Bowoto v. Chevron.*

80. The December 2004 settlement of the *Unocal* case included the dismissal of the state action, so these issues will not be resolved at the appellate level in that case.

81. The possibilities of bringing tort claims in various international and comparative contexts are explored in depth in Craig Scott, ed., *Torture Is Tort: Comparative Perspectives on the Development of Transnational Human Rights Litigation* (Oxford: Hart, 2001).

82. See, generally, Beth Stevens, "Translating Filartiga: A Comparative and International Law Analysis of Domestic Remedies for International Human Rights Violations," *Yale Journal for International Law* 27, no. 1 (2002): 1–57.

83. See 107 I.L.R. 536, 538–539 (Eng. C.A. 1996). See also *Al-Adsani v. United Kingdom,* ECHR 35763/97 (Eu.Ct.Hum.Rts. 2001), affirming dismissal of the case on immunity grounds.

84. In *Jones v. Ministry of Interior,* a magistrate rejected a similar torture claim brought against Saudi officers.

85. See Halina Ward, "Securing Transnational Corporate Accountability through National Courts: Implications and Policy Options," *Hastings International and Comparative Law Review* 24, no. 3 (2001): 451–474, at p. 456. See also Richard Meeran, "Accountability of Transnationals for Human Rights Abuses," Part 1, *New Law Journal* 148, no. 6864 (November 13, 1998): 1686–1687; Part 2., 148, no. 6865 (November 20, 1998): 1706–1708.

86. Ward, "Securing Transnational Corporate Accountability," pp. 457–458.

87. The House of Lords refused to dismiss the case in favor of litigation in South Africa because the laws there would not provide them relief: *Lubbe v. Cape PLC* (no. 2), 1 E.L.R. 1545 (H.L. 2000).

88. *Doe v. Unocal,* 248 F. 3d 915 (9th Cir. 2001).

89. "Activists Keep Up Pressure on Myanmar Investors," Energy Compass, May 10, 2002.

90. Ward, "Securing Transnational Corporate Accountability," pp. 460–461.

91. Ibid., p. 457.

92. Stevens, "Translating Filartiga," p. 32.

93. See *Tel Oren v. Libyan Arab Republic,* 726 F. 2d 774, 799, 822 (D.C. Cir. 1984), opinions of Judges Bork and Robb.

94. See Tom Carter, "Old Law Finds New Use against Oppressors; Victims of Repression, Torture Can Sue," *Washington Times,* March 17, 2003, p. A12; and Paul K. Driessen, "Repeal This Ill-Used Law," editorial, *Sun-Sentinel,* February 12, 2003, p. 29A. USA Engage, the group leading the movement for ATCA repeal, is a lobby group representing multinational corporate interests. See www.usaengage. org. See also Gary C. Hufbauer and Nicholas K. Mitrokostas, *Awakening Monster: The Alien Tort Statute of 1789* (Washington, D.C.: Institute for International Economics, 2003).

95. See, generally, Jim VandeHei, "GOP Plans New Caps on Court Awards," *Washington Post,* December 29, 2002, p. A5. After the Senate rejected a tort reform bill in 2002 that would have, among other provisions, limited noneconomic damages to $250,000, it was reintroduced and passed in the House in 2003. It faces a much better chance of passing through the now Republican-controlled Senate. The bill is H.R. 5 (Greenwood).

96. See *Crosby v. National Foreign Trade Council,* 530 U.S. 363 (2000).

97. See Samson Mulugeta, "Apartheid Victims Suing for Payments," *Seattle Times,* September 17, 2002; and Patti Waldmeir, "An Abuse of Power: U.S. Courts Should Not Punish Companies for Human Rights Violations Committed Overseas," *Financial Times* (London), March 14, 2003, p. 12. The companies being sued include Citibank, Union Bank of Switzerland, Credit Suisse, IBM, and General Motors. The South African government has made submissions to the court in the pending cases, asking that they be dismissed.

98. The South African cases raise some difficult complicity issues to the extent that they are based on the theory that doing business in apartheid South Africa automatically made foreign corporations complicit in apartheid-era human rights abuses.

99. *Roe v. Unocal,* 70 F. Supp. 2d 1073, 1076–1078 (C.D. Cal. 1999).

100. In re *Estate of Ferdinand Marcos,* 103 F. 3d 789 (9th Cir. 1996); *Hilao v. Estate of Marcos,* 25 F. 3d 1994 (9th Cir. 1995); *Republic of Philippines v. Marcos,* 862 F. 2d 1355 (9th Cir. 1988).

101. Transcript of oral argument, *Sosa v. Alvarez-Machain,* 124 S.Ct. 807 (2003), no. 03-339.

102. 124 S. Ct. 2739 (2004). This summary of the *Alvarez* decision does not begin to address the many issues raised by the decision, many of which are already being hotly debated and litigated across the country.

103. 25 F.3d 1467 (9th Cir 1994). The Court's citation to *Filártiga* and *Marcos* suggests that norms like torture, extrajudicial execution, disappearances, prolonged arbitrary detention, genocide, slavery, war crimes, and crimes against humanity are clearly actionable under the ACTA.

104. 124 S. Ct. at 2766. Justice Souter also cited to Judge Edwards's concurring opinion in *Tel-Oren v. Libyan Arab Republic,* 726 F.2d. 774, 781 (D.C. Cir. 1984) (Edwards, J., concurring).

105. The handful would have included piracy, attacks on ambassadors, violations of safe conduct. 124 S. Ct. at 2761.

106. 124 S. Ct. at 2761.

17

War Economies, Economic Actors, and International Criminal Law

William A. Schabas

A newly elected chief prosecutor of the International Criminal Court (ICC), in one of his first public declarations dealing with prosecutorial strategies and orientations, on July 16, 2003, focused on the role of economic actors in armed conflict. After indicating that the crisis in the Ituri region of the Democratic Republic of Congo would be the likely target of his initial investigations, he turned to what were described as "money-laundering and other crimes committed outside the Democratic Republic of Congo which may be connected with the atrocities." According to Chief Prosecutor Luis Moreno Ocampo:

> Various reports have pointed to links between the activities of some African, European and Middle Eastern companies and the atrocities taking place in the Democratic Republic of Congo. The alleged involvement of organized crime groups from Eastern Europe has also been mentioned. Their activities allegedly include gold mining, the illegal exploitation of oil, and the arms trade. There is general concern that the atrocities allegedly committed in the country may be fueled by the exploitation of natural resources there and the arms trade, which are enabled through the international banking system. Although the specific findings of these reports have not been confirmed, the Prosecutor believes that investigation of the financial aspects of the alleged atrocities will be crucial to prevent future crimes and for the prosecution of crimes already committed. If the alleged business practices continue to fuel atrocities, these would not be stopped even if current perpetrators were arrested and prosecuted. The Office of the Prosecutor is establishing whether investigations and prosecutions on the financial side of the alleged atrocities are being carried out in the relevant countries.[1]

The prosecutor's declaration had been anxiously awaited by those who follow the unfolding work of the new institution, because the Rome Statute of the International Criminal Court gives the prosecutor an enormous amount of individual discretion in deciding to launch cases. That economic factors would figure so prominently on his agenda was quite astonishing and utterly unexpected, especially because the court's jurisdictional framework seems to leave it very few, if any, tools with which to address economic dimensions of armed conflict, including money laundering, illicit natural resource exploitation, and the illicit arms trade.

Indeed, to date, private-sector actors, such as transnational corporations, have been highly invisible in armed conflict, fueling war and atrocity yet operating deep within the shadows and often from remote and privileged environments. At best, they are conceptualized as secondary participants in international crimes, in a world where impunity, amnesty, and immunity ensure that even the central architects of systematic human rights violations are still about as likely to be held accountable as they are to be struck by lightning. Chief Prosecutor Ocampo is surely aware of the obstacles in his way, created by the shortcomings of current legal norms and mechanisms capable of snaring the economic actors who contribute to conflict. Two paths lie open: strengthening the inadequate norms and mechanisms that currently exist and beginning to contemplate the creation of a new legal regime better adapted to tackle these problems.

Economic agendas may contribute significantly to the outbreak and the perpetuation of war. It seems that in our post–Cold War context, civil wars are often little more than campaigns to acquire access to natural resources and markets, although somewhere in the distant past it may be possible to identify a role for ideological factors and political objectives.[2] Prosecutor Ocampo's laconic statement nevertheless highlighted some of the complexities in that economic actors in armed conflict correspond to a variety of profiles. His reference to the "international banking system," the exploitation of natural resources, the arms trade, and companies from various parts of the world seems to point to classic white-collar criminals ensconced within wood-paneled boardrooms in major capitals and financial centers. These forces are cloaked in legality and legitimacy, largely beyond the reach of existing law. But note was also made of "organized crime groups," whose activities—usually more clandestine—situate them in a different legal paradigm, one that is probably more within the grasp of existing international regulation. For this latter category, the problem may be more a question of implementation and enforcement. Finally—and here the law is perhaps most robust—there are the economic dimensions of war crimes themselves, the well-recognized international offenses of pillage and plunder, condemned by customary law for centuries and expressly prohibited in one of the first great humanitarian law treaties, the Hague Convention of 1907.[3]

Catching the Accomplices

Only days after the adoption of the Rome Statute of the International Criminal Court at the conclusion of the Rome Conference in July 1998, the prestigious British business daily the *Financial Times* published an article warning "commercial lawyers" that the treaty's accomplice liability provision "could create international criminal liability for employees, officers and directors of corporations." Writer Maurice Nyberg referred to condemnation of violations of human rights involving multinational corporations by nongovernmental organizations like Human Rights Watch, adding that "it takes little imagination to jump from complicity with human rights violations to complicity with crimes covered under the ICC Treaty."[4]

Certainly, to the extent that economic actors, including international businesses, are involved in war crimes and crimes against humanity, there is much potential, and the law is, as the analysis below demonstrates, quite adequate. Their participation will almost invariably be indirect, as financiers, merchants of weapons and other war paraphernalia, or traders in the spoils of war. International criminal law may apply to the extent that illegal means or methods of war are being employed or that civilian noncombatants are being victimized. Note that the liability of economic actors would not be for *economic* crimes, as these are essentially absent from the Rome Statute, save for the war crime of "pillage and plunder." Rather, economic actors would be held responsible as accomplices in the "classic" international crimes: torture, disappearance, apartheid, and so on.

There are a variety of definitions of "complicity" in international criminal law, of which the most widely accepted, and arguably the broadest, is that found in article 25 of the Rome Statute.[5] An individual can be prosecuted for war crimes or crimes against humanity if he or she

(c) For the purpose of facilitating the commission of such a crime, aids, abets or otherwise assists in its commission or its attempted commission, including providing the means for its commission;
(d) In any other way contributes to the commission or attempted commission of such a crime by a group of persons acting with a common purpose. Such contribution shall be intentional and shall either:

(i) Be made with the aim of furthering the criminal activity or criminal purpose of the group, where such activity or purpose involves the commission of a crime within the jurisdiction of the Court; or
(ii) Be made in the knowledge of the intention of the group to commit the crime.

It should be relatively easy to understand how an economic actor might fall within the reach of these provisions.[6] Although the subject has received little or no attention from the ad hoc International Criminal Tribunals for the former Yugoslavia (ICTY) and Rwanda (ICTR), there are precedents in the post–World War II prosecutions. In concentration-camp prosecutions, personnel at Belsen were found to be "in violation of the laws and usages of war [and to be] together concerned as parties to the ill-treatment of certain persons."[7] The judge advocate who successfully prosecuted the case conceded that "mere presence on the staff was not of itself enough to justify a conviction" but insisted that "if a number of people took a part, however small in an offence, they were parties to the whole."[8] Nuremberg prosecutors also succeeded in obtaining a conviction of three I. G. Farben executives who were involved in the construction of the slave-labor factory at Auschwitz.[9] Two of them, Friedrich Flick and Otto Steinbrinck, were found guilty of complicity because of their financial support of SS leader Heinrich Himmler's activities and, more generally, those of the SS.[10] The ruling did not, however, extend to the corporation itself.

Since 1999, judges at the ICTY in The Hague have been fine-tuning a brand of complicity known as "joint criminal enterprise," by which even relatively remote accomplices to an atrocity can be found guilty of crimes committed by others to the extent that the acts themselves were an objectively foreseeable outcome of the conspiracy.[11] Now applied to war crimes and crimes against humanity, the concept has proved most effective in the prosecution of organized crime. Even the terminology itself—*enterprise*—suggests an economic context. The prosecutor of the Special Court for Sierra Leone is promising to explore this territory more thoroughly. For example, the indictments issued in March 2003 against, among others, the late rebel leader Foday Sankoh and his ally former Liberian president Charles Taylor allege a "joint criminal enterprise" whose objective was "to gain and exercise political power and control over the territory of Sierra Leone, in particular the diamond mining areas. The natural resources of Sierra Leone were to be provided to persons outside Sierra Leone in return for assistance in carrying out the joint criminal enterprise."[12]

Although criminal prosecution of economic participants in armed conflict for their role in assisting grave violations of international criminal law has much potential, it is not without its problems. First, if the objective is to choke off the conflict by depriving combatants of funds or in some other way to stymie the economic agendas that are at work, the alleged wrongs that are committed rarely fall within the scope of international criminal law. For example, although the Rome Statute prohibits use of certain weapons, such as poison, asphyxiating gas, and hollow-tip bullets, it does not at present challenge the use of the arms that are most common, especially in civil wars: automatic rifles and other forms of small arms, machetes, antipersonnel mines, and cluster bombs. Antipersonnel mines were widely used in the conflict in the former Yugoslavia, yet there have been no prosecutions alleging that this was contrary to the laws or customs of war and therefore prohibited by article 3 of the statute. In other words, while it may be possible to convict an arms manufacturer or trafficker who knowingly contributes to the use of prohibited weapons—an analogy here would be the conviction of those who supplied Zyklon-B gas to Nazi extermination camps[13]—most of the lethal weapons are not prohibited by international law. When such prohibitions exist, such as the Ottawa Convention on antipersonnel mines, they are neither comprehensive nor universal.

While the principles of complicity liability seem straightforward enough, most of the existing experiments in international criminal law have limited them in one way or another. The case law of the ad hoc tribunals for the former Yugoslavia and Rwanda has required that participation in a crime be "substantial."[14] This may discourage prosecution of economic actors, whose involvement in crimes, though undisputed, may seem to be too remote. The prosecutors of the ICTY and ICTR have shown little interest in pursuing economic actors, although there is an outstanding indictment for Rwandan businessman Felicien Kabuga for his role in financing the Rwandan *génocidaires*.[15]

Similarly, the jurisdiction of the Special Court for Sierra Leone is confined to "persons who bear the greatest responsibility" for serious violations of international humanitarian law.[16] Determining who bears the greatest responsibility would appear to belong essentially to the realm of the discretion of the prosecutor. Theoretically, he might determine that transnational diamond merchants, such as De Beers, fall within this category,[17] but this is not the direction that prosecutions have taken, and the initial indictments have been directed at military and political leaders.

Finally, while it may be of considerable interest to pursue private businesses for their complicity in war crimes, and not just the individuals who work within them as managers and directors, this is not always possible. For example, the jurisdiction of the International Criminal Court is confined to "natural persons."[18] Provisions on corporate bodies and legal persons were excluded from the Rome Statute for essentially practical reasons. For the ICC to operate fairly as a complementary regime, it was believed necessary to find a common denominator of all major criminal justice systems, many of which do not provide for criminal prosecution of corporate bodies or legal persons.[19]

Shortcomings of Existing Law

International law endeavors to regulate armed conflict in a number of ways. First and foremost, it prohibits the use of force except in two extraordinary circumstances: enforcement action pursuant to Chapter VII of the UN

Charter and the inherent right of self-defense. Its success in this area is debatable, and prevention of conflicts may well have more to do with the political and the diplomatic than it does with any legal prohibition. Nobody has been prosecuted for "crimes against peace" since the 1940s. Attempts to make aggression an international criminal offense punishable by the International Criminal Court are proceeding, but at a leisurely pace, and there is no assurance that they will succeed. Two issues make progress difficult in this area: there is no agreement among states about how to define aggression, and there are possible conflicts with the UN Security Council should the ICC attempt to determine issues of aggression, because article 39 of the Charter gives this prerogative to the council.

The law is considerably more developed and sophisticated in the area of *jus in bello,* the legal regime governing the conduct of armed conflict, irrespective of whether a given war is unlawful. In addition to a weighty repertoire of treaties, with the 1949 Geneva Conventions as the centerpiece, international law brings a rich body of customary norms to bear in this area. As recently as 1996, the world's supreme judicial body, the International Court of Justice, declared that the "cardinal principles" of international humanitarian law are the obligation to distinguish between combatants and noncombatants, never to make civilians the object of attack, and to eschew the use of weapons that cause unnecessary suffering to combatants.[20]

International humanitarian law provides a relatively sophisticated body of legal rules and principles to govern international armed conflict, many of them customary in nature and developed virtually from antiquity, but it has rather less to say with respect to intrastate armed conflict.[21] This is explained partly by historical reasons and partly by the reluctance of states to allow international law to pry into an area of great sensitivity to them— their conduct in putting down armed challenges to their own authority. To the extent that rules exist to govern the conduct of internal armed conflict, their applicability is conditional on certain threshold definitions. These exclude many low-level conflicts of great seriousness, as well as riots, disturbances, and terrorist acts. Although there are important exceptions, such as the interventions in Kosovo, Afghanistan, and Iraq in the 1990s and 2000s, most contemporary armed conflicts are internal in nature.

In parallel with international humanitarian law is the more modern regime of international human rights law. It is said to apply without exception in both peacetime and wartime and without any interest in whether a conflict is international or internal in scope. Nevertheless, certain principles of human rights law, such as the right to a fair trial and freedom of expression, can be suspended or derogated from in time of war.[22] Moreover, courts continue to debate whether human rights law and humanitarian law operate together, reinforcing each other, or whether one supersedes the other. The International Court of Justice seems to consider that humanitarian law displaces human rights law because it is a specialized body of principles intended to govern situations of armed conflict (*lex specialis*).[23] Finally, there is an ongoing debate among scholars and practitioners as to what extent international human rights law does apply to "nonstate actors," such as transnational corporations and other economic entities.

But aside from what may seem highly technical issues of the application of these two bodies of law, the real problems reside with the substance of the norms, which do not generally deal with economic matters. They are targeted at the core issues of threats to bodily integrity, such as killings, mutilations, summary executions, sexual assaults, and pillage. Of course, economic actors who are directly involved in such violations and abuses fall within the ambit of these bodies of law as much as traditional combatants do. Generally, though, the role of economic actors is more indirect. For example, while it is widely agreed that trade in diamonds helped to fuel conflict in places like Sierra Leone,[24] unless it can be established that diamond traders were actual accomplices in the atrocities committed against civilians, there is little that existing law can contribute. If it were actually an unlawful act to buy and sell diamonds while knowing that somewhere along the chain of possession they had been bartered for small arms or antipersonnel mines that were then turned on the innocent, most jewelers in the developed world would have to close their doors.

Finally, if the purpose of the exercise is to prevent conflict rather than to regulate it, to ensure that wars do not happen instead of ensuring that they are conducted with respect for rules of chivalry, international law is woefully inadequate. The prohibition of the use of force within the UN Charter, coupled with the punishability of crimes against peace or aggression for those individuals who actually participate in a breach of the peace, relates only to international armed conflict. By and large, international law has nothing to say about the *jus ad bellum* of internal wars. There is even acknowledgment of the legitimacy of resort to use of force in some circumstances. The preamble to the Universal Declaration of Human Rights accepts "recourse, as a last resort, to rebellion against tyranny and oppression," while the humanitarian law instruments nod benignly at "armed conflicts in which peoples are fighting against colonial domination and alien occupation and against racist regimes in the exercise of their right of self-determination."[25]

Illegal use of force may provoke political intervention by bodies like the Security Council of the United Nations, but it continues to elude such forums as the international criminal tribunals. For example, the ICTY is powerless to prosecute those who actually started the wars in Croatia, Bosnia and Herzegovina, and Kosovo; its subject-matter jurisdiction is confined to violations committed after the wars had begun. Although the

Security Council imposed an arms embargo on the region, the tribunal cannot prosecute those who defied the prohibition, because this is not an offense within its jurisdiction. In what was a last-minute and inadequate drafting compromise, the Rome Statute of the International Criminal Court has jurisdiction over the crime of aggression, but only to the extent that the offense is subsequently defined and the tension with article 39 of the UN Charter, which appears to reserve determination of cases of aggression for the Security Council, is resolved.[26] Unless state parties to the statute can agree on a legal formula, prosecutions for aggression cannot take place. At present, they seem far indeed from any agreement.[27]

While perhaps commonplace, it deserves repeating that wars, especially civil wars, are often rooted in social tensions and dislocations that result from violations of economic and social rights. The "rebel war" in Sierra Leone (1991–2002) may have been launched by individuals who were trained in Libya and funded by Liberia, but it drew its initial support from a stratum of the country's youth who were quite understandably dissatisfied with endemic corruption, poverty, and underdevelopment. This portrait of the conflict, already noted by some observers, is becoming increasingly evident as the hearings of Sierra Leone's Truth and Reconciliation Commission unfold. Economic actors, including corrupt officials and greedy transnational corporations involved in mining and other areas of commercial activity, contributed to the overall misery and wretchedness of the country in the decades since independence in 1961. Weak notions of social responsibility among local elites as well as transnational commercial operators must be strengthened if what may be little more than a cease-fire is to be transformed into a lasting peace. Blaming the war on meddling by Muammar Qaddafi and Charles Taylor is to some extent a distraction from the underlying economic causes of the war, to which both national and transnational businesses contributed.

Corporate Responsibility and Civil Liability

While rebel groups and shadowy criminal networks are the most central actors in civil war economies, the operations and investments of legitimate business entities can also be implicated. The corporation dates to the early stages of capitalist economies and facilitates business activities in a number of ways, not the least of which is the protection of the personal assets of the individuals who direct and profit from such a body. One means of regulating economic agendas in armed conflict may well be through standards of corporate responsibility. This area is receiving an increasing amount of attention, mainly with regard to human rights abuses suffered by persons in the South at the hands of commercial corporations directed from the North.

Labor standards and environmental protection are at the core of contemporary concerns, but there is no reason the approaches undertaken in these areas cannot and should not be extended to the context of armed conflict.

Most efforts in the area of corporate responsibility belong to the realm of "soft law" initiatives or "corporate social responsibility" (CSR). These are codes of conduct and best practice, adhered to voluntarily by businesses, sometimes in exchange for public relations and marketing advantages in one form or another. The prospect of a consumer boycott may often be a realistic encouragement to compliance. It seems likely that negative publicity about the international diamond market and its contribution to conflict in Angola, Sierra Leone, and elsewhere may well have influenced the behavior of the international diamond industry. Labeling requirements whose objective is to unleash the forces of consumers have had a nod of acceptance from the World Trade Organization's dispute resolution system.[28]

Yet one needs to distinguish between different types of corporations with operations in the area of armed conflict. Large, transnational companies in the extractive industries, which through their operations may become complicit in violations of international law, are typically legitimate entities and relatively amenable to CSR initiatives. Where the corporations involved are arms dealers and shadowy commodity traders, however, benevolent corporate culture is unlikely to be at its highest. Most of the relevant operators are not particularly vulnerable to "naming and shaming." Their activities are more analogous to those of organized crime than to the activities of innocent merchants and traders whose products and services are inadvertently put to evil use.

One of the justifications for persuasion rather than coercion when transnational corporations are involved revolves around the legal difficulties associated with regulation. International norms of human rights and humanitarian law are addressed to states, not individuals or corporations, it is argued. In response, a growing body of law that holds states responsible for "horizontal violations" of human rights is invoked. Although nonstate actors may not be directly liable under international law, states are responsible for ensuring that corporations under their jurisdiction behave in accordance with certain minimum standards.

This argument helps to a point but then confronts the additional obstacle of extraterritoriality. States argue that to the extent that they are obliged to ensure responsible behavior on the part of their corporate citizens, this duty is confined to their own territory. Anything further might be taken as a violation of the sovereignty of other states. Wealthy countries that attempt to regulate the conduct of their own nationals, corporate and other, in poorer countries may even find themselves charged with neocolonialism.

Here too, though, there is a potent answer. States are increasingly prepared to enact legislation governing conduct of their nationals abroad when this involves serious violations of human rights. Examples include the statutes adopted by many developed countries aimed at sexual tourism by their own nationals in countries where the justice system is overwhelmed, or simply corrupt, and therefore unwilling or unable to address the exploitation of children. Similarly, many states have antitrust and anti-bribery legislation with extraterritorial effect. In other words, there are significant exceptions to the general rule of discouraging legislation with extraterritorial effect. Consequently, in countries that are home to transnational corporations, robust national legislation aimed at commercial activity that contributes to armed conflict abroad could well have a meaningful impact.

There has already been at least one attempt to legislate in this area. In 1996, Massachusetts adopted what was known as its "Burma/Myanmar law," which attempted to regulate state contracts with companies doing business with or in Burma/Myanmar.[29] The statute was struck down as unconstitutional by the U.S. Supreme Court, but only because the field was deemed to come under federal jurisdiction, not because such initiatives are impermissible per se.

The real problem, of course, is defining the line beyond which commercial activity is no longer legitimate and acceptable. In many ways, this is the same problem faced in the criminal sphere with respect to complicity in war crimes and crimes against humanity. In that context, the diamond merchant who trades with armed groups engaged in notorious atrocities may be considered close enough to the offense to be criminally complicit. However, the jeweler in a foreign city who only suspects that the products he or she is dealing with are "blood diamonds" may be deemed rather too remote from the offense.

When corporate responsibility is being addressed within the context of civil liability, however, the rigorous standards that apply to criminal prosecution need not be observed. Justice systems balk at punishing a foreign jeweler who is merely suspicious as to the origin of diamonds, but they have rather less difficulty imposing various civil consequences, such as fines or confiscation, in such circumstances. The burden of proof has to do with preponderance of evidence and not the daunting reasonable-doubt standard of criminal trials. In many respects, then, a legal regime focused upon corporate accountability and responsibility, with civil or administrative but not criminal consequences, has much to recommend it.

Model legislation might be devised indicating how such a system could operate. Commercial corporations with their head office in a given country, or perhaps substantial assets or activities or some other significant nexus, would be required by law to abstain from acts that might facilitate a conflict. These could be defined in a general sense, or applicability might be triggered by some determination by a national or an international body concerning a state of armed conflict. Upon proof that the norms of conduct had been breached, a variety of sanctions could be contemplated, including fines, confiscation of assets, personal liability for directors, and ultimately, company closure.

Economic Truth Commissions

Political compromises associated with conflict resolution have often involved some form of pardon or amnesty. The premier legal instrument governing noninternational armed conflict, Protocol Additional II to the Geneva Conventions of 1949, actually says that "at the end of hostilities, the authorities in power shall endeavor to grant the broadest possible amnesty to persons who have participated in the armed conflict."[30] But to ensure that amnesty does not equal amnesia, and out of concerns that enforced silence about perpetration of atrocities leaves postconflict societies with festering sores that are fundamentally destabilizing, many countries have convened truth and reconciliation commissions. The most well known, of course, is that of postapartheid South Africa. But more than twenty-five others have been cataloged in recent decades.[31] By and large, truth commissions focus on violent breaches of civil and political rights or of international humanitarian law. They attempt to bring together victims and perpetrators and thereby promote reconciliation, but with frank and candid recognition of the truth as a prerequisite. Generally, they try to assess responsibilities for the conflict and to make recommendations aimed at preventing a recurrence.

There is no reason that truth commissions cannot also address the economic causes of conflict, the role of economic agendas during the conflict, and the possible ways to deal with them in a postconflict setting. The South African Truth and Reconciliation Commission has done this, but very much as an afterthought. Its initial report, in 1998, did not delve into the economic and social issues. Five years later, in its final report, the commission laid a share of the blame for apartheid upon the role of business, including transnational corporations, and called for companies to finance programs of compensation out of existing assets and future profits. Citing "decades of profits [that] were based on systematic violations of human rights," the 2003 report proposed a levy of 3 billion rand on South African companies, including the Anglo-American Mining Corporation (which is itself a shareholder in the De Beers diamond business), and criticized an 800 million rand trust fund established by business interests as "paltry." As a model, the commission pointed to a wealth tax levied in West Germany in order to rebuild East Germany following reunification.

The Sierra Leone Truth and Reconciliation Commission, which began work in July 2002, had a broad mandate enabling it to explore the role of economic actors, including those involved in the diamond trade, which did so much to fuel the ten-year civil war. Its enabling statute charged it with creating "an impartial historical record of violations and abuses of human rights and international humanitarian law related to the armed conflict in Sierra Leone."[32] This allowed it to examine violations and abuses of economic and social rights as well as civil and commercial rights. Moreover, it was also charged with determining whether the "violations and abuses were the result of deliberate planning, policy or authorization by any government, group or individual, and the role of both internal and external factors in the conflict."[33] The commission conducted detailed research into the role of economic factors generally, as well as the role played by the exploitation and trade in diamonds in the conflict. According to its Final Report, delivered to the UN Security Council on October 27, 2004, the commission found "that the exploitation of diamonds was not the cause of the conflict in Sierra Leone, but rather fuelled the conflict as diamonds were used by most of the armed forces to finance and support their war efforts."[34] While singling out the RUF, the AFRC, and the CDF as most responsible for targeting diamond areas, and for the human rights violations that accompanied these actions, the commission also charged successive government authorities for the endemic corruption and mismanagement of the country's natural resources that contributed to the outbreak of hostilities, as well as their participation, alongside rebel groups, in the endemic looting of the country. Elites of neighboring countries, particularly former Liberian president Charles Taylor, were named as having aided and abetted as well as having benefited from the illicit diamond trade. Perhaps most notably, the commission rebuked the international diamond industry for being "largely indifferent to the origin of 'conflict diamonds' even at a time when reports of atrocities relating to the conflict in Sierra Leone were widely disseminated in the global media. These lapses significantly promoted the trade in illicit conflict diamonds and thereby encouraged the prolonging of local wars, including the conflict in Sierra Leone."[35] While the commission did recommend that the ill-gotten assets that Charles Taylor acquired from the conflict be traced, recorded, and placed in a war victims fund, it did not urge any reparations from the international diamond industry. Instead, it urged the participants of the Kimberley Process to deepen the implementation of diamond certification and to assist the government of Sierra Leone to establish transparent and socially beneficial management of the country's diamond industry. In all, the work of the Sierra Leone Truth and Reconciliation Commission went far in attributing responsibility to those whose economic activities facilitated the conflict.

There have been suggestions that truth commissions might also provide an appropriate framework to address property disputes of various types resulting from armed conflict. They do not seem to be particularly appropriate for this area, however. Truth commissions are best at speaking to phenomena of human rights abuse committed on a large scale, by states or rebel groups, and often in contexts where it is difficult to identify the specific perpetrator. It might trivialize their significance were they to be reduced to arbitration of individual claims, rather like ordinary civil courts. Initial assessments of the information gathered by the Sierra Leone Truth and Reconciliation Commission indicate that victims were not so interested in achieving individual justice, in terms of restitution or compensation, as they were in seeing a new political regime that ensures to them basic economic and social rights, such as housing, work, education, and healthcare.

Generally, one of the great advantages of truth commissions is their flexibility. They do not establish guilt, and they do not impose punishment or other sanctions. Nevertheless, they are fact-finding bodies that can attribute responsibilities. By and large, their rules of evidence are extremely liberal. The sorts of jurisdictional issues that plague judicial solutions rarely arise with truth commissions. Of course, they are usually powerless to implement their findings and recommendations; this is left to political bodies. But overall, it would seem desirable that in future truth commissions the possible role of business in the conflict be flagged openly in the enabling instruments and that truth commissions be persuaded that no analysis will be complete if this dimension is not studied and considered.

A New International Instrument?

Traditionally, international legal and regulatory instruments are both created by states and addressed to them. They establish obligations incumbent upon states, often in the form of binding requirements, by multilateral treaty or convention, or, alternatively, as programmatic or aspirational visions, in declarations, guidelines, or some other "soft law" model. Within the context of the international protection of human rights and its translation into domestic legislation, the distinctions between hard and soft law may be overdone. In practice, both bodies of law establish norms that influence national policy and jurisprudence. Whether it is by hard or soft law measures, the initial objection to attempting to regulate economic behavior in conflict will be that the principal area of concern is the private sector and that economic forces are "nonstate actors."

But it has become increasingly accepted that international law also speaks to nonstate actors, not only indirectly but also directly. This trend is reflected in the development of international criminal justice, which holds individuals liable for what are essentially human rights violations, and the growing focus on corporate responsibility. Of course, that individuals are not only beneficiaries of the international human rights law obligations of states but are also required to observe duties to society is recognized in the penultimate provision of the Universal Declaration of Human Rights.[36] This concept is further developed in some of the regional human rights instruments. Thus there is nothing terribly innovative about an international instrument that would impose duties upon economic actors with respect to armed conflict.

That economic actors operate collectively, generally in the form of commercial corporations or similar structures, also justifies special measures in the field of international law. Most legal systems, including international law, recognize that there is something special about "groups," that they are more than simply collections of individuals, the sum of their parts. For this reason, international law has made it a crime to conspire to commit genocide, an offense committed when two or more people meet and agree to destroy an ethnic group, even if no action is ever taken.[37] In other words, while one person may decide individually to carry out genocide, without incurring criminal responsibility, once two people do this together it becomes a punishable act. Similarly, part of the definition of crimes against humanity enshrined in the Rome Statute of the International Criminal Court is that they are committed "pursuant to or in furtherance of a State or organizational policy" to attack a civilian population.[38] Thus it is not unprecedented for international law to establish a special regime to deal with organized activity, even where the organizations are not states but some other type of structure.

That commercial corporations present a special challenge to international regulation, particularly in an era of globalization, is not a matter of dispute. It seems obvious enough that these powerful organizations, operating internationally, often through complex webs of interlocking subsidiaries, have resources that are equal or even superior to those of many small states. But the technical issues involved in efforts to control their operations are all capable of solution. The real obstacle to progress in this area is political in nature and relates to the possible content of an international instrument addressing economic conduct during armed conflict.

The existing international humanitarian law instruments stay clear of the private sector and generally do not have much to contribute in the area of economic activity. What little exists focuses upon the obligations of an occupying power and involves nothing more than respect for minimum standards of labor and children's rights and prohibitions of confiscation of private property. Certain features of contemporary armed conflicts, particularly those of an intrastate nature, such as plundering of natural resources, invite attempts at standard setting. But will wealthy states, most of them former colonial powers whose economies still depend to a large extent upon the exploitation of the natural resources of developing countries, accept a prohibition in wartime of something that they consider it their right to do in peacetime? Agreement upon an international instrument in this area would seem unlikely given the difficulty in elaborating any general principles regarding resource exploitation during armed conflict that either developed or developing countries would be prepared to accept.

Given the implausibility of an international agreement, the alternative is case-by-case intervention by the UN Security Council. Indeed, Security Council initiatives have already occurred, for example with respect to "conflict diamonds" in Sierra Leone and elsewhere. Unfortunately, the Security Council is a highly politicized body that, moreover, insulates its five permanent members when measures may concern their own interests. While effective up to a point, Security Council intervention in this area will be uneven at best. Inevitably, it will invite attack as being uneven and discriminatory.

Conclusion

International law has proved to be modestly successful at regulating the conditions under which the use of force is acceptable as well as the means and methods of warfare. It has not been particularly good at controlling the phenomenon of weapons that cause unnecessary suffering or that are indiscriminate, subject to a few rather archaic exceptions, such as dum-dum bullets and poisonous gas. As a result, the most significant economic actors in armed conflict—arms producers and traders—largely escape legal sanction. Sometimes there are efforts to choke a conflict by means of arms embargo, of course, but these efforts have been notoriously unsuccessful, as the cases of the former Yugoslavia and Rwanda bear out.

As for other economic activities, such as trade in mineral and other resources, there can be no doubt that such ventures fuel armed conflict. They are probably as old as armed conflict itself. Traditionally, armies live off the land. Where there is nothing left to plunder, they wither and die, as Napoleon discovered at the gates of Moscow. The Nazi armies were finally reversed when they could not quite extend their front lines enough to include the rich oil fields of the north Caucasus, necessary to fuel the war literally as well as figuratively. How different are these historical examples from the case of Sierra Leone's Revolutionary United Front's occupying the country's fabulous alluvial diamond fields?

The adoption of a new international instrument would seem unlikely in the near future, principally because of the difficulty in reaching agreement upon general principles applicable to commercial activity during armed conflict. Everybody wants to prohibit trading with the enemy, but they first want to know who the enemy is. To the extent that there will be any international legal intervention in this area, the most likely option is Security Council action, pursuant to Chapter VII of the UN Charter, in the form of embargoes or specific efforts to regulate particular industries that are associated with conflict.

More hopeful, perhaps, is the arena of national legislation. Pressure from civil society is already leading to the development of legal instruments, most of them soft rather than hard, aimed at improving corporate social responsibility. To date, the focus has been mainly on labor and environmental standards, but there is no reason this should not extend to the specific concerns of armed conflict. In Canada, pressure from nongovernmental organizations and industrial unions induced the petroleum company Talisman to abandon its interests in Sudan, where its activities had allegedly been associated with war crimes or crimes against humanity in the context of one of the world's longest civil wars.

Commercial corporations that are involved in armed conflicts to one extent or another may find themselves—or their directors and managers—exposed to criminal prosecution as accomplices in international crimes. This is an area that deserves to be explored much further. In 1997, when women's organizations perceived that the International Criminal Tribunal for Rwanda was neglecting gender crimes, an intense lobbying campaign essentially changed the prosecutorial agenda and resulted in the first significant international judgments on the role of rape in armed conflict.[39] A serious concerted effort to encourage prosecution of the economic accomplices to conflict-related crimes might also be undertaken, to similar effect.

International prosecutors have a great deal of discretion in the targets that they choose. At Nuremberg, there were efforts to establish the role that the German business community played in the rise of Nazism. These met with varying degrees of success. Walther Funk was found guilty of war crimes and crimes against humanity principally for his role in the German financial establishment (he was president of the Reichsbank), and he was sentenced to life imprisonment. But in the more recent crop of international prosecutions—Yugoslavia, Rwanda—there has been little interest in developing cases that highlight the economic dimensions of the conflicts. The reason for this probably lies less in the inherent difficulty in preparing such cases than in prosecutorial strategy. The efforts of the prosecutor of the Special Court for Sierra Leone, who has referred to economic issues in several of his indictments, may signal a change in this respect. The chief prosecutor of the International Criminal Court has also manifested an interest in economic matters.

Perhaps the best way forward, in terms of bringing international law to bear on economic agendas in armed conflict, would be to assist the chief prosecutor of the new International Criminal Court in focusing on this area.

One or two convictions of those involved in the business of war, rather than in a war itself, will surely make headlines in the *Financial Times* or the *Wall Street Journal*. The deterrent effect could be worth more than a score of Security Council resolutions.

Notes

1. International Criminal Court, "Communications Received by the Office of the Prosecutor of the ICC," press release no. pids.009.2003-EN, The Hague, July 16, 2003, pp. 3–4.

2. Mats Berdal and David M. Malone, eds., *Greed and Grievance: Economic Agendas in Civil Wars* (Boulder: Lynne Rienner, 2000).

3. *Prosecutor v. Kunarac et al.,* Case no. IT-96-23-T and IT-96–23/1-T, Decision on Motion for Acquittal, July 3, 2000. Prohibitions of pillage and plunder can be found in Convention (IV) Respecting the Laws and Customs of War by Land (1910), U.K.T.S. 9, annex, arts. 28, 47; Agreement for the Prosecution and Punishment of Major War Criminals of the European Axis and Establishing the Charter of the International Military Tribunal (I.M.T.), annex (1951), 82 U.N.T.S. 279, art. VI(b); Convention (IV) Relative to the Protection of Civilian Persons in Time of War (1950), 75 U.N.T.S. 287, art. 33; Statute of the International Criminal Tribunal for the Former Yugoslavia, S/RES/827 (1993), annex, art. 2(d); Rome Statute of the International Criminal Court, A/CONF.183/9, arts. 8(2)(a)(iv).

4. Maurice Nyberg, "At Risk from Complicity with Crime," *Financial Times,* July 27, 1998, p. 15.

5. Complicity is also included in other instruments, such as Convention on the Prevention and Punishment of the Crime of Genocide (1951), 78 U.N.T.S. 277, art. III(e); Convention against Torture and Other Cruel, Inhuman, or Degrading Treatment or Punishment (1987), 1465 U.N.T.S. 85, art. 4(1); Statute of the International Criminal Tribunal for the Former Yugoslavia, arts. 4(3)(e), 7(1); Statute of the International Criminal Tribunal for Rwanda, S/RES/955, annex, arts. 2(3)(e), 6(1); Statute of the Special Court for Sierra Leone, art. 6(1).

6. See William A. Schabas, "Enforcing International Humanitarian Law: Catching the Accomplices," *International Review of the Red Cross* 83, no. 439 (2001): 439–459; Tom Farer, "Shaping Agendas in Civil Wars: Can International Criminal Law Help?" in Berdal and Malone, *Greed and Grievance,* pp. 205–232 (see note 2).

7. *United Kingdom v. Kramer et al.* ("Belsen Trial," 1947), 2 *Law Reports of the Trials of the War Criminals* 1, British Military Court, p. 4.

8. Ibid., pp. 109, 120.

9. *United States of America v. Carl Krauch et al.* ("I. G. Farben Case," 1948), 8 *Trials of the War Criminals,* p. 1169.

10. *United States of America v. Friedrich Flick et al.* ("Flick Case," 1948), 6 *Trials of the War Criminals,* pp. 1217–1221.

11. *Prosecutor v. Tadic,* Case no. IT-94-1-A, Judgment, July 15, 1999. See also *Prosecutor v. Krnojelac,* Case no. IT-97-25-PT, Decision on Form of Second Amended Indictment, May 11, 2000; *Prosecutor v. Brdjanin & Talic,* Case no. IT-99-36-PT, Decision on Form of Further Amended Indictment and Prosecution Application to Amend, June 26, 2001; *Prosecutor v. Krnojelac,* Case no. IT-97-25-T, Judgment, March 15, 2002.

12. For example, *Prosecutor v. Sankoh,* Case no. SCSL 2003-02-I, Indictment, March 7, 2003, para. 27; *Prosecutor v. Sesay,* Case no. SCSL 2003-5-I, Indictment, March 7, 2003, para. 23; *Prosecutor v. Koroma,* Case no. SCSL 2003-3-I, Indictment, March 7, 2003, para. 24; *Prosecutor v. Brima,* Case no. SCSL 2003-6-I, Indictment, March 7, 2003, para. 23; *Prosecutor v. Taylor,* Case no. SCSL 2003-03-I, Indictment, March 7, 2003, paras. 20, 23.

13. *United Kingdom v. Tesch et al.* ("Zyklon B Case," 1947), 1 *Law Reports of the Trials of the War Criminals* (British Military Court), pp. 93–101.

14. *Prosecutor v. Tadic,* Case no. IT-94-1-T, Opinion and Judgment, May 7, 1997, paras. 691, 692. See also *Prosecutor v. Delalic et al.,* Case no. IT-96-21-T, Judgment, November 16, 1998, para. 326; *Prosecutor v. Furundzija,* Case no. IT-95-17/1-T, Judgment, December 10, 1998, paras. 223, 234; *Prosecutor v. Aleksovski,* Case no. IT-95-14/1-T, Judgment, June 25, 1999, para. 61.

15. *Prosecutor v. Bizimana et al.,* Case no. ICTR-98-44-I, Prosecutor's Amended Indictment Pursuant to the Decision of Trial Chamber II on the Defence Motion, November 21, 2001, paras. 4.24–4.25.

16. Statute of the Special Court for Sierra Leone, art. 1.

17. Lucinda Sanders, "Rich and Rare Are the Gems They War: Holding De Beers Accountable for Trading Conflict Diamonds," *Fordham International Law Journal* 24, no. 4 (2001): 1402–1476.

18. Rome Statute of the International Criminal Court, art. 25(1).

19. For discussion of the debates leading to the exclusion of corporate bodies, Per Saland, "International Criminal Law Principles," in Roy Lee, ed., *The International Criminal Court: The Making of the Rome Statute, Issues, Negotiations, Results* (The Hague: Kluwer Law International, 1999), pp. 189–216; Kai Ambos, "General Principles of Law in the Rome Statute," *Criminal Law Forum* 10 (1999): 1–23; Andrew Clapham, "The Question of Jurisdiction Under International Criminal Law over Legal Persons: Lessons from the Rome Conference on an International Criminal Court," in Menno T. Kamminga and Saman Zia-Zarifi, eds., *Liability of Multinational Corporations under International Law* (The Hague: Kluwer Law International, 2000), pp. 139–195.

20. International Court of Justice, "Legality of the Threat or Use of Nuclear Weapons (Advisory Opinion)," ICJ Reports 226, 1996, para. 78.

21. However, a pioneering study by the International Committee of the Red Cross shows that Customary International Humanitarian Law is applicable to conduct in noninternational armed conflicts. See Jean-Marie Henckaert and Louise Doswald-Beck, *Customary International Humanitarian Law* (Oxford: ICRC and Oxford University Press, 2005).

22. For example, International Covenant on Civil and Political Rights (1976), 999 U.N.T.S. 171, art. 4. On this subject, see the recent "General Comment no. 29" of the UN Human Rights Committee, HRI/GEN/1/Rev.6, p. 186.

23. International Court of Justice, "Legality of the Threat or Use of Nuclear Weapons," para. 26.

24. John L. Hirsch, *Sierra Leone: Diamonds and the Struggle for Democracy* (Boulder: Lynne Rienner, 2001).

25. Universal Declaration of Human Rights, G.A. Res. 217 A (III), UN Doc. A/810, preamble; Protocol Additional to the 1949 Geneva Conventions of 12 August 1949, and Relating to the Protection of Victims of International Armed Conflicts (Protocol I), 1125 U.N.T.S. 3 (1979), art. 1.

26. Rome Statute of the International Criminal Court, art. 5(2). See Theodor Meron, "Defining Aggression for the International Criminal Court," *Suffolk Transnational Law Review* 25, no.1 (2001): 1–15.

27. Sylvia A. de Gurmundi Fernandez, "The Working Group on Aggression at the Preparatory Commission for the International Criminal Court," *Fordham International Law Journal* 25, no. 3 (2002): 589–605.

28. World Trade Organization Appellate Body, "United States Import Prohibition of Certain Shrimp and Shrimp Products (October 12, 1998)," *International Legal Materials* 38, no. 1 (January 1999): 118–175.

29. An Act Regulating State Contracts with Companies Doing Business with, or in Burma (Myanmar), Mass. Acts 239, chap. 130, 1996 (codified as Mass. Gen. Laws secs. 7:22G–7:22M, 40 F (1997).

30. Protocol Additional to the 1949 Geneva Conventions and Relating to the Protection of Victims of Non-international Armed Conflicts (1979), 1125 U.N.T.S. 609.

31. Priscilla B. Hayner, *Unspeaking Truths: Facing the Challenge of Truth Commissions* (New York: Routledge, 2002).

32. Truth and Reconciliation Commission Act 2000, no. 4 (2000), sec. 6.

33. Ibid., sec. 7.

34. "Findings in Respect of Mineral Resources: A Fuelling Factor," vol. 2, chap. 2, para. 509, *Sierra Leone Truth and Reconciliation Commission Final Report,* October 27, 2004, available at http://www.usip.org/library/tc/tc_regions/tc_sl.html#rep.

35. "Findings in Respect of Mineral Resources: The Role of the Global Diamond Industry," vol. 2, chap., 2, para. 549, *Sierra Leone Truth and Reconciliation Commission Final Report,* October 27, 2004, available at http://www.usip.org/library/tc/tc_regions/tc_sl.html#rep.

36. Universal Declaration of Human Rights, G.A. Res. 217 A (III), UN Doc. A/810, art. 29(1).

37. Convention on the Prevention and Punishment of the Crime of Genocide, art. III(b).

38. Rome Statute of the International Criminal Court, art. 7(2)(a).

39. *Prosecutor v. Akayesu,* Case no. ICTR-96-4-T, Judgment, September 2, 1998.

PART 4

Conclusion

18

Peace Before Profit: The Challenges of Governance

Karen Ballentine

When the issue of "conflict diamonds" in Angola and Sierra Leone first focused the attention of policymakers to the economic activities that sustain armed conflict, many viewed the policy problem simply as one of curtailing resource and revenue flows to targeted rebel groups. Since then, however, scholarly and policy analysis has revealed a much more complex picture. The predatory exploitation of natural resources and the criminal trade in lucrative commodities by armed insurgents and criminal networks are now understood not as isolated acts but as the most visible symptoms of a broader systemic problem. It is a problem by which the unfettered forces of economic globalization and the pathologies of underdevelopment conspire against the creation of effective states, and seemingly, too, against an international order predicated upon them.

Indeed, in an era of free trade and market deregulation, the rise of the warlord-cum-entrepreneur is just the most potent symbol of the concurrent privatization and commercialization of armed conflict. While war making was never the complete preserve of states, the increased ease of access to decentralized global financial and commodity markets has created transnational support networks that make a variety of nonstate actors more crucial players than ever. As Mark Duffield has explained: "Market deregulation has deepened all forms of parallel and transborder trade and allowed warring parties to forge local-global networks and shadow economies as a means of asset realization and self-provisioning. . . . Instead of conventional armies, the new wars typically oppose and ally the transborder resource networks of state incumbents, social groups, diasporas, strongmen, and so on."[1] While many of these networks are criminal, they depend on the established infrastructure of licit global trade and finance. Further, and as many contributions to this volume underscore, whether passively or actively, the routine trade and investment practices of "otherwise legitimate" businesses can be as corrosive to the peace and prosperity of developing countries as is the criminal trade.

Understood from this perspective, then, the task of managing the conflict impacts of economic activity is, as Macartan Humphreys has stressed, not limited to curtailing illicit financial flows to rebels, nor even to disrupting transnational criminal networks. As important as these efforts are, and as important as it is to strengthen them, alone they cannot address the larger problem. To quote Jonathan Winer, the larger problem is that "governance has not kept pace with globalization." By definition globalization is a transborder phenomenon, one that has opened up a vast range of decentralized economic opportunities for private actors. By contrast, governance is still largely viewed as the preserve of states, whose authority and jurisdiction, where it exists at all, still ends at their sovereign borders. The result, as Winer explains, is that "no single authority is responsible for regulating cross-border activity or enforcing legal regimes applying to cross-border activity."[2] In this sense, the challenge of reducing conflict-promoting aspects of trade and investment is both territorial and extraterritorial, requiring not only strategies to assist weak and failing states to govern their own natural resource endowments but also strategies to strengthen and harmonize interstate efforts to govern cross-border economic transactions.

Blending as it does both licit economic activities and illicit flows at the global and local levels, the political economy of contemporary armed conflict is a complex and multidimensional phenomenon. Policymakers seeking to devise regulatory and policy mechanisms to reduce the pernicious, conflict-promoting effects of commerce confront what Leiv Lunde and Mark Taylor have described as a "malign problem structure." This structure consists of a heterogeneous set of actors with strong incentives to evade regulation, a lack of empirical and normative consensus as to which activities are legitimate and which illegitimate, competing and ill-defined regulatory jurisdictions and frameworks, and asymmetrical costs and benefits of regulation.[3] The multidimensionality of the problem also means that there is no obvious, single, and authoritative international forum or agency that could provide a "policy home" in which diverse initiatives could be brought together. As the contributions to this volume show, however, this complexity is not insuperable. There are a variety of existing and emerging technical, legal, market-based and policy mechanisms that, however partial, can and do contribute to more effective regulation of conflict-promoting economic activities, both licit and illicit. Whether these initiatives can be deployed by policymakers to contribute to a more comprehensive and coordinated global regulatory framework is an open and, fundamentally, political question.

It is the purpose of this concluding discussion to highlight promising policy options and opportunities as well as to assess the prospects for harmonizing them into a more coherent international normative and regulatory framework. I begin by briefly mapping out several dimensions of the current governance deficit and how it perpetuates the political economy of armed intrastate conflict. The discussion then turns to a consideration of policy options under three broad but interrelated issue areas: strengthening efforts to curtail conflict trade and finance; improving responsible management of natural resource extraction; and enhancing international norms and frameworks for promoting compliance and accountability of economic actors in unstable and war-torn settings. We conclude with a consideration of the contributions that the United Nations and its member states can make toward a more concerted strategy for managing the resource dimensions of armed conflict.

Commerce and Conflict: The Governance Deficit

As already indicated, efforts to reduce the conflict-exacerbating effects of economic activities in conflict-prone and war-torn states by targeting specific commodities and agents need to be complemented by policies that address the broader opportunity and incentive structures that enable and even encourage them to continue. Currently, these structures make for an environment that is highly permissive of illicit natural resource exploitation and economic predation in weak and war-torn states. On the one hand, given the high global demand for oil, gas, precious gems, and minerals, their often strategic importance, the competitive nature of these markets, and the profits to be had, many business actors are willing to accept the security risks of undertaking extractive operations in war-affected countries. On the other hand, even where these activities directly support warring groups, benefit corrupt elites, or contribute to human insecurity, the constraints against them are few because regulation is effectively absent.

This governance deficit is manifest on all levels. Most obviously and most urgently, it is an endemic characteristic of war-torn countries. Particularly in those countries that are dependent upon natural resources and vulnerable to that host of evils known as the "resource curse," the collapse of effective governance has been both cause and consequence of violent conflict.[4] Where the preoccupation is with regime survival, besieged state authorities have few resources and still less capacity to combat the predatory exploitation of natural resource endowments and the criminal trade in conflict commodities by nonstate actors, let alone to prevent rent-seeking and corrupt officials from colluding in these activities for their own

benefit. Given the prevailing incentive structures, it is a wonder that anyone should expect them to act otherwise.

It may be true that most businesses prefer a stable and predictable
investment environment, but not all do. First, there are a variety of opportunistic commercial actors—notably arms traders, private security firms,
and smugglers—for whom the anarchy of war opens up a range of lucrative, often irresistible economic possibilities. But business actors that are
undeterred by violent conflict also include multinational extractive industry corporations and their affiliates.[5] While these "otherwise legitimate"
businesses may prefer to work in peaceful, law-governed countries, they
seldom leave when things go bad. The reason is simple: however unstable, developing countries possess the last untapped reservoirs of a variety
of natural resources—some strategic, some just lucrative—that are in
high demand throughout world markets. This is a trend that cannot but
continue. Indeed, in Africa alone, oil companies are set to invest 50 billion dollars in resource-rich countries such as Nigeria, Angola, Equatorial
Guinea, Gabon, Sudan, Cameroon, and São Tomé and Príncipe.
Cumulatively, this is the largest investment in African history and is
expected to double the continent's oil production by 2015.[6] In an ideal
world, host states in the developing world would be both capable and
willing to responsibly husband their natural resource wealth for the collective well-being of their citizens and to protect them against predatory
economic actors. In the context of "really existing" globalization, however, they are patently not.

These considerations expose broader international governance failures
that deepen the dire predicament of weak, failing, and war-torn countries.
First, despite the wealth and robust institutional endowments of developed
states, and despite—or perhaps because of—the obvious benefits they
derive from home companies that deliver the desired resources of developing states, very few among them possess the needed regulatory influence
over the economic activities of their individual or corporate citizens
abroad.[7] Here, preoccupations with sovereign authority are as imposing an
obstacle to extraterritorial regulation as are economic self-interests in
ensuring their commercial advantage. Thus far, most home governments
have placed their hopes for remedy on the self-interest of their home companies to voluntarily adopt corporate codes of conduct that are conflict-sensitive, respect human rights, protect the environment, and support the rule
of law in conflict-affected and conflict-vulnerable countries.[8]

In so doing, however, governments in developed states are relying on
an ideal of global corporate social responsibility that does not yet exist.
While a number of disparate and partial codes of responsible business conduct are emerging, few companies yet endorse them, and fewer still actually comply.[9] This observation is not meant as a blanket indictment against

all companies in the extractive industry with operations in unstable or war-affected countries. Much to their credit, an increasing number of companies, under pressure by development, human rights, and peace advocates, now understand that calculations of political risk, previously factored only in terms of their own profit margin, must also incorporate, anticipate, and reduce the potential negative impacts of their investment and operational decisions on unstable and war-affected countries. But these companies are still a minority, and a minority that must compete for lucrative concessions in a field dominated by others who are less concerned with the human, social, and political costs of their activities and less exposed to the reputational risks that attend their conflict-promoting activities. In short, there is no level playing field for conflict-sensitive businesses. Nor can there be in the absence of concerted multilateral state action.

Curtailing Conflict Trade and Finance: Bridging Regulatory Gaps

At first glance, curtailing the global market exchanges that transform natural resource wealth into weaponry might not appear as difficult an undertaking as it actually is. Many of these transactions involve theft, smuggling, tax evasion, money laundering, bribery, and unauthorized arms sales, all of which are widely recognized as economic crimes, duly codified in domestic law as well as in a number of international conventions.[10] Where these activities involve commodities whose extraction has been accompanied by violent plunder, forced displacement of civilian communities, property destruction, or slave labor, they may also constitute war crimes or crimes against humanity.[11] And where they involve commodities or individuals proscribed under Security Council sanctions, they are in clear violation of the UN Charter.

Despite these prohibitions, and despite some significant recent efforts to strengthen them, the trade in conflict commodities and related financial flows remains a thriving business in which sanctions busters, transnational criminal cartels, and warlords continue to profit with relative impunity. Here, the major regulatory problems are incomplete coverage and inadequate monitoring and enforcement.

Extending Regulatory Coverage

The scope of regulation is incomplete in several respects. First, many of the relevant international instruments, such as those regarding corruption, money laundering, and organized crime, were designed for other purposes and do not explicitly address the kinds of economic actors and activities that finance armed conflict. Moreover, these instruments are managed by financial regulators and law enforcement officials who are prone to a conservative interpretation of their mandates and who view conflict prevention and conflict resolution as the responsibility of others.[12] The same sort of institutional parochialism has stymied those who are mandated to promote international peace and security; indeed, it is only very recently that the United Nations has understood the need to integrate criminal law enforcement and the protection of natural resources into conflict prevention and multidimensional peace operations.[13] As Phil Williams and John Picarelli underscore, tackling the transnational criminal aspects of the conflict trade requires "a more creative combination of conflict management and law enforcement."[14] In order to make the most of existing instruments, then, there is a need to analyze their potential synergies and develop institutional mechanisms that enable regular intra-agency cooperation among the United Nations, other multilateral regulatory economic and trade agencies, and law enforcement bodies. For a start, the UN Office for Drugs and Crime and Interpol could establish dedicated units to coordinate UN-wide efforts to curtail conflict trade and finance with ongoing policies to strengthen the enforcement of existing national and international prohibitions on the trade in narcotics, money laundering, and smuggling of arms and other contraband.

Second, those regulatory instruments that do target conflict trade and finance, most notably UN sanctions, have been ad hoc and partial. Tellingly, there is no common, comprehensive definition of what constitutes a "conflict commodity." For its part, the United Nations has defined conflict diamonds as "rough diamonds which are used by rebel movements to finance their military activities."[15] While this notion has since been applied to other commodities such as timber, by making the critical element one of agency rather than activity, it addresses only rebel financing. It does not address the full dimensions of the conflict trade, which in many settings also includes participation by government officials and the state security apparatus. As Jonathan Winer has suggested, a comprehensive definition of conflict commodities would include "all commodities that are sold by any participant in a conflict to generate resources that can be used for political or military purposes in connection with the conflict and on which taxes have not been paid." In his view, "the failure to pay taxes is a key element of the definition, as with this element the sellers of such commodities are engaged in illicit activity, regardless of their official status."[16] Given the broad international consensus against smuggling and tax evasion, defining conflict commodities in this way would go far to allay some of the political sensitivities over sovereignty that have so far impeded a more inclusive norm. Were this to be given authoritative backing, whether by UN Security Council resolutions or by the amendment of relevant international conventions, it would also provide a common normative framework for the type of interagency cooperation proposed above.

Strengthening Monitoring and Enforcement Capacities

The problem of inadequate enforcement of existing laws and regulatory mechanisms to curtail conflict trade and financing likewise has two main dimensions: one technical, the other political. On the technical side, the issue is weak legal, administrative, and intelligence capacity at the level of national governments. As has been recognized by those seeking to strengthen multilateral efforts to suppress terrorist financing and by Security Council sanctions committees, a major impediment to improved state compliance has been a lack of financial and human resources to design enabling domestic legislation, adequately equip law enforcement, financial regulators, and customs agents for investigation and monitoring, and support judicial prosecutions.[17]

Enhancing UN sanctions capacity. The creation of UN expert panels and monitoring mechanisms by the Security Council was largely in response to poor state performance in monitoring and reporting back on the relative progress of sanctions implementation and on continuing sanctions violations in Angola, Sierra Leone, Liberia, Somalia, and elsewhere. The expert panels were also a reflection of a new Security Council determination "to continue to take resolute action in areas where the illegal exploitation and trafficking of high-value commodities contributes to the escalation or continuation of conflict."[18]

The expert panels reports have made a singular contribution to UN sanctions monitoring. They have improved the understanding of sanctions-busting networks and practices and have identified sanctions violators and others who have benefited from the illicit exploitation of natural resources in conflict zones. In the process, they have also pointed to the lack of capacity for sanctions implementation at the national, regional, and international levels and identified other obstacles to more systematic compliance, thereby enhancing the UN's overall capacity to refine and tighten targeted sanctions.

Several reports have noted that the work of the expert panels has been hampered by a number of operational limitations, including their ad hoc nature and composition, unclear or partial Security Council mandates, lack of intrapanel communication and coordination, unclear standards of evidence, lack of consistent procedures for listing and delisting of sanctions targets, and lack of broader administrative and technical support. As enthusiasm for the expert panels grew, so too did suggestions for ways to strengthen and extend them: improve the criteria for expert selection;

strengthen the standards of evidence for naming and shaming those identified as violators of UN sanctions or other resolutions under Chapter VII of
the UN Charter; provide better structural support for the process and the
results of the investigations so that a database of accumulated findings can
be made available to key UN actors; and consider establishing some type of
permanent sanctions-monitoring capacity within the United Nations.[19]
While some of these proposals have been taken on board, the future role of
the expert panels remains uncertain. As one expert panel member noted in
2004, enthusiasm for the panels, as with sanctions more generally, appears
to be on the wane.[20]

From the outset, the expert panels' practice of publicly "naming and
shaming" sanctions violators, including state actors, has been as controversial as it has been innovative. On the one hand, naming and shaming has
pressed member states to take demonstrable steps to improve their compliance and, in some cases, to launch investigations of their nationals suspected of participating in the prohibited activities. Naming and shaming has
also served to empower civil society actors in their efforts to make their
governments and companies accountable—particularly in the case of the
Democratic Republic of Congo (DRC), where civil society groups, armed
with expert panel reports, were able to place the issue of illicit resource
exploitation on the agenda of the Inter-Congolese Dialogue.[21] As a result of
the combined efforts of the expert panels, UN sanctions have been taken
more seriously than ever before. While the expert panel reports did not end
sanctions busting, by helping to uncover and disrupt clandestine networks,
they contributed to the costs of doing so. Arguably, by identifying ways for
governments to disrupt illicit arms and commodity flows in Sierra Leone,
Angola, and the Liberian government, they may have also contributed to
the end of armed conflict in these countries.[22] Overall, the achievements of
the expert panels attest to the significant gains that can be achieved from
marginal innovations in UN policy design and implementation.

On the other hand, naming and shaming by the expert panels ignited a
number of political controversies that damaged their credibility while also
eliciting the Security Council's traditional caution. This caution may be one
reason for the council's lack of consistent follow-through on expert panel
recommendations. Indeed, with few exceptions—notably the long-overdue
imposition of timber sanctions against Charles Taylor's government in
Liberia—the vast majority of panel recommendations have not been taken
up by the Security Council. As Patricia Feeney and Tom Kenny detail, still
other recommendations, such as the investigation of companies named as
complicit in the illicit exploitation of resources in the DRC, have been
undertaken in a closed, perfunctory, and incomplete manner.[23] Unlike the
other expert panels, the DRC Experts Panel on the illicit exploitation of
natural resources was established independently of sanctions—already a

telling sign of the Security Council's growing reliance on naming and shaming as a substitute for more decisive action. Deprived of subpoena power and lacking any enforcement capacity of their own, however, expert panels can be only a poor and partial substitute for determined Security Council and member-state action. Even at its most robust, naming and shaming has had little impact on criminal sanctions busters, who are impervious to reputational standing. As the well-known sanctions buster Victor Bout told the *New York Times Magazine,* "Maybe I should start an arms-trafficking university and teach a course on U.N. sanctions busting."[24] Moreover, in the absence of concerted follow-up action, even the demonstrated deterrent effect of naming and shaming on reputationally sensitive governments and private actors is likely to suffer further diminishing returns.

Promoting criminal prosecution of sanctions violators by national governments. Several contributors to this volume have highlighted a number of other ways to strengthen the technical and administrative requisites of improved enforcement efforts in curtailing conflict trade and financing—both for national laws and international conventions and statutes to which many states are signatories. In his discussion of UN sanctions, Pierre Kopp observes that, like other resolutions enacted under Chapter VII of the UN Charter, Security Council sanctions only proscribe designated activities and actors; they do not criminalize them. Doing so is the responsibility of member states, which are also obliged by Chapter VII to ensure sanctions enforcement. Yet a surprising number of countries, including otherwise institutionally robust jurisdictions in developed states, have not created the needed enabling legislation and have not criminalized international sanctions busting in domestic statutes.[25] Kopp shows how, in at least one case, legislative lacunae allowed a notorious arms trader and sanctions buster, Leonid Minin, to escape judicial prosecution in Italy despite the accumulated and otherwise actionable evidence against him.

Where states are delinquent in undertaking national legislation and administrative reform to comply with UN sanctions, more decisive action is needed. While the Security Council has traditionally relied on diplomatic persuasion to promote member-state compliance, it has the power to do more. Building on the precedent established by the Security Council's counterterrorism Resolution 1373 and extended through its resolution on combating the proliferation of weapons of mass destruction, the council could require member states to enact enabling domestic legislation in support of sanctions and could require more detailed reporting on their progress in sanctions implementation.[26] Alternatively, as Sue Eckert suggests, the council could act on the remit of 1373, which includes not only the sequestration of terrorists' bank accounts but also the interdiction of their "other financial assets or economic resources."[27] As terrorist groups have been found to have parasitically exploited the conflict trade, this route offers another means of enhanced enforcement.

In the realm of UN sanctions, these would constitute radical steps that, in the current sanctions-shy atmosphere, are unlikely to be taken. In that event, the task of pressing member states to live up to their UN sanctions obligations could again be taken up by civil society and shareholder activists.

Improving modalities of technical assistance. Alongside persuasion and obligation, the United Nations could strengthen sanctions enforcement against conflict trade and finance by supporting improved modalities of technical assistance. Here, the work of the UN Counter-Terrorism Committee (CTC) offers a viable and promising model. As Eckert details, a major innovation of the CTC has been to create a standing body and elaborate on working methods to assist member states to build the needed legal and administrative capacity to identify and prosecute financiers of global terrorism within their domestic jurisdictions. The result, as Eckert details, has been an unprecedented degree of legislative and administrative reform that enables member states to better monitor, identify, and prosecute terrorist financing and related activities. Encouragingly, some proactive sanctions committees have already adopted some of the technical assistance and detailed reporting practices of the CTC, but without further support by the UN and member states, their impact is likely to be haphazard at best.

Policy opportunities for strengthened monitoring and enforcement are not limited to UN venues. In many respects, UN efforts to combat illicit conflict trade and finance could be strengthened by the creative development of new mechanisms as well as the adaptation and extension of modalities established by other multilateral mechanisms. The system for the certification of rough diamonds established by the Kimberley Process is by far the most robust mechanism for combating conflict trade. By establishing a common method of certification, backed by a documented chain of warranties and supported by national legislation of all diamond-producing, -trading, and -consuming states, Kimberley has, as Ian Smillie explains, effectively created an inclusive and integrated regime for regulating the diamond trade. Indeed, by December 2004 some forty-three countries, representing 98 percent of the rough diamond trade, were part of the Kimberley regime.[28] While some questions remain about monitoring provisions, the Kimberley Process provides a solid model of collaboration by governments, NGOs, and the private sector to create common standards to regulate problematic commodity flows as well as to build the requisite legal and technical capacities in participating countries to enforce them.

In his discussion of ways to improve methods for monitoring and interdicting conflict commodities and finance, Jonathan Winer details how the integration of the forensic criteria developed to detect money laundering by regulators such as the OECD Financial Action Task Force and the Egmont Group could be combined with policies adopted in response to the threat of terrorist smuggling of weapons of mass destruction by the World Customs Organization and the U.S. government's Container Security Initiative. The objective would be to create a unified international system of documentation that tracks and reports the physical movement of transborder shipments together with the financial transactions behind them.[29] As Winer notes, while none of these mechanisms are currently coordinated nor directed at conflict trade and finance, they could be readily adapted to this end, provided that the United Nations or states make the case. Recognizing that the implementation of a unified commodity and financial tracking regime would need the cooperation of private shipping and financial companies, Winer recommends the creative use of market inducements and preferred government contracts to reward private-sector actors for demonstrated compliance. Because of its potential to monitor and regulate all forms of transborder exchange, Winer's proposed unified tracking system promises a cost-efficient alternative to regulatory efforts, such as the Kimberley Process, that focus on a single problematic commodity and a single kind of security threat.

The Limitations of Prohibition

Even the most robust measures against conflict trade and finance share the inherent limitations of interdiction policies that rely exclusively on "supply-side" controls. Chief among them is the problem of moral hazard. As explained by Kopp and by Williams and Picarelli, while commodity and trade bans may raise the cost of engaging in the prohibited activity, they also raise its value and its attractiveness to risk takers, thereby deepening the involvement of international criminal networks well suited to high-risk ventures. Typically, too, the proscription of the exploitation of, production of, or trade in a particular commodity has predictable displacement effects: belligerents and criminal groups intent on raising revenues respond by shifting their attention to other accessible commodities, much in the way that Liberia's Taylor shifted to timber exploitation in response to the UN embargo on conflict diamonds. Geographic displacement follows the same logic. One effect of drug interdiction efforts has been the relocation of cultivation and processing to neighboring states. Likewise the original impact of diamond certification in Sierra Leone was simply to reverse the flows of laundered diamonds.[30]

Another problem, elaborated by Stephen Jackson, is that, contrary to some perceptions, no matter how targeted they may be, commodity bans do have unintended humanitarian impacts on those civilians whose livelihoods have, as a consequence of wartime economic dislocation, become dependent on the illicit extraction and trade in these valuable commodities. While this sort of civilian dependence is difficult to measure directly, available evidence suggests that in some settings, such as Afghanistan and DRC, it is widespread. In these contexts, Jackson explains, embargoes and interdiction "risk creating perverse incentives that may intensify the economic activity they seek to curtail, displacing rather than disincentivizing production, widening the gap between rich and poor, and sometimes furthering economic violence."[31] Accordingly, he recommends that commodity bans be made more sensitive to their potential negative welfare effects and that they be accompanied by remedial measures to preserve productive assets (of all kinds, not merely physical), protect dependents (by weaning them away from conflict-dependent livelihoods rather than abruptly severing them through ill-designed measures), and encourage economic actors to move away from techniques of violence. More broadly, these recommendations point to the need for a wider range of policy interventions to protect and promote the responsible management of natural resource endowments in weak and war-torn countries.

Promoting the Responsible Management of Natural Resource Endowments: The Role of Aid, Trade, and Investment

Few international challenges are more in need of integrated policy responses than the economic dimensions of civil war. Just as efforts to curtail conflict trade and finance call for improved coordination of conflict management and international law enforcement, so too addressing the structural underpinnings that link natural resource wealth and conflict will require closer integration of aid, trade, and security policies. The demonstrated role that the mismanagement and inequitable distribution of resource wealth have played in perpetuating a vicious cycle of underdevelopment and violent conflict is fundamentally a problem of governance. Governance reforms are already difficult enough in developing and transitional countries seeking to avoid the scourge of armed conflict.[32] Rebuilding the capacity of domestic institutions and promoting the responsible management of natural resource extraction after years, if not decades, of war—and in contexts where the militarization, criminalization, and systemic corruption of the economy continues—is by far the more daunting challenge. Much can be done by development agencies to provide practical assistance to war-affected states to adopt fiscal transparency of resource revenues, devise equitable resource-sharing policies, and ensure that extractive projects benefit civilian communities, yet the governance agenda does not end at the borders of vulnerable and war-torn states. The redirection of natural resource wealth to sustainable peace and development also requires funda- mental reforms at the global level. This makes improved cooperation among international financial institutions, state lending agencies, private companies, development agencies, and UN peace missions essential. As long as the global marketplace in valuable resources remains unregulated, any effort to build viable economic institutions in weak and failing states risks falling victim to the contrary pulls of international trade and invest- ment.[33]

For both conflict prevention and postconflict reconstruction, the pro- motion of responsible resource management entails two broad policy objec- tives: the creation of transparent, accountable methods of managing and distributing resource wealth by host countries and measures to ensure that extractive operations are conducted in a sustainable and conflict-sensitive manner.

Managing Resource Wealth for Peace and Prosperity

Several contributions to this volume highlight a number of practical policy options that may help resource-rich but governance-poor countries to escape the predations of the resource curse. In highlighting what can be done, they also point to a variety of existing and emerging modalities whose potential has not yet been fully exploited.

Transparency of natural resource revenues. In addition to the well- established connection between resource wealth and corrosive rent seeking, policymakers have become increasingly aware of the ways that the unac- countable use of resource revenues by governments has directly financed war-making activities in a number of contemporary conflicts. In response, the promotion of revenue transparency has become a central feature of advocacy campaigns, multistakeholder initiatives, and international finan- cial institution (IFI) lending policies, as well as a growing priority for multinational extractive corporations. While revenue transparency is not a panacea, there is growing consensus that gaining a clear picture of actual natural resource revenues that accrue to national governments is an essen- tial prerequisite for making them accountable to their citizens for public expenditure decisions made in their name. The publication of official resource revenues would not only reduce the scope for rent seeking but may also, as Macartan Humphreys observes, reduce the potential for alle- gations of official corruption to become a motive for violent contestation of the state.[34]

Despite the broad normative consensus that exists, secrecy remains the order of the day. Efforts to translate this norm into practice face a variety of technical and political challenges. Technically, the problem consists in devising methods to reconcile disparate, and sometimes impenetrable, accounting systems into a reliable mechanism by which an accurate estimate of resource revenues can be made and in creating the national capacities to implement it. As Gavin Hayman and Corene Crossin detail, here development agencies could help by designing long-term training and capacity-building programs for both government administrators and civil society monitors. In the short to medium term, revenue monitoring could be undertaken through independent audits by private accounting firms or by the International Monetary Fund.[35]

The political challenges are far less tractable. Past efforts to determine accurate accounts of resource revenues—notably the ill-fated IMF-sponsored Oil Diagnostic exercise in Angola—have run up against the resistance of government officials eager to maintain wide fiscal discretion.[36] As Humphreys notes, the problem here is not only endemic corruption but also the desire of host governments to retain maximum bargaining power vis-à-vis international investors. Government intransigence has led some to advocate an alternative route to transparency and to demand that multinational extractive companies disclose all concessionary and bonus payments they make to host governments, just as they are already required to do in their home jurisdictions. This is the raison d'être of the Publish What You Pay campaign (PWYP), a coalition of NGOs founded in 2002. As Hayman and Crossin explain, financial disclosure by companies would increase incentives for host governments to demonstrate fiscal probity while also providing better information to civil society groups seeking to hold their government accountable. Predictably, many companies have objected that the campaign unfairly targets them for the malfeasance of state officials. The more fundamental problem, however, is one of collective action. With few exceptions, companies are loath to undertake steps that not only may reveal less than salutary business deals but also may reduce their market standing vis-à-vis less scrupulous rivals.[37]

To date, this is an obstacle that has not yet been overcome. The UK-sponsored Extractive Industry Transparency Initiative, relying as it does on voluntary corporate cooperation, may enjoy the support of progressive companies and governments, but for the same reason it is ill designed to resolve the larger collective action problems that they face. For its part, the PWYP campaign has sought to extend a common playing field by insisting on mandatory disclosure by companies. This approach would be backed by making such disclosure a condition for getting listed on stock exchanges. As many extractive companies are shareholder-based, such a requirement would help address the collective action problems among them by exposing publicly listed extractive companies to a common requirement. One consequence of the highly publicized corporate accounting scandals in the early 2000s is that reform of listing requirements for improved financial transparency has gained increased attention by experts and advocacy organizations.[38] As Mark Mansley details, private investors and shareholders have already begun to lobby for an expansion of listing requirements and corporate reporting practices to include issues of human rights and environmental protection. Seen from this perspective, extending listing requirements to include disclosure of payments to host governments made by extractive companies is far from being a radical proposition. Still, as company representatives rightly point out, such listing requirements would do little to alter the practices of state-owned or privately owned companies, with whom they must nonetheless compete.

As these shortcomings illustrate, if revenue transparency is to become as widespread in practice as it currently is in rhetoric, more leverage needs to be brought to bear to alter the prevailing incentive structures. One option would be to supplement ongoing transparency initiatives by making resource revenue transparency standards a condition of all multilateral and bilateral development aid. The IMF has already made regular safeguards assessment a feature of its lending policies and is increasingly insisting that governments demonstrate transparency as a condition of IMF engagement.[39] National donor agencies should do likewise. As James Boyce observes, however, even were donor agencies to arrive at a coordinated policy—itself a perennial open question—development conditionality may have limited impact on governments whose resource endowments equal or outstrip the amount of aid on offer and who may, in any case, place little priority on promoting sustainable development. It may also unfairly penalize those countries most in need of development assistance.[40] This was the situation that has occurred in Angola and one that also holds in Equatorial Guinea, where a suspension of IMF support, in part for poor natural resource revenue management, has effected little change.[41]

A far more promising avenue would be to make the disclosure of resource revenues a mandatory requirement for all lending, insurance, and project finance by national export credit agencies (ECAs) in companies' home countries. Often an indispensable source of finance for extractive industry projects, ECAs have significant potential to leverage transparent and accountable resource management among them.[42] As detailed by Nicholas Hildyard, however, the mandate of ECAs is investment protection. Incredibly, most ECAs are not required to consider the wider social or conflict impacts of the overseas investment projects they support, nor are they direct participants in current multistakeholder transparency initiatives.[43] This represents an egregious omission and one which national governments—both individually and together—must take serious action to redress. At a minimum, ECAs should be made principal participants in the

EITI. More broadly, ECA reform should be placed high on the agendas of the G-8, the OECD, and regional initiatives such as the New Partnership for Africa's Development (NEPAD), all of which have stated commitments to promoting fiscal transparency.[44] Substantively, ECAs should undertake policies requiring that conflict-sensitive measures, such as conflict-impact assessments and transparency standards, are integrated into the production sharing and concessionary agreements of the extractive projects that they finance.

Equitable distribution of resource benefits. A related issue by which natural resource wealth has been identified with conflict risk is the real or perceived inequitable distribution of benefits, both to affected communities and to society at large. The failure of host governments to share resource wealth more broadly, or to direct it to the provision of needed public goods, has been a powerful source of popular grievance that has fed violent unrest and outright war in a number of settings, such as Nigeria, Bougainville, Aceh, and Sudan.[45] In many instances, too, this governance failure has left extractive company operations vulnerable to community demands for compensation, some of which have been expressed violently. Faced with threats to the security of their plant and personnel as well as to the high costs that these threats pose, many companies have come to accept the need for some form of community compensation as essential to obtaining their "social license to operate." As Luc Zandvliet details, however, company compensation practices often take the form of crude cash payments or of poorly conceived community development projects, both of which can create more tensions than they solve and neither of which contributes to a coherent and viable development strategy.[46]

Among those concerned with conflict prevention and postconflict peacebuilding, an increasingly popular option is to promote more equitable resource distribution through the use of natural resource funds (NRFs). Traditionally, NRFs were devised as a macroeconomic and fiscal tool to preserve balanced economic growth and guard against price volatility in resource-dependent economies. Increasingly, they are viewed as a tool of revenue sharing that can contribute to conflict-sensitive development. According to one observer, "The real value of a NRF is not its effectiveness as a fiscal tool but as a political instrument. . . . NRFs can commit governments to treat revenues as public monies, not as private income veiled from public scrutiny."[47] The idea behind them is simple: natural resource revenues, or a portion thereof, are paid into an escrow account or other special fund, separate from the regular national budget and dedicated to social expenditures. Central to their effectiveness is the provision of independent oversight. Depending on the country, this oversight may be provided by the parliament, financial auditors, or a specially created mechanism that includes civil society monitors and externally appointed experts. As Humphreys' survey indicates, there are different modalities of revenue sharing, from a direct per capita distribution to all citizens, to the earmarking of revenues to the needs of affected communities in resource-producing regions, to the designation of funds for specific public goods and infrastructure projects. As each model contains its own trade-offs, only careful consideration of the particular institutional and social context can determine which model is most likely to have the desired social and economic impact.[48]

Earmarking social revenues to resource-producing areas under multistakeholder oversight is at the core of the World Bank–sponsored Chad-Cameroon Pipeline Project. Due in part to its experimental nature, this revenue-sharing scheme is flawed in many respects; among other things, it does not apply to these countries' major natural resource endowments, it is time bound, and it lacks the needed capacity to effectively implement designated social expenditures at the local level.[49] These flaws excepted, however, the Chad-Cameroon project has become an attractive model for those seeking quick ways to restore natural resource management in the early stages of postconflict recovery, when the need is urgent and when home governments may be more willing to accept the conditionality and intrusiveness that such schemes entail. One proposal is for the creation of a multistakeholder trust fund for the Ituri region in eastern DRC to collect, monitor, and allocate the revenues generated from the region's valuable natural resources for the purpose of infrastructure and social investments.[50]

Whether or not this or a similar proposal for social revenue sharing will become more widespread largely depends on the receptivity of resource-dependent states, both to the very desirability of the purposes of such schemes and to the loss of sovereign discretion over revenue distribution that they imply. As has been noted by James Boyce, countries that are rich in resources and weak in governance typically have few incentives to accept intrusive regulation of this sort and may even reject it as another form of donor neoimperialism. In this respect, the particular incentives that led the government of Chad to accept revenue sharing as part of the pipeline project, primarily the combined leverage of the World Bank and the oil consortium, may seldom obtain elsewhere. This said, in postconflict settings where development and reconstruction needs are great and donor and investment leverage is relatively strong, there may be further opportunities for revenue-sharing mechanisms to be established.[51]

A final issue concerns the sustainability of such funds. While premised on the unreliability of host governments to ensure responsible and equitable distribution of resource revenues through normal institutional channels, insulated and externally managed social funds that bypass existing structures may in fact deprive states of needed revenues, relieve them of the need to undertake regular social spending, undermine the potential for a strengthened social contract, and ultimately perpetuate state weakness. As Terry Karl elsewhere has observed, the long-term sustainability of social funds requires that they can function once international oversight is phased out, which in turn "presuppose(s) the prior existence of an independent and workable judicial system that can cope with corruption and theft, the acceptance of transparent budgetary practices, [and] a relatively independent central bank."[52] To prevent worse outcomes, then, there is a need for parallel multistakeholder efforts that encourage and support national governments in undertaking fiscal and administrative reforms of core institutions, particularly in the areas of financial oversight, budgeting, accounting, and public expenditure review, as an integral part of wider governance reforms and programs.[53]

Conflict-Sensitive Extractive Operations

The inequitable distribution of resource benefits is not limited to revenues. Where extractive projects are undertaken in populated regions, they bring predictable distributional impacts on traditional economies, environmental conditions, landholding patterns, employment structures, and other aspects of human welfare, thereby creating new winners and losers and new faultlines for conflict. In conditions of endemic violence, these problems are often compounded by the security priorities of companies, which, however legitimate, often involve the use of security forces that at best, have scant concern for the safety and well-being of local populations.

As both Humphreys and Zandvliet make clear, the fact that these impacts are predictable does not mean that companies are either fully aware or well equipped to deal with them. At the level of individual company operations in zones of weak governance or violent conflict, progress on integrating conflict-sensitive business practices into management routines has been uneven at best. Because of both their reputational exposure and their greater capacity, large multinational corporations generally have been more conflict sensitive than smaller, less visible "juniors." For the most part, however, even these efforts have been reactive rather than proactive, undertaken only once violence has been visited upon company plant and personnel or once their problematic activities have been brought to light by advocacy groups.

According to Zandvliet, part of the problem has been a corporate culture and reward structure within the extractive industry in which conflict is seen as an external problem that poses risks to company operations, which are thus best managed by minimizing local engagement. Because of the failure of companies to understand the conflict-exacerbating potential of their own activities, they have been slow to develop the capacities and know-how to accurately diagnose and anticipate problems and to take preemptive action. Yet an increasing number of progressive companies are now keenly attuned to the business case for adopting conflict-sensitive business practices, and their efforts in that direction could be greatly strengthened by supportive multistakeholder engagement.

Improving community engagement. There can be little doubt of the importance to conflict prevention of active company engagement with the communities in which its operations are located. Not only can such engagement provide much-needed welfare benefits to populations that are often economically marginalized, but it can also build trust that gives a company a "social license to operate," providing the secure environment needed for what are often long-term operations. In practice, however, not enough companies have made community engagement an important priority, while those that have done so often pursue the wrong sorts of engagement.

Typically, companies have sought to build good community relations through social investment projects, ranging from traditional philanthropy, to creating local employment, to making strategic investments in local infrastructure, such as roads, hospitals, schools, and in other public goods.[54] Very often, however, these otherwise salutary initiatives address the symptom rather than the disease. Where the main fuel for conflict stems not from local operations but from resource-related payments by companies to unaccountable and repressive state elites who are using the revenues to benefit themselves or to finance war, investments in community development may do little to mitigate armed conflict. As *The Economist* pointedly observed of Talisman Energy in Sudan: "For all its concern for ethical business, human rights and development, the ugly truth is that Talisman is helping the government to extract oil, and oil is paying for the war."[55] Further, as Zandvliet details, in many cases some well-intended company efforts can actually create new sources of conflict. For example, in settings where intergroup inequalities are already contentious, otherwise fair-minded, merit-based hiring practices may in fact deepen local divisions by rewarding those who have greatest access to education.[56] Not only do company social investment initiatives frequently fail on their own terms, but— because they are so often targeted to quick-impact projects that the company deems important—they fail to contribute to sustainable development.[57] Indeed, according to Zandvliet, the more that companies undertake the role of public service provider, the more they risk "emphasizing the inadequacies of government agencies, undermining existing or potential government and civil servant capacities, and further feeding into antigovernment sentiments."[58] In the worst case, the company risks becoming a de facto government and a primary target of local grievance, while the already unaccountable host government is relieved of the burdens of public service provision that properly belong to it.

For companies operating in weak governance zones or in areas of full-scale violent conflict, this presents a difficult dilemma. The first step in confronting it is for companies to recognize that managing political risk requires understanding the potential of their own activities on conflict dynamics. According to Zandvliet's own survey of field operations, this is an area where engaging with other stakeholders can be particularly useful, as companies frequently lack a full understanding of the local context. Through various partnerships with NGOs and with the UN Global Compact, companies have begun to develop and apply "conflict impact assessments" to better ascertain the potential negative effects of their operations on local dynamics and to identify opportunities for mutually beneficial engagement.

These approaches could be strengthened in a number of ways. At a minimum, conflict impact assessments should be made a requirement for all IFI, ECA, and shareholder financing of extractive and extractive-related projects in vulnerable and war-torn states. At the same time, companies should be encouraged to do more than share their "best practices" and document what has gone wrong and why. As Humphreys notes, thus far the cumulative knowledge available to companies as to which sorts of social investment projects work and which do not is largely based on anecdotal and incomplete evidence. If conflict impact assessments are to be a reliable instrument for companies, then what is needed is a more systematic, comparative assessment of the effects of the broad range of company interventions in different conflict settings—an undertaking that would require companies to work together with researchers with expertise in conflict analysis.

Efforts to assist companies to adopt conflict-sensitive practices in areas of operation, however, should not stop there. As important as the particular local policies and social investment projects companies deploy to mitigate conflict or to contribute to peacebuilding may be, they are, as Zandvliet stresses, far less consequential to reducing conflict than the overall manner in which they are undertaken. As his research indicates, affected communities have made clear that, while specific benefits are desired, what is more valuable to them is that their voices are being heard and taken seriously. Here, the main problem is a lack of genuine community engagement. Company engagement with local communities is a process, not an outcome. To be effective, engagement requires not only that conflict impact assessments be continually updated but also that company interactions with affected communities be better assisted by partnerships with other local stakeholders, notably UN country teams and peace missions, international donors, and locally active NGOs, all of which often have a better sense of the local context, changing conflict dynamics, and development opportunities than individual companies can or do possess on their own.[59] Precisely because the main interlocutors of UN actors and international donor agencies are host governments, undertaking strategic engagement and regular consultations with companies may not only facilitate improved company-community relations but also help companies to design policies that contribute to, rather than subtract from, host-country governance capacities.

Securing resource endowments and sustainable livelihoods in post-conflict settings. Given that many of the armed intrastate conflicts that featured violent contests over natural resources have formally ended, whether by military conquest or internationally mediated peace agreements, some observers may be tempted to conclude that natural resources are no longer a conflict issue. Such a conclusion, however, would be sorely misguided. Despite the termination of large-scale war in places such as Afghanistan, Sierra Leone, Liberia, and DRC, these nations' war economies continue. Indeed, in the immediate aftermath of conflict, efforts to implement peace are often hostage to the interests of local, national, regional, and global actors whose economic and political power has been gained through armed violence. Particularly where there is continued access to "lootable resources" such as alluvial gems and minerals and timber or illicit commodities such as poppy and coca, there is a high potential for greedy spoilers to undermine already fragile peace accords.[60]

An awareness of these risks has prompted both the United Nations and international donors engaged in postconflict reconstruction to make the restoration of effective governance of natural resource endowments an important priority. As Boyce explains about the case of Cambodia, a recognition of the continued conflict trade in timber that benefited the Khmer Rouge and created incentives for them to subvert the peace agreement prompted the UN Security Council in 1992 to mandate the UN Transitional Authority (UNTAC) to monitor the border with Thailand as a means to control the timber smuggling between the two countries that provided the Khmer Rouge with important revenues. Ultimately, the successful curtailing of this conflict trade required a supplementary effort of the World Bank to threaten sanctions against the Thai government for its complicity—an action that underscores both the need to systematically address the regional dynamics of conflict trade and the leverage that donor agencies can bring to UN peace implementation efforts. More recently, the UN Security Council mandated the UN Mission in Liberia "to assist the transitional government in restoring proper administration of natural resources" as part of its wider efforts in support of peace implementation.[61] This has required close cooperation with other UN and donor efforts to regulate the regionally embedded conflict trade in West Africa.

A central component of these efforts is to assist legitimate authorities to develop the administrative and legal capacity to counter illicit and predatory exploitation and trade in valuable commodities, by supporting reforms of customs and law enforcement agencies and by assisting in the implementation of certification schemes. Given that lootable resources are by definition decentralized and highly accessible to illicit exploitation, efforts to secure physical control over their production and trade are bound to fall short.[62] This is especially the case where civilian livelihoods are broadly dependent on these resources. Referring to Sierra Leone's artisanal diamond mining, for instance, the International Crisis Group has stressed that "'mining' in these areas is more like 'farming' that involves tens of thousands of persons and is virtually impossible to control. . . . It remains literally the only source of income for large parts of the country."[63] As Stephen Jackson highlights, these informal livelihoods have often existed already before conflict erupted. They may change and mutate during war, but typically they persist in the "postconflict" context.

In addition to enforcement capacity, then, securing effective governance of resource endowments in postconflict settings requires strategies that address the demand side of the problem. With otherwise legal commodities such as timber and diamonds, much can be gained by policies that give local laborers a formal stake in sustainable and legal production. In Sierra Leone, for example, innovative donor-funded programs such as the Kono Peace Diamonds Alliance and the Campaign for Just Mining seek to establish an "integrated diamond management system," whereby local mining cooperatives work together with local leaders and state authorities to ensure the legal, transparent, and socially responsible production and marketing of alluvial diamonds. In return for ensuring a legal chain of custody for diamond sales, miners are licensed and are assured fair prices for their labor.[64] While these programs have yet to achieve significant environmental, educational, and other social benefits for affected communities, they represent an important start in formalizing heretofore informal economic activities, thereby rendering them less vulnerable to violent and criminal capture.[65]

Where war economies rely on the production of and trade in illicit commodities such as poppy in Afghanistan or coca in Colombia, the challenges of transformation are considerably more difficult. By definition, markets in illicit narcotics are both highly lucrative and dominated by criminal violence, regardless of whether this criminal violence is tied to large-scale armed conflict. Because of the domestic problems posed by illicit drug consumption in the developed world, northern governments, whose populations are the chief consumers of illicit drugs, can gain political capital at home by adopting tough prohibitionist policies. As the respective analyses of Boyce and of Williams and Picarelli demonstrate, however, the tough interdiction policies favored by donor governments are seldom successful in reducing the production of these crops in war-torn and other areas of the developing world, where local authorities lack the requisite enforcement capacity, where producers have few other livelihood options, and where risk-taking traffickers are lured by huge profits. In fact, interdiction efforts not only reinforce criminalized economies but also increase the risk that such actors will undermine simultaneous efforts to build sustainable peace. If the international community is serious about remedying the source of the problem, then it must take more seriously the priority of investing in the creation of alternative livelihoods for producers in sectors that are lucrative yet legal. Achieving this objective means that donor governments must give more attention to reevaluating the deleterious impacts on developing economies of their own protectionist trade policies, while also devoting more funds to developing realistic economic alternatives for producers.[66]

Promoting alternative economic opportunities is also a critical component of more effective efforts at disarmament, demobilization, and reintegration (DDR). While policymakers are increasingly sensitive to this need, there has been little concerted academic and policy focus on the specific challenges for DDR in conflict settings beset by violent economic struggles over natural resource wealth and where systematic predation is well entrenched. Anecdotal evidence, however, suggests that where fighters are remunerated through pillage of lucrative natural resources or civilian predation, the possession of arms is not just a function of ongoing insecurity but also an economic asset. For some fighters, the economic opportunities and rewards available through violent predation may exceed those expected to be available after conflict, and this will influence a combatant's decision whether to voluntarily disarm and return to a civilian life. DDR may also be hampered by a lack of discipline and fractionalization of combatant groups, which makes it more difficult for leaders to convince rank-and-file soldiers to disarm and demobilize. In Sierra Leone, for instance, many ex-combatants not adequately assisted by the reintegration program became a serious security threat, mobilizing for protest and moving to the diamond areas, where they challenged local groups and were recruited as mercenaries for the war in Liberia.[67]

As Jackson's analysis makes clear, in such settings DDR is as much an economic challenge as a security imperative. Yet current practice continues to be largely security driven, focusing resources and attention on weapons-buyback programs and cantonment of ex-combatants while neglecting longer-term strategies for reintegration. Training programs to assist ex-combatants in their transition back to civilian life remain underfunded. More problematic is that little effort is made to match skills with available economic opportunities or with longer-term job creation programs in the private sector. The DDR program in Afghanistan in the early 2000s, for instance, directed the majority of ex-combatants to take the "rural option" despite the fact that the agricultural sector was not large enough to absorb the considerable numbers of former combatants. If DDR is to be sustainable, then reintegration must be pursued in parallel with disarmament and demobilization. To ensure the maximal reabsorption of ex-fighters into legal and peaceful economic life, DDR programming also needs to be better coordinated with and integrated into long-term development strategies.[68]

Establishing Accountability, Ending Impunity: Improving International Regulation of Private-Sector Actors in Armed Conflict

As discussed at the outset, because the economic forces that underpin armed intrastate conflict are deeply embedded in the prevailing international economic order, transforming war economies at the national level will accomplish little unless the global regulatory deficit is also addressed. Indeed, in the prevailing climate of international trade and investment, transnational private sector actors, with few exceptions, are not accountable for the negative social impacts of their investments and operations abroad. This state of virtual impunity is enjoyed not only by clearly criminal actors such as smugglers, money launderers, sanctions busters, and warlords but also by otherwise legitimate and powerful business actors that make enormous profits from commerce and investment in war-torn countries and other places where effective local regulation is absent. Numerous reports have made clear that otherwise legal companies have engaged in unscrupulous business deals with repressive governments and elites that perpetrate massive human rights violations against civilian populations, often in the context of armed conflict.[69] More troubling, there have also been documented cases of companies' dealing in what one analyst has dubbed "booty futures": direct company financing of rebel groups in anticipation that their victory will reward the company with lucrative resource concessions.[70] The willingness of some companies to engage in these sorts of dubious enterprise is a function not only of the profits to be had but also of a weak regulatory environment in which the costs and penalties for misconduct are few.

The Limited Promise of Self-Regulation

Thus far, efforts to address the permissive opportunity structure that perpetuates these sorts of activities have relied largely upon naming and shaming and other sorts of suasion by advocacy groups and UN expert panels, as well as exhortations to companies to regulate themselves by adopting and adhering to corporate codes of responsible business conduct. Each of these approaches has, in its own way, made an indispensable contribution.

Naming and shaming actions were the essential impetus to improved sanctions enforcement, the Kimberley Process for the certification of rough diamonds, and, more recently, the attention being paid to the need for transparency in natural resource revenues.[71] Without the pressure of bad publicity, many more companies would likely be conducting "business as usual," in complete disregard of their own negative impacts on conflict dynamics, and would have little incentive to align themselves with conflict-sensitive codes of conduct. In turn, the decision by some companies to incorporate ethical standards on security, human rights, and transparency into their corporate social responsibility policies has helped to sensitize corporate cultures as well as make these companies more receptive to developing safeguards to ensure that their activities in vulnerable and war-torn settings contribute to sustainable peace.

As highlighted in the respective analyses of Hayman and Crossin and of Feeney and Kenny, however, despite these important developments, overall progress on achieving improved business conduct through company self-regulation has been slow and partial. The most commonly cited weakness of company self-regulation is the voluntary nature of business codes of conduct. Whether industry driven or as part of public-private initiatives such as the U.S.-UK Principles on Security and Human Rights, the Extractive Industry Transparency Initiative, the ten principles of the UN Global Compact, or the OECD *Guidelines for Multinational Enterprises,* corporate standards of good conduct are not binding. With the exception of the OECD *Guidelines,* performance assessments depend largely on self-reporting by companies.[72] These reports are typically selective and nonverifiable. This leaves companies vulnerable to the criticism that pledges of responsible business conduct are a function of expediency and self-promotion rather than a long-term commitment to corporate responsibility. More problematic, even where reports indicate noncompliance, companies typically incur no penalty beyond reputational cost, a factor of sensitivity to only the most progressive of companies. In short, voluntary self-regulation may make companies more responsible, but it does not necessarily make them accountable.

As the history of the Kimberley Process shows, voluntary efforts at self-regulation can be made binding on participants. The credibility and effectiveness of other voluntary codes could be greatly improved if shareholders and NGOs encouraged the companies that have adopted them to commit themselves to the creation of clear, common, and verifiable performance obligations.[73] Strengthened self-enforcement not only would demonstrate a serious commitment to conflict-sensitive business practices but would also enable more reliable assessments of actual progress. Not least, the inclusion of performance obligations would help to identify noncompliers, thereby enhancing the reputational rewards to progressive companies.

Even assuming such a step were undertaken, however, voluntary self-regulation would still fall short. Changing internal corporate and industry cultures, though necessary, can do little to address the uneven playing field in which companies compete. As indicated in the above analysis, self-regulation is based on self-selection; it is attractive only to those companies eager to safeguard their reputational value or those genuinely convinced of the business case for conflict-sensitive policies. It is hardly surprising that large transnational companies have proved most responsive: they are based in developing countries where large and vocal NGOs are based, and they make good targets for advocacy campaigns and costly lawsuits. By contrast, being insulated from reputational costs that might translate into consumer or shareholder sanction, large state-owned enterprises (SOEs) and smaller "junior" companies based in countries with little interest in human rights and weak civil societies are conspicuously absent from such initiatives and are thus less constrained to enter into business deals that could have a negative impact on conflict dynamics. Needless to add, self-regulation has no attraction for those rogue and criminal business actors that specialize in making business from war.[74]

This disparity between socially progressive large multinationals and socially indifferent companies in less-regulated home countries creates free-rider and collective action problems that expose more progressive companies to possible loss of competitive advantage to the benefit of less scrupulous rivals. Here, the experiences of Talisman Energy in Sudan and Premier Oil in Burma/Myanmar are instructive. Faced with concerted protests from NGOs and shareholders concerning their alleged complicity in human rights abuses committed by the governments of Sudan and Burma/Myanmar, both companies ultimately chose to divest from the oil projects. However, they did so by selling their assets to their joint-venture partners, the state-owned oil companies of India and Malaysia respectively, which did not face the same domestic pressures. For the civilian victims of the Sudanese war, the withdrawal of the Western companies did nothing to change the violent conditions they faced. This is a situation that voluntary approaches alone cannot remedy.

Supplemental Regulation

Addressing the collective action problems that impede the development of conflict-sensitive trade and investment requires the creation of regulatory policies that correct the current imbalance of rewards and penalties. Improved regulation need not entail a full-scale abandonment of voluntary initiatives in favor of hard regulation. As Leiv Lunde and Mark Taylor make clear, the "voluntary-mandatory" dichotomy is as unhelpful as it is false.[75] Where the objective is to limit the role of business actors in contributing to conflict, what matters is not whether the approach is voluntary or mandatory, industry monitored or legally sanctioned, but whether it can effect positive change.[76] The voluntary/mandatory dichotomy risks obscuring the full range of regulatory mechanisms that fall between pure voluntarism and hard law. Indeed, hybrid forms of regulation, such as the Kimberley Process on the Certification of Rough Diamonds, can be highly effective; despite being a voluntary agreement, Kimberley has—through a combination of law and market inducements—created binding effects on participating members, while also reshaping the industry-wide incentive structure in favor of certification.

Enhancing market inducements. There are a number of ways that market inducements could be better designed to promote and reward conflict-sensitive business practices while also increasing the costs to businesses that continue to disregard them. Where companies are publicly held, shareholder associations, institutional investors, and private banks have significant financial leverage that can be brought to bear upon company policies and practices in conflict zones. Indeed, shareholder activism has been a central determinant in making individual companies more accountable and in compelling them to end problematic investments in war-torn countries, as well as to support initiatives such as the Voluntary Principles and the EITI. As Mark Mansley observes, however, while ethical investment is a growing force, it has been driven by shareholder activism at the company or fund level. Making adherence to transparency standards, verifiable conflict-impact assessments, and other integrity instruments a listing requirement of international securities and exchange rules would provide additional leverage to investor efforts over a larger number of companies. Further, because institutional investors and shareholders are not the only, nor even the primary, source of project finance in the extractive industry, the same sorts of conditionality need to be integrated into the policies of public financial institutions. The private-sector financing arms of the World Bank, notably the International Finance Corporation (IFC), have strengthened their lending safeguards to ensure that projects meet a variety of environmental and development standards. However, as Hildyard describes in depressing detail, most national export credit agencies, which together provide the lion's share of project financing and overseas risk insurance to the extractive industry, continue to place investment protection ahead of responsible business conduct. With a few minor exceptions, current ECA lending policies entail no social, environmental, or transparency obligations upon companies; such permissiveness actually protects rather than penalizes companies whose international investments and operations may exacerbate corruption, human rights abuse, environmental degradation, and conflict. This is a glaring deficiency that severely compromises the credibility and effectiveness of parallel bilateral and multilateral efforts to promote peace and sustainable development. If governments are serious about the latter, then they must reconcile their competing commercial and security interests and reform their export credit policies accordingly.

Strengthening legal sanction. Alongside measures to strengthen the commercial rewards for demonstrated commitments to conflict-sensitive trade and investment, there is a need to enhance the national and international legal instruments for regulating corporate conduct in vulnerable and war-torn settings. As discussed in relation to the conflict trade, weak and uneven law enforcement has permitted clearly criminal actors to continue to profit from the business of war. At a minimum, then, the scope for impunity could be reduced by strengthened domestic enforcement of existing international laws against corruption, bribery, money laundering, and smuggling; the criminalization in domestic law of violating UN sanctions; and improved mutual legal assistance efforts between states. As many contributors to this volume stress, however, even with robust enforcement, existing international legal provisions designed for other purposes do not cover the full range of economic activities that sustain armed conflict. Nor do they amount to a coherent and binding legal framework with global coverage that could address the conflict-promoting activities of otherwise legal business enterprise.

The case for a comprehensive international legal framework is compelling, not least because of the deterrent effects of hard law. In principle, a universal legal framework would also eliminate jurisdictional discrepancies and help to create a level playing field for all companies, thereby resolving the twin problems of collective action and free riding that currently impede the meaningful implementation of voluntary initiatives for conflict-sensitive business practice. Further, the creation of a common and authoritative set of legal standards would assist companies, governments, and civil society groups in sorting through competing and contradictory codes of conduct, thereby ending the present state of confusion. The setting of common expectations will provide greater predictability for companies, while also providing international legal sanction that will make progressive companies less vulnerable to retaliation by unaccountable host-government partners and perhaps increase their leverage to promote host government accountability. Importantly, though perhaps less obviously, an international legal framework for responsible business conduct in vulnerable and war-torn states would help to clarify the balance of responsibilities between companies and governments, which is currently muddied by the proliferation of competing codes of corporate conduct.[77]

As detailed in the contributions of William Schabas and of Lunde and Taylor, a central challenge is to define the normative content of this legal framework. Under international law, there are few provisions that directly address economic activities that profit from or promote conflict. The most robust provisions are those concerning the economic dimensions of war crimes—pillage, plunder, and spoliation—which are recognized by the Rome Statute of the International Criminal Court as international offenses.[78] While companies have been prosecuted under these provisions in the past, the narrow scope and the high legal thresholds of these offenses will continue to make such prosecution rare. Several voluntary instruments, such as the Voluntary Principles on Security and Human Rights, the OECD *Guidelines for Multinational Enterprises,* and the UN Subcommission on Human Rights' Norms on the Responsibilities of Transnational Corporations and Other Business Enterprises, represent an emerging corpus of norms regarding acceptable and unacceptable business practices that could serve as a reference for clarifying the legal obligations of companies operating in weak and war-torn settings. However, there is as yet little consensus among governments, corporations, and international authorities either on the precise scope of unacceptable activities or on the extent to which business actors should be legally obliged to refrain from them.

Given these difficulties, and given that many of the economic activities that exacerbate conflict do so indirectly, few would support the idea of criminalizing specific sorts of economic activities in war zones that are unproblematic in peacetime contexts. For many international jurists and legal theorists, a more promising approach lies in making companies liable when their activities are complicit in others' commission of war crimes, crimes against humanity, and gross violations of international human rights, such as torture, extrajudicial killings, forced displacement, and slavery. Because international crimes and international human rights are extensively codified, have comprehensive international coverage, and enjoy broad international acceptance, they may provide a more reliable basis for concerted action to hold companies accountable for some of the harmful impacts of their investment and operational decisions. While the notion of complicity is subject to differing interpretations in different jurisdictions, a common legal definition has been codified by the Rome Statute concerning war crimes and crimes against humanity and further extended by the notion of "joint criminal enterprise" invoked in indictments by the International Criminal Tribunal for Yugoslavia and the Sierra Leone Special Court.[79] While as yet there have been no international criminal prosecutions against the perpetrators of economic war crimes or against economic actors for aiding and abetting war crimes, crimes against humanity, and grave violations of human rights, both the chief prosecutor of the International Criminal Court and the Special Court of Sierra Leone have signaled that such prosecutions are within their remit.[80] While unlikely at this time, the successful prosecution of Charles Taylor for his violent plunder of West African diamond wealth would do much to dissuade his various business associates, however remote, from engaging in commercial relations with others of his ilk. To reduce the current climate of impunity, such prosecutions deserve greater support from the international community.

Holding companies liable for actions that aid and abet violations of international criminal and human rights law is also within the power of national governments. Several cases are now pending in France, Belgium, and the United States that seek to prosecute companies for their complicity in violations undertaken by others in foreign jurisdictions.[81] Ironically, one of the most robust national statutes regarding liability for complicity in violations of international human rights law, the U.S. Alien Torts Claims Act (ATCA), exists in a country that has steadfastly opposed the creation of the International Criminal Court. As Paul Hoffman details, ATCA provides civil redress in American courts to non-U.S. citizens for violations of customary international law—including torture, summary execution, disappearance, prolonged arbitrary detention, genocide, some war crimes (including those that occur in intrastate conflicts), crimes against humanity, and slavery or forced labor—wherever they are committed. A wave of litigation since the mid-1990s has focused on holding corporations accountable for their complicity in crimes against humanity or war crimes, such as the case against Unocal for its alleged role in aiding and abetting forced labor and forced displacement of civilians in connection with its joint-venture pipeline project with the government of Burma/Myanmar. Similar ATCA cases are pending that seek to hold other extractive corporations civilly liable for their complicity in violations of international criminal and human rights law in Sudan, Colombia, and Indonesia. The judicial determinations of these cases have the potential to create precedents for establishing clearer legal standards as well as signaling to companies in conflict zones that commercial activities that aid and abet violations of international law can no longer be conducted with impunity. In the absence of international consensus, governments that are seriously committed to reducing the conflict-exacerbating activities of their home companies might consider enacting the kind of extraterritorial legislation embodied by ATCA.

Combating War Economies:
The Role of the United Nations, the Role of States

The current policy consideration of the problematic role of international trade and investment in conflict settings owes much to the attention given it by the United Nations. The Security Council's promotion of targeted sanctions against conflict commodities and support for the Kimberley Process, the monitoring and naming and shaming by expert panels, and various reports of the Secretary-General[82] have been instrumental in giving greater normative authority and policy priority to efforts to reduce the negative linkages between commerce and conflict. In its report, the UN High-level Panel on Threats, Challenges, and Change recommended that the UN should work closely with national governments, civil society actors, IFIs, and the private sector to develop norms that help govern the management of natural resources in countries emerging from or at risk of conflict.[83] Likewise, through its policy dialogue on the private sector in zones of conflict, the UN Global Compact has provided a forum of learning and dialogue between companies and the broader peace and security community, while also developing practical tools by which companies can become more conflict sensitive.

As these studies have highlighted, there is much that the United Nations could do to strengthen these initiatives, both normatively and practically. On the normative level, the UN Security Council could build on its earlier resolutions on conflict diamonds and illicit timber to provide a broader, authoritative prohibition against conflict trade, backed by the kinds of robust enforcement requirements for member states that have been developed in resolutions to combat terrorist financing and the proliferation of weapons of mass destruction.[84] Yet in view of the Security Council's decreasing appetite for commodity sanctions, as well as its traditional reluctance to pass resolutions of a general nature, such bold steps may not be realistic at present. In the interim, the council could use its norm-setting power to endorse more modest multistakeholder initiatives, such as the EITI and the UN Subcommission on Human Rights' Norms on the Responsibilities of Transnational Corporations and Other Business Enterprises. Given the currently dismissive attitude of business actors toward the UN Norms, a Security Council endorsement could provide the impetus for greater cooperation in the determination of legitimate business responsibilities in relation to human rights as well as to critical issues of peace and security. As Ian Smillie has stressed, the Security Council's endorsement of the Kimberley Process played an important part in legitimizing it in the eyes of private-sector actors.[85]

To date, the task of practical policy development in the area of business and conflict has been largely left to the UN Global Compact. The compact has provided an important forum for engaging businesses and for developing practical guidance in the ways that business can support broader conflict prevention and postconflict reconstruction efforts. As of yet, however, these efforts have not had a cumulative, systemwide impact. In part, this is due to the relative isolation of the compact from the day-to-day work of other UN agencies, particularly the UN Development Programme and the Department of Peacekeeping; in part, also, it is due to the compact's primary focus on improving business practice.[86] There is a parallel need for mainstream UN agencies and departments to develop complementary policies and practices. The Senior Management Group's creation of the Informal Working Group on the Political Economy of Armed Conflict was undertaken with just this objective in mind. The contributions to this volume suggest a variety of practical steps that the working group could consider to help UN actors to address the economic dimensions of armed conflict, including improved coordination among international law enforcement, development, and peace and security bodies in regulating conflict trade and the integration into UN country programs and peace missions of programs to build local capacity for the responsible management of natural resources. Doing so, however, will require that UN agencies first contend with an institutional culture that regards private-sector actors as an alternative source of donor funding at best and, at worst, as alien to peace and development. Given the centrality of the private sector in contemporary international relations, the United Nations needs to make a more concerted effort to embrace private-sector actors as full partners in the design and implementation of development and security policy.

Any expectations placed on the United Nations to decisively address the economic dimensions of armed conflict must be tempered by realism. Here, it bears repeating that the United Nations is an organization of sovereign states and for that very reason is often less than the sum of its parts. For too long member states, particularly northern governments, have shied away from undertaking the kinds of legal and technical reforms of their aid, trade, and investment policies that, as these chapters have discussed, could provide inducements and sanctions that are presently lacking. A repeated theme of the contributions to this volume is the familiar problem of "lack of political will." Properly speaking, the problem is not a lack of will to promote conflict-sensitive trade and investment but the presence of seemingly stronger competing commercial and strategic interests. While many governments have stated a commitment to curtailing conflict trade and finance, they yet remain eager to protect and promote overseas trade and investment by their companies and to ensure their access to the strategic natural resource endowments of the developing world. In some cases, these strategic and economic considerations have even led governments to tolerate if not protect criminal sanctions busters.[87]

While the invocation of "political will" is often a counsel of despair, this need not be the case. Neither interests nor agendas are fixed. The political will to undertake more effective regulation of conflict trade and finance can be summoned. As Smillie underscores, "The real question about . . . [regulating any] conflict-related commodity, is whether they are associated with a problem that governments and the industry in question *want* to solve."[88] In the case of conflict diamonds, the Kimberley Process succeeded despite the initial resistance of companies and timidity of governments.

Critical to this success was the role of advocacy NGOs in widely publicizing the corrosive effects of the diamond trade on human security and in pressuring governments and companies to take action. This external push, backed by a tacit threat of consumer boycott, created a sense of urgency that compelled De Beers and other diamond companies to reevaluate their calculations of commercial and reputational self-interest, while also prompting governments to champion certification as an essential component of conflict prevention and mitigation. As Smillie also stresses, the transformation of interests and agendas that made Kimberley possible also owes much to its inclusive, consensual, multistakeholder process, which, though often fraught with tension, permitted the creation of a certification scheme that both governments and companies could support. Given the complexity of interests and activities involved, the task of building political will among governments to address conflict trade and finance more broadly is bound to be difficult. However, where the problem is clear, the threat to peace and security is urgent, and public pressure is brought to bear, decisive action is possible. The success of the Kimberley Process shows what can be achieved when governments put peace before profit.

Notes

1. Mark Duffield, *Global Governance and the New Wars: The Merging of Development and Security* (London: Zed Books, 2001), p. 14.

2. See Chapter 4 by Jonathan Winer in this volume.

3. See Chapter 13 by Leiv Lunde and Mark Taylor in this volume.

4. See Chapter 2 by Macartan Humphreys and Chapter 11 by Gavin Hayman and Corene Crossin in this volume; William Reno, *Corruption and the State in Sierra Leone* (Cambridge: Cambridge University Press, 1995); Arvind Ganesan and Alex Vines, *Engine of War: Resources, Greed, and the Predatory State* (Washington, D.C.: Human Rights Watch, 2004); Duffield, *Global Governance and the New War*; Paul Collier et al., *Breaking the Conflict Trap: Civil War and Development Policy* (Washington, D.C.: World Bank, 2003).

5. Karen Ballentine and Heiko Nitzschke, "Business and Armed Conflict: An Assessment of Issues and Options," *Die Friedens-Warte, Journal of International Peace and Organization* 79, nos. 1–2 (2004): 35–56.

6. Ian Gary and Terry Karl, *Bottom of the Barrel: Africa's Oil Boom and the Poor* (Baltimore: Catholic Relief Services, 2003), p. 1.

7. Leiv Lunde and Mark Taylor, with Anne Huser, *Commerce or Crime? Regulating Economies of Conflict,* Fafo Report 424 (Oslo: Fafo Institute, 2003); Philippe Le Billon, "Getting It Done: International Instruments of Enforcement," in Ian Bannon and Paul Collier, eds., *Natural Resources and Violent Conflict: Options and Actions* (Washington, D.C.: World Bank, 2003), pp. 215–286.

8. Jessica Banfield, Virginia Haufler, and Damien Lilly, *Transnational Corporations in Conflict Prone Zones: Public Policy Responses and a Framework for Action* (London: International Alert, 2003).

9. Jason Switzer and Halina Ward, "Enabling Corporate Investment in Peace:

An Assessment of Voluntary Principles Addressing Business and Violent Conflict," IISD IIED Discussion Paper, (International Institute for Sustainable Development and International Institute for Environment and Development), Geneva and London, February 2004; International Council on Human Rights Policy (ICHRP), *Beyond Voluntarism: Human Rights and the Developing International Legal Obligations of Companies* (Geneva: ICHRP, 2002).

10. These include the UN Convention against Transnational Organized Crime (2000), the UN Convention for the Suppression of the Financing of Terrorism (1999), the UN Convention against the Illicit Traffic in Narcotic Drugs and Psychotropic Substances (1988), and the UN Convention against Corruption (2003).

11. See Chapter 16 by Paul Hoffman and Chaptaer 17 by William Schabas in this volume; International Peace Academy and Fafo Institute, *Business and International Crimes: Assessing the Liability of Business Entities for Grave Violations of International Law* (Oslo: Fafo Institute, 2005).

12. Witness the initial protest by the Committee on International Investment and Multinational Enterprises (CIME) against the DRC Expert Panel's efforts to apply the OECD *Guidelines for Multinational Enterprises* to company activities in the DRC. Witness, too, the virtual absence of human rights and conflict prevention standards in the policies of national export credit agencies. See Chapter 14 by Patricia Feeney and Tom Kenny and Chapter 10 by Nicholas Hildyard in this volume.

13. Notable developments include the creation of an Anti–Economic Crime Unit and Organized Crime Intelligence in 2001 by UN Interim Administration Mission in Kosovo (UNMIK) (www.unmikonline.org/pub/focuskos/focusklaw3. html) and the inclusion of assistance to "the transitional government in restoring proper administration of natural resources" in the mandate of UN peace support operations in Liberia. See UN doc. S/1509/2003, September 19, 2003.

14. See Chapter 6 by Phil Williams and John Picarelli in this volume.

15. United Nations, "The Role of Diamonds in Fuelling Conflict," Resolution adopted by the General Assembly, A/RES/55/56, January 29, 2001.

16. See Chapter 4 by Winer in this volume.

17. See Peter Wallensteen, Carina Staibano, and Mikael Eriksson, eds., *Making Targeted Sanctions Effective: Guidelines for the Implementation of UN Policy Options*. Final Report of the Stockholm Process on the Implementation of Targeted Sanctions (Uppsala: Uppsala University, 2002); and David Cortright and George Lopez, eds., *Smart Sanctions: Targeting Economic Statecraft* (Lanham, Md.: Rowman and Littlefield, 2002).

18. "Declaration on the More Effective Role for the Security Council in the Maintenance of International Peace and Security," S/RES/1318(2000), p. 3.

19. Peter Wallensteen, Carina Staibano, and Mikael Eriksson, eds., *Making Targeted Sanctions Effective: Guidelines for the Implementation of UN Policy Options* (Uppsala: Uppsala University, 2004); Simon Chesterman and Béatrice Pouligny, "Are Sanctions Meant to Work? The Politics of Creating and Implementing Sanctions through the United Nations," *Global Governance* 9, no. 4 (2003): 503–518; David Cortright and George A. Lopez, *Sanctions and the Search for Security: Challenges for UN Action*, Project of the International Peace Academy (Boulder: Lynne Rienner, 2002).

20. Alex Vines, "Monitoring UN Sanctions in Africa: The Role of Panels of Experts," in Trevor Findlay, ed., *Verification Yearbook 2003* (London: Vertic, 2004).

21. François Grignon, "Economic Agendas in the Congolese Peace Process," in *The Democratic Republic of Congo: Economic Dimensions of War and Peace,*

Michael Nest, with François Grignon and Emizet F. Kisangani (Boulder: Lynne Rienner, 2005).

22. Vines, "Monitoring UN Sanctions in Africa."

23. See Chapter 14 by Feeney and Kenny in this volume.

24. Quoted in Peter Landesman, "Arms and the Man," *New York Times Magazine,* August 17, 2003.

25. See Chapter 15 by Pierre Kopp in this volume.

26. The defining statement on counterterrorism is contained in Security Council Resolution 1373, S/1373(2001), September 28, 2001. Resolution 1540 requires that states establish and enforce legal barriers to acquisition of weapons of mass destruction, whether by nonstate actors or by states. It makes strong national controls and enforcement requirements rather than options. See "Resolution to Prevent the Proliferation of Weapons of Mass Destruction," S/1540(2004), April 28, 2004.

27. See Chapter 5 by Sue Eckert in this volume.

28. For current documents on the progress of the Kimberley Process, see: www.kimberleyprocess.com.

29. See Chapter 4 by Winer in this volume.

30. While rough diamonds from Sierra Leone used to be "laundered" through Liberia, it became profitable to "launder" Liberian diamonds by exporting them as "clean" under the Sierra Leone certification regime. Michael Pugh and Neil Cooper with Jonathan Goodhand, *War Economies in a Regional Context: The Challenges of Transformation* (Boulder: Lynne Rienner, 2003), pp. 118–120.

31. See Chapter 7 by Stephen Jackson in this volume.

32. See, e.g., Merilee S. Grindle and John W. Thomas: *Public Choices and Policy Change: The Political Economy of Reform in Developing Countries* (Baltimore: Johns Hopkins University Press, 1991).

33. A unique and promising initiative to promote the deeper integration of aid, trade, and security in conflict-sensitive development has been launched by the International Institute for Sustainable Development. See Mark Halle, Jason Switzer, and Sebastian Winkler, *Aid, Trade, and Security: Towards a Positive Paradigm* (Geneva: International Institute for Sustainable Development and World Conservation Union, 2004).

34. See Chapter 2 by Humphreys in this volume.

35. See Chapter 11 by Hayman and Crossin in this volume.

36. Human Rights Watch, *The Oil Diagnostic in Angola: An Update* (Washington, D.C.: Human Rights Watch, 2001).

37. Jake Sherman, *Options for Promoting Corporate Responsibility in Conflict Zones: Perspectives from the Private Sector,* IPA Conference Report (New York: International Peace Academy, 2002).

38. See Cynthia A. William, "The Securities and Exchange Commission and Corporate Social Transparency," *Harvard Law Review* 112, no. 6 (1999): 1197-1311.

39. UN Integrated Regional Information Network, "Liberia: IMF and World Bank Demand More Transparency in Public Finances," Monrasia. October 26, 2004.

40. See Chapter 12 by James Boyce in this volume.

41. International Monetary Fund, "Angola: Memorandum of Economic and Financial Policies," April 3, 2000, available at www.imf.org/external/np/loi/2000/ago/01/index.htm.

42. In 2000, ECAs were providing a total of $500 billion in guarantees and

insurance to companies operating in developing countries, issuing $58.8 billion worth of new export credits that year alone, sums that far outstripped both the $60 billion in global overseas development assistance and the $41 billion provided as loans by multilateral development banks in the same period. World Bank, *Global Development Finance 2002* (Washington, D.C.: World Bank, 2002), chap. 4, p. 107; OECD, "Officially Supported Export Credits: Levels of New Flows and Stocks," data from 1999 and 2000, in OECD and Development Assistance Commimttee; *Statistics and US Treasury Note on Multilateral Development Banks,* available at www.ustreas.gov/omdb/tab9.pdf.

43. See Chapter 10 by Hildyard and Chapter 11 by Hayman and Crossin in this volume.

44. The G-8 has pledged to work with participating governments to achieve high standards of transparent public revenue management, including the processes for awarding contracts and concessions, and to provide capacity-building support where needed: "Fighting Corruption and Improving Transparency. A G8 Declaration," June 2003. Under its corporate and economic governance initiative, NEPAD proposes the adoption of minimum standards for corporate and economic governance, whereby member governments pledge to uphold fiscal, monetary, and budgetary transparency, adopt guidelines to manage public debt and corporate governance, use international accounting and auditing standards, and provide supervision to banks. See New Partnership for Africa's Development (NEPAD), "Declaration on Democracy, Political, Economic and Corporate Governance," June 18, 2002, paras. 16–19, available at www.avmedia.at/nepad/indexgh.html.

45. Anthony Regan, "The Bougainville Conflict: Political and Economic Agendas," in Karen Ballentine and Jake Sherman, eds., *The Political Economy of Armed Conflict: Beyond Greed and Grievance* (Boulder: Lynne Rienner, 2002); Jeffrey Herbst, "The Politics of Revenue Sharing in Resource Dependent States," Discussion paper no. 2001/43. (Helsinki: UNU/Wider, 2001).

46. See Chapter 8 by Luc Zandvliet in this volume.

47. Svetlana Tsalik, *Caspian Oil Windfalls: Who Will Benefit?* (New York: Open Society Institute, 2003), p. 2.

48. See Chapter 2 by Humphreys in this volume.

49. Gary and Karl, "Bottom of the Barrel."

50. Thomas Heller, Stephen Krasner, and John McMillan, "A Trust Fund for Ituri," unpubl., Center for Democracy, Development, and the Rule of Law, Stanford University, Stanford, Calif., December 7, 2003, accessible at www.faculty-gsb.stanford.edu/mcmillan/personal_page/documents/Ituri.pdf.

51. Philippe Le Billon, "Getting It Done: Instruments of Enforcement," in Ian Bannon and Paul Collier, eds., *Natural Resources and Conflict: Options and Actions* (Washington, D.C.: World Bank, 2003), pp. 252–256.

52. Terry Lynn Karl, *The Paradox of Plenty: Oil Booms and Petro-States* (Berkeley: University of California Press, 1997).

53. Collier et al., *Breaking the Conflict Trap.*

54. Kathryn McPhail and Aidan Davy, "Integrating Social Concerns into Private Sector Decisionmaking: A Review of Corporate Practices in the Mining, Oil, and Gas Sectors," World Bank Discussion Paper no. 384 (Washington, D.C.: World Bank, 1998).

55. "Sudan's Oil: Fueling a Fire," *The Economist,* August 31, 2000.

56. See Chapter 8 by Zandvliet in this volume.

57. Christian Aid, *Behind the Mask: The Real Face of Corporate Social Responsibility* (London: Christian Aid, 2004), available at www.christianaid.org.uk

/indepth/0401csr/. See also Switzer and Ward, "Enabling Corporate Investment in Peace."

58. See Chapter 8 by Zandvliet in this volume. I wish to thank Heiko Nitzschke for contributing his research and ideas to this discussion on natural resource funds.

59. Michael Warner, *Tri-sector Partnerships for Social Investment within the Oil, Gas, and Mining Sectors: An Analytical Framework,* Business Partners for Development Working Paper no. 2 (London: Business Partners for Development, n.d.); Aidan Davy, *Companies in Conflict Situations: A Role for Tri-sector Partnerships?* Business Partners for Development Working Paper no. 9 (London: Business Partners for Development, 2001).

60. George Downs and Stephen J. Stedman. "Evaluation Issues in Peace Implementation," in Stephen J. Stedman, Donald Rothchild, and Elizabeth M. Cousens, eds., *Ending Civil Wars: The Implementation of Peace Agreements* (Boulder: Lynne Rienner, 2003), pp. 43–69.

61. UN Security Council Resolution on Liberia, S/1509/2003, September 19, 2003.

62. Michael Ross, "Oil, Drugs, and Diamonds: The Varying Roles of Natural Resources in Civil War," in Karen Ballentine and Jake Sherman, eds., *The Political Economy of Armed Conflict: Beyond Greed and Grievance* (Boulder: Lynne Rienner, 2003), pp. 47–70.

63. International Crisis Group, *Sierra Leone: Managing Uncertainty*, Africa Report no. 5 (Freetown and Brussels: ICG, 2001).

64. For more information on these initiatives, see www.peacediamonds.org and www.nmjd.org. For more discussion of these issues, see Heiko Nitzschke, *Transforming War Economies: Challenges for Peacemaking and Peacebuilding.* Report of the 725th Wilton Park Conference in association with the International Peace Academy, October 27–29, 2003 (New York: International Peace Academy, 2003).

65. See Michael Pugh and Neil Cooper, with Jonathan Goodhand, *War Economies in a Regional Context: Challenges of Transformation* (Boulder: Lynne Rienner, 2004); Peter Andreas, "The Clandestine Political Economy of War and Peace in Bosnia," *International Studies Quarterly* 48 (2004): 29–51.

66. Susan Woodward, "Economic Priorities for Successful Peace Implementation," in Stephen John Stedman, Donald Rothchild, and Elizabeth M. Cousens, eds., *Ending Civil Wars: The Implementation of Peace Agreements* (Boulder, Lynne Rienner, 2002), pp. 183–214; Pugh, Cooper, and Goodhand, *War Economies in a Regional Context*, pp. 118–120.

67. William J. Durch et al., *The Brahimi Report and the Future of UN Peace Operations* (Washington, D.C.: Henry L. Stimson Center, 2003), p. 30.

68. Mark Sedra, *Challenging the Warlord Culture: Security Sector Reform in Post-Taliban Afghanistan,* Bonn International Center for Conversion Paper 25 (Bonn: BICC, 2002); and Irma Specht, "Jobs for Rebels and Soldiers," in Eugenia Date-Bah, ed., *Jobs after War: A Critical Challenge in the Peace and Reconstruction Puzzle* (Geneva: International Labour Office, 2003).

69. International Crisis Group, *God, Oil, and Country: The Changing Logic of War in Sudan,* Africa Report no. 39 (Brussels: ICG, 2002); Rights and Accountability in Development (RAID), *Unanswered Questions: Companies, Conflict, and the Democratic Republic of Congo* (London: RAID, 2004); "Shell Admits Fueling Corruption," BBC News, June 11, 2004, available at www.news.bbc.co.uk/2/hi/business/3796375.stm.

70. Michael Ross, "Booty Futures: Africa's Civil Wars and the Futures Market for Natural Resources," unpubl., UCLA, December 18, 2002, available at www.polisci.ucla.eou/faculty/ross/bootyfutures.pdf.

71. See Chapter 3 by Ian Smillie, Chapter 11 by Hayman and Crossin, and Chapter 14 by Feeney and Kenny in this volume.

72. In some cases, such as Shell Oil, companies have established independent social audits.

73. On the achievements of shareholder activism in promoting improved corporate conduct, see Chapter 9 by Mark Mansley in this volume.

74. Ballentine and Nitzschke, "Business and Armed Conflict."

75. See Chapter 13 by Lunde and Taylor in this volume.

76. Ingrid Samset, "Conflict of Interest or Interest in Conflict? Diamonds and War in the DRC," *Review of African Political Economy,* no. 93/94 (2002): 466.

77. Ballentine and Nitzschke, "Business and Armed Conflict"; ICHRP, *Beyond Voluntarism*; Gilles Carbonnier, "Corporate Responsibility and Humanitarian Actions: What Relations between the Business and Humanitarian Worlds?" *International Review of the Red Cross* 83, no. 844 (2001): 947–968.

78. See Chapter 17 by Schabas in this volume.

79. Ibid.

80. International Criminal Court, "Communications Received by the Office of the Prosecutor of the ICC," press release no. pids.009.2003-EN, July 16, 2003, pp. 3–4; see also indictments of the Special Court of Sierra Leone: *Prosecutor v. Sankoh,* Case no. SCSL 2003-02-I, Indictment, March 7, 2003, para. 27; *Prosecutor v. Sesay,* Case no. SCSL 2003-5-I, Indictment, March 7, 2003, para. 23; *Prosecutor v. Koroma,* Case no. SCSL 2003-3-I, Indictment, March 7, 2003, para. 24; *Prosecutor v. Brima,* Case no. SCSL 2003-6-I, Indictment, March 7, 2003, para. 23; *Prosecutor v. Taylor,* Case no. SCSL 2003-03-I, Indictment, March 7, 2003, paras. 20, 23.

81. "Activists Keep Up Pressure on Myanmar Investors," *Energy Compass,* May 10, 2002.

82. See, for example, "Report of the Secretary-General to the Security Council on the Protection of Civilians in Armed Conflict," S/2002/1300, November 26, 2002.

83. United Nations, *A More Secure World: Our Shared Responsibility.* Report of the High-level Panel on Threats, Challenges, and Change (New York: United Nations, 2004), p. 35.

84. S/1459(2003), January 28, 2003; S/1373(2001), September 28, 2001; S/1540(2004), April 28, 2004.

85. See Chapter 3 by Smillie in this volume.

86. In recognition of the need for supportive public policy that complements company efforts, the Global Compact held a series of dialogues in 2004. See the resulting report: Karen Ballentine and Virginia Haufler, *Enabling Economies of Peace: Public Policy for Conflict-Sensitive Business Practice. A Report of the UN Global Compact* (New York: United Nations, April 2005).

87. As has been the fate of the erstwhile merchant of death, Victor Bout: once on the U.S. Treasury's most-wanted list, now the recipient of Defense Department contracts in Iraq. See Chapter 15 by Kopp in this volume.

88. See Chapter 3 by Smillie in this volume.

Acronyms

ABI	Association of British Insurers
ACTF	OGP Anti-corruption Task Force
ATCA	U.S. Alien Tort Claims Act
AUC	Autodefensas Unidas de Colombia (United Self-Defense Forces of Colombia)
BIAC	OECD's Business and Industry Advisory Committee
BP	British Petroleum
CARICOM	Caribbean Community
CEP	Corporate Engagement Project
CIME	Committee on International Investment and Multinational Enterprises
CITES	Convention on International Trade in Endangered Species of Wild Fauna and Flora
COTCO	Cameroon Oil Transportation Company
CPP	Cambodian People's Party
CSI	Container Security Initiative
CSR	corporate social responsibility
CTAG	Counter-Terrorism Action Group (G-8)
CTC	Counter-Terrorism Committee (UN)
C-TPAT	Customs Trade Partnership against Terrorism
DAC	OECD's Development Assistance Committee
DDR	demobilization, disarmament, and reintegration
DRC	Democratic Republic of Congo
EACW	Economic Agendas in Civil Wars Program (IPA)
ECA	export credit agency
ECCR	Ecumenical Council for Corporate Responsibility

ECG	OECD's Export Credits Group
ECGD	Export Credits Guarantee Department (UK)
ECOWAS	Economic Community of West African States
EIA	Environmental Impact Assessment
EIR	extractive industries review
EITI	Extractive Industry Transparency Initiative
FARC	Revolutionary Armed Forces of Colombia
FATF	Financial Action Task Force against Money Laundering
FSIA	Foreign Sovereign Immunities Act
FTCA	Federal Tort Claims Act
GAAP	generally accepted accounting principles
GAO	U.S. Government Accountability Office
GATT	General Agreement on Tariffs and Trade
GRECO	Group of States Against Corruption (Council of Europe)
HSBC	Hong Kong Shanghai Banking Corporation
IAS	International Accounting Standards
ICAEW	Institute for Chartered Accountants in England and Wales
ICBL	International Campaign to Ban Land Mines
ICC	International Criminal Court
ICCR	Interfaith Center on Corporate Responsibility
ICFTU	International Confederation of Free Trade Unions
ICHRP	International Council on Human Rights Policy
ICRC	International Committee of the Red Cross
ICTR	International Criminal Tribunal for Rwanda
ICTY	International Criminal Tribunal for the Former Yugoslavia
IFC	International Financial Corporation
IFI	international financial institution
IIED	International Institute of Environment and Development
IISD	International Institute for Sustainable Development
IMF	International Monetary Fund
INCSR	International Narcotics Control Strategy Report (U.S. State Department)
IOSCO	International Organization of Securities Commissions
IRC	International Rescue Committee
ISAF	International Security Assistance Force
JEXIM	Japan's Export-Import Bank
KLA	Kosovo Liberation Army
KPCS	Kimberley Process Certification Scheme
LTTE	Liberation Tigers of Tamil Eelam
MDB	Multilateral Development Bank
MDRP	Multi-country Demobilization and Reintegration Program
MIGA	Multilateral Investment Guarantee Agency

MMSD	Global Mining Initiative's Mining Minerals and Sustainable Development project
MOGE	Moattama Oil and Gas Enterprise (Burma)
MONUC	UN Mission in the Democratic Republic of Congo
MPLA	Movement for the Liberation of Angola
MTCR	Missile Technology Control Regime
NCCTs	noncooperative countries and territories
NCPs	National Contact Points (OECD)
NEPAD	New Partnership for Africa's Development
NGO	nongovernmental organization
NPT	Nuclear Nonproliferation Treaty
NRF	natural resource fund
ODA	official development assistance
OECD	Organization for Economic Cooperation and Development
OGP	International Association of Oil and Gas Producers
OII	overseas investment insurance
OSCE	Organization for Security and Cooperation in Europe
PNG	Papua New Guinea
PPP	Public-Private Partnership
PSA	Production Sharing Agreement
PWYP	Publish What You Pay campaign
RAID	Rights and Accountability in Development
RCD	Rassemblement Congolais pour la Démocratie
RICO	Racketeer Influenced Corrupt Organizations Act
RUF	Revolutionary United Front (Sierra Leone)
SADEC	Southern African Development Community
SCSL	special court for Sierra Leone
SEC	U.S. Securities and Exchange Commission
SLTRC	Sierra Leone Truth and Reconcilitation Commission
SMP	IMF Staff-Monitored Program
SRI	socially responsible investment
TCCR	Taskforce on the Churches and Corporate Responsibility
TraCCC	Transnational Crime and Corruption Center
TSS	Transitional Support Strategy (World Bank)
TUAC	OECD's Trade Union Advisory Committee
TVPA	Torture Victims Protection Act (U.S.)
UCR	Unique Consignment Reference
UNAMSIL	UN Mission in Sierra Leone
UNEP	UN Environmental Programme
UNEPFI	UN Environmental Programme's Financial Institutions Initiative
UNITA	National Union for the Total Independence of Angola

UNMIK	UN Interim Administration Mission in Kosovo
UNODC	UN Office on Drugs and Crime
UNSMA	UN Special Mission to Afghanistan
UNTAC	UN Transitional Authority in Cambodia
VPs	Voluntary Principles on Security and Human Rights
WBG	World Bank Group
WCO	World Customs Organization
WPD	OECD's Working Party on the Declaration

Selected Bibliography

Abbot, Kenneth, and Duncan Snidal. "Hard Law and Soft Law in International Governance." *International Organization* 54, no. 3 (Summer 2000): 421–456.

Aceves, William, and Paul Hoffman. "Pursuing Crimes Against Humanity in the United States: The Need for a Comprehensive Regime." In Philippe Sands and Mark Lattimer, eds., *Justice for Crimes Against Humanity: International Law After Pinochet.* Oxford: Hart, 2004, pp. 239–270.

Addison, Tony, Philippe Le Billon, and S. Mansoob Murshed. "Finance in Conflict and Reconstruction." *Journal of International Development* 13, no. 7 (2001): 951–964.

Addison, Tony, and S. Mansoob Murshed, eds. "Explaining Violent Conflict: Going Beyond Greed versus Grievance." *Journal of International Development* 15, no. 4, special issue (May 2003).

Ahmed, Ismail I. "Remittances and Their Economic Impact in Post-war Somaliland." *Disasters* 24, no. 4 (2000): 380–389.

Alao, Abiodum, and Funmi Olonusakin. "Economic Fragility and Political Fluidity: Explaining Natural Resources and Conflicts." *International Peacekeeping* 7, no. 4 (Winter 2000): 23–36.

Ambos, Kai. "General Principles of Law in the Rome Statute." *Criminal Law Forum* 10 (1999): 1–23.

Amnesty International. *Democratic Republic of Congo: Making a Killing; The Diamond Trade in Government-Controlled DRC.* London: Amnesty International, 2002.

Anderson, Jon Lee. "Oil and Blood." *The New Yorker,* August 14, 2000, pp. 46–59.

Anderson, Mary B. *Do No Harm: How Aid Can Support Peace—or War.* Boulder: Lynne Rienner, 1999.

Anderson, Mary B., Doug Fraser, and Luc Zandvliet. *Porgera Joint Venture (PJV) Gold Mining Operation.* Corporate Engagement Project. Cambridge, Mass.: Collaborative for Development Action, 2001.

Anderson, Mary B., and Luc Zandvliet. *Corporate Options for Breaking Cycles of Conflict.* Corporate Engagement Project. Cambridge, Mass.: Collaborative for Development Action, 2001.

Anderton, C. H. "Economics of Arms Trade." In Keith Hartley and Todd Sandler, eds., *The Handbook of Defense Economics,* vol. 1. Amsterdam: North-Holland, 1995.

Andreas, Peter. "The Clandestine Political Economy of War and Peace in Bosnia." *International Studies Quarterly* 48 (2004): 29–51.

Angelet, Nicolas. "Criminal Liability for the Violation of United Nations Economic Sanctions." *European Journal of Crime, Criminal Law, and Criminal Justice* 7, no. 2 (1999): 89–102.

Angell, David J. R. "The Angola Sanctions Committee." In David M. Malone, ed., *The UN Security Council: From the Cold War to the Twenty-first Century.* Boulder: Lynne Rienner, 2004, pp. 195–204.

Aning, Emmanuel Kwesi. "Regulating Illicit Trade in Natural Resources: The Role of Regional Actors in West Africa." *Review of African Political Economy,* no. 95 (2003): 99–107.

Arlen, Jennifer. "The Potentially Perverse Effects of Corporate Criminal Liability." *Journal of Legal Studies* 23, no. 2 (1994): 833–868.

Armstrong, Andrea, and Barnett Rubin. *Policy Approaches to Regional Conflict Formations.* New York: Center on International Cooperation, 2002.

Arquilla, John, and David Ronfeldt, eds. *Networks and Netwars: The Future of Terror, Crime, and Militancy.* Santa Monica, Calif.: RAND, 2001.

Ascher, William. *Why Governments Waste Natural Resources: Policy Failures in Developing Countries.* Baltimore: Johns Hopkins University Press, 1999.

Atmar, Haneef, and Jonathan Goodhand. "Coherence or Cooption? Politics, Aid, and Peacebuilding in Afghanistan." *Journal of Humanitarian Assistance,* July 30, 2001. Available at www.jha.ac/articles/a069.htm.

Ballentine, Karen. "Beyond Greed and Grievance: Reconsidering the Economic Dynamics of Armed Conflict." In Karen Ballentine and Jake Sherman, eds., *The Political Economy of Armed Conflict: Beyond Greed and Grievance.* Boulder: Lynne Rienner, 2003, pp. 259–283.

———. *Program on Economic Agendas in Civil War: Principal Research Findings and Policy Recommendations.* Final Report. New York: International Peace Academy, 2004.

Ballentine, Karen, and Heiko Nitzschke. *Beyond Greed and Grievance: Policy Lessons from Studies in the Political Economy of Armed Conflict.* IPA Policy Report. New York: International Peace Academy, 2003.

———. "Business and Armed Conflict: An Assessment of Issues and Options." *Die Friedens-Warte: Journal of International Peace and Organization* 79, nos. 1–2 (2004): 35–56.

———. "The Political Economy of Civil War and Conflict Transformation." In Martina Fischer and Beatrix Schmelzle, eds., *Transforming War Economies: Dilemmas and Strategies.* Berlin: Berghof Research Center for Constructive Conflict Management, 2005.

Ballentine, Karen, and Jake Sherman, eds. *The Political Economy of Armed Conflict: Beyond Greed and Grievance.* Boulder: Lynne Rienner, 2003.

Ballentine, Karen, and Virginia Haufler. *Enabling Economies of Peace: Public Policy for Conflict-Sensitive Business Practice. A Report of the UN Global Compact.* New York: United Nations, April 2005.

Banfield, Jessica, Virginia Haufler, and Damien Lilly. *Transnational Corporations in Conflict Prone Zones: Public Policy Responses and a Framework for Action.* London: International Alert, 2003.

Bannon, Ian, and Paul Collier, eds. *Natural Resources and Violent Conflict: Options and Actions.* Washington, D.C.: World Bank, 2003.

Bayart, Jean-François. *The State in Africa: The Politics of the Belly.* New York: Longman, 1993.

Bayart, Jean-François, Stephen Ellis, and Beatrice Hibou. *The Criminalization of the State in Africa.* Bloomington: Indiana University Press, 1999.

Bennett, Juliette. "Multinational Companies, Social Responsibility, and Conflict." *Journal of International Affairs* 55, no. 2 (2002): 393–410.

Berdal, Mats. "How 'New' Are 'New Wars'? Global Economic Change and the Study of Civil War." *Global Governance* 9, no. 4 (2003): 477–502.

Berdal, Mats, and David Keen. "Violence and Economic Agendas in Civil Wars: Some Policy Implications." *Millennium: Journal of International Studies* 26, no. 3 (1997): 795–818.

Berdal, Mats, and David M. Malone, eds. *Greed and Grievance: Economic Agendas in Civil Wars.* Boulder: Lynne Rienner, 2000.

Berdal, Mats, and Mónica Serrano, eds. *Transnational Organized Crime and International Security: Business as Usual?* Boulder: Lynner Rienner, 2002.

Blumberg, Phillip I. "Accountability of Multinational Corporations: The Barriers Presented by Concepts of the Corporate Judicial Entity." *Hastings International and Comparative Law Review* 24, no. 3 (Spring 2001): 297–320.

Boyce, James K., ed. *Economic Policy for Building Peace: The Lessons of El Salvador.* Boulder: Lynne Rienner, 1996.

———. *Investing in Peace: Aid and Conditionality After Civil Wars.* Adelphi Paper no. 351. Oxford: Oxford University Press, 2002.

Bray, John. "Attracting Reputable Companies to Risky Environments: Petroleum and Mining Companies." In Ian Bannon and Paul Collier, eds., *Natural Resources and Violent Conflict: Options and Actions.* Washington, D.C.: World Bank, 2003, pp. 287–352.

Brömmelhörster, Jörg, and Wolf Christian Paes, eds. *The Military as an Economic Actor: Soldiers in Business.* Basingstoke, UK: Palgrave, 2003.

Buzan, Barry, and Eric Herring. *The Arms Dynamic in World Politics.* Boulder: Lynne Rienner, 1998.

Campbell, Ashley. *The Private Sector and Conflict Prevention Mainstreaming: Risk Analysis and Conflict Impact Assessment Tools for Multinational Corporations.* Ottawa, Ont.: Country Indicators for Foreign Policy, 2002.

Carbonnier, Gilles. "Corporate Responsibility and Humanitarian Actions: What Relations Between the Business and Humanitarian Worlds?" *International Review of the Red Cross* 83, no. 844 (2001): 947–968.

Center for Environment and Development et al. *Broken Promises: The Chad Cameroon Oil and Pipeline Project—Profit at Any Cost?* Yaounde/Amsterdam: Center for Environment and Development and Friends of the Earth International, 2001.

Chesterman, Simon. "Oil and Water: Regulating the Behavior of Multinational Companies Through Law." *International Law and Politics* 36 (2004): 307–329.

Chesterman, Simon, and Béatrice Pouligny. "Are Sanctions Meant to Work? The Politics of Creating and Implementing Sanctions through the United Nations." *Global Governance* 9, no. 4 (2003): 503–518.

Christian Aid. *Fuelling Poverty: Oil, War, and Corruption.* London: Christian Aid, 2003.

———. *The Scorched Earth: Oil and War in Sudan.* London: Christian Aid, 2001.

Cilliers, Jakkie, and Christian Dietrich, eds. *Angola's War Economy: The Role of Oil and Diamonds.* Pretoria: Institute for Security Studies, 2000.

Cilliers, Jakkie, and Peggy Mason, eds. *Peace, Profit, or Plunder? The*

Privatization of Security in War-Torn African Societies. Pretoria: Institute for Security Studies, 1999.

Clapham, Andrew. *Human Rights in the Private Sphere*. Oxford: Oxford University Press, 1998.

———. "The Question of Jurisdiction Under International Criminal Law over Legal Persons: Lessons from the Rome Conference on an International Criminal Court." In Menno T. Kamminga and Saman Zia-Zarifi, eds., *Liability of Multinational Corporations Under International Law*. The Hague: Kluwer Law International, 2000, pp. 139–195.

Clapham, Andrew, and Scott Jerbi. "Categories of Corporate Complicity in Human Rights Abuses." *Hastings International and Comparative Law Review* 24, no. 3 (2001): 339–349.

Clapham, Christopher. *African Guerrillas*. Bloomington: Indiana University Press, 1998.

Collier, Paul. "Conditionality, Dependence, and Coordination: Three Current Debates in Aid Policy." In Christopher L. Gilbert and David Vines, eds., *The World Bank: Structures and Policies*. Cambridge: Cambridge University Press, 2000, pp. 299–324.

———. "Doing Well out of War: An Economic Perspective." In Mats Berdal and David M. Malone, eds., *Greed and Grievance: Economic Agendas in Civil War*. Boulder: Lynne Rienner, 2000, pp. 91–111.

———. "Economic Causes of Civil Conflict and Their Implications for Policy." In Chester A. Crocker, Fen Osler Hampson, and Pamela Aall, eds., *Turbulent Peace: The Challenges of Managing International Conflict*. Washington, D.C.: United States Institute of Peace Press, 2001, pp. 143–161.

———. "Rebellion as a Quasi-Criminal Activity." *Journal of Conflict Resolution* 44, no. 6 (2000): 839–853.

Collier, Paul, and Anke Hoeffler. *Greed and Grievance in Civil Wars*. Policy research paper no. 2355. Washington, D.C.: World Bank, 2000.

———. "On Economic Causes of Civil War." *Oxford Economic Papers* 50 (1998): 563–573.

Collier, Paul, Lani Elliott, Havard Hegre, Anke Hoeffler, Marta Reynal-Querol, and Nicholas Sambanis. *Breaking the Conflict Trap: Civil War and Development Policy*. Washington, D.C.: World Bank, 2003.

Collier, Paul, and Nicholas Sambanis. "Understanding Civil War: A New Agenda." *Journal of Conflict Resolution* 46, no. 1 (2002): 3–12.

Collinson, Sarah, ed. *Power, Livelihoods, and Conflict: Case Studies in Political Economy Analysis for Humanitarian Action*. ODI Humanitarian Policy Group Report no. 13. London: Overseas Development Institute, 2003.

Commission for Africa. *Our Common Interest*. London: Commission for Africa, 2005.

Cooper, Neil. "State Collapse as Business: The Role of Conflict Trade and the Emerging Control Agenda." *Development and Change* 33, no. 5 (2002): 935–955.

Cortright, David, and George A. Lopez. *Sanctions and the Search for Security: Challenges for UN Action*. Boulder: Lynne Rienner, 2002.

———. *The Sanctions Decade: Assessing UN Strategies in the 1990s*. Boulder: Lynne Rienner, 2000.

———, eds. *Smart Sanctions: Targeting Economic Statecraft*. Boston: Rowman and Littlefield, 2002.

Cramer, Christopher. "*Homo Economicus* Goes to War: Methodological

Individualism, Rational Choice, and the Political Economy of War." *World Development* 30, no. 11 (2002): 1845–1864.

Crawford, Gordon. "Foreign Aid and Political Conditionality: Issues of Effectiveness and Consistency." *Democratization* 4, no. 3 (1997): 69–108.

Crossin, Corene, Gavin Hayman, and Simon Taylor. "Where Did It Come From? Commodity Tracking Systems." In Ian Bannon and Paul Collier, eds., *Natural Resources and Violent Conflict: Options and Actions.* Washington, D.C.: World Bank, 2003, pp. 97–160.

Cuvelier, Jeroen, and Tim Raeymaekers. *Supporting the War Economy in the DRC: European Companies and the Coltan Trade.* Brussels: International Peace Information Service, 2002.

Davy, Aidan. *Companies in Conflict Situations: A Role for Tri-sector Partnerships?* Business Partners for Development Working Paper no. 9. London: Business Partners for Development, 2001.

De Soto, Alvaro, and Graciana del Castillo. "Obstacles to Peacebuilding." *Foreign Policy*, no. 94 (1994): 69–83.

De Soysa, Indra. "Paradise Is a Bazaar? Greed, Creed, and Governance in Civil War, 1989–99." *Journal of Peace Research* 39, no. 4 (2002): 395–416.

Dietrich, Christian. *Hard Currency: The Criminalized Diamond Economy of the Democratic Republic of the Congo and Its Neighbours.* Occasional Paper no. 4. Ottawa, Ont.: Partnership Africa Canada, 2002.

Dodge, William S. "The Historical Origins of the Alien Tort Statute: A Response to the Originists." *Hastings International and Comparative Law Review* 19, no. 221 (1996): 221–258.

Doornbos, Martin. "Good Governance: The Rise and Decline of a Policy Metaphor?" *Journal of Development Studies* 37, no. 6 (2001): 93–108.

Downs, George, and Stephen J. Stedman. "Evaluation Issues in Peace Implementation." In Stephen J. Stedman, Donald Rothchild, and Elizabeth M. Cousens, eds., *Ending Civil Wars: The Implementation of Peace Agreements.* Boulder: Lynne Rienner, 2003, pp. 43–69.

Doyle, Michael, and Nicholas Sambanis. "International Peacebuilding: A Theoretical and Quantitative Analysis." *American Political Science Review* 94, no. 4 (2000): 779–801.

Drew, Kristine. *Analysis of the Working Party on Export Credits and Credit Guarantees Responses to the 2002 Survey of Measures Taken to Combat Bribery in Officially Supported Export Credits: As of 3rd October 2003.* London: Public Services International Research Unit, 2003.

Duffield, Mark. *Global Governance and the New Wars: The Merging of Development and Security.* London: Zed Books, 2001.

———. "Globalization and War Economies: Promoting Order or the Return of History?" *Fletcher Forum of World Affairs* 23, no. 2 (1999): 21–38.

———. "War as a Network Enterprise: The New Security Terrain and Its Implications." *Cultural Values* 6, nos. 1–2 (2002): 153–166.

Durch, William J., et al. *The Brahimi Report and the Future of UN Peace Operations.* Washington, D.C.: Henry L. Stimson Center, 2003.

Ebbe, Obi N. I. "The Political-Criminal Nexus: The Nigerian Case." *Trends in Organized Crime* 4, no. 3 (Spring 1999): 29–59.

Ellis, Stephen. *The Mask of Anarchy: The Roots of Liberia's War.* New York: New York University Press, 1999.

Estrin, Saul, Stephen Powell, Pinar Bagci, Simeon Thornton, and Peter Goate. *The Economic Rationale for the Public Provision of Export Credit Insurance by*

ECGD: A Report for the Export Credit Guarantee Department. London: National Economic Research Associates, 2000.

Everett, Richard, and Andrew Gilboy. "Impact of the World Bank's Social and Environmental Policies on Extractive Companies and Financial Institutions." Report submitted to the Extractive Industry Review Secretariat. Washington, D.C.: Associates for Global Change, June 2003.

Farah, Douglas. *Blood from Stones: The Secret Financial Network of Terror.* New York: Broadway Books, 2004.

Farer, Tom. "Shaping Agendas in Civil Wars: Can International Criminal Law Help?" In Mats Berdal and David M. Malone, eds., *Greed and Grievance: Economic Agendas in Civil Wars.* Boulder: Lynne Rienner, pp. 205–232.

Fearon, James D. "Primary Commodities Exports and Civil Wars." October 25, 2004, forthcoming in Journal of Conflict Resolution available at www.stanford.edu/~jfearon/papers/sxpfinal.pdf.

Fearon, James D., and David Laitin. "Ethnicity, Insurgency, and Civil War." *American Political Science Review* 97, no. 1 (2003): 75–91.

Findlay, Mark. *The Globalisation of Crime: Understanding Transnational Relationships in Context.* London: Cambridge University Press, 1999.

FitzGerald, Valpy. *Global Financial Information, Compliance Incentives, and Conflict Funding.* Queen Elizabeth House Working Paper no. 96. Oxford: University of Oxford, February 2003.

Forcese, Craig. "ATCA's Achilles Heel: Corporate Complicity, International Law, and the Alien Tort Claims Act." *Yale Journal of International Law* 26, no. 2 (2001): 487–515.

Frisch, Dieter. *Expert Credit Insurance and the Fight Against International Corruption.* Transparency International Working Paper no. 26. Berlin: Transparency International, 1999.

Frynas, Jedrzej George. "Corporate and State Responses to Anti-oil Protests in the Niger Delta." *African Affairs* 100, no. 398 (2001): 27–54.

Frynas, Jedrzej George, and Geoffrey Wood. "Oil and War in Angola." *Review of African Political Economy* 28, no. 90 (2001): 587–606.

Gaedtke, Jens-Christian. "Der US-amerikanische Alien Tort Claims Act und der Fall Doe v. Unocal: Auf dem Weg zu einer Haftung transnationaler Unternehmen für Menschenrechtsverletzungen?" *Archiv des Völkerrechts* 42, no. 2 (2004): 241–260.

Ganesan, Arvind, and Alex Vines. *Engine of War: Resources, Greed, and the Predatory State.* Washington, D.C.: Human Rights Watch, 2004.

Garapon, A. *Des crimes qu'on ne peut ni punir ni pardoner.* Paris: Odile Jacob, 2003.

Gary, Ian, and Terry Lynn Karl. *Bottom of the Barrel: Africa's Oil Boom and the Poor.* Baltimore: Catholic Relief Services, 2003.

Gberie, Lansana. *War and Peace in Sierra Leone: Diamonds, Corruption, and the Lebanese Connection.* Occasional Paper no. 6, Diamonds and Human Security Project. Ottawa, Ont.: Partnership Africa Canada, 2002.

Gelb, Leslie, et al. *Oil Windfalls: Blessing or Curse?* Washington, D.C.: World Bank, 1988.

Global Witness. *All the Presidents' Men: The Devastating Story of Oil and Banking in Angola's Privatized War.* London: Global Witness, 2000.

———. *Conflict Diamonds: Possibilities for Identification, Certification, and Control of Diamonds.* London: Global Witness, 2000.

———. "A Crude Awakening: The Role of the Oil and Banking Industries in

Angola's Civil War and the Plunder of State Assets." London: Global Witness, 1999.

———. "Deforestation without Limits: How the Cambodian Government Failed to Tackle the Untouchables." London, July 2002. Available at www.globalwitness.org/reports/show.php/en.00007.html.

———. "Forests, Famine, and War: The Key to Cambodia's Future." London, March 1995. Available at www.globalwitness.org/reports/show.php/en.00037.html.

———. *Logs of War: The Timber Trade and Armed Conflict.* Fafo Report no. 379. Oslo: Fafo Institute, 2002.

———. *A Rough Trade: The Role of Diamond Companies and Governments in the Angolan Conflict.* London, 1998.

———. *Same Old Story: A Background Study on Natural Resources in the DRC.* London: Global Witness, 2004.

———. "Thai–Khmer Rouge Links and the Illegal Trade in Cambodia's Timber." London, July 1995. Available at www.globalwitness.org/reports/show.php/en.00036.html.

———. *Time for Transparency: Coming Clean on Oil, Mining, and Gas Revenues.* London: Global Witness, 2004.

Godson, Roy. "Transnational Crime, Corruption, and Security." In Michael E. Brown, ed., *Grave New World: Security Challenges in the Twenty-first Century.* Washington, D.C.: Georgetown University Press, 2003, pp. 259–278.

Gomes Porto, João. "Contemporary Conflict Analysis in Perspective." In Jeremy Lind and Kathryn Sturman, eds., *Scarcity and Surfeit: The Ecology of African Conflicts.* Pretoria: Institute of Security Studies, 2002, pp. 1–49.

Goodhand, Jonathan. "Aiding Violence or Building Peace? The Role of International Aid in Afghanistan." *Third World Quarterly* 23, no. 5 (2002): 837–859.

———. "Enduring Disorder and Persistent Poverty: A Review of the Linkages Between War and Chronic Poverty." *World Development* 31, no. 3 (2003): 629–646.

———. "From Holy War to Opium War? A Case Study of the Opium Economy in North Eastern Afghanistan." *Disasters* 24, no. 2 (2000): 87–102.

Gowlland-Debbas, Vera. "The Review of the Security Council by Member States." In Vera Gowlland-Debbas, ed., *National Implementation of United Nations Sanctions: A Comparative Study.* Leiden: Martinus Nijhoff, 2004, pp. 63–76.

Grant, J. Andrew, and Ian Taylor. "Global Governance and Conflict Diamonds: The Kimberley Process and the Quest for Clean Gems." *Round Table* 93, no. 375 (2004): 385–401.

Grignon, François. "Legacies of the War Economy: Challenges for Peacemaking." In Michael Nest, with François Grignon and Emizet F. Kisangani, *The Democratic Republic of Congo: Economic Dimensions of War and Peace.* Boulder: Lynne Rienner, forthcoming.

Grindle, Merilee S., and John W. Thomas. *Public Choices and Policy Change: The Political Economy of Reform in Developing Countries.* Baltimore: Johns Hopkins University Press, 1991.

Guáqueta, Alexandra. "The Colombian Conflict: Political and Economic Dimensions. " In Karen Ballentine and Jake Sherman, eds., *The Political Economy of Armed Conflict: Beyond Greed and Grievance.* Boulder: Lynne Rienner, 2003, pp. 73–106.

Gwozdecky, Mark, and Jill Sinclair. "Landmines and Human Security." In Rob

McRae and Don Hubert, eds., *Human Security and the New Diplomacy: Protecting People, Promoting Peace.* Montreal: McGill-Queen's University Press, 2001, pp. 28–41.

Hagman, Lotta, and Zoe Nielsen. *A Framework for Lasting Disarmament, Demobilization, and Reintegration of Former Combatants in Crisis Situations.* New York: International Peace Academy, 2002.

Halle, Mark, Jason Switzer, and Sebastian Winkler. *Aid, Trade, and Security: Toward a Positive Paradigm.* Geneva: International Institute for Sustainable Development and World Conservation Union, 2004.

Hansen, Annika. *From Congo to Kosovo: Civilian Police in Peace Operations.* New York: Oxford University Press, 2002.

Haufler, Virginia. *Is There a Role for Business in Conflict Management?* In Chester A. Crocker, Fen Osler Hampson, and Pamela Aall, eds., *Turbulent Peace: The Challenges of Managing International Conflict.* Washington, D.C.: United States Institute of Peace Press, 2001, pp. 659–676.

Hawley, James P., and Andrew T. Williams. *The Rise of Fiduciary Capitalism: How Institutional Investors Can Make Corporate America More Democratic.* Philadelphia: University of Pennsylvania Press, 2000.

Hawley, Susan. *Turning a Blind Eye: The UK ECGD and Corruption.* London: Corner House, 2003.

Hayner, Priscilla B. *Unspeaking Truths: Facing the Challenge of Truth Commissions.* New York: Routledge, 2002.

Heine-Ellison, Sofia. "The Impact and Effectiveness of Multilateral Economic Sanctions: A Comparative Study." *International Journal of Human Rights* 5, no. 1 (2001): 81–112.

Heller, Thomas, Stephen Krasner, and John McMillan. "A Trust Fund for Ituri." Center for Democracy, Development, and the Rule of Law, Stanford University, December 7, 2003; accessible at www.faculty-gsb.stanford.edu/mcmillan/personal_page/documents/Ituri.pdf.

Henckaert, Jean-Marie, and Louise Doswald-Beck. *Customary International Humanitarian Law.* Oxford: ICRC and Oxford University Press, 2005.

Hendrickson, Dylan, and Nicole Ball. *Off-Budget Military Expenditures and Revenue: Issues and Policy Perspectives for Donors.* CSDG Occasional Papers no. 1. London: Conflict, Security, and Development Group, King's College, 2002.

Herbst, Jeffrey. "Economic Incentives, Natural Resources, and Conflict in Africa." *Journal of African Economies* 9, no. 3 (2000): 270–294.

———. *The Politics of Revenue Sharing in Resource-Dependent States.* UNU/WIDER Discussion Paper no. 2001/43. Helsinki: United Nations University, World Institute for Development Economics Research, 2001.

Heywood, Linda. *Contested Power in Angola, 1840s to the Present.* Rochester, N.Y.: University of Rochester Press, 2000.

Hildyard, Nicholas. *Snouts in the Trough: Export Credit Agencies, Corporate Welfare, and Policy Incoherence.* Corner House Briefing no. 14. London, Corner House, 1999; available at www.thecornerhouse.org.uk.

Hildyard, Nicholas, and Mark Mansley. *A Campaigners' Guide to Lobbying Financial Markets.* London: Corner House, 2001.

Hirsch, John L. *Sierra Leone: Diamonds and the Struggle for Democracy.* Boulder: Lynne Rienner, 2001.

Hoffman, Paul, and Daniel Zaheer. "The Rules of the Road: Federal Common Law and Aiding and Abetting Under the Alien Tort Claims Act." *Loyola International Comparative Law Review* 26, no. 1 (2003): 47–48.

Hufbauer, Gary C., and Nicholas K. Mitrokostas. *Awakening Monster: The Alien Tort Statute of 1789.* Washington, D.C.: Institute for International Economics, 2003.

Hufbauer, Gary C., Jeffrey J. Schott, and Kimberley Ann Elliot. *Economic Sanctions Reconsidered: History and Current Policy.* 2nd ed. Washington, D.C.: Institute for International Economics,1990.

Human Rights Watch. "Afghanistan, Crisis of Impunity: The Role of Pakistan, Russia, and Iran in Fueling the Civil War." Washington, D.C., July 2001; available at www.hrw.org/reports/2001/afghan2.

———. "The Oil Diagnostic in Angola: An Update." Washington, D.C., March 2001; available at www.hrw.org/backgrounder/africa/angola.

———. *The Price of Oil: Corporate Responsibility and Human Rights Violations in Nigeria's Oil Producing Communities.* New York: Human Rights Watch, 1999.

———. *Some Transparency, No Accountability: The Use of Oil Revenue in Angola and Its Impact on Human Rights.*Washington, D.C.: Human Rights Watch, 2004.

———. *Sudan, Oil, and Human Rights.* New York: Human Rights Watch, 2003.

Humphreys, Macartan. "Natural Resources, Conflict, and Conflict Resolution." Working paper, Columbia University, New York, 2004.

Humphreys, Macartan, and Jeremy Weinstein. *What the Fighters Say: A Survey of Ex-Combatants in Sierra Leone, June–August 2003. Interim Report.* New York: Earth Institute, July 2004.

Hutchful, Eboe, and Kwesi Aning, "The Political Economy of Conflict." In Adekeye Adebajo and Ismael Rashid, eds., *West Africa's Security Challenges: Building Peace in a Troubled Region.* Boulder: Lynne Rienner, 2004, pp. 195–222.

International Council on Human Rights Policy (ICHRP). *Beyond Voluntarism: Human Rights and the Developing International Legal Obligations of Companies.* Geneva: ICHRP, 2002.

International Crisis Group. "Angola's Choice: Reform or Regress." April 7, 2003. Available at www.crisisweb.org/projects/showreport.cfm?reportid=935.

———. *Disarmament and Reintegration in Afghanistan.* ICG Asia Report no. 65. Kabul: ICG, 30 September 2003.

———. *God, Oil, and Country: Changing the Logic of War in Sudan.* ICG Africa Report no. 39. Brussels: ICG, 2002.

———. *Sierra Leone: Managing Uncertainty.* Africa Report no. 35. Freetown/Brussels: ICG, 2001.

International Institute for Strategic Studies. "Transnational Control of Money-Laundering." In *Strategic Survey, 2001/2002.* Oxford: Oxford University Press, 2002.

International Peace Academy and Fafo Institute. *Business and International Crimes: Assessing the Liability of Business Entities for Grave Violations of International Law.* Oslo: Fafo Institute, 2005.

International Rescue Committee (IRC). *Mortality in the Democratic Republic of Congo: Results from a Nationwide Survey.* New York: IRC, 2003.

International Right to Know Campaign. *International Right to Know: Empowering Communities through Corporate Transparency.* Washington, D.C.: International Right to Know Campaign, 2003.

Jackson, Stephen. "Fortunes of War: The Coltan Trade in the Kivus." In Sarah Collinson, ed., *Power, Livelihoods, and Conflict: Case Studies in Political Economy Analysis for Humanitarian Action.* ODI Humanitarian Policy Group Report no. 13. London: Overseas Development Institute, 2003, pp. 21–36.

———. "Making a Killing: Criminality and Coping in the Kivu War Economy." *Review of African Political Economy* 29, nos. 93/94 (2002): 517–536.

———. "Nos richesses sont pillées: Economies de guerre et rumeurs de crime dans les Kivus, République Démocratique du Congo." *Politique Africaine,* no. 84 (December 2001): 117–135.

Jackson, Stephen, and François Grignon. "The Kivus: Forgotten Crucible of the Congo Conflict." ICG Report no. 56. Brussels/Nairobi: International Crisis Group, 2003.

Jean, François, and Jean-Christophe Rufin, eds. *Economies des guerres civiles.* Paris: Hachette, 1996.

Kaldor, Mary. *New and Old Wars: Organized Violence in a Global Era.* Stanford, Calif.: Stanford University Press, 1999.

Karl, Terry Lynn. *The Paradox of Plenty: Oil Booms and Petro-states.* Berkeley: University of California Press, 1997.

Keen, David. *The Best of Enemies: Conflict and Collusion in Sierra Leone.* London: James Curry, 2005.

———. *The Economic Functions of Violence in Civil Wars.* Adelphi Paper no. 320. Oxford: Oxford University Press, 1998.

———. "Incentives and Disincentives for Violence." In Mats Berdal and David M. Malone, eds., *Greed and Grievance: Economic Agendas in Civil Wars.* Boulder: Lynne Rienner, 2000, pp. 19–41.

———. "War and Peace: What's the Difference?" In Adekeye Adebajo and Chandra Lekha Sriram, eds., *Managing Armed Conflicts in the Twenty-first Century.* London: Frank Cass, 2001, pp. 1–22.

Khuri, Fuad I. "The Social Dynamics of the 1975–1977 War in Lebanon." *Armed Forces and Society* 7, no. 3 (1981): 383–408.

Klare, Michael T. *Resource Wars: The New Landscape of Global Conflict.* New York: Henry Holt, 2001.

Kopp, Pierre. *The Political Economy of Illegal Drugs.* London: Routledge, 2004.

Le Billon, Philippe. "Angola's Political Economy of War: The Role of Oil and Diamonds, 1975–2000." *African Affairs* 100 (2001): 55–80.

———. "Buying Peace or Fuelling War: The Role of Corruption in Armed Conflicts." *Journal of International Development* 15, no. 4 (2003): 413–426.

———. "Getting It Done: International Instruments of Enforcement." In Ian Bannon and Paul Collier, eds., *Natural Resources and Violent Conflict: Options and Actions.* Washington, D.C.: World Bank, 2003, pp. 215–286.

———. "The Political Ecology of Transition in Cambodia, 1989–1999: War, Peace, and Forest Exploitation." *Development and Change* 31, no. 4 (2000): 785–805.

———. "The Political Ecology of War: Natural Resources and Armed Conflicts." *Political Geography* 20, no. 5 (2001): 561–584.

———. *The Political Economy of War: What Relief Agencies Need to Know.* Humanitarian Practice Network Paper no. 33. London: Overseas Development Institute, 2000.

———. "Thriving on War: The Angolan Conflict and Private Business." *Review of African Political Economy,* no. 90 (2001): 629–652.

Leighton, Michelle, Naomi Roht-Arriaza, and Lyuba Zarsky. *Beyond Good Deeds: Case Studies and a New Policy Agenda for Corporate Accountability.* Berkeley: California Global Corporate Accountability Project, 2002.

Leite, Carlos, and Jens Weidmann. "Does Mother Nature Corrupt? Natural Resources, Corruption, and Economic Growth." IMF Working Paper no. 99/85. Washington, D.C.: International Monetary Fund, 1999.

Lilly, Damian, and Philippe Le Billon. *Regulating Business in Zones of Conflict: A Synthesis of Strategies*. London: Overseas Development Institute, July 2002.

Lindsay, J. M. "Trade Sanctions as Policy Instruments: A Re-examination." *International Studies Quarterly* 30 (1986): 153–173.

Litan, Robert E. "Economics: Global Finance." In P. J. Simmons and Chantal de Jonge Oudraat, eds., *Managing Global Issues: Lessons Learned*. Washington, D.C.: Brookings Institution, 2001, pp. 196–233.

Lunde, Leiv, and Mark Taylor, with Anne Huser. *Commerce or Crime? Regulating Economies of Conflict*. Fafo Report no. 424. Oslo: Fafo Institute, 2003.

MacDonald, Gary, and Timothy McLaughlin. "Extracting Conflict." In Rory Sullivan, ed., *Business and Human Rights: Dilemmas and Solutions*. Sheffield, UK: Greenleaf, 2003, pp. 232–242.

MacGaffey, Janet. "Evading Male Control: Women in the Second Economy in Zaire." In Sharon B. Stichter and Jane L Parpart, eds., *Patriarchy and Class*. Boulder: Westview, 1998, pp. 161–176.

Mack, Andrew, and Asif Khan. "The Efficacy of UN Sanctions." *Security Dialogue* 31, no. 2 (2000): 279–292.

Malan, Mark, et al. *Sierra Leone: Building the Road to Recovery*. ISS Monograph no. 80. Pretoria: Institute for Security Studies, 2003.

Malaquias, Assis. "Making War and Lots of Money: The Political Economy of Protracted Conflict in Angola." *Review of African Political Economy* 28, no. 90 (2001): 521–536.

Malone, David M., and Heiko Nitzschke, "Economic Agendas in Civil War: What We Know, What We Need to Know." UNU-WIDER Discussion Paper, Helsinki: UNU-WIDER, 2005.

Mansley, Mark. "Building Tomorrow's Crisis? The Baku-Tbilisi-Ceyhan Pipeline and BP: A Financial Analysis." London: Claros Consulting, May 2003.

———. *Open Disclosure: Sustainability and the Listing Regime*. London: Claros Consulting, 2003.

Mbembe, Achille. "At the Edge of the World: Boundaries, Territoriality, and Sovereignty in Africa." In Arjun Appadurai, ed., *Globalization*. Durham, N.C.: Duke University Press, 2001, pp. 22–51.

McPhail, Kathryn. "The Revenue Dimension of Oil, Gas, and Mining Projects: Issues and Practices." Paper presented at the Society of Petroleum Engineers International Conference on Health, Safety, and Environment in Oil and Gas Exploration and Production, Kuala Lumpur, March 20–22, 2002.

McPhail, Kathryn, and Aidan Davy. "Integrating Social Concerns into Private Sector Decisionmaking: A Review of Corporate Practices in the Mining, Oil, and Gas Sectors." World Bank Discussion Paper no. 384. Washington, D.C.: World Bank, 1998.

Meagher, Kate. "A Back Door to Globalisation? Structural Adjustment, Globalisation, and Transborder Trade in West Africa." *Review of African Political Economy* 30, no. 95 (2003): 57–75.

Meeran, Richard. "Accountability of Transnationals for Human Rights Abuses, Part 1." *New Law Journal* 148, no. 6864 (November 13, 1998): 1686–1687.

———. "Accountability of Transnationals for Human Rights Abuses, Part 2." *New Law Journal* 148, no. 6865 (November 20, 1998): 1706–1708.

Milieu Defensie et al. International NGO Training and Strategy Seminar on the OECD *Guidelines for Multinationals*: A Tool to Combat Violations of Environmental and Workers' Rights. Friends of the Earth/IRENE, Amsterdam, February 2003.

Misol, Lisa. "Weapons and War Crimes: The Complicity of Arms Suppliers." Human Rights Watch report, Washington, D.C., January 1994.

Mitchell, John, ed. *Companies in a World of Conflict*. London: Earthscan, 1998.

Monks, Robert A. G. *The New Global Investors: How Shareholders Can Unlock Prosperity Worldwide*. Oxford: Capstone, 2001.

Moyers, Reese. *The Feasibility of Establishing a Formal Credit Delivery Mechanism for Small-Scale Diamond Miners in Kono District, Sierra Leone*. Washington, D.C.: Management Systems International, May 2003.

Nafziger, Wayne E. "Economic Development, Inequality, War, and State Violence." *World Development* 30, no. 2 (February 2002): 153–163.

Nafziger, Wayne E., and Juna Auvinen. *Economic Development, Inequality, and War: Humanitarian Emergencies in Developing Countries*. Houndmills, UK: Palgrave, 2003.

Naylor, R. Thomas. "The Insurgent Economy: Black Market Operations of Guerilla Organizations." *Crime, Law, and Social Change* 20, no. 1 (1993): 13–51.

———. *Patriots and Profiteers: On Economic Warfare, Embargo Busting, and State-Sponsored Crime*. Toronto: McClelland and Stewart, 1999.

Ndikumana, Léonce, and Kisangani Emizet. "The Economics of Civil War: The Case of the Democratic Republic of Congo." Political Economy Research Institute Working Paper no. 63, University of Massachusetts, Amherst, 2003; available at www.umass.edu/peri/pdfs/WP63.pdf.

Nelson, Jane. *The Business of Peace: The Private Sector as a Partner in Conflict Resolution*. London: International Alert and Prince of Wales Business Leaders Forum, 2000.

Nest, Michael, with François Grignon and Emizet F. Kisangani. *The Democratic Republic of Congo: Economic Dimensions of War and Peace*. Boulder: Lynne Rienner, forthcoming.

Nichols, Philip M. "Regulating Transnational Bribery in Times of Globalization and Fragmentation." *Yale Journal of International Law* 24, no. 1 (1999): 257–303.

Nitzschke, Heiko. *Transforming War Economies: Challenges for Peacemaking and Peacebuilding*. Report of the 725th Wilton Park Conference in association with the International Peace Academy, October 27–29, 2003. New York: International Peace Academy, 2003.

Nitzschke, Heiko, and Kaysie Studdard. "The Legacies of War Economies: Challenges and Options for Peacemaking and Peacebuilding." *International Peacekeeping* 12, no. 2 (2005): 1–18.

Office for the Coordination of Humanitarian Affairs (OCHA). *Consolidated Interagency Appeal for the Democratic Republic of the Congo 2003: Mid-year Review*. New York: OCHA, 2003.

Organization for Economic Cooperation and Development (OECD). *Behind the Corporate Veil: Using Corporate Entities for Illicit Purposes*. Paris: OECD, 2001.

———. *Harmful Tax Competition: An Emerging Global Issue*. Paris: OECD, 1998.

———. *Multinational Enterprises in Situations of Violent Conflict and Widespread Human Rights Abuse*. Background Note. Paris: OECD, 2002.

———. *The OECD Guidelines for Multinational Enterprises*. Paris: OECD, 2000.

———. *OECD Guidelines for Multinational Enterprises: Enhancing the Role of Business in the Fight Against Corruption; Annual Report 2003*. Paris: OECD, 2003.

———. *OECD Guidelines for Multinational Enterprises: Focus on Responsible Supply Chain Management; Annual Report 2002*. Paris: OECD, 2002.

————. *Recommendation on Common Approaches on Environment and Officially Supported Export Credits*. Paris: OECD, 2003.

Orr, Robert C. "Building Peace in El Salvador: From Exception to Rule." In Elizabeth M. Cousens and Chetan Kumar, eds., *Peacebuilding as Politics: Cultivating Peace in Fragile Societies*. Boulder: Lynne Rienner, 2001, pp. 153–181.

Partnership Africa Canada. *Diamond Industry Annual Review: Sierra Leone, 2004*. Ottawa, Ont.: Partnership Africa Canada, 2004.

Pastor, Manuel, and Michael E. Conroy. "Distributional Implications of Macroeconomic Policy: Theory and Applications to El Salvador." In James K. Boyce, ed., *Economic Policy for Building Peace: The Lessons of El Salvador*. Boulder: Lynne Rienner, 1996, pp. 155–176.

Pegg, Scott. "The Cost of Doing Business: Transnational Corporations and Violence in Nigeria." *Security Dialogue* 30, no. 4, 1999: 473–484.

Picarelli, John T., and Louise Shelley. "Methods, Not Motives: Implications of the Convergence of International Organized Crime and Terrorism." *Police Practice and Research* 3, no. 4 (2002): 305–318.

Pole Institute. *The Coltan Phenomenon: How a Rare Mineral Has Changed the Life of the Population of War-Torn North Kivu Province in the Democratic Republic of Congo*. Goma, DRC: Pole Institute, 2002.

Pole Institute and International Alert. *Natural Resource Exploitation and Human Security in the Democratic Republic of Congo*. London: International Alert, 2004.

Pugh, Michael. "Postwar Political Economy in Bosnia and Herzegovina: The Spoils of Peace." *Global Governance* 8, no. 4 (2002): 467–482.

Pugh, Michael, and Neil Cooper, with Jonathan Goodhand. *War Economies in a Regional Context: Challenges of Transformation*. Boulder: Lynne Rienner, 2004.

Raeymaekers, Timothy. *Network War: An Introduction to Congo's Privatized War Economy*. Brussels: International Peace Information Service, 2002.

Ramasastry, Anita. "Corporate Complicity from Nuremberg to Rangoon: An Examination of Forced Labor Cases and Their Impact on the Liability of Multinational Corporations." *Berkeley Journal of International Law* 20, no. 1 (2002): 91–151.

Randall, Kenneth C. "Federal Jurisdiction over International Law Claims: Inquiries into the Alien Tort Statute." *New York University Journal of International Law and Politics* 18, no. 1 (1985): 1–72.

Rangel, Alfredo. "Parasites and Predators: Guerrillas and the Insurrection Economy of Colombia." *Journal of International Affairs* 53, no. 2 (2000): 577–601.

Rashid, Ahmed. *Taliban: Militant Islam, Oil, and Fundamentalism in Central Asia*. New Haven, Conn.: Yale University Press, 2000.

Ratner, Steven R. "Corporations and Human Rights: A Theory of Legal Responsibility." *Yale Law Journal* 111, no. 3 (2001): 443–545.

————. "The Security Council and International Law." In David M. Malone, ed., *The UN Security Council: From the Cold War to the Twenty-first Century*. Boulder: Lynne Rienner, 2004, pp. 591–605.

Regan, Anthony J. "The Bougainville Conflict: Political and Economic Agendas." In Karen Ballentine and Jake Sherman, eds., *The Political Economy of Armed Conflict: Beyond Greed and Grievance*. Boulder: Lynne Rienner, 2003, pp. 133–166.

Renner, Michael. *The Anatomy of Resource Wars*. Worldwatch Paper no. 162. Washington, D.C.: Worldwatch Institute, 2002.

Reno, William. *Corruption and the State in Sierra Leone*. Cambridge: Cambridge University Press, 1995.

———. "The Politics of Insurgency in Collapsing States." *Development and Change* 33, no. 5 (2002): 837–858.

———. "Shadow States and the Political Economy of Civil War." In Mats Berdal and David M. Malone, eds., *Greed and Grievance: Economic Agendas in Civil Wars*. Boulder: Lynne Rienner, 2000, pp. 43–68.

———. *Warlord Politics and the African State*. Boulder: Lynne Rienner, 1998.

Reyes, David, and Luc Zandvliet. *A Look at the Operational Activities of Logging Companies in Cameroon*. Corporate Engagement Project Case Study. Cambridge, Mass.: Collaborative for Development Action, 2002.

Rich, Bruce, Korinna Horta, and Aaron Goldzimer. *Export Credit Agencies in Sub-Saharan Africa: Indebtedness for Extractive Industries, Corruption, and Conflict*. Washington, D.C.: Environmental Defense Fund, n.d.

Richani, Nazih. *Systems of Violence: The Political Economy of War and Peace in Colombia*. Albany: State University of New York Press, 2000.

Rights and Accountability in Development (RAID). *Unanswered Questions: Companies, Conflict, and the Democratic Republic of Congo*. London: RAID, 2004.

Ross, Michael L. "Booty Futures: Africa's Civil Wars and the Futures Market for Natural Resources." Unpubl., University of California at Los Angeles (UCLA), available at www.polisci.ucla.edu/faculty/ross/bootyfutures.pdf. December 18, 2002.

———. *Extractive Sectors and the Poor*. Oxfam America Report. Washington, D.C.: Oxfam America, 2001.

———. "How Do Natural Resources Influence Civil War? Evidence from Thirteen Cases." *International Organization* 58, no. 1 (2004): 35–67.

———. "Oil, Drugs, and Diamonds: The Varying Roles of Natural Resources in Civil War." In Karen Ballentine and Jake Sherman, eds., *The Political Economy of Armed Conflict: Beyond Greed and Grievance*. Boulder: Lynne Rienner, 2003, pp. 47–70.

———. "The Political Economy of the Resource Curse." *World Politics* 51, no. 2 (1999): 297–322.

———. "What Do We Know About Natural Resources and Civil War?" *Journal of Peace Research* 41, no. 3 (2004): 337–356.

Rotberg, Robert I., ed. *State Failures and State Weakness in a Time of Terror*. Cambridge, Mass.: World Peace Foundation, 2003.

Rubin, Barnett. *Blood on the Doorstep: The Politics of Preventive Action*. New York: Century Foundation Press, 2002.

———. *The Fragmentation of Afghanistan: State Formation and Collapse in the International System*. New Haven, Conn.: Yale University Press, 1995.

———. "The Political Economy of War and Peace in Afghanistan." *World Development* 28, no. 10 (2000): 1789–1803.

———. *Road to Ruin: Afghanistan's Booming Opium Industry*. New York: Center on International Cooperation, 2004.

Rubin, Barnett, Ashraf Ghani, William Maley, Ahmed Rashid, and Olivier Roy. "Afghanistan: Reconstruction and Peacebuilding in a Regional Framework." Bern: Center for Peacebuilding (KOFF), Swiss Peace Foundation, June 2001.

Rubin, Barnett, Humayun Hamidzada, and Abby Stoddard. "Through the Fog of Peace Building: Evaluating the Reconstruction of Afghanistan." New York: New York University, Center on International Cooperation, June 2003.

Sachs, Jeffrey D., and Andrew M. Warner, "The Curse of Natural Resources." *European Economic Review* 45 (2001): 827–838.

Sala-i-Martin, Xavier, and Arvind Subramanian. "Addressing the Natural Resource Curse: An Illustration from Nigeria." Working Paper no. 9804. Cambridge, Mass.: National Bureau for Economic Research, 2003.

Saland, Per. "International Criminal Law Principles." In Roy S. K. Lee, ed., *The International Criminal Court: The Making of the Rome Statute.* The Hague: Kluwer Law International, 1999, pp. 189–216.

Sambanis, Nicholas. "A Review of Recent Advances and Future Directions in the Literature on Civil War." *Defense and Peace Economics* 13 (2002): 215–243.

Samset, Ingrid. "Conflict of Interest or Interest in Conflict? Diamonds and War in the DRC." *Review of African Political Economy,* nos. 93/94 (2002): 466.

Sandbu, Martin. "Taxable Resource Revenue Distributions: A Proposal For Alleviating the Natural Resource Curse." Center on Government and Sustainable Development (CGSD) Working Paper 21. New York: Columbia University, 2004.

Sanders, Lucinda. "Rich and Rare Are the Gems They War: Holding De Beers Accountable for Trading Conflict Diamonds." *Fordham International Law Journal* 24, no. 4 (2001): 1402–1476.

Save the Children Fund. *War Brought Us Here: Protecting Children Displaced within Their Own Countries by Conflict.* London: Save the Children Fund, 2000.

Schabas, William A. "Enforcing International Humanitarian Law: Catching the Accomplices." *International Review of the Red Cross* 83, no. 439 (2001): 439–459.

Schloss, Miguel. "Does Petroleum Procurement and Trade Matter?" *Finance and Development,* March 1993, pp. 44–46.

Scoones, Ian. *Sustainable Rural Livelihoods: A Framework for Analysis.* IDS Working Paper no. 72. Brighton: Institute for Development Studies, 1998.

Scott, Craig, ed. *Torture Is Tort: Comparative Perspectives on the Development of Transnational Human Rights Litigation.* Oxford: Hart, 2001.

Sedra, Mark. *Challenging the Warlord Culture: Security Sector Reform in Post-Taliban Afghanistan.* Bonn International Center for Conversion Paper no. 25. Bonn: BICC, 2002.

Sherman, Jake. "Burma: Lessons from the Cease-Fires." In Karen Ballentine and Jake Sherman, eds., *The Political Economy of Armed Conflict: Beyond Greed and Grievance.* Boulder: Lynne Rienner, 2003, pp. 225–255.

———. *Options for Promoting Corporate Responsibility in Conflict Zones: Perspectives from the Private Sector.* IPA Conference Report. New York: International Peace Academy, 2002.

———. *Policies and Practices for Regulating Resource Flows to Armed Conflict.* IPA Conference Report. New York: International Peace Academy, 2002.

———. *Private Sector Actors in Zones of Conflict: Research Challenges and Policy Responses.* IPA-Fafo Institute Conference Report. New York: International Peace Academy, 2001.

Sierra Leone Truth and Reconciliation Commission Final Report. October 27, 2004. Available at http://www.usip.org/library/tc/tc_regions/tc_sl.html#rep

Smillie, Ian. *Dirty Diamonds: Armed Conflict and the Trade in Rough Diamonds.* Fafo Report no. 377. Oslo: Fafo Institute, 2002.

———. *The Kimberley Process: The Case for Proper Monitoring.* Occasional Paper no. 5. Ottawa, Ont.: Partnership Africa Canada, 2002.

Smillie, Ian, Lansana Gberie, and Ralph Hazelton. *The Heart of the Matter: Sierra Leone, Diamonds, and Human Security*. Ottawa, Ont.: Partnership Africa Canada, 2000.

Smith, A. *East West Trade. Embargoes and Expectations*. Center for Economic Policy Research Discussion Paper no. 139. London, Center for Economic Policy, 1986.

Social Investment Forum (SIF). *2003 Report on Socially Responsible Investing Trends in the United States*. Washington, D.C.: SIF, 2003.

Sparkes, Russell. *Socially Responsible Investment: A Global Revolution*. London: John Wiley, 2002.

Specht, Irma. "Jobs for Rebels and Soldiers." In Eugenia Date-Bah, ed., *Jobs After War: A Critical Challenge in the Peace and Reconstruction Puzzle*. Geneva: International Labour Office, 2003.

Sriram, Chandra Lekha. "Contemporary Practice of Universal Jurisdiction: Disjointed and Disparate, Yet Developing." *International Journal of Human Rights* 6 (Fall 2002): 49–76.

Stauber, John, and Sheldon Rampton. *Toxic Sludge Is Good for You: Lies, Damn Lies, and the Public Relations Industry*. London: Common Courage, 1995.

Stedman, Stephen John. Introduction to Stephen John Stedman, Donald Rothchild, and Elizabeth M. Cousens, eds., *Ending Civil Wars: The Implementation of Peace Agreements*. Boulder: Lynne Rienner, 2002, pp. 1–40.

———. "Spoiler Problems in Peace Processes." *International Security* 22, no. 2 (1997): 5–53.

Steering Committee for the Joint Evaluation of Emergency Assistance to Rwanda. *The International Response to Conflict and Genocide: Lessons from the Rwanda Experience; Synthesis Report*. Copenhagen: Author, 1996.

Steinhardt, Ralph, and Anthony D'Amato, eds. *The Alien Tort Claims Act: An Analytical Anthology*. Ardsley, N.Y.: Transnational, 1999.

Stephens, Beth. "Translating Filártiga: A Comparative and International Law Analysis of Domestic Remedies for International Human Rights Violations." *Yale Journal for International Law* 27, no. 1 (2002): 1–57.

Stephens, Beth, and Michael Ratner. *International Human Rights Litigation in U.S. Courts*. Ardsley, N.Y.: Transnational, 1996.

Stewart, Frances. "Crisis Prevention: Tacking Horizontal Inequalities." *Oxford Development Studies* 28, no. 3 (2000): 245–262.

———. "Horizontal Inequalities as a Source of Conflict." In Fen Osler Hampson and David M. Malone, eds., *From Reaction to Conflict Prevention: Opportunities for the UN System*. Boulder: Lynne Rienner, 2002, pp. 105–136.

Studdard, Kaysie. *War Economies in a Regional Context: Overcoming the Challenges of Transformation*. IPA Policy Report. New York: International Peace Academy, 2004.

Suberu, Rotimi T. *Federalism and Ethnic Conflict in Nigeria*. Washington, D.C.: United States Institute of Peace Press, 2001.

Swanson, Philip. *Fuelling Conflicts: The Oil Industry and Armed Conflict*. Fafo Report no. 378. Oslo: Fafo Institute, 2002.

Swanson, Philip, Mai Olgard, and Leiv Lunde. "Who Gets the Money? Reporting Resource Revenues." In Ian Bannon and Paul Collier, eds., *Natural Resources and Violent Conflict: Options and Actions*. Washington, D.C.: World Bank, 2003, pp. 43–96.

Switzer, Jason. *Armed Conflict and Natural Resources: The Case of the Minerals Sector*. London: International Institute for Environment and Development, 2001.

Switzer, Jason, and Halina Ward. "Enabling Corporate Investment in Peace: An Assessment of Voluntary Principles Addressing Business and Violent Conflict." IISD (International Institute for Sustainable Development) Discussion Paper, Chatelaine, February 2004.

Szasz, Paul C. "The Security Council Starts Legislating." American Journal of International Law 96, (2002): 901ff.

Tamm, Ingrid J. Diamonds in Peace and War: Severing the Conflict-Diamond Connection. World Peace Foundation Report no. 30. Cambridge, Mass.: Carr Center for Human Rights Policy, 2002.

Taylor, Mark. Conflict Trade: The Private Sector and Contemporary Wars. London: Pluto Press, 2004.

————. "Public Sector Finance in Post-Conflict Situations." Report of the Peace Implementation Network Forum, FAFO AIS, Washington, D.C., April 1999.

Tebtebba Foundation and Forest Peoples Programme. Extracting Promises: Indigenous Peoples, Extractive Industries, and the World Bank. Baguio City, Philippines: Tebtebba Foundation, 2003.

Transnational Crime and Corruption Center. Transnational Crime and Peacekeeping: Comparative Perspectives. Conference Report. Washington, D.C.: TraCCC, 2002.

Transparency International. Global Corruption Report 2003. Berlin: Transparency International, 2003.

Tsalik, Svetlana. Caspian Oil Windfalls: Who Will Benefit? New York: Open Society Institute, 2003.

Uvin, Peter. Aiding Violence: The Development Enterprise in Rwanda. West Hartford, Conn.: Kumarian, 1998.

Van Acker, Frank, and Koen Vlassenroot. "Youth and Conflict in Kivu: 'Komona clair.'" Journal of Humanitarian Assistance, July 21, 2000; available at www.jha.ac/greatlakes/b004.htm.

Van Bergeaux, P. "Success and Failure of Economic Sanctions." Kyklos 42, no. 3 (1989): 385–404.

Verschave, François-Xavier. Noir silence. Paris: Éditions des Arènes, 2000.

Vines, Alex. "Monitoring UN Sanctions in Africa: The Role of Panels of Experts." In Trevor Findlay, ed., Verification Yearbook 2003. London: Vertic, 2004.

Vlassenroot, Koen, and Timothy Raeymaekers. Conflict and Social Transformation in Eastern DR Congo. Ghent, Belgium: University of Gent, Conflict Research Group, 2004.

Vlassenroot, Koen, and Hans Romkema. "The Emergence of a New Order? Resources and War in Eastern Congo." Journal of Humanitarian Assistance, October 28, 2002; available at www.jha.ac/articles/a111.htm.

Von Brabant, Konrad, and Tony Killick. "The Use of Development Incentives and Disincentives in Influencing Conflict or Civil Violence: Afghanistan Case Study." Paper prepared for the OECD Development Assistance Committee, Paris, March 1999.

Vwakyanakazi, Mukohya. "Import and Export in the Second Economy in North Kivu." In Janet MacGaffey, ed., The Real Economy of Zaire: The Contribution of Smuggling and Other Unofficial Activities to National Wealth. Philadelphia: University of Pennsylvania Press, 1991, pp. 43–71.

Wallensteen, Peter, Carina Staibano, and Mikael Eriksson, eds. Making Targeted Sanctions Effective: Guidelines for the Implementation of UN Policy Options. Uppsala: Uppsala University, 2004.

Wang, Hongying, and James N. Rosenau. "Transparency International and

Corruption as an Issue of Global Governance." *Global Governance* 7, no. 1 (2001): 25–49.

Ward, Curtis A. "Building Capacity to Combat International Terrorism: The Role of the United Nations Security Council." *Journal of Conflict and Security Law* 8, no. 2 (2003): 289–305.

Ward, Halina. "Securing Transnational Corporate Accountability through National Courts: Implications and Policy Options." *Hastings International and Comparative Law Review* 24, no. 3 (2001): 451–474.

Warner, Michael. *Tri-sector Partnerships for Social Investment within the Oil, Gas, and Mining Sectors: An Analytical Framework.* Business Partners for Development Working Paper no. 2. London: BPD, n.d.

Weiss, Thomas. "Sanctions as a Foreign Policy Tool: Weighing Humanitarian Impulses." *Journal of Peace Research* 36, no. 5 (September 1999): 499–510.

Weissbrodt, David, and Muria Kruger. "Norms on the Responsibilities of Transnational Corporations and Other Business Enterprises with Regard to Human Rights." *American Journal of International Law* 97, no. 4 (2003): 901–922.

Wenger, Andreas, and Daniel Möckli. *Conflict Prevention: The Untapped Potential of the Business Sector.* Boulder: Lynne Rienner, 2003.

Williams, Cynthia A. "The Securities and Exchange Commission and Corporate Social Transparency." *Harvard Law Review* 112, no. 6 (1999): 1197–1311.

Williams, Phil. "Criminalization and Stability in Central Asia and South Caucasus." In Olya Oliker and Thomas Szayna, eds., *Faultlines of Conflict in Central Asia and the South Caucasus: Implications for the US Army.* Santa Monica, Calif.: RAND, 2003, pp. 71–107.

Winer, Jonathan M. *Illicit Finance and Global Conflict.* Fafo Report no. 380. Oslo: Fafo Institute, 2002.

Winer, Jonathan M., and Trifin J. Roule. "The Finance of Illicit Resource Extraction." In Ian Bannon and Paul Collier, eds., *Natural Resources and Violent Conflict: Options and Actions.* Washington, D.C.: World Bank, 2003, pp. 161–214.

Wood, Elisabeth J. "The Peace Accords and Postwar Reconstruction." In James K. Boyce, ed., *Economic Policy for Building Peace: The Lessons of El Salvador.* Boulder: Lynne Rienner, 1996, pp. 73–105.

Woodward, Susan. "Economic Priorities for Successful Peace Implementation." In Stephen John Stedman, Donald Rothchild, and Elizabeth M. Cousens, eds., *Ending Civil Wars: The Implementation of Peace Agreements.* Boulder: Lynne Rienner, 2002, pp. 183–214.

World Bank. *Assessing Aid: What Works, What Doesn't, and Why.* New York: Oxford University Press, 1998.

———. *Global Development Finance 2002: Financing the Poorest Countries.* Washington, D.C.: World Bank, 2002.

———. *Greater Great Lakes Regional Strategy for Demobilization and Reintegration.* Report no. 23869-AFR. Washington D.C.: World Bank, 2002.

———. *The World Bank's Experience with Post-conflict Reconstruction.* Vol. 3, *El Salvador Case Study.* Washington, D.C.: World Bank, 1998.

Zahar, Marie-Joëlle. "Reframing the Spoiler Debate." In Rolf Habbel, John Darby and Roger MacGinty, eds., *Contemporary Peacemaking: Conflict, Violence and Peace Processes.* Houndmills, UK, Palgrave, 2003, pp. 114–124.

Zandvliet, Luc, and Ibiba Don Pedro. *Oil Company Policies in the Niger Delta.* Corporate Engagement Project. Cambridge, Mass.: Collaborative for

Development Action, 2002; available at www.cdainc.com/cep/publications/reports/Visit03Nigeria.pdf.

Key United Nations Documents and Resolutions

United Nations. *A More Secure World: Our Shared Responsibility.* Report of the High-level Panel on Threats, Challenges, and Change. New York: United Nations, 2004.

United Nations Environmental Program (UNEP). *Finance, Mining, and Sustainability: Exploring Sound Investment Decision Processes.* Paris: UNEP, 2002.

United Nations General Assembly. "The Role of Diamonds in Fuelling Conflict: Breaking the Link Between the Illicit Transaction of Rough Diamonds and Armed Conflict as a Contribution to Prevention and Settlement of Conflicts." A/RES/55/56, January 29, 2001.

———. "The Role of Diamonds in Fuelling Conflict: Breaking the Link Between the Illicit Transaction of Rough Diamonds and Armed Conflict as a Contribution to Prevention and Settlement of Conflicts." A/RES/56/263, April 9, 2002.

———. United Nations Convention Against Transnational Organized Crime. A/RES/55/25, January 8, 2001.

United Nations Office on Drugs and Crime (UNODC). *Afghanistan: Opium Survey 2003.* Vienna: United Nations Office on Drugs and Crime, 2003.

———. *The Opium Economy in Afghanistan: An International Problem.* New York: United Nations, 2003; available at www.reliefweb.int/library/documents/2003/unodc-afg-31jan.pdf.

United Nations Security Council. *Addendum to the Report of the Panel of Experts on the Illegal Exploitation of Natural Resources and Other Forms of Wealth of the Democratic Republic of the Congo.* S/2001/1072, November 13, 2001.

———. *Final Report of the Panel of Experts on the Illegal Exploitation of Natural Resources and Other Forms of Wealth in the Democratic Republic of the Congo.* S/2002/1146, October 16, 2002.

———. *Final Report of the Panel of Experts on the Illegal Exploitation of Natural Resources and Other Forms of Wealth in the Democratic Republic of Congo.* S/2003/1027, October 23, 2003.

———. *Report of the Panel of Experts Appointed pursuant to Security Council Resolution 1306 (2000), Paragraph 19, in Relation to Sierra Leone.* S/2000/1195, December 20, 2000.

———. *Report of the Panel of Experts on Violations of Security Council Sanctions Against UNITA.* S/2000/203, March 10, 2000.

———. *Report of the Panel of Experts pursuant to Security Council Resolution 1343 (2001), Paragraph 19, concerning Liberia.* S/2001/1015, October 26, 2001.

———. "Report of the Policy Working Group on the United Nations and Terrorism." S/2002/875, August 6, 2002.

———. "Report of the Secretary-General to the Security Council on Angola." S/2002/834, July 26, 2002.

———. "Report of the Secretary-General to the Security Council on the Protection of Civilians in Armed Conflict." S/2002/1300, November 26, 2002.

————. *Report of the UN Panel of Experts on the Illegal Exploitation of Natural Resources and Other Forms of Wealth of the Democratic Republic of the Congo.* S/2001/357, April 12, 2001.

————. "Role of Business in Conflict Prevention, Peacekeeping, and Post-conflict Reconstruction." S/PV/4943, April 15, 2004.

————. "Supplementary Report of the Monitoring Mechanism on Sanctions Against UNITA." S/2001/966, October 12, 2001.

The Contributors

Karen Ballentine is senior consultant with the New Security Program of the Fafo Institute in Norway. In 2000–2003, she was senior associate with the International Peace Academy, directing the program on Economic Agendas in Civil Wars, and she was research associate for the Commission on the Prevention of Deadly Conflict at the Carnegie Corporation of New York from 1994 to 2000. She has also served as a consultant for the UN Global Compact, the Human Security Report, and the Millennium Development Goals. She is coauthor (with Jack Snyder) of *Nationalism and the Marketplace of Ideas* and coeditor (with Jake Sherman) of *The Political Economy of Armed Conflict: Beyond Greed and Grievance.*

James K. Boyce is professor of economics at the University of Massachusetts, Amherst, where he directs the program on development, peacebuilding, and the environment at the Political Economy Research Institute. He is author of an Adelphi Paper, *Investing in Peace: Aid and Conditionality after Civil Wars,* editor of *Economic Policy for Building Peace: The Lessons of El Salvador,* and author of *The Political Economy of the Environment.*

Corene Crossin is campaigns researcher at Global Witness, where she works on research projects relating to the governance of natural resources, particularly in the Democratic Republic of Congo. She has also worked on a World Bank forestry governance initiative examining the political, sociological, and technical aspects of "conflict timber" in sub-Saharan Africa and is coauthor (with Gavin Hayman and Simon Taylor) of "Where Did It

Come From? Commodity Tracking Systems," a contribution to *Natural Resources and Violent Conflicts* (edited by Ian Bannon and Paul Collier).

Sue E. Eckert is senior fellow at the Thomas J. Watson Jr. Institute for International Studies at Brown University. Her current research focuses on terrorist financing, targeted sanctions, and critical infrastructure issues. From 1993 to 1997, she served as assistant secretary of commerce for export administration, administering a range of U.S. security export control and defense industrial base programs. Previously, she served on the professional staff of the U.S. House of Representatives' Committee on Foreign Affairs. Her most recent publication is *Targeting Financial Sanctions: Harmonizing National Legislation and Regulatory Practices.*

Patricia Feeney is the director of Rights and Accountability in Development (RAID), an Oxford-based nongovernmental organization that conducts research into corporate accountability, human rights, and extractive industries, particularly in the Democratic Republic of Congo. She is also the policy coordinator for OECD WATCH and research affiliate of Queen Elizabeth House at the University of Oxford. Previously she was senior policy adviser for Oxfam on aid, trade, investment, and human rights and a researcher in Amnesty International's Latin American Department. She is the author of numerous reports and articles, as well as *Accountable Aid,* published by Oxfam in 1998.

Gavin Hayman is the lead campaigner and investigator for Global Witness working on oil revenue misappropriation and corporate malfeasance. Prior to this, he was associate fellow of the Sustainable Development Programme at the Royal Institute of International Affairs, where he wrote extensively on environmental crime and commodity-tracking issues. In 1996–1998, he was a campaigner and investigator at the Environmental Investigation Agency. He is coauthor of "Where Did It Come From? Commodity Tracking Systems."

Nicholas Hildyard works with the Corner House, a UK-based research and solidarity group focusing on human rights, environment, and development. He has been monitoring development impacts of the major international financial institutions since 1980. He is author or coauthor of a number of books on environment and development issues, including *A Campaigners' Guide to Financial Markets* (with Mark Mansley). He is active in the international NGO campaign to reform the lending practices of the OECD's export credit agencies.

Paul L. Hoffman is a partner in the law firm of Schonbrun, De Simone,

Seplow, Harris and Hoffman and cooperating attorney with the Center for Constitutional Rights. He is the former legal director of the American Civil Liberties Union (ACLU) Foundation of Southern California and has litigated numerous cases brought under the Alien Tort Claims Act, including as one of the lead counsel in *Doe v. Unocal*. He currently chairs the International Executive Committee of Amnesty International and teaches international human rights law at University of Southern California Law School and Oxford University.

Macartan Humphreys is assistant professor of political science at Columbia University and research scholar at the Earth Institute's Center for Globalization and Development. He is principal adviser on the Earth Institute's São Tomé and Príncipe Oil Management Law project and member of the Millennium Project Task Force on Poverty and Economic Development. His publications include (with Robert Bates) *Political Institutions and Economic Policies: Lessons from Africa;* (with Jeremy Weinstein) *What the Fighters Say: A Survey of Ex-Combatants in Sierra Leone;* and (with Ashutosh Varshney) *Violent Conflict and the Millennium Development Goals: Diagnosis and Recommendations.*

Stephen Jackson is associate director of the Conflict Prevention and Peace Forum at the Social Science Research Council, with particular responsibility for programming related to African conflicts. From 1998 to 2002, he was the founding director of the International Famine Centre at the National University of Ireland, Cork. Between 1997 and 2002, he conducted anthropological fieldwork in the eastern Democratic Republic of Congo. Prior to that, he worked as a relief worker in Somalia, Rwanda, and Angola. His publications include *Fortunes of War: The Coltan Trade in the Kivus* and *Making a Killing: Criminality and Coping in the Kivu War Economy.*

Tom Kenny is a researcher and consultant on human rights, development, and the private sector. He has written on the social cost of privatization in Zambia and has advised on submissions to the UN Committee on Economic, Social, and Cultural Rights and under the OECD *Guidelines for Multinational Enterprises*. He has written handbooks on the use of economic and social rights instruments by NGOs, including *Securing Social Rights across Europe.*

Pierre Kopp is professor of public policy and the economy of law at the Université du Panthéon-Sorbonne (Paris I), where he is director of the research program on Public Decisions, Institutions, and Organizations. He is author of numerous books and journal articles on the political economy of drug control, organized crime, and money laundering, including *The*

Political Economy of Illegal Drugs, Embargo et criminalisation de l'economie, and *Organized Crime: Strategies and Counter-Measures; An Economic Analysis.*

Leiv Lunde is a partner and senior policy analyst with ECON Analysis in Oslo, Norway. He is a political scientist with broad experience in research and policy analysis in areas such as international development, humanitarian policy and conflict resolution, human rights, corporate social responsibility, environmental policy, and climate change. From 1997 to 2000 he was deputy minister for international development and human rights in the Norwegian Ministry of Foreign Affairs. His is coauthor of *Nepal: Economic Drivers of the Maoist Insurgency* (with John Bray and S. Mansoob Murshed), *Who Gets the Money? Reporting Resource Revenues* (with Philip Swanson and Mai Oldgard), and *Commerce or Crime? Regulating Economies of Conflict* (with Mark Taylor).

Mark Mansley is responsible for strategy and communication at Rathbone Greenbank Investments, the specialist ethical investment unit of Rathbone Brothers PLC. Prior to that, he was director of Claros Consulting, advising institutional investors and pension fund managers on environmentally and socially responsible investment. He has acted as an expert adviser on financial issues to the UN Commission on Sustainable Development and served on the external panel of experts to the financial working group of the World Business Council for Sustainable Development. He is a lead author of the Special Report on Technology Transfer for the Intergovernmental Panel on Climate Change and coauthor of *Socially Responsible Investment: A Guide for Pension Funds and Institutional Investors.*

Heiko Nitzschke was senior program officer for the International Peace Academy's research program Economic Agendas in Civil Wars from 2002 to 2004. He has also worked with the World Bank, Transparency International, and Oxfam America. He is the author of several IPA policy reports and articles on the political economy of armed conflict, including *Transforming War Economies: Challenges for Peacemaking and Peacekeeping,* as well as (with Karen Ballentine) of *Business and Armed Conflict: An Assessment of Issues and Options* and *The Political Economy of Civil War and Conflict Transformation.*

John T. Picarelli is research lecturer and Ph.D. candidate at the Center for the Study of Transnational Crime and Corruption (TraCCC), American University, where he is lead analyst on a study of the convergence and divergence of organized crime and terrorism. Prior to joining TraCCC, he served as an analyst at Pacific-Sierra Research Corporation, preparing briefings for the defense and intelligence communities on organized crime, terrorism, and the proliferation of weapons of mass destruction. His publications include *Global Crime Inc.* (with Louise Shelley and Chris Corpora) and *Information Technologies and Transnational Organized Crime* (with Phil Williams).

William A. Schabas is director of the Irish Centre for Human Rights at the National University of Ireland, Galway, where he also holds a professorship in human rights law. Prior to that, he was professor of human rights law and criminal law at the University of Québec. In 2002, he was appointed to the Sierra Leone Truth and Reconciliation Commission by President Abdul Tejan Kabbah. He is editor-in-chief of *Criminal Law Forum* and author of numerous articles and books, including *International Human Rights Law and the Canadian Charter, The Abolition of the Death Penalty in International Law, An Introduction to the International Criminal Court,* and *Genocide in International Law: The Crime of Crimes.*

Ian Smillie is an Ottawa-based development consultant and an associate of the Humanitarianism and War Project at Tufts University in Boston. He currently serves as research coordinator on Partnership Africa Canada's Diamonds and Human Security Project and is an NGO participant in the intergovernmental Kimberley Process. During 2000 he served on the UN Security Council Expert Panel investigating the links between illicit weapons and the diamond trade in Sierra Leone. His latest books are *Patronage or Partnership: Local Capacity Building in Humanitarian Crises* and *Managing for Change: Leadership, Strategy, and Management in Asian NGOs* (with John Hailey).

Mark Taylor is the deputy managing director at the Fafo Institute for Applied International Studies (Fafo AIS), Oslo, where he directs the New Security Program. Prior to that he worked in Palestine for a number of years, carrying out economic and human rights analysis for the United Nations and nongovernmental organizations. He is coauthor of *Commerce or Crime? Regulating Economies of Conflict* and *Security, Development and Economies of Conflict: Problems and Responses* and author of Conflict Trade: The Private Sector and Contemporary Wars, as well as editor of Fafo's Economies of Conflict research and policy papers.

Phil Williams is professor of international security in the Graduate School of Public and International Affairs at the University of Pittsburgh, where he was director of the Matthew B. Ridgway Center for International Security Studies from 1992 to 2001. He has been a consultant to both the United Nations and U.S. government agencies on organized crime. He has published extensively in the field of international security, international relations, and international organized crime, most recently as editor of *Russian Organized Crime,* author of *Illegal Immigration and Commercial Sex: The New Slave Trade,* and coeditor of *Combating Transnational Crime.*

Jonathan M. Winer practices law at Alston and Bird LLP in Washington, D.C. and is a former U.S. deputy assistant secretary of state for international law enforcement. Previously, he served for ten years as chief counsel and principal legislative assistant to Senator John F. Kerry. He is a member of the independent task force of the Council on Foreign Relations on Terrorist Financing and the Center for Strategic and International Studies Task Force on Transnational Threats. His publications include *The Finance of Illicit Resource Extraction, Globalization, Terrorist Finance, and Global Conflict,* and *International and Domestic Efforts to Combat Terrorist Finance since 9/11.*

Luc Zandvliet is director of the Corporate Engagement Project at the Cambridge-based Collaborative for Development Action (CDA), working with companies on a "do no harm" approach to business operations in conflict zones. In this capacity, he has conducted social and political risk assessments of extractive industry operations in Papua New Guinea, Nigeria, Cameroon, Sri Lanka, Myanmar, Nepal, and Indonesia. Previously he worked for Doctors without Borders (MSF) and the International Committee of the Red Cross in multiple complex emergencies in Africa.

Index

Abuja Joint Declaration, 28
Accountability, of economic actors in conflict: corporate responsibility and civil liability in armed conflict, 432–435; establishing accountability, ending impunity, 12–16, 315–330, 430–435, 476; evolution of ATCA, 397–399; postconflict punishment of conflict actors, 38, 84. *See also* Civil liability; Corporate social responsibility; International Criminal Court; International law, criminal liability; Naming and shaming; OECD *Guidelines for Multinationals, Regulation and Enforcement;* UN expert panels; UNSC sanctions
Act of state doctrine, 406–407
Afghan Development Forum, 304
Afghanistan: conflict commodities, 299–304; conflict dependents, 180(n52); conflict reduction and crime reduction efforts, 145–146; DDR programs, 469–470; sanctions escalating violence, 170; timber exports, 312(n60)
Afghan Support Group, 301
Aggregated disclosure, 273–274
Aggression, crime of, 429–432
Agricultural products, 164
Aguinda v. Texaco, 400

Aid. *See* Development assistance
Aiding and abetting, 475–476; under the Rome Statute, 341(n47), 392(n22), 427. *See also* Accountability; International Criminal Court; Joint Criminal Enterprise
Alaska Permanent Fund, 30
Algeria, 253(n6)
Alien Tort Claims Act. *See* ATCA
Al-Qaida, 104, 108
Alternative livelihoods. *See* Livelihoods
Amnesty, applicability to economic accomplices in war, 426, 435
Amnesty International, 243, 322–323
Anglo-American Mining Corporation, 435
Angola: British Petroleum disclosure, 312(n54); conflict commodities, 49–52, 129,295–299; effectiveness of UN sanctions, 329, 341(n43), 454; IMF conditionality, 327; Kimberley Process, 56; need for mandatory disclosure, 271; OECD *Guidelines,* 350–351; oil wealth, corruption and conflict, 264; pilot diamond certification systems, 62. *See also* Revenue transparency
Angola Sanctions Committee, 49–50. *See also* Fowler Report; UN expert panels
Annan, Kofi, 14, 18, 322

About the Book

In contemporary civil wars, combatants' access to lucrative natural resources has been both a means and a motive for armed conflict and thus has often served to counter incentives for peace. *Profiting from Peace* offers the first comprehensive assessment of practical strategies and tools that might be used by both international and state actors to help reduce the illicit exploitation of natural resources and the related financial flows that sustain violence.

Karen Ballentine is senior consultant for the New Security Program at the FAFO Institute for Applied International Studies, where she undertakes research and policy development to improve global efforts to address economic activities in conflict zones. Her publications include *The Political Economy of Armed Conflict: Beyond Greed and Grievance,* coedited with Jake Sherman (Lynne Rienner 2002). **Heiko Nitzschke** was a senior program officer with the International Peace Academy's Economic Agendas in Civil Wars program. He is the author of several IPA reports on the political economy of armed conflict.